Trends in Computational Social Choice

Ulle Endriss (editor)
ILLC, University of Amsterdam

Published by

AI Access

AI Access is a not-for-profit publisher with a highly respected scientific board that publishes open access monographs and collected works. Our texts are available electronically for free and in hardcopy at close to cost. We welcome proposals for new texts.

© The Authors 2017

ISBN 978-1-326-91209-3

AI Access
Managing editor: Toby Walsh
Monograph editor: Kristian Kersting
Collected works editor: Pascal Poupart
URL: aiaccess.org

Supported by

COST

This volume is the result of the work of COST Action IC1205 on Computational Social Choice, funded by COST (European Cooperation in Science and Technology). COST is an EU-funded programme that enables researchers to set up their interdisciplinary research networks in Europe and beyond. We provide funds for organising conferences, meetings, training schools, short scientific exchanges, or other networking activities on a wide range of scientific topics. By creating open spaces where people and ideas can grow, we unlock the full potential of science.

www.cost.eu

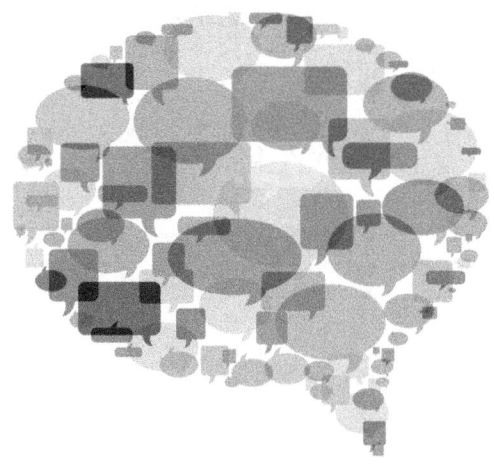

Cover Illustration by VLADGRIN/Shutterstock.com

Contents

Preface	vii
Contributors	xvii

PART I: SCENARIOS

1 Rolling the Dice: Recent Results in Probabilistic Social Choice — 3
Felix Brandt

2 Multiwinner Voting: A New Challenge for Social Choice Theory — 27
Piotr Faliszewski, Piotr Skowron, Arkadii Slinko, and Nimrod Talmon

3 The Mathematics of Seat Allocation and Political Districting — 49
Federica Ricca, Andrea Scozzari, and Paolo Serafini

4 Iterative Voting — 69
Reshef Meir

5 Group Activity Selection Problems — 87
Andreas Darmann and Jérôme Lang

6 Popular Matchings — 105
Ágnes Cseh

7 Belief Merging and its Links with Judgment Aggregation — 123
Patricia Everaere, Sébastien Konieczny, and Pierre Marquis

8 Strategic Behavior in Judgment Aggregation — 145
Dorothea Baumeister, Jörg Rothe, and Ann-Kathrin Selker

9 Social Choice and Social Networks — 169
Umberto Grandi

PART II: TECHNIQUES

10 Structured Preferences — 187
Edith Elkind, Martin Lackner, and Dominik Peters

11 Having a Hard Time? Explore Parameterized Complexity! — 209
Britta Dorn and Ildikó Schlotter

12 Approximation Algorithms and Hardness Results for Fair Division   231
Evangelos Markakis

13 Computer-aided Methods for Social Choice Theory   249
Christian Geist and Dominik Peters

14 An Introduction to Voting Rule Verification   269
Bernhard Beckert, Thorsten Bormer, Rajeev Goré, Michael Kirsten, and Carsten Schürmann

15 A PREFLIB.ORG Retrospective: Lessons Learned and New Directions   289
Nicholas Mattei and Toby Walsh

PART III: APPLICATIONS

16 US vs. European Apportionment Practices   309
László Á. Kóczy, Péter Biró, and Balázs Sziklai

17 Recent Advances in Large-Scale Peer Grading   327
Ioannis Caragiannis

18 Applications of Matching Models under Preferences   345
Péter Biró

19 School Placement of Trainee Teachers: Theory and Practice   375
Katarína Cechlárová

20 Social Choice on the Web   387
Sylvain Bouveret

Preface

Ulle Endriss

Computational Social Choice

Computational social choice is an area of research at the interface of Computer Science and Economics that is concerned with the design and analysis of methods for collective decision making. The central question studied in the field is that of how best to aggregate the individual points of view of several agents, so as to arrive at a reasonable compromise.

For example, each individual agent might be a voter in a political election, using her ballot sheet to express her individual views regarding the candidates, i.e., to report her preferences. In this context, the relevant methods of social choice are the various voting rules we could use to aggregate the individual preferences to arrive at an election outcome that appropriately represents the preferences of society as a whole. But those individual points of view could also be very different things, such as the recommendations of different experts on climate change, the choices made by the participants of a marketing survey, or the legal opinions of the members of a panel of judges. In fact, the agents whose points of view are to be aggregated need not even be human beings, but could also be, say, machines (e.g., robots that need to agree on a joint plan of action), institutions (e.g., schools that need to agree how to divide a pool of applicants amongst them), or abstract entities such as algorithms (e.g., different search engines producing alternative rankings of websites that need to be aggregated into a single view).

The design of methods for collective decision making has a long and proud history. Many well-known historical figures have pondered the question of how groups of people should make collective decisions (McLean and Urken, 1995). For instance, in the late 13th century, the Catalan missionary, writer, and philosopher Ramon Llull suggested to first hold a majority contest between any two alternatives and to then select the alternative that wins the largest number of these pairwise contests. A few hundred years later, in the late 19th century, the English writer and mathematician Charles Lutwidge Dodgson—better known as Lewis Carroll, the author of *Alice's Adventures in Wonderland*—instead proposed to choose the alternative that would minimise the degree to which the agents would have to change their preferences before the chosen alternative would win *all* pairwise majority contests. From the middle of the 20th century onwards, questions of social choice started to get studied systematically and in mathematically precise terms. This development initially occurred in the Economics literature, sparked by the seminal contribution of the American economist Kenneth J. Arrow, who analysed what kinds of desirable properties we can possibly hope to see satisfied by a rule for aggregating individual preferences into a collective preference relation (Arrow, 1963). Political scientists, philosophers, and mathematicians joined soon afterwards. Finally, in the early years of the 21st century, social choice theory got established as a mainstream research topic in Computer Science. This development is due to two reasons. First, several application domains studied in Computer Science involve collective decision making (between autonomous computer systems rather than between people) and, maybe even more importantly, the tools and techniques of Computer Science turned out to be helpful in better understanding the intricacies of collective decision making.

The state of the art in computational social choice is represented by the *Handbook of Computational Social Choice* (Brandt et al., 2016). The present volume builds on this body of knowledge and offers insights into some of the latest research trends in the field that have developed since the conception of the *Handbook*. This concerns both novel scenarios in which methods for collective decision making are required and novel techniques for the analysis of those methods. The book also introduces a number of innovative applications of the insights obtained and techniques developed in recent research in computational social choice.

COST Action IC1205

This volume has been produced by *COST Action IC1205 on Computational Social Choice*, a European research network set up to advance the state of the art in computational social choice by supporting the international research community in this domain. It was running for four years, from November 2012 to November 2016, and received a about two-thirds of a million euros in funding. COST (*Cooperation in Science and Technology*), founded in 1971, is the longest-running European framework facilitating the cooperation of scientists, engineers, and scholars across national borders. COST funds networking activities rather than research itself. It does so by allowing researchers, in a bottom-up fashion, to set up *Actions*, i.e., research networks, on specific innovative themes that are of emerging importance and that have a certain scientific and societal urgency.

COST Action IC1205 has been one of the largest such networks funded in the history of COST. The Action's *Memorandum of Understanding*, outlining a research agenda on computational social choice in broad terms, was signed by the governments of 32 European countries: Austria, Belgium, Croatia, Cyprus, the Czech Republic, Denmark, Estonia, Finland, France, Germany, Greece, Hungary, Iceland, Ireland, Israel, Italy, Luxembourg, Macedonia, Malta, the Netherlands, Norway, Poland, Portugal, Romania, Serbia, Slovakia, Slovenia, Spain, Sweden, Switzerland, Turkey, and the United Kingdom. Furthermore, a small number of individual institutions from Australia, New Zealand, Russia, Singapore, South Africa, the Ukraine, and the United States joined the network as associate partners. In total, over 500 people got involved—around 25% of them female and at least 70% of them early-career researchers.

Preface

Activities of COST Action IC1205

The activities of the Action were plentiful and wide-ranging. First, there were the large Action Meetings, organised around the formal gatherings of the Action's Management Committee in the form of 3-day workshops with 10–12 invited speakers each. For every such meeting, the Action was able to fund the participation of 40-50 individuals, with participation being open to (and free of charge for) others as well. These meetings enabled in-depth scientific interaction between the participants, without the usual pressures of quickly getting through as many presentations as possible, as is often the case at regular scientific conferences. Such meetings were held in Oxford (April 2013), Barcelona (October 2013), Maastricht (April 2014), Sibiu (October 2014), Glasgow (April 2015), and Istanbul (November 2015). In addition, a *Workshop on Future Directions in Computational Social Choice* was held in Budapest in November 2016.

The Action also organised four one-week Action Summer Schools, each attracting between 40 and 80 participants—typically PhD students, but also a few Master's students, postdoctoral researchers, and senior faculty members. This included the *Summer School on Matching Problems, Markets and Mechanisms* in Budapest in June 2013, the *Summer School on the Interdisciplinary Analysis of Voting Rules* in Caen in July 2014, and the *Summer School on Fair Division* in Grenoble in July 2015, each of which focused on a specific topic within computational social choice. It also included the *Summer School on Computational Social Choice* in San Sebastián in July 2016, which provided a broader overview of several of these individual topics.

In addition to these two main types of events, the Action also organised several smaller workshops on specific topics, such as simple games, network formation, iterative voting, and logical models of collective decision making. The Action also contributed to the organisation of events chiefly organised by others, e.g., by providing a keynote speaker or by financially supporting early-career researchers to allow them to attend the event. This included two summer schools on autonomous agents and multiagent systems (in Chania in 2013 and 2014), the *International Workshop on Matching under Preferences* in Glasgow in 2015, two editions of the *International Workshop on Computational Social Choice* (in Pittsburgh in 2014 and in Toulouse in 2016), and the *Meeting of the Society for Social Choice and Welfare* in Lund in 2016.

While the focus of the Action and its activities has been on scientific foundations, it also reached out to stakeholders outside of the academic community and to the general public. For instance, in June 2014 the Action organised a panel session on *Democracy in the Digital Age* at the EuroScience Open Forum in Copenhagen. And in June 2016 the Action organised an *Industry Day* in Toulouse, with a technical programme consisting of invited keynote talks by practitioners, from both the private and the public sector, who make innovative use of collective decision making technologies for which computational social choice provides the scientific foundations. These keynote talks were delivered by representatives of Google Research, Orange Labs, the Association for Interactive Democracy, National Matching Services Inc., and NHS Blood and Transplant.

On top of organising this diverse range of events, the Action also made prominent use of another networking instrument available to a COST Action, namely the facilitation of so-called *short-term scientific missions*. A short-term scientific mission is a research visit, of between one week and three months, of an individual researcher to an institution in another country. COST Action IC1205 financed over 130 individual research visits of this kind.

Resources Collected by COST Action IC1205

Another important aspect of the mission of COST Action IC1205 has been the dissemination of knowledge on computational social choice. The production of this volume forms an important part of these efforts. In addition, the Action collected a number of resources, all of which are available via its public website:

```
http://research.illc.uva.nl/COST-IC1205/
```

These resources include information on social choice mechanisms used in practice, particularly information on voting rules used in different European countries and information on matching schemes used around the world for student admission, job markets, and kidney exchange. The website also lists links to datasets available to researchers in computational social choice and to several online software tools for experimenting with different types of social choice mechanisms. Finally, the website makes available a list of surveys, books, and expository articles, and it provides access to educational resources that can be used for teaching computational social choice at a variety of levels.

Overview of the Book

This book consists of three parts. Part I is dedicated to *scenarios* in which some form of collective decision making is required, Part II reviews a number of *techniques* that are useful for the analysis of such scenarios, and Part III presents several innovative *applications* that illustrate the wide-ranging relevance of the field of computational social choice.

Part I: Scenarios

The scenarios that have most commonly been studied in the literature on computational social choice to date include the election of a single official on the basis of the preferences of a group of voters, the fair allocation of a set of goods to a number of agents, and the partitioning of a group of agents into coalitions in a manner that satisfies some notion of stability. The chapters in Part I go beyond these familiar scenarios in a number of ways.

In Chapter 1, Felix Brandt gives an introduction to probabilistic social choice and reviews a number of recent results in this domain. Here the outcome of an election may not always be a winning alternative, but rather a lottery over alternatives. This is important, given that some level of randomness may be unavoidable in case of ties, at least if we want to guarantee certain basic fairness properties. In Chapter 2, Piotr Faliszewski, Piotr Skowron, Arkadii Slinko, and

Nimrod Talmon introduce the topic of multiwinner voting. In this setting, the outcome of an election is a set of winning alternatives rather than a single winning alternative. Gaining a better understanding of multiwinner voting is important for a number of scenarios in which people vote, e.g., when shortlisting job applicants (rather than choosing one applicant to offer the job to) or when electing a parliament (rather than a president). In Chapter 3, Federica Ricca, Andrea Scozzari, and Paolo Serafini address a specific instance of multiwinner voting in great detail by reviewing several algorithmic methods for the apportionment problem, i.e., for the problem of allocating parliamentary seats to political parties in a manner that reflects, as best as possible, the vote share each party received. They also discuss the related problem of political districting, i.e., the problem of dividing the land, and thus the voters living on it, into electoral districts in a manner that does not give one party an undue advantage.

The next two chapters also deal with voting, but move away from the standard scenario even further. In Chapter 4, Reshef Meir discusses a model of iterative voting, where voters can inspect the outcome of an election and choose to respond to that outcome by changing their vote. If we iterate this process, a number of interesting questions arise, the most fundamental of which is whether such a process can be guaranteed to terminate eventually. Iterative voting can model, for instance, the deliberations of the members of a committee who take a number of straw polls before coming to a final decision. In Chapter 5, Andreas Darmann and Jérôme Lang introduce the family of group activity selection problems, where the members of a group each have to vote on a number of joint activities they may wish to participate in. Their preferences depend not only on the activities as such, but also on the number of fellow group members choosing the same activity. Thus, this novel scenario is related both to voting and to coalition formation.

In Chapter 6, Ágnes Cseh gives an introduction to popular matchings. In matching theory, the goal is to find a way of pairing up agents with either each other or with objects in a way that is socially optimal in some sense, such as not giving anyone an incentive to look for an alternative match. In the context of popular matchings, optimality is defined in terms of the preferences of the majority of the agents, i.e., we are looking for a matching such that no majority of agents would rather implement a different matching.

The next two chapters deal with the aggregation of judgments and beliefs, rather than with the aggregation of preferences. In Chapter 7, Patricia Everaere, Sébastien Konieczny, and Pierre Marquis compare the frameworks of propositional belief merging and judgment aggregation. While both frameworks offer means to aggregate the views of several agents regarding the truth of a number of logically related statements, the approaches taken to formalise this scenario and the types of results obtained differ significantly. In Chapter 8, Dorothea Baumeister, Jörg Rothe, and Ann-Kathrin Selker focus on one specific family of questions within judgment aggregation, namely those that relate to the strategic behaviour of agents. For instance, an agent may try to obtain a more favourable outcome by misrepresenting her own judgments, or an outside party may seek to do the same by bribing some of the agents.

Finally, in Chapter 9, Umberto Grandi gives an overview of the various opportunities for fruitful interaction between social choice theory and social network analysis. This symbiosis goes two ways: we may try to take the social structure of a group into account when designing (or reasoning about) a collective decision making rule for them, and we may use aggregation rules, as studied in social choice theory, to model the manner in which agents on a social network update their opinions based on those of their neighbours.

Part II: Techniques

Research in computational social choice makes use of a wide-ranging set of techniques from a variety of disciplines, including in particular Mathematics, Economics, and Computer Science, whilst also regularly looking for inspiration to Philosophy and Political Science. Part II of this book presents a number of techniques, particularly techniques of a computational nature, that have gained prominence in computational social choice research in recent years.

In Chapter 10, Edith Elkind, Martin Lackner, and Dominik Peters review recent work on structured preferences. While social choice in its most general form is notoriously difficult, both from a normative and a computational point of view, positive results are often within reach when we can assume that the preferences of the agents share some underlying structure. The most famous example is the condition of 'single-peakedness', which is satisfied in case all agents agree that the alternatives can be arranged on some common axis (e.g., modelling how 'rightwing' a given party is on the political spectrum) and the plot of each agent's preferences relative to that common axis only has a single peak.

The analysis of the computational complexity of problems arising in the context of collective decision making has always had an important place in computational social choice. The next two chapters introduce the reader to two specific sets of techniques within this broad domain. In Chapter 11, Britta Dorn and Ildikó Schlotter give an introduction to parameterized complexity analysis and review how this technique has been applied to a variety of problems in computational social choice. The central idea in parameterized complexity theory is that computational intractability of a problem is often due to specific parameters only, and if these parameters can be held relatively small, then practical algorithm design may still be feasible. In Chapter 12, Evangelos Markakis shows how approximation techniques can be put to good use in computational social choice, and specifically so in the context of computing approximately fair allocations of goods to agents when finding a (not just approximately) fair allocation is computationally intractable. Besides such positive results, the chapter also discusses inapproximability results, i.e., cases where even finding an approximately fair solution is intractable.

The next two chapters illustrate how one can use techniques developed in the field of automated reasoning to tackle problems in computational social choice. In Chapter 13, Christian Geist and Dominik Peters report on recent results where automated reasoning tools, particularly highly optimised satisfiability solvers for propositional logic, have been used to both verify existing proofs of theorems in social choice theory and to assist in the discovery of new such theorems. This concerns, in particular, impossibility theorems that show that certain combinations of desirable properties may be impossible to realise in a mechanism for social choice, such as a voting rule. In Chapter 14, Bernhard Beckert, Thorsten Bormer, Rajeev Goré, Michael Kirsten, and Carsten Schürmann show how logic-based program verification technology can be used to formally verify that a given implementation of a voting rule satisfies a given property of interest. This, crucially, is a different question from the question traditionally studied by social choice theorists, namely whether a given voting rule (a mathematical object, rather than a piece of software) satisfies a given property.

Concluding this part of the book, in Chapter 15, Nicholas Mattei and Toby Walsh, the creators of PREFLIB, an online reference library for preference data, reflect on some of the lessons learned from building this important resource. PREFLIB provides the computational social choice researcher with a host of data on people's preferences in real-world decision making scenarios, ranging from voter preferences in political elections, to ratings of athletes in sports competitions, to reviewer choices when bidding for papers to review for a conference.

Part III: Applications

Questions of social choice are directly relevant to a wide range of applications. The obvious one is the analysis of political elections and the systems by which we conduct such elections, but it goes much further than that. Part III of this book discusses several examples.

In Chapter 16, László Kóczy, Péter Biró, and Balázs Sziklai survey the apportionment methods used in different countries for allocating parliamentary seats to parties, given the vote shares received by these parties. They then discuss how these different methods fare in view of the recommendations of the European Commission for Democracy through Law, better know as the Venice Commission. They also demonstrate how some of these policy recommendations can conflict with basic monotonicity requirements. Thus, work in computational social choice can help clarify what are and what are not reasonable requirements to impose when designing electoral laws.

In Chapter 17, Ioannis Caragiannis explains how ideas from computational social choice can be helpful in designing systems for large-scale peer grading. Such systems are needed, for instance, in the context of massive online open courses (MOOC's), where there are too many students for it to be feasible for the work of the students to get graded by teaching assistants. The setting is similar to a voting scenario, except that the set of voters (the graders) and the set of alternatives (the students) coincide. One of the main challenges here is to arrive at an accurate ranking of the full student population, even though each grader only gets to see the assignments of a tiny subset of that population.

In Chapter 18, Péter Biró offers an overview of the application of matching mechanisms, i.e., algorithms for matching agents with either other agents or objects on the basis of the preferences of those agents. These applications include matching students with college places, children with kindergarten spots, and kidney patients with donors. The chapter covers a large number of specific case studies, explaining the intricacies of designing algorithmic solutions that account for specific legal or cultural requirements in different countries of the world.

In Chapter 19, Katarína Cechlárová focuses on one specific use of matching technology, namely the placement of trainee teachers into schools. The chapter specifically focuses on the case of trainee teacher allocation in Slovakia, where each trainee specialises in two disciplines, say, Mathematics and French, and thus a school needs to be found where there is a teachers who is formally qualified to act as the supervisor of a trainee teacher for each of the two disciplines in question. This combinatorial feature of the problem significantly increases the computational complexity of finding a good match for all trainees. Nevertheless, it turns out that designing algorithms that work well in practice is possible.

Finally, in Chapter 20, Sylvain Bouveret points out the enormous potential for using social choice theory in helping people with their everyday problems. This potential is created by the Internet in combination with the ubiquity of mobile devices. It is nowadays feasible to implement sophisticated collective decision making methods that are grounded in social choice theory and that can be used by anyone with very little effort through their own personal mobile device. The chapter exemplifies these possibilities by reviewing one such online tool, WHALE, and by reviewing some of the lessons learned in designing and fielding it.

Acknowledgments

I owe a debt of gratitude to a great many people. First and foremost, there are the authors of this volume: thank you very much for agreeing to provide a chapter at such short notice and for delivering such outstanding work! Zoi Terzopoulou did an excellent job as editorial assistant. Thank you! I also would like to acknowledge the various organisations that have made the publication of this book possible: thanks to COST for financing the production of the book; thanks to the AI Access Foundation for creating a community-driven open-access publishing outlet that seems ideal for book projects such as this one; and thanks to my own research institute, the Institute for Logic, Language and Computation (ILLC) at the University of Amsterdam, for providing administrative support.

This book is the final piece of output produced by COST Action IC1205, so this seems like a good place to also acknowledge my gratitude to everyone who helped make this enterprise a success. To start with, I would like to thank my good friends and colleagues who, in 2010, encouraged me to put together a proposal for a COST Action on Computational Social Choice. History is somewhat murky on this point, and it is not entirely clear anymore how the idea was born exactly. What I do remember is that Iannis Caragiannis was, if not its earliest, then certainly its most persistent supporter. I also recall warming to the idea during a get-together in Coimbra, just before the eruption of the Eyjafjallajökull left several of us stranded all over Southern Europe. Coincidentally, that get-together in Coimbra was happening thanks to a meeting of another COST Action, COST Action IC0602 on Algorithmic Decision Theory. I'm very grateful to Alexis Tsoukiàs, the chair of that Action, for his advice and his support of the idea to create a new Action. And, of course, I wholeheartedly want to thank the dozens of people who have contributed to or have given feedback on the proposals I wrote in 2010 and 2011 to get the project funded.

Once the Action was up and running, every single one of its over 500 participants has made a valuable contribution, including Management Committee members, organisers and attendees of workshops and summer schools, and people who carried out or hosted short-term scientific missions. Still, a few people deserve a special mention. Mike Wooldridge, Péter Biró, Flip Klijn, Hans Peters, Annick Laruelle, Vincent Merlin, Constantin-Bala Zamfirescu, David Manlove, Bahar Rastegari, Sylvain Bouveret, Nicolas Maudet, Murat Ali Çengelci, Umberto Grandi, Elena Iñarra, Jérôme Lang, and Ági Cseh were the organisers of one or more of our main meetings and summer schools. I was personally present at most of them and remember them fondly. Bettina Klaus, Britta Dorn, Annick Laruelle, Nicolas Maudet, Jérôme Lang, Péter Biró, and myself formed the Steering Committee of the Action, and I was most fortunate to be able to rely on their advice and counsel. Special thanks are due to Britta, who invested many, many hours into running the Action's short-term scientific mission programme.

At the ILLC in Amsterdam, which hosted the grant from COST used to run the Action, I was lucky to be able to count on the support of Andreea Achimescu, Inés Crespo, and Laura Biziou-Van Pol, who all spent some time working on the project as administrative assistants. Special thanks to Jan-Willem Bleeker for his most efficient handling of all financial matters during these four years.

At the COST Office in Brussels, our Action was supported by Ralph Stübner, Giuseppe Lugano, Rose Cruz Santos, Aranzazu Sanchez, Philippe Callens, Svetlana Voinova, and François Riccobene. I thank them all for their contribution.

Finally, I would like to express my gratitude to the wise men and women who have set up the COST framework and ensured its continued thrive throughout the years. If used the right way, a COST Action is an exceptionally effective means for doing scientific networking. I find it difficult to imagine a funding instrument that would have greater impact on scientific activity 'on the ground' at this scale and for such a relatively modest price.

Bibliography

K. J. Arrow. *Social Choice and Individual Values*. John Wiley and Sons, 2nd edition, 1963. First edition published in 1951.

F. Brandt, V. Conitzer, U. Endriss, J. Lang, and A. D. Procaccia, editors. *Handbook of Computational Social Choice*. Cambridge University Press, 2016.

I. McLean and A. B. Urken, editors. *Classics of Social Choice*. University of Michigan Press, Ann Arbor, 1995.

Contributors

Dorothea Baumeister
Institut für Informatik
Heinrich-Heine-Universität Düsseldorf

Bernhard Beckert
Institute of Theoretical Informatics
Karlsruhe Institute of Technology

Péter Biró
Institute of Economics
Centre for Economic and Regional Studies
Hungarian Academy of Sciences

Thorsten Bormer
Institute of Theoretical Informatics
Karlsruhe Institute of Technology

Sylvain Bouveret
Laboratoire d'Informatique de Grenoble
Université Grenoble-Alpes

Felix Brandt
Institut für Informatik
Technische Universität München

Ioannis Caragiannis
Department of Computer Engineering and Informatics
University of Patras

Katarína Cechlárová
Institute of Mathematics
P.J. Šafárik University Košice

Ágnes Cseh
Institute of Economics
Centre for Economic and Regional Studies
Hungarian Academy of Sciences

Andreas Darmann
Institute of Public Economics
University of Graz

Britta Dorn
Department of Computer Science
University of Tübingen

Edith Elkind
Department of Computer Science
University of Oxford

Ulle Endriss
Institute for Logic, Language and Computation
University of Amsterdam

Patricia Everaere
Centre de Recherche en Informatique Signal et Automatique de Lille
Université de Lille

Piotr Faliszewski
Department of Computer Science
AGH University of Science and Technology

Christian Geist
Institut für Informatik
Technische Universität München

Rajeev Goré
Research School of Computer Science
The Australian National University

Umberto Grandi
Institut de Recherche en Informatique de Toulouse (IRIT)
University of Toulouse

Michael Kirsten
Institute of Theoretical Informatics
Karlsruhe Institute of Technology

László Á. Kóczy
Institute of Economics
Centre for Economic and Regional Studies
Hungarian Academy of Sciences

Sébastien Konieczny
Centre de Recherche en Informatique de Lens
CNRS and Université d'Artois

Martin Lackner
Department of Computer Science
University of Oxford

Jérôme Lang
Laboratoire d'Analyse et de Modélisation des Systèmes pour l'Aide à la Décision
CNRS and Université Paris-Dauphine, PSL Research University

Evangelos Markakis
Department of Informatics
Athens University of Economics and Business

Pierre Marquis
Centre de Recherche en Informatique de Lens
Université d'Artois

Nicholas Mattei
Cognitive Computing Group
IBM Thomas J. Watson Research Center

Reshef Meir
Faculty of Industrial Engineering and Management
Technion—Israel Institute of Technology

Dominik Peters
Department of Computer Science
University of Oxford

Federica Ricca
Dipartimento di Metodi e Modelli per l'Economia, il Territorio e la Finanza
Università degli Studi di Roma, La Sapienza

Jörg Rothe
Institut für Informatik
Heinrich-Heine-Universität Düsseldorf

Ildikó Schlotter
Department of Computer Science and Information Theory
Budapest University of Technology and Economics

Carsten Schürmann
Computer Science Department
IT University of Copenhagen

Andrea Scozzari
Faculty of Economics
Università degli Studi Niccolò Cusano, Roma

Ann-Kathrin Selker
Institut für Informatik
Heinrich-Heine-Universität Düsseldorf

Paolo Serafini
Dipartimento di Scienze Matematiche, Informatiche e Fisiche
Università di Udine

Piotr Skowron
Electrical Engineering and Computer Science
Technische Universität Berlin

Arkadii Slinko
Department of Mathematics
University of Auckland

Balázs Sziklai
Institute of Economics
Centre for Economic and Regional Studies
Hungarian Academy of Sciences

Nimrod Talmon
Faculty of Mathematics and Computer Science
The Weizmann Institute of Science

Toby Walsh
University of New South Wales and Data61

PART I
SCENARIOS

CHAPTER 1

Rolling the Dice: Recent Results in Probabilistic Social Choice

Felix Brandt

Casting the lot puts an end to disputes and decides between powerful contenders.
— Solomon, c. 900 BC (Proverbs 18:18, RSV)

1.1 Introduction

When aggregating the preferences of multiple agents into one collective choice, it is easily seen that certain cases call for randomization or other means of tie-breaking. For example, if there are two alternatives, a and b, and two agents such that one prefers a and the other one b, there is no deterministic way of selecting a single alternative without violating one of two basic fairness conditions known as *anonymity* and *neutrality*. Anonymity requires that the collective choice ought to be independent of the agents' identities whereas neutrality requires impartiality towards the alternatives.[1] Allowing lotteries as social outcomes hence seems like a necessity for impartial collective choice. Indeed, most common "deterministic" social choice functions such as plurality rule, Borda's rule, or Copeland's rule are only deterministic as long as there is no tie, which is usually resolved by drawing a lot. The use of lotteries for the selection of officials interestingly goes back to the world's first democracy in Athens, where it was widely regarded as a principal characteristic of democracy (Headlam, 1933), and has recently gained increasing attention in political science (see, e.g., Goodwin, 2005; Dowlen, 2009; Stone, 2011; Guerrero, 2014).

It turns out that randomization—apart from guaranteeing impartiality—allows the circumvention of well-known impossibility results such as the Gibbard-Satterthwaite Theorem. Important questions in this context are how much "randomness" is required to achieve positive results and which assumptions are made about the agents' preferences over lotteries. In this chapter, I will survey some recent axiomatic results in the area of probabilistic social choice.

Probabilistic social choice functions (PSCFs) map collections of individual preference relations over alternatives to lotteries over alternatives and were first for-

---
[1] Moulin (1983, pp. 22–25) has provided a complete characterization that shows for which numbers of alternatives and agents there are deterministic single-valued social choice functions that satisfy anonymity and neutrality when individual preferences are strict.

mally studied by Zeckhauser (1969), Fishburn (1972), and Intriligator (1973). Perhaps one of the best known results in this context is Gibbard's characterization of strategyproof (i.e., non-manipulable) PSCFs (Gibbard, 1977). An important corollary of Gibbard's characterization, attributed to Hugo Sonnenschein, concerns the most studied PSCFs: *random dictatorships*. In random dictatorships, one of the agents is picked at random and his most preferred alternative is implemented as the social choice. Gibbard (1977) has shown that *random dictatorships* are the only strategyproof and *ex post* efficient PSCFs. While Gibbard's result might seem as an extension of classic negative results on strategyproof non-probabilistic social choice functions (Gibbard, 1973; Satterthwaite, 1975), it is in fact much more positive (see also Barberà, 1979b). In contrast to deterministic dictatorships, the uniform random dictatorship (henceforth, *RD*), in which every agent is picked with the same probability, enjoys a high degree of fairness and is in fact used in many subdomains of social choice that are concerned with the fair assignment of objects to agents (see, e.g., Abdulkadiroğlu and Sönmez, 1998; Bogomolnaia and Moulin, 2001; Che and Kojima, 2010; Budish et al., 2013).

One may wonder how Gibbard defined strategyproofness for PSCFs since, in his framework, agents submit their preferences over alternatives, but no preferences over lotteries. Preferences over lotteries are often defined by assuming the existence of a *von Neumann-Morgenstern (vNM) utility function* which assigns cardinal utility values to alternatives. A lottery is preferred to another lottery if the former yields more expected utility than the latter. The notion of strategyproofness considered by Gibbard is a rather strong one. According to his definition, a PSCF is strategyproof if, for *all* vNM utility functions that are compatible with the ordinal preferences, submitting one's true preferences yields at least as much expected utility as submitting any other preference relation. This notion of strategyproofness is sometimes also referred to as *strong SD-strategyproofness* (see Section 1.3.2). According to strong *SD*-strategyproofness, a PSCF may be deemed manipulable just because it can be manipulated for some contrived and highly unlikely vNM utility representations. While it is good to know that *RD* satisfies such a high degree of strategyproofness, an interesting question is whether there are other—perhaps more attractive and "less randomized"—PSCFs that satisfy weaker notions of strategyproofness.

Since there are various problems associated with asking agents to submit their complete preference relations over all lotteries, a common approach to defining axiomatic properties of PSCFs is to systematically extend the agents' preferences over alternatives to (possibly incomplete) preferences over lotteries via so-called *lottery extensions*.[2] In Section 1.3, I will define a number of lottery extensions, which will in turn lead to varying notions of strategyproofness, efficiency, and participation. On top of that, I will discuss several consistency conditions, which are not based on the individual preferences over lotteries. One such condition is *population-consistency* which requires that whenever a PSCF

---

[2]Preference relations over lotteries may, for example, not allow for a concise representation. Moreover, and perhaps more importantly, agents are in many cases not even aware of their complete preferences over lotteries. Even if they *think* they can competently assign vNM utilities to alternatives, these assignments are prone to be based on arbitrary choices.

returns the same lottery for two disjoint electorates, then this lottery should also be returned for the union of both electorates. In Section 1.4, I will review positive and negative axiomatic results for PSCFs. Particular attention will be paid to the case of weak individual preferences, i.e., preferences that may contain ties. Allowing weak preferences can lead to results that significantly differ from those for strict preferences; positive results may turn into impossibilities and easy computational problems may become intractable. In many important subdomains of social choice such as assignment, matching, and coalition formation, ties are unavoidable because agents are indifferent among all outcomes in which their allocation, match, or coalition is the same.

It is impossible to completely cover the topic of probabilistic social choice in this chapter. The selection of results is certainly biased towards work that I was involved in and I apologize in advance for any omissions. In particular, there has been interesting computational work on establishing hardness of manipulation via randomization (Conitzer and Sandholm, 2003; Elkind and Lipmaa, 2005; Walsh and Xia, 2012), approximating deterministic voting rules (Procaccia, 2010; Birrell and Pass, 2011; Service and Adams, 2012), and measuring the worst-case utilitarian performance of randomized voting rules (Anshelevich et al., 2015; Anshelevich and Postl, 2016; Gross et al., 2017).

1.2 Probabilistic Social Choice Functions

Let $N = \{1, \ldots, n\}$ be a set of agents and A a finite set of m alternatives. Every agent $i \in N$ is equipped with a complete and transitive *preference relation* $\succsim_i \subseteq A \times A$, the strict (or asymmetric) part of which is denoted by $\succ_i$. A preference relation $\succsim_i$ is called *strict* if it is antisymmetric, i.e., it is identical to its strict part up to reflexivity. Otherwise, the preference relation is said to be *weak*. A *preference profile* maps each agent $i \in N$ to a preference relation.

The set of all *lotteries* (or *probability distributions*) over A is denoted by $\Delta(A)$, i.e.,

$$\Delta(A) = \left\{ p \in \mathbb{R}^m : p(x) \geq 0 \text{ for all } x \in A \text{ and } \sum_{x \in A} p(x) = 1 \right\}.$$

For convenience, I will also write lotteries as convex combinations of alternatives, e.g., $1/2\, a + 1/2\, b$ denotes the uniform distribution over $\{a, b\}$.[3] A lottery p is *degenerate* if its support is of size 1, i.e., it puts all probability on a single alternative.

Our central object of study are PSCFs, i.e., functions that map a preference profile to a non-empty convex subset of lotteries.[4] A PSCF is *anonymous* if its outcome is invariant under permutations of the agents. Similarly, a PSCF is *neutral* if permuting alternatives in the preference profile leads to lotteries in which alternatives are permuted accordingly.

---

[3]The lotteries returned by PSCFs do not necessarily have to be interpreted as probability distributions. They can, for instance, also be seen as fractional allocations of divisible objects such as time shares or monetary budgets.
[4]We consider set-valued PSCFs because RSD and ML may return more than one lottery. If there are sufficiently many agents, this is however almost never the case (see also Brandl et al., 2016c). Single-valued PSCFs are called *social decision schemes* (Gibbard, 1977).

In this chapter, we will consider four exemplary PSCFs, all of which are anonymous and neutral: random dictatorship, two probabilistic variants of Borda's rule, and maximal lotteries.[5]

Random Dictatorship (RD). Perhaps the most-studied PSCF is *random dictatorship*, where one of the agents is picked uniformly at random and this agent's most-preferred alternative is selected. Thus, the probabilities assigned by RD are directly proportional to the number of agents who top-rank a given alternative (or, in other words, the alternative's plurality score). RD is only well-defined for strict preferences. In order to be able to deal with ties in the preferences, RD is typically extended to *random serial dictatorship (RSD)*. RSD selects a permutation of the agents uniformly at random and then sequentially allows agents in the order of the permutation to narrow down the set of alternatives to their most preferred of the remaining ones. This will always result in a single alternative unless there are two alternatives among which all agents are indifferent.[6] While implementing RSD is straightforward, computing the resulting RSD probabilities is #P-complete and therefore intractable (Aziz et al., 2013a). Also, checking whether the RSD probability of a given alternative exceeds some fixed value from the interval $(0, 1)$ is NP-complete. Subsequent work has studied the parameterized complexity of these problems (Aziz and Mestre, 2014).

The remaining three PSCFs considered in this chapter are based on pairwise majority comparisons between alternatives. For a given profile of preferences, the $m \times m$ matrix of *majority margins* M is defined by

$$M_{xy} = |\{i \in N : x \succsim_i y\}| - |\{i \in N : y \succsim_i x\}|.$$

If the output of a neutral PSCF f only depends on M, f is called *pairwise*. Pairwiseness is an informational requirement and is formally defined by demanding that the output for two preference profiles, which give rise to the same majority margin matrix, has to be identical. An advantage of pairwise PSCFs is that they are applicable even when individual preferences are incomplete or intransitive.

Borda's Rule. Traditionally, Borda's rule is defined as a scoring rule in which each agent assigns a score of $m - 1$ to his most-preferred alternative, $m - 2$ to his second-most preferred alternative, etc. The alternatives with maximal accumulated score win. Alternatively, Borda scores can be obtained from the majority margin matrix.[7] The Borda score of alternative x is $\sum_{y \in A} M_{xy}/2 + n$. We will discuss two probabilistic variants of Borda's rule. The first one, $Borda_{max}$ yields all lotteries that randomize over alternatives with *maximal* Borda score. The second one, $Borda_{pro}$, involves much more randomness and assigns probabilities to

---

[5]Other PSCFs not covered in this chapter include the recently proposed *maximal recursive rule* (Aziz, 2013), *egalitarian simultaneous reservation rule* (Aziz and Stursberg, 2014), and *2-Agree* (Gross et al., 2017).

[6]Simpler extensions of RD to weak preferences such as returning a uniform lottery over all first-ranked alternatives of a randomly selected agent typically suffer from a lack of *ex post* efficiency.

[7]This also yields a natural generalization of Borda's rule for preferences that fail to be antisymmetric, complete, or even transitive. Borda's rule is the only pairwise scoring rule.

the alternatives that are *proportional* to their Borda scores. Examples are given below.

One of the most influential notions in social choice theory is that of a *Condorcet winner*, i.e., an alternative that is preferred to every other alternative by some majority of agents. Formally, M admits a *Condorcet winner* if it contains a row in which all entries but one are strictly positive. Example 2 below shows that Borda's rule may fail to select a Condorcet winner. It is well-known that Condorcet winners do not exist in general (see Example 3 below). In fact, the absence of Condorcet winners—the so-called *Condorcet paradox*—is the root cause for central impossibility theorems in social choice theory such as Arrow's Theorem or the Gibbard-Satterthwaite Theorem. The essence of Condorcet's paradox is that there are voting situations in which *no matter* which alternative is selected, there will always be another alternative that is preferred by a majority of the agents. In other words, it is impossible to select an outcome that cannot be overturned by an organized majority of agents who all agree with which alternative it should be replaced.

Maximal Lotteries (ML). Maximal lotteries were first considered by Kreweras (1965) and independently rediscovered and studied in detail by Fishburn (1984a).[8] A lottery p is *maximal* iff $p^T M \geq 0$. A maximal lottery p can thus be seen as a "randomized weak Condorcet winner", i.e., a lottery that is weakly preferred to every other lottery by an *expected* majority of agents: $p^T M q \geq 0$ for all $q \in \Delta(A)$.[9] See Example 3 below for a profile with no Condorcet winner, but a unique maximal lottery. Maximal lotteries are equivalent to the mixed maximin strategies (or Nash equilibria) of the symmetric zero-sum game given by M. In contrast to Condorcet winners, maximal lotteries are thus guaranteed to exist by von Neumann's Minimax Theorem. Moreover, most profiles admit a *unique* maximal lottery. This is, for example, the case when there is an odd number of agents with strict preferences (see Laffond et al., 1997; Le Breton, 2005). More generally, if the number of agents goes to infinity, the number of profiles with multiple maximal lotteries goes to zero. Maximal lotteries can be found in polynomial time by solving a linear feasibility problem.[10]

---

[8] Interestingly, maximal lotteries or variants thereof have been rediscovered again by economists (Laffond et al., 1993), mathematicians (Fisher and Ryan, 1995), political scientists (Felsenthal and Machover, 1992), and computer scientists (Rivest and Shen, 2010). In particular, the support of maximal lotteries, called the *bipartisan set* or the *essential set*, has received considerable attention. A number of scholars have recommended maximal lotteries for practical use (Felsenthal and Machover, 1992; Rivest and Shen, 2010; Brandl et al., 2016c; Hoang, 2017). Within the domain of random assignment, maximal lotteries are known as popular mixed matchings (see Chapter 6 of this book).

[9] $p^T M q > 0$ iff the expected number of agents who prefer the alternative returned by p to that returned by q is at least as large as the expected number of agents who prefer the outcome returned by q to that returned by p. This is reminiscent of the *PC* lottery extension (see Section 1.3.2). However, when not taking the expectation over the number of agents and directly comparing lotteries using lottery extensions such as *SD* or *PC*, all lotteries can be overturned by some majority of agents in the absence of Condorcet winners (see, also Zeckhauser, 1969; Aziz, 2015).

[10] Brandt and Fischer (2008, Thm. 5) have shown that deciding whether an alternative receives positive probability in some maximal lottery is P-complete and therefore not amenable to parallelization.

Example 1. In the case of only two alternatives, a and b, the four considered PSCFs break down to two prototypical rules: the proportional lottery (left) and the simple majority rule (right).

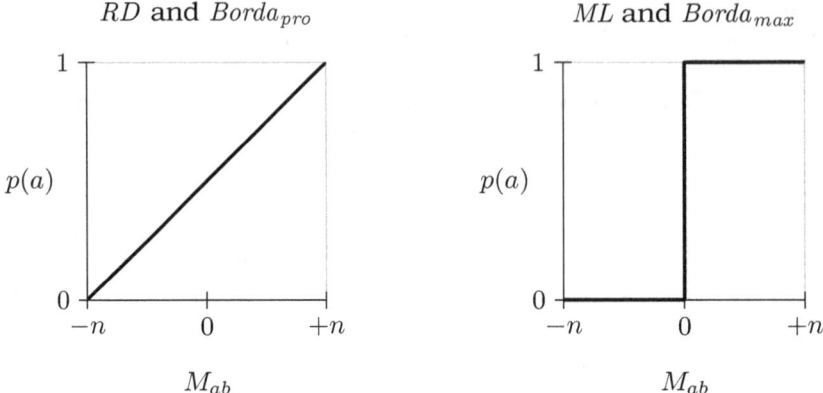

It is easily seen that the simple majority rule maximizes the agents' average *ex ante* satisfaction (Fishburn and Gehrlein, 1977). For example, consider three agents, two of which prefer a to b and one of which prefers b to a. Then, under the proportional rule, the former two will be satisfied with probability $2/3$ and the latter one with probability $1/3$. Hence, the average probability of satisfaction is $5/9$, which is lower than that of the simple majority rule ($2/3$). This gap widens when agents are risk-averse.

The proportional rule, on the other hand, steers clear of the "tyranny of the majority" by giving agents with a minority opinion at least the chance of being satisfied. Depending on the concrete setting, this can be very desirable. However, one should be aware that the proportional rule (and, in fact, any rule different from the simple majority rule) can return alternatives that are majority-dominated and therefore subject to strong opposition or even resistance. In other words, there is the possibility of *ex post* majority dissatisfaction.[11]

Example 2. Consider the following preference profile and its corresponding majority margin matrix.

$$\begin{array}{cc} 3 & 2 \\ \hline a & b \\ b & c \\ c & a \end{array} \qquad M = \begin{array}{c} \\ a \\ b \\ c \end{array} \begin{pmatrix} a & b & c \\ 0 & 1 & 1 \\ -1 & 0 & 5 \\ -1 & -5 & 0 \end{pmatrix}$$

The RD lottery is $3/5\,a + 2/5\,b$. The Borda score of a is $(0+1+1)/2 + 5 = 6$, that of b is $(-1+0+5)/2 + 5 = 7$, and that of c is $(-1-5+0)/2 + 5 = 2$. Hence, $Borda_{max}$ returns b and $Borda_{pro}$ returns $6/15\,a + 7/15\,b + 2/15\,c$. The profile admits a Condorcet

---

[11]Note that this is not possible when the outcomes of PSCFs are implemented as fractional allocations rather than actual lotteries (see Footnote 3).

winner because the first row of M is positive, except for the first entry. ML thus (uniquely) returns a because

$$\begin{pmatrix} 1 & 0 & 0 \end{pmatrix} \cdot M = \begin{pmatrix} 0 & 1 & 1 \end{pmatrix} \geq 0.$$

Example 3. Consider the following preference profile and its corresponding majority margin matrix.

$$\begin{array}{ccc} 2 & 2 & 1 \\ \hline a & b & c \\ b & c & a \\ c & a & b \end{array} \qquad M = \begin{array}{c} \\ a \\ b \\ c \end{array} \begin{pmatrix} a & b & c \\ 0 & 1 & -1 \\ -1 & 0 & 3 \\ 1 & -3 & 0 \end{pmatrix}$$

In this example, RD yields $2/5\,a + 2/5\,b + 1/5\,c$. The Borda scores of a, b, and c are 5, 6, and 3, respectively. Hence, $Borda_{max}$ returns b and $Borda_{pro}$ $5/14\,a + 6/14\,b + 3/14\,c$. The pairwise majority relation is cyclic and there is no Condorcet winner. The unique maximal lottery returned by ML is $3/5\,a + 1/5\,b + 1/5\,c$ because

$$\begin{pmatrix} 3/5 & 1/5 & 1/5 \end{pmatrix} \cdot M = \begin{pmatrix} 0 & 0 & 0 \end{pmatrix} \geq 0.$$

1.3 Axioms

The axioms considered in this chapter can be roughly divided into two subgroups: those that are independent of the agents' preferences over lotteries and those that do require preferences over lotteries.[12]

1.3.1 Consistency

We first discuss consistency axioms belonging to the first category. Non-probabilistic versions of these axioms have been widely studied in the literature.

Condorcet-consistency. A PSCF is *Condorcet-consistent* if it uniquely returns a lottery that puts probability 1 on the Condorcet winner whenever a Condorcet winner exists. Condorcet-consistency, which goes back to the 18th century, is one of the oldest formal axioms in social choice theory and considered by many to be desirable (see, e.g., Black, 1958; Fishburn, 1977; Campbell and Kelly, 2003; Dasgupta and Maskin, 2008).

Agenda-consistency. Part of the motivation of Condorcet-consistency is that an alternative that emerges as the unequivocal winner in all pairwise comparisons should also be chosen from the entire set of alternatives. Rational choice theory continues this train of thought by specifying a number of axioms that

---

[12]Apart from the axioms considered here, some authors have proposed "fairness" conditions for PSCFs such as an axiom that prescribes that every agent should receive positive probability on at least one alternative he does not rank last (Bogomolnaia et al., 2005; Duddy, 2015).

deal with choices from variable subsets of alternatives and postulating whether these choices are consistent with each other. These axioms can be transferred to probabilistic social choice simply by restricting the preference profile in question to a subset of alternatives and observing which lotteries a PSCF returns for the reduced profile. Let p be a lottery and A, B two subsets of alternatives such that p's support is contained in both A and B. Then, what we call *agenda-consistency* requires that p is returned for A and B iff it is returned for the union of A and B. The implication from left to right is known as Sen's γ or *expansion*, whereas the implication from right to left is Sen's α or *contraction* (see Sen, 1971, 1977, 1986; Schwartz, 1976).

Population-consistency. A PSCF is *population-consistent* if, whenever it returns the same lottery for two preference profiles (defined on disjoint sets of agents), it also returns the same lottery for a profile that results by merging both profiles.[13] Population-consistency is merely a statement about abstract sets of outcomes, which makes no reference to lotteries whatsoever. It was first considered independently by Smith (1973), Young (1974), and Fine and Fine (1974) and features prominently in the characterization of scoring rules by Smith (1973) and Young (1975) as well as the characterization of Kemeny's rule by Young and Levenglick (1978).

Cloning-consistency and Composition-consistency. *Cloning-consistency* requires that the probability that an alternative receives is unaffected by introducing new variants of another alternative. Alternatives are variants of each other if they form a component, i.e., they bear the same relationship to all other alternatives and therefore constitute a contiguous interval in each agent's preference ranking. This condition was first considered by Tideman (1987) (see also Zavist and Tideman, 1989). Cloning-consistency imposes no restrictions on the relative probabilities of alternatives within a component. *Composition-consistency* is stronger than cloning-consistency and additionally requires that the probability of an alternative within a component should be directly proportional to the probability that the alternative receives when the component is considered in isolation. It was first considered by Laffond et al. (1996) and has been analyzed from a computational point of view by Brandt et al. (2011). Cloning-consistency implies neutrality (Brandl et al., 2016c, Lem. 1).

Apart from their intuitive appeal, these axioms can be motivated by the desire to prevent a central planner from strategically tampering with the set of feasible alternatives (e.g., by removing irrelevant alternatives or by introducing variants of alternatives) and the set of agents (e.g., by partitioning the electorate into subelectorates). For formal definitions and examples, the reader is referred to Brandl et al. (2016c).

---

[13] A slightly stronger variant of this axiom is also known as *reinforcement*.

1.3.2 Efficiency, Strategyproofness, and Participation

Several important axioms require the specification of preferences over lotteries. We will generate these preferences by systematically lifting a preference relation over alternatives to possibly incomplete preferences over lotteries. Formally, for any given preference relation $\succsim$ on A and any pair of lotteries $p, q \in \Delta(A)$, a lottery extension $\mathcal{E}$ prescribes whether $p \succsim^{\mathcal{E}} q$. The strict part $\succ^{\mathcal{E}}$ of $\succsim^{\mathcal{E}}$ is defined by letting $p \succ^{\mathcal{E}} q$ iff $p \succsim^{\mathcal{E}} q$ and not $q \succsim^{\mathcal{E}} p$. We will consider five different lottery extensions in this section. For all examples we assume that the underlying preference relation is $a \succ b \succ c$.

The first, and most conservative, lottery extension we consider is called *deterministic dominance (DD′)* and postulates that p is preferable to q iff any alternative possibly returned by p is strictly better than any alternative possibly returned by q. In other words,

$$p \succsim^{DD'} q \quad \text{iff} \quad \forall x, y \colon [p(x) \cdot q(y) > 0 \Rightarrow x \succ y]. \tag{DD′}$$

A variant of this extension can be defined using the weak preference relation rather than the strict one.

$$p \succsim^{DD} q \quad \text{iff} \quad \forall x, y \colon [p(x) \cdot q(y) > 0 \Rightarrow x \succsim y]. \tag{DD}$$

Hence, $p \succ^{DD} q$ iff every alternative returned by p is at least as good as every alternative returned by q with at least one strict preference. An agent may thus strictly prefer one lottery to another even though he is eventually indifferent between particular instantiations of the lotteries. Clearly, whether $p \succ^{DD} q$ or $p \succ^{DD'} q$ only depends on the supports of p and q.[14] DD' only allows the comparison of lotteries with disjoint supports whereas the supports may overlap for DD as long as the agent is indifferent between all alternatives contained in the intersection of both supports. For example, $2/3\,a + 1/3\,b \succ^{DD'} c$ and $2/3\,a + 1/3\,b \succ^{DD} 1/2\,b + 1/2\,c$. DD' and DD may seem rather crude, but very risk-averse agents who seek to avoid uncertainty under any circumstances may subscribe to these preference extension. Furthermore, many PSCFs based on deterministic social choice functions already violate DD'-strategyproofness.

The second extension we consider is called *bilinear dominance (BD)* and requires that, for every pair of alternatives, the probability that p yields the more preferred alternative and q the less preferred alternative is at least as large as the other way round. Formally,

$$p \succsim^{BD} q \quad \text{iff} \quad \forall x, y \in A \colon [(x \succ y \Rightarrow p(x) \cdot q(y) \geq p(y) \cdot q(x)]. \tag{BD}$$

Apart from its intuitive appeal, the main motivation for BD is that p bilinearly dominates q iff p is preferable to q for every skew-symmetric bilinear (SSB) utility function consistent with $\succsim$ (cf. Fishburn, 1984b; Aziz et al., 2015).[15] For example, $1/2\,a + 1/2\,b \succ^{BD} 1/3\,a + 1/3\,b + 1/3\,c$.

---

[14]Within the context of set-valued social choice functions, DD is known as Kelly's preference extension (see, e.g., Kelly, 1977; Brandt, 2015).

[15]SSB utility theory is a generalization of von Neumann and Morgenstern's linear expected utility theory, which does not require the controversial independence axiom and transitivity (see, e.g., Fishburn, 1988).

Perhaps the best-known lottery extension is *stochastic dominance (SD)*, which prescribes that, for each alternative $x \in A$, the probability that p selects an alternative that is at least as good as x is greater or equal than the probability that q selects such an alternative. Formally,

$$p \succsim^{SD} q \quad \text{iff} \quad \forall x\colon \sum_{y\colon y \succsim x} p(y) \geq \sum_{y\colon y \succsim x} q(y). \qquad (SD)$$

For example, $1/2\, a + 1/2\, c \succ^{SD} 1/2\, b + 1/2\, c$. It is well-known that $p \succsim^{SD} q$ iff, for every vNM utility function compatible with $\succsim$, the expected utility for p is at least as large as that for q (see, e.g., Brandl et al., 2016a, Lem. 2).

The last lottery extension we consider is called *pairwise comparison (PC)* and postulates that p should be preferred to q iff the probability that p yields a better alternative than q is at least as large as the other way round (Aziz et al., 2015). Formally,

$$p \succsim^{PC} q \quad \text{iff} \quad \sum_{x,y\colon x \succ y} p(x) \cdot q(y) \geq \sum_{x,y\colon x \succ y} q(x) \cdot p(y). \qquad (PC)$$

For example, $2/3\, a + 1/3\, c \succ^{PC} b$. The terms in the inequality above can be associated with the probability of *ex ante* regret. Then, a lottery is PC-preferred to another lottery if its choice results in less *ex ante* regret. The PC extension can alternatively be defined using canonical SSB utility functions. Blavatskyy (2006) gave a characterization of the PC extension which relies on the axioms that characterize SSB utility functions (cf. Fishburn, 1982, 1988) plus an additional axiom that singles out PC. In contrast to the previous three extensions, PC yields *complete* preference relations over lotteries.

The five lottery extensions introduced here form a hierarchy, i.e., for any preference relation $\succsim$,

$$\succsim^{DD'} \subseteq \succsim^{DD} \subseteq \succsim^{BD} \subseteq \succsim^{SD} \subseteq \succsim^{PC}.$$

The examples mentioned also show that these inclusions are strict if $m \geq 3$.

Other extensions that have been considered in the literature include the downward lexicographic (DL), the upward lexicographic (UL) (Cho, 2016), and the sure-thing (ST) (Aziz et al., 2013b) extensions.

Standard axioms such as efficiency, strategyproofness, and participation can now be defined in varying degrees depending on the underlying lottery extension.

Efficiency. Arguably one of the most fundamental axioms in microeconomic theory, Pareto efficiency prescribes that social outcomes should be "optimal" in a well-defined weak way. For a lottery extension $\mathcal{E}$, p $\mathcal{E}$-*dominates* q if $p \succsim_i^{\mathcal{E}} q$ for all $i \in N$ and $p \succ_i^{\mathcal{E}} q$ for some $i \in N$. A PSCF is $\mathcal{E}$-*efficient* if it never returns $\mathcal{E}$-dominated lotteries. A common efficiency notion that cannot be formalized using lottery extensions is *ex post* efficiency. *Ex post* efficiency requires that whenever $x \succsim_i y$ for all $i \in N$ and $x \succ_i y$ for some $i \in N$ (i.e., y is *Pareto dominated* by x) then y should receive probability 0. It can be shown that SD-efficiency implies *ex post* efficiency and *ex post* efficiency implies BD-efficiency (Aziz et al., 2015).

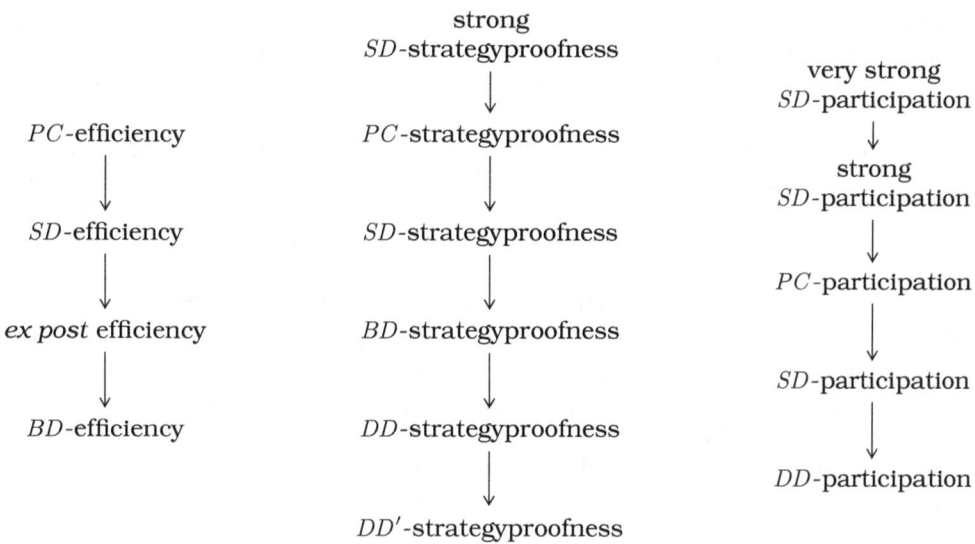

Figure 1.1: Logical relationships between varying degrees of efficiency, strategyproofness, and participation. PC-efficiency, for example, implies SD-efficiency. A PSCF is *ex post* efficient if it puts probability 0 on all Pareto dominated alternatives. Strong SD-strategyproofness is equivalent to the strategyproofness notion considered by Gibbard (1977). Very strong SD-participation requires that a participating agent is always *strictly* better off (unless he already obtains a most preferred outcome).

Strategyproofness. *Strategyproofness* demands that agents cannot benefit from misrepresenting their preferences. Since most lottery extensions return incomplete preference relations, there are two fundamentally different ways how to define strategyproofness. Consider a preference profile, a resulting lottery p, and a lottery extension $\mathcal{E}$. The strong notion of strategyproofness, first advocated by Gibbard (1977), requires that every misreported preference relation of an agent will result in a lottery q such that $p \succsim^{\mathcal{E}} q$. According to the weaker notion, first used by Postlewaite and Schmeidler (1986) and then popularized by Bogomolnaia and Moulin (2001), no agent can misreport his preferences to obtain a lottery q such that $q \succ^{\mathcal{E}} p$. In other words, the strong version always interprets incomparabilities in the worst possible manner (such that they violate strategyproofness) while the weak version interprets them as actual incomparabilities that cannot be resolved. In the following, strategyproofness (without qualifier) will refer to weak strategyproofness. Note that due to the completeness of the PC extension, strong PC-strategyproofness and PC-strategyproofness coincide. Moreover, strong SD-strategyproofness is stronger than PC-strategyproofness while (weak) SD-strategyproofness is weaker. A PSCF is *group-strategyproof* for some lottery extension if no group of agents can jointly misrepresent their preferences such that all of them are strictly better off.

Participation. Like population-consistency, *participation* is a variable-electorate condition. It requires that no agent is ever better off by *abstaining* from an election or—equivalently—that an agent can never be worse off by participating in an election. Again each preference extension yields a corresponding notion of weak and strong participation. On top of that, we define the notion of *very strong participation*, which demands that a participating agent is always *strictly* better off (unless he already obtains a most preferred lottery). While prohibitive in non-probabilistic social choice, this condition is satisfiable by reasonable PSCFs because incentives can be arbitrarily small. In analogy to group-strategyproofness, a PSCF satisfies *group-participation* if no group of agents is individually strictly better off by abstaining from an election.

In principle, every lottery extension leads to corresponding notions of efficiency, weak and strong strategyproofness, and weak, strong, and very strong participation. The relationships between the most relevant concepts are depicted in Figure 1.1. Some combinations such as DD-efficiency or strong BD-strategyproofness are omitted because they are extremely weak or prohibitively strong.

The sets of efficient lotteries for the various lottery extensions given above already constitute an interesting research subject (see Aziz et al., 2015). For example, it has been shown that whether a lottery is BD-efficient or whether it is SD-efficient only depends on its support. Perhaps surprisingly, the set of SD-efficient lotteries and the set of PC-efficient lotteries may fail to be convex. As a consequence, the convex combination of two SD-efficient PSCFs may violate SD-efficiency. Finding and verifying BD-, SD-, and PC-efficient lotteries can be achieved in polynomial time.

1.4 Results

A complete overview of which properties are satisfied by which PSCF is given in Table 1.1. Interestingly, some combinations of these axioms are prohibitive in *deterministic* social choice while they can be satisfied by reasonable PSCFs. This is, for example, the case for population-consistency and Condorcet-consistency (Young and Levenglick, 1978), participation and Condorcet-consistency (Moulin, 1988), and population-consistency and cloning-consistency (Brandl et al., 2016c). Each of agenda-consistency and very strong participation is prohibitive on its own when paired with minimal further assumptions.

Gibbard (1977) provided a complete characterization of strongly SD-strategyproof PSCFs for strict preferences in terms of convex combinations of so-called *unilaterals* (where only one agent affects the outcome) and *duples* (where only two alternatives may receive positive probability). The most well-known consequence of this result is known as the *Random Dictatorship Theorem*.

Theorem 1.1 (Gibbard, 1977). *RD is the only anonymous, strongly SD-strategyproofness, and* ex post *efficient PSCF when preferences are strict.*

Subsequent research has provided alternative proofs for this theorem (Duggan, 1996; Nandeibam, 1997; Tanaka, 2003) as well as various extensions and

	RSD (RD)	$Borda_{max}$	$Borda_{pro}$	ML
efficiency	*ex post* (SD)	SD	–	PC
strategyproofness	strong SD	–	strong SD	DD' (DD)
group-strategyproofness	DD (SD)	–	DD (BD)	DD' (DD)
participation	very strong SD	strong SD	strong SD	PC
group-participation	DD	SD	DD (BD)	PC
Condorcet-consistency	–	–	–	✓
population-consistency	– (✓)	✓	✓	✓
agenda-consistency	✓	–	–	✓
composition-consistency	–	–	–	✓
cloning-consistency	✓	–	–	✓
pairwiseness	–	✓	✓	✓
computational complexity	#P-complete (in P)	in P	in P	in P
randomness	*a lot*	*little*	*a lot*	*some*

Table 1.1: Properties of PSCFs. In general, results hold for weak preferences. A property that is only satisfied for strict preferences is given in parentheses. All results are tight in the sense that each cell contains the strongest version of a satisfied property. The cells of PSCFs that satisfy the strongest version of the corresponding property are highlighted in gray. Non-trivial results are due to Gibbard (1977); Barberà (1979b); Aziz et al. (2013a,b); Brandl et al. (2015b, 2016b,c); Brandt (2015).

variations (e.g., Gibbard, 1978; Barberà, 1979a; Hylland, 1980; Barberà et al., 1998; Benoît, 2002; Dutta et al., 2002, 2007; Nandeibam, 2008; McLennan, 2011; Nandeibam, 2013; Picot and Sen, 2012; Chatterji et al., 2014).[16]

Since $Borda_{max}$ and ML are *ex post* efficient, Theorem 1.1 entails that these PSCFs violate strong SD-strategyproofness (in fact, ML fails to satisfy BD-strategyproofness while $Borda_{max}$ does not even satisfy DD'-strategyproofness). Another, less obvious, consequence of Gibbard's characterization is that $Borda_{pro}$ satisfies strong SD-strategyproofness (Barberà, 1979b).[17] While the results on strongly SD-strategyproof PSCFs are encouraging, these PSCFs involve an enormous amount of randomization (it follows from Theorem 1.1 that $Borda_{pro}$ even fails to put probability 0 on Pareto dominated alternatives). In general, there appears to be a pervasive tradeoff between efficiency and strategyproofness. For example, it quickly follows from Theorem 1.1 that PC-efficiency and strong SD-strategyproofness are incompatible, even when preferences are strict: since PC-efficiency is stronger than *ex post* efficiency, the only candidate for such a PSCF would be RD, which is easily seen to violate PC-efficiency. A number of impossibilities illustrating this tradeoff (and other incompatibilities) are given in Table 1.2. Among these, the following result deserves special mention.

---

[16]See also Barberà (2010, Section 7).

[17]This result has been rediscovered several times (see Heckelman, 2003; Procaccia, 2010; Heckelman and Chen, 2013).

axioms			prefs	$m \geq$	$n \geq$	source
SD-eff.	SD-strategypr.	anon. & neutr.	weak	4	4	c
PC-eff.	PC-strategypr.	anon. & neutr.	weak	3	3	a
ex post-eff.	BD-group-strategypr.	anon. & neutr.	weak	3	3	a
ex post-eff.	DD-strategypr.	pairwise	weak	3	3	f
Cond.-cons.	DD-strategypr.	—	weak	3	$3m$	d
Cond.-cons.	strong SD-part.	—	strict	4	12	e
ex post-eff.	very strong SD-part.	pairwise	strict	2	3	b

a: Aziz et al., 2014, b: Brandl et al., 2015b, c: Brandl et al., 2016a, d: Brandt, 2015, e: Brandt et al., 2017a, f: Unpublished work with C. Saile and C. Stricker

Table 1.2: Impossibility theorems. The first row corresponds to Theorem 1.2.

Theorem 1.2 (Brandl et al., 2016a). *There is no anonymous, neutral, SD-efficient, and SD-strategyproof PSCF when $m, n \geq 4$.*

Alternatively, the theorem can be phrased as follows: let f be an anonymous and neutral PSCF which does not return lotteries that are Pareto dominated for *all* vNM utility representations compatible with the agents' preferences. Then f can be manipulated for *all* vNM utility representations compatible with the manipulator's preferences. This sweeping impossibility was obtained with the help of a computer and the proof is long and tedious to verify for humans. It has been verified by the interactive theorem prover Isabelle/HOL (see also Chapter 13 of this book). When preferences are strict, the axioms are compatible (and satisfied by RD). Theorem 1.2 implies that RD cannot be extended to weak preferences without giving up SD-efficiency or SD-strategyproofness (Brandl et al., 2016d). When restricting attention to pairwise PSCFs, SD-efficiency and SD-strategyproofness can be weakened to *ex post* efficiency and BD-strategyproofness (see Table 1.2).

Perhaps surprisingly, even the lowest degree of strategyproofness (DD'-strategyproofness) is violated by many PSCFs. In particular, $Borda_{max}$ (and PSCFs that randomize over plurality winners, Copeland winners, Nanson winners, etc.) violate DD'-strategyproofness. However, a handful of interesting PSCFs are DD'-strategyproof. A sufficient condition for DD'-strategyproofness is *set-monotonicity*, which requires that weakening alternatives that receive probability 0 does not affect the support of the resulting lottery.

Theorem 1.3 (Brandt, 2015, Brandl et al., 2015a). *Every set-monotonic PSCF satisfies DD'-group-strategyproofness and DD'-group-participation (if completely indifferent agents do not affect the outcome). When preferences are strict, set-monotonicity implies DD-group-strategyproofness.*

As a consequence, PSCFs that randomize arbitrarily over the choice sets of some well-known set-valued social choice functions such as the *top cycle*, the *minimal covering set*, or the *bipartisan set* (see, e.g., Brandt et al., 2016) are DD'-group-strategyproof and satisfy DD'-group-participation. It is easily seen that a PSCF is DD'-group-strategyproof if, for every preference profile, it returns a lottery whose support contains the support of the lottery returned by another DD'-group-strategyproof PSCF. This implies that, apart from the PSCFs mentioned above, randomizing over elements of the *uncovered set* is DD'-group-strategyproof (even though the corresponding PSCF violates set-monotonicity). ML was shown to satisfy ST-strategyproofness, a minor strengthening of DD'-strategyproofness (Aziz et al., 2013b).

DD-strategyproofness, on the other hand, is already prohibitive when paired with further assumptions such as Condorcet-consistency or pairwiseness and *ex post* efficiency (see Table 1.2). Other impossibility theorems involving DD-strategyproofness were given by Kelly (1977) and Barberà (1977).

Let us now turn to consistency conditions. As mentioned above, population-consistency and composition-consistency are incompatible in deterministic social choice. When allowing lotteries as outcomes, these axioms uniquely characterize ML.[18]

Theorem 1.4 (Brandl et al., 2016c). *ML is the only anonymous PSCF satisfying population-consistency and composition-consistency when preferences are strict.*

RD satisfies population-consistency, but violates composition-consistency. When replacing composition-consistency with the weaker property of cloning-consistency (which is satisfied by RD) and adding Condorcet-consistency (which is violated by RD), the previous characterization remains intact.

Theorem 1.5 (Brandl et al., 2016c). *ML is the only anonymous PSCF satisfying population-consistency, cloning-consistency, and Condorcet-consistency when preferences are strict.*

Since population-consistency has been identified as the defining property of Borda's scoring rule (Young, 1974; Nitzan and Rubinstein, 1981; Saari, 1990), this theorem can be seen as one possible resolution of the well-documented dispute between the founding fathers of social choice theory, the Chevalier de Borda and the Marquis de Condorcet, which dates back to the 18th century (see, e.g., Black, 1958; Young, 1988, 1995; McLean and Hewitt, 1994). In this sense, Theorem 1.5 resembles the characterization of Kemeny's rule by Young and Levenglick (1978).[19]

On top of population-consistency and composition-consistency, ML also satisfies agenda-consistency. Agenda-consistency, the contraction part of which is at the heart of virtually all choice-theoretic Arrovian impossibility theorems (see, e.g., Sen, 1977, 1986), is also satisfied by RD. Pattanaik and Peleg (1986) considered a significantly stronger version of contraction-consistency, which demands that probabilities cannot decrease when removing arbitrary alternatives (by contrast, we require lotteries to be *unaffected* when removing alternatives *that receive probability 0*). Together with *ex post* efficiency and an independence

---

[18]The formal statement was shown for a framework using fractional profiles which requires PSCFs to be continuous, decisive, and unanimous (see Brandl et al., 2016c). These are mild technical assumptions that are satisfied by every reasonable PSCF.

[19]Interestingly, all three rules—Borda's rule, Kemeny's rule, and maximal lotteries—maximize aggregate score in a well-defined sense. For maximal lotteries, this is the case because they maximize social welfare according to the PC SSB utility functions representing the agents' ordinal preferences (Brandl et al., 2016b).

condition, this stronger contraction-consistency condition characterizes RD in a variable-agenda framework. It is violated by $Borda_{max}$, $Borda_{pro}$, and ML.

Recently, ML has also been characterized using a strengthening of PC-group-participation and additional technical properties (Brandl et al., 2016b).

1.5 Discussion and Future Work

Whether randomization is inadmissible, acceptable, or even desirable strongly depends on the application. While electing a political leader via lottery would probably be controversial, randomly selecting an employee of the day, a restaurant to go to, or background music for a party seems quite natural. Important factors in this context are how frequently elections are repeated and how much randomization is entailed by the voting procedure. The degree of randomization of the PSCFs considered in this chapter greatly differs (see Table 1.1). This can, for example, be illustrated by considering the precise circumstances under which these PSCFs return a degenerate lottery. While $Borda_{pro}$ *never* returns a degenerate lottery (if $m > 2$), RD and RSD do so only if all agents favor the same alternative, and ML only if there is a weak Condorcet winner. Interestingly, there is strong empirical evidence that most real-world preference profiles for *political* elections do admit a Condorcet winner (see, e.g., Feld and Grofman, 1992; Regenwetter et al., 2006; Laslier, 2010; Gehrlein and Lepelley, 2011). Hence, the actual degree of randomization of ML might be relatively low. For a more comprehensive discussion of the acceptability of randomization in social choice, the reader is referred to Brandl et al. (2016c, pp. 1841–1843).

Many topics in probabilistic social choice deserve further study. For example, to the best of my knowledge, there is no formal analysis of the degree of randomization of specific PSCFs. Furthermore, while strong SD-strategyproofness and weak notions of efficiency such as *ex post* efficiency are well understood, this is not the case for the other two extremes. Only little is known about the structure of the set of PC-efficient lotteries (Aziz et al., 2015) and there is no coherent picture of which PSCFs are DD-strategyproof and which ones are not (see, e.g., Brandt, 2015). There are a number of concrete open problems for strict preferences:

- Are there PC-efficient and BD-strategyproof (or even SD-strategyproof or PC-strategyproof) PSCFs?

- Are there Condorcet-consistent and PC-strategyproof PSCFs?

- Are there PC-efficient PSCFs that satisfy very strong PC-participation?

Similarly, there are challenging questions for weak preferences:

- Are there SD-efficient PSCFs that satisfy very strong SD-participation?

- Are there SD-efficient and DD-strategyproof (or even BD-strategyproof) PSCFs?

- Is neutrality required for the first three impossibilities in Table 1.2?

Just like in non-probabilistic social choice, considering restricted domains of preferences such as dichotomous or single-peaked preferences opens up new avenues for intriguing results (see Ehlers et al., 2002; Bogomolnaia et al., 2005). Also, economic domains such as random assignment, random matching, or random coalition formation may allow for positive results as well as strengthened impossibilities (e.g., Bogomolnaia and Moulin, 2001, 2004; Aziz et al., 2013a,c, 2017; Brandt et al., 2017b; Brandl et al., 2017)

Finally, one of the main appeals of RD is its association with a natural voting procedure that implements the RD outcome. Apart from its simplicity, this procedure has the advantage of minimal preference elicitation. It would be interesting to study similarly natural procedures or cryptographic protocols that implement other PSCFs. Such procedures and protocols are particularly important in probabilistic social choice because agents not only need to be convinced that the outcome was computed correctly, but also that the randomization was performed faithfully.

Acknowledgments

Thanks to Haris Aziz, Florian Brandl, Markus Brill, Christian Geist, Johannes Hofbauer, and Hans Georg Seedig for many illuminating discussions. I am furthermore grateful to Ulle Endriss and Dominik Peters for helpful feedback on drafts of this chapter. This work is supported by the Deutsche Forschungsgemeinschaft under grant BR 2312/11-1.

Bibliography

A. Abdulkadiroğlu and T. Sönmez. Random serial dictatorship and the core from random endowments in house allocation problems. *Econometrica*, 66(3):689–701, 1998.

E. Anshelevich and J. Postl. Randomized social choice functions under metric preferences. In *Proceedings of the 25th International Joint Conference on Artificial Intelligence (IJCAI)*, pages 46–59. AAAI Press, 2016.

E. Anshelevich, O. Bhardwaj, and J. Postl. Approximating optimal social choice under metric preferences. In *Proceedings of the 29th AAAI Conference on Artificial Intelligence (AAAI)*, pages 777–783, 2015.

H. Aziz. Maximal Recursive Rule: A New Social Decision Scheme. In *Proceedings of the 23nd International Joint Conference on Artificial Intelligence (IJCAI)*, pages 34–40. AAAI Press, 2013.

H. Aziz. Condorcet's paradox and the median voter theorem for randomized social choice. *Economic Theory Bulletin*, 35(1), 2015.

H. Aziz and J. Mestre. Parametrized algorithms for random serial dictatorship. *Mathematical Social Sciences*, 72:1–6, 2014.

H. Aziz and P. Stursberg. A generalization of probabilistic serial to randomized social choice. In *Proceedings of the 28th AAAI Conference on Artificial Intelligence (AAAI)*, pages 559–565. AAAI Press, 2014.

H. Aziz, F. Brandt, and M. Brill. The computational complexity of random serial dictatorship. *Economics Letters*, 121(3):341–345, 2013a.

H. Aziz, F. Brandt, and M. Brill. On the tradeoff between economic efficiency and strategyproofness in randomized social choice. In *Proceedings of the 12th International Conference on Autonomous Agents and Multiagent Systems (AAMAS)*, pages 455–462. IFAAMAS, 2013b.

H. Aziz, F. Brandt, and P. Stursberg. On popular random assignments. In *Proceedings of the 6th International Symposium on Algorithmic Game Theory (SAGT)*, volume 8146 of *Lecture Notes in Computer Science (LNCS)*, pages 183–194. Springer-Verlag, 2013c.

H. Aziz, F. Brandl, and F. Brandt. On the incompatibility of efficiency and strategyproofness in randomized social choice. In *Proceedings of the 28th AAAI Conference on Artificial Intelligence (AAAI)*, pages 545–551. AAAI Press, 2014.

H. Aziz, F. Brandl, and F. Brandt. Universal Pareto dominance and welfare for plausible utility functions. *Journal of Mathematical Economics*, 60:123–133, 2015.

H. Aziz, F. Brandt, E. Elkind, and P. Skowron. Computational social choice: The first ten years and beyond. In B. Steffen and G. Woeginger, editors, *Computer Science Today*, volume 10000 of *Lecture Notes in Computer Science (LNCS)*. Springer-Verlag, 2017. Forthcoming.

S. Barberà. The manipulation of social choice mechanisms that do not leave "too much" to chance. *Econometrica*, 45(7):1573–1588, 1977.

S. Barberà. A note on group strategy-proof decision schemes. *Econometrica*, 47(3):637–640, 1979a.

S. Barberà. Majority and positional voting in a probabilistic framework. *Review of Economic Studies*, 46(2):379–389, 1979b.

S. Barberà. Strategy-proof social choice. In K. J. Arrow, A. K. Sen, and K. Suzumura, editors, *Handbook of Social Choice and Welfare*, volume 2, chapter 25, pages 731–832. Elsevier, 2010.

S. Barberà, A. Bogomolnaia, and H. van der Stel. Strategy-proof probabilistic rules for expected utility maximizers. *Mathematical Social Sciences*, 35(2):89–103, 1998.

J.-P. Benoît. Strategic manipulation in voting games when lotteries and ties are permitted. *Journal of Economic Theory*, 102(2):421–436, 2002.

E. Birrell and R. Pass. Approximately strategy-proof voting. In *Proceedings of the 22nd International Joint Conference on Artificial Intelligence (IJCAI)*, pages 67–72. AAAI Press, 2011.

D. Black. *The Theory of Committees and Elections*. Cambridge University Press, 1958.

P. R. Blavatskyy. Axiomatization of a preference for most probable winner. *Theory and Decision*, 60(1):17–33, 2006.

A. Bogomolnaia and H. Moulin. A new solution to the random assignment problem. *Journal of Economic Theory*, 100(2):295–328, 2001.

A. Bogomolnaia and H. Moulin. Random matching under dichotomous preferences. *Econometrica*, 72(1):257–279, 2004.

A. Bogomolnaia, H. Moulin, and R. Stong. Collective choice under dichotomous preferences. *Journal of Economic Theory*, 122(2):165–184, 2005.

F. Brandl, F. Brandt, C. Geist, and J. Hofbauer. Strategic abstention based on preference extensions: Positive results and computer-generated impossibilities. In *Proceedings of the 24th International Joint Conference on Artificial Intelligence (IJCAI)*, pages 18–24. AAAI Press, 2015a.

F. Brandl, F. Brandt, and J. Hofbauer. Incentives for participation and abstention in probabilistic social choice. In *Proceedings of the 14th International Conference on Autonomous Agents and Multiagent Systems (AAMAS)*, pages 1411–1419. IFAAMAS, 2015b.

F. Brandl, F. Brandt, and C. Geist. Proving the incompatibility of efficiency and strategyproofness via SMT solving. In *Proceedings of the 25th International Joint Conference on Artificial Intelligence (IJCAI)*, pages 116–122. AAAI Press, 2016a.

F. Brandl, F. Brandt, and J. Hofbauer. Welfare maximization entices participation. 2016b. Working paper.

F. Brandl, F. Brandt, and H. G. Seedig. Consistent probabilistic social choice. *Econometrica*, 84(5):1839–1880, 2016c.

F. Brandl, F. Brandt, and W. Suksompong. The impossibility of extending random dictatorship to weak preferences. *Economics Letters*, 141:44–47, 2016d.

F. Brandl, F. Brandt, and J. Hofbauer. Random assignment with optional participation. In *Proceedings of the 16th International Conference on Autonomous Agents and Multiagent Systems (AAMAS)*, pages 326–334. IFAAMAS, 2017.

F. Brandt. Set-monotonicity implies Kelly-strategyproofness. *Social Choice and Welfare*, 45(4):793–804, 2015.

F. Brandt and F. Fischer. Computing the minimal covering set. *Mathematical Social Sciences*, 56(2):254–268, 2008.

F. Brandt, M. Brill, and H. G. Seedig. On the fixed-parameter tractability of composition-consistent tournament solutions. In *Proceedings of the 22nd International Joint Conference on Artificial Intelligence (IJCAI)*, pages 85–90. AAAI Press, 2011.

F. Brandt, M. Brill, and P. Harrenstein. Tournament solutions. In F. Brandt, V. Conitzer, U. Endriss, J. Lang, and A. D. Procaccia, editors, *Handbook of Computational Social Choice*, chapter 3. Cambridge University Press, 2016.

F. Brandt, C. Geist, and D. Peters. Optimal bounds for the no-show paradox via SAT solving. *Mathematical Social Sciences*, 2017a. Special Issue in Honor of Hervé Moulin. Forthcoming.

F. Brandt, J. Hofbauer, and M. Suderland. Majority graphs of assignment problems and properties of popular random assignments. In *Proceedings of the 16th International Conference on Autonomous Agents and Multiagent Systems (AAMAS)*, pages 335–343. IFAAMAS, 2017b.

E. Budish, Y.-K. Che, F. Kojima, and P. Milgrom. Designing random allocation mechanisms: Theory and applications. *American Economic Review*, 103(2): 585–623, 2013.

D. E. Campbell and J. S. Kelly. A strategy-proofness characterization of majority rule. *Economic Theory*, 22(3):557–568, 2003.

S. Chatterji, A. Sen, and H. Zeng. Random dictatorship domains. *Games and Economic Behavior*, 86:212–236, 2014.

Y.-K. Che and F. Kojima. Asymptotic equivalence of probabilistic serial and random priority mechanisms. *Econometrica*, 78(5):1625–1672, 2010.

W. J. Cho. Incentive properties for ordinal mechanisms. *Games and Economic Behavior*, 95:168–177, 2016.

V. Conitzer and T. Sandholm. Universal voting protocol tweaks to make manipulation hard. In *Proceedings of the 18th International Joint Conference on Artificial Intelligence (IJCAI)*, pages 781–788. Morgan Kaufmann, 2003.

P. Dasgupta and E. Maskin. On the robustness of majority rule. *Journal of the European Economic Association*, 6(5):949–973, 2008.

O. Dowlen. Sorting out sortition: A perspective on the random selection of political officers. *Political Studies*, 57(2):298–315, 2009.

C. Duddy. Fair sharing under dichotomous preferences. *Mathematical Social Sciences*, 73:1–5, 2015.

J. Duggan. A geometric proof of Gibbard's random dictatorship theorem. *Economic Theory*, 7(2):365–369, 1996.

B. Dutta, H. Peters, and A. Sen. Strategy-proof probabilistic mechanisms in economies with pure public goods. *Journal of Economic Theory*, 106(2):392–416, 2002.

B. Dutta, H. Peters, and A. Sen. Strategy-proof cardinal decision schemes. *Social Choice and Welfare*, 28(1):163–179, 2007.

L. Ehlers, H. Peters, and T. Storcken. Strategy-proof probabilistic decision schemes for one-dimensional single-peaked preferences. *Journal of Economic Theory*, 105(2):408–434, 2002.

E. Elkind and H. Lipmaa. Hybrid voting protocols and hardness of manipulation. In *Proceedings of the 16th International Symposium on Algorithms and Computation (ISAAC)*, volume 3827 of *Lecture Notes in Computer Science (LNCS)*, pages 206–215. Springer-Verlag, 2005.

S. L. Feld and B. Grofman. Who's afraid of the big bad cycle? Evidence from 36 elections. *Journal of Theoretical Politics*, 4(2):231–237, 1992.

D. S. Felsenthal and M. Machover. After two centuries should Condorcet's voting procedure be implemented? *Behavioral Science*, 37(4):250–274, 1992.

B. Fine and K. Fine. Social choice and individual ranking I. *Review of Economic Studies*, 41(127):303–323, 1974.

P. C. Fishburn. Lotteries and social choices. *Journal of Economic Theory*, 5(2): 189–207, 1972.

P. C. Fishburn. Condorcet social choice functions. *SIAM Journal on Applied Mathematics*, 33(3):469–489, 1977.

P. C. Fishburn. Nontransitive measurable utility. *Journal of Mathematical Psychology*, 26(1):31–67, 1982.

P. C. Fishburn. Probabilistic social choice based on simple voting comparisons. *Review of Economic Studies*, 51(4):683–692, 1984a.

P. C. Fishburn. Dominance in SSB utility theory. *Journal of Economic Theory*, 34(1):130–148, 1984b.

P. C. Fishburn. *Nonlinear preference and utility theory*. The Johns Hopkins University Press, 1988.

P. C. Fishburn and W. V. Gehrlein. Towards a theory of elections with probabilistic preferences. *Econometrica*, 45(8):1907–1924, 1977.

D. C. Fisher and J. Ryan. Tournament games and positive tournaments. *Journal of Graph Theory*, 19(2):217–236, 1995.

W. V. Gehrlein and D. Lepelley. *Voting Paradoxes and Group Coherence*. Studies in Choice and Welfare. Springer-Verlag, 2011.

A. Gibbard. Manipulation of voting schemes: A general result. *Econometrica*, 41(4):587–601, 1973.

A. Gibbard. Manipulation of schemes that mix voting with chance. *Econometrica*, 45(3):665–681, 1977.

A. Gibbard. Straightforwardness of game forms with lotteries as outcomes. *Econometrica*, 46(3):595–614, 1978.

B. Goodwin. *Justice by Lottery*. University of Chicago Press, 2005. 1st edition 1992.

S. Gross, E. Anshelevich, and L. Xia. Vote until two of you agree: Mechanisms with small distortion and sample complexity. In *Proceedings of the 31st AAAI Conference on Artificial Intelligence (AAAI)*, pages 544–550, 2017.

A. Guerrero. Against elections: The lottocratic alternative. *Philosophy and Public Affairs*, 42(2):135–178, 2014.

J. W. Headlam. *Election by Lot at Athens*. Cambridge University Press, 1933.

J. C. Heckelman. Probabilistic Borda rule voting. *Social Choice and Welfare*, 21: 455–468, 2003.

J. C. Heckelman and F. H. Chen. Strategy proof scoring rule lotteries for multiple winners. *Journal of Public Economic Theory*, 15(1):103–123, 2013.

L. N. Hoang. Strategy-proofness of the randomized Condorcet voting system. *Social Choice and Welfare*, 48(3):679–701, 2017.

A. Hylland. Strategyproofness of voting procedures with lotteries as outcomes and infinite sets of strategies. Mimeo, 1980.

M. D. Intriligator. A probabilistic model of social choice. *Review of Economic Studies*, 40(4):553–560, 1973.

J. S. Kelly. Strategy-proofness and social choice functions without single-valuedness. *Econometrica*, 45(2):439–446, 1977.

G. Kreweras. Aggregation of preference orderings. In *Mathematics and Social Sciences I: Proceedings of the seminars of Menthon-Saint-Bernard, France (1–27 July 1960) and of Gösing, Austria (3–27 July 1962)*, pages 73–79, 1965.

G. Laffond, J.-F. Laslier, and M. Le Breton. The bipartisan set of a tournament game. *Games and Economic Behavior*, 5(1):182–201, 1993.

G. Laffond, J. Lainé, and J.-F. Laslier. Composition-consistent tournament solutions and social choice functions. *Social Choice and Welfare*, 13(1):75–93, 1996.

G. Laffond, J.-F. Laslier, and M. Le Breton. A theorem on symmetric two-player zero-sum games. *Journal of Economic Theory*, 72(2):426–431, 1997.

J.-F. Laslier. In silico voting experiments. In J.-F. Laslier and M. R. Sanver, editors, *Handbook on Approval Voting*, chapter 13, pages 311–335. Springer-Verlag, 2010.

M. Le Breton. On the uniqueness of equilibrium in symmetric two-player zero-sum games with integer payoffs. *Économie publique*, 17(2):187–195, 2005.

I. McLean and F. Hewitt. *Condorcet: Foundations of Social Choice and Political Theory*. Edward Elgar Publishing, 1994.

A. McLennan. Manipulation in elections with uncertain preferences. *Journal of Mathematical Economics*, 47(3):370–375, 2011.

H. Moulin. *The Strategy of Social Choice*. North-Holland, 1983.

H. Moulin. Condorcet's principle implies the no show paradox. *Journal of Economic Theory*, 45:53–64, 1988.

S. Nandeibam. An alternative proof of Gibbard's random dictatorship result. *Social Choice and Welfare*, 15(4):509–519, 1997.

S. Nandeibam. A note on the structure of stochastic social choice functions. *Social Choice and Welfare*, 30(3):447–455, 2008.

S. Nandeibam. The structure of decision schemes with cardinal preferences. *Review of Economic Design*, 17(3):205–238, 2013.

S. Nitzan and A. Rubinstein. A further characterization of Borda ranking method. *Public Choice*, 36(1):153–158, 1981.

P. K. Pattanaik and B. Peleg. Distribution of power under stochastic social choice rules. *Econometrica*, 54(4):909–921, 1986.

J. Picot and A. Sen. An extreme point characterization of random strategy-proof social choice functions: The two alternative case. *Economics Letters*, 115(1):49–52, 2012.

A. Postlewaite and D. Schmeidler. Strategic behaviour and a notion of ex ante efficiency in a voting model. *Social Choice and Welfare*, 3(1):37–49, 1986.

A. D. Procaccia. Can approximation circumvent Gibbard-Satterthwaite? In *Proceedings of the 24th AAAI Conference on Artificial Intelligence (AAAI)*, pages 836–841. AAAI Press, 2010.

M. Regenwetter, B. Grofman, A. A. J. Marley, and I. M. Tsetlin. *Behavioral Social Choice: Probabilistic Models, Statistical Inference, and Applications*. Cambridge University Press, 2006.

R. L. Rivest and E. Shen. An optimal single-winner preferential voting system based on game theory. In *Proceedings of the 3rd International Workshop on Computational Social Choice (COMSOC)*, pages 399–410, 2010.

D. G. Saari. The Borda dictionary. *Social Choice and Welfare*, 7(4):279–317, 1990.

M. A. Satterthwaite. Strategy-proofness and Arrow's conditions: Existence and correspondence theorems for voting procedures and social welfare functions. *Journal of Economic Theory*, 10(2):187–217, 1975.

T. Schwartz. Choice functions, "rationality" conditions, and variations of the weak axiom of revealed preference. *Journal of Economic Theory*, 14:414–427, 1976.

A. K. Sen. Choice functions and revealed preference. *Review of Economic Studies*, 38(3):307–317, 1971.

A. K. Sen. Social choice theory: A re-examination. *Econometrica*, 45(1):53–89, 1977.

A. K. Sen. Social choice theory. In K. J. Arrow and M. D. Intriligator, editors, *Handbook of Mathematical Economics*, volume 3, chapter 22, pages 1073–1181. Elsevier, 1986.

T. C. Service and J. A. Adams. Strategyproof approximations of distance rationalizable voting rules. In *Proceedings of the 11th International Conference on Autonomous Agents and Multiagent Systems (AAMAS)*, pages 569–576. IFAAMAS, 2012.

J. H. Smith. Aggregation of preferences with variable electorate. *Econometrica*, 41(6):1027–1041, 1973.

P. Stone. *The Luck of the Draw: The Role of Lotteries in Decision Making*. Oxford University Press, 2011.

Y. Tanaka. An alternative proof of Gibbard's random dictatorship theorem. *Review of Economic Design*, 8:319–328, 2003.

T. N. Tideman. Independence of clones as a criterion for voting rules. *Social Choice and Welfare*, 4(3):185–206, 1987.

T. Walsh and L. Xia. Lot-based voting rules. In *Proceedings of the 11th International Conference on Autonomous Agents and Multiagent Systems (AAMAS)*, pages 603–610. IFAAMAS, 2012.

H. P. Young. An axiomatization of Borda's rule. *Journal of Economic Theory*, 9(1):43–52, 1974.

H. P. Young. Social choice scoring functions. *SIAM Journal on Applied Mathematics*, 28(4):824–838, 1975.

H. P. Young. Condorcet's theory of voting. *The American Political Science Review*, 82(4):1231–1244, 1988.

H. P. Young. Optimal voting rules. *Journal of Economic Perspectives*, 9(1):51–64, 1995.

H. P. Young and A. Levenglick. A consistent extension of Condorcet's election principle. *SIAM Journal on Applied Mathematics*, 35(2):285–300, 1978.

T. M. Zavist and T. N. Tideman. Complete independence of clones in the ranked pairs rule. *Social Choice and Welfare*, 6(2):167–173, 1989.

R. Zeckhauser. Majority rule with lotteries on alternatives. *Quarterly Journal of Economics*, 83(4):696–703, 1969.

CHAPTER 2

Multiwinner Voting: A New Challenge for Social Choice Theory

Piotr Faliszewski, Piotr Skowron, Arkadii Slinko, and Nimrod Talmon

2.1 Introduction

There are many reasons why societies run elections. For example, a given society may need to select its leader (e.g., a president), members of a team may need to find an appropriate meeting time, or referees may need to decide which candidate should receive an award in a contest. Each of these settings may call for a different type of election and a different voting rule. For example, Plurality with Runoff is used for presidential elections in France and Poland, Approval is used by Doodle, a popular website for scheduling meetings, and rules very similar to Borda are used to select winners in the Eurovision song contest, in ski-jumping competitions, and in Formula 1 racing. Nonetheless, the general goal of finding a single candidate that is judged as highly as possible by as many people as possible is the same in each of these settings. The differences stem from a tension between the desire to select a candidate judged "as highly as possible" and supported "by as many people as possible" (e.g., in presidential election the focus is on the former requirement and it is considered acceptable that large minorities are dissatisfied with the elected president; in the scheduling example the focus is on the latter and it is perfectly fine to have a meeting time that is not optimal for anyone, provided that a large number of team members can attend). Other differences between the settings can be explained through practical considerations (e.g., choosing a president and choosing an award recipient are similar in spirit, but the latter carries much less weight for the society, is not constrained by laws, and so societies are willing to experiment with more sophisticated voting rules). Nonetheless, a rule that is very good for one of the above settings will likely do well for the others (for example, Laslier and Van der Straeten (2008) have shown the feasibility of using approval voting for presidential elections).

However, there is also another family of elections, where instead of choosing a single best candidate, the goal is to choose a group of candidates, i.e., a committee. Such elections are even more ubiquitous than the single-winner ones, and include parliamentary elections, various business decisions (e.g., an Internet store has to decide which products to show on its homepage), or shortlisting tasks (prior to deciding who should receive an award, typically there is a procedure that finds the finalists). These elections are far more varied than the single-winner ones, and different scenarios may require rules which follow different principles. Indeed, a rule that is good for shortlisting would, likely, select a poorly representative parliament, if a society were to use it for that purpose.

Following Elkind et al. (2017b), we distinguish the following three main types of multiwinner elections:[1]

Excellence-Based Elections. In this case the voters correspond to experts acting as judges, referees, or reviewers. They have their opinions on the quality of the candidates (or on their suitability for the position that candidates have applied for) and the goal is to select the "finalists." The finalists are then evaluated far more accurately (e.g., invited for an interview) and, say, a single one of them is eventually chosen; making this final choice is beyond the scope of excellence-based committee elections. Thus, multiwinner rules that focus on candidate excellence should simply pick the individuals of the highest quality, independently and without regard to any interactions between them. For example, two very similar candidates should either both be selected or should both be rejected (with possible exceptions for boundary cases). Thus excellence-based elections resemble single-winner elections. (Note that we use the term "excellence" to refer to expert evaluation by a particular group of voters, and not to imply that there necessary exists an objectively correct ranking of the candidates.)

Selecting a Diverse Committee. Consider the task of selecting locations for a number of facilities, such as fire stations in a city. Even though a location in the city center minimizes the average driving time to all other points in the city, and thus this is objectively the best location if we were to build just a single fire station, we do not want to build all fire stations in the central area; rather, we would prefer to distribute them more uniformly, so that each point in the city is in a close proximity to some fire station.[2] Similarly, consider an Internet store that has to choose what products to display on its homepage. One of the best strategies is to present a set of options which is as diverse as possible, keeping in mind that each customer should see something appealing to him or her. Selecting a diverse committee is guided by very different principles than excellence-based elections. It is no longer possible to evaluate the candidates separately and, e.g., if there are two similar candidates then we may either select one of them or neither of them (if there are better options), but we should not select them both.

Proportional Representation. Parliamentary elections are perhaps the best known type of multiwinner elections. In this case the goal is to select a

---

[1] Some elements of this classification existed, of course, prior to the work of Elkind et al. (2017b). For example, Barberà and Coelho (2008) considered shortlisting tasks (similar to our excellence-based tasks), and Chamberlin and Courant (1983) and Monroe (1995) (and many others) have considered committees providing optimal proportional representation.

[2] The facility location problem is often studied without regard to multiwinner elections and with somewhat different assumptions (e.g., optimizing locations in Euclidean spaces and not with respect to preferences of potential users). We point the reader to the book of Farahani and Hekmatfar (2009) for a detailed discussion of facility location problems.

committee (say, members of the parliament) in such a way that the views of the society are represented proportionally. Thus the main objective of proportional representation is to find a committee of, say, k representatives, each associated with an equally sized constituency of approximately n/k voters (where n is the total number of voters). Importantly, this constituency may be territorial or virtual (i.e., depending on either geography or preferences). The requirement of constituencies of equal size is the incarnation of 'one man, one vote' principle for representative democracies, but sometimes it precludes electing the most diverse committee possible.

Naturally, there are also other, often more involved, settings where multiwinner elections are useful, but discussing them is beyond the scope of this chapter.

Multiwinner elections lead to a number of challenges, of which we discuss two in this chapter. The first one pertains to the problem of choosing a voting rule for a particular election type. How can we predict if a given rule would provide good results for a given setting? One approach, which we pursue, is to seek axiomatic properties useful for judging the suitability of a multiwinner rule for a particular application, and to analyze different rules with respect to these properties. For instance, we may check whether a rule that is meant for excellence-based elections extends the selected committee (without removing anyone from it) when we increase the target committee size (Elkind et al., 2017b; Barberà and Coelho, 2008), or we may check whether a rule for finding a proportional committee satisfies Dummett's proportionality (Dummett, 1984), the Droop Proportionality Criterion (Woodall, 1994), as well as other similar notions (Elkind et al., 2017b; Aziz et al., 2017a). Other approaches, which we mostly omit due to space restrictions, include considering what various rules do on certain simpler domains, where their behavior can be interpreted intuitively (Elkind et al., 2017a; Brill et al., 2017), and various types of other theoretical and experimental evaluations (Diss and Doghmi, 2016; Caragiannis et al., 2016).

The second challenge regards our ability to compute the results of multiwinner elections. In the single-winner setting, almost all prominent voting rules are polynomial-time computable (although there are important exceptions, such as the rules of Dodgson, Young, and Kemeny (Bartholdi et al., 1989; Hemaspaandra et al., 1997; Rothe et al., 2003; Hemaspaandra et al., 2005)). For the multiwinner setting, the situation is much more complex. There is a number of polynomial-time computable rules, but many interesting ones are NP-hard. There are several ways in which we can deal with this problem. For elections of small enough size, we may be able to compute a winning committee either through FPT winner-determination algorithms (which are efficient when certain parameters, such as the number of voters or the number of candidates, are small), or through fast heuristics.[3] If this approach is infeasible, then we may use (deterministic or randomized) approximation algorithms. Such algorithms can be viewed as new, easy to compute, rules, which even sometimes correspond to previously known

---

[3]Fortunately, "small enough" does not need to mean "impractically small". For example, Elkind et al. (2017a) routinely compute results for several NP-hard rules for elections with 200 candidates and 200 voters each.

voter	ordinal ballot	approval ballot
v_1:	$a \succ b \succ c \succ d \succ e$	$\{a,b,c\}$
v_2:	$e \succ a \succ b \succ d \succ c$	$\{a,e\}$
v_3:	$d \succ a \succ b \succ c \succ e$	$\{d\}$
v_4:	$c \succ b \succ d \succ e \succ a$	$\{b,c,d\}$
v_5:	$c \succ b \succ e \succ a \succ d$	$\{b,c\}$
v_6:	$b \succ c \succ d \succ e \succ a$	$\{b\}$

Table 2.1: Two sample elections for candidate set $A = \{a,b,c,d,e\}$ and 6 voters, one with ordinal ballots and one with approval ballots (the approval ballots are formed by taking the top-ranked candidates from the ordinal ballots, for each voter choosing individually how many candidates to approve).

voting rules. Thus, we study axiomatic properties of the rules defined by such approximation algorithms, just as we do for the original voting rules.

This chapter is organized as follows. First, in Section 2.2, we introduce formal notions regarding the theory of multiwinner elections and discuss three important groups of multiwinner rules: committee scoring rules, approval-based rules, and rules based on the Condorcet principle. In Section 2.3 we discuss rules from these families, as well as some other relevant rules, for our three main tasks: excellence-based elections, selecting a diverse committee, and finding a committee that represents the voters proportionally. We conclude in Section 2.4, where we mention some further challenges regarding multiwinner voting.

2.2 Preliminaries

An election is a pair (A, R), where A is a set of candidates and R is a profile of the voters' preferences. In the ordinal model, R consists of linear orders $\succ_v$, one for each voter v (order $\succ_v$ ranks all the candidates and is often referred to as the preference order or the ordinal ballot of voter v). In the approval (or dichotomous) model, the profile contains, for each voter v, the set A_v of those candidates that this voter approves of (often referred to as the approval ballot of this voter). We show an example of both types of elections in Table 2.1.

A single-winner voting rule is a function that, given an election (A, R), returns a set of candidates that tie as winners. For example, the Plurality rule selects those candidates that are ranked first by the largest number of voters (formally, we assume the voters have ordinal preferences; in practice, each voter provides its top candidate only). Analogously, a multiwinner voting rule is a function f that, given an election (A, R) and a positive integer k, $1 \leqslant k \leqslant |A|$, returns a nonempty family of size-k subsets of A, referred to as the winning committees. In practice, there always is some tie-breaking scheme that selects a single winning committee, but for simplicity we will disregard this issue. Unless specified otherwise, we assume the parallel-universe tie-breaking model (Conitzer et al., 2009), where a voting rule outputs all the committees that could end up winning for some way of resolving ties that occur while executing the rule. If a rule always selects a single committee (e.g., because it is already combined with some tie-breaking scheme), then we say that it is resolute.

One of the most famous examples of multiwinner voting rules is the single transferable vote rule (STV) for ordinal elections, defined next.

Single Transferable Vote (STV) Rule. Consider an election with m candidates, n voters, and with the target committee size k. STV proceeds in rounds, until k candidates are elected. A single round proceeds as follows: We check if there is a candidate ranked first by at least $q = \lfloor \frac{n}{k+1} \rfloor + 1$ voters. If so, then such a candidate is included in the winning committee, q voters that rank him or her first are removed from the election, and he or she is removed from all the remaining preference orders. If such a candidate does not exist, then a candidate that is ranked first by the smallest number of voters is removed. (Note that this description strongly relies on parallel-universe tie-breaking).

Example 2.1. *Consider the ordinal election from Table 2.1 with the target committee size $k = 2$. STV uses the quota value $q = \lfloor \frac{6}{3} \rfloor + 1 = 3$. No candidate is ranked first by at least three voters so in the first round STV removes one candidate from $\{a, b, d, e\}$ (each of whom is ranked first only once, whereas c is ranked first twice). If we remove a, then in the next round still no candidate is ranked first by at least three voters and we need to remove either d or e. Say that we remove d. Then, in the next round b is ranked first by three voters (v_1, v_3, and v_6), so we add b to the committee, remove b from the election, and remove these three voters. In the next two rounds we first remove e from the election and then add c to the committee. Thus $\{b, c\}$ is among the winning committees for this election under STV.*

In what follows, we describe several families of multiwinner rules, starting with multiwinner analogues of single-winner scoring rules, through rules for approval elections, to rules based on the Condorcet principle. For a positive integer t, we write $[t]$ to denote the set $\{1, \ldots, t\}$.

2.2.1 Committee Scoring Rules

Let us consider a setting with a set A of m candidates and with ordinal ballots. For a preference order $\succ$ and candidate c, we write $\text{pos}_\succ(c)$ to denote the position of c in $\succ$ (the candidate ranked first has position 1, the candidate ranked last has position m). A single-winner scoring function γ_m, $\gamma_m \colon [m] \to \mathbb{R}$, is a function that associates each position in a vote with a number of points, such that if $i < j$ then $\gamma_m(i) \geqslant \gamma_m(j)$. The two best-known examples of single-winner scoring functions are the Borda scoring function, $\beta_m(i) = m - i$, and the t-Approval family of scoring functions (where t is a positive integer; 1-Approval is known as Plurality):

$$\alpha_t(i) = \begin{cases} 1 & \text{if } i \leqslant t, \\ 0 & \text{otherwise.} \end{cases}$$

A family $\gamma = (\gamma_m)_{m \in \mathbb{N}}$ of single-winner scoring functions defines a rule f_γ as follows. The score of candidate c in an election $E = (A, R)$, where $R = (\succ_1, \ldots, \succ_n)$, is $\text{score}(c, E) = \sum_{i=1}^{n} \gamma_{|A|}(\text{pos}_{\succ_i}(c))$. The rule selects the candidate(s) with the highest score (for example, the Borda rule uses the scoring functions β_m while the

t-Approval rule uses α_t). Committee scoring rules are defined analogously, but for an extended notion of *position*.

Let S be a size-k committee and let $\succ$ be a preference order. By the *position* of S in $\succ$, denoted $\text{pos}_\succ(S)$, we mean the sequence of positions of the members of S sorted in an increasing order; we write $[m]_k$ to denote the set of all size-k increasing sequences of elements from $[m]$. For two committee positions $I = (i_1, \ldots, i_k)$ and $J = (j_1, \ldots, j_k)$ from $[m]_k$, we say that I dominates J (denoted $I \succ J$) if for each t we have that $i_t \leq j_t$.

Elkind et al. (2017b) defined committee scoring rules as follows. A *committee scoring function* $\gamma_{m,k}: [m]_k \to \mathbb{R}$ for m candidates and committee size k, is a function that associates each committee position with a score in such a way that if $I, J \in [m]_k$ are two committee positions such that $I \succ J$, then $\gamma_{m,k}(I) \geq \gamma_{m,k}(J)$.

Definition 2.1 (Elkind et al., 2017b). *Let $\gamma = (\gamma_{m,k})_{k \leq m}$ be a family of committee scoring functions (one for each number m of candidates and committee size k). A committee scoring rule f_γ is a multiwinner rule that for election $E = (A, R)$, with $R = (\succ_1, \ldots, \succ_n)$, and committee size k outputs those committees W for which* $\text{score}(W, E) = \sum_{i=1}^{n} \gamma_{|A|,k}(\text{pos}_{\succ_i}(W))$ *is the highest.*

Many well-known multiwinner rules are, in fact, committee scoring rules:

Single Non-Transferable Vote (SNTV). Under SNTV, a committee receives a point from a voter if this committee contains the voters' most preferred candidate. That is, SNTV uses the scoring functions $\gamma_{m,k}^{\text{SNTV}}(i_1, \ldots, i_k) = \alpha_1(i_1)$.

Bloc. Under Bloc, each voter names his or her k favorite candidates and the winning committee consists of those mentioned most frequently. In other words, Bloc uses the scoring functions $\gamma_{m,k}^{\text{Bloc}}(i_1, \ldots, i_k) = \sum_{t=1}^{k} \alpha_k(i_t)$.

k-Borda. k-Borda outputs committee(s) that consist of k candidates with the highest (individual) Borda scores. That is, k-Borda uses the scoring functions $\gamma_{m,k}^{k\text{-Borda}}(i_1, \ldots, i_k) = \sum_{t=1}^{k} \beta_m(i_t)$.

Chamberlin–Courant (β-CC). The Chamberlin–Courant rule (β-CC) uses the scoring functions $\gamma_{m,k}^{\beta\text{-CC}}(i_1, \ldots, i_k) = \beta_m(i_1)$. This means that the score that a committee receives from a voter is the Borda score of the committee member that the voter ranks highest (among all the committee members). One possible interpretation is that each voter chooses a representative from the committee (clearly, a voter chooses the candidate that he or she likes the most) and gives the committee the Borda score of his or her representative. The rule was introduced by Chamberlin and Courant (1983).

Example 2.2. *Let us again consider the ordinal election from Table 2.1. Under SNTV, every winning committee contains the candidate c and one other candidate. Under Bloc, the two winning committees are $\{a, b\}$ and $\{b, c\}$. Under k-Borda, the winning committee is $\{b, c\}$. The winning committee under β-CC is $\{a, c\}$, with a representing the voters v_1, v_2, v_3 and c representing the voters v_4, v_5, v_6 (it is a coincidence that each candidate represents the same number of voters).*

Naturally, there are many other interesting committee scoring rules. For an overview of the internal structure of such rules we point the reader to the works of Faliszewski et al. (2016a,b); axiomatic characterization of these rules is due to Skowron et al. (2016b).

2.2.2 Approval-Based Rules

Let us now consider the approval model of elections. For the single-winner case, the approval rule simply selects those candidates that are approved by the largest number of voters. For the multiwinner setting, Aziz et al. (2017a) defined the following class of rules (which generalizes many previously studied ones; see the overview of Kilgour (2010) for more details regarding approval-based multiwinner rules, and the work of Aziz et al. (2015) for a computational perspective). Let A be a set of m candidates, let k be the committee size, and let $w^{(k)} = (w_1^{(k)}, \ldots, w_k^{(k)})$ be a vector of k real numbers. The $w^{(k)}$-AV score that a voter with approval ballot A_i assigns to a committee S is $\sum_{j=1}^{|S \cap A_i|} w_j^{(k)}$.

Definition 2.2 (Thiele, 1895; Kilgour, 2010). *Let $w = (w^{(i)})_{i \in \mathbb{N}}$ be a sequence of real-valued vectors (where each w^i has i coordinates). Given an election (A, R) and a committee size k, the w-AV rule outputs those committees for which the sum of the $w^{(k)}$-AV scores assigned by the voters is the highest.*

Quite amazingly, these rules were first defined and studied at the end of the nineteenth century by Thiele (1895), thus we refer to them as Thiele methods. Examples of Thiele methods include the following rules.

Approval Voting (AV). AV uses vectors $w^{(k)}$ of the form $(1, \ldots, 1)$. That is, AV outputs committees of those k candidates that are approved most frequently.

Approval-Based Chamberlin–Courant rule (α-CC). Under the α-CC rule we use vectors of the form $(1, 0, \ldots, 0)$. As in the case of the ordinal-based Chamberlin–Courant rule (β-CC), a possible interpretation is that each voter chooses a representative from the committee and, thus, increases the score of the committee by one if there is at least one committee member that this voter approves.

Proportional Approval Voting (PAV). The PAV rule uses vectors of the form $(1, 1/2, 1/3, \ldots, 1/k)$. This rule satisfies strong axioms pertaining to the proportionality of election results. We discuss this in more detail in Section 2.3.3.

Example 2.3. *Let us consider the approval election from Table 2.1. The AV rule selects the committee $\{b, c\}$ (b is approved four times, c is approved three times, each other candidate is approved at most twice). The winning committee under α-CC is $\{a, b\}$ (with score five, where only v_3 does not approve any committee member), and the winning committees under PAV are $\{a, b\}$, $\{b, c\}$, and $\{b, d\}$, each obtaining 5.5 points (e.g., $\{a, b\}$ receives 1.5 points from v_1 and one point from each of the other voters except v_3, who assigns zero points to this committee).*

There is a relation between Thiele methods and committee scoring rules (for the ordinal election model). For example, given a preference order and a commitee size k, we might say that a voter approves his or her top k candidates. Then, a w-AV rule generates the following family of committee scoring functions,

$$\gamma_k^{w\text{-AV}}(i_1, \ldots, i_k) = w_1 \alpha_k(i_1) + w_2 \alpha_k(i_2) + \cdots + w_k \alpha_k(i_k),$$

and, thus, the corresponding committee scoring rule. For example, AV generates the Bloc rule. The choice of the approval threshold, k in this case, is quite arbitrary, but Faliszewski et al. (2016b) suggest reasons why it is natural: they refer to these committee scoring rules as top-k-counting rules and argue that only rules of this form can have certain axiomatic properties.

There are many multiwinner rules for the approval setting that are based on other principles than the Thiele methods. While the discussion of those is beyond the scope of this chapter, we do mention the Minimax approval voting rule (Brams et al., 2007), which, together with its generalizations (Amanatidis et al., 2015), received substantial attention from the research community.

2.2.3 Condorcet Committees and Related Rules

One of the most important notions regarding single-winner elections (in the ordinal model) is that of a Condorcet winner. A candidate c is a Condorcet winner if, for every other candidate d, a majority of the voters prefer c to d. A single-winner rule is Condorcet-consistent if it selects the Condorcet winner whenever one exists. Two prominent examples of Condorcet-consistent rules include the Copeland rule and the Maximin rule, defined next.

Consider an election $E = (A, R)$. For each two candidates c and d, we define $N_E(c, d)$ to be the number of voters that prefer c to d. The Copeland score of candidate c is the number of candidates d such that $N_E(c, d) > N_E(d, c)$ (i.e., the number of candidates that c defeats in a head-to-head majority contest[4]), whereas the Maximin score of c is defined as $\min_{d \in A \setminus \{c\}} N_E(c, d)$. The Copeland rule selects the candidates with the highest Copeland score and the Maximin rule selects those with the highest Maximin score.

The notion of the Condorcet winner was adapted to the multiwinner setting by Fishburn (1981a,b) as follows: A committee C is a Condorcet committee if for every other committee D (of the same size) a majority of voters prefers C to D. However, for this definition to be meaningful one has to either assume that the voters have explicit preferences over the committees, or that there is an accepted mechanism for lifting preferences over candidates to those over committees. For example, Fishburn considered the latter possibility for approval elections (he assumed that a voter prefers committee C over committee D if it contains more approved candidates). Recently, Darmann (2013) considered Condorcet committees for ordinal elections, where voters use Borda scores to compare committees (i.e., a voter prefers committee C to committee D if the sum of the Borda scores that the voter assigns to the members of C is greater than that of the members

---

[4]If it happens that for some two candidates c and d we have $N_E(c, d) = N_E(d, c)$ then, typically, each of them receives some $\alpha \in [0, 1]$ points. Values 0, 0.5, and 1 are the most typical ones.

of D). Darmann (2013) showed computational hardness of deciding whether a given set is a Condorcet committee (both for the approval and ordinal settings; in fact, under some preference extensions even computing a Pareto optimal committee may be hard (Aziz et al., 2016)).

Gehrlein (1985) and Ratliff (2003) provided another interpretation of Condorcet consistency for the case of multiwinner elections, based directly on the preferences over the candidates (Kaymak and Sanver (2003) showed that their notion can be understood in terms of Fishburn's Condorcet committees as well).

Definition 2.3 (Gehrlein, 1985; Ratliff, 2003). *Let (A, R) be an election, let k be a committee size, and let S be some committee of size k. We say that S is a (weak) Condorcet set if for every candidate c in S and every candidate d in $A \setminus S$ it holds that more than half (at least half) of the voters prefer c to d.*

Following Barberà and Coelho (2008), we say that a multiwinner rule is stable if it outputs a weak Condorcet set of a given size k whenever such a set exists. For example, Coelho (2004) proposed the following weakly stable rules.

Number of External Defeats (NED). Under the NED rule, the score of a committee S is the number of pairs (c, d) of candidates such that $c \in S$, $d \in A \setminus S$, and at least half of the voters prefer c to d. The committee(s) with the highest score are the winners.

Minimum Size of External Opposition (SEO). Under the SEO rule, the score of a committee S in an election $E = (A, R)$ is defined as $\min_{c \in S, d \in A \setminus S} N_E(c, d)$ (i.e., the score of a committee S is the smallest number of voters that prefer some committee member to a committee nonmember). The committee(s) with the highest score are the winners.

These rules are natural analogues of the Copeland and Maximin rules (for a particular way of handling the cases where $N_E(c, d) = N_E(d, c)$ under the Copeland rule). Other single-winner Condorcet-consistent rules were adapted to the multiwinner setting by Ratliff (2003) and Kamwa (2017).

Example 2.4. *In the (ordinal) election from Table 2.1, the committee $\{b, c\}$ is a weak Condorcet set of size two. Indeed, exactly half of the voters prefer b to a, half of the voters prefer c to a, and strict majorities of the voters prefer each of b and c to each of d and e. In fact, $\{b, c\}$ is the unique weak Condorcet set of size two for this election and, so, is the unique winning committee under both NED and SEO.*

A completely different idea for extending the notion of a Condorcet winner to the multiwinner setting was introduced by Elkind et al. (2015). Briefly put, they said that committee S is a θ-winning set if for every candidate d not in S, more than a θ-fraction of the voters prefer some member of S to d; they refer to $1/2$-winning sets as Condorcet winning sets. Unfortunately, Condorcet winning sets cannot be easily interpreted as Condorcet committees in the sense of Fishburn (specifically, Elkind et al. considered several standard means of extending preferences over candidates to preferences over committees and under neither of them Condorcet winning sets turned out to be Fishburn's Condorcet committees). Nonetheless, the notion of a θ-winning set leads to an interesting multiwinner rule: Elkind et al. propose to output those committees S (of a given committee size k) that are θ-winning sets for the largest value of θ. For $k = 1$ this rule degenerates to the Maximin rule.

Example 2.5. *Under the rule of Elkind et al. (2015), the unique size-two winning committee for the (ordinal) election from Table 2.1 is $\{a, c\}$. For each candidate x from the set $\{b, d, e\}$, exactly five voters prefer either a or b to x; e.g., v_1, v_2 and v_3 prefer a to b, v_4 and v_5 prefer c to b, and only v_6 prefers b to both a and c.*

2.3 Three Main Types of Multiwinner Elections

We now discuss the three main types of multiwinner elections mentioned in the introduction. For each of them, we consider formal properties that multiwinner rules for these elections should satisfy, mention rules that do satisfy these properties (and sometimes those that fail them), and discuss the computational complexity of identifying the winning committees under these rules.

2.3.1 Excellence-Based Elections

Excellence-based rules (also called screening rules by Barberà and Coelho (2008)) are those multiwinner rules that can be thought of as preliminary selection of candidates for the subsequent ultimate choice of, say, a single candidate; since only one candidate will be ultimately selected, it must be the 'best' one and any dependencies or similarities between candidates should not matter.[5] It is implicitly assumed that the final choice can be made by other voters and will be based on other principles so any candidate from the selection can be ultimately chosen. Thus the main normative principle which any excellence-based rule should satisfy is *committee monotonicity* (or *enlargement consistency* (Barberà and Coelho, 2008)). For simplicity, throughout this section we assume that our voting rules are resolute, i.e., that $f(E, k)$ is a singleton for each E and k.

Definition 2.4 (Elkind et al., 2017b; Barberà and Coelho, 2008). *Let f be a multiwinner voting rule. It is said to be* committee monotone *if for any election $E = (A, R)$ and any size of the target committee $k < |A|$ we have $f(E, k) \subset f(E, k+1)$.*

The idea is that if a candidate was good enough to be included in the list of k best ones, then it should be good enough to be included in the list of $k + 1$ best ones. For some rules committee monotonicity follows from their definition as for the following rule.

Sequential Plurality (Barberà and Coelho, 2008). We proceed in rounds. The first selected candidate is the Plurality winner (i.e., the candidate ranked

---

[5]Excellence-based elections are closely connected to shortlisting tasks, but some shortlisting scenarios are more complicated. For example, when shortlisting a group of people considered for a job, it may be necessary to maintain a certain level of diversity of the committee, to ensure that minorities are not discriminated against. In this chapter we do not consider this requirement: If such diversity is necessary, one should seek voting rules that strike a balance between candidate excellence and committee diversity.

first by the largest number of voters). Then this candidate is removed and the procedure is repeated. This is done k times.

Each committee monotone rule f produces a ranking of the candidates. Let us consider some election $E = (A, R)$ and take the convention that $f(E, 0) = \emptyset$. If for each k we let $\{a_k\} = f(E, k) \setminus f(E, k-1)$, then we obtain the ranking $a_1 \geq a_2 \geq \cdots \geq a_m$. In other words, a committee monotone rule f generates a social welfare function F which, given an election E, produces the ranking $F(E)$ constructed above. Moreover, $f(E, k)$ is the set of top k elements of $F(E)$ (relative to some tie-breaking mechanism). Analogously, if F is a social welfare function and E is an election, then we can define a multiwinner voting rule f by setting $f(E, k)$ to be the top k candidates of $F(E)$ (relative to some fixed tie-breaking rule). Elkind et al. (2017b) refer to such rules as *best-k rules*. Some examples follow.

Best-k rules for positional scoring SWFs. Let $\gamma = (\gamma_m)_{m \in \mathbb{N}}$ be a single-winner scoring function. The social welfare function associated with γ ranks the candidates (in a given election) according to their γ scores. For example, k-Borda is a best-k rule from this family.

Best-k rules based on non-positional scoring SWFs. Sometimes scores of candidates come from other sources. For example, a social welfare function can output a ranking of candidates according to their Maximin scores. This leads to a best-k rule that we call k-Maximin.

Best-k rules based on the majority relation. Suppose for simplicity that n is odd and, given an election $E = (A, R)$ with $R = (\succ_1, \ldots, \succ_n)$, define the majority relation $\succ_E$ as:

$$a \succ_E b \iff |\{i \in [n] \mid a \succ_i b\}| > |\{i \in [n] \mid b \succ_i a\}|.$$

Notice that this majority relation is a tournament. We can now define the score of a candidate c as the outdegree of c (considered as a vertex in this tournament). This score is, in fact, the Copeland score of c and, so, we refer to the corresponding best-k rule as k-Copeland.

Barberà and Coelho (2008) noticed that no committee monotone (excellence-based) rule can be stable (see Section 2.2.3); to this end, they presented a simple profile which possesses a unique Condorcet set with two elements and a disjoint unique Condorcet set with three elements. This is disappointing because an unstable excellence-based rule can produce a committee that contains some candidate c such that a majority of the voters prefers to it another candidate d who is not in the committee. Another consequence of this result is that the NED rule is different from k-Copeland and the SEO rule is different from k-Maximin. Indeed, the former two rules are NP-hard to compute (as all stable rules (Aziz et al., 2017b)), whereas the latter two are polynomial-time computable.

On the other hand, Elkind et al. (2017b) identified a subclass of committee scoring rules that are committee monotone.

Definition 2.5 (Elkind et al., 2017b). *A committee scoring rule f is* separable *if there exists a family of committee scoring functions $\gamma = (\gamma_{m,k})_{k \leqslant m}$ and a family of* single-winner scoring functions $\delta = (\delta_m)_{m \in \mathbb{N}}$ such that $f = f_\gamma$ and for each m, k ($k \leqslant m$), and a committee position $I = (i_1, \ldots, i_k) \in [m]_k$ we have that

$$\gamma_{m,k}(i_1, \ldots, i_k) = \delta^m(i_1) + \ldots + \delta^m(i_k).$$

For example, k-Borda is a separable committee scoring rule, whereas Bloc is not (while at first it seems to be defined in an appropriate way, the single-winner scoring functions used in its definition depend on k and this is not allowed in separable committee scoring rules). In particular, Bloc is not committee monotone (Staring, 1986).

Theorem 2.1 (Elkind et al., 2017b). *Every separable committee scoring rule is committee monotone.*

It also holds that every separable committee scoring rule is polynomial-time computable, provided that its underlying single-winner scoring functions are.

2.3.2 Selecting a Diverse Committee

In the introduction we provided examples of settings where a diverse committee is a desirable outcome of a voting rule. Throughout this section we will focus on yet another one, due to Elkind et al. (2017b),[6] considering an airline which designs the content of its in-flight entertainment system for the airplanes. There are numerous movies, TV programs, and sports competitions to choose from and, due to technical and financial reasons, only a small selection can be chosen. The airline would like to maximize the satisfaction of the passengers and, thus, a diversity among the selected entertainment items is highly desirable.

Specifically, we assume that each passenger chooses a single movie[7] (the one that he or she likes best among the available ones).[8] If every passenger has only a single favorite movie and does not wish to watch anything else (as might be the case for a group of small children), then it is natural for the airline to use the SNTV rule. This way, the largest number of passengers will get their favorite movie (while the rest will be left dissatisfied). On the other hand, if each passenger has a set of good movies and is satisfied if at least one of these movies is available, then it is natural to model the problem as an approval election and to use the α-CC rule. Finally, if every passenger has a ranking of the movies and the appreciation that a passenger has for a movie decreases linearly as its position in the ranking grows,[9] then β-CC is our rule of choice.

The above rules are either committee scoring rules (SNTV and β-CC) or can be interpreted as such (recall the discussion below Example 2.3). Elkind et al.

---

[6] Originally presented in the conference version of their paper.

[7] For simplicity, we speak only of movies, omitting other types of entertainment.

[8] It would also be quite natural to assume that every passenger chooses two best movies, or that he or she watches the best movie with some high probability, the second best with a lower probability, the third best with even lower one, and so on. Skowron et al. (2016a) study such settings and identify an interesting class of rules based on ordered weighted average (OWA) operators (these rules can also be interpreted as committee scoring rules).

[9] This is a very idealized assumption. In practice, no passenger can possibly have an opinion about all movies.

(2017b) refer to committee scoring rules where the score depends only on the position of the most preferred candidate as *representation-focused* rules.

Definition 2.6 (Elkind et al., 2017b). *A committee scoring rule f is representation-focused if there exists a family of committee scoring functions $\gamma = (\gamma_{m,k})_{k \leqslant m}$ and a family of single-winner scoring function $\delta = (\delta_{m,k})_{k \leqslant m}$ such that $f = f_\gamma$ and for each m, k ($k \leqslant m$), and a committee position $I = (i_1, \ldots, i_k) \in [m]_k$ we have $\gamma_{m,k}(i_1, \ldots, i_k) = \delta_{m,k}(i_1)$.*

Let us now consider which axiomatic properties should be satisfied by rules that are appropriate for selecting diverse committees (we focus on the ordinal setting). Somewhat surprisingly, the literature does not offer many choices. Firstly, such a rule must satisfy the following criterion which is a straightforward adaptation of the notion of a *consensus committee* of Elkind et al. (2017b).

Definition 2.7. *A voting rule f satisfies the* narrow-top *criterion if for each election $E = (A, R)$ and each positive integer $k \leq |A|$ the following holds: if there exists a committee W of size k such that each voter ranks some member of W on top, then $W \in f(E, k)$.*

Secondly, the following condition requires that if a rule selects some committee W then this committee should still win if any voter shifts his or her most preferred member of W forward.

Definition 2.8 (Faliszewski et al., 2016a). *We say that a voting rule f is* top-member monotone *if for every election E, positive integer k, committee $W \in f(E, k)$, and election E' obtained from E by shifting forward in some vote the top ranked member of W, it holds that $W \in f(E', k)$.*

All representation-focused committee scoring rules satisfy the narrow-top criterion and are top-member monotone (Faliszewski et al., 2016a).

Unfortunately, among the three rules that we discussed here only SNTV is polynomial-time computable (and this rule suffers from being dependant on each voter's first choice only). As for the other rules, Procaccia et al. (2008) showed that both α-CC and β-CC are NP-hard to compute. On the other hand, Betzler et al. (2013) used the framework of parameterized complexity to show that winner determination for these rules can be solved efficiently for elections with few voters or with few alternatives. They also showed that these rules are polynomial-time computable for single-peaked elections, whereas Skowron et al. (2015b) have shown the same for single-crossing elections.

There are approximation algorithms which efficiently find committees whose score is close to the optimal one. For example, the greedy algorithm of Lu and Boutilier (2011) executes k greedy iterations, in each selecting a candidate whose inclusion brings the greatest marginal increase to the total committee score; this algorithm achieves approximation ratio of $1 - 1/e$ (this holds for both α-CC and β-CC; unless P = NP, this is the best possible polynomial-time approximation for α-CC (Skowron and Faliszewski, 2015)). Skowron et al. (2015a) describe several other approximation algorithms for β-CC, all of which are somewhat based on the greedy approach, that achieve better approximation guarantees in certain situations, including a polynomial-time approximation scheme (PTAS). Skowron and Faliszewski (2015) give an FPT approximation scheme for α-CC (parameterized by the committee size). While using approximation algorithms for computing outcomes of voting rules in political elections may be controversial (but see the discussion of Faliszewski et al. (2016c)), in any business-related application of voting rules the use of approximation algorithms is fully justified.

In practice, for up to medium-sized elections, finding a winning committee under α-CC and β-CC can be done by solving a certain integer linear program (ILP), as described by Lu and Boutilier (2011). Currently the best heuristic solution is to use a clustering algorithm by Faliszewski et al. (2016c).

2.3.3 Proportional Representation

Black (1958) defines proportionality of a voting rule as the ability to reflect "all shades of political opinion" of a society within the winning committee. Commonly, parliaments—or any other committees that are meant to represent voters proportionally—are elected using the first-past-the-post (FPTP) voting system, where the voters and candidates are divided into electoral districts, and a representative of each district is elected via Plurality voting. This is practical because typically it is easier for voters to compare candidates from their districts only, but it might lead to large disproportionality. For example, if there are two main opposing political views, X and Y, and 49% of the voters in each district support view X while 51% support view Y, then each district elects a Y supporter, and nearly half of the population is not represented.

Under SNTV each voter also votes for a single person, but the voters are not divided into electoral districts. If a committee of size k is to be elected, then the k candidates with the best plurality scores form it. Both under FPTP and SNTV the voters only reveal their top-preferred candidates, yet, often the preferences of the voters are much more complex and they are rarely apathetic about the candidates different from their top choice. Thus, it is natural and important to study forms of proportionality which take into account full preferences of the voters; this idea is often referred to as *fully proportional representation*. Dummett (1984) was among the first to initiate such a study for the case of ordinal preferences, formulating the following axiom.

Definition 2.9 (Dummett, 1984). *Consider a setting with n voters, where we want to select a committee of size k. If there exists some $\ell \in [k]$ and a group of $\ell \cdot n/k$ voters who all rank the same ℓ candidates on top of their preference orders, then these ℓ candidates should all belong to all the winning committees.*

For $\ell = 1$, Elkind et al. (2017b) refer to this property as the *solid coalitions* property and show that both STV and SNTV, among others, satisfy it. There is also a variant of Dummett's proportionality which uses the Droop quota (i.e., $\lfloor n/k+1 \rfloor + 1$) instead of the value n/k (Woodall, 1994). A variant of the STV rule which is used, e.g., for electing the Australian senate satisfies this version of Dummett's proportionality. Indeed, STV is often considered to be very well-suited for tasks that require proportional representation (Tideman and Richardson, 2000; Elkind et al., 2017b,a).

Monroe (1995) suggested another interesting rule that takes full ordinal ballots as input and aims at achieving proportional representation.

Monroe. Consider an election $E = (A, R)$, with $R = (\succ_1, \ldots, \succ_n)$, and let k be the size of committee to be elected. For a committee S, an *assignment* is a function $\Phi\colon [n] \to S$ that maps voters to committee members. We interpret $\Phi(i)$ as the member of S that represents voter i (under the assignment Φ). We say that Φ is *balanced* if for each $c \in S$ we have $\lfloor n/k \rfloor \leqslant |\Phi^{-1}(c)| \leqslant \lceil n/k \rceil$. We define the score of assignment Φ as $\mathrm{score}(\Phi) = \sum_{i=1}^n \beta(\mathrm{pos}_{\succ_i}(\Phi(i)))$, i.e., as the total Borda score of the voters' representatives. The score of a committee S is the score of the best balanced assignment of voters to the members of S. The Monroe rule selects the committee(s) with the highest score.

Monroe's rule resembles the Chamberlin and Courant rule, which also implicitly defines an assignment of voters to their representatives in a winning committee, and both are based on the concept of satisfaction which both rules maximize. However, Monroe's rule additionally requires that each committee member represents roughly the same number of voters. This makes a meaningful difference—the Monroe's rule is proportional while the Chamberlin–Courant's is not. Unfortunately, finding winners according to the Monroe rule is computationally hard (Procaccia et al., 2008), even when certain natural parameters of the election are small (Betzler et al., 2013) or when preferences of the voters are single-crossing (Skowron et al., 2015b) (hardness for single-peaked elections is known only for a more general variant of the rule (Betzler et al., 2013)). Yet, recently, Skowron et al. (2015a) proposed a greedy variant of this rule:

Greedy Monroe (Skowron et al., 2015a). The rule executes k iterations as follows. In iteration i, we find a group V_i of n/k voters and a candidate c for which the total Borda score that the voters from V_i assign to c is maximal. Then, we add c to the winning committee, assigns c as a representative to the voters from V_i, and remove these voters from further consideration.

The Greedy Monroe rule can be viewed as an approximation algorithm for the original rule, but it also exhibits some new interesting properties. For example, it satisfies the solid coalitions property, whereas the original Monroe rule does not (Elkind et al., 2017b).

To conclude the discussion of proportional representation in the ordinal election model, let us recall that Elkind et al. (2015) introduced the concept of θ-winning sets (see Section 2.2.3 for the definition) which combines the ideas behind proportional representation and the Condorcet principle.

Now, let us move to the rules which take approval ballots as input. We start by considering the following illustrative example.

Example 2.6. *Consider an approval election where the set of 30 standing candidates can be split into three disjoint sets, C_1, C_2, and C_3 of equal size, such that 50 voters approve all candidates in C_1, 30 voters—all candidates in C_2, and 20 voters—all candidates in C_3. If our goal is to select a committee of size $k = 10$, then we would expect any proportional rule to choose 5 candidates from C_1, 3 candidates from C_2, and 2 candidates from C_3.*

Of course, usually we cannot hope for such a nice structure of the voters' preferences, but Example 2.6 is helpful in understanding the behavior of approval-based voting rules. Let us consider RAV, the greedy variant of the PAV rule:

Reweighted Approval Voting (RAV). Consider an election with n voters, where the i-th voter approves candidates in the set A_i. RAV starts with an empty committee S and executes k rounds. In each round it adds to S a candidate c with the maximal value of $\sum_{i:\ c \in A_i} \frac{1}{|S \cap A_i|+1}$, i.e., a candidate c which maximizes the PAV score of $S \cup \{c\}$.

Let us discuss how RAV works for the election from Example 2.6. Before the first round S is empty, so adding a candidate from C_1 to S would increase the total PAV score of S by 50; adding a candidate from C_2 and C_3 would increase the total score by 30 and 20, respectively. Thus, in the first round a candidate from C_1 is selected. The following rounds proceed analogously. Eventually, after 7 rounds, S contains 4 candidates from C_1, 2 candidates from C_2 and 1 candidate from C_3. In the eighth step, 50 voters have already 4 representatives so adding a candidate from C_1 to S (which would become their fifth approved candidate) would increase the PAV score of each of them by $1/5$, increasing the total score by 10. Similarly, adding a candidate from C_2 or from C_3 to S would also increase the total score of S by 10. We see that in the next three steps RAV selects one candidate from each of the sets C_1, C_2, and C_3, forming a proportional committee.

Interestingly, the harmonic sequence of weights $w^{(k)} = (1, 1/2, \ldots, 1/k)$ is the unique sequence which results in proportionality on such nicely structured preferences as in Example 2.6. This was formalized by Aziz et al. (2017a) and Brill et al. (2017). In particular, Aziz et al. (2017a) defined two properties, called justified representation and extended justified representation, defined next.

Definition 2.10 (Aziz et al., 2017a). *A rule satisfies* extended justified representation *(EJR) if for each approval election with n voters, each committee size k, and each $\ell \in [k]$, the following holds: There is no group of $\lceil \ell \cdot n/k \rceil$ voters that all approve at least ℓ common candidates, but neither of whom approves ℓ or more members of each winning committee. A rule satisfies* justified representation *(JR) if it satisfies EJR for $\ell = 1$.*

Intuitively, justified representation requires that, if there is a group of at least n/k voters whose approval ballots have at least one candidate in common, then it cannot be the case that neither of these voters is represented in the committee. EJR extends this reasoning to larger groups of voters and larger sets of jointly approved candidates. Aziz et al. (2017a) showed that PAV is the only w-AV rule which satisfies EJR. Brill et al. (2017), on the other hand, discussed a relation between multiwinner voting rules and methods of apportionment, which allows to view PAV and RAV as extensions of the d'Hondt method of apportionment to the multiwinner setting (see Chapter 3 of this book for more details on seat allocations). Similarly, the Monroe rule can be adapted to work on approval ballots—such variant of the Monroe rule can be viewed as a generalization of the Hamilton method. Unfortunately, finding winners according to PAV is NP-hard (Aziz et al., 2015; Skowron et al., 2016a). Yet, RAV can be viewed as a good approximation algorithm for PAV (Skowron et al., 2016a) which can be even better approximated when certain natural parameters are low (Skowron, 2016).

So far, we only referred to "linear proportionality". There exist other interesting concepts, such as degressive proportionality (Koriyama et al., 2013) which says that smaller groups of voters should be given more representatives than the traditional proportionality suggests. Thus, degressive proportionality recommends taking a step from traditional proportionality towards diversity. Also, we only discussed proportionality with respect to voters' preferences. Other forms of proportional representation can be considered as well—for instance, where different candidates have different attributes (e.g., gender, age, nationality, affiliation), and where our goal is to select a representative committee with respect to each of the attributes (Lang and Skowron, 2016).

2.4 Further Challenges

We discussed axiomatic and algorithmic properties of various multiwinner rules for our three main tasks. Yet, these are not the only challenges regarding electing committees. For instance, many voting rules require full preference rankings provided by voters, and with a large number of candidates obtaining such information might be infeasible. It is thus natural to study multiwinner voting for the case where only partial preference information is available. Other challenges include the problem of convincing societies to adopt new rules, the problem of modeling political parties (Brill et al., 2017 provide some very initial studies in this respect), the problem of presenting the election results (it is easy to tell who won, but candidates may wish to know how well they did even if they lost), and many others. These are very important and we believe that addressing them will at least partially shape future studies of multiwinner voting.

Acknowledgments

Piotr Faliszewski was supported by the National Science Centre, Poland, under project 2016/21/B/ST6/01509. Piotr Skowron was supported by ERC-StG 639945 (ACCORD) and by a Humboldt Research Fellowship for Postdoctoral Researchers. Arkadii Slinko was supported by the Royal Society of NZ Marsden Fund 3706352.

Bibliography

G. Amanatidis, N. Barrot, J. Lang, E. Markakis, and B. Ries. Multiple referenda and multiwinner elections using Hamming distances: Complexity and manipulability. In *Proceedings of the 14th International Conference on Autonomous Agents and Multiagent Systems (AAMAS)*, pages 715–723, 2015.

H. Aziz, S. Gaspers, J. Gudmundsson, S. Mackenzie, N. Mattei, and T. Walsh. Computational aspects of multi-winner approval voting. In *Proceedings of the*

14th International Conference on Autonomous Agents and Multiagent Systems (AAMAS), pages 107–115, 2015.

H. Aziz, J. Lang, and J. Monnot. Computing Pareto optimal committees. In *Proceedings of the 25th International Joint Conference on Artificial Intelligence (IJCAI)*, pages 60–66, 2016.

H. Aziz, M. Brill, V. Conitzer, E. Elkind, R. Freeman, and T. Walsh. Justified representation in approval-based committee voting. *Social Choice and Welfare*, 48(2):461–485, 2017a.

H. Aziz, E. Elkind, P. Faliszewski, M. Lackner, and P. Skowron. The Condorcet principle for multiwinner elections: From shortlisting to proportionality. In *Proceedings of the 26th International Joint Conference on Artificial Intelligence (IJCAI)*, 2017b.

S. Barberà and D. Coelho. How to choose a non-controversial list with k names. *Social Choice and Welfare*, 31(1):79–96, 2008.

J. Bartholdi, III, C. Tovey, and M. Trick. Voting schemes for which it can be difficult to tell who won the election. *Social Choice and Welfare*, 6(2):157–165, 1989.

N. Betzler, A. Slinko, and J. Uhlmann. On the computation of fully proportional representation. *Journal of Artificial Intelligence Research*, 47:475–519, 2013.

D. Black. *The Theory of Committees and Elections*. Cambridge University Press, 1958.

S. Brams, M. Kilgour, and R. Sanver. A minimax procedure for electing committees. *Public Choice*, 132(3–4):401–420, 2007.

M. Brill, J. Laslier, and P. Skowron. Multiwinner approval rules as apportionment methods. In *Proceedings of the 31st AAAI Conference on Artificial Intelligence (AAAI)*, pages 414–420, 2017.

I. Caragiannis, S. Nath, A. D. Procaccia, and N. Shah. Subset selection via implicit utilitarian voting. In *Proceedings of the 25th International Joint Conference on Artificial Intelligence (IJCAI)*, pages 151–157, 2016.

B. Chamberlin and P. Courant. Representative deliberations and representative decisions: Proportional representation and the Borda rule. *American Political Science Review*, 77(3):718–733, 1983.

D. Coelho. *Understanding, Evaluating and Selecting Voting Rules Through Games and Axioms*. PhD thesis, Universitat Autònoma de Barcelona, 2004.

V. Conitzer, M. Rognlie, and L. Xia. Preference functions that score rankings and maximum likelihood estimation. In *Proceedings of the 21st International Joint Conference on Artificial Intelligence (IJCAI)*, pages 109–115, 2009.

A. Darmann. How hard is it to tell which is a Condorcet committee? *Mathematical Social Sciences*, 66(3):282–292, 2013.

M. Diss and A. Doghmi. Multi-winner scoring election methods: Condorcet consistency and paradoxes. Technical Report WP 1613, GATE Lyon Saint-Étienne, Mar. 2016.

M. Dummett. *Voting Procedures*. Oxford University Press, 1984.

E. Elkind, J. Lang, and A. Saffidine. Condorcet winning sets. *Social Choice and Welfare*, 44(3):493–517, 2015.

E. Elkind, P. Faliszewski, J. Laslier, P. Skowron, A. Slinko, and N. Talmon. What do multiwinner voting rules do? An experiment over the two-dimensional euclidean domain. In *Proceedings of the 31st AAAI Conference on Artificial Intelligence (AAAI)*, pages 494–501, 2017a.

E. Elkind, P. Faliszewski, P. Skowron, and A. Slinko. Properties of multiwinner voting rules. *Social Choice and Welfare*, 48(3):599–632, 2017b.

P. Faliszewski, P. Skowron, A. Slinko, and N. Talmon. Committee scoring rules: Axiomatic classification and hierarchy. In *Proceedings of the 25th International Joint Conference on Artificial Intelligence (IJCAI)*, pages 250–256, 2016a.

P. Faliszewski, P. Skowron, A. Slinko, and N. Talmon. Multiwinner analogues of the plurality rule: Axiomatic and algorithmic views. In *Proceedings of the 30th AAAI Conference on Artificial Intelligence (AAAI)*, pages 482–488, 2016b.

P. Faliszewski, A. Slinko, K. Stahl, and N. Talmon. Achieving fully proportional representation by clustering voters. In *Proceedings of the 15th International Conference on Autonomous Agents and Multiagent Systems (AAMAS)*, pages 296–304, 2016c.

F. Z. Farahani and M. Hekmatfar, editors. *Facility Location: Concepts, Models, and Case Studies*. Springer, 2009.

P. Fishburn. Majority committees. *Journal of Economic Theory*, 25(2):255–268, 1981a.

P. Fishburn. An analysis of simple voting systems for electing committees. *SIAM Journal on Applied Mathematics*, 41(3):499–502, 1981b.

W. Gehrlein. The Condorcet criterion and committee selection. *Mathematical Social Sciences*, 10(3):199–209, 1985.

E. Hemaspaandra, L. Hemaspaandra, and J. Rothe. Exact analysis of Dodgson elections: Lewis Carroll's 1876 voting system is complete for parallel access to NP. *Journal of the ACM*, 44(6):806–825, 1997.

E. Hemaspaandra, H. Spakowski, and J. Vogel. The complexity of Kemeny elections. *Theoretical Computer Science*, 349(3):382–391, 2005.

E. Kamwa. Stable rules for electing committees and divergence on outcomes. *Group Decision and Negotiation*, 26(3):547–564, 2017.

B. Kaymak and R. Sanver. Sets of alternatives as Condorcet winners. *Social Choice and Welfare*, 20(3):477–494, 2003.

M. Kilgour. Approval balloting for multi-winner elections. In J. Laslier and R. Sanver, editors, *Handbook on Approval Voting*. Springer, 2010. Chapter 6.

Y. Koriyama, J. F. Laslier, A. Macé, and R. Treibich. Optimal Apportionment. *Journal of Political Economy*, 121(3):584–608, 2013.

J. Lang and P. Skowron. Multi-attribute proportional representation. In *Proceedings of the 30th AAAI Conference on Artificial Intelligence (AAAI)*, pages 530–536, 2016.

J. Laslier and K. Van der Straeten. A live experiment on approval voting. *Experimental Economics*, 11(1):97–105, 2008.

T. Lu and C. Boutilier. Budgeted social choice: From consensus to personalized decision making. In *Proceedings of the 22nd International Joint Conference on Artificial Intelligence (IJCAI)*, pages 280–286, 2011.

B. Monroe. Fully proportional representation. *American Political Science Review*, 89(4):925–940, 1995.

A. Procaccia, J. Rosenschein, and A. Zohar. On the complexity of achieving proportional representation. *Social Choice and Welfare*, 30(3):353–362, 2008.

T. Ratliff. Some startling inconsistencies when electing committees. *Social Choice and Welfare*, 21(3):433–454, 2003.

J. Rothe, H. Spakowski, and J. Vogel. Exact complexity of the winner problem for Young elections. *Theory of Computing Systems*, 36(4):375–386, 2003.

P. Skowron. FPT approximation schemes for maximizing submodular functions. In *Proceedings of the 12th Conference on Web and Internet Economics (WINE)*, pages 324–338, 2016.

P. Skowron and P. Faliszewski. Fully proportional representation with approval ballots: Approximating the MaxCover problem with bounded frequencies in FPT time. In *Proceedings of the 29th AAAI Conference on Artificial Intelligence (AAAI)*, pages 2124–2130, 2015.

P. Skowron, P. Faliszewski, and A. Slinko. Achieving fully proportional representation: Approximability result. *Artificial Intelligence*, 222:67–103, 2015a.

P. Skowron, L. Yu, P. Faliszewski, and E. Elkind. The complexity of fully proportional representation for single-crossing electorates. *Theoretical Computer Science*, 569:43–57, 2015b.

P. Skowron, P. Faliszewski, and J. Lang. Finding a collective set of items: From proportional multirepresentation to group recommendation. *Artificial Intelligence*, 241:191–216, 2016a.

P. Skowron, P. Faliszewski, and A. Slinko. Axiomatic characterization of committee scoring rules. Technical report, arXiv:1604.01529 [cs.GT], Apr. 2016b.

M. Staring. Two paradoxes of committee elections. *Mathematics Magazine*, 59: 158–159, 1986.

T. N. Thiele. Om flerfoldsvalg. In *Oversigt over det Kongelige Danske Videnskabernes Selskabs Forhandlinger*, pages 415–441. København: A.F. Høst., 1895.

N. Tideman and D. Richardson. Better voting methods through technology: The refinement-manageability trade-off in the Single Transferable Vote. *Public Choice*, 103(1–2):13–34, 2000.

D. Woodall. Properties of preferential election rules. *Voting Matters*, 3:Paper 4, 1994.

CHAPTER 3

A Guided Tour of the Mathematics of Seat Allocation and Political Districting

Federica Ricca, Andrea Scozzari, and Paolo Serafini

3.1 Introduction

This chapter focuses on Seat Allocation and Political Districting, two of the main topics in the study of electoral systems. Models and algorithms from discrete mathematics and combinatorial optimization are used to formalize the problems and find solutions that meet some fairness requirements. The first problem concerns the assignment of seats to parties in political elections. In particular, we discuss the well-known Biproportional Apportionment Problem (BAP), that is, the problem of assigning the House seats in those countries that adopt a two-level proportional system. The problem is difficult also from a mathematical viewpoint, since it combines a matrix feasibility problem with the requirement of double proportionality. The second topic, Political Districting (PD), is a territorial problem in which electoral districts must be designed so that each voter is univocally assigned to one district. This is a relevant problem, since, given the same vote outcome of an election, depending on the district shape and size, the final seat allocation to parties could be drastically different. For this reason, PD procedures have been proposed to output district maps that meet a set of criteria aimed at avoiding district manipulation by parties.

Both BAP and PD are extensively studied in the literature, the first one starting from the seminal paper by Balinski and Demange (1989a,b), the second dating back to 1960's when the paper by Hess et al. (1965) formulated for the first time the problem as an optimization one. The chapter is organized in two parts, the first related to BAP, the second to PD.

3.2 Biproportional Apportionment Problem

3.2.1 Proportional Apportionments

Before describing the Biproportional Apportionment Problem it is necessary to briefly introduce the simpler Proportional Apportionment Problem in which the fixed number of seats of the House has to be divided among constituencies. A mathematically equivalent problem consists in dividing the seats of the House among parties. This second problem presents additional features of candidate selections which are clearly not present in the first problem. In this section we limit ourselves to outlining the main features of the first problem. We refer the reader to the monograph by Balinski and Young (2001) for a comprehensive review of apportionment problems.

Let H be the number of the seats of the House and let I be the set of constituencies, with $m = |I|$. Let p_i be the population of constituency i and let $P = \sum_{i \in I} p_i$ be the total population. In almost all nations the seats assigned to each constituency are required to be proportional to the populations, a notable exception being the European Parliament where the so-called degressive proportionality requirement is called for (see Grimmett (2012), Serafini (2012) and other papers in the same issue).

Ideally, exact proportionality would be obtained by assigning the number of seats $q_i := p_i H/P$ to constituency i, but q_i is in general a fractional number that must be rounded in some way. The question of how to round these numbers presents several subtle features and no univocal answer exists as the history of the US House of Representatives has shown (an interesting account can be found at the site https://www.census.gov/history/www/reference/apportionment/).

Perhaps the simplest method of rounding q_i is the Largest Remainder Rule, also known under the names of Hamilton, Vinton, Hare or Hare-Niemayer. First, to each constituency the number of seats $s_i := \lfloor q_i \rfloor$ is assigned. Then the remaining seats are assigned to those constituencies that have been most penalized by the rounding, namely the ones with largest remainders. It can be easily shown that this method finds the point in $\mathbb{R}^m$ with integral coordinates at minimum distance from the point $q \in \mathbb{R}^m$, where the distance can be measured with any norm.

In spite of the simplicity of the method and this important minimum norm property, the method is questionable for other reasons. First, it considers the absolute deviation while the relative deviation could be perceived more important. Second, it is prone to some anomalous behaviors, that are respectively known as the Alabama Paradox, the Population Paradox and the New State Paradox (Balinski and Young, 2001). For these reasons the method is avoided in many countries. In Italy the Largest Remainder Rule is stated in the Constitution.

The paradoxes are avoided by the divisor methods. A 'modern' way to present a divisor method is as follows. First, a *signpost* function is defined

$$\delta : \mathbb{Z} \to \mathbb{R}, \quad \text{with} \quad \delta(z) \in [z, z+1]$$

that assigns to each integer z a real number between z and $z+1$. The function $\delta(z)$ specifies how to round a real $a \in [z, z+1)$. The rounding, denoted as $[\![a]\!]$, is given by

$$[\![a]\!] = \begin{cases} \lfloor a \rfloor & \text{if } a \leq \delta(z) \\ \lceil a \rceil & \text{if } \delta(z) < a < z+1 \end{cases}$$

This definition implies $[\![a]\!] = \lfloor a \rfloor$ if $a = \delta(z)$. Actually, we have a tie since we might as well define $[\![a]\!] = \lceil a \rceil$ if $a = \delta(z)$. This ambiguity is exploited in the Tie-

and-Transfer method for BAP as we shall see. In the Proportional Apportionment Problem the probability that $a = \delta(z)$ is almost negligible.

Then a multiplier λ is looked for such that the seats

$$s_i = [\![\lambda\, p_i]\!]$$

sum up to H. The crucial aspect of a divisor method is the choice of the signpost function. These are the choices that have been proposed and also implemented in some cases:

$$\delta(z) = z \qquad \text{Adams method}$$
$$\delta(z) = \frac{2}{\frac{1}{z} + \frac{1}{z+1}} \qquad \text{Dean method}$$
$$\delta(z) = \sqrt{z\,(z+1)} \qquad \text{Huntington-Hill method}$$
$$\delta(z) = z + 0.5 \qquad \text{Webster method}$$
$$\delta(z) = z + 1 \qquad \text{Jefferson or D'Hondt method}$$

We just recall that the Adams method favors the small constituencies, while the opposite happens for the Jefferson method. The Huntington-Hill method is the one currently employed to apportion the seats of the US House of Representatives.

3.2.2 Biproportional Apportionment Problem: Introduction

A common feature of many parliaments is the presence of a house of representatives whose seats are not only *a priori* divided among constituencies but also, after the election, among the various competing lists. In these systems the vote assigned to a list is of primary importance and the choice of the actual representatives is done after having assigned the seats to the lists at national level. In other systems the seats assigned to a list are a consequence of the seats won by the candidates.

In this chapter we deal with the problem in which the seats allotted to each constituency are fixed, typically before the elections, the seats allotted to the lists are preliminarily computed on the basis of the votes received in the whole nation, and we have to compute the seats to assign to each list in each constituency. Clearly, we have to respect the previous seat assignments and try to have seats as much as possible proportional to the votes.

Formally, let m be the number of constituencies, H the total number of seats in the house, and R_i the seats allotted to constituency i (obviously $\sum_i R_i = H$). Let n be the number of lists. Let v_{ij} be the votes obtained by list j in constituency i. Let $V_j := \sum_i v_{ij}$ be the votes obtained by list j at national level and let $V := \sum_j V_j$ be the total number of votes. Let P_j be the total number of seats in the house assigned to list j (obviously $\sum_j P_j = H$). The computation of the numbers R_i (before the election) and the numbers P_j (after the election) is done by one of the methods seen in the previous section. Then we have to compute the seats s_{ij} to assign to list j in constituency i subject to:

1. $\sum_{i=1}^m s_{ij} = P_j$, for every list j;

2. $\sum_{j=1}^{n} s_{ij} = R_i$, for every constituency i;

3. If $v_{ij} = 0$ for some list j in some constituency i, then $s_{ij} = 0$;

4. The seats s_{ij} have to be "as proportional as possible" to the votes v_{ij}.

This is the so-called Biproportional Apportionment Problem. The first three requirements are clear. The crucial issue is the last requirement. Exact proportionality of the seats to both the lists and the constituencies cannot be achieved in general if we must satisfy requirements 1, 2 and 3. Therefore, we have to clearly define the goal we want to pursue. In addition we require integrality of the final outcome. The BAP is not a simple problem and one needs *ad hoc* mathematical tools to solve it.

Let us first note that the constraints 1, 2 and 3 are linear programming constraints whose underlying matrix is totally unimodular. Therefore, the feasible set of (where $E = \{(i,j) \in I \times J : v_{ij} > 0\}$)

$$\sum_{j:(i,j)\in E} x_{ij} = R_i \quad i \in I$$

$$\sum_{i:(i,j)\in E} x_{ij} = P_j \quad j \in J \qquad (3.1)$$

$$x_{ij} \geq 0 \quad (i,j) \in E$$

is a polyhedron whose vertices have integral coordinates and therefore a seat apportionment can be found among its vertices. This is a fundamental property that allows to solve the BAP problem as a tractable linear programming problem. The property holds also if we bound each x_{ij} within an interval with integral extremes, i.e.,

$$l_{ij} \leq x_{ij} \leq u_{ij} \qquad (3.2)$$

where l_{ij} and u_{ij} are integral. Hence the existence of a feasible fractional solution to (3.1) and (3.2) implies the existence of an integral solution to the same constraints.

Let us call *quotas* real numbers q_{ij} that would represent an 'ideal' seat apportionment if we were allowed to relax the integrality requirement and maybe also requirements 1 and 2. The definition of ideal is up to the lawmakers. For instance we might define as quotas the numbers $v_{ij} H/V$ that fully satisfy the proportionality requirement to both lists and constituencies, but they do not satisfy requirements 1 and 2.

In some nations (e.g., Italy and Belgium) the following quotas, called *regional quotas*, are used

$$q_{ij} = \frac{v_{ij}}{\sum_k v_{ik}} R_i$$

These quotas guarantee exact proportionality among lists within each constituency. By definition we have $\sum_j q_{ij} = R_i$, but in general $\sum_i q_{ij} = P_j$ does not hold and there is no proportionality among constituencies within each list.

It is possible to define quotas such that both requirements 1 and 2 are satisfied at the expense of losing exact proportionality. Such quotas are called *fair share quotas* and are defined in the next section. Let us note that a slight shift of votes in one constituency has the effect of propagating to the overall set of quotas if both sums must be satisfied. This may be not desirable if we want to preserve some form of autonomy among constituencies. For this reason the regional quotas, that are independent of each constituency, may be preferred. However, fair share quotas exhibit important mathematical properties and this is considered an important factor in favor of using the fair share quotas.

If the seats of an apportionment are obtained from the quotas by rounding each quota either up or down, we say that the apportionment *stays within the quotas*.

By and large there are two approaches to the BAP. In the first approach a set of axioms that every reasonable apportionment should satisfy is designed and then a method aimed at satisfying the axioms is looked for. Typically such a method is unique. This is the approach proposed by Balinski and Demange (1989a,b). The other approach consists in defining fractional ideal quotas and then finding a seat apportionment that minimizes some measure of deviation with respect to the ideal quotas (Ricca et al., 2012). A detailed comparison of the two approaches is discussed by Ricca et al. (2012) and we refer the reader to this paper for a more comprehensive understanding of the various issues.

3.2.3 Divisor Methods: Axioms

An apportionment method can be seen as a function S that maps the problem data, i.e., the vote matrix v_{ij} and the values H, R_i and P_j, into an integral non-negative matrix. It is convenient to denote the data as a pair (v, w) where v is the vote matrix and w is the set of numbers H, R_i and P_j. Then $S(v, w)$ is the particular matrix output by the apportionment method defined by the function S.

We may also relax the integrality requirement and consider fractional apportionments. In this case a fractional apportionment method can be seen as a function Q that maps (v, w) into a fractional non-negative matrix $Q(v, w)$.

Let us consider the following axioms that a fractional apportionment method Q for BAP should satisfy (Balinski and Demange, 1989b). Here $q = Q(v, w)$.

1. Exactness: if the v_{ij} satisfy $H \sum_j v_{ij} = R_i V$ and $H \sum_i v_{ij} = P_j V$, then $q = Hv/V$.

2. Uniformity: let I be a subset of constituencies and J a subset of lists, and let v_{IJ} and q_{IJ} be the matrix restrictions to $I \times J$ of v and q, respectively. Moreover, let

$$\hat{R}_i := \sum_{j \in J} q_{ij}, \quad i \in I, \qquad \hat{P}_j := \sum_{i \in I} q_{ij}, \quad j \in J, \qquad \hat{H} = \sum_{i \in I} \sum_{j \in J} q_{ij}$$

These values define the data w_{IJ}. Then q_{IJ} must be an admissible apportionment output by Q if directly applied to the data (v_{IJ}, w_{IJ}).

3. Monotonicity: if v' and v are two vote matrices that are different only for one pair (h, k) where $v'_{hk} > v_{hk}$ and $q' = Q(v', w)$ then we must have $q'_{hk} \geq q_{hk}$.

4. Homogeneity: if two rows h and k of the vote matrix are proportional, i.e.,

$v_{hj} = \lambda v_{kj}$ for all j, and $R_h = R_k$, then the apportionment on the two rows must be the same, i.e., $q_{hj} = q_{kj}$ for all j. The same principle must hold for the columns.

We report here the axioms in a restricted framework with respect to Balinski and Demange (1989b), who consider R and P variable numbers within specified bounds. Another axiom (Relevance) is introduced by Balinski and Demange (1989b), that becomes void when R and P are fixed data.

It can be shown that Homogeneity and Uniformity imply together uniqueness of the apportionment. Uniqueness is clearly a necessary requirement for every apportionment method. We may invoke the same axioms also for an integral apportionment method. In addition a new axiom is introduced that calls for a 'continuity' property. To state this axiom we need to assume that the votes v_{ij} are real numbers. Then we require:

5. Completeness: let v^k be a sequence such that $v^k \to \bar{v}$ and let $s = S(v^k, w)$ for all k. Then $s = S(\bar{v}, w)$.

This axiom may be too restrictive if we allow zero votes for some pair (i, j). In this case it might happen that $v_{ij}^k > 0$, $v_{ij}^k \to 0$ and $s_{ij} = 1$. Since $S(\bar{v}, w)$ must output $s_{ij} = 0$, the axiom cannot be fulfilled. We may take the point of view that zero votes happen only because a certain list is not present in a particular constituency. In this case $v_{ij}^k = 0$ for any k.

The fundamental result by Balinski and Demange is that the unique fractional apportionment that satisfies the axioms 1–4 is a matrix F denoted *fair share* that can be expressed as

$$F_{ij} = \lambda_i v_{ij} \mu_j, \qquad i \in I, \; j \in J,$$

where $\lambda_i > 0$ and $\mu_j > 0$ are multipliers chosen to satisfy the constraints

$$\sum_{j \in J} F_{ij} = R_i, \quad i \in I, \qquad \sum_{i \in I} F_{ij} = P_j, \quad j \in J.$$

The existence of the fair share matrix is always granted if the vote matrix is strictly positive. If the vote matrix contains some zeros the fair share matrix might not exist as it happens in this simple example

$$v = \begin{pmatrix} 1 & 1 \\ 0 & 1 \end{pmatrix}, \quad R = \begin{pmatrix} 1 \\ 1 \end{pmatrix}, \qquad P = \begin{pmatrix} 1 & 1 \end{pmatrix}$$

Since $v_{ij} = 0$ implies $F_{ij} = 0$ the only matrix satisfying the sum constraint is the identity matrix. However, there are no positive multipliers such that $\lambda_1 v_{12} \mu_2 = 0$.

An existence result even with some zero elements is provided by the following theorem (Bachem and Korte, 1979; Rothblum and Schneider, 1989; Kalantari et al., 2008).

Theorem 3.1. *A fair share matrix exists if and only if there exists a feasible solution to the constraints*

$$\sum_{j:(i,j) \in E} x_{ij} = R_i, \; i \in I, \quad \sum_{i:(i,j) \in E} x_{ij} = P_j, \; j \in J, \quad x_{ij} \geq \frac{1}{|E|}, \; (i,j) \in E. \qquad (3.3)$$

The feasibility of (3.3) can be checked in polynomial time by standard network flow techniques. However, it is simpler to use the so-called RAS algorithm to compute F. This algorithm alternately scales rows and columns in order to satisfy in turn either row or column sum. Formally the following computation has to be carried out starting from the initial solution $F^0 = v$, $\lambda_i^0 = 1$ and $\mu_j^0 = 1$:

$$\alpha_i := \frac{R_i}{\sum_j F_{ij}^k}, \qquad \lambda_i^{k+1} = \alpha_i \lambda_i^k, \qquad \bar{F}_{ij}^k = \alpha_i F_{ij}^k \qquad j = 1, \ldots, n, \quad i = 1, \ldots m,$$

$$\beta_j := \frac{P_j}{\sum_i \bar{F}_{ij}^k}, \qquad \mu_j^{k+1} = \beta_j \mu_j^k, \qquad F_{ij}^{k+1} = \beta_j \bar{F}_{ij}^k \qquad i = 1, \ldots, m, \quad j = 1, \ldots n.$$

One important property of the fair share matrix is that there always exists an apportionment obtained by rounding each matrix entry either down or up, i.e., it stays within the quotas. We have already observed that the existence of a feasible fractional solution to (3.1) and (3.2) implies the existence of an integral solution to the same constraints and F is feasible for (3.1) and (3.2) with $l_{ij} = \lfloor F_{ij} \rfloor$ and $u_{ij} = \lceil F_{ij} \rceil$.

3.2.4 Divisor Methods: TT and DAS Methods

Like in the Proportional Apportionment Problem, once a signpost function $\delta(z)$ is defined, we have to find multipliers λ_i and μ_j such that the seats obtained by

$$s_{ij} = [\![\lambda_i \, v_{ij} \, \mu_j]\!]$$

satisfy row and column sums. If we round the fair share matrix, it is unlikely that the sums are respected. Hence we have to find out other multipliers.

The Tie-and-Transfer method (TT) by Balinski and Demange (1989a) cleverly exploits the idea that if $\lambda_i v_{ij} \mu_j = \delta(\lfloor \lambda_i v_{ij} \mu_j \rfloor)$ then the matrix entry can be rounded either up or down because there is a tie. Hence the multipliers must be continuously updated in order to have a series of ties that allow a simultaneous transfer of seats in order to satisfy the sum constraints. Explaining in detail the TT method is beyond the scope of this short survey due to its many technical details. The reader is directed to the literature. The remarkable fact about the method is that it is polynomial and satisfies the axioms.

The Discrete Alternating Scaling Algorithm (DAS) by Pukelsheim (2004) is similar in the sense that it aims at finding multipliers λ_i and μ_j such that the rounding is consistent with the sum constraints. However, it differs in the way the multipliers are computed. Furthermore, the algorithm may stall, although with very low probability. However, its simplicity is an important pro toward a possible adoption and indeed it has been adopted in the Cantons of Zürich, Schaffhausen and Aargau (Switzerland) (Pukelsheim and Schuhmacher, 2004).

The DAS method works as the RAS algorithm for the computation of the fair share matrix. The only difference is that the sum constraint is enforced by using a divisor method applied to either the rows or to the columns in an alternate way.

In more detail let λ_i^k and μ_j^k be the multipliers obtained at the k-th step and let $q^k = \lambda_i^k v_{ij} \mu_j^k$. Starting with $\lambda_i^0 = 1$ and $\mu_j^0 = 1$ we iterate as

1. Let λ_i^k such that $s_{ij} = [\![\lambda_i^k q_{ij}^{k-1}]\!]$ and $\sum_j s_{ij} = R_i$. Compute $q_{ij}^k = \lambda_i^k q_{ij}^{k-1}$.
   If $\sum_i s_{ij} = P_j$ stop, otherwise $k := k+1$ and go to 2.

2. Let μ_j^k such that $s_{ij} = [\![q_{ij}^{k-1} \mu_j^k]\!]$ and $\sum_i s_{ij} = P_j$. Compute $q_{ij}^k = q_{ij}^{k-1} \mu_j^k$.
   If $\sum_j s_{ij} = R_i$ stop, otherwise $k := k+1$ and go to 1.

The final multipliers are given by

$$\lambda_i = \prod_k \lambda_i^k, \qquad \mu_j = \prod_k \mu_j^k.$$

3.2.5 Minimum Deviation Methods

Given ideal quotas the seats can be computed by finding those that minimize an appropriate measure of deviation from the quotas. Since there can be many different ways of measuring the deviation we may consequently define different apportionment methods. Which one to choose in practice is a decision of the lawmakers.

The important framework common to all methods is that the constraint matrix is (3.1) with the possible addition of (3.2) and therefore a linear objective function will always produce a seat apportionment. In particular, these problems can be cast as network flow problems for which fast and reliable algorithms are available.

One natural way of measuring the deviation of the computed seats s_{ij} from the ideal quotas q_{ij} considers an L_ρ-norm, so that the objective function is

$$\min_s \sum_{ij} |s_{ij} - q_{ij}|^\rho$$

The typical values for ρ are $\rho = 1$, $\rho = 2$ or $\rho = \infty$ (that corresponds to $\min_s \max_{ij} |s_{ij} - q_{ij}|$ and we speak of *minimax* solutions). In addition we may also require that the seats stay within the quotas. Other ways of measuring the deviation not directly linked to a norm may be also defined. For instance we may consider 'fair' a rounding of the quotas to the closest integer and 'unfair' to the second closest integer. If we want to find an apportionment within the quotas we necessarily round each entry in the table either fairly or unfairly. A possible objective could be the minimization of the number of unfair roundings. The apportionment found this way might be called a *Best Rounding apportionment*.

Since we want to model the problems as linear programming problems on the constraint set (3.1) with the possible addition of (3.2), the only modeling issue that remains to be solved is how to express the various minimizations as linear functions. For the L_1-norm we note that the function $f_{ij}(x) = |x - q_{ij}|$ is convex and piece-wise linear. The function

$$g_{ij}(x) = \begin{cases} q_{ij} - x & \text{if } x \le \lfloor q_{ij} \rfloor \\ (1 - 2\langle q_{ij} \rangle)(x - \lfloor q_{ij} \rfloor) + \langle q_{ij} \rangle & \text{if } \lfloor q_{ij} \rfloor \le x \le \lceil q_{ij} \rceil \\ x - q_{ij} & \text{if } x \ge \lceil q_{ij} \rceil. \end{cases} \qquad (3.4)$$

(where $\langle a \rangle = a - \lfloor a \rfloor$ is the fractional part of a) is also convex and piece-wise linear with integral breakpoints. Furthermore, $g_{ij}(x) = f_{ij}(x)$ on the breakpoints of g.

Hence, if we minimize $\sum_{ij} g_{ij}(x_{ij})$ we obtain integral values for x. The function (3.4) can be turned into linear programming by expressing each x_{ij} as a sum of three additional variables

$$x_{ij} = \xi_{ij}^1 + \xi_{ij}^2 + \xi_{ij}^3$$

subject to $0 \leq \xi_{ij}^1 \leq \lfloor q_{ij} \rfloor$, $0 \leq \xi_{ij}^2 \leq 1$, $0 \leq \xi_{ij}^3$ and having the following objective function

$$\min \sum_{(ij) \in E} q_{ij} - \xi_{ij}^1 + (1 - 2 \langle q_{ij} \rangle) \xi_{ij}^2 + \langle q_{ij} \rangle + \xi_{ij}^3 + 1 - \langle q_{ij} \rangle$$

that is equivalent up to a constant shift to

$$\min \sum_{(ij) \in E} -\xi_{ij}^1 + (1 - 2 \langle q_{ij} \rangle) \xi_{ij}^2 + \xi_{ij}^3$$

The objective function coefficients are such that $\xi_{ij}^2 > 0$ only if $\xi_{ij}^1 = \lfloor q_{ij} \rfloor$ and $\xi_{ij}^3 > 0$ only if $\xi_{ij}^2 = 1$.

The same trick of substituting a piece-wise linear function with another one which has integral breakpoints and is equal to the first function on these breakpoints can work with any convex objective function. There is however a subtle theoretical issue that should not be neglected. For each breakpoint we have to introduce a new variable. Hence we should know if the number of breakpoints is polynomial. A trivial bound, based on the values R_i or P_j is only pseudo-polynomial.

Although in practice a naive implementation of this technique works well, because the vast majority of instances have optimal apportionments within the bounds $\lfloor q_{ij} \rfloor - 1$ and $\lceil q_{ij} \rceil + 1$, and therefore we do not need in practice more than five additional variables, yet we wonder whether exists a polynomial algorithm to solve the problem. The answer is affirmative thanks to a scaling procedure due to Minoux (1984).

For the L_2 norm we substitute the function $f_{ij}(x) = (x - q_{ij})^2$ with the function

$$g_{ij}(x) = (\lfloor x \rfloor - q_{ij})^2 + \langle x \rangle (1 + 2(\lfloor x \rfloor - q_{ij}))$$

which can be linearized by introducing additional variables ξ_{ij}^k subject to

$$x_{ij} = \sum_k \xi_{ij}^k, \qquad 0 \leq \xi_{ij}^k \leq 1, \qquad k = 0, \ldots, \min\{P_j, R_i\}, \qquad (i,j) \in E$$

with objective function

$$\sum_{ij} \sum_k (1 + 2(k - q_{ij})) \xi_{ij}^k$$

Optimal apportionments for either norm L_1 or L_2 do not necessarily stay within the quotas. Counterexamples can be given (see, for instance, Ricca et al., 2012). If we want an apportionment within the quotas we simply add to (3.1) the constraints $\lfloor q_{ij} \rfloor \leq x_{ij} \leq \lceil q_{ij} \rceil$. In this case we can solve for any L_ρ-norm ($\rho < \infty$) by simply using the objective function (see Cox and Ernst, 1982)

$$\min \sum_{ij} \left((1 - \langle q_{ij} \rangle)^\rho - \langle q_{ij} \rangle^\rho \right) x_{ij}$$

The norms L_1 and L_2 tend to produce the same optimal apportionment. Indeed it is possible to prove the following result:

Theorem 3.2. *If an optimal apportionment with respect to the L_1-norm stays within the quotas, then the same apportionment is optimal with respect to the L_2-norm.*

If we have in mind a Best Rounding apportionment, we can count the unfair rounding and minimize this count by defining the sets

$$E^+ := \{(i,j) \in E : \langle q_{ij} \rangle < 0.5\}, \qquad E^- := \{(i,j) \in E : \langle q_{ij} \rangle > 0.5\},$$

and using the objective function

$$z = \min \sum_{(ij) \in E^+} x_{ij} - \sum_{(ij) \in E^-} x_{ij}$$

The actual count of unfair roundings is given by $z - \sum_{(ij)\in E^+} \lfloor q_{ij} \rfloor + \sum_{(ij)\in E^-} \lceil q_{ij} \rceil$. It is interesting to note that the TT and DAS methods obtain *a posteriori* quotas $\lambda_i v_{ij} \mu_j$ and an apportionment $[\![\lambda_i v_{ij} \mu_j]\!]$ that is necessarily a Best Rounding with respect to these quotas.

The approach for the L_∞-norm is different because it is not based on the direct solution of a linear programming minimization problem, rather on the solution of a sequence of feasibility problems. A thorough investigation of this approach can be found in Serafini and Simeone (2012a). Let us fix a deviation τ from the quotas. An apportionment that is also feasible for the constraints

$$q_{ij} - \tau \leq s_{ij} \leq q_{ij} + \tau$$

has maximum deviation not greater than τ. Since an apportionment must be integral, these constraints are equivalent to

$$\lceil q_{ij} - \tau \rceil \leq s_{ij} \leq \lfloor q_{ij} + \tau \rfloor \tag{3.5}$$

that, moreover, guarantee integrality of a feasible apportionment. Finding a feasible apportionment, or determining that the problem is infeasible, with respect to (3.1), (3.2) and (3.5) can be done via a Max Flow problem. We have to find the minimum value τ^* such that a feasible apportionment exists. This search can be done in a binary search fashion. The details of three different implementations can be found in Serafini and Simeone (2012a). We recall here that an optimal apportionment can be found in strongly polynomial time.

3.2.6 Other Issues

Non-uniqueness of the optimal apportionment is a serious issue and any method must be robust enough to prevent such circumstance. Uniqueness cannot be always guaranteed. One can construct examples in which the votes are so symmetrically distributed that there may be many equivalent apportionments. However, these circumstances may be considered extremely unlikely in a real election. There are other causes of non-uniqueness that some methods can exhibit that are inherent to the method itself and one has to find a way to fix them.

The L_∞-norm minimization has many equivalent optimal solutions because minimax solutions are insensitive to deviations for some pairs (i, j) which are less than the maximum deviation. A stronger form of L_∞-norm optimality to refine the choice among the optima is as follows: for a given apportionment x^* let $\tau_{hk}^* := |q_{hk} - x_{hk}^*|$ be the deviation for the pair (h, k). Let

$$L(h, k) := \{(i, j) \neq (h, k) : \tau_{ij}^* \leq \tau_{hk}^*\}, \qquad U(h, k) := \{(i, j) : \tau_{ij}^* > \tau_{hk}^*\}.$$

$L(h, k)$ is the set of pairs with deviation not larger than τ_{hk}^* and $U(h, k)$ is the complement set, excluding (h, k) itself. Then we say that the apportionment x^* is *strongly optimal* if, for any pair (h, k), there is no apportionment with deviation $\tau_{hk} < \tau_{hk}^*$, $\tau_{ij} \leq \tau_{hk}^*$ for $(i, j) \in L(h, k)$ and $\tau_{ij} \leq \tau_{ij}^*$ for $(i, j) \in U(h, k)$.

Strongly optimal solutions are unique and a refinement of the previously stated binary search can be given that produces a strongly optimal solution (Serafini and Simeone, 2012a).

L_2-norm optimal solutions are robust in terms of uniqueness while L_1-norm optimal solutions can exhibit many equivalent solutions. It is shown in Ricca et al. (2012) that this undesirable circumstance is likely to happen if the apportionment does not stay within the quotas (compare with Theorem 3.2) and this in turn is a rare circumstance if fair share quotas are used.

We quote from Serafini and Simeone (2012b): "Electoral systems are usually quite complex and they are assembled out of many interacting components, ... it may happen that only mathematically sophisticated algorithms are available for solving a certain design problem. Are they "writable" as an actual law? Citizens rightly demand simple, easy to understand, voting systems. ... Which is better? To have simple, but unsound electoral laws, or sound, but complex ones?"

The way out from this dilemma is to "leave to a mathematically sophisticated algorithm the task of PRODUCING a sound solution, but attach to it a certificate of guarantee, that is, describe a simple procedure whereby ANYBODY CAN CHECK, through some elementary operations, that the solution output by the algorithm indeed satisfies all the requirements sought for."

Since the minimization methods described are linear programming problems, strong duality holds for all of them and the certificate is indeed based on duality properties. Checking the claim that a solution is indeed optimal does not however require knowledge of mathematical programming theory. Only some elementary mathematical notions are needed. Describing the certificates in detail is out of the scope of this chapter and the reader is referred to Serafini and Simeone (2012b) and Serafini (2015).

3.3 Political Districting

Political Districting (PD) is particularly important in plurality systems with single-member districts. When only one seat is at stake in each district, the size and the shape of the districts may influence the outcome of the election, since even a single vote can produce the majority for one of the candidates. *Gerrymandering* is the name of the malpractice of designing biased electoral districts for favoring one preferred political party or candidate. But, even if gerrymandering is banned, the design of the districts remains a crucial technical issue in the definition of an electoral law, and it needs to be solved by using appropriate models and procedures. For this reason, many papers in the Operations Research (OR) literature studied this problem since the 1960's, providing different models and solution techniques (Grilli di Cortona et al., 1999, Ricca and Simeone, 1997 and Ricca et al., 2013).

3.3.1 Problem Definition

PD is a territorial partition problem which requires the discretization of the territory and imposes criteria related to spatial contiguity and population size. Here we assume that the territory is composed of a set of n elementary units, each identified by its geographical center and its population (*population units*).

Let $k < n$ be the total number of districts. We denote by p_i the size of the population of unit i, $i = 1, \ldots, n$, and by $P = \sum_{i=1}^{n} p_i$ the total population of the territory. The average district population is given by $\bar{P} = P/k$. A distance measure between units i and j is denoted by d_{ij}. The PD problem can be formulated as *finding a partition of the n units into k districts according to a specific set of criteria*. The main PD criteria are:

1. Integrity: each territorial unit cannot be split between two or more districts.

2. Contiguity: the units of each district should be geographically contiguous, that is, one can walk from any point in the district to any other without ever leaving the district.

3. Population balance: all districts should have the same portion of representation (*one person-one vote* principle); therefore single-member districts should have nearly the same populations.

4. Compactness: each district should be compact, that, according to the Oxford Dictionary, is, "closely and neatly packed together" (for example a round-shaped district).

An additional criterion frequently used in PD is the **respect of existing administrative subdivisions of the territory**. There are other PD criteria which are seldom used since there is no unanimous consensus on their legitimacy (e.g., *respect of natural boundaries, representation of ethnic minorities* and *respect of integrity of communities*). Broad discussions about political districting criteria can be found in Bozkaya et al. (2003), Grilli di Cortona et al. (1999), Kalcsics et al. (2005) and Ricca and Simeone (1997).

Traditionally, PD is formulated as an Integer Linear/Nonlinear Program (see, e.g., Hess et al. (1965), Garfinkel and Nemhauser (1970)), depending on the criterion selected for the objective function. From the seminal paper by Hess et al. (1965), works published in the 1960's and 1970's focused on location/allocation and transportation models and methods. Later, agglomerative techniques were mainly developed following Garfinkel and Nemhauser (1970) who proposed a set partitioning approach (Nygreen, 1988; Mehrotra et al., 1998).

Starting from the 1990's, local search methods became pervasive for PD (see

Bozkaya et al. (2003) and Ricca and Simeone (2008)), as well as techniques borrowed from the field of genetic and evolutionary algorithms. More recently, interesting approaches based on computational geometry were proposed (Kalcsics et al., 2005; Ricca et al., 2008).

In recent years, there was also a wide variety of papers basically describing the application of some known PD techniques (or slight variants) for the design of the electoral district map of a specific country. We note that PD can be seen as a particular case of the more general *territory design problem*, related to applications in public services like transportation districts, healthcare and school zoning, etc. On this topic, there is a rich and lively production of papers where PD is cited as one possible application, even if it is not the original motivation.

Many authors adopt a graph-theoretic model representing the territory as a connected n-node graph $G = (N, E)$ (*contiguity graph*, see Bodin (1973); Simeone (1978)), where the nodes correspond to the elementary territorial units and an edge between two nodes exists if and only if the two corresponding units are neighboring. To each node is assigned a weight representing its population.

In this case, the PD problem is formulated as follows: *find a compact partition of G into k connected components such that the weight of each component (sum of the weights of its nodes) is as close as possible to $\bar{P}$.*

It is well-known that the partition of a graph G into k connected components that minimizes population imbalance measured by an L_1-norm objective function is NP-hard even when $k = 2$ and G is a 2-spider, i.e., a tree with only one node with degree greater than 2 (De Simone et al., 1990). The problem remains NP-hard on spiders also for the L_ρ-norm with $2 \leqslant \rho < \infty$ and $k > 2$ (Schroeder, 2001).

In the following, we provide a brief overview of the PD mathematical models and methods of the last fifty years. Two main approaches emerge in our analysis of the literature, namely the *exact approach* (Section 3.3.2), and the *heuristic approach* (Section 3.3.3). The strength of the exact approach is that the problem is formulated by an algebraic optimization model. Therefore, in principle, any PD criterion can be modeled by a set of constraints, or it can be implemented in the objective function.

The drawback is that indicators adopted to measure the criteria may be highly non-linear (like for compactness), or even not computable by a formula, as it may happen for example for the respect of existing administrative subdivisions. In addition, the constraints in the PD model might be too many, i.e., their number may grow exponentially with the number of elementary units of the territory. This is the case of order constraints provided in Apollonio et al. (2008), by which contiguity of the districts is guaranteed, but at the cost of introducing an exponential number of constraints.

The power of the heuristic approach is that feasible solutions are characterized in a conceptually simple way so that they can evaluate a huge number of solutions in few seconds. As a counterpart, a loss in the quality of the solution must be accepted w.r.t. the exact approach. For both approaches, we discuss both the papers that are commonly considered milestones in this research field and also the ones that we deem to be the most representative, since, in our opinion, they produced innovative ideas or fixed drawbacks of previous works.

3.3.2 Exact Approach

In this section we review some classical mathematical models and solution techniques presented in the literature starting from the paper by Hess et al. (1965), which is generally considered the earliest OR paper in political districting. Here PD is formulated as a discrete location problem and the idea is to identify k units representing the centers of the k districts, so that each territorial unit must be assigned to exactly one center. The model has the following binary variables:

$$x_{ij} = \begin{cases} 1 & \text{if unit } i \text{ is assigned to center } j \\ 0 & \text{otherwise} \end{cases} \quad i,j = 1,\ldots,n$$

and, in particular, $x_{jj} = 1$ if unit j is chosen as one of the centers and $x_{jj} = 0$ otherwise. The political districting problem is formulated as follows:

$$\begin{aligned}
\min \quad & \sum_{i=1}^{n} \sum_{j=1}^{n} d_{ij}^2 \, p_i \, x_{ij} \\
& \sum_{j=1}^{n} x_{ij} = 1 & i = 1,\ldots,n \\
& \sum_{j=1}^{n} x_{jj} = k \\
& a \bar{P} x_{jj} \leqslant \sum_{i=1}^{n} p_i \, x_{ij} \leqslant b \bar{P} x_{jj} & j = 1,\ldots,n \\
& x_{ij} \in \{0,1\} & i,j = 1,\ldots,n
\end{aligned} \quad (3.6)$$

where a and b define the minimum and the maximum allowable district population, calculated as a percentage of the average district population $\bar{P}$ ($a < 1$, $b > 1$). By the first n constraints, each unit must belong to exactly one district. The next one imposes that the total number of districts is k. The $2n$ inequalities impose upper and lower bounds on the population of the districts. This type of constraint is frequently used to control population balance, since it is easy to read and understand also by non OR experts and lawmakers. The objective function measures compactness by the moment of inertia w.r.t. the district centers. The main drawback of the above integer programming model is that it does not take into account spatial contiguity of the districts at all. Therefore, an *a posteriori* revision may be necessary for assessing contiguity of the solution with an unavoidable loss in optimality.

In Garfinkel and Nemhauser (1970) a two-phase procedure based on a set partitioning approach is proposed. Phase I generates the set J of all possible feasible districts w.r.t. contiguity, population balance and compactness. In phase II the following set partitioning model is formulated that minimizes the overall deviation of district populations from $\bar{P}$.

$$\begin{aligned}
\min \quad & \sum_{j \in J} f_j \, x_j \\
& \sum_{j \in J} a_{ij} \, x_j = 1 & i = 1,\ldots,n \\
& \sum_{j \in J} x_j = k \\
& x_j \in \{0,1\} & j \in J
\end{aligned} \quad (3.7)$$

where $f_j = (|P_j - \bar{P}|)/(\alpha \bar{P})$, and $\alpha \in [0,1]$ is the tolerance on the percentage of deviation from $\bar{P}$ for the population of a district; $a_{ij} = 1$ if unit i is in district j and $a_{ij} = 0$ otherwise; $x_j = 1$ if district $j \in J$ is included in the partition and $x_j = 0$ otherwise. The same implicit enumeration strategy is followed to find all the feasible solutions in phase I and to find an optimal solution for (3.7) in phase II (for details the interested reader can refer to Geoffrion (1967)).

In this approach compactness is taken into account only in phase I, when districts are generated individually. It is measured on each single district separately with an index based on both the maximum distance between two territorial units in the district and the district area. A district is deemed compact if its index value is less than or equal to a fixed threshold. Then, the set partitioning problem in phase II does not consider any compactness measure for the whole district map, which, in fact, at the end, may result non-compact under different viewpoints. Note that, as suggested by Young (1988), there are many measures of compactness, and any good measure must apply both to the district map as a whole and to each district individually (for a classification of compactness measures see, e.g., Horn et al. (1993)).

The set partitioning approach in Garfinkel and Nemhauser (1970) was followed by other authors (Nygreen, 1988; Mehrotra et al., 1998) who suggested variants of model (3.7) aimed at improving the performance w.r.t. compactness. Both papers rely on a graph representation of the territory.

In Nygreen (1988) the innovative idea is that phase I is formulated in terms of spanning forests of G in which each subtree is rooted at some units playing the role of a district's center. Compactness is then controlled by imposing that the trees of the spanning forest have depth at most equal to two.

In Mehrotra et al. (1998) the problem is formulated as a constrained graph partitioning problem and a specialized branch-and-price solution methodology is developed. To take into account compactness properly, a cost function, based on distances computed between nodes in G, is defined on the set of possible districts, and the objective function of the set partitioning problem (*master problem*) is given by the sum of these costs. At each step, each new-generated district is priced with the same cost function used in the master problem, and this allows for controlling compactness of the whole map during the procedure.

The idea of formulating PD in terms of spanning forests is also exploited in Apollonio et al. (2008) and Lari et al. (2016), where the authors investigate *centered* graph partitioning problems, i.e., partitions of G into k of connected components, each including exactly one fixed center. They consider a class of objective functions based on unit-center costs that are independent of the topology of G (*flat costs*). For PD, population constraints are relaxed via a Lagrangean objective function, and flat costs correspond to the coefficients of such objective function. The problem becomes: *finding a spanning forest of G such that each tree in the forest contains exactly one center and the total cost is minimized*. The problem is shown to be NP-hard even on planar bipartite graphs (Apollonio et al., 2008; Lari et al., 2016), while it is polynomially solvable on trees. For this case, an interesting formulation is proposed where district contiguity is explicitly formulated by a set of order constraints. Unfortunately, these results cannot be directly exploited in PD applications, since the tree structure is too poorly connected to represent any real territory. In spite of this, the availability of efficient algorithms on trees leads to the idea of developing effective heuristics for finding a good district map on G through the (optimal) solution of a sequence of restrictions of the problem to spanning trees of G. It is worth noticing how contiguity is imposed in the above models by the use of order constraints. Since the district centers are fixed in advance, in a tree $T = (N, E)$ contiguity can be accomplished by imposing that if unit i is included in the district centered in s, then all units in G lying in the unique path $P_{i,s}$ from i to s must be included in the same district as i. The model has $O(n^2 k)$ order constraints in total. This can be further improved to $O(n\,k)$ if one imposes order constraints on successive adjacent nodes in $P_{i,s}$ and exploits transitivity. Thus, the constraints of the PD model become:

$$\begin{aligned} & \sum_{s \in S} y_{is} = 1 & & i \in U \\ & y_{is} \leqslant y_{j(i,s),s} & & i \in U,\, s \in S,\, (i,s) \notin E \\ & y_{is} \in \{0,1\} & & i \in U,\, s \in S \end{aligned} \qquad (3.8)$$

where $S \subset N$, is the set of centers, with $|S| = k$, and $U = N \setminus S$. The binary variables y_{is} are defined as follows:

$$y_{is} = \begin{cases} 1 & \text{if unit } i \text{ belongs to the district centered in } s \\ 0 & \text{otherwise} \end{cases} \qquad i \in U,\, s \in S$$

Node $j(i,s)$ is the adjacent to i in the unique path from i to s. The feasible polytope described by (3.8) is integral. This could be exploited when the PD problem on a graph G is solved by the heuristic sketched above, that at each step can rely on linear programming for solving the problem on a spanning tree of G.

From the above discussion, two critical aspects emerge in the exact approach: i) guaranteeing contiguity, that needs to be formulated as a hard constraint; ii) measuring the other PD criteria, which may be a difficult task if an explicit analytic expression does not exist for some criteria. In this view, a heuristic approach may help, since the solution procedure is free from the rigid formulation of an algebraic model. In addition, the graph-theoretic model for the representation of the territory, that cannot be always fully exploited in a mathematical formulation, appears to be particularly fitting in a heuristic framework, as the papers reviewed in the following section show.

3.3.3 Heuristic Methods

In the last two decades, the use of heuristic techniques has taken a growing place in the study of PD problems. The main contributions in the literature are aimed at the evaluation of the performance of those meta-heuristics, like Tabu Search (TS), Simulated Annealing (SA), Threshold Algorithms (TA), Genetic Algorithms (GA), that have already shown to be successful for other difficult combinatorial optimization problems. Two extensive methodological works are provided in Ricca and Simeone (2008) and Bozkaya et al. (2003), both testing different versions of Local Search (LS) algorithms. LS is a powerful general purpose technique with a special capability of evaluating a huge number of different solutions in short times. The basic features of LS are: the *starting feasible solution*; the *(local) move*;

the *neighborhood* of a feasible solution. In PD the initial solution is generally easy to find since one can always rely on an already available administrative territorial division, or, in case of redistricting problems, even on the previous electoral district map which is going to be updated. A move operates a slight perturbation of a feasible solution. Given the current solution s, a neighboring solution of s is defined as any solution that can be obtained from s by performing a move. Although the variety of moves that can be thought of is wide, the principle of simplicity is in generally recommended, in order to avoid too sophisticated implementations which might slow down the computation. This principle is followed in both Ricca and Simeone (2008) and Bozkaya et al. (2003) where a move corresponds to the migration of one unit from a district to an adjacent one.

In Ricca and Simeone (2008) the aim is to investigate the intrinsic nature and potential of LS strategies like TS, SA, and TA. Therefore, streamlined versions of the algorithms are implemented. The authors rely on a graph-theoretic model to guarantee integrity and contiguity. PD is formulated as a multi-criteria optimization problem via a weighted objective function combining population balance, compactness, and conformity to administrative boundaries. In particular, good district maps are provided by *Old Bachelor Acceptance* (Hu et al., 1995), a threshold-based heuristic that is able to avoid premature stops in local optima by the use of a non-monotonic updating scheme.

In Bozkaya et al. (2003) a territory graph model is adopted and an enhanced LS procedure based on TS is developed within an adaptive memory search framework. During the procedure several 'good' district maps are generated, their districts are evaluated singularly by a performance function, and the best ones are recorded in order to be used again for restarting TS. This is, in fact, a mean for implementing both fitness selection, typical of GA, and a multi-start approach, that is generally recommended in LS. Beside the basic PD criteria, socio-economic homogeneity and integrity of communities are considered in a single weighted objective function.

A relatively new field of research on PD borrows notions and techniques from the computational geometry area. For the more general *territory design problem*, Kalcsics et al. (2005) propose an algorithm based on a continuous spatial model. The novelty is that discrete elementary territorial units are still considered but they are represented in the continuous space by the coordinates of their geographical centers. The algorithm repeatedly partition the territory into two halfspaces by drawing a straight line (*successive dichotomy strategy*). At each step, this generates two new subsets of territorial units. The benefit of the algorithm is that it is conceptually simple and easy to implement. This approach naturally satisfies contiguity, but which portion of territory must be divided next, and which straight line must be drawn, remain two substantial issues from which the performance of the algorithm strongly depends. In spite of this, in our opinion, the approach is worth to be investigated for further developments.

Ricca et al. (2008) apply to PD a heuristic approach based on Voronoi Regions (VR). The underlying idea is that VR are inherently compact, so that one may overcome the problem of choosing a measure of compactness. They refer to the graph representation of the territory and assign weights to the edges which represent distances between units. They introduce the notion of *weighted discrete*

Voronoi Regions that can be seen as the graph-theoretic counterpart of the ordinary VR in the continuous space. The authors propose algorithms that feature an iterative updating of the distances (according to different rules) in order to balance district populations as much as possible. In this model the authors exploit contiguity conditions formulated in Apollonio et al. (2008). Even if the graph is not a tree, these conditions can be used in the following way in the heuristic procedure. At each iteration contiguity of the districts is maintained thanks to the *geodesic consistency* property: if unit i belongs to district s and j lies on the geodesic between i and s, then j also belongs to district s, the geodesic being the shortest path between two nodes in G. By admitting a slight perturbation of the edge lengths, it can be assumed that there is a unique geodesic between any two nodes. Under this assumption, the authors prove that geodesic consistency implies contiguity. Actually, geodesic consistency can be seen as a way to formalize the order constraints in (3.8).

3.3.4 Practical and Application Issues

To conclude, we point out one main issue in the design of the electoral districts, that is: *if* and *how* the above discussed methods can be practically exploited in a law. It is generally difficult that formal models are accepted by lawmakers. However, differently from BAP, there is a general awareness that PD is a difficult problem. This could make computer based procedures more acceptable by lawmakers. Therefore, besides the study of new and more efficient methods, it is important to diffuse the already existing tools among the institutions. This would certainly help the administrative staff who has the (hard) task of executing all the procedures related to the political elections of a country. We believe that human contribution must not be excluded in the district definition process, but, when possible, it is recommended to take advantage from the power of mathematical modeling and automatic elaboration.

Bibliography

N. Apollonio, I. Lari, F. Ricca, B. Simeone, and J. Puerto. Polynomial algorithms for partitioning a tree into single-center subtrees to minimize flat service costs. *Networks*, 51:78–89, 2008.

A. Bachem and B. Korte. On the RAS- algorithm. *Computing*, 23:189–198, 1979.

M. L. Balinski and G. Demange. Algorithms for proportional matrices in reals and integers. *Mathematical Programming*, 45:193–210, 1989a.

M. L. Balinski and G. Demange. An axiomatic approach to proportionality between matrices. *Mathematics of Operations Research*, 14:700–219, 1989b.

M. L. Balinski and H. Young. *Fair Representation – Meeting the Ideal of One Man, One Vote.* Brookings Institution Press; second edition, 2001.

L. Bodin. A districting experiment with a clustering algorithm. *Annals of the New York Academy of Sciences*, 219(1):209–214, 1973.

B. Bozkaya, E. Erkut, and G. Laporte. A tabu search heuristic and adaptive memory procedure for political districting. *European Journal of Operational Research*, 144(1):12–26, 2003.

L. Cox and L. Ernst. Controlled rounding. *INFOR—Information Systems and Operational Research*, 20:423–432, 1982.

C. De Simone, M. Lucertini, S. Pallottino, and B. Simeone. Fair dissections of spiders, worms, and caterpillars. *Networks*, 20(3):323–344, 1990.

R. Garfinkel and G. Nemhauser. Optimal political districting by implicit enumeration techniques. *Management Science*, 16(8):495–508, 1970.

A. M. Geoffrion. Integer programming by implicit enumeration and Balas' method. *SIAM Review*, 9:178–190, 1967.

P. Grilli di Cortona, C. Manzi, A. Pennisi, F. Ricca, and B. Simeone. *Evaluation and optimization of electoral systems.* Society for Industrial and Applied Mathematics (SIAM), Philadelphia, PA, 1999.

G. R. Grimmett. European apportionment via the Cambridge compromise. *Mathematical Social Sciences*, 63(2):68–73, 2012.

S. Hess, J. Weaver, H. Siegfeldt, J. Whelan, and P. Zitlau. Nonpartisan political redistricting by computer. *Operations Research*, 13(6):998–1006, 1965.

D. L. Horn, C. R. Hampton, and A. J. Vandenberg. Practical application of district compactness. *Political Geography*, 12(2):103–120, 1993.

T. C. Hu, A. B. Kahng, and C. W. A. Tsao. Old bachelor acceptance: A new class of non-monotone threshold accepting methods. *ORSA Journal on Computing*, 7(4):417–425, 1995.

B. Kalantari, I. Lari, F. Ricca, and B. Simeone. On the complexity of general matrix scaling and entropy minimization via the ras algorithm. *Mathematical Programming, Series A*, 112:371–401, 2008.

J. Kalcsics, S. Nickel, and M. Schröder. Towards a unified territorial design approach-applications, algorithms and gis integration. *Top*, 13(1):1–56, 2005.

I. Lari, F. Ricca, J. Puerto, and A. Scozzari. Partitioning a graph into connected components with fixed centers and optimizing cost-based objective functions or equipartition criteria. *Networks*, 67(1):69–81, 2016.

A. Mehrotra, E. Johnson, and G. Nemhauser. An optimization based heuristic for political districting. *Management Science*, 44(8):1100–1114, 1998.

M. Minoux. A polynomial algorithm for minimum quadratic cost flow problems. *European Journal of Operational Research*, 18:377–387, 1984.

B. Nygreen. European assembly constituencies for Wales - comparing of methods for solving a political districting problem. *Mathematical Programming*, 42(1-3): 159–169, 1988.

F. Pukelsheim. Bazi – a Java program for proportional representation. Reports 1, Oberwolfach, 2004.

F. Pukelsheim and C. Schuhmacher. Das neue Zürcher Zuteilungsverfahren für Parlamentswahlen. *Aktuelle Juristische Praxis – Pratique Juridique Actuelle*, 13: 505–522, 2004.

F. Ricca and B. Simeone. Political redistricting: Traps, criteria, algorithms, and trade-offs. *Ricerca Operativa*, 27:81–119, 1997.

F. Ricca and B. Simeone. Local search algorithms for political districting. *European Journal of Operational Research*, 189(3):1409–1426, 2008.

F. Ricca, A. Scozzari, and B. Simeone. Weighted Voronoi region algorithms for political districting. *Mathematical and Computer Modelling*, 48(9-10):1468–1477, 2008.

F. Ricca, A. Scozzari, P. Serafini, and B. Simeone. Error minimization methods in biproportional apportionment. *TOP*, 20:547–577, 2012.

F. Ricca, A. Scozzari, and B. Simeone. Political districting: from classical models to recent approaches. *Annals of Operations Research*, 204:271–299, 2013.

U. G. Rothblum and H. Schneider. Scaling of matrices which have prescribed row sums and column sums via optimization. *Linear Algebra Applications*, 114: 737–764, 1989.

M. Schroeder. *Gebiete optimal aufteilen - OR-Verfahren für die Gebietsaufteilung als Anwendungsfall gleichmäßiger Baumzerlegung*. PhD thesis, Universität Karlsruhe, 2001.

P. Serafini. Allocation of the EU parliament seats via integer linear programming and revised quotas. *Mathematical Social Sciences*, 63:107–113, 2012.

P. Serafini. Certificates of optimality for minimum norm biproportional apportionments. *Social Choice and Welfare*, 44:1–12, 2015.

P. Serafini and B. Simeone. Parametric maximum flow methods for minimax approximation of target quotas in biproportional apportionment. *Networks*, 59: 191–208, 2012a.

P. Serafini and B. Simeone. Certificates of optimality: the third way to biproportional apportionment. *Social Choice and Welfare*, 38:247–268, 2012b.

B. Simeone. Optimal graph partitioning. *Atti giornate di lavoro AIRO, Urbino*, pages 57–73, 1978.

H. Young. Measuring the compactness of legislative districts. *Legislative Studies Quarterly*, 13(1):105–115, 1988.

CHAPTER 4

Iterative Voting

Reshef Meir

4.1 Introduction

In typical theoretical models of voting, all voters submit their vote at once, without an option to change or revise their decision. While this assumption fits some political voting settings, it fails to hold in most realistic scenarios: committees often follow an informal voting process where members are free to revise their votes or hold noncommittal straw votes; online voting tools such as Facebook and Doodle allow voters to see previous votes and to change their vote by logging in later on; and even in traditional political voting, polls broadcast in the media may prompt voters to change their vote.

Iterative voting games aim to capture such settings. We assume voters have fixed preferences and start from some announcement (e.g., they might sincerely report their preferences). Votes are aggregated via some predefined rule (e.g., Plurality), but voters may change their votes after observing the current announcements and outcome. The game proceeds in turns, where a single voter changes his vote at each turn, until no voter has objections and the final outcome is announced. Crucially, the outcome of iterative voting (like the strategies themselves) may depend on the *order* of voters, which may be affected by external constraints (such as voters' availability to answer an online poll), internal incentives (such as voting early to signal other voters) or other factors.

The lack of a well-defined voting order prevents solutions such as a backward-induction that are common in game theory, even if we are willing to assume that voters are fully rational.

The common assumption in iterative voting is that voters do not know the other voters' preferences or who might change their vote, and thus act in a *myopic way*. That is, vote in every round as if it is the last one, since there is no reliable information for any future prediction. In game-theoretic terms, each voter will play a best reply to the *current action profile* of the other voters. If no voter wants to change his vote, then by definition the current profile is a pure Nash equilibrium (PNE). Voters who are more sophisticated on the one hand, or have less accurate information about the current state on the other hand, may not follow their best reply and instead use other heuristics, in which case equilibria (profiles where no voter wants to move) may not correspond to Nash equilibria.

For any voting rule and type of behavior we are interested in the following questions:

- Are voters guaranteed to converge to an equilibrium? If so, how fast?
- What are all the equilibria reachable from a particular initial state?
- Is the iterative process leading the society to a socially good outcome?

In order to answer these questions, we will first introduce formal game-theoretic definitions for equilibrium and convergence (Section 4.2). Section 4.3 shows how these notions apply in the simple Plurality rule and demonstrates some analysis techniques. Section 4.4 overviews most known results on convergence of iterative voting for myopic rational agents with complete information. In Section 4.5 we relax the model to allow various voting heuristics for iterative voting, focusing on some selected models and convergence results. Section 4.6 concludes and suggests future research directions.

4.2 Preliminaries

For a finite set X, we denote by $\mathcal{L}(X)$ the set of all linear (strict) orders over X. For $L \in \mathcal{L}(X)$, denote by $top(L)$ the first element of L.

A *voting instance* is defined by a set of *candidates*, or *alternatives*, A, a set of *voters* N, and a *preference profile* $\boldsymbol{L} = (L_1, \ldots, L_n)$, where each $L_i \in \mathcal{L}(A)$. For $a, b \in A, i \in N$, candidate a precedes b in L_i (denoted $a \succ_i b$) if voter i prefers candidate a over candidate b. Thus $top(L_i) \in A$ is i's most preferred candidate. In this chapter we assume a voter is never indifferent, i.e., $a \succeq_i b$ means that either $a \succ_i b$ or $a = b$.

A *voting rule* (or, in the game theory literature, *game form*) defines a set of actions A_i for each player, and a function $f : \times_{i \in N} A_i \to A$ from joint actions to alternatives. However most common voting rules assume a certain structure on the action sets. Typically, that the possible actions are preferences over alternatives.

Following Zwicker (2016), a *social choice function* (SCF) is a function that accepts a preference profile $\boldsymbol{L}$ as input, and outputs a nonempty set of winning candidates. Formally: $f : \mathcal{L}(A)^n \to 2^A \setminus \{\emptyset\}$. An SCF f is *resolute* if $|f(\boldsymbol{L})| = 1$ for all $\boldsymbol{L}$. In this chapter we mainly discuss resolute SCFs, which we also refer to as *standard voting rules* or *standard game forms*. However all definitions, except for the notion of truthful vote, naturally extend to non-standard voting rules.[1] See Figure 4.1 for examples of standard and non-standard game forms.

A pair $\langle f, \boldsymbol{L} \rangle$ defines an *ordinal game*, where players' actions are preference orders. The preference of player i over outcomes is given by L_i. In the case of Plurality (or Veto), the set of actions is the set of alternatives A, rather than $\mathcal{L}(A)$. Since A is a coarsening of $\mathcal{L}(A)$, Plurality is still a well-defined SCF.

---

[1] We emphasize that game forms or voting rules where the actions are not permutations over A (or coarsenings of such permutations) cannot be written as an SCF. An example of a common voting rule that is non-standard is Approval voting.

Iterative Voting

f_1	a	b	c
a	a	a	a
b	b	b	b
c	c	c	c

f_2	a	b	c
a	a	a	a
b	a	b	b
c	a	b	c

f_3	$\emptyset$	a	b	c	ab	ac	bc	abc
a	a	a	a	a	a	a	a	a
b	b	a	b	b	a	a	b	a
c	c	a	b	c	a	a	b	a

f_4	x	y
a	a	b
b	b	c
c	c	a

Figure 4.1: Four examples of game forms with two agents. f_1 is a dictatorial game form with 3 candidates (the row agent is the dictator). f_2 is the Plurality voting rule with 3 candidates and lexicographic tie-breaking. f_3 and f_4 are non-standard game forms. In f_3 player 1 has a single vote, whereas player 2 may approve any subset of candidates. f_4 is a non-standard game form, where the action sets are $A_1 = A = \{a, b, c\}, A_2 = \{x, y\}$.

Convergence and Equilibrium. Any game G induces a directed graph whose vertices are all action profiles (states) $\mathcal{A}$, and edges are all local improvement steps (better replies) (Young, 1993; Andersson et al., 2010). That is, there is an edge from profile a to profile a' if there is some agent i and some action a'_i such that $a' = (a_{-i}, a'_i)$ and i prefers $f(a')$ to $f(a)$. A better reply $a_i \xrightarrow{i} a'_i$ is called a *best reply* if i has no better reply at profile (a_{-i}, a'_i).

The *sinks* of G are all states with no outgoing edges. Clearly, a state is a sink iff it is a PNE. Since a state may have multiple outgoing edges, we need to specify which one is selected in a given play: in particular, *which player i makes a move* and *which of i's available better replies is selected*.

Much attention has been given in the game theory literature to the question of *convergence*, and several notions of convergence have been defined (Monderer and Shapley, 1996; Milchtaich, 1996; Kukushkin, 2011; Apt and Simon, 2012). For more detailed definitions using schedulers see Meir et al. (2017).

A game G has the *finite individual improvement property* (we say that G has FIP), if the corresponding improvement graph has no cycles.

In other words, any sequence of better replies from any initial state a^0 reaches a PNE. Games that have FIP are also known as *acyclic games* and as *generalized ordinal potential games* (Monderer and Shapley, 1996). Two weaker notions of acyclicity are as follows.

- A game G has *weakly-FIP* if from any initial state a^0 there is *some* path in the improvement graph that reaches a PNE. Such games are known as *weakly acyclic*.

- A game G has *restricted-FIP* (Kukushkin, 2011) if from any initial state a^0 and *any order of players* there is *some* path in the improvement graph that reaches a PNE. We refer to such games as *order-free acyclic*.

Intuitively, restricted FIP means that there is some restriction players can adopt such that convergence is guaranteed regardless of the order in which they play. Kukushkin identifies a particular restriction of interest, namely restriction to best reply improvements, and defines the *finite best reply property* (FBRP) and its weak and restricted analogs. The *Finite direct reply property* (FDRP) is only

```
FBRP f.t.   ⇐   FBRP            restricted-FBRP  ⇒  weak-FBRP
   ⇑            ⇑                      ⇓                ⇓
FIP f.t.    ⇐   FIP      ⇛     restricted-FIP   ⇒  weak-FIP   ⇒  pure Nash
   ⇓            ⇓                      ⇑                ⇑         exists
FDRP f.t.   ⇐   FDRP           restricted-FDRP  ⇒  weak-FDRP
```

Figure 4.2: A double arrow X ⇒ Y means that any game or game form with the X property also has the Y property. A triple arrow means that any property on the premise side entails all properties on the conclusion side. 'f.t.' means 'from truth.' The third row is only relevant for Plurality/Veto, where direct reply is well defined.

relevant for certain voting rules and is defined later on. Figure 4.2 demonstrates entailment relations among the various acyclicity properties.

We emphasize that the playing agent *must* select an available action, if one exists. For example, we can imagine a dynamics where a voter that only votes for a candidate that is much more preferred than the current winner (say, ranked at least 3 positions above). Such a voter may not move even though he has available better replies. Thus convergence of this dynamic does not imply restricted-FIP.

We say that a game G has *FIP from state a* if all paths from $a \in \mathcal{A}$ reach a PNE. G has *FIP from the truth* if it has FIP from the truthful state $a^* = L$ (for standard rules). We say that a voting rule f has FIP if for *any* preference profile L the induced game $\langle f, L \rangle$ has FIP. The definitions for all other notions of finite improvement properties are analogous.

4.3 Iterative Plurality Voting

Plurality is a particularly simple voting rule, where f returns the candidate ranked at the top position by the largest number of voters.

The *final score* of c for a given profile $a \in A^n$ in the Plurality game form f^{PL} is the total number of voters that vote c. We denote the final score vector by s_a (often just s when the other parameters are clear from the context), where $s(c) = |\{i \in N : a_i = c\}|$. Thus the Plurality rule f^{PL} selects the candidate from $W = \text{argmax}_{c \in A}\, s_a(c)$ with the lowest lexicographic index.

Unfortunately, Plurality is not acyclic, and this holds even if voters are restricted to best replies.

Proposition 4.1. *f^{PL} does not have FBRP. In particular it does not have FIP.*

Proof. There are three candidates $A = \{a, b, c\}$ and three voters. We have a single fixed voter voting for a whose preferences are irrelevant. The preference profile of the two other voters is defined as $a \succ_1 b \succ_1 c$, $c \succ_2 b \succ_2 a$. The following cycle consists of better replies ((a_1, a_2) are the votes at time t, the winner appears in curly brackets): $(b,c)\{a\} \xrightarrow{2} (b,b)\{b\} \xrightarrow{1} (c,b)\{a\} \xrightarrow{2} (c,c)\{c\} \xrightarrow{1} (b,c)\{a\}$. □

Direct Replies. Meir et al. (2010, 2017) identify a different restriction, namely *direct reply*, which is well defined under the Plurality rule. Formally, a step $a \xrightarrow{i} a'$ is a direct reply if $f(a') = a'_i$, i.e., if i votes for the new winner. An example of an indirect step is when a voter who votes for the winner changes the outcome by moving to a candidate with a low score (e.g., the steps of voter 1 in the example above).

Theorem 4.2 (Meir et al. 2010, 2017). f^{PL} *has FDRP. Moreover, any path of direct replies will converge after at most $m^2 n^2$ steps. In particular, Plurality is order-free acyclic.*

The number of steps until convergence drops to $O(mn)$ if players start from the initial truthful state (Meir et al., 2010) or follow their (unique) direct best reply (Reyhani and Wilson, 2012).

We will demonstrate some of the ideas often used in such proofs, by proving a *weaker* result, namely that any sequence of direct best replies (FDBRP) from the truth converges.

Proof of FDBRP from the truth. Denote by $w^t = f^{PL}(a^t)$ the winner after step t, and by W^t all candidates that can become winners by at most one additional vote. Denote $a = a_i^{t-1}$. We claim that at any step $a \xrightarrow{i} a_i^t$, the following invariants hold:

(1) $a \neq w^{t-1}$ (the manipulator never leaves the current winner);

(2) a_i^t is i's most preferred candidate in $W^{t-1} \setminus \{a\}$;

(3) $a_i^t = w^t$ (vote goes to the new winner);

(4) $a_i^{t-1} \succ_i a_i^t$ (voter always compromises for a less preferred candidate);

(5) $W^t \subseteq W^{t-1}$ (set of possible winners always shrinks); and

(6) For any voter j, either $a_j^t \notin W^t$, or a_j^t is j's most preferred candidate in W^t.

Assume all of (1)-(6) hold until time $t-1$ and consider step t. We prove by induction that all invariants still hold after step t.

Due to (6), we know that either $a \notin W^{t-1}$, or a is i's most preferred in W^{t-1}. Suppose that $a = w^{t-1}$, then we are in the latter case (a is most preferred in W^{t-1}), which means that $w^t = f(a_{-i}^{t-1}, a_i^t) \prec_i a = w^{t-1}$. Thus this cannot be a manipulation step, and $a \neq w^{t-1}$. That is, invariant (1) holds.

Now, since $a \neq w^{t-1}$ the score of the winner after step t does not decrease, only voting candidates in W^{t-1} may change the outcome. Then, invariant (2) follows immediately from our direct best reply assumption.

Invariant (3) follows immediately from the definition of direct replies.

As for (4), either t is the first move of i, in which case $a = top(L_i) \succ_i a_i^t$, or there had been a step $a' \xrightarrow{i} a$ at some time $t' < t$, in which case a is the most preferred in $W^{t'}$. By inductively applying (5), we have that $W^{t-1} \subseteq W^{t'}$, and thus $a \succ_i c$ for all $c \in W^{t-1} \setminus \{a\}$, and in particular $a \succ_i a'$. Thus (4) holds at step t.

We have $s_{a^t}(w^t) \geq s_{a^t}(w^{t-1}) = s_{a^{t-1}}(w^{t-1})$ (the equality is due to (1)), which means that the score of the winner weakly increased. Thus the threshold to become a possible winner also weakly increased, whereas the score of all $c \neq a_i^t$ weakly decreased. This means that for any $c \neq a_i^t$ we have $c \notin W^{t-1} \Rightarrow c \notin W^t$, and (5) holds at step t.

Invariant (6) holds at a^0 by our assumption of truthful initial vote, and continues to hold as long as (5) does, since a more preferred candidate cannot join W^t. Thus (6) holds at step t. Finally, note that by (3), each voter can move at most $m-1$ times, and thus convergence is achieved in at most $n(m-1)$ steps. □

4.4 Myopic Rational Voters

We overview most of the known results on convergence of iterative voting under various notions of acyclicity, summarized in Table 4.1. Some of the results we cite require some tweaks, for details see Meir et al. (2017). We then study whether equilibria of iterative voting are beneficial for the society.

4.4.1 Strongly Acyclic Voting Rules

It is not hard to see that any *dictatorial rule* (where a single voter determines the outcome) has FIP, due to transitivity of preferences. Interestingly, dictatorships are not the only FIP rules.

In the *direct kingmaker* voting rule (Dutta, 1984) all voters $i \in N \setminus \{1\}$ specify a single candidate $a \in A$, whereas voter 1 selects $i \in N \setminus \{1\}$ to be a "dictator of the day." Note that the direct kingmaker is a non-standard voting rule.

Theorem 4.3. *The direct kingmaker has FIP.*

Proof. Denote $d^t = a_1^t$ as the dictator in a^t. In every state a^t, only agents 1 and d^t may have a better reply. Further, any better reply of d^t is selecting a more-preferred candidate, i.e., $a_{d^t}^{t+1} \succ_{d^t} a_{d^t}^t$. Thus any agent except agent 1 may move at most $m-1$ times. Since any cycle implies an unlimited number of steps by at least 2 agents, there can be no cycles. □

Characterizing all FIP voting rules is an important and nontrivial problem. For some partial results, see Boros et al. (2010); Kukushkin (2011); Meir et al. (2017).

4.4.2 Order Free and Weak Acyclicity

Veto was shown to converge under direct replies from any initial state (Lev and Rosenschein, 2012; Reyhani and Wilson, 2012). For other common voting rules, results are not as rosy: it is usually possible to construct examples of cycles, even when voters start by voting truthfully. Table 4.1 summarizes known results.

Further, even variations of the Plurality rule, such as adding voters' weights and/or changing the tie-breaking method may result in games with cycles. At least for Plurality with a random tie-breaking rule, it can be shown that it is *weakly acyclic*, thereby providing partial explanation to the fact that simulations almost never hit a cycle (Meir et al., 2017). Whether other common voting rules are also weakly acyclic is an open question, which is particularly of interest for a large number of voters.

Iterative Voting

Other Notions of Convergence. The above model only considers voters who change their vote one-by-one. Other iterative models exist, that make different assumptions. For example, we can consider voters that make coordinated coalitional moves (Kukushkin, 2011; Gourvès et al., 2016), simultaneous (non-coordinated) moves (Meir, 2015), or a different dynamic where in each step a voter proposes one alternative to replace the current winner using a Majority vote (Airiau and Endriss, 2009).

4.4.3 Reachable Equilibria

Depending on the initial profile and the order of voters, the game may reach one of several equilibria (or none at all, for some voting rules), possibly with different winners. We want to know what these equilibria are. Also, in those cases where an iterative voting game converges, we would like to know "how good" the outcome is to the society. As with other game-theoretic analyses of voting outcomes, there are at least two different approaches to measure outcome quality:

- with respect to the particular voting rule in question,

- with respect to an objective measure, such as social welfare, Condorcet efficiency, etc.

Characterization. The structure of equilibria attained under iterative Plurality voting was studied by Rabinovich et al. (2015), who considered both the model above, and variations where voters are truth-biased (weakly prefer to vote truthfully) or lazy (weakly prefer to abstain). In general, they show that finding whether a particular outcome is reachable via iterative voting from the truthful state, is NP-complete, suggesting that a simple characterization may not exist. In contrast, they provide an efficient algorithm to test which equilibrium states are reachable when the voters a truth-biased or lazy. In fact, when voters are lazy, then in equilibrium at most one voter remains active.

We emphasize that under truth-bias or lazyness, the equilibrium outcomes do not coincide with Nash equilibria.

Dynamic Price of Anarchy. A common way to measure the inefficiency in a game due to strategic behavior is the *Price of Anarchy*: the ratio between the quality of the outcome in the worst Nash equilibrium, and the optimal outcome (Christodoulou and Koutsoupias, 2005). In the context of voting, this translates to the question of how far the equilibrium outcome can be from the truthful voting outcome (seeing the truthful outcome as "optimal" according to the voting rule in use).

As we have seen, Nash equilibria in most voting rules can be arbitrarily far from the truth. Thus, Brânzei et al. (2013) suggested instead to restrict attention to the set of Nash equilibria that are the outcome of some iterative voting procedure, starting from the truthful vote.

Formally, consider a score-based voting rule f, and denote by $s_f(c, L)$ the score of candidate c in action profile L. The *reachable equilibria* of f, denoted $EQ^T(f, L)$, are the set of all profiles L' s.t. :

- There is a path of best-replies from the truthful profile L to L'.
- L' is a Nash equilibrium of $\langle f, L \rangle$.

The dynamic Price of Anarchy is defined as

$$\text{DPoA}(f) = \min_{L} \min_{L' \in EQ^T(f,L)} \frac{s_f(f(L'), L)}{s_f(f(L), L)}.$$

Brânzei et al. (2013) show that the DPoA of Plurality is close to 1 (i.e., a winner in equilibrium must have a very close score to the truthful winner); and that the DPoA in Veto depends on the number of candidates m. In particular for $m \leq 3$ the DPoA in Veto is constant, regardless of n. The DPoA in Borda, on the other hand, is $\Omega(n)$, meaning that equilibria can be arbitrarily bad.

Objective Quality Metrics. The fact that we chose to use a particular voting rule does not necessarily mean that this rule represents the optimal outcome for every profile. The selection of the rule might be affected by the simplicity of the rule, due to tradition, and so on. We may thus have multiple criteria for a "good outcome," and ask how well a given voting rule satisfies them in equilibrium.

For example, we may be interested in the social welfare of the voters (as measured by Borda score), in the likelihood of finding the Condorcet winner when one exists, or avoiding the Condorcet loser, and so on.

This question was studied using extensive simulations by Meir et al. (2014) for the Plurality rule, where it was shown that equilibria outcomes are *better* than the truthful outcome under most metrics observed. Koolyk et al. (2017) performed similar simulations for several other voting rules, and obtained mixed results w.r.t. the the social welfare. More interestingly, rules that are not Condorcet consistent (Plurality, Bucklin, STV) are more likely to find the Condorcet winner under rational play (i.e., in equilibrium) than under truthful voting, whereas the Condorcet efficiency of Condorcet-consistent rules only slightly declines.

That said, when the number of voters is large, the initial outcome is almost always an equilibrium (whether truthful or not), and thus in most games no voter will move, and the positive effect of best reply dynamics becomes negligible.

4.5 Voting Heuristics

The equilibrium analysis and the best reply dynamics considered in the previous sections makes the following implicit assumptions.

- Voters know exactly how other voters currently vote.
- Voters are myopic: always vote as if the game ends after the current turn.
- Voters are rational: always vote in a way that improves or maximizes their utility.

4.5.1 Ad hoc Heuristics

Most heuristics are similar to best reply in that they only assume the voter knows his own preferences, and has some information about the current voting profile (e.g., the score of each candidate, or their current ranking). However in contrast to best or better reply, a heuristic step may or may not change the outcome. It thus reflects the belief of the voter that she might be pivotal even if this is not apparent from the current state. In the next subsection we will look more closely into such a rational (or bounded-rational) justification, but for now we will be satisfied with just describing some heuristics that have been proposed.

In the following description, we assume f is some score-based rule, unless specified otherwise. Let L_i be the real preferences of voter i, and let $a = (a_1, \ldots, a_n)$, $s = (s_1, \ldots, s_m)$ be the current action profile and current scores of all candidates. We denote by c_j the candidate with the j'th highest score in s.

Crucially, some of these heuristics depend on some internal private parameters, which can be used to explain behavioral differences among voters.

- "k-pragmatist" (Reijngoud and Endriss, 2012): Here, each voter has a parameter k_i, and ranks candidates $W = \{c_1, \ldots, c_{k_i}\}$ at the top according to her real preferences L_i. All other candidates are ranked below W according to their order in L_i.[2]

- "Threshold": Similar to k-pragmatist, except instead of a fixed parameter k_i, the set of "possible winners" W consists of all candidates whose score s_j is above some threshold $T_i(a)$ (i.e., the threshold may depend both on i and on the current state).

- "Second Chance" (Grandi et al., 2013): If the current winner is not i's best or second-best choice according to L_i, she moves her second-best alternative to the top position.

- "Best Upgrade" (Grandi et al., 2013): This is a restriction of best reply to candidates that are ranked above the current winner $f(a)$ in L_i.

- "Upgrade" (Obraztsova et al., 2015): Similar to Best Upgrade, except the upgraded candidate is not necessarily placed first (only high enough to win).

- "Unit Upgrade" (Obraztsova et al., 2015): Similar to Upgrade, except the upgraded candidate is moved exactly one step up (if this is enough to win).

Simulations show that these heuristics almost always lead to convergence when applied in an iterative voting setting (Grandi et al., 2013).

4.5.2 Strict Uncertainty and Bounded Rationality

A different approach to derive heuristic voting behavior is to consider a formal way to model voter's *uncertainty* regarding the outcome. Then, based on his beliefs, the voter selects the action (ballot) that is best for him.

---

[2]There is another variation where only the most preferred candidate in W is moved to the top, without other changes.

To see why this may differ from a purely rational behavior, note that:

1. The beliefs of the voter may not be correct or justified.

2. The response of the voter may not maximize his expected utility, which may not even be well-defined.

Thus we can think of such approaches as models of voters with *bounded rationality*. In contrast to Bayesian game-theoretic models of strategic voting (Myerson and Weber, 1993; Messner and Polborn, 2005), voters may not assign exact probabilities to outcomes, and in particular cannot compute expected utilities.[3]

Several papers studied beliefs based on strict uncertainties. One that we already mentioned is (Reijngoud and Endriss, 2012), which assumes the voter may only be aware of the current winner, the order of candidates according to scores, etc. Similar models are considered in other papers without studying iterative moves or convergence (Conitzer et al., 2011; van Ditmarsch et al., 2013). We can also think of voters whose beliefs depend on some internal parameter, which we can think of as their *uncertainty level*. Intuitively, as the voter is more uncertain, she considers more outcomes as possible.

Two such models based on voter's optimism were suggested by Reyhani et al. (2012) and Obraztsova et al. (2016), where in the first paper the optimism is regarding the actual unknown scores, and in the second it is about the voter's ability to prompt other voters into supporting the same candidate. In both models, more optimistic voters will consider a larger set of candidates as possible winners, and will vote strategically to one of them.

Local Dominance. A third model of strict uncertainty is based on local dominance (Meir et al., 2014; Meir, 2015), and can be applied to scoring-based rules. This model explicitly separates the beliefs of the voter on candidates' scores and his strategic actions:

- All voters share some prospective score vector $s = (s_1, \ldots, s_m)$.

- Each voter i has an uncertainty parameter r_i.

- Voter i considers as *possible* all outcomes s' such that $|s_c - s'_c| \leq r_i$ for all $c \in A$.[4] Denote all possible states in voting profile a by $S_i(a) = \{s' : \|s' - s_a\|_{\ell_\infty} \leq r_i\}$.

- Given this belief, voter i will change his action from a_i to a'_i if action a'_i *dominates* action a_i. Formally, if $f(s', a'_i) \succeq_i f(s', a_i)$ for all states $s' \in S_i(a)$, and $f(s'', a'_i) \succ_i f(s'', a_i)$ for at least one state $s'' \in S_i(a)$.

This behavior encodes bounded rationality under *loss aversion*: the voter will make a strategic move only if certain (according to his beliefs) that this move will not hurt him, and might be beneficial.

---

[3]Also note that expected utility is undefined for a voter with ordinal preferences, even if we have such a distribution.

[4]The paper also considers other distance metrics, but the ℓ_∞ metric is the simplest one.

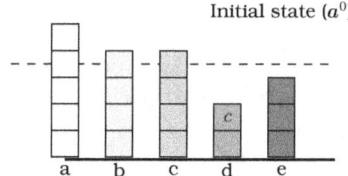 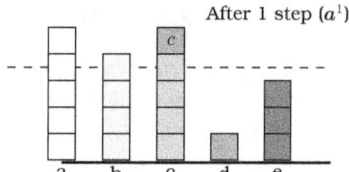

Figure 4.3: A single Local-Dominance step. The letter inside a voter is his *second* preference, thus the highlighted voter has preferences $d \succ_i c \succ_i \{a,b,e\}$. The dashed line marks the threshold of possible winners W_i for voters of type $r_i = 2$. Although $d \xrightarrow{i} c$ is not a better reply (since it does not change the outcome), it is a valid LD move according to Lemma 4.4: $d = a_i^0 \notin W_i$, $c = a_i^1 \in W_i$, and there is a candidate $a \in W_i$ such that $c \succ_i a$.

Denote by $W_i \subseteq A$ the set of candidates whose Plurality score (without voter i) is at least $max_c s(c) - 2r_i$. Note that these are exactly the candidates considered as possible winners by voter i, since there is a possible state s' where $j \in W_i$ gets r_i more votes, and the current winner gets r_i votes less. See Figure 4.3 for an example of a Local-Dominance move.

Local dominance is in fact a special case of π-manipulation (Reijngoud and Endriss, 2012), where in the general case $S_i(a)$ may be an arbitrary set of "possible profiles." One other special case of interest is W-manipulation, where the manipulator is assumed to know only the identity of the winner, i.e., $S_i(a) = \{a' \text{ s.t. } f(a) = f(a')\}$.

Worst-Case Regret minimization (WCR) (Meir, 2015) and Non-Myopic voting (NM) (Obraztsova et al., 2016) are similar to local dominance in the way they derive the set of possible winners W_i, but then make some different behavioral assumptions on action selection, which we will not specify explicitly here.

It turns out that the local dominance provides a (bounded) rational justification to the threshold heuristic we described above, at least for Plurality.

Lemma 4.4 (Meir et al. 2014; Meir 2015). *a_i' locally dominates a_i only if:*

1. *either $a_i \notin W_i$, or a_i is the least preferred candidate in W_i;*

2. *$a_i' \in W_i$;*

3. *there is some $c \in W_i$ that is less preferred than a_i'.*

In addition, if the above conditions apply, then the most preferred candidate $a_i' \in W_i$ always locally dominates a_i.

Therefore, a voter that simply follows the threshold heuristics is essentially strategizing according to local dominance.[5] If the voter selects a step *minimizing his worst-case regret* rather than following local dominance moves, then this coincides with the threshold heuristics exactly (Meir, 2015).

Local dominance is strongly related to models based on modal logic and epistemology (Chopra et al., 2004; van Ditmarsch et al., 2013).

---

[5]Note that while any LD move is consistent with the threshold heuristics, the converse does not always hold. E.g., if there are 5 possible winners above the threshold, then a move from the third-preferred to the most preferred is not a local dominance move.

4.5.3 Equilibrium and Convergence

Given a voting rule f and a population of voters with well defined heuristics, a *voting equilibrium* is simply a profile of valid votes a, such that for each $i \in N$, the heuristic action of i in profile a is his current action a_i. That is, a state where no voter wants to change his vote.

Observation 4.5. *Consider an arbitrary voting rule f, and any restricted better reply dynamics (including best reply and better reply). Then for any preference profile L, a state a is a voting equilibrium if and only if a is a pure Nash equilibrium of the game $\langle f, L \rangle$.*

Given a voting rule and a heuristic, two important questions are: (a) does an equilibrium exist? and (b) will voters converge to equilibrium? The latter question can be further split to whether convergence is guaranteed from arbitrary initial states or from the truthful state.

Recall that the FIP property means that convergence is guaranteed regardless of the initial state, the order of the voters, and which available reply they choose. As any heuristic simply replaces the (possibly empty) set of better replies with some other set, we can modify the definition of FIP, or FIP from the truth, accordingly.

These questions were studied in several recent papers. Some heuristics are very easy to analyze. For example, when voters start from the truthful vote, then voters using the k-pragmatist or the Second Chance heuristics will move at most once (Reijngoud and Endriss, 2012; Grandi et al., 2013). Therefore, FIP from the truth is immediate. Obraztsova et al. (2015) identified some common structure for heuristic dynamics, which can be used to prove convergence for various combinations of voting rules and heuristics. This was further developed by Endriss et al. (2016) to prove convergence under W-manipulation.

However, all these studies are restricted to voters that start by reporting the truth, and use exactly the same heuristics. Results are summarized in Table 4.2.

Uncertainty-based Heuristics. Uncertainty-based heuristics are more involved, especially when the society is composed of voters with different uncertainty levels. Therefore, they have been studied mostly for the Plurality rule. On the other hand, it turns out that the Local Dominance heuristics has very strong convergence properties. An example of a Plurality game where voters use the Local Dominance heuristics is given in Figure 4.4.

Theorem 4.6 (Meir et al. 2014; Meir 2015). *Plurality with the Local Dominance heuristics has FIP. This holds for any population of voters with either homogeneous or diverse uncertainty levels.*

Limited convergence properties were also shown for other uncertainty-based heuristics. We summarize them in Table 4.2.

4.5.4 Equilibrium Properties

Equilibrium properties are typically studied using simulations, so that uncommon or unlikely equilibria can be ignored. Simulations are carried out by gen-

Iterative Voting

Voting rule	FIP	FBRP	restricted-FIP	Weak-FIP
Dictator	✓	✓	✓	✓
Direct Kingmaker	✓[M16]	✓	✓	✓
Plurality	✗	✗[MP+10]	✓[MP+10,MP+17]	✓
Veto	✗	✗[M16]	✓[RW12,LR12]	✓
k-approval ($k \geqslant 2$)	✗	✗[LR12,L15]	✗	✗[M16]
Borda	✗	✗[RW12,LR12]	✗	✗[RW12]
PSRs (except k-approval)	✗	✗[LR12,L15]	?	?
Approval	✗	✗[M16]	✓[M16]	✓
Other common rules	✗	✗[KT+17]	?	?

Table 4.1: Positive results carry over to the righthand side, negative to the lefthand side. All rules in the table use lexicographic tie-breaking. Reference codes: MP+10 (Meir et al., 2010), RW12 (Reyhani and Wilson, 2012), LR12 (Lev and Rosenschein, 2012) (see (Lev and Rosenschein, 2016) for the full version), M15 (Meir, 2015), L15 (Lev, 2015), M16 (Meir, 2016), KS+17 (Koolyk et al., 2017), MP+17 (Meir et al., 2017).

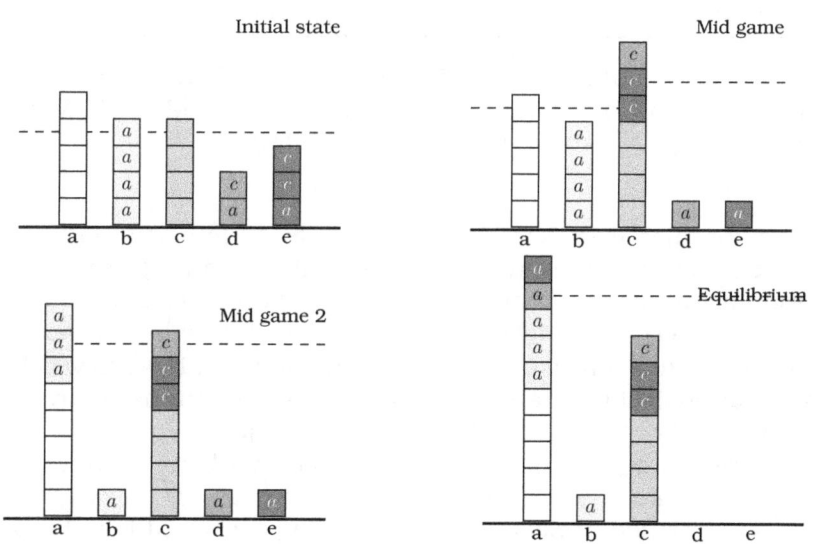

Figure 4.4: Convergence under Local-Dominance. The top left figure shows the initial (truthful) state of the game. The letter inside a voter is his second preference. The dashed line marks the threshold of possible winners W_i for voters of type $r_i = 2$. Note that due to tie breaking it is not the same for all candidates. For example, since a beats b in tie-breaking, b needs 2 more votes to win in the initial state. In the next two figures we can see voters leaving their candidates (who are not possible winners for them) to join one of the leaders. The last figure shows an equilibrium that was reached.

Voting rule	k-prag. [RE12]	Second Chance [GL+13]	Best Upgrade [GL+13]	Upgrade [OM+15]	Unit Upgrade [OM+15]	W-manip. [EO+16]
PSRs	✓	✓	✓	?	✓*	✓#
Maximin	✓	✓	✓	✓	✓	✓
Copland	✓	✓	✓	?	?	✓
Bucklin	-	✓	?	?	✓	?
all rules	-	✓	?	?	?	?

Table 4.2: Positive results mean FIP from the truth for uniform population. * - common PSRs including Borda and Plurality. # - means restricted-FIP. Reference codes: RE12 (Reijngoud and Endriss, 2012), GL+13 (Grandi et al., 2013), OM+15 (Obraztsova et al., 2015), EO+16 (Endriss et al., 2016).

Heuristic	Population	FIP	FIP from truth	equilibrium exists
LD	uniform	✓[M15]	✓[MLR14]	✓
LD	uniform + truth bias	?	✓[MLR14]	✓
LD	diverse	✓[M15]	✓	✓
WCR	uniform	?	✓[M15]	✓
WCR	diverse	×	×	×[M15]
NM	uniform	?	✓[OL+16]	✓
NM	diverse	×	×[OL+16]	?

Table 4.3: Convergence results for Local-Dominance and Worst-Case Regret minimization. All results are for Plurality. Reference codes: MLR14 (Meir et al., 2014), M15 (Meir, 2015), OL+16 (Obraztsova et al., 2016).

erating preference profiles from some distribution (e.g., Impartial culture, Urn, Plackett-Luce, etc.), setting the initial profile (truthful or other), and then sampling voters randomly to make a heuristic move, until an equilibrium is reached. For some heuristics voters' parameters should also be decided up front.

It should first be noted that convergence to equilibrium is achieved in practice (i.e., in simulations) almost always, whether or not this is guaranteed by theorems. Moreover, this convergence is typically very quick.

The *ad hoc* heuristics we mentioned typically lead to a better winner in terms of Condorcet efficiency and Borda score (Grandi et al., 2013). As with the best reply simulations mentioned in Section 4.4.3, this improvement is mild, possibly since the aforementioned heuristics give rise to a small amount of strategic behavior, and thus in many profiles the equilibrium is simply the initial state (note that some of these heuristics are just restrictions of best reply).

Extensive simulations of Plurality voting with Local Dominance heuristics show the following (Meir et al., 2014):

- As uncertainty level r increases, there is more strategic interaction among voters (more moves) until a certain point, from which strategic interaction declines.

- With more strategic interaction, the welfare measures (including Borda score, Condorcet consistency and others) tend to improve, reaching a significant improvement around the peak of strategic activity.

- With more strategic interaction, votes are more concentrated around two candidates (Duverger Law).

These findings are consistent among a broad class of preference distributions, and for different numbers of voters and candidates. Therefore, at least for Plurality, it seems that equilibria reached under Local Dominance resemble outcomes we observe in reality, and avoids unreasonable or highly inefficient Nash equilibria.

4.6 Conclusion

Iterative voting provides a natural tool to analyze strategic voting, which avoids the need to introduce cardinal utilities and probabilities, yet allows for flexible models of bounded rationality and restricted information. It turns out that iterative voting can also be a useful tool for automated systems that aggregate information from many sources (Hassanzadeh et al., 2013).

Theoretical analysis can be used to characterize the conditions under which convergence is expected, as well as properties of the attained equilibria. Future work could focus on general properties of voting rules that lead to positive results, and on designing simple iterative mechanisms that improve efficiency and welfare.

Theory alone, however, cannot settle the question of *which models and assumptions are more plausible*, especially when heuristics are involved. To answer these questions, theoretical models should be combined with empirical data and behavioral experiments (Forsythe et al., 1996; Palfrey, 2009; Kearns et al., 2009; Mattei et al., 2012; Tal et al., 2015; Bassi, 2015). Such interdisciplinary study would help social choice researchers to better understand iterative voting and design better voting mechanisms.

Acknowledgments

The author thanks Nick Jennings, Omer Lev, Svetlana Obraztsova, Maria Polukarov, and Jeffrey S. Rosenschein for many helpful discussions and useful comments.

Bibliography

S. Airiau and U. Endriss. Iterated majority voting. In *Proceedings of the 1st International Conference on Algorithmic Decision Theory (ADT)*, 2009.

D. Andersson, V. Gurvich, and T. D. Hansen. On acyclicity of games with cycles. *Discrete Applied Mathematics*, 158(10):1049–1063, 2010.

K. R. Apt and S. Simon. A classification of weakly acyclic games. In *Proceedings of the 5th International Symposium on Algorithmic Game Theory (SAGT)*, 2012.

A. Bassi. Voting systems and strategic manipulation: An experimental study. *Journal of Theoretical Politics*, 27(1):58–85, 2015.

E. Boros, V. Gurvich, K. Makino, and D. Papp. Acyclic, or totally tight, two-person game forms: Characterization and main properties. *Discrete Mathematics*, 310 (6):1135–1151, 2010.

S. Brânzei, I. Caragiannis, J. Morgenstern, and A. D. Procaccia. How bad is selfish voting? In *Proceedings of the 27th AAAI Conference on Artificial Intelligence (AAAI)*, 2013.

S. Chopra, E. Pacuit, and R. Parikh. Knowledge-theoretic properties of strategic voting. In *Proceedings of the 9th European Conference On Logics In Artificial Intelligence (JELIA)*, 2004.

G. Christodoulou and E. Koutsoupias. The price of anarchy of finite congestion games. In *Proceedings of the 37th Annual ACM Symposium on the Theory of Computing (STOC)*, 2005.

V. Conitzer, T. Walsh, and L. Xia. Dominating manipulations in voting with partial information. In *Proceedings of the 25th AAAI Conference on Artificial Intelligence (AAAI)*, 2011.

B. Dutta. Effectivity functions and acceptable game forms. *Econometrica: Journal of the Econometric Society*, 52(5):1151–1166, 1984.

U. Endriss, S. Obraztsova, M. Polukarov, and J. S. Rosenschein. Strategic voting with incomplete information. In *Proceedings of the 25th International Joint Conference on Artificial Intelligence (IJCAI)*, 2016.

R. Forsythe, T. Rietz, R. Myerson, and R. Weber. An experimental study of voting rules and polls in three candidate elections. *International Journal of Game Theory*, 25(3):355–383, 1996.

L. Gourvès, J. Lesca, and A. Wilczynski. Strategic voting in a social context: Considerate equilibria. In *Proceedings of the 22nd European Conference on Artificial Intelligence (ECAI)*, 2016.

U. Grandi, A. Loreggia, F. Rossi, K. B. Venable, and T. Walsh. Restricted manipulation in iterative voting: Condorcet efficiency and Borda score. In *Proceedings of the 3rd International Conference on Algorithmic Decision Theory (ADT)*, 2013.

F. F. Hassanzadeh, E. Yaakobi, B. Touri, O. Milenkovic, and J. Bruck. Building consensus via iterative voting. In *Proceedings of the IEEE International Symposium on Information Theory Proceedings (ISIT)*, 2013.

M. Kearns, S. Judd, J. Tan, and J. Wortman. Behavioral experiments on biased voting in networks. *Proceedings of the National Academy of Sciences*, 106(5): 1347–1352, 2009.

A. Koolyk, T. Strangway, O. Lev, and J. S. Rosenschein. Convergence and quality of iterative voting under non-scoring rules. In *Proceedings of the 26th International Joint Conference on Artificial Intelligence (IJCAI)*, 2017.

N. S. Kukushkin. Acyclicity of improvements in finite game forms. *International Journal of Game Theory*, 40(1):147–177, 2011.

O. Lev. *Agent Modeling of Human Interaction: Stability, Dynamics and Cooperation*. PhD thesis, The Hebrew University of Jerusalem, 2015.

O. Lev and J. S. Rosenschein. Convergence of iterative voting. In *Proceedings of the 11th International Conference on Autonomous Agents and Multiagent Systems (AAMAS)*, 2012.

O. Lev and J. S. Rosenschein. Convergence of iterative scoring rules. *Journal of Artificial Intelligence Research*, 57:573–591, 2016.

N. Mattei, J. Forshee, and J. Goldsmith. An empirical study of voting rules and manipulation with large datasets. *Proceedings of the 4th International Workshop on Computational Social Choice (COMSOC)*, 2012.

R. Meir. Plurality voting under uncertainty. In *Proceedings of the 29th AAAI Conference on Artificial Intelligence (AAAI)*, 2015.

R. Meir. Strong and weak acyclicity in iterative voting. In *Proceedings of the 9th International Symposium on Algorithmic Game Theory (SAGT)*, 2016.

R. Meir, M. Polukarov, J. S. Rosenschein, and N. Jennings. Convergence to equilibria of plurality voting. In *Proceedings of the 24th AAAI Conference on Artificial Intelligence (AAAI)*, 2010.

R. Meir, O. Lev, and J. S. Rosenschein. A local-dominance theory of voting equilibria. In *Proceedings of the 15th ACM Conference on Electronic Commerce (ACM-EC)*, 2014.

R. Meir, M. Polukarov, J. S. Rosenschein, and N. R. Jennings. Acyclic games and iterative voting. *Artificial Intelligence*, 2017. Forthcoming.

M. Messner and M. Polborn. Robust political equilibria under plurality and runoff rule. *IGIER Working Paper*, 2005.

I. Milchtaich. Congestion games with player-specific payoff functions. *Games and Economic Behavior*, 13(1):111–124, 1996.

D. Monderer and L. S. Shapley. Potential games. *Games and Economic Behavior*, 14(1):124–143, 1996.

R. B. Myerson and R. J. Weber. A theory of voting equilibria. *The American Political Science Review*, 87(1):102–114, 1993.

S. Obraztsova, E. Markakis, M. Polukarov, Z. Rabinovich, and N. R. Jennings. On the convergence of iterative voting: How restrictive should restricted dynamics be? In *Proceedings of the 29th AAAI Conference on Artificial Intelligence (AAAI)*, 2015.

S. Obraztsova, O. Lev, M. Polukarov, Z. Rabinovich, and J. S. Rosenschein. Non-myopic voting dynamics: An optimistic approach. In *Proceedings of the 10th Multidisciplinary Workshop on Advances in Preference Handling (M-PREF)*, 2016.

T. Palfrey. Laboratory experiments in political economy. *Annual Review of Political Science*, 12:379–388, 2009.

Z. Rabinovich, S. Obraztsova, O. Lev, E. Markakis, and J. S. Rosenschein. Analysis of equilibria in iterative voting schemes. In *Proceedings of the 29th AAAI Conference on Artificial Intelligence (AAAI)*, 2015.

A. Reijngoud and U. Endriss. Voter response to iterated poll information. In *Proceedings of the 11th International Conference on Autonomous Agents and Multiagent Systems (AAMAS)*, 2012.

R. Reyhani and M. C. Wilson. Best-reply dynamics for scoring rules. In *Proceedings of the 20th European Conference on Artificial Intelligence (ECAI)*, 2012.

R. Reyhani, M. C. Wilson, and J. Khazaei. Coordination via polling in plurality voting games under inertia. In *Proceedings of the 20th European Conference on Artificial Intelligence (ECAI)*, 2012.

M. Tal, R. Meir, and Y. Gal. A study of human behavior in voting systems. In *Proceedings of the 14th International Conference on Autonomous Agents and Multiagent Systems (AAMAS)*, 2015.

H. van Ditmarsch, J. Lang, and A. Saffidine. Strategic voting and the logic of knowledge. In *Proceedings of the 14th Conference on Theoretical Aspects of Rationality and Knowledge (TARK)*, 2013.

H. P. Young. The evolution of conventions. *Econometrica: Journal of the Econometric Society*, 61(1):57–84, 1993.

W. S. Zwicker. Introduction to the theory of voting. In F. Brandt, V. Conitzer, U. Endriss, J. Lang, and A. D. Procaccia, editors, *Handbook of Computational Social Choice*. Cambridge University Press, 2016.

CHAPTER 5

Group Activity Selection Problems

Andreas Darmann and Jérôme Lang

5.1 Introduction

Group activity selection consists in selecting one or several activities for a set of participants (agents) and of assigning these agents to one of the different selected activities (or possibly to no activity at all), according to the agents' preferences. The specificity of the group activity selection problem is that agents' preferences bear both on activities and on the number of participants for a given activity. As a concrete example of a group activity selection problem consider the organisers of a workshop[1] who are planning to have a set of group activities taking place during a free afternoon:

- Activities are held in parallel, so that each participant can take part in at most one activity.

- The possible activities include a hike, a bus trip to a nearby historic city, and a table tennis competition.

- There can be several hiking groups, and similarly, several buses can be rented for the trip; however, there can be only one group for the table tennis competition, as there is only one table.

- The cost of renting a bus (or several buses) has to be shared between the participants of the trip, therefore the participants generally prefer a bus trip with more participants over one with few participants.

- As for the table tennis competition, a plausible preference about the number of participants would be that the number should neither be too small nor too large; typically, the players will neither want to wait to long for their turn nor wish to play permanently (without reasonable breaks).

There are several natural variations over this problem. For instance, there may be only one activity (say, a dinner or another social event) and we look for a set of invitees, where potential invitees have preferences about the number of invitees, and possibly also about the other invitees: this variant is called the

---

[1]This example is adapted from a real scenario that took place at a Dagstuhl Seminar on Computation and Incentives in Social Choice in 2012. The problem is apparently known by the Dagstuhl staff as the 'Dagstuhl group activity selection problem'!

stable invitation problem (Lee and Shoham, 2015). This problem can also be extended to a setting in which the preferences of the invitees depend also on the date the event takes place (Lee and Shoham, 2014).

If activities are not typed (or equivalently, if it is known beforehand that every group will be assigned to the same activity), then we have an *anonymous hedonic game*, where agents' preferences bear only on the size in their group; if, on the other hand, agents can have preferences about the identity of the other participants in their group (and not only about its size) then we have more generally a *hedonic game*.

The goal of this chapter is to describe these problems formally, to show how solution concepts that have been well-studied for hedonic games also apply to group activity selection problems, and to consider additional solution concepts from social choice theory to group activity selection. As there is a recent and detailed survey chapter about hedonic games (Aziz and Savani, 2016), we do not cover general hedonic games here.

In this chapter we hence consider the model for group activity selection problems in which the agents' preferences are over pairs "(activity, group size)", and the above mentioned related problems/variations. In Section 5.2 we describe the different problems formally, and we clarify the relationships between them. In Section 5.3 we discuss natural assumptions that one might make about agents or activities (domain restrictions). In Section 5.4 we review several solution concepts from the literature on hedonic games, show how they specialize or adapt to group activity selection along with some concrete examples, and apply solution concepts from social choice theory to group activity selection. In Section 5.5 we address the computational issues for these solution concepts and in Section 5.6 we briefly consider strategic issues. Section 5.7 gives a short conclusion and some further links to other fields of research.

5.2 Models

In this section, we present models of different classes of group activity selection problems. We begin with some basic definitions.

5.2.1 Basic Definitions

For the various models below we describe only the input, with various possible assumptions about the nature of preferences. In the whole chapter, we will consider a set of *agents* $N = \{1, \ldots, n\}$. We now consider in sequence activities, assignments, alternatives, and preference profiles.

Activities and Assignments. We consider a set of *activities* $A = A^* \cup \{a_\emptyset\}$, where $A^* = \{a_1, \ldots, a_m\}$. Activity $a_\emptyset$ is called the *void activity*; an agent being assigned to $a_\emptyset$ means that the agent will not participate in any concrete activity.

An *assignment* for (N, A) is a mapping $\pi : N \to A$. We denote by π^0 the set of agents i such that $\pi(i) = a_\emptyset$ and for each $j \leqslant m$, π^j the set of agents i such that

$\pi(i) = a_j$. Finally, the coalition structure induced by π is defined as $CS_\pi = \{\{i\} \mid i \in \pi^0\} \cup \{\pi^j \mid 1 \leqslant j \leqslant m, \pi^j \neq \emptyset\}$.

In addition, we may consider a more general version of the problem with constraints (especially, cardinality constraints) restricting the set of possible sets of activities that can be jointly organised, as well as constraints concerning the number of participants to an activity. In this case, we denote the set of all constraints by Γ, and an assignment is *feasible* if it satisfies the constraints in Γ.

Alternatives and Preference Profiles. Agents have preferences that bear both on the activity they will be assigned to, and on the set of agents who will participate in the same activity. An *alternative for agent* i is either $a_\emptyset$ or a pair $(a, S) \in A^* \times N_i$, where N_i is the set of all subsets of N containing i. The set of *alternatives* for i is X_i.

Each agent i has some preferences over X_i. A *preference relation for agent* i $\succsim_i$ is a reflexive and transitive order over X_i; the strict part and the indifference parts of $\succsim_i$ are denoted respectively by $\succ_i$ and $\sim_i$. A *preference profile* is an n-tuple $P = (\succsim_1, \ldots, \succsim_n)$ where $\succsim_i$ is a preference relation for i.

Recall that agent i is assigned to $a_\emptyset$ if she is not assigned to any activity (and will stay alone). If $(a, S) \succsim_i a_\emptyset$ then i likes being assigned to a with coalition S at least as much as staying alone: in this case we say that alternative (a, S) is *admissible* for i. When (a, S) is not admissible for i, i.e., $a_\emptyset \succ_i (a, S)$, then i would prefer to 'leave the game' and stay alone. An assignment is *individually rational* if it admissible for all agents. Individual rationality is the most basic and most important stability criterion for assignments (more complex stability notions will be defined in Section 5.4.)

A simple preference restriction is one where agents simply approve alternatives that are admissible for them, without ranking them. If, in addition, no agent is indifferent between being alone and some other activity, we will say that the agent has *trichotomous* preferences: in this case, agent i specifies a set of alternatives S_i, which induces a partition of the set of alternatives in three clusters, ranked in this order: S_i, then $\{a_\emptyset\}$, and last, $X_i \setminus (S_i \cup \{a_\emptyset\})$. Another preference restriction consists in requiring that each agent expresses a *strict order* over X_i.

Finally, a *group activity selection problem* is a triple (N, A, P). If, in addition, we have feasibility constraints, then we have a *constrained group activity selection problem*. We now consider several classes of group activity selection problems, depending on the nature of the preference relations in P.

5.2.2 Classes of Group Activity Selection Problems

Hedonic Games. We say that $\succsim_i$ is activity-independent if $(a, S) \sim_i (a', S)$ for all activities a, a' and coalitions S: i's preference relation $\succsim_i$ depends only on the set of agents in i's coalition, and not on the activity to which i is assigned. When $P = (\succsim_1, \ldots, \succsim_n)$ is such that every $\succsim_i$ is activity-independent, (N, A, P) degenerates into a *hedonic game*, where agents only care about which agents are in their coalition (Drèze and Greenberg, 1980; Banerjee et al., 2001; Bogomolnaia and Jackson, 2002).

If, in addition to being activity-independent, $\succsim_i$ depends only on the *cardinality* of i's coalition, $\succsim$ is said to be *anonymous*; if every $\succsim_i$ in P is activity-independent and anonymous, then (N, A, P) is an *anonymous hedonic game*.

The input of an anonymous hedonic game thus consists, without loss of generality, of a preference relation $\succsim_i^*$ over $\{1, \ldots, n\}$ for each agent, where $k \succsim_i^* k'$ if and only if $S \succsim_i S'$ for some (and, equivalently, for all) S and S' containing i such that $|S| = k$ and $|S'| = k'$, meaning that agent i likes being in a coalition of k agents at least as much as in a coalition of k' agents. Anonymous hedonic games have been studied by Ballester (2004).

While the input of an anonymous hedonic game can be represented succinctly in $O(n^2)$, the input of a hedonic game (and *a fortiori* of a group activity selection problem) needs in general an exponentially large space. Because of this, some restrictions of hedonic games have been considered: apart of anonymous hedonic games, we find *additive* hedonic games (each agent specifies a utility value for each other agent, and the utility of a coalition for i is the sum of the values of agents in it), *fractional* hedonic games (similar to additive hedonic games, except that the utility of a coalition for i is the *average* of the values of agents in it), *friends-and-enemies* hedonic games (an agent partitions N between two sets, corresponding to friends and enemies, and his preference relation depends on the number of friends and the number of enemies in his coalition), *optimistic* (respectively, *pessimistic*) hedonic games (each agent ranks other agents and values a coalition according to the best (respectively, worst) agent in his coalition), or *Boolean* hedonic games (each agent specifies the set of coalitions he approves, possibly succinctly, using a propositional formula). A recent survey on hedonic games, with a focus on how they can be represented succinctly and how various forms of equilibria can be computed, is that of Aziz and Savani (2016).

The extension to hedonic games studied by Spradling et al. (2013) considers agents who have preferences over pairs consisting of the role they will play in their coalition and of the composition of roles in their coalition. See the work of Darmann et al. (2012) for a discussion on the relation of this model to group activity selection.

Anonymous Group Activity Selection. Anonymous group activity selection is to non-anonymous (or general) activity selection what anonymous hedonic games are to hedonic games: agents care only about the activity they belong to and the number of participants to that activity (this number, of course, depends on the activity). To keep the terminology consistent with existing papers, the general model (where agents care about the assigned activity and the identity of the agents in their coalitions) will be called *generalised group activity selection* and the anonymous model will be called, simply, *group activity selection*. Therefore, without loss of generality, a group activity selection problem (GASP) is a triple (N, A, P), where P consists of n preference relations over $\{a_\emptyset\} \cup (A \times \{1, \ldots, n\})$. If, furthermore, all agents have approval-based preferences, then we will say that P is an *approval-based group activity selection problem*, for short a-GASP (Darmann et al., 2012): in such a problem, P consists in n subsets of $A \times \{1, \ldots, n\}$, namely the *approval sets* S_i, $i \in N$; and if all agents have strict preferences (without any ties between alternatives), then we will say that P is an *ordinal group activity selection problem*, for short o-GASP (Darmann, 2015).

Example 5.1. *We have two non-void activities: $A^* = \{a, b\}$, and 5 agents with the following preferences (which we truncate at $a_\emptyset$, because, as we will be interested in individually rational assignments, preferences below $a_\emptyset$ will not play any role).*

$$
\begin{aligned}
1: & \quad (a,1) \succ (a,2) \succ (a,3) \succ a_\emptyset \succ \ldots \\
2: & \quad (b,5) \succ (a,1) \succ (a,2) \succ (b,4) \succ (b,3) \succ (b,2) \succ a_\emptyset \succ \ldots \\
3: & \quad (b,5) \succ (b,4) \succ (b,3) \succ (b,2) \succ (a,1) \succ a_\emptyset \succ \ldots \\
4: & \quad (b,5) \succ (b,4) \succ (b,3) \succ (b,2) \succ (a,1) \succ (a,2) \succ a_\emptyset \succ \ldots \\
5: & \quad (a,1) \succ (a,2) \succ (b,5) \succ (b,4) \succ a_\emptyset \succ \ldots
\end{aligned}
$$

There is no feasibility constraint so we have here a (non-constrained) anonymous group activity selection problem, and more precisely an instance of o-GASP. Two individually rational assignments are π and λ with

$$
\begin{aligned}
\pi: & \quad 1, 2 \mapsto a; \quad 3, 4 \mapsto b; \quad 5 \mapsto a_\emptyset \\
\lambda: & \quad 1 \mapsto a; \quad 2, 3, 4, 5 \mapsto b
\end{aligned}
$$

An analogue of the above example in the approval-based setting of a-GASP would be the following.

Example 5.2. *In the setting of a-GASP, note that we only need to take into account the approval sets of the agents. These are given by*

$$
\begin{aligned}
S_1 = & \quad \{(a,1), (a,2), (a,3)\} = \{a\} \times [1,3] \\
S_2 = & \quad \{b\} \times [2,5] \cup \{a\} \times [1,2] \\
S_3 = & \quad \{b\} \times [2,5] \cup \{(a,1)\} \\
S_4 = & \quad \{b\} \times [2,5] \cup \{a\} \times [1,2] \\
S_5 = & \quad \{b\} \times [4,5] \cup \{a\} \times [1,2].
\end{aligned}
$$

Clearly, both assignments π and λ defined in Example 5.1 are individually rational also in this example.

Lu and Boutilier (2012) discuss a model of cooperative group buying, which can be embedded into GASP (more specifically, GASP with decreasing preferences, see Section 5.3). See Darmann et al. (2012) for further discussion.

Stable Invitations. If there is only one non-void activity, i.e., $A^* = \{a\}$, where a is called the *event*, then we have a *stable invitation* problem: in an invitation problem, agent i's preferences bear on $a_\emptyset \cup \{(a, S) \mid S \in N_i\}$. If moreover, preferences are anonymous, then we have an *anonymous stable invitation problem*, for short ASIP (Lee and Shoham, 2015): in this case, each agent has a preference over $\{0, \ldots, n\}$, where 0 means that the agent is not attending the event, while if $t > 0$ then t means that the agent attends together with $t - 1$ other agents. Lee and Shoham (2015) also define a *general stable invitation problem*, for short GSIP, in which agents preferences are restricted and given as follows: each agent i has a preference relation over $\{0, \ldots, n\}$ as before, together with an *acceptance set* $F_i \subseteq N \setminus \{i\}$ and a *rejection sets* $R_i \subseteq N \setminus \{i\}$; i is willing to attend only if all agents of F_i attend, no agent in R_i attends, and the number of attendees is preferred to 0 (that is, to not attending); among such acceptable coalitions, i prefers (a, S) to (a, S') if she prefers $|S|$ to $|S'|$.

Example 5.3. *Here is an anonymous stable invitation problem, with 6 agents and the following preferences (which we truncate at 0, because again we will be interested only in individually rational assignments (invitations)).*

$$
\begin{aligned}
1 &: \ 6 \succ 5 \succ 4 \succ 0 \\
2 &: \ 6 \succ 5 \succ 4 \succ 3 \succ 2 \succ 0 \\
3 &: \ 3 \succ 4 \succ 0 \\
4 &: \ 2 \succ 3 \succ 0 \\
5 &: \ 6 \succ 5 \succ 4 \succ 0 \\
6 &: \ 1 \succ 2 \succ 3 \succ 4 \succ 5 \succ 6 \succ 0
\end{aligned}
$$

Some individually rational invitations are $\{1, 2, 3, 5\}$, $\{1, 2, 5, 6\}$ and $\{2, 3, 4\}$.

Group Activity Selection on Social Networks. Igarashi et al. (2017) and Igarashi et al. (2017) consider a constrained group activity selection problem where the agents are linked through an undirected graph G (representing social interactions) and assigning a coalition of agents to an activity is feasible only if this coalition is connected with respect to this graph. Although the global feasibility constraint Γ_G pays attention to the identity of agents, their preferences are anonymous. We denote by gGASP such a game. Note that GASP is obtained as a special case where G is a complete graph.

Relation between the Classes of Problems. We end the section by a diagram showing the inclusion relationship between the different problems. In the diagram we have added one more class: *simplified* GASP, in which the agents' preferences depend only of the activity they are assigned to (this problem, of course, is nontrivial only if there are feasibility constraints).

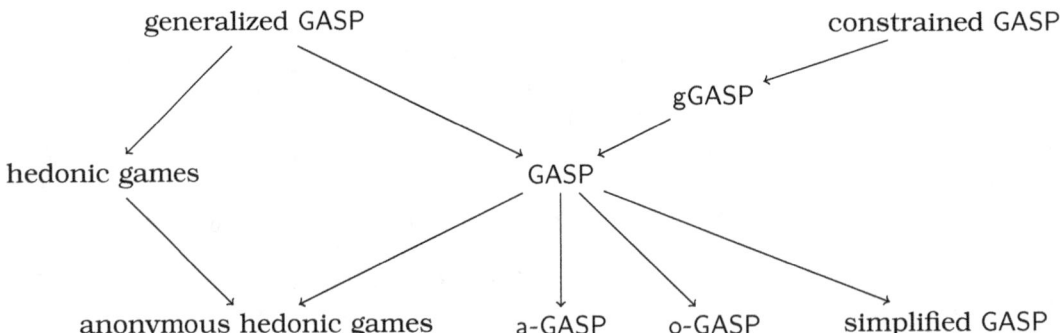

5.3 Domain Restrictions

Now that we have defined group activity selection and some interesting subproblems, it is worth going further and to consider restrictions of the problem obtained either by assuming specific assumptions on the agents' preferences or on the available activities.

5.3.1 Restrictions on Preferences

For any activity $a \in A^*$ and any agent i with preference relation $\succsim_i$, let $\succsim_i^{\downarrow a}$ denote the projection of $\succsim_i$ on a defined by: for all subsets of agents S, S' containing i, $S \succsim_i^{\downarrow a} S'$ if $(S, a) \succsim_i^{\downarrow a} (S', a)$. Now, we say that $\succsim_i$ is *monotonic* with respect to a if $\succsim_i^{\downarrow a}$ is monotonic, that is, if $S \supseteq S'$ implies $S \succsim_i^{\downarrow a} S'$. Likewise, $\succsim_i$ is *antimonotonic* with respect to a if $\succsim_i^{\downarrow a}$ is antimonotonic, that is, if $S \supseteq S'$ implies $S' \succsim_i^{\downarrow a} S$.

When group activity selection is anonymous, then monotonicity and antimonotonicity – called increasingness and decreasingness in the setting of GASP (see Darmann et al., 2012; Darmann, 2015) – simplifies into the following:

The preferences of agent i are

- *increasing* with respect to activity $a \in A^*$ if $(a, k) \succsim_i (a, k-1)$ for any $k \in \{2, \ldots, n\}$
- *decreasing* with respect to activity $a \in A^*$ if $(a, k-1) \succsim_i (a, k)$ for any $k \in \{2, \ldots, n\}$.

An instance $\mathcal{I} = (N, A, P)$ of GASP is called increasing (respectively, decreasing) if for each $a \in A^*$ and each agent $i \in N$ the preferences of agent i are increasing (respectively, decreasing) with respect to a. An instance is called *mixed increasing/decreasing*, if there is a set $A' \subseteq A^*$ such that for each agent $i \in N$ her preferences are increasing with respect to each $a \in A'$ and decreasing with respect to each $a \in A^* \setminus A'$.

Clearly, for the setting of o-GASP these definitions translate in a straightforward way. For a-GASP, however, these definitions can be simplified by considering only the set of approved alternatives. Informally, in a-GASP an agent i has increasing preferences with respect to activity a, if the set of group sizes k for which agent i approves (a, k) forms an interval with upper bound n; formally, in a-GASP agent i has *increasing preferences* with respect to activity a, if there is a threshold ℓ_i^a such that $\{k \mid (a, k) \in S_i\} = [\ell_i^a, n]$. Analogously, in a-GASP agent i has *decreasing preferences* with respect to activity a, if there is a threshold u_i^a such that $\{k \mid (a, k) \in S_i\} = [1, u_i^a]$.

Observe that the instances in Example 5.1 and Example 5.2, respectively, are mixed increasing/decreasing.

5.3.2 Restrictions on Activities

Among the non-void activities, some of them might be organised in several 'copies': for instance, if there are three guides in the local museum, up to three guided tours can be organised concurrently. Formally, we say that two activities

a and a' are *copies* of each other if for each agent i and subset S containing i, i is indifferent between (a, S) and (a', S). We say that A^* contains k copies of a (or, a is k-copyable) if there exists $k-1$ other activities in A^* that are copies of a.

Sometimes, an activity can exist in as many copies as we like (for instance, a hike). In this case it will be said to be *infinitely copyable*; since there are only n agents and considering more than n copies would be irrelevant, an activity is infinitely copyable just if it is n-copyable. An activity is said to be *simple* if it is not k-copyable for any $k > 1$. Unless stated otherwise, an activity is assumed to be simple.

5.4 Solution Concepts

We define solution concepts for hedonic games first and show how these specialize to the model of GASP and the stable invitation problem respectively. To simplify notation, in hedonic games we consider assignment π as a partition of the set of agents and identify $\pi(i)$ with the coalition to which i is assigned under π.

5.4.1 Maximum Individual Rationality and Pareto Optimality

A *maximum individually rational* assignment is one among the individually rational ones that maximizes the number of agents assigned to a non-void activity. E.g., in the instance considered in Example 5.1 assignment λ is a maximum individually rational assignment; in particular, λ assigns each agent to an activity different from $a_\emptyset$.

The next concept considered is the one of *Pareto optimality*. In a hedonic game, a partition π is called Pareto optimal, if there is no partition π' such that $\pi'(i) \succsim \pi(i)$ holds for each $i \in N$ and for at least one agent $j \in N$ we have $\pi'(i) \succ \pi(i)$. Translating the concept to GASP, an individually rational assignment π is *Pareto optimal* if there is no assignment π' such that for at least one $i \in N$ $(\pi'(i), |\pi'_i|) \succ_i (\pi(i), |\pi_i|)$ holds and there is no $i \in N$ with $(\pi'(i), |\pi'_i|) \prec_i (\pi(i), |\pi_i|)$. Note that in the approval-scenario of a-GASP, a maximum individually rational assignment is also Pareto optimal.

As particular examples for o-GASP, both assignments π and λ are Pareto optimal with respect to Example 5.1.

5.4.2 Stability Notions

In this subsection, we consider the aspect of stability with respect to agents' incentive to deviate from the considered assignment. In this respect, we distinguish between single agent deviations and group deviations. We first introduce the concepts for the hedonic game framework and translate them to the group activity selection problems afterwards. At the end of this section, we consider the stable invitation problem.

Starting with single agents' deviations, a very basic stability concept is Nash stability. In the hedonic game framework, a partition is Nash stable, if no agent benefits by moving from her coalition to another coalition. A partition is individually stable, if there is no agent such that the agent benefits by moving from her coalition to another coalition and all members of the new coalition agree with the agent joining. Finally, a partition is contractually individually stable, if it is not the case that a deviating agent is better off and both the old and new coalition agrees with the deviation of the agent.

In the group deviations case, the most famous solution concept is the core. Here, we distinguish between strong and weak group deviations. A *strong group deviation* is beneficial for each member of the deviating group; in a *weak group deviation* at least one member of the group is better off while the deviation does not harm any of the group members. These notions lead to the concepts of the core and the strict core, respectively.

Formally, in a *hedonic game*, a partition π is said to be

- *Nash stable*, if there is no $i \in N$ such that for some $S \in \pi \cup \{\emptyset\}$ we have $S \cup \{i\} \succ_i \pi(i)$.

- *individually stable*, if there is no $i \in N$ such that for some $S \in \pi \cup \{\emptyset\}$ we have $S \cup \{i\} \succ_i \pi(i)$ and $S \cup \{i\} \succsim_j S$ for each $j \in S$.

- *contractually individually stable*, if there is no $i \in N$ such that (i) for some $S \in \pi \cup \{\emptyset\}$ we have $S \cup \{i\} \succ_i \pi(i)$ and $S \cup \{i\} \succsim_j S$ for each $j \in S$ and (ii) $\pi(i) \setminus \{i\} \succsim_{j'} \pi(i)$ holds for each $j' \in \pi(i)$.

- *core stable*, if there is no subset $S \subseteq N$ such that for each $i \in S$ we have $S \succ_i \pi(i)$.

- *strictly core stable*, if there is no subset $S \subseteq N$ such that for each $i \in S$ we have $S \succsim_i \pi(i)$ and for at least one $j \in S$ we have $S \succ_j \pi(j)$.

For the setting of GASP these concepts translate as follows. An individually rational assignment π is called

- *Nash stable*, if

  (1) for every agent $i \in N$ with $\pi(i) \neq a_\emptyset$ and every $a_j \in A^* \setminus \{\pi(i)\}$ it holds that $(\pi(i), |\pi(i)|) \succsim_i (a_j, |\pi^j| + 1)$, and

  (2) for every agent $i \in N$ with $\pi(i) = a_\emptyset$ and every $a_j \in A^*$ it holds that $a_\emptyset \succsim (a_j, |\pi^j| + 1)$.

For the approval-setting of a-GASP, note that an agent only has an incentive to deviate if she is currently assigned to $a_\emptyset$. In that setting the definition of Nash stability thus simplifies as follows: An individually rational assignment π is Nash stable, if for each $i \in N$ with $\pi(i) = a_\emptyset$ and each $a_j \in A^*$ it holds that $(a_j, |\pi^j| + 1) \notin S_i$.

In the strict preference setting of o-GASP, the weak preferences in the above definition are replaced by strict preferences. With respect to Example 5.1 λ is not Nash stable, since, for instance, agent 2 wants to deviate from λ in order to join the single agent assigned to a (i.e., agent 2 prefers $(a, 2)$ to $(b, 4)$). In contrast, assignment π is Nash stable.

- *individually stable*, if

    (1) for every agent $i \in N$ with $\pi(i) \neq a_\emptyset$ and every $a_j \in A^* \setminus \{\pi(i)\}$ such that $(a_j, |\pi^j| + 1) \succ_i (\pi(i), |\pi(i)|)$ there exists an agent $i' \in \pi^j$ with $(a_j, |\pi^j|) \succ_{i'} (a_j, |\pi^j| + 1)$, and

    (2) for every agent $i \in N$ with $\pi(i) = a_\emptyset$ and every $a_j \in A^*$ such that $(a_j, |\pi^j| + 1) \succ_i a_\emptyset$ there exists an agent $i' \in \pi^j$ with $(a_j, |\pi^j|) \succ_{i'} (a_j, |\pi^j| + 1)$.

    For a-GASP, this boils down to the following definition: π is individually stable if for each agent $i \in N$ with $\pi(i) = a_\emptyset$ and each $a_j \in A^*$ it holds that $(a_j, |\pi^j| + 1) \notin S_{i'}$ for some $i' \in \pi^j \cup \{i\}$.

    As a particular example for the setting o-GASP, in Example 5.1 both λ and π are individually stable. For instance, considering assignment λ it is sufficient to verify that agent 1 has neither an incentive to leave activity a nor does she want other agents to join a.

- *contractually individually stable*, if

    (1) for every agent $i \in N$ with $\pi(i) = a_\ell$ for some $a_\ell \in A^*$ and every $a_j \in A^* \setminus \{\pi(i)\}$ such that $(a_j, |\pi^j| + 1) \succ_i (\pi(i), |\pi(i)|)$ there exists an agent $i' \in \pi^j$ with $(a_j, |\pi^j|) \succ_{i'} (a_j, |\pi^j| + 1)$ or an agent $i'' \in \pi^\ell \setminus \{i\}$ with $(a_\ell, |\pi(i)|) \succ_{i''} (a_\ell, |\pi(i)| - 1)$, and

    (2) for every agent $i \in N$ with $\pi(i) = a_\emptyset$ and every $a_j \in A^*$ such that $(a_j, |\pi^j| + 1) \succ_i a_\emptyset$ there exists an agent $i' \in \pi^j$ with $(a_j, |\pi^j|) \succ_{i'} (a_j, |\pi^j| + 1)$.

    Note that in a-GASP for individually rational assignments the concepts of contractual individual stability and individual stability coincide, because no agent assigned to a non-void activity has an incentive to deviate.

    As a particular example for the setting o-GASP, in Example 5.1 consider assignment μ with $\mu(1, 4) = a$, $\mu(2, 3) = b$ and $\mu(5) = a_\emptyset$. μ is not individually stable, because agent 4 would like to join b and agents 2, 3 are better off with agent 4 joining since they prefer $(b, 3)$ over $(b, 2)$. However, μ is contractually individually stable, since agent 1 objects to agent 4 leaving a.

- *core stable* (or in the core), if there is no $E \subseteq N$, $E \neq \emptyset$, such that for some $a_j \in A^*$ with $\pi^j \subseteq E$ it holds that $(a_j, |E|) \succ_i (\pi(i), |\pi(i)|)$ for all $i \in E$.

    In the setting of a-GASP, given that the initial assignment is individually rational, only agents assigned to $a_\emptyset$ can benefit from forming a coalition (in order to deviate to a non-void activity). Hence, the above definition simplifies as follows: an individually rational assignment π is core stable if there is no $E \subseteq \pi^0$ such that for some $a_j \in A^*$ with $\pi^j = \emptyset$ it holds that $(a_j, |E|) \in S_i$ for all $i \in E$.

- *strictly core stable* (or in the strict core), if there is no $E \subseteq N$ such that for some $a_j \in A^*$ with $\pi^j \subseteq E$ it holds that $(a_j, |E|) \succsim_i (\pi(i), |\pi(i)|)$ for all $i \in E$ and $(a_j, |E|) \succ_i (\pi(i), |\pi(i)|)$ for some $i \in E$.

    For a-GASP, note that now also agents assigned to a non-void activity may be part of the deviating group E of agents as long as E contains at least one agent assigned to $a_\emptyset$ (which thus benefits from the deviation). In that setting, the definition can hence be simplified as follows: an individually rational assignment π is strictly core stable if there is no $E \subseteq N$ with $E \cap \pi^0 \neq \emptyset$ such that for some $a_j \in A^*$ with $\pi^j \subseteq E$ it holds that $(a_j, |E|) \in S_i$ for all $i \in E$. The condition $E \cap \pi^0 \neq \emptyset$ makes sure that at least one member of the deviating group E strictly prefers the new outcome.

We point out that in the setting of o-GASP the concepts of the core and the strict core coincide (Darmann, 2015). Consider again Example 5.1. Assignments π and λ are both core stable. In contrast, assignment η with $\eta(1) = a$, $\eta(3) = \eta(4) = b$ and $\eta(2) = \eta(5) = a_\emptyset$ is not core stable, since each member of the group $E = \{2, 3, 4, 5\} \supset \{3, 4\}$ is better off with $(b, |E|) = (b, 4)$.

Finally, in the stable invitation problem the concept of stability considered is the one of Nash stability. Formally, we have the following:

- In ASIP, an invitation S (i.e., a subset of agents) is *stable*, if it is individually rational and for each $i \in N \setminus S$ we have $|S| + 1 \prec_i 0$.

- In GSIP, an invitation S is *stable*, if it is individually rational and for each $i \in N \setminus S$ at least one of the following holds: $F_i \not\subseteq (S \cup \{i\})$, $R_i \cap (S \cup \{i\}) \neq \emptyset$, or $|S| + 1 \prec_i 0$.

Consider the instance of ASIP presented in Example 5.3. The invitation $\{1, 2, 3, 5\}$ is not stable, since agent 6 prefers a group size of 5 over 0. Similarly, neither is the invitation $\{2, 3, 4\}$ stable because agent 1 would like to join the group. However, it is not difficult to verify that the invitation $\{1, 2, 5, 6\}$ is stable.

5.4.3 Social Choice Based Concepts

In addition to these game-theory based stability concepts also concepts from social choice theory have been applied to GASP. These concepts are positional scores (in particular approval and Borda scores) on the one hand, and the Condorcet criterion on the other.

Given an instance of GASP, a scoring function f maps an assignment to a non-negative real number by means of $f(\pi) := \sum_{i \in N} f_i(\pi(i), |\pi_i|)$ with $f_i : X_i \to \mathbb{R}_0^+$. The value $f(\pi)$ is called *score of* π. The goal now would be to find an individually rational assignment of maximum total score.

In *Approval scores*, for $i \in N$ let $f_i(x) = 1$ if $x \in S_i$ and $f_i(x) = 0$ if $x \notin S_i$. Approval scores in the case $|S_i| = k$ for each $i \in N$ are called *k-approval scores* ($k \in \mathbb{N}$). In an instance of o-GASP, *Borda scores* are given by $f_i(x) = |\{x' \in X_i : x \succ_i x'\}|$ for $i \in N$.

Note that approval scores take back the setting to the one of a-GASP; in particular, an individually rational assignment of maximum approval score corresponds to a maximum individually rational assignment.

An alternative approach is to adapt the Condorcet criterion to GASP. This leads to the following two solution concepts: (*i*) a Condorcet-winner among the individually rational assignments, and (*ii*) a Condorcet-winner among the maximum individually rational assignments.

Comparing two individually rational assignments $\pi, \bar{\pi}$ in an instance (N, A, P) of GASP, we say that agent i *prefers* π over $\bar{\pi}$ (denoted by $\pi \triangleright_i \bar{\pi}$), if $\pi(i) = a_j$ for some $a_j \in A^*$ and either

(1) $\bar{\pi}(i) = a_\emptyset$ and $(a_j, |\pi^j|) \succ_i a_\emptyset$ or

(2) $\bar{\pi}(i) = a_\ell$ for some $a_\ell \in A^*$ and $(a_j, |\pi^j|) \succ_i (a_\ell, |\bar{\pi}^\ell|)$ holds.

Then, an assignment π is called

- *IR-Condorcet*, if π is individually rational and for all individually rational assignments $\pi' \neq \pi$ we have $|\{i \in N : \pi \triangleright_i \pi'\}| > |\{i \in N : \pi' \triangleright_i \pi\}|$.

- *MIR-Condorcet*, if π is maximum individually rational and for all maximum individually rational assignments $\pi' \neq \pi$ we have $|\{i \in N : \pi \triangleright_i \pi'\}| > |\{i \in N : \pi' \triangleright_i \pi\}|$.

5.5 Computational Issues

In this section we provide some computational complexity results for GASP, and in particular a-GASP and o-GASP; we also refer to the stable invitation problem where appropriate. We begin with the concept of maximum individual rationality.

Maximum Individually Rational Assignments

Clearly, an individually rational assignment always exists; e.g., the assignment which assigns each agent to the void activity $a_\emptyset$ is individually rational. One natural goal, especially in the setting of a-GASP, is to assign the maximum number of agents to non-void activities. However, this task of finding a maximum individually rational assignment turns out to be computationally hard. In particular, even for restricted instances of a-GASP it is hard to decide whether a *perfect assignment* exists, i.e., an assignment that assigns each agent to a non-void activity.

Theorem 5.1 (Darmann et al., 2012). *It is NP-complete to decide whether a-GASP admits a perfect assignment, even when all activities in A^* are simple and all agents have increasing preferences.*

Theorem 5.2 (Darmann et al., 2012). *It is NP-complete to decide whether a-GASP admits a perfect assignment, even when all activities in A^* are simple and all agents have decreasing preferences.*

The latter theorem also holds if restricted to instances in which either (*i*) each agent $i \in N$, in any of her approved alternatives, accepts a group size of at most 2, or (*ii*) each agent i's approval set is "made up" of at most 3 different activities, i.e., $|\{a \mid (a, k) \in S_i \text{ for some } k \in \mathbb{N}\}| \leq 3$ holds for each $i \in N$.
On the positive side, it can be shown that a polynomial time algorithm to find a maximum individually rational assignment exists, if the number of agents or the number of activities are bounded by a constant ((Darmann et al., 2012); note that this also implies that in the anonymous stable invitation setting, a maximum

individually rational invitation can be determined efficiently). Alternatively, if the number of approved alternatives is bounded by a constant (i.e., in the case of k-approval scores), then for the case of all agents having increasing preferences a maximum individually rational assignment can be found efficiently; for the case of all agents having decreasing preferences this holds if and only if the number of approved alternatives is at most three for each agent (see Darmann, 2015).

Considering copyable activities, the decision problem whether a perfect assignment exists turns out to be NP-complete even when all activities in A^* are equivalent, i.e., A^* consists of a single infinitely copyable activity a only. However, on the positive side, there is a $\mathcal{O}(\sqrt{n})$ approximation algorithm in this case. For details and further results we refer the reader to Darmann et al. (2012).

Maximum Score Assignments and Condorcet Assignments

As mentioned in Section 5.4, a maximum individually rational assignment corresponds to one that maximizes total approval score among the individually rational assignments. In the setting of o-GASP it might seem plausible to use other solution concepts to compare different outcomes. For instance, other types of scores such as Borda scores could be applied. However, finding an individually rational assignment maximizing Borda score is NP-hard, both for the special cases of increasing and decreasing preferences (Darmann, 2016b).

Instead of using scores, an alternative solution concept from social choice theory would be the one of a Condorcet winner. This approach again leads to negative complexity results for restricted instances of o-GASP already: It turns out to be coNP-hard to decide whether an IR-Condorcet assignment or MIR-Condorcet assignment exists even in the case of increasing preferences. In contrast, in the case of decreasing preferences, an IR-Condorcet assignment is guaranteed to exist and can be determined efficiently. If a similar result holds also for MIR-Condorcet assignments is an interesting open question. For details we refer to Darmann (2016b).

Stable Assignments

For both hedonic and non-hedonic games, Ballester (2004) shows that it is NP-complete to decide whether a partition exists that is Nash stable, (contractually) individually stable, or core stable. We will not discuss the results for hedonic games in detail here, for an overview we refer to Aziz and Savani (2016).

In a-GASP, a Nash stable assignment does not always exist, as the following example (taken from Darmann et al. (2012)) shows.

Example 5.4. *Let $\mathcal{I} = (N, A, P)$ be an instance of a-GASP with $N = \{1, 2\}$, $A^* = \{a\}$, and induced approval votes $S_1 = \{(a, 1)\}$ and $S_2 = \{(a, 2)\}$. There are two individually rational assignments: π with $\pi(1) = a$ and $\pi(2) = a_\emptyset$ and λ with $\lambda(1) = \lambda(2) = a_\emptyset$. Neither of these assignments is Nash stable, since in π agent 2 would like to join a, and in λ agent 1 wants to engage in a.*

In particular, it turns out that the related decision problem whether a-GASP admits a Nash stable assignment is NP-complete (Darmann et al. (2012)). On the positive side, in a mixed increasing-decreasing instance of a-GASP a Nash stable assignment is guaranteed to exist; this case even allows for an efficient computation of such an assignment.

Theorem 5.3 (Darmann et al., 2012). *Given a mixed increasing-decreasing instance (N, A, P) of a-GASP, we can find a Nash stable assignment in polynomial time.*

However, in o-GASP an analogous result does not hold. In particular, even if all agents have increasing preferences a Nash stable assignment does not always exist as shown by the following example (taken from Darmann (2015)).

Example 5.5. *The following instance with 6 agents $N = \{1, 2, 3, 4, 5, 6\}$ and 3 activities $A^* = \{a, b, c\}$ is given by:*

1	2	3	4	5	6
$(b,6)$	$(a,6)$	$(c,6)$	$(b,6)$	$(a,6)$	$(c,6)$
$(b,5)$	$(a,5)$	$(c,5)$	$(b,5)$	$(a,5)$	$(c,5)$
$(b,4)$	$(a,4)$	$(c,4)$	$(b,4)$	$(a,4)$	$(c,4)$
$(b,3)$	$(a,3)$	$(c,3)$	$(b,3)$	$(a,3)$	$(c,3)$
$(a,6)$	$(a,2)$	$(b,6)$	$(b,2)$	$(c,6)$	$(c,2)$
$(a,5)$	$a_\emptyset$	$(b,5)$	$a_\emptyset$	$(c,5)$	$a_\emptyset$
$(a,4)$		$(b,4)$		$(c,4)$	
$(a,3)$		$(b,3)$		$(c,3)$	
$(a,2)$		$(b,2)$		$(c,2)$	
$(a,1)$		$(b,1)$		$(c,1)$	
$a_\emptyset$		$a_\emptyset$		$a_\emptyset$	

Consider an assignment π. Assume π is Nash stable. Then, π must assign each of the agents $1, 3, 5$ to a non-void activity, since otherwise the agents would like to join a, b and c respectively.

Assume agent 1 is assigned to b. This implies that also agents $3, 4$ must be assigned to b. Agent 5, who has to be assigned to a non-void activity, cannot be assigned to a since this would imply that also agent 1 is assigned to a. Thus, agent 5 must be assigned to c. Hence, agent 6 must also be assigned to c due to the Nash stability of π. This, however, implies that agent 3 would like to deviate from π in order to join c because agent 3 prefers $(c, 3)$ to $(a, 3)$, and π cannot be Nash stable.

Assume agent 1 is assigned to a. By Nash stability, this implies that agent 2 has to be assigned to a, and in turn, also agent 5 needs to be assigned to a. Agent 3, who needs to be assigned to a non-void activity, must hence be assigned to c since agent 1 is already assigned to a (and not to b). This, however, implies that exactly 3 agents are assigned to c which is not possible since agent 5 is already assigned to a.

In o-GASP, it turns out that even for increasing instances the decision problem whether a Nash stable assignment exists is NP-complete (Darmann, 2015). For the general setting of GASP, this decision problem is even W[1]-hard with respect to the number of activities (Igarashi et al., 2017).

Turning to the variant of GASP with only one activity, i.e., the stable invitation problem, we get different complexity results for the two versions ASIP and GSIP.

For the anonymous variant ASIP, it can be decided in polynomial time whether a (Nash) stable invitation exists; if it does, then a stable invitation maximizing the number of invitees can also be determined efficiently. In GSIP, however, in general the corresponding decision problem is computationally hard, even if the size of all rejection sets and acceptance sets is at most one. For details and further complexity results with respect to the size of these sets we refer the reader to Lee and Shoham (2015).

Considering further stability concepts, we point out that in a-GASP an individually stable assignment (and thus a contractually assignment) always exists and can be determined efficiently. For o-GASP, even in the restricted case of increasing preferences this does not hold, since in that special case individual stability coincides with Nash stability. In addition, recall that in o-GASP the concepts of core and strict core are equivalent; the core might be empty and the decision problem whether a core stable assignment exists is computationally hard even for increasing preferences. In contrast, for decreasing preferences, a stable assignment can be determined efficiently for each of these stability concepts. Also, we point out that in a-GASP both the core and the strict core are always non-empty, and an assignment in the core can be determined efficiently. For details we refer to Darmann et al. (2012) and Darmann (2015).

Finally, Igarashi et al. (2017) show that in GASP deciding whether a core stable assignment exists is NP-complete even for instances with only 4 activities. Further, they provide a number of complexity and fixed parameter tractability results for gGASP, for different types of underlying networks.

5.6 Strategic Issues

From a strategic viewpoint the question arises whether there is a deterministic mechanism (that for each instance of GASP outputs an assignment of agents to activities) which is robust against strategic manipulation. Darmann (2016a) shows that even in the single activity case a strategy-proof mechanism that outputs a maximum individually rational assignment in general does not exist. While it is not hard to see that restricting the single activity case to increasing preferences rules out strategic manipulation, also for increasing preferences there does not exist a strategy-proof mechanism that finds a maximum individually rational assignment if there are two or more activities. For further results and an analysis of strategic manipulability of the aggregation correspondence which outputs, for an instance of GASP, all maximum individually rational assignments, we refer to Darmann (2016a).

In a similar spirit, Lee and Shoham (2015) show that for ASIP there is no strategy-proof mechanism that always finds a stable assignment (if it exists); for the increasing preferences case, however, there is such a mechanism that even finds a stable invitation of maximum size in polynomial time.

5.7 Conclusion

We have provided an overview over variants of group activity selection problems, with the focus on the setting of GASP. We have discussed its relation to the literature and, in particular, hedonic games, and have shown how the stability concepts in hedonic games translate to GASP and its two variants a-GASP and o-GASP. Since it can also be understood as a kind of voting problem, we have adapted solution concepts from voting theory as well. For these concepts, both negative and positive computational complexity results have been provided; in addition, we have briefly pointed towards strategic issues.

We end by mentioning three areas that are related to group activity selection:

- *Congestion games* (Rosenthal, 1973): agents choose routes (which sort of play the same role as activities) and have decreasing preferences on the number of users who take the same route, which may conflict with their intrinsic preferences over routes (for instance, most agents prefer shorter routes, which then tend to be congested).

- *Committee elections* in the style of Monroe (1995): agents express preferences on single candidates, and a committee of k representatives has to be selected. The Monroe rule assigns every agent to one of the member of the committee, who is supposed to represent her; this is similar to group activity selection, with candidates playing the role of activities, and where agents have preferences that depend only on the activity they are assigned to, and not the number of participants.

- *Course assignment* (Gale and Shapley, 1962): Courses play a similar role as activities: each course has a capacity, we can only open a limited number of courses, and agents are assigned either to one course (in which case we have an instance of group activity selection with preferences over activities only) or to multiple courses, which can be seen as a generalization of group activity selection where the agent-activity assignment is many-to-many, and where agents have preferences over sets of activities.

Bibliography

H. Aziz and R. Savani. Hedonic games. In F. Brandt, V. Conitzer, U. Endriss, J. Lang, and A. D. Procaccia, editors, *Handbook of Computational Social Choice*, chapter 15. Cambridge University Press, 2016.

C. Ballester. NP-completeness in hedonic games. *Games and Economic Behavior*, 1(49):1–30, 2004.

S. Banerjee, H. Konishi, and T. Sönmez. Core in a simple coalition formation game. *Social Choice and Welfare*, 18:135–153, 2001.

A. Bogomolnaia and M. O. Jackson. The stability of hedonic coalition structures. *Games and Economic Behavior*, 38:201–230, 2002.

A. Darmann. Group activity selection from ordinal preferences. In *Proceedings of the 4th International Conference on Algorithmic Decision Theory (ADT)*, pages 35–51, 2015.

A. Darmann. Manipulation in group activity selection. *Available at SSRN: https://ssrn.com/abstract=2757100*, 2016a.

A. Darmann. Borda, Condorcet, and Pareto optimality in ordinal group activity selection. In *Proceedings of the 6th International Workshop on Computational Social Choice (COMSOC)*, 2016b.

A. Darmann, E. Elkind, S. Kurz, J. Lang, J. Schauer, and G. Woeginger. Group activity selection problem. In *Proceedings of the 8th Workshop on Internet and Network Economics (WINE)*, pages 156–169, 2012.

J. H. Drèze and J. Greenberg. Hedonic coalitions: Optimality and stability. *Econometrica*, 48(4):987–1003, 1980.

D. Gale and L. Shapley. College admissions and the stability of marriage. *The American Mathematical Monthly*, 69(1):9–15, 1962.

A. Igarashi, R. Bredereck, and E. Elkind. On parameterized complexity of group activity selection problems on social networks. In *Proceedings of the 16th International Conference on Autonomous Agents and Multiagent Systems (AAMAS)*, pages 1575–1577, 2017.

A. Igarashi, D. Peters, and E. Elkind. Group activity selection on social networks. In *Proceedings of the 31st AAAI Conference on Artificial Intelligence (AAAI)*, pages 565–571, 2017.

H. Lee and Y. Shoham. Stable group scheduling. In *Proceedings of the 13th International Conference on Autonomous Agents and Multiagent Systems (AAMAS)*, pages 1347–1348, 2014.

H. Lee and Y. Shoham. Stable invitations. In *Proceedings of the 29th AAAI Conference on Artificial Intelligence (AAAI)*, pages 965–971, 2015.

T. Lu and C. Boutilier. Matching models for preference-sensitive group purchasing. In *Proceedings of the 13th ACM Conference on Electronic Commerce (ACM EC)*, pages 723–740, 2012.

B. Monroe. Fully proportional representation. *The American Political Science Review*, 89(4):925–940, 1995.

R. Rosenthal. A class of games possessing pure-strategy Nash equilibria. *International Journal of Game Theory*, 2(1):65–67, 1973.

M. Spradling, J. Goldsmith, X. Liu, C. Dadi, and Z. Li. Roles and teams hedonic game. In *Proceedings of the 3rd International Conference on Algorithmic Decision Theory (ADT)*, pages 351–362, 2013.

CHAPTER 6

Popular Matchings

Ágnes Cseh

6.1 Introduction

Matching problems lie at the heart of discrete mathematics. Their rich history reaches back over 100 years (Kőnig, 1916), including some milestones of complexity and algorithms, such as perfect, maximum weight and minimum cost matchings, together with their connection to network flow and vertex cover problems.

In this chapter we focus on matching markets under preferences, where each market participant expresses their preferences as an ordered list of possible scenarios. Our task is to find a matching that is optimal with respect to these preferences. If the agents express their preferences in a cardinal manner, then the most common aim is to maximize the total utility of the agents. This yields the concept of *maximum weight* or *minimum cost matchings*. If preferences are ordinal, one might want to guarantee that no two agents are inclined to form a coalition in order to deviate from the given solution. This concept corresponds to the well-known notion of *stable matchings*. In coordinated allocation mechanisms, the central authority of control usually aims at a solution that matches a large number of agents. Thus, negotiating the size and the optimality of the matching with respect to agents' preferences is a problem that occurs naturally.

Popularity is a concept that offers an attractive trade-off between these two notions. In short, a popular matching M guarantees that no matter what alternative matching is offered on the market, the majority of the agents will opt for M. Moreover, $|M|$ is relatively close to the size of the maximum matching in the market. The notion was first defined by Gärdenfors (1975) and surprisingly, it comes from cognitive science, where such a majority decision is a well-motivated potential focus of investigation. After Gärdenfors' paper, decades passed without any achievement in the topic. Recently, an impressive amount of top-tier publications have demonstrated the importance of popular matchings.

6.1.1 Definition of Popular Matchings

Popular matchings can be defined in various market settings. For the sake of generality we assume that we are given a not necessarily complete and not necessarily bipartite graph with n vertices and m edges, where each vertex represents an agent and each edge stands for an acceptable agent-agent pair. Each agent expresses her preferences over her adjacent agents in the form of a strictly ordered list—every time ties are allowed, we explicitly say so. Figure 6.2 depicts such an instance. The ranking of each vertex can be seen on the edges incident to it. Lower numbers mean a better rank: for instance, agent a_1's top choice is b_2, her second choice is b_1, her third choice is b_3, while she finds b_4 unacceptable. To the left of the figure, the preference lists are shown. A matching is a set of edges in the graph so that no agent is matched to more than one other agent.

We compare matchings M_1 and M_2 in the following manner. Each vertex casts a vote for M_1 or M_2 or abstains from voting. If vertex v is matched to a better partner in M_1 than in M_2 or it is matched in M_1 and unmatched in M_2, then v votes for M_1. Analogous rules specify when v votes for M_2. Finally, v abstains from voting if its situation is the same in both matchings: either because it is matched to a vertex with the same rank or because it is unmatched in both matchings. If the number of votes for M_1 is at least as large as the number of votes for M_2, then we say that M_1 is *at least as popular as* M_2. If M_1 receives strictly more votes than M_2, then M_1 *defeats* M_2, in other words, M_1 is more popular than M_2. Note that the notion of defeat here is not transitive. Figure 6.2 shows an instance in which four matchings defeat each other in a circular manner.

Matching M is *popular* if it is at least as popular as any other matching in the instance. In other words, M does not get defeated by any matching in a comparison.

Besides the aforementioned roots in cognitive science, an approach to motivate the notion of popularity comes from voting theory. If we consider all possible matchings in an instance as the set of alternatives and let the agents vote, then it turns out that popular matchings form a well-defined subset of alternatives, namely the set of weak Condorcet winners (Condorcet, 1785). This set consists of the alternatives that beat or tie with every other alternative in a pairwise comparison.

In a similar spirit, popular matchings can be viewed as a special case of *maximal lotteries*, defined by Kreweras (1965) and Fishburn (1984) and rediscovered by several other researchers since then (Felsenthal and Machover, 1992; Laffond et al., 1993; Rivest and Shen, 2010). Chapter 1 of this book elaborates on maximal lotteries and points out the connection to popular mixed matchings, which we will discuss in Section 6.3.2.

6.1.2 Models and Chapter Structure

The most general setting involves an arbitrary graph representing a set of agents and the possible connections between them. We will refer to this setting as the non-bipartite model. Bipartite graphs play a distinguished role in matching markets. In bipartite graphs, the popular matching problem has been studied in the following two models.

- *One-sided model.* One side of the graph consists of agents who have preferences and votes, while the other side is formed by objects with no preferences or votes. This setting is analogous to the house allocation market model.

- *Two-sided model.* Vertices on both sides are agents, so they all have preferences and cast votes. This setting is analogous to the stable marriage model and it is a subcase of the non-bipartite model.

The remainder of this chapter is structured as follows. We start in Section 6.2 with a literature review of optimality concepts that can be seen as alternatives of popularity. After this, the two main building blocks follow in Sections 6.3 and 6.4, centered around the two above described bipartite models. Finally, in Section 6.5 we discuss results in the non-bipartite setting. Our approach is mainly algorithmic, but at the end of each section we also elaborate on more applied studies in the literature. The aim of this chapter is to give a structured overview of the rapidly growing field of the theory of popular matchings.

6.2 Related Literature

Defining optimality on markets with ordinal preferences is far from straightforward. In this subsection we sketch a number of alternative optimality concepts to popularity. These concepts are grouped based on the model they are most common to be used in.

6.2.1 One-sided Model

A number of optimality concepts for one-side markets have been studied in the literature. The most prevalent concept is *Pareto-optimality*. Informally, a matching is Pareto-optimal if there is no other matching in which at least one agent is better off, whilst no agent is worse off. Pareto-optimal matchings always exist in the one-sided model and at least one can be found using the strategyproof *Random Serial Dictatorship* mechanism, as shown by Abdulkadiroğlu and Sönmez (1998). The shortcomings of Pareto-optimal matchings are that even the largest one of them can be as small as half the size of a maximum matching. Moreover, the definition allows all but one agents to receive poor choices in order to avoid a single agent to be allocated to a slightly worse object than she has.

Other optimality concepts are defined based on the *profile* of the matching. This is a array of numbers, where the ith element is the number of agents who are matched to their ith choice object. Matchings that maximize the profile in a lexicographic sense are called *rank-maximal* matchings, defined by Irving (2003). Similarly to Pareto-optimal matchings, rank-maximal matchings always exist and can be found in polynomial time (Irving et al., 2006). On the other hand, even the largest rank-maximal matchings can be as small as half the size of a maximum matching asymptotically. To overcome this disadvantage, *greedy maximum matchings* (Michail, 2007) and *generous maximum matchings* (Abraham et al., 2006) were also defined, both of them are based on the profile of the matching.

6.2.2 Two-sided Model

The literature on two-sided markets is clearly dominated by *stable matchings* first discussed by Gale and Shapley (1962). A matching is called stable if it is not blocked by any pair of agents. A *blocking pair* comprises two agents not matched to each other who are either single or prefer to be matched to one another than to their respective partners in the matching. By their well-known deferred acceptance algorithm, Gale and Shapley showed that a stable matching always exists and can be found in linear time. A characteristic feature of stable matchings is the so called Rural Hospitals Theorem (Roth, 1984), part of which states that the set of matched agents is identical in all stable matchings. In particular, all stable solutions have the same cardinality.

Pareto-optimal matchings can be defined in two-sided markets analogously to one-sided markets. Clearly every stable matching in a market with strict preferences is Pareto optimal, but Pareto optimal matchings can be twice as large as stable matchings. Sng (2008) showed that a maximum Pareto optimal matching can be found in polynomial time. Profile-based optimality concepts were studied in the paper of Huang and Kavitha (2012).

6.2.3 Non-bipartite Model

The non-bipartite version of the stable matching problem is usually referred at as the *stable roommates problem*, which is quite different from its classical variant from an algorithmic point of view. First of all, a stable solution is not guaranteed to exist, which was pointed out by Gale and Shapley (1962) already, but there is a polynomial algorithm to find one, or a proof for its nonexistence (Irving, 1985).

The definition of Pareto-optimal matchings carries over to this setting. Just as in the simpler models, a Pareto-optimal matching always exists and a largest Pareto-optimal matching can be found in polynomial time (Abraham and Manlove, 2004). Profile-based optimality concepts were studied by Abraham et al. (2008).

The detailed study of existing literature on popular matchings is spread thorough the upcoming sections. Nevertheless, we would like to point out earlier surveys on the topic, such as those of Kavitha (2008), Mestre (2008) and Chapter 7 in the book of Manlove (2013).

6.3 One-sided Model

We start the study of popular matchings in one-sided models, where the two sides of the bipartite graph $G = (A \cup B, E)$ represent agents (A) and objects (B), respectively. The defining property of this setting is that only vertices in A cast votes, the objects have neither preferences nor a right to vote. Such one-sided markets are particularly suitable for modeling object allocation, such as in the well-known house allocation problem.

This section starts with the existence of popular matchings and the problem of finding a maximum size popular matching. Then we turn to the most important extensions of the problem from a theoretical point of view. Finally, we discuss some more applied approaches, such as computational studies and fairness concepts.

6.3.1 Finding a Max Size Popular Matching

As we have already mentioned, the initial paper of Gärdenfors (1975) was followed by decades of silence in the matching community. The notion of popular matchings in bipartite graphs reappeared in 2005, in the conference version of a paper by Abraham et al. (2007), who worked on the one-sided model. The main result of their paper is a polynomial algorithm for deciding whether a popular matching exists.

$a_1 : b_1 \quad b_2$
$a_2 : b_1 \quad b_2$
$a_3 : b_1 \quad b_2$

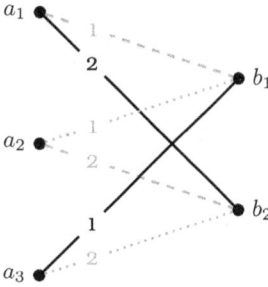

Figure 6.1: No popular matching exists in this instance. The dotted gray matching $\{a_2b_1, a_3b_2\}$ is more popular than the dashed gray matching $\{a_1b_1, a_2b_2\}$, because both a_2 and a_3 prefer it. Similarly, the black matching $\{a_1b_2, a_3b_1\}$ defeats the dotted gray, and the dashed gray defeats the black.

In the one-sided model, the existence of a popular matching is not guaranteed. Figure 6.1 depicts an instance equivalent to the famous voting paradox of Condorcet (1785), where none of the matchings is popular. In this context, the following result answers the most striking algorithmic question of the topic.

Theorem 6.1 (Abraham et al., 2007). *There is an $O(n+m)$ algorithm that outputs either a largest cardinality popular matching or a proof for its nonexistence.*

Note that this result not only answers the question on the existence of a popular matchings but it also guarantees a maximum cardinality solution, if any exists. Maximizing the cardinality of the outputted matching is particularly important, since the main motivation behind popular matchings is that the concept unites preference-optimality and large size.

The notion of first and second choice objects plays a crucial role in the algorithm of Abraham et al. (2007). The object ranked highest by agent a_i is called a_i's *first choice object*. The *second choice object* of agent a_i is the object that was not marked as a first object by anyone and it is ranked the highest among such objects in a_i's preference list. The following lemma sheds light to the importance of these two definitions.

Lemma 6.2. *M is popular in an instance of the one-sided model if and only if*

1. *every first choice object is assigned in M and*

2. *each agent is matched to either their first or second choice object.*

From this lemma, it is easy to see how to search for a popular matching. First we need to construct the graph, where each agent is adjacent to their first and second choice objects only and then check for a matching that matches all agents and all first choice objects. To reach a maximum cardinality popular matching, one needs to ensure that as few agents are matched to their dummy last resort object as possible. This can be done by a simple augmenting path algorithm, for example.

A slightly modified version of the above described algorithm serves to solve the general case in which preference lists may contain ties. This is also presented by Abraham et al. (2007), who gave an $O(\sqrt{nm})$ time algorithm for the maximum cardinality one-sided popular matching problem with ties.

6.3.2 Theoretical Results

This subsection is built up by three parts, each of them centered around capacitated instances, the relaxation of popular matchings and weighted instances, respectively.

Capacitated Extension

The many-to-one matching case clearly belongs to the most intuitive generalizations of the popular matching problem. In this setting, each object is assigned a positive capacity, which is the upper bound on the number of agents who can get this object allocated to them. On the other hand, each agent is allowed to receive one object at most. Due to this latter point, the notion of comparing two matchings does not need to be modified at all.

A characterization analogous to the one in Lemma 6.2 was given by Sng and Manlove (2010). They also presented the following results on the complexity of finding a popular matching.

Theorem 6.3 (Sng and Manlove, 2010). *There is an $O(\sqrt{C}n + m)$ algorithm to determine if an instance of the capacitated popular matching problem admits a popular matching, and if so, to find a largest such matching, where C is the total capacity of the objects. If ties are allowed, the time complexity of the algorithm changes to $O((\sqrt{C} + n)m)$.*

Defining a voting rule in the many-to-many setting is complex, and as a matter of fact, there are several legitimate options to study. Lexicographic order was studied by Paluch (2014). She provided a characterization of popular matchings and showed that finding a popular matching or a proof for its nonexistence is NP-hard.

Relaxing Popular Matchings

Having established in Theorem 6.1 that we can distinguish instances with and without popular matchings in polynomial time, the relaxation of popularity is the next intuitive move. We will now sketch the two most common relaxations, namely least unpopular matchings and popular mixed matchings.

Least unpopular matchings. First, the notion of *least unpopular* matchings was proposed to deal with instances that had no popular matchings (McCutchen, 2008). Assume that M_1 and M_2 are two matchings in the same instance. We say that M_2 dominates M_1 by a factor of $\frac{u}{v}$, if u is the number of agents who strictly prefer M_2 to M_1 and v is the number of agents who strictly prefer M_1 to M_2. For instance, matching $\{a_2b_1, a_3b_2\}$ in Figure 6.1 dominates matching $\{a_1b_1, a_2b_2\}$ by a factor of 2. The *unpopularity factor* of a matching M is the maximum factor by which it is dominated by any other matching, ignoring matchings that give $u = v = 0$. According to this definition, a matching is popular if and only if its unpopularity factor is exactly 1.

McCutchen (2008) also defined an alternative concept to measure the degree of popularity, called the *unpopularity margin*. This is defined in the same manner as the unpopularity factor, except that one subtracts the numbers of votes instead of dividing them. More precisely, M_2 dominates M_1 by a margin of $u - v$, if u is the number of agents who strictly prefer M_2 to M_1 and v is the number of agents who strictly prefer M_1 to M_2. Returning to the same example in Figure 6.1, we can state that $\{a_2b_1, a_3b_2\}$ dominates $\{a_1b_1, a_2b_2\}$ by a margin of 1. The *unpopularity margin* of M is the maximum margin by which M is dominated by any other matching. According to this definition, a matching is popular if and only if its unpopularity margin is exactly 0.

Theorem 6.4 (McCutchen, 2008, Manlove, 2013). *There is an $O(m\sqrt{n})$ time algorithm to find the unpopularity factor of a matching and there is an $O(m\sqrt{n} \cdot \log n)$ time algorithm to find the unpopularity margin of a matching. These algorithms work even in the presence of ties.*

Theorem 6.5 (McCutchen, 2008). *The problems of finding a least unpopularity factor matching and a least unpopularity margin matching are NP-hard.*

McCutchen (2008) also showed that the unpopularity factor of any matching is always an integer. In particular, if G does not admit a popular matching, then the unpopularity factor is at least 2 for all matchings in G.

Note that matchings with least unpopularity factor are exactly the matchings with least unpopularity margin. The least unpopularity margin is equivalent to the Simpson-Kramer voting rule (Kramer, 1977; Simpson, 1969), which selects as the winner the candidate whose greatest pairwise defeat is smaller than the greatest pairwise defeat of any other candidate.

Popular mixed matchings. The second optimality concept proposed for instances without popular matchings is *popular mixed matchings* (Kavitha et al., 2011). The notion of popularity is kept intact here, while the matching condition is relaxed. A mixed matching is a probability distribution over matchings in the input graph. The vote of an agent can be adjusted in a straightforward manner to this setting. For instance, taking each of the three matchings of cardinality 2 in Figure 6.1 with probability $\frac{1}{2}$ is a mixed matching that defeats matching $\{a_1b_1, a_2b_2\}$ by exactly one vote, because a_1 casts half a vote for $\{a_1b_1, a_2b_2\}$, a_1 casts half a vote for the mixed matching and finally, a_3 fully votes for the mixed matching.

Theorem 6.6 (Kavitha et al., 2011). *Popular mixed matchings exist even in the presence of ties in preference lists, and they can be found in polynomial time.*

Kavitha et al. (2011) presented two algorithms for the problem. Interestingly, one of them relies on the algorithm of McCutchen (2008) to determine the unpopularity margin of a matching, while the other one uses linear programming techniques.

Optimizing over Weights

A natural extension of the popular matching problem is to consider graphs with edge or vertex weights and search for the weight-optimal popular solution.

Edge weights. McDermid and Irving (2011) gave a structural characterization of popular matchings, and efficient algorithms to enumerate them. This led to the following result.

Theorem 6.7 (McDermid and Irving, 2011). *In the presence of edge weights, a maximum weight maximum cardinality popular matching or a proof for its nonexistence can be found in $O(n+m)$ time.*

Presenting a reduction to the minimum cost assignment problem Matsui and Hamaguchi (2016) proposed a polynomial time algorithm for finding a maximum weight popular matching, irrespective of its cardinality.

Vertex weights. Another intuitive extension of the problem is to assign an arbitrary positive weight to each agent. The vote of that agent then counts with the multiplicity given by this weight. Mestre (2014) considered this extension and showed the following.

Theorem 6.8 (Mestre, 2014). *In the presence of vertex weights, a maximum weight maximum cardinality popular matching or a proof for its nonexitence can be found in polynomial time even in the presence of ties.*

6.3.3 Applied Approaches

Upon establishing the characterization of popular matchings in the one-sided model, Abraham et al. (2007) ran experiments to test the probability of the existence of a popular matching in randomly generated instances with $|A| = |B|$. Their results show that the ratio of solvable instances drops radically as the length of preference lists increase. Obviously, if every list is of length 1, a popular matching is guaranteed to exist. Out of 1000 instances with 100 agents and lists of length 10 only 2 were solvable, while the same setting with preference list of length 20 or more did not allow a single instance to admit a popular matching. The intuition behind this phenomenon is that dummy posts as second choice objects increase the probability of a matching assigning all agents. Due to Lemma 6.2, this latter is a necessary condition for the existence of a popular matching. To complement these slightly discouraging results, Mahdian (2006) showed that a popular matching exists with high probability, if $|B|$ is a small multiplicative factor larger than $|A|$.

Popular mixed matchings were studied from the view of fairness concepts by Aziz et al. (2013). They showed that in some instances, popularity and envy-freeness are incompatible if $n \geq 3$. On the other hand, if a popular and envy-free assignment exists, it can be computed in polynomial time. The also proved that there is no strategyproof popular random assignment rule if $n \geq 3$. Weaker notions of envy-freeness and strategyproofness were also showed to be incompatible with popularity by Brandt et al. (2017), for $n \geq 5$ and $n \geq 7$, respectively.

Nasre (2013) studied strategyproofness in the classical integral matching case. She assumed that a_1 is the sole manipulative agent who is aware of the true preference lists of all other agents and that a central authority chooses an arbitrary popular matching. Thus, the goal of a_1 is to falsify her preference list to weakly improve the post she gets matched to in the falsified instance with any chosen popular outcome. She showed that the optimal cheating strategy for a single agent to get better always can be computed in $O(n + m)$ time when preference lists are all strict and in $O(\sqrt{n}m)$ time when preference lists are allowed to contain ties.

6.4 Two-sided Model

In this section we turn to bipartite graphs with preferences on both sides. Such instances model situations where vertices on both sides represent agents and thus are given the right to vote. Initially, Gärdenfors (1975) defined the notion of popularity for these two-sided markets with preferences on both sides. He also showed that if all preference lists are strict, then any stable matching is popular; thus a popular matching always exists and can be found in linear time using the well-known deferred acceptance algorithm of Gale and Shapley (1962). Huang and Kavitha (2013) later gave a characterization of popular matchings based on augmenting paths. They also came up with an $O(m)$ algorithm to test whether a given matching is popular.

This section is structured similarly to Section 6.3. It starts with the problem of finding a maximum size popular matching, then we elaborate on extensions of the problem, such as the case of ties or maximum weight popular matchings. Finally, we discuss some more applied approaches.

6.4.1 Finding a Max Size Popular Matching

Popular matchings of the same instance can differ in size, as illustrated by a sample instance from Kavitha (2015) in Figure 6.2. Besides the two stable matchings $M_1 = \{a_1b_1, a_2b_2\}$ and $M_2 = \{a_1b_2, a_2b_1\}$ the perfect matching $M_3 = \{a_1b_3, a_2b_4, a_3b_2, a_4b_1\}$ is also popular. This gives us popular matchings of size 2 and 4. None of the four matchings of size 3 is popular, because they defeat each other in a circular manner. Note one more nicety of this instance: no popular matching defeats any of these size 3 matchings strictly in a comparison.

$a_1 : b_2 \; b_1 \; b_3$ $\quad b_1 : a_1 \; a_2 \; a_4$
$a_2 : b_1 \; b_2 \; b_4$ $\quad b_2 : a_2 \; a_1 \; a_3$
$a_3 : b_2$ $\quad\quad\quad\quad b_3 : a_1$
$a_4 : b_1$ $\quad\quad\quad\quad b_4 : a_2$

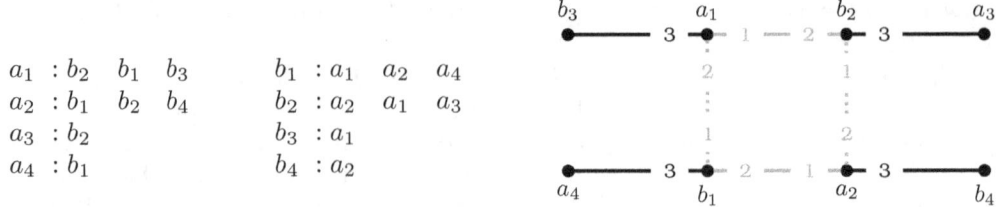

Figure 6.2: Sample instance with popular matchings of size 2 and 4.

As demonstrated by this instance, a strikingly important feature of popular matchings is that they beat stable matchings in size. As a matter of fact, any stable matching is a minimum size popular matching (Huang and Kavitha, 2013). The size of a stable matching in G can be as small as $|M_{\max}|/2$, where $M_{\max}$ is a maximum matching in G. Relaxing stability to popularity yields larger matchings and it is easy to show that a largest popular matching has size at least $\frac{2}{3} \cdot |M_{\max}|$. This result begs for the question about finding a maximum size popular matching.

Efficient algorithms for computing a maximum size popular matching were given by Huang and Kavitha (2013) and Kavitha (2014). Here we present the latter one.

The algorithm can be seen as a 2-round Gale-Shapley algorithm. Each man in the instance can have two states: unpromoted or promoted. At start, every man is unpromoted and the deferred acceptance rounds of the Gale-Shapley algorithm begin. According to the rules of that, each man proposed to his most preferred woman. As a response, each woman temporarily accepts the offer she ranks highest and rejects the rest of the proposing men. Rejected men now proceed to their second-choice woman and compete for her by submitting a proposal. Later proposals can result in the rejection of the earlier temporarily accepted man. The Gale-Shapley algorithm terminates with a stable matching.

At this stage, all men in the instance are unpromoted. The second round of the algorithm starts with the promotion of all men who remained unmatched at the end of the Gale-Shapley algorithm. These men now get the chance to walk through their original preference list one more time, from the top to the bottom. Women find promoted me more attractive than unpropoted men, irrespective of their original preferences. Two men of the same state will always be compared according to the original list of the woman. It is easy to see that the proposals of promoted men can result in some other men becoming single. Every time a man reaches the end of his preference list for the first time, he gets promoted. If a man reaches the end of his preference list for a second time as well, he is deactivated.

This algorithm outputs a maximum size popular matching, moreover, its time-complexity is the same as of the Gale-Shapley algorithm.

Theorem 6.9 (Huang and Kavitha, 2013, Kavitha, 2014). *In the two-sided model with strictly ordered lists there is an $O(m)$ algorithm that outputs a largest cardinality popular matching.*

It is easy to see that once a woman got a proposal in this algorithm, she will never become single. In particular, women matched in the output of the Gale-Shapley algorithm will be matched in the computed popular matching. As Hirakawa et al. (2015) have shown, more is true: every maximum cardinality popular matching assigns the same set of agents, which is a superset of the agents matched in any stable matching.

Naturally, one could allow men to be promoted after the second round as well. Kavitha (2014) showed that more Gale-Shapley rounds yield an even larger matching, but this increment in size comes at a price of an increased unpopularity factor. This latter can be defined in the two-sided model analogously as in the one-sided model.

Theorem 6.10 (Kavitha, 2014). *For every k where $2 \leqslant k \leqslant n$, there is a matching M_k such that $|M_k| \geqslant \frac{k}{k+1}|M_{\max}|$ and $u(M_k) \leqslant k - 1$, where $M_{\max}$ is a maximum matching in G and $u(M_k)$ is the unpopularity factor of M_k. This matching can be computed in $O(km)$ time via a k-round Gale-Shapley procedure.*

6.4.2 Theoretical Results

Popularity among Maximum Matchings

Motivated by the search for a matching that is of largest cardinality among popular matchings, Kavitha (2014) investigated the question of finding a maximum cardinality matching that is never defeated by any other maximum cardinality matching.

Theorem 6.11 (Kavitha, 2014). *A matching that is popular among maximum cardinality matchings always exists and can be found in $O(nm)$ time.*

Ties in Preference Lists

It turns out that ties have a massive effect on the complexity of popular matching problems in the two-sided model. When ties are allowed in preference lists on both sides, Biró et al. (2010) showed that deciding whether a popular matching exists is NP-complete. This result was further strengthened by Cseh et al. (2015) who also studied an intermediate variant between the 1-and 2-sided models with strict lists, namely if only agents in A have ordered preference lists ranking their neighbors, however agents on both sides cast votes—in this case, agents in B only care about being matched. Their results can be summarized as follows.

Theorem 6.12 (Cseh et al., 2015). *If one side of the bipartite graph has strict preference lists while on the other side each agents either puts its neighbors into a single tie or into a strict list, then deciding whether a popular matching exists is NP-complete.*

If one side of the bipartite graph has strict preference lists while on the other side each agents puts its neighbors into a single tie, then a popular matching or a proof for its nonexistence can be found in $O(n^2)$ time.

Optimizing over Weights

Currently there is no known method to find a maximum weight popular matching in a graph equipped with edge weights. Several results point in this direction, which justifies that the problem is clearly among the most riveting open questions in the area.

Cseh and Kavitha (2016) investigated the case of a forced edge in the graph. This refers to the problem in which there is a given forced edge e and we seek popular matchings that contain e. The problem is equivalent to searching for a maximum weight matching with weight function 1 on e and 0 elsewhere.

Theorem 6.13 (Cseh and Kavitha, 2016). *A popular matching containing a given forced edge e or a proof for its nonexistence can be found in $O(m)$ time.*

The same authors investigated the maximum-weight popular matching problem with complete lists.

Theorem 6.14 (Cseh and Kavitha, 2016). *If all preference lists are complete, then a maximum weight popular matching can be found in polynomial time.*

Besides considering special weight functions or preference lists, another approach is to relax the matching condition by permitting mixed matchings. A special case of those is half-integral matchings, in which edges are allowed to occur with value 0, $\frac{1}{2}$ or 1.

Theorem 6.15 (Kavitha, 2016). *The maximum weight popular half-integral matching problem can be solved in polynomial time.*

Most recently, Huang and Kavitha (2017) achieved remarkable structural results using LP techniques. Alongside other results they showed that there is always a half-integral popular matching among the maximum weight fractional popular matchings.

Theorem 6.16 (Huang and Kavitha, 2017). *The popular fractional matching polytope is half-integral and in the special case where a stable matching in the graph is a perfect matching, it is integral.*

6.4.3 Applied Approaches

Bhattacharya et al. (2015) studied a dynamic matching scenario, when agents and edges of the graph arrive and depart iteratively over time. The question is whether one can maintain a popular matching after each timeslot by modifying the given matching only in a few edges. They showed that maintaining popularity requires an amortized number of $\Omega(n)$ changes to the matching per round. Their result also answers an algorithmic question of independent interest. No algorithm is known for finding a popular matching by gradually building it up from a given matching, stepping from one matching to a more popular matching in each round. The negative result about maintaining popularity implies that two-sided instances might have no such paths to a popular matching, even for complete and strict preferences.

Popular Matchings

Chisca et al. (2016) propose the first constraint programming formulation of the popular matching problem. They encode preferences using the global cardinality constraint (Régin, 1996).

Popular matchings were proposed as a solution concept for task allocation in multi-camera networks by Cui and Jia (2013). According to users priority and task nature, different tasks are prioritized. For example, routine patrolling may have the lowest rank, while tasks that are triggered by motion detection are ranked highest. The authors run extensive simulations and demonstrate that popular matchings offer an attractive and efficient alternative to baseline approaches based on various greedy matching procedures.

6.5 Non-bipartite Model

The notion of popularity can be defined in not necessarily bipartite instances by a straightforward adjustment of the definition introduced in Section 6.1.1. We assume that all vertices represent agents and cast votes.

This section also follows the outline of the previous two sections. Due to the smaller volume, we do not separate the parts on existence, theoretical and applied approaches.

Chung (2000) was the first to observe that stable matchings are popular even in the non-bipartite case. Thus, if an instance with strict lists admits a stable matching, then the existence of a popular matching is also guaranteed. Some instances of the stable roommates problem do not admit a stable solution, yet they admit a popular matching, as demonstrated by Figure 6.3, first presented by Biró et al. (2010). Surprisingly, the complexity of deciding whether a non-bipartite instance admits a popular matching is unknown. Biró et al. (2010) proved that validating whether a given matching is popular can be done in polynomial time, even if ties are present in the preference lists.

$a_1 : a_2 \quad a_3 \quad a_4$
$a_2 : a_3 \quad a_1 \quad a_4$
$a_3 : a_1 \quad a_2 \quad a_4$
$a_4 : a_3 \quad a_2 \quad a_1$

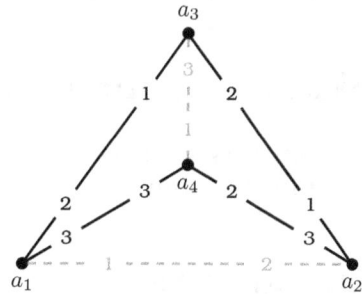

Figure 6.3: The dotted gray edges mark the unique popular matching $M = \{a_1a_2, a_3a_4\}$. It is blocked by the edge a_2a_3. The instance admits no stable matching.

Even though the main complexity question about popular matchings in non-bipartite instances has not been answered yet, there is a number of results marking a promising path towards it.

Huang and Kavitha (2017) showed that the polytope of popular fractional matchings is half-integral in the non-bipartite case, analogously to Theorem 6.16. This means that one can compute a maximum weight popular half-integral matching in polynomial time. They also showed that the problem of computing an integral maximum weight popular matching in a non-bipartite instance is NP-hard. Note that this still does not answer the open question on finding a largest cardinality popular matching, if any exists in the instance.

Some studies about extensions of the problem are also present in the literature. Huang and Kavitha (2013) have proved that the problem of computing a least unpopularity factor matching is NP-hard and presented instances where every matching has unpopularity factor $\Omega(\log n)$. On the positive side, they proved that every instance admits a matching whose unpopularity factor is $O(\log n)$, and such a matching can be computed in linear time.

6.6 Conclusion

In this chapter we have discussed the popular matching problem from an algorithmic point of view. We discussed existence, maximum size popular matchings, various theoretical and applied contributions in the cases of a bipartite market with one-sided and two-sided preferences, and finally in non-bipartite instances.

We have posed three open questions.

1. What is the complexity of finding a maximum weight popular matching in the two-sided model?

2. What is the complexity of finding a popular matching in the non-bipartite model?

3. What is the complexity of finding a largest cardinality popular matching in the non-bipartite model, if any exists in the instance?

Acknowledgment

This work was supported by the Hungarian Academy of Sciences under its Momentum Programme (LP2016-3/2016) and OTKA grant K108383.

Bibliography

A. Abdulkadiroğlu and T. Sönmez. Random serial dictatorship and the core from random endowments in house allocation problems. *Econometrica*, 66(3):689–701, 1998.

D. J. Abraham and D. F. Manlove. Pareto optimality in the Roommates problem. Technical Report TR-2004-182, University of Glasgow, Department of Computing Science, December 2004.

D. J. Abraham, N. Chen, V. Kumar, and V. S. Mirrokni. Assignment problems in rental markets. In *Proceedings of the 2nd International Workshop on Internet and Network Economics (WINE)*, volume 4286 of *Lecture Notes in Computer Science*, pages 198–213. Springer, 2006.

D. J. Abraham, R. W. Irving, T. Kavitha, and K. Mehlhorn. Popular matchings. *SIAM Journal on Computing*, 37:1030–1045, 2007.

D. J. Abraham, A. Levavi, D. F. Manlove, and G. O'Malley. The stable roommates problem with globally-ranked pairs. *Internet Mathematics*, 5:493–515, 2008.

H. Aziz, F. Brandt, and P. Stursberg. On popular random assignments. In *Proceedings of the 6th International Symposium on Algorithmic Game Theory (SAGT)*, pages 183–194. Springer, 2013.

S. Bhattacharya, M. Hoefer, C.-C. Huang, T. Kavitha, and L. Wagner. Maintaining near-popular matchings. In *Proceedings of the 42nd International Colloquium on Automata, Languages, and Programming (ICALP)*, pages 504–515, 2015.

P. Biró, R. W. Irving, and D. F. Manlove. Popular matchings in the marriage and roommates problems. In *Proceedings of the 7th International Conference on Algorithms and Complexity (CIAC)*, volume 6078 of *Lecture Notes in Computer Science*, pages 97–108. Springer, 2010.

F. Brandt, J. Hofbauer, and M. Suderland. Majority graphs of assignment problems and properties of popular random assignments. *Proceedings of the 16th International Conference on Autonomous Agents and Multiagent Systems (AAMAS)*, 2017.

D. S. Chisca, M. Siala, G. Simonin, and B. O'Sullivan. A CP-based approach for popular matching. In *Proceedings of the 30th AAAI Conference on Artificial Intelligence*. AAAI Press, 2016.

K. S. Chung. On the existence of stable roommate matchings. *Games and Economic Behavior*, 33(2):206–230, 2000.

M. Condorcet. *Essai sur l'application de l'analyse à la probabilité des décisions rendues à la pluralité des voix*. L'Imprimerie Royale, 1785.

Á. Cseh and T. Kavitha. Popular edges and dominant matchings. In *Proceedings of the 18th International Conference on Integer Programming and Combinatoral Optimization (IPCO)*, Lecture Notes in Computer Science, pages 138–151. Springer, 2016.

Á. Cseh, C.-C. Huang, and T. Kavitha. Popular matchings with two-sided preferences and one-sided ties. In *Proceedings of the 42nd International Colloquium on Automata, Languages, and Programming (ICALP)*, volume 9134 of *Lecture Notes in Computer Science*, pages 367–379. Springer, 2015.

L. Cui and W. Jia. Weighted capacitated popular matching for task assignment in multi-camera networks. In *Proceedings of the 25th International Teletraffic Congress (ITC)*, pages 1–4. IEEE, 2013.

D. S. Felsenthal and M. Machover. After two centuries, should Condorcet's voting procedure be implemented? *Behavioral Science*, 37(4):250–274, 1992.

P. C. Fishburn. Probabilistic social choice based on simple voting comparisons. *The Review of Economic Studies*, 51(4):683–692, 1984.

D. Gale and L. S. Shapley. College admissions and the stability of marriage. *American Mathematical Monthly*, 69:9–15, 1962.

P. Gärdenfors. Match making: assignments based on bilateral preferences. *Behavioural Science*, 20:166–173, 1975.

M. Hirakawa, Y. Yamauchi, S. Kijima, and M. Yamashita. On the structure of popular matchings in the stable marriage problem - Who can join a popular matching? In *Proceedings of the 3rd International Workshop on Matching Under Preferences (MATCH-UP)*, 2015.

C.-C. Huang and T. Kavitha. Weight-maximal matchings. In *Proceedings of the 2nd International Workshop on Matching Under Preferences (MATCH-UP)*, pages 87–98, 2012.

C.-C. Huang and T. Kavitha. Popular matchings in the stable marriage problem. *Information and Computation*, 222:180–194, 2013.

C.-C. Huang and T. Kavitha. Popularity, mixed matchings, and self-duality. In *Proceedings of the 28th Annual ACM-SIAM Symposium on Discrete Algorithms (SODA)*, pages 2294–2310. SIAM, 2017.

R. W. Irving. An efficient algorithm for the "stable roommates" problem. *Journal of Algorithms*, 6(4):577–595, 1985.

R. W. Irving. Greedy matchings. Technical report, TR-2003-136. University of Glasgow, Glasgow, UK, 2003.

R. W. Irving, T. Kavitha, K. Mehlhorn, D. Michail, and K. Paluch. Rank-maximal matchings. *ACM Transactions on Algorithms*, 2(4):602–610, 2006.

T. Kavitha. Ranked Matching. In *Encyclopedia of Algorithms*, pages 744–748. Springer, 2008.

T. Kavitha. A size-popularity tradeoff in the stable marriage problem. *SIAM Journal on Computing*, 43:52–71, 2014.

T. Kavitha. Popular matchings. Talk given at COST Action IC1205 meeting on Matching and Fair Division, 2015. URL http://www.optimalmatching.com/COST2015/slides/KavithaTelikepalli.pdf.

T. Kavitha. Popular half-integral matchings. In *Proceedings of the 43rd International Colloquium on Automata, Languages, and Programming (ICALP)*, volume 55, pages 22:1–22:13, Dagstuhl, Germany, 2016.

T. Kavitha, J. Mestre, and M. Nasre. Popular mixed matchings. *Theoretical Computer Science*, 412:2679–2690, 2011.

D. Kőnig. Über Graphen und ihre Anwendung auf Determinantentheorie und Mengenlehre. *Mathematische Annalen*, 77(4):453–465, 1916.

G. H. Kramer. A dynamical model of political equilibrium. *Journal of Economic Theory*, 16(2):310–334, 1977.

G. Kreweras. Aggregation of preference orderings. In *Mathematics and Social Sciences I: Proceedings of the seminars of Menthon-Saint-Bernard, France (1–27 July 1960) and of Gösing, Austria (3–27 July 1962)*, pages 73–79, 1965.

G. Laffond, J.-F. Laslier, and M. Le Breton. The bipartisan set of a tournament game. *Games and Economic Behavior*, 5(1):182–201, 1993.

M. Mahdian. Random popular matchings. In *Proceedings of the 7th ACM Conference on Electronic Commerce (EC)*, pages 238–242. ACM, 2006.

D. F. Manlove. *Algorithmics of Matching Under Preferences*. World Scientific, 2013.

T. Matsui and T. Hamaguchi. Characterizing a set of popular matchings defined by preference lists with ties. *arXiv preprint arXiv:1601.03458*, 2016.

R. M. McCutchen. The least-unpopularity-factor and least-unpopularity-margin criteria for matching problems with one-sided preferences. In *Proceedings of the 8th Latin-American Theoretical Informatics Symposium (LATIN)*, volume 4957 of *Lecture Notes in Computer Science*, pages 593–604. Springer, 2008.

E. McDermid and R. W. Irving. Popular matchings: Structure and algorithms. *Journal of Combinatorial Optimization*, 22(3):339–358, 2011.

J. Mestre. Weighted popular matchings. In *Encyclopedia of Algorithms*, pages 1023–1024. Springer, 2008.

J. Mestre. Weighted popular matchings. *ACM Transactions on Algorithms*, 10(1): 2:1–2:16, 2014.

D. Michail. Reducing rank-maximal to maximum weight matching. *Theoretical Computer Science*, 389(1-2):125–132, 2007.

M. Nasre. Popular matchings: Structure and cheating strategies. In *Proceedings of the 30th International Symposium on Theoretical Aspects of Computer Science (STACS)*, pages 412–423. Citeseer, 2013.

K. Paluch. Popular and clan-popular b-matchings. *Theoretical Computer Science*, 544:3–13, 2014.

J.-C. Régin. Generalized arc consistency for global cardinality constraint. In *Proceedings of the 13th AAAI Conference on Artificial Intelligence*, pages 209–215. AAAI Press, 1996.

R. L. Rivest and E. Shen. An optimal single-winner preferential voting system based on game theory. In *Procedings of the 3rd International Workshop on Computational Social Choice (COMSOC)*, pages 399–410. University of Düsseldorf, 2010.

A. E. Roth. The evolution of the labor market for medical interns and residents: a case study in game theory. *Journal of Political Economy*, 92(6):991–1016, 1984.

P. B. Simpson. On defining areas of voter choice: Professor Tullock on stable voting. *The Quarterly Journal of Economics*, pages 478–490, 1969.

C. T. S. Sng. *Efficient Algorithms for Bipartite Matching Problems with Preferences*. PhD thesis, University of Glasgow, Department of Computing Science, 2008.

C. T. S. Sng and D. F. Manlove. Popular matchings in the weighted capacitated house allocation problem. *Journal of Discrete Algorithms*, 8(2):102–116, 2010.

CHAPTER 7

An Introduction to Belief Merging and its Links with Judgment Aggregation

Patricia Everaere, Sébastien Konieczny,
and Pierre Marquis

7.1 Introduction

Belief merging aims at defining the beliefs of a group of agents from their individual beliefs and some integrity constraints to be respected. This objective appears as non-trivial as soon as some conflicts between the individual beliefs and possibly involving the constraints exist. For this reason, the belief merging issue has raised much attention in artificial intelligence for more than two decades. Many results of various nature have been obtained, including belief merging operators (based on several intuitions), postulates for delineating the rational ones, representation theorems establishing constructive ways of defining some belief merging operators, the identification of the complexity of some operators, some comparisons of their inferential powers, some implementations, and other results connected to several issues which are often addressed in social choice, like strategy-proofness or truth-tracking.

The main goal of this chapter is to give an introduction to propositional belief merging and to stress some of the links and differences between propositional belief merging (BM) and judgment aggregation (JA). While BM and JA have been developed mainly independently, they are two logically-founded theories of logical aggregation, with similar objectives. Accordingly, some connections between the two have already been exploited in some previous works. Thus, Pigozzi (2006) shows how one can take advantage of a BM operator for defining a JA one. Studying what make BM and JA close and what make them different is useful for a better understanding of the pros and the cons of the two theories.

Let us illustrate what a belief merging process is on a simple scenario. Consider three agents 1, 2 and 3, each of them associated with a belief base K_1, K_2 and K_3 (respectively), as given in Figure 7.1 (we do not consider any integrity constraints — stated otherwise, the integrity constraint is a tautology).

The objective of belief merging is to define the beliefs of the group of agents (the merged base) from the individual beliefs of its members. For this example,

$$\begin{array}{ccc} K_1 & K_2 & K_3 \\ a,\ b \to c & a,\ b & \neg a \end{array}$$

Figure 7.1: An example of belief merging: $\Delta(K_1, K_2, K_3) =\ ?$

one cannot simply consider the conjunction (union) of the bases as the result of the merging process since this conjunction is not consistent. A closer look at the bases shows that a is a conflicting piece of belief, while no conflict involves b or $b \to c$. If b and $b \to c$ are kept in the merged base, then c can be inferred at the group level, though none of the agents can draw such a conclusion alone. Accordingly, "new" pieces of belief, i.e., beliefs that no agent can infer alone, can be generated during the merging process. Now, if one wants to go further in the merging process and get some information about a, a majority argument can be used. Indeed, two out of the three agents believe that a is true, and this can be considered as a sufficient reason for considering a also as a piece of belief at the group level. Note that in belief merging adhering to such a majority principle is not mandatory, but there is a subclass of majority merging operators which are based on it. Similarly, there also exists a subclass of so-called arbitration operators, which aim at defining a merged base which is as close as possible to the base of each agent.

In the following, after a presentation of BM and JA which aims at introducing a number of key concepts and postulates, we focus on the relations and differences between BM and JA. For this purpose, we investigate the question of how to define the judgment set of an agent given her belief base and an agenda. On this ground, we show that the beliefs produced by a BM operator and those produced by a JA one can easily be incompatible, even if the two operators satisfy some rationality conditions. Interestingly, in the restricted case when the two approaches are equally informed (i.e., when the agenda is the set of all interpretations), every merging operator can be associated with a judgment aggregation operator, and *vice versa*. We show that some close connections can be established, linking the satisfaction of some postulates by the pairs of operators that correspond to each other.

7.2 On Belief Merging

We consider a propositional language $\mathcal{L}$ defined from a finite set $\mathcal{P}$ of propositional symbols and the usual connectives, including the Boolean constants $\top$ and $\bot$.

An interpretation (or state of the world) ω is a total function from $\mathcal{P}$ to $\{0, 1\}$. The set of all interpretations is denoted by $\mathcal{W}$. An interpretation ω is usually represented by a bit vector whenever a strict total order on $\mathcal{P}$ is specified. It can also be viewed as the complete formula $\bigwedge_{p \in \mathcal{P} | \omega(p)=1} p \wedge \bigwedge_{p \in \mathcal{P} | \omega(p)=0} \neg p$.

The symbol $\models$ denotes the logical entailment relation and $\equiv$ the logical equivalence relation. The set of models of a formula φ is denoted by $[\varphi]$, i.e., $[\varphi] = \{\omega \in \mathcal{W} \mid \omega \models \varphi\}$.

A *belief base* K is a finite set of propositional formulae $\{\varphi_1, \ldots, \varphi_k\}$. We denote by $\bigwedge K$ the conjunction of the formulae of K, i.e., $\bigwedge K = \varphi_1 \wedge \ldots \wedge \varphi_k$. In order to simplify the notation, we often identify[1] a base K with the formula $\bigwedge K$. We suppose that each belief base is consistent, and denote by $\mathcal{K}$ the set of all bases.

A *profile* E represents the beliefs of a group of n agents involved in the merging process; formally E is given by a vector $(K_1, \ldots, K_n)$ of belief bases, where K_i is the belief base of agent i (different agents are allowed to exhibit identical bases). The conjunction of all elements of E is denoted $\bigwedge E$, i.e., $\bigwedge E = \bigwedge K_1 \wedge \ldots \wedge \bigwedge K_n$ and if $E = (K_1, \ldots, K_i)$ and $E' = (K'_1, \ldots, K'_j)$, $E \sqcup E'$ denotes the profile $(K_1, \ldots, K_i, K'_1, \ldots, K'_j)$. $\mathcal{E}$ is the set of all profiles. A profile E is said to be consistent if and only if $\bigwedge E$ is consistent.

We denote by E^p the profile $E^p = \underbrace{E \sqcup \ldots \sqcup E}_{p}$. Two profiles $E = (K_1, \ldots, K_n)$ and $E' = (K'_1, \ldots, K'_n)$ are equivalent, denoted $E \equiv E'$, if there exists a permutation π over $\{1, \ldots, n\}$ such that for each $i \in 1, \ldots, n$, we have $K_i \equiv K'_{\pi(i)}$. If $\leqslant$ is a preorder on $\mathcal{W}$ (i.e., a reflexive and transitive relation), then $<$ denotes the associated strict order defined by $\omega < \omega'$ if and only if $\omega \leqslant \omega'$ and $\omega' \not\leqslant \omega$. A preorder is *total* if $\forall \omega, \omega' \in \mathcal{W}, \omega \leqslant \omega'$ or $\omega' \leqslant \omega$. A preorder that is not total is called *partial*. If $\leqslant$ is a preorder on A, and $B \subseteq A$, then $\min(B, \leqslant) = \{b \in B \mid \nexists a \in B\ a < b\}$.

An *integrity constraint* μ is a consistent formula restricting the possible results of the merging process.

Merging operators are mappings from the set of profiles and the set of propositional formulae (that represent integrity constraints) to the set of bases, i.e. $\Delta : \mathcal{E} \times \mathcal{L} \to \mathcal{K}$. We use the notation $\Delta_\mu(E)$ instead of $\Delta(E, \mu)$. $\Delta(E)$ is short for $\Delta_\top(E)$.

We first present the main logical properties pointed out for characterizing the IC merging operators and recall a representation theorem for them, expressed in terms of preorders on interpretations. Some of these properties had been proposed by Revesz (1997) in order to define *model fitting* operators. They have been extended by Konieczny and Pino Pérez (2002b).

Definition 7.1. *A merging operator Δ is an* IC merging operator *if it satisfies the following properties (the so-called IC postulates):*

(IC0) $\Delta_\mu(E) \models \mu$

(IC1) *If μ is consistent, then $\Delta_\mu(E)$ is consistent*

(IC2) *If $\bigwedge E \wedge \mu$ is consistent, then $\Delta_\mu(E) \equiv \bigwedge E \wedge \mu$*

(IC3) *If $E_1 \equiv E_2$ and $\mu_1 \equiv \mu_2$, then $\Delta_{\mu_1}(E_1) \equiv \Delta_{\mu_2}(E_2)$*

(IC4) *If $K_1 \models \mu$ and $K_2 \models \mu$, then $\Delta_\mu((K_1, K_2)) \wedge K_1$ is consistent if and only if $\Delta_\mu((K_1, K_2)) \wedge K_2$ is consistent*

(IC5) $\Delta_\mu(E_1) \wedge \Delta_\mu(E_2) \models \Delta_\mu(E_1 \sqcup E_2)$

(IC6) *If $\Delta_\mu(E_1) \wedge \Delta_\mu(E_2)$ is consistent, then $\Delta_\mu(E_1 \sqcup E_2) \models \Delta_\mu(E_1) \wedge \Delta_\mu(E_2)$*

(IC7) $\Delta_{\mu_1}(E) \wedge \mu_2 \models \Delta_{\mu_1 \wedge \mu_2}(E)$

---
[1] This identification is done when the BM operator under consideration is not sensitive to the syntactical representation of the bases. Otherwise, it is important to make a distinction between a base K and the conjunction of its formulae (see e.g., Konieczny et al., 2004).

(IC8) *If $\Delta_{\mu_1}(E) \wedge \mu_2$ is consistent, then $\Delta_{\mu_1 \wedge \mu_2}(E) \models \Delta_{\mu_1}(E)$*

The meaning of the postulates is as follows: when satisfied, (IC0) ensures that the merged base satisfies the integrity constraints. (IC1) states that if the integrity constraints are consistent, then the merged base is consistent as well. (IC2) states that the merged base is the conjunction of the belief bases with the integrity constraints when this conjunction is consistent. (IC3) is the principle of irrelevance of syntax, i.e., if two profiles are equivalent and two integrity constraints bases are logically equivalent then the corresponding merged bases are logically equivalent. (IC4) is a fairness postulate: when two belief bases are merged, no preference has to be given to one of them. (IC5) expresses the following idea: if two profiles E_1 and E_2 agree on some models then these models must be chosen if the two profiles are joined. (IC5) and (IC6) together state that if the merged bases corresponding to two profiles agree on some models, then if the two profiles are joined, the models of the corresponding merged base must be those models for which there is an agreement. (IC7) and (IC8) can be viewed as a direct generalization of the (R5-R6) postulates for belief revision (Katsuno and Mendelzon, 1991). They state some conditions about conjunctions of integrity constraints. Actually, they ensure that the notion of *closeness* one wants to capture is well-behaved. If a model ω is chosen in the set of possible models $[\mu]$, then if the set of possible models is narrowed but ω still belongs to the resulting set, it still must be selected. Similar properties to this quite natural requirement appear in different social choice theories.

The IC properties are the basic ones one could expect for BM operators. Some additional requirements can be considered for constraining further the behavior of the merging operators. Especially, two important subclasses of IC merging operators consist of the majority operators and the arbitration operators. First of all, a *majority merging operator* is an IC merging operator that satisfies the following *majority* postulate:

(Maj) $\exists n \; \Delta_\mu(E_1 \sqcup E_2^n) \models \Delta_\mu(E_2)$

This postulate expresses the fact that if a subgroup is repeated sufficiently many times in a profile then the opinion of this subgroup must prevail. Majority merging operators aim at satisfying the group of agents as a whole. Contrastingly, arbitration operators aim at satisfying each agent of the group as far as possible. Formally, an *arbitration operator* is an IC merging operator that satisfies the following *arbitration* postulate:

(Arb) If $\Delta_{\mu_1}(K_1) \equiv \Delta_{\mu_2}(K_2), \Delta_{\mu_1 \leftrightarrow \neg \mu_2}((K_1, K_2)) \equiv (\mu_1 \leftrightarrow \neg \mu_2), \mu_1 \not\models \mu_2,$ and $\mu_2 \not\models \mu_1,$
then $\Delta_{\mu_1 \vee \mu_2}((K_1, K_2)) \equiv \Delta_{\mu_1}(K_1)$

This property, which is much more intuitive when it is expressed in a model-theoretical way (cf. condition 8 of a fair syncretic assignment in Definition 7.2), roughly states that "median models" must be preferred.

We now present some representation theorems that give more constructive ways to define rational BM operators than the previous postulates. Such theorems show that each IC merging operator corresponds to a family of preorders on interpretations. First, one needs to define the notion of *syncretic assignment*.

Definition 7.2. *A* **syncretic assignment** *is a mapping associating with each profile E a total preorder $\leqslant_E$ over W such that for any profile E, E_1, E_2 and for any belief base K, K' the following conditions hold:*

1. *If $\omega \models E$ and $\omega' \models E$, then $\omega \simeq_E \omega'$*
2. *If $\omega \models E$ and $\omega' \not\models E$, then $\omega <_E \omega'$*
3. *If $E_1 \equiv E_2$, then $\leqslant_{E_1} = \leqslant_{E_2}$*
4. *$\forall \omega \models K \ \exists \omega' \models K' \ \omega' \leqslant_{(K,K')} \omega$*
5. *If $\omega \leqslant_{E_1} \omega'$ and $\omega \leqslant_{E_2} \omega'$, then $\omega \leqslant_{E_1 \sqcup E_2} \omega'$*
6. *If $\omega <_{E_1} \omega'$ and $\omega \leqslant_{E_2} \omega'$, then $\omega <_{E_1 \sqcup E_2} \omega'$*

A **majority syncretic assignment** *is a syncretic assignment which satisfies the following condition:*

7. *If $\omega <_{E_2} \omega'$, then $\exists n \ \omega <_{E_1 \sqcup E_2^n} \omega'$*

A **fair syncretic assignment** *is a syncretic assignment which satisfies the following condition:*

8. *If $\omega <_{K_1} \omega'$, $\omega <_{K_2} \omega''$, and $\omega' \simeq_{(K_1,K_2)} \omega''$, then $\omega <_{(K_1,K_2)} \omega'$*

The two first conditions ensure that the models of the conjunction of the bases from the profile (if any) are the most plausible interpretations for the preorder associated with the profile. The third condition states that two equivalent profiles are associated with the same preorders. These first three conditions are very close to the ones considered in belief revision for defining faithful assignments (Katsuno and Mendelzon, 1991). The fourth condition states that, when merging two belief bases, for each model of the first one, there is a model of the second one that is at least as good as the first one. It ensures that the two bases receive equal treatments in the merging process. The fifth condition states that if an interpretation ω is at least as plausible as an interpretation ω' for a profile E_1 and if ω is at least as plausible as ω' for a profile E_2, and if one then joins the two profiles, then ω must be at least as plausible as ω'. The sixth condition strengthens the previous condition by stating that if an interpretation ω is at least as plausible as an interpretation ω' for a profile E_1 and if ω is strictly more plausible than ω' for a profile E_2, then if the two profiles are joined, ω must be strictly more plausible than ω'. These two conditions are very close the to Pareto conditions in social choice. The seventh condition states that if an interpretation ω is strictly more plausible than an interpretation ω' for a profile E_2, then there is a quorum n of repetitions of the profile E_2 such that ω is more plausible than ω' for the larger profile $E_1 \sqcup E_2^n$. This condition seems to be the weakest form of "majority" condition one could state. Finally, the eighth condition states that "median choices" must be preferred by the group. More precisely, if an interpretation ω is more plausible than an interpretation ω' for a belief base K_1, if ω is more plausible than ω'' for another base K_2, and if ω' and ω'' are equally plausible for the joint profile (K_1, K_2), then ω has to be more plausible than ω' and ω'' for (K_1, K_2).

The following representation theorems have been established:

Proposition 7.1 (Konieczny and Pino Pérez, 2002a). *A merging operator Δ is an IC merging operator (resp. a majority merging operator, an arbitration operator) if and only if there exists a syncretic assignment (resp. a majority syncretic assignment, a fair syncretic assignment) that maps each profile E to a total preorder $\leqslant_E$ over $\mathcal{W}$ such that $mod(\Delta_\mu(E)) = \min(mod(\mu), \leqslant_E)$*

7.3 On Distance-Based Merging Operators

Let us now give some examples of IC merging operators from the family of distance-based merging operators (Konieczny et al., 2004). For such operators, the total preorders $\leqslant_E$ generated by the corresponding assignments are induced from a distance between interpretations and an aggregation function: an interpretation ω is at least as close to E as an interpretation ω', i.e., $\omega \leqslant_E \omega'$, if the (aggregated) distance of ω to E is lower than or equal to the (aggregated) distance of ω' to E. Formally:

Definition 7.3. *A (pseudo-)distance between interpretations is a mapping $d : \mathcal{W} \times \mathcal{W} \to \mathbb{R}^+$ such that for any $\omega_1, \omega_2 \in \mathcal{W}$:*

- $d(\omega_1, \omega_2) = d(\omega_2, \omega_1)$
- $d(\omega_1, \omega_2) = 0$ *if and only if* $\omega_1 = \omega_2$

Typical distances are the Hamming distance d_H, that is the number of propositional letters on which the two interpretations differ and the drastic distance d_D, defined as $d_D(\omega_1, \omega_2) = 0$ if $\omega_1 = \omega_2$, and $= 1$ otherwise.

Definition 7.4. *An aggregation function is a mapping[2] f from $\mathbb{R}^m$ to $\mathbb{R}$, which satisfies:*

- *if $x_i \geqslant x'_i$, then $f(x_1, ..., x_i, ..., x_m) \geqslant f(x_1, ..., x'_i, ..., x_m)$* **(non-decreasingness)**
- *$f(x_1, ..., x_m) = 0$ if $\forall i, x_i = 0$* **(minimality)**
- *$f(x) = x$* **(identity)**
- *If σ is a permutation over $\{1, ..., m\}$, then $f(x_1, ..., x_m) = f(x_{\sigma(1)}, ..., x_{\sigma(m)})$* **(symmetry)**

Some additional properties can also be considered for f, especially:

- *if $x_i > x'_i$, then $f(x_1, ..., x_i, ..., x_m) > f(x_1, ..., x'_i, ..., x_m)$* **(strict non-decreasingness)**
- *If $f(x_1, ..., x_n) \leqslant f(y_1, ..., y_n)$, then $f(x_1, ..., x_n, z) \leqslant f(y_1, ..., y_n, z)$* **(composition)**
- *If $f(x_1, ..., x_n, z) \leqslant f(y_1, ..., y_n, z)$, then $f(x_1, ..., x_n) \leqslant f(y_1, ..., y_n)$* **(decomposition)**
- *If $\forall i, z > y_i$, then $f(z, x_1, ..., x_n) > f(y_1, ..., y_{n+1})$* **(strict preference)**

Standard aggregation functions are Σ (sum), $Gmax$ (also referred to as *leximax*), $Gmin$ (also referred to as *leximin*), and Σ^n (sum of the nth powers).

---
[2] Strictly speaking, it is a family of mappings, one for each integer $m \geqslant 1$.

Definition 7.5. *Let d and f be a distance between interpretations and an aggregation function, respectively. The* distance-based merging operator $\Delta^{d,f}$ *is defined semantically by*

$$[\Delta^{d,f}_\mu(E)] = \min([\mu], \leqslant^{d,f}_E)$$

where the total preorder $\leqslant_E$ on $\mathcal{W}$ is defined in the following way :

- $\omega \leqslant^{d,f}_E \omega'$ *if and only if* $d^{d,f}(\omega, E) \leqslant d^{d,f}(\omega', E)$
- $d^{d,f}(\omega, (K_1, \ldots, K_n)) = f(d(\omega, K_1), \ldots, d(\omega, K_n))$
- $d(\omega, K) = \min_{\omega' \models K} d(\omega, \omega')$

Example 7.1. *As a matter of illustration, consider the three belief bases:* $K_1 = \{\neg a \wedge \neg b \wedge \neg c\}$, $K_2 = \{(a \wedge b) \vee (\neg a \wedge \neg b \wedge c)\}$ *and* $K_3 = \{a \wedge b \wedge c\}$. *We have* $[K_1] = \{000\}$, $[K_2] = \{001, 110, 111\}$ *and* $[K_3] = \{111\}$. *Suppose that the integrity constraints are* $\mu = (a \vee c) \wedge (a \wedge c \to b)$.

The following table reports the merged bases corresponding to the merging of the profile (K_1, K_2, K_3) under μ for some of the most usual distance-based operators. The lines of the table correspond to the available interpretations. In this example, three propositional symbols a, b and c are considered, so there are 8 interpretations (6 being models of μ). The first three columns give the Hamming distance of the models to each base, the last four columns indicate the aggregated distances of the models to E, depending on the chosen aggregation function. The selected interpretations (depending on the chosen aggregation function) are boldfaced.

This example clearly shows that different BM operators can lead to different merged bases. Δ^{Gmin,d_H} and Δ^{Σ,d_H} are majority merging operators, so they tend to select interpretations satisfying a maximal number of bases. Δ^{Gmax,d_H} is an arbitration operator, so it tends to select "median interpretations".

	K_1	K_2	K_3	Δ^{Gmax,d_H}	Δ^{Gmin,d_H}	Δ^{Σ,d_H}	Δ^{Σ^2,d_H}
001	1	0	2	**210**	012	3	5
011	2	1	1	211	112	4	6
100	1	1	2	211	112	4	6
110	2	0	1	**210**	012	3	5
111	3	0	0	300	**003**	**3**	9

On this example, 111 is selected by the operators based on $Gmin$ or Σ because they are majoritarian operators, and $\Delta^{Gmin,d_H} \equiv a \wedge b \wedge c$. 001 or 110 are selected by the operators based on $Gmax$ or Σ^2, because these interpretations are more consensual than the other ones. Thus, we have $\Delta^{Gmax,d_H} \equiv (\neg a \wedge \neg b \wedge c) \vee (a \wedge b \wedge \neg c)$.

For usual aggregation functions, whatever the chosen distance, the corresponding distance-based BM operators exhibit good logical properties:

Proposition 7.2 (Konieczny and Pino Pérez, 2002b). *For any distance d, if f is equal to Σ, $Gmax$, $Gmin$, or Σ^n, then $\Delta^{d,f}$ is an IC merging operator.*

More generally, in (Konieczny et al., 2004), a necessary and sufficient condition on the chosen aggregation function f is identified, ensuring that the corresponding distance-based BM operators $\Delta^{d,f}$ are IC ones (whatever the distance d):

Proposition 7.3. *Let d and f be a distance between interpretations and an aggregation function respectively. The operator $\Delta^{d,f}$ satisfies the postulates (IC0-IC8) iff the aggregation function f satisfies composition and decomposition.*

To conclude this introduction to BM, we sketch some alternative approaches. Though we mainly focused on model-based BM operators in this introduction, it must be noted that formula-based BM operators have also been defined (Baral et al., 1991, 1992). The general principle underlying them is to select some preferred consistent subsets of formulae from the union of all the bases of the input profile. One important limitation of the formula-based BM approaches is to possibly forget some important pieces of information available in the input profile, such as the number of bases supporting each formula. On the other hand, inconsistent belief bases can be taken into account easily by such approaches. Formula-based BM operators have been shown to satisfy less postulates than the model-based ones (Konieczny, 2000). Konieczny et al. (2004) generalize the family of distance-based BM operators to so-called DA^2 operators, in order to take advantage of the pros offered by distance-based BM operators and by formula-based operators. Thus, DA^2 operators can deal with inconsistent belief bases and are based on two aggregation functions: the first one is used to extract pieces of belief from inconsistent bases and the second one to aggregate the resulting pieces of belief.

Everaere et al. (2008) have defined and studied conflict-based merging operators. These operators refine the distance-based ones by computing conflicts. They aim at minimizing the conflicts between the beliefs of the agents. Default-based merging operators have also been introduced by Delgrande and Schaub (2007). In this work, inconsistencies are fixed by renaming some propositional symbols, and the merged bases are characterized as those requiring "as few renamings as possible".

Additional merging postulates have also been pointed out in the literature. Let us mention the work of Everaere et al. (2010) where a **Unanimity** postulate for BM operators has been introduced. This postulate can be considered either for formulae or for models: if all agents share a common piece of belief, it should be the case that the merged base also supports this piece of belief. Everaere et al. (2010) also define a **Disjunction** postulate, which is in a certain sense a counterpoint to the arbitration postulate **(Arb)**. This postulate ensures that every logical consequence of the merged base is among the logical consequences of at least one input base. Other properties inspired by similar conditions in social choice have been translated into the BM framework. This led to the definitions of various notions of interest for merging, like truth tracking by Everaere et al. (2007), rationalization by Konieczny et al. (2011), or egalitarianism by Everaere et al. (2014a). Recently, a study of voting properties in the context of BM has also been conducted by Haret et al. (2016).

Merging has also been studied in other representation frameworks than the purely propositional one. When all the pieces of information belonging to the bases do not have the same importance, weighted approaches must be considered. Many frameworks have been defined and studied to take account of the relative plausibility of pieces of belief, including *possibilistic logic* (Dubois et al., 1994) and *ordinal conditional functions* (Spohn, 1987). Thus, Delgrande et al.

(2006) define prioritized merging operators, in order to merge sets of weighted formulae. Benferhat, Dubois, Kaci and Prade point out several merging operators suited to representations in possibilistic logic (Kaci et al., 2000; Benferhat et al., 2002).

Bloch and Lang (2000) define model-based merging operators using maximum as aggregation function ($\Delta^{d,\max}$) and show how the corresponding merged bases can be characterized via a *dilation* process. Gorogiannis and Hunter (2008) extend this approach in order to define other model-based merging operators, based on a dilation process. The interest of the dilation-based approach is that it can be extended to first-order logic without much efforts.

The issue of merging logic programs under ASP semantics has also been considered. The approach to merging given in (Hué et al., 2009) relies on the deletion of a set of formulae in the union of the bases, characterized using a selection function (the idea is close to the one considered in (Konieczny, 2000)). The corresponding operators satisfy only some IC postulates. Let us also mention the work of Delgrande et al. (2009), where the merging operators pointed out are based on the definition of a distance between stable models.

Condotta et al. (2009) studied the merging of qualitative constraint networks. Finally, Coste-Marquis et al. (2007) and Delobelle et al. (2016) study the problem of *merging argumentation frameworks*, where the arguments are distributed among several agents.

7.4 On Judgment Aggregation

Let us now briefly present some definitions and notation used in the following. An *agenda* $X = \{\varphi_1, \ldots, \varphi_m\}$ is a finite, non-empty and totally ordered set of contingent (i.e., consistent but not valid) propositional formulae. A *judgment* on a formula φ_k of X is an element of $D = \{1, 0, \star\}$, where 1 means that φ_k is supported, 0 that $\neg \varphi_k$ is supported, $\star$ that neither φ_k nor $\neg \varphi_k$ is supported. A *judgment set* on X is a mapping γ from X to D, also viewed as an m-vector over D, when the cardinality of X is m, or alternatively as the set of formulae such that $\varphi_k \in \gamma$ when $\gamma(\varphi_k) = 1$, $\neg\varphi_k \in \gamma$ when $\gamma(\varphi_k) = 0$, for every $\varphi_k \in X$. For each φ_k of X, γ is supposed to satisfy $\gamma(\neg\varphi_k) = \neg\gamma(\varphi_k)$, where $\neg\gamma$ is given by $\neg\gamma(\varphi_k) = \star$ if $\gamma(\varphi_k) = \star$, $\neg\gamma(\varphi_k) = 1$ if $\gamma(\varphi_k) = 0$, and $\neg\gamma(\varphi_k) = 0$ if $\gamma(\varphi_k) = 1$.

Judgment sets are often asked to be consistent and complete, where a judgment set is *complete* if $\forall \varphi_k \in X$, $\gamma(\varphi_k) = 0$ or $\gamma(\varphi_k) = 1$, and a judgment set γ on X is *consistent* if the associated formula (judgment) $\widehat{\gamma} = \bigwedge_{\{\varphi_k \in X | \gamma(\varphi_k) = 1\}} \varphi_k \wedge \bigwedge_{\{\varphi_k \in X | \gamma(\varphi_k) = 0\}} \neg\varphi_k$ is consistent.

Aggregating judgments consists in associating a set of collective judgment sets with a profile containing n individual judgment sets (one per agent): a *profile* $\Gamma = (\gamma_1, \ldots, \gamma_n)$ of judgment sets on X is a non-empty vector of judgments sets on X. Γ is *consistent* (resp. *complete*) when each judgment set in it is consistent (resp. complete).

For each agenda X, a *JA operator* Ag associates with a consistent profile Γ on X a non-empty set Ag_Γ of collective judgment sets γ_Γ on X, also viewed as a formula (the collective judgment) $\widehat{Ag_\Gamma} = \bigvee_{\gamma_\Gamma \in Ag_\Gamma} \widehat{\gamma_\Gamma}$. For $\varphi_k \in X$, we note $Ag_\Gamma(\varphi_k) =$

1 (resp. $Ag_\Gamma(\varphi_k) = 0$) if and only if $\forall \gamma_\Gamma \in Ag_\Gamma$, $\gamma_\Gamma(\varphi_k) = 1$ (resp. $\forall \gamma_\Gamma \in Ag_\Gamma$, $\gamma_\Gamma(\varphi_k) = 0$), and $Ag_\Gamma(\varphi_k) = \star$ in the remaining case.

When Ag_Γ is a singleton for each Γ, the JA operator Ag is called a resolute JA rule, and it is called an irresolute JA rule (or a JA correspondence in (Lang et al., 2011)) otherwise.

Here are some common properties for JA rules that have been identified in the literature:

Universal domain. The domain of Ag is the set of all consistent profiles.

This property is often relaxed, as in (List and Pettit, 2002), to:

C-universal domain. The domain of Ag is the set of all profiles which are consistent and complete.

Some properties also state that the result should be consistent and complete:

Collective rationality. For any profile Γ in the domain of Ag, Ag_Γ is a set of consistent collective judgment sets.

Collective completeness. For any profile Γ in the domain of Ag, Ag_Γ is a set of complete collective judgment sets.

For obvious equity reasons, agents and issues are expected to play symmetric roles:

Anonymity. For any two profiles $\Gamma = (\gamma_1, \ldots, \gamma_n)$ and $\Gamma' = (\gamma'_1, \ldots, \gamma'_n)$ in the domain of Ag which are permutations one another, we have $Ag_\Gamma = Ag_{\Gamma'}$.

Neutrality. For any φ, φ' in the agenda X and profile Γ in the domain of Ag, if $\forall i$ $\gamma_i(\varphi) = \gamma_i(\varphi')$, then $Ag_\Gamma(\varphi) = Ag_\Gamma(\varphi')$.

A more demanding property is:

Independence. For any φ in the agenda X and profiles $\Gamma = (\gamma_1, \ldots, \gamma_n)$ and $\Gamma' = (\gamma'_1, \ldots, \gamma'_n)$ in the domain of Ag, if $\forall i$ $\gamma_i(\varphi) = \gamma'_i(\varphi)$, then $Ag_\Gamma(\varphi) = Ag_{\Gamma'}(\varphi)$.

Systematicity. For any φ, φ' in the agenda X and profiles $\Gamma = (\gamma_1, \ldots, \gamma_n)$ and $\Gamma' = (\gamma'_1, \ldots, \gamma'_n)$ in the domain of Ag, if $\forall i$ $\gamma_i(\varphi) = \gamma'_i(\varphi')$, then $Ag_\Gamma(\varphi) = Ag_{\Gamma'}(\varphi')$.

Clearly, **Systematicity** is equivalent to **Independence** and **Neutrality**.

The above properties are quite standard ones, but unfortunately they are jointly incompatible:

Proposition 7.4 (List and Pettit, 2002). *There exists no JA rule that satisfy* **C-universal domain**, **Collective rationality**, **Collective resoluteness**, **Systematicity**, *and* **Anonymity**.

This impossibility theorem relies on some strong assumptions. First is the completeness assumptions of the individuals (**C-universal domain**), that can be criticized, since in many cases one cannot reasonably expect all agents to have an opinion on all possible issues; this is also the case of the **Collective completeness** property, that is helpful for making decisions, but forces to make some choices even when it is not possible to do so (Gärdenfors, 2006). Thus the **Collective completeness** requirement imposes sometimes to discriminate further some judgment sets, using additional information not given in the input profile,

Γ	φ_1	φ_2	φ_3	φ_4	φ_5	φ_6
1	1	1	0	1	1	1
2	1	1	1	0	1	1
3	1	1	1	1	0	1
4	1	1	1	1	1	0
5	1	0	1	1	1	1
6	1	0	1	1	1	1

Γ'	φ_1	φ_2	φ_3	φ_4	φ_5	φ_6
1'	0	1	1	1	1	1
2'	0	1	1	1	1	1
3'	0	1	1	1	1	1
4'	0	1	1	1	1	1
5'	1	0	0	0	0	0
6'	1	0	0	0	0	0

Table 7.1: Example of the need of a non-isolated decision on φ_2

and as such, it conflicts with the **Anonymity** and **Neutrality** conditions. Suppose for instance a perfect tie (say, about a unique issue φ in the agenda, with 4 votes for and 4 votes against it), why and how to make a distinction between φ and $\neg\varphi$? The **Systematicity** property is also highly criticizable, as shown by Everaere et al. (2014b). Indeed, it prevents from viewing JA as an optimization process, trying to achieve a best compromise. The following example illustrates this:

Example 7.2. *Let us consider an agenda X composed of the following six formulae: $\varphi_1 = (\neg a \vee \neg b \vee \neg c \vee \neg d \vee \neg e)$, $\varphi_2 = a$, $\varphi_3 = b$, $\varphi_4 = c$, $\varphi_5 = d$, $\varphi_6 = e$. Let us consider the profiles Γ and Γ' on this agenda, as given by Table 7.1. In the (resolute) profile Γ, every formula has a majority of votes, so using simple majority vote all the formulae have to be selected, which would lead to an inconsistent collective judgment set. So (at least) one of the six formulae has to be rejected by the judgment aggregation correspondence. There is a unanimity for accepting φ_1, so it seems sensible to select φ_1 in the result. All the other formulae except φ_2 are quasi-unanimous (they get all votes but one). The least supported formula is φ_2, so we can consider that the most sensible result should be $\gamma_\Gamma = \{\varphi_1, \neg\varphi_2, \varphi_3, \varphi_4, \varphi_5, \varphi_6\}$.*

*Consider now the profile Γ'. The simple majority vote leads to a consistent collective judgment set $\gamma_{\Gamma'} = \{\neg\varphi_1, \varphi_2, \varphi_3, \varphi_4, \varphi_5, \varphi_6\}$, which thus appears as the expected result (a requirement of the majority preservation property that we will recall below). So, although the individual judgments for φ_2 are the same ones in the two profiles Γ and Γ', $\neg\varphi_2$ is selected when Γ is considered, whereas φ_2 is selected when Γ' is considered. Since φ_2 gets the same votes pros and cons in the two profiles, no judgment aggregation method satisfying **Systematicity** can make such a distinction.*

This example illustrates that the individual judgments on an issue should not be considered independently from those for the other issues.

Lang et al. (2011) and Everaere et al. (2014b) study other attractive properties for JA operators, such as **Unanimity** or **Majority preservation**.

Unanimity. For any $\varphi_k \in X$, for any profile Γ in the domain of Ag, if $\exists x \in \{0, 1\}$ s.t. $\forall \gamma_i \in \Gamma$, $\gamma_i(\varphi_k) = x$, then for every $\gamma_\Gamma \in Ag_\Gamma$, we have $\gamma_\Gamma(\varphi_k) = x$.

Note that a unanimity condition is not required when $x = \star$, since in this case it makes sense to let the acceptance of φ_k depend on the acceptance of other (logically related) formulae.

Majority preservation. If the judgment set obtained using the majority rule[3] is consistent and complete, then Ag_Γ is a singleton which consists of this set.

Majority preservation (Lang et al., 2011) (called strong majority preservation by Slavkovik (2012)) is a very natural property, stating that if the simple majority vote on each issue leads to a consistent judgment set, then the JA operator must output precisely this set. Indeed, it is sensible to stick to the result furnished by a simple majority vote when no doctrinal paradox occurs.

Many JA operators that have been defined in the literature, but most of them, following the requirements given by the **Systematicity/Independence** properties, do not allow to consider the collective judgment sets as the results of some optimization process, aiming at making decision on each issue by taking the context (i.e., the other issues) into account. Nonetheless, Lang et al. (2011) introduce several families of JA operators based on minimization, inspired by operators considered in voting theory or in artificial intelligence. Majority preservation is presented as a natural requirement for such operators. Everaere et al. (2014b) define another family of operators, called ranked majority operators, that exploit the number of votes received by each formula of the agenda.

7.5 BM vs. JA

A fundamental difference between BM and JA concerns the nature of the input and the nature of the output considered in the two settings. Propositional BM mainly considers the beliefs of individual agents from a group. Beliefs are typically encoded by belief bases, i.e., sets of propositional formulae over a finite set of atoms, or, equivalently, by sets of interpretations. Interpretations are independent and mutually conflicting views of the same world, and each agent believes that the true world is one of the interpretations in her beliefs. Belief bases are often supposed to be consistent. In many approaches to BM, the notion of interpretation is a key notion, since the interpretations are the "candidates" of the decision process (in a nutshell, belief merging can be defined as a process which aims at finding the most plausible interpretations given the beliefs of the agents of the group). The selection of the most plausible interpretations relies on a number of principles. The notion of majority can play a role here (i.e., one can focus on interpretations shared by a majority of agents) but this is not mandatory, some BM operators can select interpretations that are rejected by every agent of the group. The belief base provided by each agent is implicitly assumed to contain all the pieces of belief to be considered in the merging process. Modifying a single base by adding/removing some pieces of belief may have a strong impact on the result furnished by the merging operator, which can be logically strengthened, weakened or become logically unrelated with the merged base obtained before the modification.

In JA, a focus is laid on a specific set of issues, encoded as propositional formulae φ, and called the agenda. The input is a set of individual judgments

---

[3]Several definitions are possible for the majority rule when abstention is allowed. Here, one considers that the majority rule gives 1 (resp. 0) when the number of agents reporting 1 (resp. 0) is strictly greater than the number of agents reporting 0 (resp. 1), and it gives $\star$ otherwise.

(0/reject or 1/accept or $\star$/abstain) from the agents of the group on the formulae of the agenda. If an agent accepts/rejects φ, then she rejects/accepts $\neg\varphi$. No assumption is made on the way individual decisions/judgments are made by each agent (but a consistency condition, stating that an agent cannot accept formulae that are jointly inconsistent, reflecting the fact that she has consistent beliefs). Each individual judgment reflects the epistemic status of each formula from the agenda in the belief base of the corresponding agent (but nothing more). The beliefs of the group are determined from the collective judgment(s) on the agenda, which is the result produced by the JA operator that is considered. The principle of majority plays an important role here. Typically, the judgment of the group on a given formula φ of the agenda is the point of view of the majority on it: if a majority of agents accept/reject it, then this is the case as well for the group. A doctrinal paradox occurs when the conjunction of the formulae accepted by the group is inconsistent. In such a case, the resulting collective judgment must be somehow weakened for recovering consistency, and several approaches can be used to this purpose (e.g., considering that some formulae of the agenda are more important than others). Modifying the agenda by adding/removing some issues in it may have a strong impact on the collective judgment(s) furnished by the JA operator. Typically, no integrity constraints are considered in a JA process, but it could be possible to do it (merely, by replacing the notion of consistency by a notion of consistency with the integrity constraints).

Unsurprisingly, since BM operators and JA operators are based on different inputs and outputs, the sets of properties of interest for BM operators and for JA operators do not coincide. In propositional BM, some sets of postulates characterize the behavior of rational operators, and representation theorems exist. In judgment aggregation, some properties (often inspired by voting theory) have been identified as well. However, these properties typically lead to impossibility theorems, showing that they are not jointly compatible. That said, some judgment aggregation operators have nevertheless been characterized by sets of properties, as the quota operators in (Dietrich and List, 2007) (the work of Grandi and Endriss (2011) gives also a characterization of quota rules using binary aggregation and suited integrity constraints).

7.6 Decision Policies

As explained previously, BM and JA consider different inputs. Notwithstanding the integrity constraints, in BM, the input is a profile of belief bases, representing the beliefs of a group of agents. In JA, the input is composed of answers "yes" (1), "no" (0) or "undetermined" ($\star$) reported by the agents for some issues (those of the agenda), and the input profile is a vector of such answers (alias judgment sets). Of course, agents might use their beliefs to answer the questions, but it is out of the scope of JA operators to specify how individual judgments are obtained.

Let us consider the following question: if the beliefs K_i of an agent i are known, given an issue φ_k, what could be the opinion of the agent on the issue?

Suppose that the agent only believes that $a \wedge b$ is true, and is questioned about a: she will probably answer "yes" to the question because she necessarily believes that a is true. If the question is $\neg b$, she will probably answer "no" because b being false is incompatible with her beliefs. Suppose now that the agent just believes that a is true, and that the question is $a \wedge b$. In this case the agent probably has no opinion on the question (the question is contingent given her beliefs), thus she will probably answer "undetermined".

What is needed to make it formal is a mapping which characterizes the answers (i.e., the judgment set) an agent can give to the issues of the agenda, depending on her belief base. We call such mapping *decision policies*, and our purpose is first to characterize them axiomatically:

Definition 7.6. *A decision policy $p : \mathcal{L} \times \mathcal{L} \to \{0, 1, \star\}$ is a mapping associating an element of $\{0, 1, \star\}$ with any pair of non-trivial formulae (K, φ) and satisfying:*
1. *if $K_1 \equiv K_2$, then $\forall \varphi, p(K_1, \varphi) = p(K_2, \varphi)$*
2. *if $\varphi_1 \equiv \varphi_2$, then $\forall K, p(K, \varphi_1) = p(K, \varphi_2)$*
3. *$p(\varphi, \varphi) = 1$*

Conditions 1 and 2 can be viewed as a formal counterpart, respectively, of a neutrality condition and of an anonymity condition for decision policies.

Given an agenda $X = \{\varphi_1, \ldots, \varphi_m\}$ and a belief base K (respectively a profile $E = (K_1, \ldots, K_n)$ of belief bases), every decision policy p induces a judgment set $p_X(K) = (p(K, \varphi_1), \ldots, p(K, \varphi_m))$ (resp. a profile of judgment sets $p_X(E) = (p_X(K_1), \ldots, p_X(K_n))$).

Examples of decision policies are the following ones:

$$p_B(K, \varphi) = \begin{cases} 1 & \text{if } K \models \varphi \\ 0 & \text{if } K \models \neg\varphi \\ \star & \text{otherwise} \end{cases} \qquad p_C(K, \varphi) = \begin{cases} 1 & \text{if } K \wedge \varphi \not\models \bot \\ 0 & \text{otherwise} \end{cases}$$

Using the *belief decision policy* p_B, an agent answers "yes" (resp. "no") to a given issue precisely when it (resp. its negation) is a logical consequence of her belief base; in the remaining case, she answers "undetermined".

Observe that with the *consistency decision policy* p_C it is possible to have together $p_C(K_i, \varphi_k) = 1$ and $p_C(K_i, \neg\varphi_k) = 1$ (for instance, a belief base equivalent to a is consistent with b and with $\neg b$). In order to avoid this problem, some additional conditions must be satisfied:

Definition 7.7. *Let $p : \mathcal{L} \times \mathcal{L} \to \{0, 1, \star\}$ be a decision policy. It is a rational decision policy if it satisfies the two following conditions:*
4. *if $p(K, \varphi) = 1$, then $p(K, \neg\varphi) = 0$*
5. *If $K_1 \wedge K_2$ is consistent and if $p(K_1, \varphi) = 1$ then $p(K_1 \wedge K_2, \varphi) = 1$*

It turns out that these two additional conditions fully characterize the belief decision policy:

Proposition 7.5. *p is a rational decision policy if and only if $p = p_B$.*

p_B also ensures individual consistency:

Proposition 7.6. *Whatever the belief base K and the agenda X, if γ is the judgment set on X induced by p_B given K, then the associated judgment $\hat{\gamma}$ is consistent.*

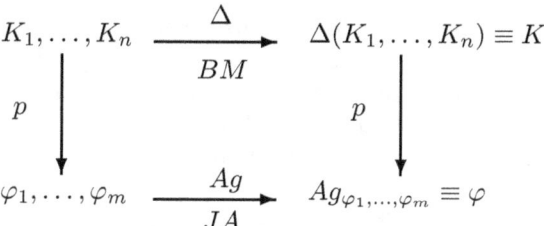

Figure 7.2: BM vs. JA

7.7 Merge-then-Project or Project-then-Aggregate?

Thanks to the rational decision policy $p = p_B$ defined in the previous section, we know how to determine the judgment set of an agent i on any agenda $X = \{\varphi_1, \ldots, \varphi_n\}$ when her belief base K_i is known. This judgment set $(p(K_i, \varphi_1), \ldots, p(K_i, \varphi_m))$ can be viewed as the "projection" of K_i onto X, and such a concept of projection was the missing link between the BM process and the JA one, as illustrated on Figure 7.2.

From it, it appears that there are two ways to define the collective judgment(s) of a group of agents on an agenda, assuming that the beliefs of the agents are known. On the one hand, belief bases can be first merged using a BM operator, then the resulting merged base can be projected onto the agenda. On the other hand, the belief bases can be first projected on the agenda, and then the resulting $0/1/\star$ matrix can be aggregated using a JA operator. The chosen approach typically has a strong influence on the output of the process.

Example 7.3. *Let us illustrate this on a simple example, with 4 agents. Suppose that the set $\mathcal{P}$ of propositional symbols is $\{a, b\}$, so that only 4 interpretations are possible: $\omega_1 = 00$, $\omega_2 = 01$, $\omega_3 = 10$, and $\omega_4 = 11$. Suppose also that the set of models of the belief base of each agent consists of a single interpretation: $[K_1] = \{\omega_1\}$, $[K_2] = \{\omega_2\}$, $[K_3] = \{\omega_3\}$, and $[K_4] = \{\omega_4\}$. Suppose finally that the agenda X consists of the three formulae $\neg a \wedge \neg b$, $\neg a \wedge b$, and $a \wedge \neg b$.*

In order to use the project-then-aggregate approach, one first need to determine the individual judgments on X. They are reported in the following table:

	$\neg a \wedge \neg b$	$\neg a \wedge b$	$a \wedge \neg b$
K_1	1	0	0
K_2	0	1	0
K_3	0	0	1
K_4	0	0	0

Since a majority of agents reject each of the issues, using a JA rule satisfying the **Majority preservation** condition leads to the collective judgment $\gamma_2 = (0, 0, 0)$ so that $\widehat{\gamma}_2 \equiv a \wedge b$ which is consistent. Hence the beliefs of the group will be computed as $a \wedge b$, despite the fact that each agent actually rejects $a \wedge b$.

This example also shows the importance of the choice of the agenda. For this example, the fact that $a \wedge b$ is accepted or rejected by any agent is fully determined by her individual judgment set on $X = \{\neg a \wedge \neg b, \neg a \wedge b, a \wedge \neg b\}$ (since judgment sets are supposed to be consistent). Stated otherwise, $a \wedge b$ is a redundant issue given X, hence asking each agent whether she accepts or rejects $a \wedge b$ should be useless when the issues from X have been considered. It turns out that this is not the case. Let us complete the agenda X with the issue $a \wedge b$ and the previous table by the individual judgments of the four agents on $a \wedge b$:

	$\neg a \wedge \neg b$	$\neg a \wedge b$	$a \wedge \neg b$	$a \wedge b$
K_1	1	0	0	0
K_2	0	1	0	0
K_3	0	0	1	0
K_4	0	0	0	1

Since a majority of agents reject each of the issues, using a JA rule satisfying the **Majority preservation** condition leads to the collective judgment $\gamma_3 = (0, 0, 0, 0)$ so that $\widehat{\gamma_3} \equiv \bot$ which is inconsistent. This conflict must thus be solved by the JA rule under consideration. Clearly enough, since the instance is fully symmetric, there is no reason here that the beliefs of the group will be computed as $a \wedge b$ again.

Contrastingly, using the merge-then-project approach (with the distance-based operator $\Delta^{d_H, \Sigma}$), one first compute $\Delta_\top^{d_H, \Sigma}((K_1, K_2, K_3, K_4))$ which is equivalent to $\top$, then the projection of this merged base on X gives the collective judgment $\gamma_1 = (\star, \star, \star)$, so that $\widehat{\gamma_1} \equiv \top$ as well, meaning that the group has no information about the issues from X. Note that the same result is obtained if the agenda is completed by the issue $a \wedge b$.

This example illustrates that the processus of judgment aggregation is very sensible to the choice of the issues, and that adding to the agenda an issue (even a redundant one) may have a huge impact on the result. This is strongly related to the problem of manipulating the agenda and as such, it has been studied in the JA literature, for example by Dietrich (2016) and by Lang et al. (2016).

Let us now give an example that illustrates that some information can be lost with the project-then-aggregate approach while it is preserved when the merge-then-project approach is considered instead.

Example 7.4. Let $K_1 = \{p \vee q\}$, $K_2 = K_1$, and $K_3 = \{p \vee \neg q\}$ and an agenda containing only p. The matrix containing the responses to p is composed of three $\star$, because no agent knows whether p is true or false. If the projection of the bases on p is computed first, then the three projected bases are equivalent to $\top$, and the result of their aggregation will be equivalent to $\top$ as well (the group does not know whether p is true or false). If the three bases are first merged using an IC merging operator, then since their conjunction is consistent, the merged base will be equivalent to p. If this merged base is then projected onto p, the conclusion will be that p is true. Thus, JA typically lead to lose much more information than BM when the input belief bases are not complete ones.

7.8 More on BM vs. JA

Let us step back to Figure 7.2 and denote by φ_{Ag} the formula obtained following the project-then-aggregate path $Ag \circ p$, and φ_Δ the formula obtained following the merge-then-project path $p \circ \Delta$. While the previous example shows that φ_Δ and φ_{Ag} can be distinct, it is important to determine whether some logical connections between φ_Δ and φ_{Ag} can be ensured whenever Δ and Ag both satisfy some rationality properties.

The answer is negative in the general case. Everaere et al. (2015) show that the two resulting formulae are not necessarily jointly consistent. More precisely, for distance-based operators, a negative result has been exhibited: φ_{Ag} and $\varphi_{\Delta^{d,f}}$ are not necessarily jointly consistent even if Ag satisfies **Majority preservation**, d is any normal[4] distance and f is any strictly non-decreasing aggregation function. The significance of the result comes from the fact that usual distances between interpretations (Hamming distance, drastic distance) are normal ones and usual aggregation functions (Σ, $Gmax$, $Gmin$, Σ^n, ...) satisfy strict non-decreasingness.

Things are different in the case when the two approaches are equally informed, i.e., when the agenda X gathers all interpretations of $\mathcal{W}$. Under these assumptions, Everaere et al. (2015) have shown that the beliefs of the group computed following the merge-then-project path are the same as the beliefs of the group obtained following the project-then-aggregate path. On this ground, an irresolute JA rule $Ag = Ag^\Delta$ can be defined from a BM operator Δ, and reciprocally, a BM operator $\Delta = \Delta^{Ag}$ can be defined from a irresolute JA rule Ag. Details of the construction are given by Everaere et al. (2015).

A natural question is then to determine whether imposing some rationality conditions on a BM operator Δ leads the induced JA operator $Ag = Ag^\Delta$ to satisfy some rationality conditions, and vice-versa, whether imposing some rationality conditions on a JA operator Ag leads the induced BM operator $\Delta = \Delta^{Ag}$ to satisfy some rationality conditions.

It has been shown that Δ^{Ag} satisfies the postulates **(IC0)**, **(IC1)** and **(IC3)** when Ag satisfies **Universal domain** and **Anonymity**. For getting **(IC2)** for Δ^{Ag}, an additional condition of **Consensuality** must be satisfied by Ag. This condition ensures that if an issue of the agenda is accepted by **all** the agents (i.e., it is a unanimous issue), then the collective judgment set computed by Ag consists exactly of those unanimous issues. Interestingly, **(IC4)** for Δ^{Ag} is not ensured by the **Neutrality** condition on Ag.

Other connections between the satisfaction of some IC postulates for BM and the satisfaction of some conditions on JA operators can be established for the operators in correspondence (Ag^Δ and Δ, and Δ^{Ag} and Ag) in the complete agenda case (i.e., when the agenda is the set of all interpretations). The **Weak consistency** condition on JA operators states that if an issue is accepted by a profile Γ of individual judgment sets and by a profile Γ' of individual judgment sets, then it must be accepted by the union of the two profiles.

The **Consistency** condition strengthens it by stating that if there is at least one issue that is accepted by two profiles Γ and Γ', then each issue that is accepted by the whole profile $\Gamma \sqcup \Gamma'$ should be accepted by each of the two profiles Γ and Γ'. It turns out that those properties correspond respectively to the IC postulates **(IC5)** and **(IC6)**. Quite surprisingly, these conditions have not been considered as standard ones for JA operators (we are only aware of (Lang et al.,

---

[4] A distance is *normal* if $d(\omega_1, \omega_2) \leqslant d(\omega_3, \omega_4)$ whenever the variables which have different truth values in ω_1 and ω_2 are included into the variables which have different truth values in ω_3 and ω_4.

2011; Slavkovik, 2012; Lang et al., 2016) which point out the **Consistency** condition, under the name "separability").

Everaere et al. (2015) give a list of properties required for a JA operator to induce an IC merging operator in the complete agenda case. A key question is whether these properties can be satisfied by some JA operator. A positive answer to this issue is given when some JA rules $\delta^{RM\oplus}$ defined by Everaere et al. (2014b) are considered. Roughly, each $\delta^{RM\oplus}$ rule consists in selecting in the set of all consistent and resolute judgment sets the best ones, where the score of each judgment set is defined as the $\oplus$-aggregation of an m-vector of values (one value per question in the agenda X, reflecting the number of agents supporting the question in the input profile Γ). When the agenda is complete, for any $\oplus$ satisfying strict non-decreasingness, the ranked majority judgment aggregation rule $\delta^{RM\oplus}$ satisfies **Universal domain**, **Collective rationality**, **Collective resoluteness**, **Anonymity**, **Neutrality**, **Unanimity**, **Consensuality**, and **Majority preservation**. It does not satisfy **Independence**. For $\oplus = \Sigma$, **Weak consistency** and **Consistency** are also satisfied.

7.9 Conclusion

BM and JA are two distinct theories for the aggregation of beliefs. They do not operate on the same inputs, and typically lead to collective beliefs that can be jointly conflicting. When focusing on the case where the inputs are equally informed (i.e., when the agenda is the set of all interpretations), some valuable connections between the two families of operators and between the corresponding rationality postulates can be established nevertheless.

Bibliography

C. Baral, S. Kraus, and J. Minker. Combining multiple knowledge bases. *IEEE Transactions on Knowledge and Data Engineering*, 3(2):208–220, 1991.

C. Baral, S. Kraus, J. Minker, and V. S. Subrahmanian. Combining knowledge bases consisting of first-order theories. *Computational Intelligence*, 8(1):45–71, 1992.

S. Benferhat, D. Dubois, S. Kaci, and H. Prade. Possibilistic merging and distance-based fusion of propositional information. *Annals of Mathematics and Artificial Intelligence*, 34(1-3):217–252, 2002.

I. Bloch and J. Lang. Towards mathematical morpho-logics. In *Proceedings of the 8th International Conference on Information Processing and Management of Uncertainty in Knowledge-Based Systems (IPMU)*, pages 1405–1412, 2000.

J.-F. Condotta, S. Kaci, P. Marquis, and N. Schwind. Merging qualitative constraint networks in a piecewise fashion. In *Proceedings of the 21st International Conference on Tools with Artificial Intelligence (ICTAI)*, pages 605–608, 2009.

S. Coste-Marquis, C. Devred, S. Konieczny, M.-C. Lagasquie-Schiex, and P. Marquis. On the merging of dung's argumentation systems. *Artificial Intelligence*, 171:740–753, 2007.

J. Delgrande and T. Schaub. A consistency-based framework for merging knowledge bases. *Journal of Applied Logic*, 5(3):459–477, 2007.

J. Delgrande, D. Dubois, and J. Lang. Iterated revision as prioritized merging. In *Proceedings of the 10th International Conference on Knowledge Representation and Reasoning (KR)*, pages 210–220, 2006.

J. Delgrande, T. Schaub, H. Tompits, and S. Woltran. Merging logic programs under answer set semantics. In *Proceedings of the 25th International Conference on Logic Programming (ICLP)*, pages 160–174, 2009.

J. Delobelle, A. Haret, S. Konieczny, J.-G. Mailly, J. Rossit, and S. Woltran. Merging of abstract argumentation frameworks. In *Proceedings of the 15th International Conference on Principles of Knowledge Representation and Reasoning (KR)*, pages 33–42, 2016.

F. Dietrich. Judgment aggregation and agenda manipulation. *Games and Economic Behavior*, 95:113–136, 2016.

F. Dietrich and C. List. Judgment aggregation by quota rules: Majority voting generalized. *Journal of Theoretical Politics*, 4(19):391–424, 2007.

D. Dubois, J. Lang, and H. Prade. Nonmonotonic reasoning and uncertain reasoning, chapt. possibilistic logic. In *Handbook of Logic in Artificial Intelligence and Logic Programming*, volume 3. Oxford Science Publications, 1994.

P. Everaere, S. Konieczny, and P. Marquis. The strategy-proofness landscape of merging. *Journal of Artificial Intelligence Research*, 28:49–105, 2007.

P. Everaere, S. Konieczny, and P. Marquis. Conflict-based merging operators. In *Proceedings of the 11th International Conference on Principles of Knowledge Representation and Reasoning (KR)*, pages 348–357, 2008.

P. Everaere, S. Konieczny, and P. Marquis. Disjunctive merging: Quota and Gmin merging operators. *Artificial Intelligence*, 174(12-13):824–849, 2010.

P. Everaere, S. Konieczny, and P. Marquis. On egalitarian belief merging. In *Proceedings of the 14th International Conference on Principles of Knowledge Representation and Reasoning (KR)*, pages 121–130, 2014a.

P. Everaere, S. Konieczny, and P. Marquis. Counting votes for aggregating judgments. In *Proceedings of the 13th International Conference on Autonomous Agents and Multiagent Systems (AAMAS)*, pages 1177–1184, 2014b.

P. Everaere, S. Konieczny, and P. Marquis. Belief merging versus judgment aggregation. In *Proceedings of the 14th International Conference on Autonomous Agents and Multiagent Systems (AAMAS)*, pages 999–1007, 2015.

P. Gärdenfors. An Arrow-like theorem for voting with logical consequences. *Economics and Philosophy*, 22(2):181–19, 2006.

N. Gorogiannis and A. Hunter. Merging first-order knowledge using dilation operators. In *Proceedings of the 5th International Symposium on Foundations of Information and Knowledge Systems (FoIKS)*, pages 132–150, 2008.

U. Grandi and U. Endriss. Binary aggregation with integrity constraints. In *Proceedings of the 22nd International Joint Conference on Artificial Intelligence (IJCAI)*, pages 204–209. AAAI Press, 2011.

A. Haret, A. Pfandler, and S. Woltran. Beyond IC postulates: Classification criteria for merging operators. In *Proceedings of the 22nd European Conference on Artificial Intelligence (ECAI)*, pages 372–380, 2016.

J. Hué, O. Papini, and E. Würbel. Merging belief bases represented by logic programs. In *Proceedings of the 10th International Conference on Symbolic and Quantitative Approaches to Reasoning with Uncertainty (ECSQARU)*, pages 371–382, 2009.

S. Kaci, S. Benferhat, D. Dubois, and H. Prade. A principled analysis of merging operations in possibilistic logic. In *Proceedings of the 16th Conference in Uncertainty in Artificial Intelligence (UAI)*, pages 24–31, 2000.

H. Katsuno and A. O. Mendelzon. Propositional knowledge base revision and minimal change. *Artificial Intelligence*, 52:263–294, 1991.

S. Konieczny. On the difference between merging knowledge bases and combining them. In *Proceedings of the 7th International Conference on Principles of Knowledge Representation and Reasoning (KR)*, pages 135–144, 2000.

S. Konieczny and R. Pino Pérez. On the frontier between arbitration and majority. In *Proceedings of the 8th International Conference on Principles of Knowledge Representation and Reasoning (KR)*, pages 109–118, 2002a.

S. Konieczny and R. Pino Pérez. Merging information under constraints: A logical framework. *Journal of Logic and Computation*, 12(5):773–808, 2002b.

S. Konieczny, J. Lang, and P. Marquis. DA^2 merging operators. *Artificial Intelligence*, 157:49–79, 2004.

S. Konieczny, P. Marquis, and N. Schwind. Belief base rationalization for propositional merging. In *Proceedings of the 22nd International Joint Conference on Artificial Intelligence (IJCAI)*, pages 951–956, 2011.

J. Lang, G. Pigozzi, M. Slavkovik, and L. van der Torre. Judgment aggregation rules based on minimization. In *Proceedings of the 13th Conference on Theoretical Aspects of Rationality and Knowledge (TARK)*, pages 238–246, 2011.

J. Lang, M. Slavkovik, and S. Vesic. Agenda separability in judgment aggregation. In *Proceedings of the 30th Conference on Artificial Intelligence (AAAI)*, pages 1016–1022, 2016.

C. List and P. Pettit. Aggregating sets of judgments: An impossibility result. *Economics and Philosophy*, 18:89–110, 2002.

G. Pigozzi. Belief merging and the discursive dilemma: An argument-based account to paradoxes of judgment aggregation. *Synthese*, 152(2):285–298, 2006.

P. Z. Revesz. On the semantics of arbitration. *International Journal of Algebra and Computation*, 7(2):133–160, 1997.

M. Slavkovik. *Judgment Aggregation in Multiagent Systems*. PhD thesis, Luxemburg University, 2012.

W. Spohn. Ordinal conditional functions: A dynamic theory of epistemic states. *Causation in Decision, Belief Change, and Statistics*, 2:105–134, 1987.

CHAPTER 8

Strategic Behavior in Judgment Aggregation

Dorothea Baumeister, Jörg Rothe, and
Ann-Kathrin Selker

8.1 Introduction

Collective decision making is concerned with aggregating information reported by a number of individuals into a collective decision appropriately capturing the individual views as a whole. Examples include, most prominently, *preference aggregation in voting* (surveyed, e.g., by Zwicker, 2016, and Baumeister and Rothe, 2015) where voters express their preferences on the candidates and the collective decision is to select a winner; *argumentation frameworks* (surveyed, e.g., by Rahwan and Simari, 2009) where individuals express arguments on an issue that can attack or support each other and while the individuals may have different assessments of which arguments are valid or which attack which, a goal is to collectively decide which arguments to select according to certain criteria (e.g., conflict-freeness); *resource allocation* and *fair division* (surveyed, e.g., by Bouveret et al., 2016, Lang and Rothe, 2015, and Moulin, 2004) where agents have individual utilities for bundles of objects and the collective decision is to allocate the objects to agents so that social welfare is maximized or certain fairness conditions (e.g., envy-freeness) are satisfied; and *judgment aggregation* (previously surveyed, e.g., by Endriss, 2016, Baumeister et al., 2015b, Grossi and Pigozzi, 2014, List, 2012, and List and Puppe, 2009) where individual judges express possibly different opinions on whether some logically connected propositions are true or false and the collective decision is to find a joint judgment on their truth.

This chapter is devoted to judgment aggregation and will in particular focus on analyzing scenarios involving strategic behavior in this context. The beginnings of the field of judgment aggregation go back to the seminal work of Kornhauser and Sager (1986) who were the first to describe a situation that they called the *doctrinal paradox*.[1] For illustration, suppose three judges—Alyson, Bill, and Cadi—are going to adjudicate upon the guilt of their colleague, judge Don, who is accused of having accepted a bribe in a previous trial where he pronounced a verdict of not guilty of murder for an alleged mafia boss. In the present trial, judge Don

---

[1]As a more general variant, Pettit (2001) introduced the *discursive dilemma*; the differences between the two notions are discussed in detail by Mongin (2012).

is to be sentenced for five years in prison if and only if he is found guilty, first, of having taken a considerable amount of money from a close associate of the alleged mafia boss and, second, of having denied a relevant piece of evidence in court that would have entailed the death sentence for sure.

"To me it's crystal-clear," judge Alyson goes first. "$3000 is a considerable amount of money that was given to Don in an envelope when he thought no one were looking. And how can he *not* allow the knife with the mafia boss's fingerprints on it as a very relevant piece of evidence? It was found stuck in the victim's body, for goodness' sake! I conclude that Don has to go to prison."

"I do agree with your second point, Your Honor," says judge Bill slowly. "However, I disagree with your first point and, therefore, with your conclusion as well. Sure enough, $3000 sounds like a lot of money, but taking into account that it's *Canadian* dollars makes it much less sizeable. I wouldn't even speak of bribery here; it's just peanuts. And we cannot sentence Don to five years of prison for bribery if all he has taken is just peanuts."

"You can't be serious, Your Honor," judge Cadi now counters. "3000 bucks, Canadian or US, *is* a considerable amount of money and *cannot* go unpunished—*if* it indeed was used to bribe judge Don and to bias his judgment toward suppressing some relevant piece of evidence. However, I do agree with your conclusion that Don should not have to go to prison, because I do not consider this knife a relevant piece of evidence. May I remind you that the victim in fact was killed by machine gun fire? The body was completely perforated! I have no idea why this knife stuck in the body, but I do know for sure that it was not causing death and, hence, it was completely irrelevant for this trial."

Judge	Considerable amount?	Relevant evidence denied?	Is Don guilty?
Alyson	true	true	true
Bill	false	true	false
Cadi	true	false	false
Majority	true	true	false

Table 8.1: Doctrinal paradox

Table 8.1 shows the three individual judgments. Note that the proposition "Don is guilty" is logically equivalent to the conjunction of the propositions that "the amount is considerable" and "a relevant piece of evidence has been denied." Now, if we aggregate the three individual judgments by the majority rule, as shown in Table 8.1, we see that, even though the individual judgments are each logically consistent, we obtain a logically inconsistent collective judgment. That is why Kornhauser and Sager (1986) called it a paradox.

In Section 8.2, we will outline the basics of judgment aggregation and will discuss various judgment aggregation rules and their properties and the complexity of winner determination. The main part of this chapter is Section 8.3 where we will deal with strategic behavior in judgment aggregation, including manipulation, bribery, and control. In particular, we will give an overview of computational complexity results for the associated problems.

8.2 Foundations of Judgment Aggregation

In this section, we present the basics of judgment aggregation, introduce the preferences that judges may have about judgment sets as well as some common judgment aggregation rules and their properties, briefly mention some complexity-theoretic notions, and discuss the complexity of winner determination.

8.2.1 Basics

We briefly recall the basic notions of judgment aggregation, starting with the *formula-based framework*. Throughout this chapter, we will essentially use the notation of Endriss (2016), Baumeister et al. (2015b), and de Haan (2016b).

For a set PS of propositional variables, let $\mathcal{L}_{PS}$ denote the set of all propositional formulas that can be built from variables in PS by using the common boolean connectives (such as $\wedge$, $\vee$, $\neg$, $\Rightarrow$, and $\Leftrightarrow$). We use $\overline{\varphi}$ to denote the *complement of* φ, i.e., $\overline{\varphi} = \neg\varphi$ if φ is not negated, and $\overline{\varphi} = \psi$ if $\varphi = \neg\psi$. An *agenda* is a finite set $\Phi \subseteq \mathcal{L}_{PS}$ of *formulas* (or *issues* or *propositions*) without doubly negated formulas that is *closed under complementation* (i.e., $\overline{\varphi} \in \Phi$ for each $\varphi \in \Phi$). Every set $J \subseteq \Phi$ is called a *judgment set*. A judgment set J is said to be *complete* if $\varphi \in J$ or $\overline{\varphi} \in J$ for each $\varphi \in \Phi$, and J is said to be *consistent* if there exists a truth assignment such that each formula in J is true. Let $\mathcal{J}(\Phi)$ denote the set of complete and consistent judgment sets. For an agenda Φ, and a set $N = \{1, \ldots, n\}$ of *judges* (or *agents*), $\boldsymbol{J} = (J_1, \ldots, J_n) \in \mathcal{J}(\Phi)^n$ denotes their *profile of (individual) complete, consistent judgment sets*. If not stated otherwise, the presented examples and results will employ the formula-based framework.

The second framework often used in judgment aggregation is the *constraint-based framework*: The agenda $\Phi = \{\varphi_1, \ldots, \varphi_m, \neg\varphi_1, \ldots, \neg\varphi_m\}$ consists of a finite set of propositional variables and their negations and we have an integrity constraint Γ, i.e., a propositional formula over these variables that can be used to restrict the judgment sets we consider. A judgment set J is Γ-*consistent* if there exists a truth assignment such that each formula in the set and Γ are true. All other terms are defined accordingly. An overview of this framework is given, e.g., by de Haan (2016b).[2]

We say that two complete judgment sets, J and J', *agree on a proposition* $\varphi \in \Phi$ if either both contain φ or none of them does; otherwise, we say J and J' *disagree on* φ; and their *Hamming distance* $H(J, J')$ is the number of disagreements between J and J'. More generally, since we will also use the Hamming distance between two consistent, but not necessarily complete judgment sets J and J', $H(J, J')$ is defined as the number of positive issues occurring in exactly one of J and J' and its negation in the other. (One can also consider the *weighted Hamming distance*, denoted by $H_\omega(J, J')$ for a weight function $\omega : \Phi \to \mathbb{N}$ with $\omega(\varphi) = \omega(\overline{\varphi})$, where we sum up the weights of the corresponding issues instead of

---

[2] He defines also the formula-based framework so as to include an integrity constraint, not necessarily an element of $\mathcal{L}_{PS}$. Results whose proofs require this constraint will be marked. A detailed comparison of the formula-based and the constraint-based framework is due to Endriss et al. (2016). They compare the succinctness of both frameworks and explore the effect on computational problems.

counting them.) Define the Hamming distance between a profile $\boldsymbol{J}$ of consistent judgment sets and a consistent judgment set J' as $H(\boldsymbol{J}, J') = \sum_{J \in \boldsymbol{J}} H(J, J')$.

Besides the common choice of using classical propositional logic to formulate judgment aggregation settings (as we do throughout this chapter), Dietrich (2007) proposes a more general model that includes problems expressed in predicate, modal, or conditional logic and some multi-valued and fuzzy logics.

8.2.2 Preferences

We will model the strategic behavior of agents—either *internal* ones (who are judges themselves) or *external* ones (who from the outside seek to influence the result of a judgment aggregation procedure to their advantage)—who want to obtain a "better" outcome than before. Therefore, in order to measure the success of an attack, the agents need to rank the possible outcomes depending on their *desired set* J; desired sets will always be assumed to be contained in a complete and consistent set. However, given an agenda Φ with m positive issues, there are up to 2^m possible (complete and consistent) outcomes. That is why we need a compact way of representing agents' preferences over judgment sets, even if—as a consequence—we may lose information about their preferences.

We now define four preference types that were introduced by Dietrich and List (2007c) and later applied by Baumeister et al. (2015a,c). Here, we only define preferences over complete and consistent judgment sets. A *weak order* over $\mathcal{J}(\Phi)$ is a transitive and total binary relation $\succsim$ by which any two judgment sets in $\mathcal{J}(\Phi)$ can be compared with one another.

For each of the following preference types, an agent is said to be *indifferent between X and Y under this type*, denoted by $X \sim Y$, if $X \succsim Y$ and $Y \succsim X$, and to *strictly prefer X to Y under this type*, denoted by $X \succ Y$, if $X \succsim Y$ and not $Y \succsim X$.

Definition 8.1 (Preference types). *For an agenda Φ, let $X, Y \in \mathcal{J}(\Phi)$, let $J \subseteq \Phi$ be an agent's desired set (consistent but possibly incomplete), and let U_J be the set of all unrestricted J-induced (weak) preferences, i.e., the set of all weak orders $\succsim_J$ over $\mathcal{J}(\Phi)$ for which $X \sim_J Y$ whenever $X \cap J = Y \cap J$.*

We say that a weak order $\succsim_J \in U_J$ is a
1. *top-respecting J-induced (weak) preference if $X \succ_J Y$ whenever $X \cap J = J$ and $Y \cap J \neq J$, i.e., all we know is that the desired set J is a subset of this agent's most preferred judgment set;*
2. *closeness-respecting J-induced (weak) preference if $X \succ_J Y$ whenever $X \cap J \supset Y \cap J$, i.e., whenever X agrees with J on the same issues as Y with J and on at least one issue more than Y with J; and*
3. *Hamming-distance-respecting J-induced (weak) preference if $X \succsim_J Y$ whenever $H(X, J) \leqslant H(Y, J)$, i.e., whenever X and J disagree on at most as many issues as Y and J. (In the weighted case, $X \succsim_J Y \iff H_\omega(X, J) \leqslant H_\omega(Y, J)$.)*

While we learn (essentially) nothing from unrestricted J-induced preferences, top-respecting J-induced preferences tell us something about an agent's most preferred judgment set: namely, that it contains J. The same is true for closeness-respecting J-induced preferences, but for them we know in addition that judgment sets having additional agreements with J are preferred. This is also the case for Hamming-distance-respecting J-induced preferences, which depend on the total number of disagreements and are the most restrictive preference type.

Let X and Y be complete and consistent judgment sets. We say that an agent with a (possibly incomplete) desired set J *possibly/necessarily weakly prefers X to Y under preference type T* if $X \succsim_J Y$ holds true in some/all J-induced weak orders of type T, and *possible/necessary preference of X to Y under type T* is defined analogously via $X \succ_J Y$. Since there is exactly one Hamming-distance-respecting J-induced weak order for each desired set J, the notions of possible and necessary preferences coincide for this type.

Example 8.1 (Preferences). *Consider the example from the introduction. Let $N = \{A, B, C\}$ denote the set of the three judges: A(lyson), B(ill), and C(adi). Let $\Phi = \{a, \neg a, e, \neg e, g, \neg g\}$ be the agenda, where a stands for* amount, *e for* evidence, *and g for* guilt *and where g is $a \wedge e$.[3] Further, let $\boldsymbol{J} = (J_A, J_B, J_C) \in \mathcal{J}(\Phi)^3$ with $J_A = \{a, e, g\}$, $J_B = \{\neg a, e, \neg g\}$, and $J_C = \{a, \neg e, \neg g\}$ be the profile of complete and consistent judgment sets (see Table 8.1). Now assume that judge Bill's desired set is $J = \{e, \neg g\}$. In addition to J_A, J_B, and J_C, the only possible complete and consistent judgment set for Φ is $J_0 = \{\neg a, \neg e, \neg g\}$. Since among these four sets, Bill's judgment set J_B is the only one containing J, Bill necessarily prefers J_B to all others (i.e., to J_A, J_C, and J_0) under top-respecting J-induced preferences. Assuming closeness-respecting J-induced preferences, Bill necessarily prefers J_B to J_C because J_B and J (of course) agree on the whole desired set J, whereas J_C and J only agree on a strict subset of J. However, Bill only possibly prefers J_A to J_C and he also possibly prefers J_C to J_A: Both judgment sets agree with J on different issues, so we do not know which set he actually prefers under closeness-respecting J-induced preferences. The situation is different when we assume Hamming-distance-respecting J-induced preferences. Since $H(J_C, J) = 1 = H(J_A, J)$, we know that—with respect to his desired set J—Bill is indifferent between these two judgment sets. Note that knowing that Bill is indifferent between these two judgment sets decisively differs from not knowing which of them he prefers to the other.*

8.2.3 Judgment Aggregation Rules and Their Properties

Having the individual judgment sets of the participating judges, a judgment aggregation rule is needed to reach a consensus. A *judgment aggregation rule* (or *procedure*) is a function F that maps any profile of judgment sets to a set of judgment sets, which we call the *(collective) outcome*. F is *complete* (*consistent*) if each $J \in F(\boldsymbol{J})$ is complete (consistent) for each profile $\boldsymbol{J} = (J_1, \ldots, J_n) \in \mathcal{J}(\Phi)^n$, and F is *resolute* if the outcome is always a singleton (and is *irresolute* otherwise). For resolute rules F, we write $F(\boldsymbol{J}) = J$ rather than $F(\boldsymbol{J}) = \{J\}$.

---

[3]This is an example of a conjunctive agenda. An agenda is *conjunctive* if it consists of premises $p_1, \ldots, p_k$, a conclusion of the form $p_1 \wedge \cdots \wedge p_k$, and their negations, and it is *disjunctive* if its conclusion is of the form $p_1 \vee \cdots \vee p_k$. Note that Dietrich and List (2007c) consider the conclusion to be just a variable c and add a "connection rule" $c \Leftrightarrow (p_1 \wedge \cdots \wedge p_k)$ or $c \Leftrightarrow (p_1 \vee \cdots \vee p_k)$ to the agenda. Note further that if we adapt our example to the constraint-based framework, g would be a propositional variable instead of the formula $a \wedge e$ and $g \Leftrightarrow (a \wedge e)$ would be the integrity constraint Γ.

The perhaps most intuitive way of judgment aggregation is the *(proposition-wise) majority rule* that was used in Table 8.1 to illustrate the doctrinal paradox. One way of circumventing the doctrinal paradox is to use a *premise-based* approach: Divide the agenda into premises and conclusions, then apply a rule on the premises and derive the outcome for the conclusions from the outcome for the premises. To generalize the majority rule, Dietrich and List (2007b) introduced the quota rules, and to guarantee complete and consistent outcomes, we use the premise-based approach and focus on the class of *uniform premise-based quota rules*. Under these rules, a premise is contained in the collective outcome if and only if the number of judges having it in their individual judgment sets exceeds the quota. The outcome for the conclusions can then be derived easily. Formally:

Definition 8.2 (Uniform premise-based quota rules). *Partition the agenda Φ into a set of premises Φ_p and a set of conclusions Φ_c, both closed under complementation, and partition Φ_p into sets Φ_1 and Φ_2 so that $\varphi \in \Phi_1$ if and only if $\overline{\varphi} \in \Phi_2$. (We assume that Φ_1 consists of all positive literals.) Let $|S|$ denote the cardinality of a set S and $\models$ the satisfaction relation. The* uniform premise-based quota rule *with quota q, $0 \leqslant q < 1$ and q rational, is a function mapping each profile $J = (J_1, \ldots, J_n)$ over Φ to the collective outcome $UPQR_q(J) = \Delta \cup \{\psi \in \Phi_c \mid \Delta \models \psi\}$, where $\Delta = \{\varphi \in \Phi_1 \mid |\{i \mid \varphi \in J_i\}| > nq\} \cup \{\varphi \in \Phi_2 \mid |\{i \mid \varphi \in J_i\}| \geqslant n(1-q)\}$.*

The special case $UPQR_{1/2}$ with an odd number of judges is simply called the premise-based procedure *(PBP, for short; see the work of Endriss et al., 2012).*

$UPQR_q$ is resolute and—if the agenda Φ is closed under propositional variables and the set of premises Φ_p consists of exactly all literals—$UPQR_q$ is also complete and consistent. In the following sections, we will assume that these restrictions hold. Note that a premise $\varphi \in \Phi_1$ is part of the collective outcome if and only if at least $\lfloor nq + 1 \rfloor$ judges accept it, whereas the outcome contains $\overline{\varphi}$ if and only if it is part of at least $\lceil n(1-q) \rceil$ judgment sets.

By contrast, in the *conclusion-based* approach, votes are taken only on the conclusions (e.g., by requiring that a conclusion $\psi \in \Phi_c$ is in the collective judgment set if a strict majority of judges have ψ in their individual judgment sets, and otherwise $\overline{\psi}$ is in the collective judgment set), and no collective judgments are made on the premises. An obvious disadvantage of conclusion-based procedures is that they always output incomplete collective judgment sets.

Another way of using majority to reach a consensus is to apply it sequentially. The input additionally contains a fixed order over the positive issues in the agenda. In each step, we check whether the current solution entails a solution for the next issue of the agenda, and if this is not the case, we apply the majority rule. Obviously, this always leads to complete and consistent outcomes, but the solution strongly depends on the chosen order, i.e., it is path-dependent (see, for example, the work by Dietrich and List, 2007b). Sequential variants of other judgment aggregation rules are defined analogously.

Yet another possibility of defining judgment aggregation rules is to consider distances between judgment sets and to choose those judgment sets that minimize the sum of the distances to the individual judgment sets. In voting theory, the method due to Kemeny (1959) also minimizes the sum of the distances to the votes to elect a winner. This approach has been transferred to judgment aggregation by Pigozzi (2006) and further extended to the Prototype-Hamming rule by Miller and Osherson (2009): The Kemeny rule in judgment aggregation picks exactly the complete and consistent judgment sets closest to the given profile.[4]

Definition 8.3 (Kemeny rule). *Let Φ be an agenda. The* Kemeny rule *maps each profile J over Φ to the collective outcome $Kemeny(\boldsymbol{J}) = \mathrm{argmin}_{J \in \mathcal{J}(\Phi)} H(\boldsymbol{J}, J)$.*

Note that the majority outcome is consistent if and only if it coincides with the Kemeny outcome.[5] The Kemeny rule is complete, consistent, and irresolute.

Example 8.2. *Consider the setting in Example 8.1. Let $\Phi_p = \{a, \neg a, e, \neg e\}$ be the set of premises and let $\Phi_c = \{g, \neg g\}$ be the set of conclusions. Then $UPQR_{1/2}(\boldsymbol{J}) = J_A$, since a majority of judges accept a and e (and g is evaluated accordingly). On the other hand, $Kemeny(\boldsymbol{J}) = \{J_A, J_B, J_C\}$, since all three judgment sets have a Hamming distance of 4 to the profile $\boldsymbol{J}$, whereas the only other complete and consistent judgment set, $J_0 = \{\neg a, \neg e, \neg g\}$, has a Hamming distance of 5 to $\boldsymbol{J}$.*

While there is a large body of literature on specific voting rules in social choice theory, the early work in judgment aggregation has focused more on the study of impossibility results. More recently, further specific judgment aggregation rules have been introduced, for example, by Lang et al. (2011). They transfer minimization concepts from voting theory and logic-based knowledge representation and reasoning to define judgment aggregation rules that in some way minimize the part of a profile that has to be removed to reach a consensus. Lang et al. (2017) survey existing judgment aggregation rules, their properties, and the relations between them.

Besides consistency and completeness, many other properties of judgment aggregation rules have been studied, for example, by List and Pettit (2002) and Dietrich and List (2007c). We will focus on properties of resolute judgment aggregation rules only. A very basic property is the *universal domain* assumption. It requires that a rule's domain consists of all possible profiles of complete and consistent judgment sets, which is the case for the rules studied here. Another basic property is *anonymity*, which says that the order of the judges should have no influence on the collective outcome. A more demanding property is *independence*. A judgment aggregation rule is *independent* if for any two profiles with the same number of judges over the same agenda, if the individual judgments are the same for any given proposition, then the collective outcomes for both profiles should agree on this proposition. That is to say that the collective judgment regarding any proposition should be independent of the collective judgments on the remaining propositions. The *neutrality* property requires that if all judges have the same opinion on any two propositions, then the collective judgments on these propositions should also be the same. Unfortunately, List and Pettit (2002) show that if the agenda contains two literals and their conjunction, then no judgment

---

[4]This rule is also referred to as *median rule* by Nehring et al. (2011), *max-weight subagenda* by Lang and Slavkovik (2014), and *distance-based procedure* by Baumeister et al. (2015b) and Endriss et al. (2012), and Dietrich (2014) shows that it coincides with what he calls the *simple scoring rule*.

[5]The majority outcome is consistent if the profile $\boldsymbol{J}$ is *unidimensionally aligned* (List, 2003), i.e., if there is an alignment of the judges from left to right so that for each proposition φ, the judges accepting φ are to the left of the ones accepting $\overline{\varphi}$ (or vice versa).

aggregation rule always returning a complete and consistent collective outcome can simultaneously satisfy anonymity, neutrality, and independence.

Example 8.3. *Consider again the setting in Example 8.1, with the set of premises $\Phi_p = \{a, \neg a, e, \neg e\}$ and the set of conclusions $\Phi_c = \{g, \neg g\}$. When Cadi changes her mind on whether the amount is considerable, her new judgment set is $J'_C = \{\neg a, \neg e, \neg g\} = J_0$, so $UPQR_{1/2}(\boldsymbol{J'}) = J_B$ for the modified profile $\boldsymbol{J'}$. But this violates independence, since the individual judgments on g do not change, but the collective judgment on g is not the same for both profiles: $g \in J_A$ but $\neg g \in J_B$.*

The *monotonicity* property informally says that a proposition should never be judged worse collectively because of receiving additional individual support: If a proposition is collectively accepted, but now some judge changes her mind from rejecting to accepting it while all other judges stick to their judgments of this proposition, then it should still be collectively accepted after this change. Dietrich and List (2007b) show that a class of judgment aggregation rules, the quota rules, can be characterized through the properties of anonymity, independence, and monotonicity. Many more characterization and impossibility results are known in judgment aggregation. For example, Dietrich and List (2007a) prove an analogue of the theorem of Arrow (1951—revised 1963) in judgment aggregation, and we will see more examples due to Dietrich and List (2007c) in Section 8.3.1 concerning strategic manipulation.

8.2.4 Winner Determination

Some desirable properties (such as completeness and consistency) of judgment aggregation rules have been described above. When used in multiagent systems with a large number of participating judges, computational aspects must also be taken into account. As judgment aggregation may be applied in security systems, it is extremely important that the collective outcome of a rule can be computed efficiently. This raises the question on the complexity of winner determination.

We assume the reader to be familiar with the basic notions of complexity theory, including the complexity classes P and NP and the notions of hardness and completeness for complexity classes. For more background on the relevant classes—namely, the classes $\Theta_2^p = P_{\|}^{NP}$ (a.k.a. "parallel access to NP"), $\Sigma_2^p = NP^{NP}$, and $\Pi_2^p = coNP^{NP}$ that constitute the second level of the polynomial hierarchy and the parameterized class W[2]—we refer to the books by Rothe (2015) (Section 1.5), Rothe (2005) (Sections 5.2 and 5.3), Downey and Fellows (2013), and Chapter 11 of this book.

For the uniform premise-based quota rules, it has to be checked for every premise whether the quota is reached or not, which is obviously possible in polynomial time. Due to the agenda being closed under propositional variables, the collective outcome for the conclusions can then also be computed efficiently.

Unfortunately, this is not the case for the Kemeny rule in judgment aggregation. To study the computational complexity, an adequate decision problem has to be formulated. For irresolute rules F, Endriss et al. (2012) propose the following definition of F-WINNER-DETERMINATION: Given an agenda Φ, a profile $\boldsymbol{J} \in \mathcal{J}(\Phi)^n$, and a subset $L \subseteq \Phi$, is there a $J^\star \subseteq \Phi$ with $L \subseteq J^\star$ such that $J^\star \in F(\boldsymbol{J})$?

Theorem 8.1 (Endriss et al., 2012). *Kemeny*-WINNER-DETERMINATION *is Θ_2^p-complete.*

In addition to the decision problems, Endriss and de Haan (2015) study search problems for winner determination in judgment aggregation. Determining the complexity of the search problem, which outputs a collective outcome, is more useful for practical purposes than determining that of the decision problem, which merely gives a yes/no answer. For the Kemeny rule, an even more fine-grained complexity analysis is given by de Haan (2016a,b): the parameterized complexity with respect to five parameters and their combinations. He studies both the formula-based and the constraint-based framework, with the surprising result that even though classical complexity results are the same in both models, the parameterized complexity results differ. In addition to the above winner determination problem, Lang and Slavkovik (2014) determine the complexity of problems that ask whether the collective outcome satisfies some given property.

8.3 Strategic Behavior in Judgment Aggregation

We now survey various scenarios of strategic behavior in judgment aggregation, namely manipulation, bribery, and control, which have been intensively studied for elections in computational social choice (see Conitzer and Walsh, 2016, Faliszewski and Rothe, 2016, and Baumeister and Rothe, 2015), and we show how to transfer these models from preference to judgment aggregation.

8.3.1 Manipulation

Example 8.4. *The court is hiring new judges. Chief judge Zoe is on a business trip officially (even though, inofficially and undercover, she is meeting with the alleged mafia boss—who was just acquitted of murder—in the underworld bar "Angels from Hell"), leaving the hiring decision to her judges Alyson, Bill, Cadi, and Don (who at present is not yet on trial for having been bribed). According to the job description, a new judge is to be hired if and only if s/he has a proven track record and expertise in at least one of the areas this court is so renowned for: drug trafficking offenses (denoted by variable d), financial crimes (f), large-scale frauds (ℓ), and organized crime (o). That is, the (disjunctive) agenda contains the premises d, f, ℓ, and o, the conclusion $h = d \lor f \lor \ell \lor o$, and their negations.*

Elena, Felix, George, and Hillevi have applied for a job as a judge. The four judges in charge, using $UPQR_{2/3}$, quickly and unanimously agree on three of these candidates: Felix and George will be hired, but Hillevi fails. Elena's case, though, is not as clear. After listening to his co-judges' arguments and reasons, Don knows their judgment sets: $J_A = \{d, f, \neg\ell, \neg o, h\}$, $J_B = \{d, \neg f, \ell, \neg o, h\}$, and $J_C = \{\neg d, \neg f, \neg\ell, \neg o, \neg h\}$.

Looking at Elena's application papers, Don's truthful judgment would be the same as Cadi's, which would result in not hiring Elena because at least one of the premises must be accepted by at least three judges for her to be hired. However, he wouldn't be Don if he'd look only at papers! Indeed, Don is looking at Elena ... and suddenly he has an agenda of his own and changes his mind. What he sees is a beautiful young lady and, being an outcome-oriented person, he doesn't care about her expertise and track record; all that matters for him is the conclusion: He wants Elena to be hired! Rather than his truthful judgment set $J_D = J_C$, *he thus reports the set* $J_D^* = \{d, f, \neg\ell, \neg o, h\} = J_A$, *just as Alyson. With three judges accepting d for Elena, instead of* $UPQR_{2/3}(\boldsymbol{J})$ *providing the collective outcome* $\{\neg d, \neg f, \neg\ell, \neg o, \neg h\}$ *for the truthful profile* $\boldsymbol{J}$, *we have the outcome* $\{d, \neg f, \neg\ell, \neg o, h\}$ *for the modified profile* $\boldsymbol{J}^*$, *which means that Elena will be hired.*

"What?" baffled Cadi looks at Don with a reproachful glance. "Didn't we have the same opinion on Elena when we discussed her application?" Then, looking again at the glossy photograph on Elena's application folder and becoming suspicious, she adds, "Shame on you, Don! You are sexist and a manipulator!"

Dietrich and List (2007c) were the first to study manipulation and strategy-proofness in judgment aggregation. In particular, they introduced the preference types presented in Definition 8.1 so as to formulate a judgment aggregation analogue of the famous Gibbard–Satterthwaite Theorem from social choice theory, which is due to Gibbard (1973) and Satterthwaite (1975) and, roughly, says that no reasonable voting rule can be strategy-proof (i.e., were it to satisfy a number of reasonable conditions including strategy-proofness, it would be dictatorial).

Dietrich and List (2007c) define a resolute judgment aggregation rule F to be *strategy-proof* if for each profile $\boldsymbol{J} = (J_1, \ldots, J_n)$ of individual judgment sets, for each judge i, and for each preference relation induced by J_i according to one of the preference types in Definition 8.1, i weakly prefers the outcome $F(\boldsymbol{J})$ (resulting, in particular, from her truthful judgment set J_i) to any outcome $F(\boldsymbol{J}_{-i}, J_i^*) = F(J_1, \ldots, J_{i-1}, J_i^*, J_{i+1}, \ldots, J_n)$ (i.e., to any outcome of F on the profile identical to $\boldsymbol{J}$ except with J_i replaced by J_i^*) with a misreported judgment set J_i^*.

By contrast, they also define a preference-free notion of *nonmanipulability*: F is *manipulable at profile* $\boldsymbol{J} = (J_1, \ldots, J_n)$ *by individual judge* i *on proposition* $\varphi \in \Phi$ if J_i disagrees with $F(\boldsymbol{J})$ on φ, but J_i agrees with $F(\boldsymbol{J}_{-i}, J_i^*)$ on φ for some misrepresented judgment set J_i^*. F is said to be *nonmanipulable* if F is not manipulable at any profile by any individual judge on any proposition in Φ.[6] The crucial difference between strategy-proofness and nonmanipulability is that the former notion is based on preferences and so expresses *incentives* of individual judges to misreport their judgment sets, whereas the latter notion is preference-free and thus merely captures the existence of an *opportunity* for individual judges to manipulate. Dietrich and List (2007c) provide the following characterization result.

Theorem 8.2 (Dietrich and List, 2007c). *Every resolute judgment aggregation rule satisfying universal domain is nonmanipulable if and only if it is independent and monotonic.*

In particular, for conjunctive and disjunctive agendas (as defined in Footnote 3), conclusion-based judgment aggregation is independent and monotonic

---

[6]More generally, Dietrich and List (2007c) define these notions on any subset of the agenda, which we will here neglect for simplicity. They also show that monotonicity in Theorem 8.2 can be replaced by a weaker form of monotonicity and the equivalence still holds true.

and therefore, by Theorem 8.2, nonmanipulable, whereas premise-based judgment aggregation rules such as *PBP* are not independent and thus are manipulable.[7] Dietrich and List (2007c) also provide an impossibility result for a large class of agendas, the so-called *path-connected agendas* that contain the conjunctive and disjunctive agendas: For them, a resolute judgment aggregation rule F satisfies universal domain, always outputs consistent and complete judgment sets, and is responsive[8] and nonmanipulable if and only if F is a dictatorship of some individual judge.[9]

This is the above-mentioned analogue of the Gibbard–Satterthwaite Theorem in judgment aggregation. However, being based on the preference-free concept of nonmanipulability, the above impossibility result does not take the judges' incentives into account. Using a game-theoretic approach, Dietrich and List (2007c) introduced the preference types stated in Definition 8.1 to model different motivations of the individual judges. Specifically, assuming *unrestricted* J-induced (weak) preferences (with J being the judge's desired set, i.e., the outcome that matters for this judge) means that this judge's preferences are not linked to her judgments in any systematic way. On the other hand, *top-respecting*, or even *closeness-respecting* or *Hamming-distance-respecting*, J-induced (weak) preferences model situations where judges want the collective judgments to be close to their own individual desired sets. Now, for each resolute judgment aggregation rule satisfying universal domain, strategy-proofness (as defined earlier) implies that judging truthfully is a weakly dominant strategy for every individual judge in a game-theoretic sense (see, e.g., the book chapter by Faliszewski et al., 2015).

Theorem 8.3 (Dietrich and List, 2007c). *Every resolute judgment aggregation rule satisfying universal domain is strategy-proof for closeness-respecting preferences if and only if it is nonmanipulable.*

From Theorems 8.2 and 8.3, we immediately have that strategy-proofness for closeness-respecting preferences is equivalent to simultaneously requiring independence and monotonicity. Another consequence is that we can replace "nonmanipulable" by "strategy-proof for closeness-respecting preferences" in the impossibility result for path-connected agendas stated above. Note that the implication from left to right in this characterization (i.e., if F satisfies these conditions then it is dictatorial) holds true for any preference type containing the closeness-respecting preferences (e.g., it also holds for top-respecting preferences), as strategy-proofness for this more general preference type implies strategy-proofness for closeness-respecting preferences and thus dictatorship. The other way round, the implication from right to left in this characterization (i.e., if F is dictatorial then it satisfies these conditions) holds for any preference type contained in the top-respecting preferences (e.g., it also holds for closeness-respecting preferences), for otherwise a dictatorship would not be strategy-proof (even though it is nonmanipulable).

---

[7] However, when we consider an agenda restricted to only the premises, this is simply the majority rule, which is independent and monotonic and thus nonmanipulable.

[8] F is said to be *responsive* if for each *contingent* proposition $\varphi \in \Phi$ (which means that both $\{\varphi\}$ and $\{\overline{\varphi}\}$ are consistent), there are profiles J and J' such that $\varphi \in F(J)$ and $\varphi \notin F(J')$.

[9] F is a *dictatorship of judge i* if i always dictates the collective outcome: $F(J) = J_i$ for each J.

For an agenda that is conjunctive or disjunctive, two special cases of closeness-respecting preferences are particularly important: outcome- and reason-oriented preferences. A judge with *outcome-oriented preferences* (such as Don in Example 8.4) is not interested in the premises; all he cares about is that the collective judgment on the conclusion matches his own (desired) judgment. A judge with *reason-oriented preferences*, by contrast, is not interested in the collective judgment on the conclusion; all she cares about is that the collective judgments on the premises match her own (desired) judgments, i.e., the reasons in support of the conclusion are what matters for her, more than the conclusion itself. While outcome-oriented preferences are often the better motivational assumption in economics, reason-oriented preferences better fit the arguments made in deliberative settings of democracy. Which kind of preference is appropriate of course depends on the situation and on the subjective goals of the agents involved.

Recall that conclusion-based judgment aggregation is nonmanipulable for conjunctive and disjunctive agendas and therefore, by Theorem 8.3, it is also strategy-proof for these agendas and closeness-respecting preferences, which immediately implies strategy-proofness for outcome- and reason-oriented preferences. However, Dietrich and List (2007c) show that, for a conjunctive or disjunctive agenda, while the premise-based procedure is not strategy-proof for outcome-oriented preferences, it is strategy-proof for reason-oriented preferences. They also show that for outcome-oriented preferences, premise- and conclusion-based judgment aggregation are strategically equivalent in a game-theoretic sense: For both rules and for each profile, there is a (weakly) dominant strategy profile in equilibrium yielding the same collective outcome on the conclusion.

From Theorems 8.2 and 8.3 we know that independence and monotonicity provide a criterion for nonmanipulability and for strategy-proofness for closeness-respecting preferences. However, what about judgment aggregation rules that are not independent or monotonic, such as the premise-based procedure? Can we at least provide some protection for them by showing that the manipulation problem is computationally intractable (i.e., NP-hard)?

Endriss et al. (2010, 2012) were the first to study strategic manipulation of judgment aggregation rules from a computational social choice perspective. They obtained the following result for *PBP* under Hamming-distance-respecting preferences. First, let us define the corresponding manipulation problem, denoted by *PBP*-*H*-MANIPULATION, as follows: Given an agenda Φ, a profile $\boldsymbol{J} = (J_1, \ldots, J_n)$ in $\mathcal{J}(\Phi)^n$, and a manipulator i, does there exist a judgment set $J_i^* \in \mathcal{J}(\Phi)$ such that $H(J_i, PBP(\boldsymbol{J}_{-i}, J_i^*)) < H(J_i, PBP(\boldsymbol{J}))$? That is, is it possible for the manipulator to report an insincere judgment set J_i^* such that the collective outcome under *PBP* is closer to her truthful judgment set J_i in terms of Hamming distance than the collective outcome under *PBP* if she had reported J_i itself?

Theorem 8.4 (Endriss et al., 2012). *PBP*-*H*-MANIPULATION *is* NP-*complete.*

Baumeister et al. (2013, 2014, 2015a) continued this study and obtained complexity results for manipulation with respect to the class of uniform premise-based quota rules (which, in particular, contains *PBP*) under unrestricted, top-respecting, closeness-respecting, and Hamming-distance-respecting preferences, considering not only complete but also incomplete desired sets so as to capture, for instance, outcome- and reason-oriented preferences. These incomplete desired sets are not restricted to the premises or the conclusions, though; all they need to satisfy is that they can be consistently extended to the whole agenda. Preferences are then restricted to the issues occurring in the desired set.

Inspired by the notions, due to Konczak and Lang (2005), of possible and necessary winners from voting theory, Baumeister et al. (2015a) consider the notions of possible and necessary strategy-proofness in judgment aggregation. Noting that *necessary strategy-proofness* captures what Dietrich and List (2007c) call strategy-proofness (as defined earlier in this section), Baumeister et al. (2015a) introduce the other notion by defining a resolute judgment aggregation rule F to be *possibly strategy-proof for unrestricted/top-respecting/closeness-respecting weak preferences* (see Definition 8.1) if for each profile $\boldsymbol{J} = (J_1, \ldots, J_n)$, for each judge i, and for each preference relation induced by i's desired set J_i according to the corresponding preference type, i possibly weakly prefers (as defined after Definition 8.1) the undoctored outcome $F(\boldsymbol{J})$ to the outcome $F(\boldsymbol{J}_{-i}, J_i^*)$ resulting from any misrepresented judgment set J_i^*.[10] Clearly, (necessary) strategy-proofness implies possible strategy-proofness for each of these preference types.

Since $UPQR_q$ is independent and monotonic whenever the agenda contains only premises, it is (necessarily) strategy-proof for closeness-respecting preferences. However, $UPQR_q$ is not strategy-proof in general (and many other judgment aggregation rules aren't either). Therefore, Baumeister et al. (2015a) have studied the computational complexity of the corresponding decision problems. For example, given a preference type T, they define the problem $UPQR_q$-T-Possible-Manipulation as follows: Given an agenda Φ, a profile $\boldsymbol{J} = (J_1, \ldots, J_n) \in \mathcal{J}(\Phi)^n$, and a consistent (not necessarily complete) set $J \subseteq J_i$ desired by manipulator i, is there a judgment set $J_i^* \in \mathcal{J}(\Phi)$ such that i possibly prefers the outcome $UPQR_q(\boldsymbol{J}_{-i}, J_i^*)$ to the undoctored outcome $UPQR_q(\boldsymbol{J})$ under preference type T? $UPQR_q$-T-Necessary-Manipulation is defined analogously, except that the manipulator necessarily (not only possibly) prefers $UPQR_q(\boldsymbol{J}_{-i}, J_i^*)$ to $UPQR_q(\boldsymbol{J})$ under preference type T (where, for the reasons mentioned in Footnote 10, we omit "Possible" and "Necessary" in the problem name under Hamming-distance-respecting preferences and simply write $UPQR_q$-H-Manipulation).

Baumeister et al. (2015a) also define an exact variant of manipulation for uniform premise-based quota rules, denoted by $UPQR_q$-Exact-Manipulation, to model situations where a manipulator wants to achieve not only a better (in terms of the preferences given in Definition 8.1) but a *best* outcome for her desired set (in the sense that everything she desires is actually contained in the collective outcome resulting from the manipulation): Given the same input as above, does there exist a set $J_i^* \in \mathcal{J}(\Phi)$ such that $J \subseteq UPQR_q(\boldsymbol{J}_{-i}, J_i^*)$? They obtained the following results for these problems.

Theorem 8.5 (Baumeister et al., 2015a). *Table 8.2 summarizes the results on the manipulation problems defined above for $UPQR_q$, q rational and $0 \leqslant q < 1$.*

---

[10]Since just one Hamming-distance-respecting weak preference order is induced by any given desired set, we simply use the term *strategy-proofness* for them, without distinguishing between possible and necessary strategy-proofness.

Preference type	POSSIBLE MANIPULATION with incomplete desired set	NECESSARY MANIPULATION with incomplete desired set	POSSIBLE MANIPULATION with complete desired set	NECESSARY MANIPULATION with complete desired set
Unrestricted	NPC	possibly sp	in P	possibly sp
Top-respecting	NPC	NPC	in P	possibly sp
Closeness-respecting	NPC	NPC	NPC[a]	possibly sp
H-respecting	NPC, W[2]-hard[c]		NPC[b], W[2]-hard[c]	
EXACT	NPC		sp	

[a] This result is due to Selker (2014).
[b] This result is due to Endriss et al. (2012) for the special case of the premise-based procedure.
[c] Parameterized by the number of changes in the premises of the manipulator's desired set.

Table 8.2: Results of Baumeister et al. (2015a) on manipulation for $UPQR_q$. Key: NPC means "NP-complete" and sp means "strategy-proof."

Recently, de Haan (2017) studied the Kemeny rule with respect to exact manipulation and manipulation under Hamming-distance-respecting preferences, for both the weighted and the unweighted case. These problems are defined analogously to the corresponding $UPQR_q$ problems above (with an additionally given weight function for the case of the weighted Hamming distance), but—since the Kemeny rule is irresolute—they require that *each* set in the new outcome is preferred to *each* set in the old outcome. The complexity of these problems is stated in the following theorem, which remains valid in the constraint-based framework.

Theorem 8.6 (de Haan, 2017). *Kemeny*-EXACT-MANIPULATION, *Kemeny*-H-MANIPULATION, *and Kemeny*-H_ω-MANIPULATION *are Σ_2^p-complete.*[11]

Having studied manipulation by a single judge so far, a natural question is whether the situation changes when more than one judge tries to manipulate. In voting theory and computational social choice, this is referred to as *coalitional manipulation*, investigated, for instance, by Conitzer et al. (2007) in the context of computational complexity (see also Conitzer and Walsh, 2016). *Group manipulation in judgment aggregation*, introduced by Botan et al. (2016), studies the corresponding setting where a group of judges tries to coordinate a manipulative action in order to improve the result. In their model, preferences over judgments are modeled via the Hamming distance, and the goal is to minimize the sum of the Hamming distances between the manipulators' judgments and the outcome. Whenever no more than two agents try to manipulate, they show that a neutral and, as they call it, "unbiased" aggregation rule is group-strategy-proof if and only if it is independent and monotonic. This does no longer hold for a group of three or more manipulators, though. They also introduce a variant of group manipulation for "fragile coalitions," where manipulators fear that perhaps not all of them will indeed execute the manipulative action.

[11] His results require an integrity constraint even in the formula-based framework. Note that the results for exact manipulation and for manipulation under weighted-Hamming-distance-respecting preferences even hold for a singleton desired set, three judges, and a unidimensionally aligned profile.

Finally, we mention the work of Grossi et al. (2009) who initialize a study of situations where manipulation in judgment aggregation is not considered to be driven by malicious intent but to be "virtuous" and thus desirable: For example, to avoid an unpleasing inconsistent collective outcome, judges may have reason to report less preferred judgment sets, even though they may not be truthful.

8.3.2 Bribery

Example 8.5. *One year earlier, at the night right before the trial against the alleged mafia boss is opened, judge Don (who has been appointed to the jury) secretly meets with a high-rank mafioso in the "Angels from Hell" bar.*

"Tomorrow we will decide which witnesses to summon in the trial, which experts to appoint, and which evidence to allow or deny for the trial," Don explains. "The good news for your boss is that we couldn't find any witness still alive. The bad news is that his knife was found stuck in the victim's body with his fingerprints all over it, and the pathologist, Dr. Slitter, told me that he believes this knife indeed was causing death. That makes your boss the prime suspect."

"Don't worry about Slitter. We've kidnapped his wife and son, he'll testify whatever we want. Make sure he'll be appointed as expert. He'll say machine gun fire killed the sleazebag. And the guy with the gun, y'know, is m... wasn't arrested."

"OK," Don says, "then I do know what to do. I'm on the jury with Bill and Cadi. I'm uncertain about him, but Cadi will for sure deny the knife as evidence if she thinks it wasn't causing death, and so will I, which means we will outvote Bill in any case. And with the knife gone, which is the only piece of evidence linking your boss to the crime, he can look forward to a verdict of not guilty. So you can give me the money: $6000, as we said."

"$6000? That's way too much. Y'know, they've frozen all our bank accounts and I still have to pay some guys' salaries! I give you $4500."

"$6000 was the deal!"

"OK, I give you half of it now," and he passes him an envelope, "and you'll get the other half tomorrow after the trial if everything runs smoothly."

"All right," says Don delighted and takes the money. "Hey!" he suddenly snaps. "That is Canadian money!" But the felon has already disappeared in the dark of the night.

Inspired by the work on bribery in voting, due to Faliszewski et al. (2009a,b) and surveyed by Faliszewski and Rothe (2016) and Baumeister and Rothe (2015), Baumeister et al. (2015a, 2011) initiated the study of bribery in judgment aggregation, focusing on $UPQR_q$ and the Hamming distance. In particular, they define the problem $UPQR_q$-BRIBERY as follows: Given an agenda Φ, a profile $\boldsymbol{J} \in \mathcal{J}(\Phi)^n$, a consistent (not necessarily complete) set $J \subseteq J' \in \mathcal{J}(\Phi)$ desired by the briber (an external agent), and a positive integer k (the briber's budget), is it possible to change up to k individual judgment sets in $\boldsymbol{J}$ such that for the resulting new profile $\boldsymbol{J}^*$ we have that $H(UPQR_q(\boldsymbol{J}^*), J) < H(UPQR_q(\boldsymbol{J}), J)$? They also consider a variant called $UPQR_q$-MICROBRIBERY (just as Faliszewski et al., 2009b, do in voting), which is defined analogously, except that the budget k is now a bound on the number of premise entries the briber can change in the given individual judgment sets in $\boldsymbol{J}$. And for both problems, they also consider an exact variant, called

$UPQR_q$-EXACT-BRIBERY and $UPQR_q$-EXACT-MICROBRIBERY, where the question in the problem is not whether the new profile is closer to the desired set according to the Hamming distance, but whether the desired set J is contained in the outcome $UPQR_q(J^*)$ for the modified profile. For the special case of PBP, we have:

Theorem 8.7 (Baumeister et al., 2015a). *PBP-BRIBERY, PBP-MICROBRIBERY, PBP-EXACT-BRIBERY, and PBP-EXACT-MICROBRIBERY are NP-complete.*

Baumeister et al. (2015a) also study this problems in terms of parameterized complexity, showing that PBP-EXACT-BRIBERY is W[2]-hard when parameterized by the number of bribes. More generally, for an in-depth treatise of the complexity of both bribery and microbribery under top- and closeness-respecting preferences for $UPQR_q$, we refer to the work of Baumeister et al. (2015c).

Further, de Haan (2017) defines the corresponding bribery and exact bribery problems for the Kemeny procedure, again for weighted and unweighted Hamming distances and with the additional requirement that *each* set in the new outcome is preferred to *each* set in the old one. In the weighted case, the input additionally contains a weight function.

The following result also holds in the constraint-based framework.

Theorem 8.8 (de Haan, 2017). *Kemeny-EXACT-BRIBERY and Kemeny-BRIBERY (weighted and unweighted) are Σ_2^p-complete.*[12]

A field closely related to judgment aggregation is that of lobbying in multiple referenda introduced by Christian et al. (2007). This problems corresponds to a judgment aggregation problem where we have only logically unconnected premises in the agenda and some external agent tries to influence some voters in order to reach a desired outcome when evaluated according to the majority rule. Hence, this problem is very closely related to the bribery problems described in this section. Such lobbying problems (and generalizations thereof) have also been studied by Bredereck et al. (2014) and Binkele-Raible et al. (2014). Also related, though in a somewhat different context, is the work by Alon et al. (2015). In their setting, voters support or reject proposals. A ballot is *accepted* by a voter if she supports at least half of the proposals in it. The task is then to find a vote that is accepted either by all voters or by a majority of them.

8.3.3 Control

Example 8.6. *As Example 8.2 shows, Don will be found guilty if the judges use $UPQR_{1/2}$ to aggregate their judgments. However, this would be detrimental to chief judge Zoe (responsible, in particular, for appointing judges to cases at this court) and her secret lover, the alleged mafia boss, because it would lead to further investigations into the matter and would most certainly result in a retrial. Therefore, Zoe decides to publicly question the authority of the three appointed judges.*

---

[12] Again, his results require an integrity constraint even in the formula-based framework, and the results for *Kemeny*-EXACT-BRIBERY and *Kemeny*-BRIBERY in the weighted case even hold for a singleton desired set, three judges, and a unidimensionally aligned profile.

"This a matter of utmost importance," Zoe exclaims. "I rule that some of our most trusted judges should assist in forming a decision, since three judges are certainly not enough to handle this intricate and delicate problem!"

Zoe needs to achieve an addition of at least two judges that both agree on $\neg a$ or $\neg e$ so that at least one of a and e does no longer exceed the quota. Fortunately for her, possible candidates for these additional judges are Elena with judgment set $J_E = \{\neg a, \neg e, \neg g\}$, Felix with $J_F = \{a, e, g\}$, and George with $J_G = \{\neg a, e, \neg g\}$, so she appoints Elena and George as additional judges, saving both her lover and Don.

It may also happen that Don will be found guilty when using the Kemeny rule (see Example 8.2). To ensure that the non-guilty verdict for her lover remains valid, Zoe has a backup plan up her sleeve for this case. If she succeeds in dropping the question of whether the amount of money taken by Don was considerable, then the new collective outcome (given the original profile) only consists of $J'_B = \{e, \neg g\}$ with a Hamming distance of 2 as opposed to the three disagreements of the other possible judgment sets (all restricted to the new agenda).

As this example shows, another possible influence on the judgment aggregation process is *control* where an external agent, commonly called the *chair* (or "*chief judge*" in the above example), is able to change the structure of the process. As surveyed by Faliszewski and Rothe (2016) and Baumeister and Rothe (2015), control in elections has been studied since the seminal paper by Bartholdi III et al. (1992) and has produced a vast number of results. Inspired by this work, Baumeister et al. (2012a,b) introduced this type of strategic behavior to judgment aggregation. In their scenarios, they focus on the judges: The chair is able (1) to add a certain number of judges to the given profile from another given profile, (2) to delete a certain number of judges, (3) to replace judges (which combines adding and deleting judges by the chair first deleting a number of judges and then adding the same number of judges from another given profile), or (4) to bundle the judges into groups so that every group of judges only decides over their own subset of issues in a partition of the agenda.[13] Here, we focus on only the first three control actions. For the resolute rules $UPQR_q$, *possible/necessary control by adding/deleting/replacing judges* asks,[14] given the chair's desired set, whether the chair possibly/necessarily prefers the new outcome to the old one under a certain preference type, and *exact control by adding/deleting/replacing judges* asks whether the desired set is a subset of the new outcome.

Theorem 8.9 (Baumeister et al., 2015c). *Possible and necessary control by adding and by deleting judges is* NP*-complete for* $UPQR_{1/2}$ *under closeness-respecting preferences, even when the desired set is complete.*

Theorem 8.10 (Baumeister et al., 2012a). *Exact control by adding and by deleting judges and control by adding and by deleting judges under Hamming-distance-respecting preferences are* NP*-complete for* $UPQR_{1/2}$.

---

[13]A variant of control by bundling judges is studied by Alon et al. (2013), yet with the bundling occurring on the issues. When several issues are bundled together, the judges have to decide whether to accept or reject the whole bundle. They show that the problems related to such bundling attacks are computationally hard when simple majority is used to aggregate the individual judgments.

[14]Since possible and necessary preferences coincide for the Hamming distance, we only consider *control by adding/deleting/replacing judges* for this preference type, dropping "*possible/necessary*."

Baumeister et al. (2015c, 2012a) further show that Theorems 8.9 and 8.10 also hold for control by replacing judges, even for a rational quota q, $0 \leqslant q < 1$.

Recently, de Haan (2017) introduced two control scenarios that focus on the issues: The chair can change the agenda by adding an arbitrary number of issues to the agenda, or by deleting an arbitrary number of issues. He then asks whether the given desired set is contained in each set of the resulting outcome, i.e., he is interested in the exact control variant.

Note that the following result also holds for the constraint-based framework.

Theorem 8.11 (de Haan, 2017). *Exact control by adding and by deleting issues is Σ_2^p-complete for* Kemeny.[15]

Dietrich (2016) also studies how to influence the outcome via the agenda. An agenda is said to be *sensitive* if the collective outcome depends on the choice of propositions that are being aggregated. Three types of agenda-insensitivity are introduced and characterized axiomatically, along with an impossibility theorem.

8.4 Conclusions and Outlook

We have surveyed strategic behavior in judgment aggregation, focusing on both axiomatic characterizations and computational complexity and distinguishing the same strategic scenarios that are well known and have been extensively studied in computational social choice: manipulation, bribery, and control. While preference and judgment aggregation have a lot in common (specifically, the *preferences* of either voters or judges), there are also crucial differences where judgment aggregation parts company from voting—for instance, due to logical constraints on and dependencies between judgments and due to the need to compactly represent the judges' preferences. Still, we suspect that computational social choice will severely keep influencing the field of judgment aggregation and will continue to shape the future of this field. One issue that we consider particularly important for future work is to model judgment aggregation as a dynamic process over time. After all, judgment aggregation often *is* a dynamically evolving process, with new judges arriving and others departing or with the outcome heavily depending on the order in which propositions are considered.

While sequential variants of judgment aggregation rules have already been studied (e.g., by Dietrich and List, 2007b, as mentioned in Section 8.2.3), it would be very interesting to adapt other approaches from computational social choice to dynamic settings in judgment aggregation, such as the work by Tennenholtz (2004) on dynamic voting, the Stackelberg voting games studied by Desmedt and Elkind (2010) and Xia and Conitzer (2010), and the work by Parkes and Procaccia (2013) who use Markov decision processes to model evolving preferences. And modeling *strategic behavior* dynamically in judgment aggregation can also be inspired by the work of Hemaspaandra et al. (2014, 2012a, 2017a, 2012b, 2017b) on online manipulation, online candidate control, and online voter control in sequential elections.

---

[15]This theorem uses the formula-based framework with an additional integrity constraint.

Acknowledgments

This work was supported in part by the NRW Ministry for Innovation, Science, and Research, DFG grant RO 1202/15-1, and an SFF grant of HHU Düsseldorf.

Bibliography

N. Alon, D. Falik, R. Meir, and M. Tennenholtz. Bundling attacks in judgment aggregation. In *Proceedings of the 27th AAAI Conference on Artificial Intelligence*, pages 39–45. AAAI Press, July 2013.

N. Alon, R. Bredereck, J. Chen, S. Kratsch, R. Niedermeier, and G. Woeginger. How to put through your agenda in collective binary decisions. *ACM Transactions on Economics and Computation*, 4(1):Article 5, 2015.

K. Arrow. *Social Choice and Individual Values*. John Wiley and Sons, 1951—revised 1963.

J. Bartholdi III, C. Tovey, and M. Trick. How hard is it to control an election? *Mathematical and Computer Modelling*, 16(8/9):27–40, 1992.

D. Baumeister and J. Rothe. Preference aggregation by voting. In J. Rothe, editor, *Economics and Computation. An Introduction to Algorithmic Game Theory, Computational Social Choice, and Fair Division*, Springer Texts in Business and Economics, chapter 4, pages 197–325. Springer-Verlag, 2015.

D. Baumeister, G. Erdélyi, and J. Rothe. How hard is it to bribe the judges? A study of the complexity of bribery in judgment aggregation. In *Proceedings of the 2nd International Conference on Algorithmic Decision Theory (ADT)*, pages 1–15. Springer-Verlag *Lecture Notes in Artificial Intelligence #6992*, October 2011.

D. Baumeister, G. Erdélyi, O. Erdélyi, and J. Rothe. Bribery and control in judgment aggregation. In F. Brandt and P. Faliszewski, editors, *Proceedings of the 4th International Workshop on Computational Social Choice*, pages 37–48. AGH University of Science and Technology, Kraków, Poland, September 2012a.

D. Baumeister, G. Erdélyi, O. Erdélyi, and J. Rothe. Control in judgment aggregation. In *Proceedings of the 6th European Starting AI Researcher Symposium*, pages 23–34. IOS Press, August 2012b.

D. Baumeister, G. Erdélyi, O. Erdélyi, and J. Rothe. Computational aspects of manipulation and control in judgment aggregation. In *Proceedings of the 3rd International Conference on Algorithmic Decision Theory (ADT)*, pages 71–85. Springer-Verlag *Lecture Notes in Artificial Intelligence #8176*, November 2013.

D. Baumeister, G. Erdélyi, O. Erdélyi, and J. Rothe. Computational aspects of manipulation and control in judgment aggregation. In A. D. Procaccia and T. Walsh, editors, *Proceedings of the 5th International Workshop on Computational Social Choice*, Pittsburgh, USA, June 2014. Carnegie Mellon University.

D. Baumeister, G. Erdélyi, O. Erdélyi, and J. Rothe. Complexity of manipulation and bribery in judgment aggregation for uniform premise-based quota rules. *Mathematical Social Sciences*, 76:19–30, 2015a.

D. Baumeister, G. Erdélyi, and J. Rothe. Judgment aggregation. In J. Rothe, editor, *Economics and Computation. An Introduction to Algorithmic Game Theory, Computational Social Choice, and Fair Division*, Springer Texts in Business and Economics, chapter 6, pages 361–391. Springer-Verlag, 2015b.

D. Baumeister, J. Rothe, and A. Selker. Complexity of bribery and control for uniform premise-based quota rules under various preference types. In *Proceedings of the 4th International Conference on Algorithmic Decision Theory (ADT)*, pages 432–448. Springer-Verlag *Lecture Notes in Artificial Intelligence #9346*, September 2015c.

D. Binkele-Raible, G. Erdélyi, H. Fernau, J. Goldsmith, N. Mattei, and J. Rothe. The complexity of probabilistic lobbying. *Discrete Optimization*, 11(1):1–21, 2014.

S. Botan, A. Novaro, and U. Endriss. Group manipulation in judgment aggregation. In *Proceedings of the 15th International Conference on Autonomous Agents and Multiagent Systems (AAMAS)*, pages 411–419. IFAAMAS, May 2016.

S. Bouveret, Y. Chevaleyre, and N. Maudet. Fair allocation of indivisible goods. In F. Brandt, V. Conitzer, U. Endriss, J. Lang, and A. D. Procaccia, editors, *Handbook of Computational Social Choice*, chapter 12, pages 284–310. Cambridge University Press, 2016.

R. Bredereck, J. Chen, S. Hartung, S. Kratsch, R. Niedermeier, O. Suchý, and G. Woeginger. A multivariate complexity analysis of lobbying in multiple referenda. *Journal of Artificial Intelligence Research*, 50:409–446, 2014.

R. Christian, M. Fellows, F. Rosamond, and A. Slinko. On complexity of lobbying in multiple referenda. *Review of Economic Design*, 11(3):217–224, 2007.

V. Conitzer and T. Walsh. Barriers to manipulation in voting. In F. Brandt, V. Conitzer, U. Endriss, J. Lang, and A. D. Procaccia, editors, *Handbook of Computational Social Choice*, chapter 6, pages 127–145. Cambridge University Press, 2016.

V. Conitzer, T. Sandholm, and J. Lang. When are elections with few candidates hard to manipulate? *Journal of the ACM*, 54(3):Article 14, 2007.

R. de Haan. Parameterized complexity results for the Kemeny rule in judgment aggregation. In U. Grandi and J. Rosenschein, editors, *Proceedings of the 6th International Workshop on Computational Social Choice*, Toulouse, France, June 2016a.

R. de Haan. Parameterized complexity results for the Kemeny rule in judgment aggregation. In *Proceedings of the 22nd European Conference on Artificial Intelligence (ECAI)*, pages 1502–1510. IOS Press, August/September 2016b.

R. de Haan. Complexity results for manipulation, bribery and control of the Kemeny judgment aggregation procedure. In *Proceedings of the 16th International Conference on Autonomous Agents and Multiagent Systems (AAMAS)*, May 2017. To appear.

Y. Desmedt and E. Elkind. Equilibria of plurality voting with abstentions. In *Proceedings of the 11th ACM Conference on Electronic Commerce (EC)*, pages 347–356. ACM Press, June 2010.

F. Dietrich. A generalised model of judgment aggregation. *Social Choice and Welfare*, 28(4):529–565, 2007.

F. Dietrich. Scoring rules for judgment aggregation. *Social Choice and Welfare*, 42(4):873–911, 2014.

F. Dietrich. Judgment aggregation and agenda manipulation. *Games and Economic Behavior*, 95:113–136, 2016.

F. Dietrich and C. List. Arrow's theorem in judgment aggregation. *Social Choice and Welfare*, 29(1):19–33, 2007a.

F. Dietrich and C. List. Judgment aggregation by quota rules: Majority voting generalized. *Journal of Theoretical Politics*, 19(4):391–424, 2007b.

F. Dietrich and C. List. Strategy-proof judgment aggregation. *Economics and Philosophy*, 23(3):269–300, 2007c.

R. Downey and M. Fellows. *Parameterized Complexity*. Springer-Verlag, 2nd edition, 2013.

U. Endriss. Judgment aggregation. In F. Brandt, V. Conitzer, U. Endriss, J. Lang, and A. D. Procaccia, editors, *Handbook of Computational Social Choice*, chapter 17, pages 399–426. Cambridge University Press, 2016.

U. Endriss and R. de Haan. Complexity of the winner determination problem in judgment aggregation: Kemeny, Slater, Tideman, Young. In *Proceedings of the 14th International Conference on Autonomous Agents and Multiagent Systems (AAMAS)*, pages 117–125. IFAAMAS, May 2015.

U. Endriss, U. Grandi, and D. Porello. Complexity of winner determination and strategic manipulation in judgment aggregation. In V. Conitzer and J. Rothe, editors, *Proceedings of the 3rd International Workshop on Computational Social Choice*, pages 139–150. Universität Düsseldorf, Düsseldorf, Germany, September 2010.

U. Endriss, U. Grandi, and D. Porello. Complexity of judgment aggregation. *Journal of Artificial Intelligence Research*, 45:481–514, 2012.

U. Endriss, U. Grandi, R. de Haan, and J. Lang. Succinctness of languages for judgment aggregation. In *Proceedings of the 15th International Conference on Principles of Knowledge Representation and Reasoning (KR)*, pages 176–185. AAAI Press, April 2016.

P. Faliszewski and J. Rothe. Control and bribery in voting. In F. Brandt, V. Conitzer, U. Endriss, J. Lang, and A. D. Procaccia, editors, *Handbook of Computational Social Choice*, chapter 7, pages 146–168. Cambridge University Press, 2016.

P. Faliszewski, E. Hemaspaandra, and L. Hemaspaandra. How hard is bribery in elections? *Journal of Artificial Intelligence Research*, 35:485–532, 2009a.

P. Faliszewski, E. Hemaspaandra, L. Hemaspaandra, and J. Rothe. Llull and Copeland voting computationally resist bribery and constructive control. *Journal of Artificial Intelligence Research*, 35:275–341, 2009b.

P. Faliszewski, I. Rothe, and J. Rothe. Noncooperative game theory. In J. Rothe, editor, *Economics and Computation. An Introduction to Algorithmic Game Theory, Computational Social Choice, and Fair Division*, Springer Texts in Business and Economics, chapter 2, pages 41–134. Springer-Verlag, 2015.

A. Gibbard. Manipulation of voting schemes. *Econometrica*, 41(4):587–601, 1973.

D. Grossi and G. Pigozzi. *Judgment Aggregation: A Primer*. Synthesis Lectures on Artificial Intelligence and Machine Learning. Morgan and Claypool Publishers, 2014.

D. Grossi, G. Pigozzi, and M. Slavkovik. White manipulation in judgment aggregation. In *Proceedings of the 21st Benelux Conference on Artificial Intelligence (BNAIC)*, October 2009.

E. Hemaspaandra, L. Hemaspaandra, and J. Rothe. Controlling candidate-sequential elections. In *Proceedings of the 20th European Conference on Artificial Intelligence (ECAI)*, pages 905–906. IOS Press, Aug. 2012a.

E. Hemaspaandra, L. Hemaspaandra, and J. Rothe. Online voter control in sequential elections. In *Proceedings of the 20th European Conference on Artificial Intelligence (ECAI)*, pages 396–401. IOS Press, Aug. 2012b.

E. Hemaspaandra, L. Hemaspaandra, and J. Rothe. The complexity of online manipulation of sequential elections. *Journal of Computer and System Sciences*, 80(4):697–710, 2014.

E. Hemaspaandra, L. Hemaspaandra, and J. Rothe. The complexity of controlling candidate-sequential elections. *Theoretical Computer Science*, 2017a. To appear. DOI: 10.1016/j.tcs.2017.03.037.

E. Hemaspaandra, L. Hemaspaandra, and J. Rothe. The complexity of online voter control in sequential elections. *Journal of Autonomous Agents and Multi-Agent Systems*, 2017b. To appear. DOI: 10.1007/s10458-016-9349-1.

J. Kemeny. Mathematics without numbers. *Dædalus*, 88:571–591, 1959.

K. Konczak and J. Lang. Voting procedures with incomplete preferences. In *Proceedings of the Multidisciplinary IJCAI-05 Workshop on Advances in Preference Handling*, pages 124–129, July/August 2005.

L. Kornhauser and L. Sager. Unpacking the court. *Yale Law Journal*, 96(1): 82–117, 1986.

J. Lang and J. Rothe. Fair division of indivisible goods. In J. Rothe, editor, *Economics and Computation. An Introduction to Algorithmic Game Theory, Computational Social Choice, and Fair Division*, Springer Texts in Business and Economics, chapter 8, pages 493–550. Springer-Verlag, 2015.

J. Lang and M. Slavkovik. How hard is it to compute majority-preserving judgment aggregation rules? In *Proceedings of the 21st European Conference on Artificial Intelligence (ECAI)*, pages 501–506. IOS Press, 2014.

J. Lang, G. Pigozzi, M. Slavkovik, and L. van der Torre. Judgment aggregation rules based on minimization. In *Proceedings of the 13th Conference on Theoretical Aspects of Rationality and Knowledge (TARK)*, pages 238–246. ACM Press, July 2011.

J. Lang, G. Pigozzi, M. Slavkovik, L. van der Torre, and S. Vesic. A partial taxonomy of judgment aggregation rules and their properties. *Social Choice and Welfare*, 48(2):327–356, 2017.

C. List. A possibility theorem on aggregation over multiple interconnected propositions. *Mathematical Social Sciences*, 45(1):1–13, 2003.

C. List. The theory of judgment aggregation: An introductory review. *Synthese*, 187(1):179–207, 2012.

C. List and P. Pettit. Aggregating sets of judgments: An impossibility result. *Economics and Philosophy*, 18(1):89–110, 2002.

C. List and C. Puppe. Judgment aggregation. In P. Anand, P. Pattanaik, and C. Puppe, editors, *The Handbook of Rational and Social Choice*, chapter 19, pages 457–482. Oxford University Press, 2009.

M. Miller and D. Osherson. Methods for distance-based judgment aggregation. *Social Choice and Welfare*, 32(4):575–601, 2009.

P. Mongin. The doctrinal paradox, the discursive dilemma, and logical aggregation theory. *Theory and Decision*, 73(3):315–355, 2012.

H. Moulin. *Fair Division and Collective Welfare*. MIT Press, 2004.

K. Nehring, M. Pivato, and C. Puppe. Condorcet admissibility: Indeterminacy and path-dependence under majority voting on interconnected decisions. Technical Report MPRA 32434, University of Munich, 2011.

D. Parkes and A. D. Procaccia. Dynamic social choice with evolving preferences. In *Proceedings of the 27th AAAI Conference on Artificial Intelligence*, pages 767–773. AAAI Press, July 2013.

P. Pettit. Deliberative democracy and the discursive dilemma. *Philosophical Issues*, 11(1):268–299, 2001.

G. Pigozzi. Belief merging and the discursive dilemma: An argument-based account to paradoxes of judgment. *Synthese*, 152(2):285–298, 2006.

I. Rahwan and G. Simari, editors. *Argumentation in Artificial Intelligence*. Springer, 2009.

J. Rothe. *Complexity Theory and Cryptology. An Introduction to Cryptocomplexity*. EATCS Texts in Theoretical Computer Science. Springer-Verlag, 2005.

J. Rothe, editor. *Economics and Computation. An Introduction to Algorithmic Game Theory, Computational Social Choice, and Fair Division*. Springer Texts in Business and Economics. Springer-Verlag, 2015.

M. Satterthwaite. Strategy-proofness and Arrow's conditions: Existence and correspondence theorems for voting procedures and social welfare functions. *Journal of Economic Theory*, 10(2):187–217, 1975.

A. Selker. Manipulative Angriffe auf Judgment-Aggregation-Prozeduren. Master's thesis, Heinrich-Heine-Universität Düsseldorf, Institut für Informatik, Düsseldorf, Germany, September 2014.

M. Tennenholtz. Transitive voting. In *Proceedings of the 5th ACM Conference on Electronic Commerce (EC)*, pages 230–231. ACM Press, July 2004.

L. Xia and V. Conitzer. Stackelberg voting games: Computational aspects and paradoxes. In *Proceedings of the 24th AAAI Conference on Artificial Intelligence*, pages 697–702. AAAI Press, July 2010.

W. S. Zwicker. Introduction to the theory of voting. In F. Brandt, V. Conitzer, U. Endriss, J. Lang, and A. D. Procaccia, editors, *Handbook of Computational Social Choice*, chapter 2, pages 23–56. Cambridge University Press, 2016.

CHAPTER 9

Social Choice and Social Networks

Umberto Grandi

9.1 Introduction

Individuals do not typically reason in isolation when confronted with collective-decision making, but rather take into consideration the preferences of like-minded individuals and engage in strategic activities such as influence, persuation and information exchange. Consider the example of a vote in a small committee, like a department meeting or a company board. Members typically have partial knowledge of other members' preferences, and before a decision is taken they will take strategic actions on which piece of information to disclose and to whom. There are important variables that they take into account: they know who are the people they can *count on*, they know who are the people whose opinion they *trust*, they also estimate whether their opinion will be *influential* and to whom. That is, they reason about the structure of various social networks that relate the individuals around them, and are able to devise and play complex strategies to achieve their goals and influence the result of the collective decision.

Similar phenomena are not restricted to collective decisions taken by small groups of people. Recent elections have shown how echo-chamber effects seem to polarise the opinions of societies, and how viral content can rapidly shift the public view, making traditional polls rather unreliable. Moreover, emerging technologies in the field of e-democracy present new challenges for designing trustworthy mechanisms for collective decisions on social media or on the Internet in general.

Social network analysis (Jackson, 2008; Easley and Kleinberg, 2010) is a burgeoning area which provides tools to analyse networks. It has proven very successful in many diverse fields, e.g., in the study of virus diffusion in biology, job market analyses, and targeted marketing. Well-established economic frameworks such as game theory the market analysis have started considering more complex models of society based on the study of networks. Social choice theory has been left relatively untouched by these new developments, and it is only recently that researchers have started to study the interplay between the networks relating members of a community and the collective decisions these individuals take.

This chapter provides an overview of novel approaches put forward in the computational social choice literature on the topic of social choice and social networks. References from outside of computer science are reduced to a minimum, but the problem is clearly of interest to political scientists and sociologists.

After briefly introducing some basic terminology and definitions in Section 9.2, we start in Section 9.3 by analysing the effects of social networks on standard collective decision scenarios. We first focus on the maximum-likelihood approach to voting, and then move to the setting of iterated strategic voting. Section 9.4 surveys a number of papers in which collective decision processes are designed to take into consideration the information coming from a network structure relating the individuals, in order to prevent strategic actions, or simply to obtain a better collective decision. In Section 9.5 we show how ideas from social choice theory have been used to devise novel models of opinion diffusion on social networks, with individual opinion updates defined by means of aggregation procedures. Section 9.6 concludes the survey pointing at a number of directions for future research.

9.2 Basic Definitions

We denote with $N = \{1, \ldots, n\}$ the set of voters and $A = \{a, b, c, \ldots\}$ the set of alternatives. We assume that voters in N are connected by a social network, represented as a directed graph identified by the set of its edges $E \subseteq N \times N$. Undirected graphs can be represented as symmetric directed graphs. We denote the neighbourhood of an individual i as $N(i) = \{j \in N \mid (j,i) \in E\}$, using a definition that can be applied to both directed and undirected networks. The structure of the network E can be constrained, e.g., to be a directed acyclic graph, a chain, a tree, or a more complex hierarchical structure. Influence or trust networks (Section 9.4.1) and delegation networks (Section 9.5) are assumed to be directed, while general social networks representing social acquaintances or information channels are assumed to be undirected. In the literature on social network analysis, graphs are typically undirected, and statistical assumptions are made on the distribution of the edges, for instance when considering random graphs or scale-free networks. While some of the papers referenced in this chapter are based on simulations and experiments, and hence make use of similar statistical assumptions, these properties are typically substituted by discrete graph properties in most algorithmic and theoretical papers.

Depending on the situation at hand, voters express their preferences in different forms. The classical approach from voting theory is that of a profile $P = (\succ_1, \ldots, \succ_n)$, where $\succ_i$ is an irreflexive, complete and transitive binary relation over alternatives in A (i.e., a linear order). Another common setting is that of binary voting, where we will assume $A = \{0, 1\}$. A profile in this case is any $P = (p_1, \ldots, p_n)$ where $p_i \in A$ is an individual ballot selecting one of the two alternatives. Further settings represent indidual opinions as real numbers, as vectors of binary views, or as propositional knowledge bases, and will be briefly introduced in the relevant sections.

A social choice mechanism will identify, in general, a procedure to obtain a collective decision from a profile of individual opinions. Examples can range from quota rules in binary voting, selecting 1 as the collective decision if the number

Social Choice and Social Networks   **171**

of individual ballots for 1 exceeds a certain quota, or a rating system proposing a collective ranking of the alternatives from the evaluations of the individuals.

We recall here that there are two complementary views when assessing a social choice mechanism. In the first approach individuals are supposed to express their tastes over the set of alternatives, without there being any objective or true judgment on which alternative is best for the group. Political elections are a classic example, as well as lower stake decisions such as deciding which movie to watch among friends. Under this interpretation, the objective of the social choice mechanism is to guarantee the representativity of the collective choice with respect to the profile of individuals' ballots. The evaluation of a procedure under this interpretation is often done by means of axiomatic properties, with the most well-know result being Arrow's Theorem (Arrow, 1963).

The second approach views social choice as a problem of reconstructing an underlying correct ordering of the alternatives from noisy estimates received from the voters. These situations can occur, for instance, when the board of a company needs to judge on what project to invest in, or a committee on which candidate to choose for a given job, or crowdsourcing applications aiming at collectively classifying images or texts. Under this interpretation, a social choice mechanism is assessed by (a) devising a suitable noise distribution, and (b) proving that the mechanism maximises the probability of recovering the correct ordering of alternatives under the given noise distribution. The simplest and most well-known result in this research area is Condorcet's Jury Theorem (Condorcet, 1785): in binary voting, the majority rule is the maximum likelihood estimator for the noise model that assumes each voter to be correct with probability $p > 0.5$.

9.3 Effects of Social Networks on Collective Choices

A social network in a voting context acts as an information filter transforming a global view (the potential winner of an election, the distribution of preferences among voters, ...) into a multiplicity of local realities, each observed by a voter in the neighbourhood defined by the network. This first observation is well explained by a simple example known as the majority illusion (Lerman et al., 2016):

Example 9.1. *The citizens of a town have to vote in a two-candidate election: those supporting the first candidate are represented with full nodes in Figure 9.1, and those supporting the second candidate with empty nodes. A couple of days before the election takes place, a polling firm asks each voter which candidate she or he thinks will win. The election will be decided by majority, and each voter's reply to the poll is based on her private observation of other voters' opinions in her own neighbourhood. That is, we assume that voters are connected by a social network, and that they only have access to the opinions of their direct neighbours.*

The situation depicted in Figure 9.1 results in a surprising failure of the poll: while only 3 individuals out of 14 support the first candidate (the full nodes), a majority of the voters respond to the poll that it is the second candidate who will win the election. To see this, take for instance the rightmost voter, marked with a ∗: she can see three full nodes and one empty node, reporting a probable victory of

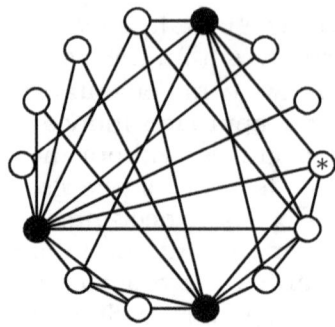

Figure 9.1: A network showing the "majority illusion".

the first candidate. The same happens to all 11 empty nodes in the graph, resulting in a poll which forecasts a victory of the first candidate with 11 votes against 3.

In this section we review a selection of recent papers from the literature on computational social choice that analyse how the information structure induced by a social network can affect the functioning of various voting mechanisms.

9.3.1 Noisy Votes

One of the first papers analysing the effects of social networks in computational social choice is the work of Conitzer (2012). This paper views voting as reconstructing a ground truth from noisy votes (i.e., the maximum likelihood estimator viewpoint described in Section 9.2), and reaches the following conclusion: if we see the probability that an individual estimates the correct alternative as an independent factor from the probability of being influenced by her neighbours' opinions, then the best mechanism to recover the ground truth simply ignores the existence of a network. Let us see this result in its simplest form.

We are in the setting of binary voting, with $A = \{0, 1\}$ as the set of alternatives, and we assume that one of the two alternatives in A is the correct one (i.e., the ground truth), and we denote it with $c \in A$. A population of voters N connected by an undirected network E receives a noisy distribution of opinions supporting either candidate 0 or candidate 1, generating a profile of binary opinions P. In the maximum likelihood approach we are interested in the probability of observing profile of votes P given that the correct alternative is c, i.e., estimating $Prob(P\,|\,c)$.

The first important assumption made by Conitzer (2012) is that such probability can be factored as $Prob(P\,|\,c) = \prod_{i \in N} f_i(p_i, P_{N(i)}\,|\,c)$, where p_i is agent i's opinion and $P_{N(i)}$ the restriction of profile P to i's influencers. That is, the overall probability of observing profile P can be factored into independent probability functions f_i, one for every individual, calculating the probability of observing opinion p_i and neighbouring opinions $P_{N(i)}$ given that the correct alternative is c. Assume now that the probability of observing an agent's ballot can be factored into (a) the probability of observing her ballot given that the correct alternative is c, and (b) the probability of observing her ballot given the profile of her influencers' opinions. In formulas, for every voter i there exist functions g_i and h_i such that $f_i(p_i, P_{N(i)} \,|\, c) = g_i(p_i \,|\, c) \cdot h_i(p_i, P_{N(i)})$.

We can now proceed to look for the maximum likelihood alternative, i.e., the $\hat{c} \in A$ maximising $Prob(P \,|\, \hat{c})$. By the formulation above, this is equivalent to maximising the product of functions h_i and g_i in c. However, since function h_i does not depend on the alternative c under consideration it can be ignored in the maximisation process. Hence, the maximum likelihood alternative can be found by only looking at functions g_i, which are independent from the structure of the network since they only depend on the current opinion p_i of individual i.

The assumptions that led to the previous result are clearly strong ones, in particular the one assuming that individuals form their views independently albeit being on a network. In a follow-up paper, Conitzer (2013) introduces a noise model for profile generation which has similarities with the models of opinion diffusion that will be introduced in Section 9.5. Such noise model is also defined for two alternatives, and assumes that the network E is such that each voter has an odd number of neighbours.[1] In the *independent conversation model*, voters have conversations with all of their neighbours, each one resulting in an argument in favour of one of the two alternatives, and will vote according to the majority of the arguments received.

In formulas, we associate with each edge $e = (i,j) \in E$ a random alternative $A_e \in \{0,1\}$, representing the result of the conversation between i and j: if $A_e = 0$, for instance, the two voters after the conversation will end up with an argument in favour of 0. A profile of conversations $A_E = (A_e \,|\, e \in E)$ is the profile of alternatives $A_e \in A$ associated with edges $e \in E$, and $n(c, A_e) = |\{e \in E \,|\, A_e = c\}|$ is the number of edges associated with alternative $c \in A$. With every profile of conversations A_E, we can associate a profile of votes P such that $p_i = maj(\{A_{(j,i)} \,|\, j \in N(i)\})$, with each voter supporting the alternative for which they obtained a majority of arguments supporting it. Assuming that alternative A_e is the correct one with probability $p > 0.5$, and is the incorrect one with probability $1 - p$, we can obtain the probability of observing a profile P given that the correct alternative is c as $Prob(P \,|\, c) = \sum_{A_E} p^{n(c, A_E)} \times (1-p)^{|E| - n(c, A_E)}$, where A_E ranges over all profiles of conversations that are consistent with the observed profile, i.e., such that $p_i = maj(\{A_{(j,i)} \,|\, j \in N(i)\})$. The maximum likelihood alternative c is therefore the one that maximises the expression above. Considering all profiles A_E that are consistent with the observed profile of votes P clearly leads to an exponential explosion and to computationally intractable problems. For instance, computing the figure above is $\#P$-hard (Conitzer, 2013).

The independent conversation model explained above has been refined and extended in related work. Tsang et al. (2015) include the assumption that agents are more easily convinced by arguments supporting the correct alternative than by those supporting the incorrect one. Procaccia et al. (2015) include multiple alternatives and a more sophisticated process of individual response to conversations, testing whether two families of voting rules are *accurate in the limit*, i.e., whether their probability of recovering the ground truth tends to 1 when the

---

[1] In social choice theory it is commonplace to assume that a collective decision is taken by an odd number of individuals. This assumption is less natural when applied to a social network, but can still be considered as realistic when the number of individuals on the network is sufficiently large.

number of voters tends to infinity (an approach in line with the Condorcet's Jury Theorem mentioned in Section 9.2).

9.3.2 Iterative Voting

Strategic voting, i.e., the possibility of misrepresenting one's vote to influence the result of an election in one's favour, is typically considered as a one-shot strategic game with perfect information. Iterative voting relaxes some of these assumptions (see, e.g., Chapter 4 of this book). In this model, an initial profile of votes is gathered, let it be P^0. Such profile can be assumed to consist of the agents' truthful preferences, but can also be a completely random preference profile. Summary information about P^0 is then broadcast to voters, for instance in the form of a poll giving the percentage of voters supporting each of the candidates. Voters can then respond to this information by submitting a new vote, to form a new profile P^1. The process is repeated until a stable state is reached, i.e., a state in which no voter has an incentive to change her voting ballot. A social network in the setting of iterative voting has the effect of filtering the information available to voters, who will then take into consideration only the partial information observed in their neighbourhood when updating their vote.

Tsang and Larson (2016) generalise the model of iterative voting by giving each voter access only to the ballots of her neighbouring voters. By associating numerical values (cardinal preferences) to voters' ordinal preferences, they monitor experimentally the evolution of a number of parameters such as the price of stability and the price of honesty, as well the effects of iterative strategic voting on the ranking of less popular alternatives.

The same underlying principle is used by Sina et al. (2015): voters in the network can see how their neighbours voted at each stage, and this information can also be complemented by a summary poll obtained from the entire profile. The authors show that a central authority that is in control of the network structure is able to easily influence the result of an election. Technically, they present a polynomial-time algorithm that makes a chosen candidate the winner of the election by only adding a linear number of edges to the network. The existence of such a central authority should not be viewed as unrealistic: consider for instance the Facebook feed, that has the ability to block the information flow from certain connections or to suggest new ones.

9.3.3 Coalitional Games and Voting Equilibria

The presence of a social network has effects on a number of other collective decision processes. One example is studied in the work of Elkind (2014) and Igarashi (2017), who analyse coalitional games on a network in which coalition formation is restricted to connected subsets of players. A similar approach is taken by Igarashi et al. (2017), who study problems of group activity selection where the allocation of activities can only consider connected subgroups of individuals, as well as by Gourvès et al. (2016), who refine the notion of equilibrium in strategic voting by restricting deviations to coalitions of players that form a clique of the network and by including a form of empathy in the behaviour of the agents.

9.4 Social Choice Mechanisms over Networks

A social choice problem typically consists in taking a collective decision starting solely from the voters' preferences. When this input is complemented with knowledge of the social network that relates the voters, novel mechanisms can be conceived to take this additional information into consideration. In this section we survey a variety of procedures for collective choice that are designed to be implemented on a network of voters.

9.4.1 Liquid Democracy

The road from representative democracy, in which voters elect representatives that later take decisions on their behalf, to direct democracy, where voters directly take decisions on the issues at stake, is full of hybrid voting systems. One of these is *proxy voting* or *liquid democracy*.

Consider a set N of voters who need to take a decision on one single issue, and who are connected by an undirected social network E. Voters are allowed to either vote directly in favour (1) or against (0) the issue, or to *delegate* their vote to any other voter in their neighbourhood $N(i)$ who will act as their proxy.[2] The crucial assumption here is that delegations are transitive, i.e., a voter who received 4 delegations can in turn delegate her vote together with the extra 4 delegations to another voter.[3] The input of this particular social choice problem consists then of a profile P of ternary ballots, with each individual i specifying a vote for 0 or 1, or a proxy $j \in N(i)$, inducing a *delegation network* on N which we shall call E_P. Observe that every node in the delegation graph E_P has outdegree at most one, since every voter can delegate to only one person, restricting considerably the type of graphs that can be encountered in this setting.

There are several possibilities to take a collective decision on such input profiles. If the principle of "one man, one vote" needs to be kept, then a weighted majority rule will be used, defining the weight of a proxy as the number of voters that have delegated their vote, either directly or via a chain of delegations, to the proxy. Formally, let a proxy be a voter i that expressed a direct vote either for 0 or for 1. Its weight can then be computed as $w_i = |\{j \in N \mid j\ E_P^*\ i\}|$, where jE_P^*i is the reflexive and transitive closure of the delegation graph E_P. Christoff and Grossi (2017b) analyse this setting through the lens of judgment aggregation, assuming that there are multiple interconnected binary issues at stake. Among the numerous problems they consider, there is the existence of cycles of delegations, which may cause a failure of the "one man, one vote" principle. They also observe that computing the result of a liquid democracy vote can be performed by finding a stable state of a suitable opinion diffusion model on the delegation network, a problem that we will analyse in detail in Section 9.5.

An alternative direction is to use off-the-shelf spectral ranking techniques to

---

[2]The assumption that delegates must be part of the social neighbourhood of a voter can be relaxed, but it is often assumed in practice to guarantee a minimal level of trust in the delegation process.

[3]Non-delegable proxy voting has been studied in the social choice literature by, e.g., Miller (1969). Moreover, recent work in computational social choice assess the use of non-delegable proxies in elections with a small number of active voters (Cohensius et al., 2017).

compute the weight of each proxy on the delegation network. This includes the well-known PageRank algorithm (Boldi et al., 2009) and the Katz index (Boldi et al., 2011). In the latter paper, the authors introduce a damping factor to limit the effect of long chains of transitive delegations. Their idea is the following: every delegation path leading to a proxy contributes to its weight with a sum that is inversely proportional to the path length. Clearly, the "one man, one vote" principle is lost, but in various settings (such as voting on online social media) the trust relation underlying a delegation may not be strong enough to justify the transfer of voting power. If $\alpha \in (0,1)$ is a damping factor, and we denote with $|p|$ the length of a path p,[4] we can define the weight of a proxy i as $w_i = \sum_{p \in Path(-,i)} \alpha^{|p|}$, where $Path(-,i)$ is the set of delegation paths ending in i. Once the weights of the proxies have been computed, a vote by weighted majority can be staged to compute the winning alternative. These methods have also been proposed and tested to construct a personalised recommender system (Boldi et al., 2015).

Non-binary versions of proxy voting give rise to a variety of other problems, as pointed out by the work of Behrens et al. (2014). For instance, when a large number of alternative proposals need to be considered and voted on, the ordering in which these competing alternatives are presented to the voters is of crucial importance. Skowron et al. (2017) mention this problem as a potential application of their work on proportionality, in which a ranking of alternatives needs to be constructed from individual approval ballots.

9.4.2 Ratings and Recommendations

Obtaining a collective rating for products or objects (classical example: the rating application TripAdvisor) is a collective decision problem that is close to that of obtaining recommendations for users (classical example: Netflix or Amazon's recommender systems). Both problems are typically solved at a global scale, considering preferences and calculating similarities over the whole of the users' data. In this section we look at three examples of how a social network can play a role in obtaining more meaningful and robust recommendations.

Let us first set some definitions. As before, let N be a set of individuals connected by a social network E. A subset of individuals $V \subseteq N$, called voters, express their opinions over a set of alternatives A, which we assume by simplicity consists of a single object. These opinions, which we denote $opinion(i)$ for $i \in N$, can take different forms, e.g., a like/dislike, a numerical rating, or an evaluation on a discrete scale. The problem of recommendation is then the following: given a target non-voter $v^* \in N \setminus V$ and the vector of individual opinions from voters in V, should the product be recommended to v^*?

One of the simplest solutions is to first calculate a collective rating for the object, perhaps as the average or the median of all the ratings expressed by voters, and recommend the object to the non-voter if the collective rating exceeds a certain threshold. This approach is not ideal for a number of reasons, one of which being its vulnerability to a variety of attacks by strategic agents. Consider for instance the problem of *false-name manipulations*: by opening multiple

---

[4] For ease of explanation we discard the case of infinite paths.

fake accounts providing the same rating as her own, a voter is able to influence both the median and the average towards her evaluation. When the social network connecting the individuals is known, a simple idea can however be used to obtain more robust rating mechanisms: instead of computing a global collective rating, recommendations should be based on a personalised form of rating, computed from the opinions of those voters that belong to a suitable notion of neighbourhood of the target user v^*. We now review three papers that formalised and studied a personalised approach to ratings and recommendations.

Andersen et al. (2008) carry out an axiomatic study of trust-based recommender systems, assuming that voters express binary opinions (like/dislike) on a single object. Let v^* be a non-voter and v a voter, and let $Prob(v^*, v)$ be the probability of reaching voter v from v^* with a random walk on the trust network E. Their *random walk* system will then recommend the product to v^* if the probability of reaching a voter from v^* whose opinion is "like" is higher than the probability of reaching a voter whose opinion is "dislike". Hence, they base recommendations on the ratings of all individuals in the connected component of E containing v^*, weighted by the network structure.

Grandi and Turrini (2016) focus instead on real-valued or discrete-scale opinions on a single object. Rather than presenting the overall average rating to all agents, the authors propose the use of *personalised ratings*, obtained by computing for each agent i the average rating of her direct neighbours on the trust network E. The strategic problem studied is that of bribery, in which an external agent tries to influence the rating of the object by bribing individuals to increase their ratings. Compared to providing the overall average of ratings, personalised ratings make bribery by an external agent more costly and, under some specific assumptions, not profitable.

Brill et al. (2016a) refine this idea by considering a broader notion of neighbourhood than the direct connections on the trust network. Their idea is the following one: let $F(u)$ be the set of users that are disconnected from the target user v^* as a result of removing node u from the network. A voter v is called *legitimate* if it does not belong to $F(u)$ for any $u \in N$, that is, if v is still reachable from v^* after the deletion of any node. They propose a recommender system based on this notion of neighbourhood, showing that it is false-name strategy-proof, i.e., it cannot be manipulated by the addition of fake users.

9.4.3 Social Polls and Empathetic Preferences

Gaspers et al. (2013) study the computational complexity of determining possible and necessary winners in the context of social polling. The key aspect of their model is that agents vote following a sequential order, observing the ballots that were previously cast by voters in their direct neighbourhood.

While voters are typically assumed to be influenced by the decisions of their neighbours, Salehi-Abari and Boutilier (2014) propose a different model in which voters' utilities on collectively decided alternatives depend positively on the utilities of their neighbours, to represent voters' desire to see others satisfied with the chosen alternative.

9.5 Opinion Diffusion

As in the introductory example of a committee decision, the addition of a network in a social choice problem is typically done to take into consideration phenomena such as social influence and the information diffusion that takes place before (or during) the decision process. The literature on social network analysis abounds with models of influence-based opinion diffusion. Two classical examples are threshold models (Granovetter, 1978), with more recent generalisations by Kempe et al. (2003, 2005), and the De Groot or Lehrer-Wagner model (de Groot, 1974; Lehrer and Wagner, 1981). With the notable exception of the recent work of Friedkin et al. (2016), these models are based on a simple representation of individual opinions as either a binary view on a single issue, or a real-valued opinion in the interval $[0, 1]$. We do not survey this literature here, pointing at the classical references in social network analysis for a detailed survey (Jackson, 2008; Easley and Kleinberg, 2010).

In this section, instead, we focus on a number of recent papers that borrowed techniques from social choice theory and knowledge representation to model the diffusion of *complex* opinions: multiple binary issues, linear orders, and belief bases. Such models are founded on the observation that influence on a social network is itself a social choice problem, since every individual uses some form of aggregation when updating her opinion based on the opinions of her influencers (e.g., her direct neighbours). This gives rise to a discrete-time iterative process in which at each point in time a number of agents on the network update their opinion using an aggregation procedure F_i that takes into account the opinions of the neighbours as well as her own one. Typical problems that can be studied are the *termination* of the iterative processes, characterising those networks or initial profiles of opinions on which the process is guaranteed to reach a stable state, and *convergence*, obtaining a characterisation of termination states. A typical example of the latter problem is convergence to consensus, i.e., the identification of properties of the network that guarantee that all agents will have unanimous opinions at the end of the diffusion process.

Example 9.2. *Consider the following example from Brill et al. (2016b). Let there be four agents on the influence network described below, and let each agent express her preferences in the form of a linear order over three alternatives a, b and c:*

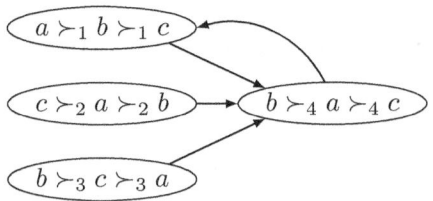

Figure 9.2: The influence of a Condorcet cycle.

The preferences of agents 1, 2, *and* 3 *form what is known as a* **Condorcet cycle**, *i.e., the majority relation of their preferences is cyclic. Assume now that opinion update process follows the opinion of the majority of an agent's influencers, by swapping* adjacent pairs of alternatives in her preferences accordingly. In the example above, we can devise a sequence of asynchronous (i.e., sequential) updates that terminates (albeit not to consensus). First, we let agent 4 update on pair ab, moving to preference $a \succ_4 b \succ_4 c$. After that, no further updates are possible: even though agent 4 disagrees with its influencers on pair ac, this pair cannot be swapped since it is no longer adjacent in $\succ_4$. In the same example, if we consider synchronous updates by the agents, then we can devise a sequence that does not terminate, namely the one where agents 1 and 4 update repeatedly on pair ab. Observe that in any update sequence agents 2 and 3 never update their preferences.

Let us start from the case of individual opinions over *multiple binary issues*. Consider a set of agents N on a directed network E, each one having a binary opinion over a set of issues I. Let for instance agent i express her opinion as $p_i = (0, 1, 0, 0)$ on a domain composed of four issues. At each point in time, an individual i has access to the opinions of its direct neighbours or influencers in $N(i)$, and updates her opinion using an aggregation function F. If P^t is the profile of individual profiles at time t, then $p_i^{t+1} = F(P^t_{|N(i)}, p_i^t)$, where $P^t_{|N(i)}$ is the restriction of profile P to the individuals in $N(i)$. The process can be *synchronous*, when all individuals update at the same time, or *asynchronous*, when individuals update one after the other. Grandi et al. (2015) provide algorithms and characterisation results for the termination of synchronous opinion diffusion models on multiple binary issues described above. Some of these results have been subsumed by the recent work of Christoff and Grossi (2017a), which focuses on aggregation procedures F that satisfy some natural choice-theoretic properties. When the aggregation procedure F is a quota rule (Dietrich and List, 2007), these models are equivalent to Granovetter's threshold functions. Goles and Olivos (1980) show that under such assumptions, every sequence of synchronous updates always terminates to a stable state or cycles with period 2. Different opinion diffusion models over multiple binary issues can be defined from any rule from the judgment aggregation literature (Endriss, 2016). Slavkovik and Jamroga (2016), for instance, explore the use of a distance-based procedure to reach consensus on a network. Finally, the addition of an integrity constraint relating the multiple issues is not a trivial generalisation, and initial results in this directions have been obtained by Botan et al. (2017).

In a voting setting, individual opinions are typically assumed to be *linear orders* over a set of alternatives, inducing more complex diffusion models studied by Brill et al. (2016b) and by Farnoud et al. (2013) (the latter for the case of a complete network). The main problem faced in these models is the presence of intransitive majorities, as presented in Example 9.2: three influencers with preferences $a \succ_1 b \succ_1 c$, $c \succ_2 a \succ_2 b$, and $b \succ_3 c \succ_3 a$, influencing a fourth individual with preferences $b \succ_4 a \succ_4 c$. Aggregating the three linear orders by majority results in a cycle: how should then the fourth agent update her preferences? One possible solution is to restrict individual updates to swapping pairs that are already adjacent in the individual ordering that is being updated. For instance, in the previous example, the fourth agent may update on pair (b, a), switching to $a \succ_4 b \succ_4 c$, which agrees on all adjacent pairs with the (intransitive) majority of her influencers. In this model, Brill et al. (2016b) provide a termination result on arbitrary networks under additional assumptions on the profile of individual preferences, and show that on directed acyclic graphs the diffusion model preserves classical domain restrictions from voting theory such as single-peakedness.

Belief bases are sets of formulas in propositional logic that are used to compactly represent the beliefs of an agent about the current state of the world. For example, if p stands for "it is raining" and q stands for "it is cold", an agent with a belief base of $p \vee q$ believes that it is raining or it is cold, or both. These mathematical objects have been used as individual opinions by Schwind et al. (2015) and Cholvy (2016), to define diffusion processes in line with those described above. Individuals on a network are assumed to have access to the belief bases of their direct neighbours, and to use this information to update their current belief base using a belief merging operator (see, e.g., Chapter 7 of this book). In particular, Schwind et al. (2015) analyses the axiomatic properties of this model, varying the belief merging technique that is used for the update of individuals' belief bases.

The strategic aspects of the diffusion models described above are of clear interest, both for individual strategic actions such as misrepresenting one's own opinion, and for external actions such as bribery or control. Some of these problems are just beginning to be explored in the case of belief bases (Schwind et al., 2016) and binary issues (Grandi et al., 2017; Brederick and Elkind, 2017).

9.6 Conclusions

In this chapter we surveyed recent work in the computational social choice literature on social choice and social networks.

First, we saw how social-network-related phenomena, such as social influence and an asymmetric distribution of information, can impact the result of standard procedures for collective decision-making. When taking a maximum likelihood approach to social choice, the structure of a network can be exploited to create novel noise models and new maximum likelihood estimators. An open question is then whether opinion diffusion models such as those defined in Section 9.5 can be interpreted as noise models, and what are the maximum likelihood estimators for them. The setting of iterative voting, when voters respond iteratively to a sequence of polls or elections, is also affected by individuals responding to local information filtered through the network. Political elections provide numerous examples to observe the consequences of network-related processes, from the majority illusion discussed in Section 9.3, to echo-chamber effects, to polarisation. Assessing the effects of social networks on the ability of taking collective decisions in society is a crucial topic for modern social choice, and a rich source of computational problems.

We then considered the problem of designing mechanisms for collective choice that are implemented on networks of voters. The classical example here is proxy voting, in which voters can delegate their voting power to a neighbour, inducing a delegation network. Various notions from spectral ranking can be used to compute the weights of voters and arrive at a collective decision. While classical weight functions from social network analysis have been tested, novel measures may be defined that are specific to a voting context. We also saw applications to the problem of obtaining ratings and recommendations of objects to users. In this setting, suitable notions of neighbourhood on the network can be used to provide personalised ratings and recommendations that are more robust against malicious strategic actions by both users and external agents.

Finally, we showed how social choice can contribute to the definition of novel models of opinion diffusion, based on the idea that individuals aggregate the views they receive from their neighbours on a social network. Depending on the application at hand, these models can be constructed using voting rules from classical social choice theory, aggregation procedures from judgment aggregation, or belief merging operators. These models present a number of open algorithmic challenges, most notably the characterisation of networks guaranteeing termination, and provide a computation-friendly representation of diffusion whose effects on social choice methods still need to be assessed.

Strategic aspects of collective decision-making on social networks are still largely unexplored. Agents may have multiple actions available, from adding or severing links on the network, to misrepresenting their opinion in different ways to different agents, to exercising their influence at various degrees. This new layer of strategic reasoning may have a significant impact on the problem of equilibrium selection in voting games, and we have seen some first studies in this direction in the area of iterative voting. Many of the ideas discussed in this chapter also have the potential to contribute to real-world applications: from ratings and recommendations on networks, to the rise of platforms for democracy and online decision making (see, e.g., Chapter 20 of this book).

Acknowledgments

The author gratefully acknowledges Markus Brill, Davide Grossi, and Arianna Novaro for their useful comments and discussions.

Bibliography

R. Andersen, C. Borgs, J. Chayes, U. Feige, A. Flaxman, A. Kalai, V. Mirrokni, and M. Tennenholtz. Trust-based recommendation systems: An axiomatic approach. In *Proceedings of the 17th International Conference on World Wide Web (WWW)*, 2008.

K. J. Arrow. *Social Choice and Individual Values*. John Wiley and Sons, 2nd edition, 1963. First edition published in 1951.

J. Behrens, A. Kistner, A. Nitsche, and B. Swierczek. *Principles of Liquid Feedback*. Interaktive Demokratie e. V., 2014.

P. Boldi, F. Bonchi, C. Castillo, and S. Vigna. Voting in social networks. In *Proceedings of the 18th ACM Conference on Information and Knowledge Management (CIKM)*, 2009.

P. Boldi, F. Bonchi, C. Castillo, and S. Vigna. Viscous democracy for social networks. *Communications of the ACM*, 54(6):129–137, 2011.

P. Boldi, C. Monti, M. Santini, and S. Vigna. Liquid FM: recommending music through viscous democracy. In *Proceedings of the 6th Italian Information Retrieval Workshop*, 2015.

S. Botan, U. Grandi, and L. Perrussel. Propositionwise opinion diffusion with constraints. In *Proceedings of the 4th AAMAS Workshop on Exploring Beyond the Worst Case in Computational Social Choice (EXPLORE)*, 2017.

R. Bredereck and E. Elkind. Manipulating opinion diffusion in social networks. In *Proceedings of the 26th International Joint Conference on Artificial Intelligence (IJCAI)*, 2017.

M. Brill, V. Conitzer, R. Freeman, and N. Shah. False-name-proof recommendations in social networks. In *Proceedings of the 15th International Conference on Autonomous Agents and Multiagent Systems (AAMAS)*, 2016a.

M. Brill, E. Elkind, U. Endriss, and U. Grandi. Pairwise diffusion of preference rankings in social networks. In *Proceedings of the 25th International Joint Conference on Artificial Intelligence (IJCAI)*, 2016b.

L. Cholvy. Diffusion of opinion and influence. In *Proceedings of the 10th International Conference on Scalable Uncertainty Management (SUM)*, 2016.

Z. Christoff and D. Grossi. Stability in binary opinion diffusion. In *Proceedings of the 6th International Conference on Logic, Rationality, and Interaction (LORI)*, 2017a.

Z. Christoff and D. Grossi. Binary voting with delegable proxy: An analysis of liquid democracy. In *Proceedings of the 16th Conference on Theoretical Aspects of Rationality and Knowledge (TARK)*, 2017b.

G. Cohensius, S. Mannor, R. Meir, E. A. Meirom, and A. Orda. Proxy voting for better outcomes. In *Proceedings of the 16th Conference on Autonomous Agents and Multiagent Systems (AAMAS)*, 2017.

Condorcet, Marie Jean Antoine Nicolas de Caritat, Marquis de. *Essai sur l'application de l'analyse à la probabilité des décisions rendues à la pluralité des voix*. Paris, 1785.

V. Conitzer. Should social network structure be taken into account in elections? *Mathematical Social Sciences*, 64(1):100–102, 2012.

V. Conitzer. The maximum likelihood approach to voting on social networks. In *Proceedings of the 51st Annual Allerton Conference on Communication, Control, and Computing*, 2013.

M. H. de Groot. Reaching a consensus. *Journal of the American Statistical Association*, 69(345):118–121, 1974.

F. Dietrich and C. List. Judgment aggregation by quota rules: Majority voting generalized. *Journal of Theoretical Politics*, 19(4):391–424, 2007.

D. Easley and J. Kleinberg. *Networks, Crowds, and Markets: Reasoning About a Highly Connected World*. Cambridge University Press, 2010.

E. Elkind. Coalitional games on sparse social networks. In *Proceedings of the 10th International Conference on Web and Internet Economics (WINE)*, 2014.

U. Endriss. Judgment aggregation. In F. Brandt, V. Conitzer, U. Endriss, J. Lang, and A. D. Procaccia, editors, *Handbook of Computational Social Choice*, chapter 17. Cambridge University Press, 2016.

F. Farnoud, E. Yaakobi, B. Touri, O. Milenkovic, and J. Bruck. Building consensus via iterative voting. In *Proceedings of the 2013 IEEE International Symposium on Information Theory*, 2013.

N. E. Friedkin, A. V. Proskurnikov, R. Tempo, and S. Parsegov. Network science on belief system dynamics under logical constraints. *Science*, 354(6310):321–326, 2016.

S. Gaspers, V. Naroditskiy, N. Narodytska, and T. Walsh. Possible and necessary winner problem in social polls. In *Proceedings of the 12th International Conference on Autonomous Agents and Multiagent Systems (AAMAS)*, 2013.

E. Goles and J. Olivos. Periodic behaviour of generalized threshold functions. *Discrete Mathematics*, 30(2):187–189, 1980.

L. Gourvès, J. Lesca, and A. Wilczynski. Strategic voting in a social context: Considerate equilibria. In *Proceedings of the 22nd European Conference on Artificial Intelligence (ECAI)*, 2016.

U. Grandi and P. Turrini. A network-based rating system and its resistance to bribery. In *Proceedings of the 25th International Joint Conference on Artificial Intelligence (IJCAI)*, 2016.

U. Grandi, E. Lorini, and L. Perrussel. Propositional opinion diffusion. In *Proceedings of the 14th International Conference on Autonomous Agents and Multiagent Systems (AAMAS)*, 2015.

U. Grandi, E. Lorini, A. Novaro, and L. Perrussel. Strategic diffusion of opinions on a social network. In *Proceedings of the 16th International Conference on Autonomous Agents and Multiagent Systems (AAMAS)*, 2017.

M. Granovetter. Threshold models of collective behavior. *American Journal of Sociology*, 83(6):1420–1443, 1978.

A. Igarashi. Supermodular games on social networks. In *Proceedings of the 16th Conference on Autonomous Agents and Multiagent Systems (AAMAS)*, 2017.

A. Igarashi, D. Peters, and E. Elkind. Group activity selection on social networks. In *Proceedings of the 31st AAAI Conference on Artificial Intelligence (AAAI)*, 2017.

M. O. Jackson. *Social and Economic Networks*. Princeton University Press, 2008.

D. Kempe, J. M. Kleinberg, and E. Tardos. Maximizing the spread of influence through a social network. In *Proceedings of the 9th ACM SIGKDD International Conference on Knowledge Discovery and Data Mining*, 2003.

D. Kempe, J. M. Kleinberg, and E. Tardos. Influential nodes in a diffusion model for social networks. In *Proceedings of the 32nd International Colloquium on Automata, Languages and Programming (ICALP)*, 2005.

K. Lehrer and C. Wagner. *Rational Consensus in Science and Society*. Springer, 1981.

K. Lerman, X. Yan, and X.-Z. Wu. The "majority illusion" in social networks. *PLoS ONE*, 11(2):1–13, 02 2016.

J. C. Miller. A program for direct and proxy voting in the legislative process. *Public Choice*, 7(1):107–113, 1969.

A. D. Procaccia, N. Shah, and E. Sodomka. Ranked voting on social networks. In *Proceedings of the 24th International Joint Conference on Artificial Intelligence (IJCAI)*, 2015.

A. Salehi-Abari and C. Boutilier. Empathetic social choice on social networks. In *International conference on Autonomous Agents and Multiagent Systems (AAMAS)*, 2014.

N. Schwind, K. Inoue, G. Bourgne, S. Konieczny, and P. Marquis. Belief revision games. In *Proceedings of the 29th AAAI Conference on Artificial Intelligence (AAAI)*, 2015.

N. Schwind, K. Inoue, G. Bourgne, S. Konieczny, and P. Marquis. Is promoting beliefs useful to make them accepted in networks of agents? In *Proceedings of the 25th International Joint Conference on Artificial Intelligence (IJCAI)*, 2016.

S. Sina, N. Hazon, A. Hassidim, and S. Kraus. Adapting the social network to affect elections. In *Proceedings of the 14th International Conference on Autonomous Agents and Multiagent Systems (AAMAS)*, 2015.

P. Skowron, M. Lackner, M. Brill, D. Peters, and E. Elkind. Proportional rankings. In *Proceedings of the 26th International Joint Conference on Artificial Intelligence (IJCAI)*, 2017.

M. Slavkovik and W. Jamroga. Iterative judgment aggregation. In *Proceedings of the 22nd European Conference on Artificial Intelligence (ECAI)*, 2016.

A. Tsang and K. Larson. The echo chamber: Strategic voting and homophily in social networks. In *Proceedings of the 15th International Conference on Autonomous Agents and Multiagent Systems (AAMAS)*, 2016.

A. Tsang, J. A. Doucette, and H. Hosseini. Voting with social influence: Using arguments to uncover ground truth (extended abstract). In *Proceedings of the 2015 International Conference on Autonomous Agents and Multiagent Systems (AAMAS)*, 2015.

PART II
TECHNIQUES

CHAPTER 10

Structured Preferences

Edith Elkind, Martin Lackner, and Dominik Peters

10.1 Introduction

In a typical social choice scenario, agents rank the available alternatives and have to collectively decide on the best alternative, or a ranking of the alternatives. If there are just two alternatives, the decision can be made by a majority vote. However, for three or more alternatives the agents may face a difficult choice. For instance, there can be a cycle in the majority preferences: it may happen that a majority of voters prefer a to b, a majority of voters prefer b to c, yet a majority of voters prefer c to a. Indeed, Arrow (1950) has shown that when there are more than two alternatives, the only social welfare function that satisfies a small set of natural axioms is a dictatorship. Moreover, essentially any reasonable voting rule is susceptible to strategic behavior: Gibbard (1973) and Satterthwaite (1975) observed that under any non-trivial voting rule there exists a scenario where some voter benefits from misrepresenting her preferences.

These classic results provide ample evidence that preference aggregation is hard from a conceptual standpoint. On the other hand, preference aggregation is also hard in a very different sense: it can be shown that for many important voting rules computing the winner(s) is NP-hard. In particular, this is the case for the Kemeny rule, which is arguably the most natural method for aggregating a set of preference rankings into a single ranking, as well as for many popular multiwinner rules, such as Proportional Approval Voting, the Chamberlin–Courant rule, and the Monroe rule (see Chapter 2 of this book for definitions).

Now, social choice theorists have observed that the first source of hardness can be circumvented by focusing on scenarios where voters' preferences share some common structure. The most famous result of this type dates back to the important early works of Black (1948) and Arrow (1951). They proved that if voters' preferences are essentially single-dimensional, then there are no cycles in the majority preferences, and there is a voting rule that is strategyproof. The specific domain of preferences considered by Black and Arrow is that of single-peaked preferences; similar results have been subsequently obtained for other restricted preference domains, such as those of preferences that are single-crossing or single-peaked on a tree (to be formally defined later in this chapter).

It is then natural to ask whether the same approach can be used to circumvent computational complexity issues as well. The first foray in this direction was made by Walsh (2007), and since then hardness and easiness results for various restricted preference domains have been obtained for a number of problems including winner determination under a variety of voting rules, preference elicitation, as well as several forms of strategic behavior in voting.

Interestingly, while purely social choice-theoretic issues (such as existence of majority cycles) vanish as soon as we assume that voters' preferences belong to a suitable restricted domain, many of the algorithms for voting-related problems rely on the knowledge of the respective structural relationship among voters/alternatives (such as the order of alternatives witnessing that the profile is single-peaked). Thus, to make use of these algorithms, one also needs an efficient procedure to determine whether a given preference profile has the required structural property and to find a respective witness. Consequently, the problem of designing such procedures has received a considerable amount of attention, too, resulting in polynomial-time algorithms for recognizing preferences that belong to several prominent restricted domains.

In this chapter, we will survey work on four specific topics that concern algorithmic properties of restricted preference domains. After defining the relevant concepts in Section 10.2, in Section 10.3 we discuss two extensions of the single-peaked domain, namely the domains of preferences that are single-peaked on *trees* and on *circles*, and show that several positive results for single-peaked preferences extend to these larger domains. In Section 10.4, we look at how the definitions of single-peaked and single-crossing preferences can be adapted to approval voting scenarios, and analyze the resulting preference domains from an algorithmic point of view. In Section 10.5, we review work on the complexity of strategic behavior in settings that are *nearly* structured. Finally, in Section 10.6, we demonstrate how assuming that voters' preferences belong to a restricted domain can make preference elicitation more efficient.

10.2 Background

Suppose that citizens of a country X are about to vote on the (flat) tax rate. The set of alternatives is $A = \{0\%, 1\%, \ldots, 100\%\}$, and it admits a natural ordering $0\% \lhd 1\% \lhd \cdots \lhd 100\%$. Consider a voter i whose most-preferred alternative (the *peak*) is 35%. Then it is plausible that i's preferences decrease as we move away from this peak: for example, we would expect $40\% \succ_i 50\%$, and $30\% \succ_i 20\%$. Such preferences are called single-peaked with respect to the ordering $\lhd$.

Formally, let $P = (\succ_1, \ldots, \succ_n)$ be a preference profile consisting of linear orders over an alternative set A, and let $N = \{1, \ldots, n\}$. Let $\text{top}(i)$ denote the most-preferred alternative of voter i. Given a linear order $\lhd$ of A, we say that $\succ_i$ is *single-peaked with respect to* $\lhd$ if for all $a, b \in A$ such that $\text{top}(i) \lhd a \lhd b$ or $b \lhd a \lhd \text{top}(i)$ we have $a \succ_i b$; we refer to $\lhd$ as an *axis* for A. In other words, $\succ_i$ is decreasing as we move in either direction from i's peak. We say that the profile P is *single-peaked* if there exists

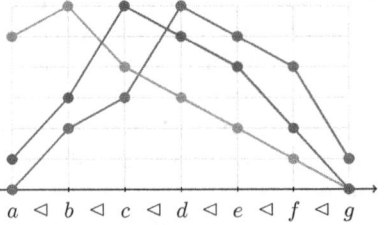

$a \lhd b \lhd c \lhd d \lhd e \lhd f \lhd g$

some axis $\lhd$ such that for each voter $i \in N$ it holds that $\succ_i$ is single-peaked with respect to $\lhd$.

The concept of single-peaked preferences was first proposed by Black (1948) and Arrow (1951), who noticed that for every single-peaked profile with an odd number of voters the majority relation is transitive and hence there exists a Condorcet winner. Further, there is a voting rule defined on single-peaked profiles that is strategyproof (see Moulin (1991, p. 263) for details). This result is known as the *median voter theorem* because of the form of this non-manipulable voting rule: it orders the voters in order of their peaks (according to $\lhd$) and then selects the median voter's peak, which is also the Condorcet winner.

Another notion of structure in voters' preferences is based on ordering the voters rather than the candidates. A profile $P = (\succ_1, \ldots, \succ_n)$ of linear orders over A is called *single-crossing* if voters can be ordered so that for all $a, b \in A$, the set of voters who prefer a to b forms an interval of this ordering. Thus, if the very first voter prefers a to b, then there is some value i, $1 \leq i \leq n$, such that the first i voters prefer a to b and the remaining $n - i$ voters prefer b to a, i.e., the voters 'switch' from $a \succ b$ to $b \succ a$ at most once. Just like a single-peaked profile, a single-crossing profile is single-dimensional; in this case it is the *voters* who are ordered on an 'ideological' spectrum. Single-crossing profiles with an odd number of voters also enjoy a transitive majority relation. In fact, they have the so-called *representative voter property*: the majority relation is identical to the preference relation of the median voter with respect to the single-crossing order (Rothstein, 1991).

$\succ_1$	$\succ_2$	$\succ_3$	$\succ_4$	$\succ_5$
a	b	b	d	d
b	a	d	b	c
c	d	a	c	b
d	c	c	a	a

The class of *one-dimensional Euclidean preferences* (Coombs, 1950) combines the ideas of single-peaked and single-crossing preferences; it is defined based on geometric considerations. Formally, a profile $P = (\succ_1, \ldots, \succ_n)$ of linear orders over A is called *1-Euclidean* if there is a mapping $x : N \cup A \to \mathbb{R}$ which assigns every voter $i \in N$ a position $x(i)$ on the real line, and assigns every alternative $a \in A$ a position $x(a)$ on the real line, so that for all $i \in N$ and all pairs $a, b \in A$ we have $a \succ_i b$ if and only if $|x(i) - x(a)| < |x(i) - x(b)|$. Thus, in a 1-Euclidean profile, voters prefer closer alternatives to those that are further away. It is easy to see that every 1-Euclidean profile is single-peaked and single-crossing; the respective orderings of candidates and voters are given by an embedding x witnessing that P is 1-Euclidean. Yet, there are profiles that are both single-peaked and single-crossing, but fail to be 1-Euclidean (Elkind et al., 2014). The geometric approach extends to higher dimensions: a profile is *d-Euclidean* if there exists an embedding $x : N \cup A \to \mathbb{R}^d$ such that voters' preferences are consistent with Euclidean distances to alternatives under this embedding.

10.2.1 Algorithmic Results

There are polynomial-time algorithms for recognizing single-peaked (Bartholdi III and Trick, 1986; Doignon and Falmagne, 1994; Escoffier et al., 2008), single-crossing (Doignon and Falmagne, 1994; Elkind et al., 2012; Bredereck et al., 2013) and 1-Euclidean (Doignon and Falmagne, 1994; Knoblauch, 2010; Elkind and Faliszewski, 2014) profiles; in contrast, Peters (2017) has shown that recognizing d-Euclidean profiles is computationally hard. For single-peaked and single-crossing profiles, the recognition problem can be reduced to the *consecutive 1s* problem, which asks whether the columns of a 0–1 matrix can be permuted so that in each row all 1s appear consecutively; this problem is polynomial-time solvable (Booth and Lueker, 1976). (Section 10.4 provides an example of such a reduction for dichotomous preferences.) Both of these domains also admit direct polynomial-time recognition algorithms; for single-peaked preferences such an algorithm runs in time $O(mn)$, which is linear in the input size.

There are many examples of NP-hard social choice problems that become easy for single-peaked and single-crossing preferences. For instance, with an odd number of voters, both of these preference restrictions guarantee that the majority relation is transitive and, in particular, there exists a Condorcet winner. This implies that for profiles that satisfy these constraints the Kemeny rank aggregation rule can be evaluated in polynomial time (since the transitive majority relation gives an optimal ranking), and winners according to the Dodgson rule and the Young rule can be found efficiently (since the Condorcet winner is the unique winner for both rules). These results can be extended to profiles with an even number of voters (Brandt et al., 2015).

Similar results hold for several NP-hard multiwinner voting rules (see Chapter 2 of this book). For example, Betzler et al. (2013) showed that, given a single-peaked profile with n voters and m alternatives, we can find a winning committee according to the Chamberlin–Courant rule (Chamberlin and Courant, 1983) in time $O(m^2 n)$ by a dynamic programming algorithm; this result can be extended to single-crossing preferences (Skowron et al., 2015) and to a few other multiwinner rules (Elkind and Ismaili, 2015; Peters, 2016). In essence, the algorithm of Betzler et al. (2013) proceeds along the axis $\lhd$ from left to right, deciding whether to add candidates to the committee being constructed; note that this means that the algorithm needs to know such an axis, i.e., it relies on the existence of efficient recognition algorithms discussed earlier in this section. Some of the computational problems associated with various forms of strategic behavior (such as manipulation, control and bribery) also become polynomial-time solvable when voters' preferences can be assumed to be single-peaked or single-crossing; we survey such results in more detail in Section 10.5.

10.3 Single-Peaked Preferences: Beyond the Line

The positive results for winner determination problems over restricted domains discussed above have a potential drawback: in practice, very few profiles are single-peaked. For example, under the impartial culture model, it is exponentially unlikely that a profile is single-peaked (Lackner and Lackner, 2017), and no real-world profile in PREFLIB (see Chapter 15 of this book) is single-peaked. One can try to address this issue by extending the existing algorithms to profiles that are "nearly" single-peaked or single-crossing, for an appropriate distance measure; we will survey a sample of such results in Section 10.5. In the rest of this section, we will pursue a different agenda: instead of considering preferences that are single-peaked with respect to an axis, i.e., a path, we consider preferences that are single-peaked on more general graphs. We focus on two classes of graphs that admit positive algorithmic and social choice-theoretic results, namely, trees and cycles. This approach allows us to capture a broader class of preference profiles and can be seen as a step towards mapping out the precise boundaries between tractable and intractable instances of winner determination problems for several important voting rules.

Preferences Single-Peaked on a Tree

Demange (1982) introduced the notion of preferences that are *single-peaked on a tree*. Fix a set of alternatives A and consider a tree $T = (A, E)$. A preference order $\succ_i$ over A is *single-peaked on T* if $a \succ_i b$ whenever a lies on the (unique) path between $\text{top}(i)$ and b. Thus, a voter's preferences decrease as we move away from her peak along any path in T. A profile $P = (\succ_1, \ldots, \succ_n)$ over a set of alternatives A is said to be *single-peaked on a tree* if there is some tree $T = (A, E)$ such that for each voter $i \in N$ the preference order $\succ_i$ is single-peaked on T. Note that this definition is equivalent to the one in Section 10.2 when T is a path.

To make sense of this definition, it is useful to consider the case where T is a *star*. Specifically, suppose that T is a star with center c, so $E = \{\{c, a\} : a \in A \setminus \{c\}\}$. Which preference orders are single-peaked on T? Consider a voter i with $\text{top}(i) = c$. No matter how she ranks the candidates in $A \setminus \{c\}$, her preferences are necessarily single-peaked on T. On the other hand, if voter i's peak is a leaf vertex $a \neq c$, then c lies on the path from a to any other vertex b, and so we must have $c \succ_i b$ for every $b \in A \setminus \{a, c\}$, i.e., c must be i's second-most-preferred alternative; the remaining alternatives may appear in $\succ_i$ in an arbitrary order. Thus, a preference order is single-peaked on T if and only if c occurs in first or second position in that order.

This analysis shows that moving from paths to arbitrary trees gives us many more profiles: there are only $\Theta(2^{m-1})$ orders that are single-peaked on a given path, but there are $\Theta((m-1)!)$ orders that are single-peaked on a given star. However, this expansion comes at a cost: Demange (1982) shows that profiles single-peaked on a tree are not guaranteed to have a transitive majority relation. On the positive side, such profiles still admit a Condorcet winner, and a strategyproof voting rule. Moreover, Trick (1989) shows that it is possible to recognize whether a given profile is single-peaked on a tree and to find a suitable tree in $O(m^2 n)$ time. A natural next question, then, is whether hard winner determination problems become easier for profiles that are single-peaked on trees.

For the Dodgson rule and the Young rule, the answer is clearly positive as long as the number of voters is odd: we can simply output the Condorcet winner. On the other hand, our characterization of profiles single-peaked on a star shows that finding a consensus ranking according to the Kemeny rule remains hard. Indeed, we can transform an arbitrary profile into one that is single-peaked on a star by adding a dummy candidate and placing it in the first position in every vote; the consensus ranking for the original profile can be easily extracted from the one for the new 'structured' profile.

For multiwinner rules, the results are somewhat disappointing as well. In particular, for a profile single-peaked on a tree, while one can efficiently compute a winning committee under the egalitarian version of the Chamberlin–Courant rule, for the more common utilitarian version, the winner determination problem remains NP-hard (Yu et al., 2013). Interestingly, however, this hardness result does not apply to profiles that are single-peaked on a star. This is because including the center of the star in the committee ensures that each voter is quite well represented; filling the rest of the committee then boils down to choosing candidates that appear most often in the top position. This argument can be generalized to show that the problem of winner determination under the Chamberlin–Courant rule for preferences that are single-peaked on trees is fixed-parameter tractable with respect to the number of non-leaf vertices of the tree (Peters and Elkind, 2016). In a similar vein, Yu et al. (2013) show that dynamic programming can be used for trees that are 'path-like', in the sense of having a few leaves; they place the Chamberlin–Courant winner determination problem into the class XP with respect to the number of leaves. Both the algorithm for trees with few leaves and the algorithm for trees with few internal nodes rely on knowing a suitable tree; Yu et al. (2013) and Peters and Elkind (2016) show that it is indeed possible to efficiently decide whether a given profile is single-peaked on some such tree.

Preferences Single-Peaked on a Circle

Peters and Lackner (2017) initiate the algorithmic study of preferences that are single-peaked on a circle. A preference profile is said to be *single-peaked on a circle* if the alternatives can be arranged on a circle in such a way that for each voter we can cut this circle so that her preferences are single-peaked on the resulting path.

An intriguing property of this class of profiles is that it is closed under preference reversal: if an order is single-peaked on a circle, then so is the reverse of this order. In particular, a profile that combines orders that are single-peaked with respect to some axis and ones that are single-caved with respect to the same axis is single-peaked on a circle. Thus, in a political context, this model allows for voters with a preferred point along the ideological left-to-right spectrum as well as for 'extremists' who dislike centrist alternatives. It can also capture other application scenarios, including some that are more explicitly cyclic, such as scheduling international meetings across time zones or placing a facility (e.g., an airport) somewhere on the boundary of a city.

Profiles that are single-peaked on a circle do not inherit nice axiomatic properties of profiles that are single-peaked on a path; indeed, the (in)famous Condorcet cycle (i.e., the three-voter profile over $\{x,y,z\}$ given by $x \succ_1 y \succ_1 z$, $y \succ_2 z \succ_2 x$, and $z \succ_3 x \succ_3 y$) is single-peaked on a circle, This means, in particular, that profiles single-peaked on a circle do not necessarily have a Condorcet winner. In fact, every majority relation can be realized by a profile that is single-peaked on a circle, as we can implement the construction in the proof of McGarvey's theorem using a profile in this domain (Peters and Lackner, 2017). This implies that the Kemeny rule remains hard to evaluate on such profiles. Furthermore, the Gibbard–Satterthwaite Theorem can be proven using only profiles single-peaked on a circle (Kim and Roush, 1980), which means that there is no analogue of the median voter procedure for circles.

However, from an algorithmic perspective, this domain restriction turns out to be quite useful. For example, given a profile single-peaked on a circle, a greedy algorithm can efficiently compute winners according to the Young rule (Peters and Lackner, 2017). Also, for such profiles we can efficiently compute a winning committee under the Chamberlin–Courant rule and its variants, by reducing this problem to solving integer linear programs with totally unimodular constraint matrices (Peters, 2016; Peters and Lackner, 2017).

Preferences Single-Peaked on Arbitrary Graphs?

In principle, for any graph $G = (A, E)$, one can formally define what it means for a preference order over A to be single-peaked on G: one can require that for each $b \in B$ the upper-contour set $\{a \in A : a \succ b\}$ is connected in G. Note that under this definition, every profile is single-peaked on the complete graph. However, as we try to move beyond trees and circles, we cannot expect many positive results: any class of graphs that contains circles would inherit the negative social choice-theoretic results for circles, and any class of graphs that contains trees would inherit the computational hardness results for trees. Moreover, the associated recognition problem may be difficult as well: e.g., a result of Gottlob and Greco (2013) implies that it is NP-hard to decide whether a profile is single-peaked on a graph of treewidth at most 3.

There are other possibilities for definitions of single-peaked preferences on arbitrary graphs, such as ones based on shortest paths (Nehring and Puppe, 2007). It would be interesting to compare them in terms of algorithmic usefulness.

10.4 Structure in Dichotomous Preferences

Approval Voting is one of social choice theorists' favorite voting rules (Brams and Fishburn, 2007; Laslier and Sanver, 2010). It asks voters to report *dichotomous preferences*, i.e., to split the alternatives into *approved* and *disapproved* choices—a dichotomy. It then selects the alternative(s) with the maximum number of approvals. This voting rule has many desirable axiomatic properties, but to a large extent its attraction stems from its input format: it is easy for voters to make up their mind about which preferences to report, it is easy to elicit such preferences, and it is easy to reason mathematically about them. However, some attractive voting rules for dichotomous preferences are still hard to evaluate, particularly in the multiwinner setting. It is therefore natural to ask what it means for dichotomous preferences to be essentially one-dimensional, and whether the respective preference restrictions are algorithmically useful.

Building on earlier work of List (2003), Dietrich and List (2010) and Faliszewski et al. (2011), a recent paper by Elkind and Lackner (2015) considers several ways of extending the definitions of single-peaked, single-crossing and 1-Euclidean preferences to the dichotomous setting. The paper studies algorithmic properties of the resulting domains, focusing on the complexity of recognizing profiles that belong to these domains and computing the outputs of well-known approval-based multiwinner rules.

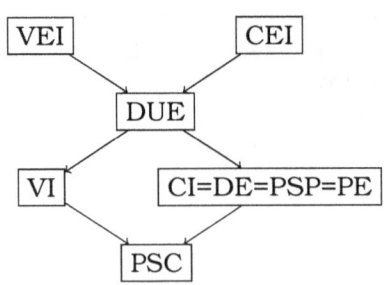

Figure 10.1: Relations between notions of structure for dichotomous preferences as established by Elkind and Lackner (2015). Arrows indicate containment; more restrictive domains are at the top.

Defining Domain Restrictions for Dichotomous Preferences

One approach that allows us to adapt any preference restriction defined for linear orders to the realm of dichotomous orders is to view dichotomies as weak orders: we can ask if it is possible to *refine* each weak order in a given dichotomous profile so as to obtain a profile of linear orders with a given structural property (Lackner, 2014; Elkind et al., 2015). Formally, we say that a linear order $\succ$ *extends* an approval ballot B if for every pair of candidates (a,b) such that a is approved in B and b is not approved in B we have $a \succ b$. We then say that a dichotomous profile belongs to the domain of *possibly single-peaked (PSP)* profiles if it can be extended to a profile of linear orders that is single-peaked. Possibly single-crossing (PSC) and possibly 1-Euclidean (PE) dichotomous profiles can be defined in a similar manner.

For linear orders, it is known that the single-peaked and the single-crossing domain overlap, but neither is contained in the other, and that the 1-Euclidean domain is strictly contained in their intersection (see, e.g., Elkind et al., 2014). Interestingly, the relationship among their approval-based cousins is different: Elkind and Lackner (2015) show that PSP coincides with PE, whereas PSC is a strict subdomain of PSP/PE (see Figure 10.1).

A more direct approach is based on the idea of contiguity: we could say that a dichotomous profile is single-peaked if there exists an ordering of candidates such that each voter's approval set forms an interval of this ordering. This definition is used by Faliszewski et al. (2011); we will say that such profiles belong to the the *candidate interval (CI)* domain. Similarly, a profile belongs to the *voter interval (VI)* domain if the voters can be ordered so that for every candidate c, the set of voters approving c forms an interval of that ordering. Stronger variants of both properties require every interval to contain the leftmost or the rightmost element of the candidate/voter ordering; this yields the *candidate/voter extremal interval (CEI/VEI)* domains.

For single-peaked preferences, the two approaches result in the same class of profiles: Elkind and Lackner (2015) show that the CI domain coincides with the PSP domain (and hence with the PE domain). In constrast, for single-crossing

$$\begin{bmatrix} a & b & c & d \\ 1 & 0 & 0 & 0 \\ 0 & 0 & 1 & 1 \\ 1 & 1 & 0 & 1 \\ 1 & 0 & 0 & 1 \end{bmatrix} \begin{matrix} \{a\} \\ \{c,d\} \\ \{a,b,d\} \\ \{a,d\} \end{matrix} \longmapsto \begin{bmatrix} b & a & d & c \\ 0 & 1 & 0 & 0 \\ 0 & 0 & 1 & 1 \\ 1 & 1 & 1 & 0 \\ 0 & 1 & 1 & 0 \end{bmatrix} \begin{matrix} \{a\} \\ \{d,c\} \\ \{b,a,d\} \\ \{a,d\} \end{matrix}$$

Figure 10.2: Detecting the candidate interval (CI) property by solving an instance of consecutive 1s problem.

preferences, this is not the case: VI is strictly contained in PSC. Further, for the interval-based approach, the relationship between CI and VI (direct analogues of the single-peaked and the single-crossing domains) is similar to that for linear orders: CI and VI do not contain each other and have a non-empty intersection, which strictly contains a dichotomous analogue of 1-Euclidean preferences (to be defined in the next paragraph).

The interval-based approach can also be applied to the 1-Euclidean domain. We say that a profile belongs to the *dichotomous Euclidean (DE)* domain if voters and candidates can be positioned on the real line so that for every voter i there exists a radius r_i such that all candidates within a distance r_i of i are approved by i. We can also require the radius r to be the same for all voters; the resulting domain is called the *dichotomous uniform Euclidean (DUE)* domain. Remarkably, DE turns out to coincide with CI: the order of candidates in a DE embedding witnesses that the profile belongs to CI, and for the converse direction we can place the candidates on the real line in a way that respects the CI ordering, and then pick a suitable position for each voter. In contrast, the DUE domain is much smaller; in particular, every DUE profile belongs to the VI domain (and similarly to the case of linear orders, there are profiles that are CI and VI, but not DUE).

So far in this section, we focused on one-dimensional preference domains. However, the approaches based on Euclidean distances can be easily generalized to higher dimensions. Let us say that a profile belongs to the d-DE domain for $d \in \mathbb{N}$ if voters and candidates can be placed in $\mathbb{R}^d$ so that for every voter i, there exists a radius r_i such that i approves exactly the candidates in the r_i-ball around i; the d-DUE domain is defined similarly, with the additional restriction that $r_i = 1$ for each voter i.

Recognition Algorithms

Elkind and Lackner (2015) show that almost all one-dimensional restricted domains defined earlier in this section can be recognized in polynomial time; the only exception is PSC, for which the complexity is open. All the polynomial-time algorithms except for the one for DUE are based on reductions to the *consecutive 1s problem*, defined in Section 10.2.

To illustrate the proof technique, we will now show how to reduce the problem of deciding if a given dichotomous profile belongs to the CI domain to an instance of the consecutive 1s problem; our reduction is illustrated in Figure 10.2. Given a dichotomous profile, we construct a binary matrix that contains a row for each voter and a column for each candidate; the entry associated with voter v and candidate c is set to 1 if v approves c and to 0 otherwise. By construction, a permutation of the columns that results in 1s appearing consecutively in each row corresponds to a permutation of candidates witnessing that the input profile belongs to the CI domain. Similar reductions work for VI, CEI, and VEI. For DUE, there is a reduction to recognizing bipartite permutation graphs.

Peters (2017) shows that detecting whether a given profile belongs to d-DE or to d-DUE is NP-hard for $d \geqslant 2$; more precisely, he shows that these problems are $\exists \mathbb{R}$-complete. In this respect, dichotomous orders behave like linear orders.

Algorithms for Approval-Based Multiwinner Rules

Let us now turn to applications of the preference restrictions considered in this section. We consider two multiwinner voting rules that are defined for dichotomous preferences (see Chapter 2 of this book for a more general discussion of multiwinner rules), namely Maximin Approval Voting (MAV) and Proportional Approval Voting (PAV). For both of these rules computing a winning committee is NP-hard (LeGrand et al., 2007; Skowron et al., 2016; Aziz et al., 2015). Hence, it is natural to ask whether focusing on restricted domains, such as CI, VI, CEI, VEI, etc. allows for faster algorithms.

We will first define the MAV rule. Let A_i denote the set of candidates approved by voter i. Given a target committee size k, MAV returns a set of candidates W, $|W| = k$, that minimizes $\max_{i \in N} |W \setminus A_i| + |A_i \setminus W|$, i.e., the maximum Hamming distance between a voter's preferences and the committee (both viewed as 0/1 strings). Liu and Guo (2016) prove that a winning committee under MAV can be computed in polynomial time for preference profiles that belong to CI or VI. This is achieved by dynamic programming algorithms that exploit the structure of the respective preferences. As a consequence, winner determination is also easy for DUE, VEI, and CEI preferences (cf. Figure 10.1).

PAV is a less egalitarian, but more proportional rule than MAV. It returns a set of candidates W, $|W| = k$, that maximizes $\sum_{i \in N} h(|A_i \cap W|)$, where $h(1) = 1$, $h(2) = 1 + \frac{1}{2}$, $h(3) = 1 + \frac{1}{2} + \frac{1}{3}$, etc. Elkind and Lackner (2015) showed that for preference profiles that belong to CEI or VEI, a winning committee under PAV can be computed in polynomial time via dynamic programming. Recently, Peters (2016) extended this result to the CI domain, using a very different approach: he shows that this problem reduces to solving an integer linear program with a totally unimodular constraint matrix. Whether a polynomial-time algorithm is also possible for the VI domain is an open problem.

10.5 Nearly Structured Preferences

While definitions in Sections 10.2 and 10.3 are mathematically appealing, we cannot expect real-world preference data to satisfy them. Indeed, for all domains we consider, the presence of a single voter with an unorthodox opinion, or a few minor errors made during the preference elicitation process, may result in a profile that does not belong to the target domain. At the same time, we do not encounter arbitrary combinations of preference orders in real-life preference data, and in many cases we expect the voters' preferences to be essentially one-dimensional. One way to formalize this intuition is to define what it means for a profile to be nearly single-peaked or nearly single-crossing, and then verify whether these definitions are satisfied by the available preference data. A related question is whether tractability results for structured domains can be extended to nearly structured domains.

Defining Nearly Structured Preferences

This research agenda was put forward by Faliszewski et al. (2014), who focused on single-peaked preferences. They proposed several measures of distance to the single-peaked domain, including, in particular, the number of voters that have to be deleted from a given profile so as to make it single-peaked. Alternatively, one can ask how many candidates need to to be removed to make a profile single-peaked; this measure was suggested by Escoffier et al. (2008). Another approach shares motivation with the definitions of the Dodgson rule and the Kemeny rule: we ask how many swaps of adjacent candidates are needed to arrive to a single-peaked profile (Erdélyi et al., 2017). An egalitarian variant of this measure, which asks what is the smallest number t such that a given profile can be made single-peaked by performing at most t candidate swaps per vote, was proposed by Faliszewski et al. (2014). We can also try to partition voters (Escoffier et al., 2008) or candidates (Erdélyi et al., 2017) into a small number of sets, so that each component forms a single-peaked profile. Yet another closeness measure is based on the idea of *decloning*. Recall that a set of candidates forms a *clone set* if each voter ranks these candidates consecutively in her vote. To make a given profile single-peaked, we can 'collapse' one or more clone sets by replacing each such set with a single candidate; the 'cost' of this operation can be measured as the overall reduction in the number of candidates (Elkind et al., 2012) or the size of the largest clone set that we collapsed (Cornaz et al., 2012). Of course, each of these approaches can also be used to measure how close a given profile is to being single-crossing, 1-Euclidean, or single-peaked on a tree.

The suitability of each of these closeness measures depends on the kind of errors we expect: for instance, the swap-based approach implicitly assumes that the preferences are fundamentally single-peaked, but small errors have been made during the elicitation process, whereas the decloning-based approach is based on the intuition that the set of available options is one-dimensional, yet some of the options are represented by several virtually indistinguishable alternatives. When several types of errors can be present, it may be useful to combine several closeness measures, e.g., to allow, say, a few candidate deletions and a small number of swaps.

Recognition of Nearly Structured Preferences

It is natural to ask if we can efficiently determine whether a given profile is nearly structured. Technically, we are interested in computing the number of modifications of a given type that are necessary to make a given profile single-peaked or single-crossing. The complexity of this task has been considered by several authors. Erdélyi et al. (2017) focus on computing the distance to the single-peaked domain, for many of the distance measures listed above. Bredereck et al. (2016) consider both the single-peaked domain and the single-crossing domain, but limit themselves to two types of modifications, namely, voter deletion and candidate deletion. The complexity of optimally decloning a given profile so as to make it single-peaked or single-crossing was investigated by Cornaz et al. (2012) and Elkind et al. (2012). Most of the results in these papers are negative: checking if a given profile is close to being single-peaked or single-crossing is typically NP-hard. However, there are several notable exceptions: it can be efficiently decided how many candidates have to be deleted to make an election single-peaked (Erdélyi et al., 2017) or how many voters need to be deleted to make an election single-crossing (Bredereck et al., 2016); also, there are several positive results for optimal decloning (Cornaz et al., 2012; Elkind et al., 2012). Moreover, Elkind and Lackner (2014) provide efficient constant-factor approximation algorithms for all computational problems considered by Bredereck et al. (2016).

Manipulation and Control with Nearly Structured Preferences

We have already seen a few examples of hard computational social choice problems that become polynomial-time solvable for single-peaked or single-crossing preferences. One may then wonder if such results extend to preferences that are nearly single-peaked or nearly single-crossing. Faliszewski et al. (2014) were the first to ask this question for coalitional manipulation and control.

An instance of the constructive coalitional manipulation problem is given by an election, a distinguished candidate p and a positive integer k; we ask if we can add k new voters (manipulators) to the election to make p an election winner. In the weighted variant of this problem (CCWM), each of the (old and new) voters is associated with an integer voting weight (encoded in binary). For $k > 1$, finding a successful manipulation is typically NP-hard (see, e.g., Conitzer and Walsh, 2016). However, if the existing voters' preferences are known to be single-peaked with respect to a given axis, and the manipulators' votes are required to be single-peaked with respect to the same axis, CCWM becomes polynomial-time solvable for several voting rules (Faliszewski et al., 2011). This is viewed as a negative result, since NP-hardness results for manipulation are often interpreted as 'barriers' to strategic behavior; thus, for single-peaked preferences these barriers may disappear. However, as argued above, while real-life preferences may be close to single-peaked, they are unlikely to be single-peaked; does this mean that we can expect manipulation to be NP-hard in practical scenarios?

Faliszewski et al. (2014) show that easiness results for CCWM with single-peaked preferences can be fragile. For instance, they identify a class of 3-candidate scoring rules for which CCWM has been shown to be NP-hard for general profiles and polynomial-time solvable for single-peaked profiles (Faliszewski et al., 2011), and show that it remains NP-hard for profiles that can be made single-peaked by deleting a single voter. They obtain a similar result for profiles that can be made single-peaked by swapping at most one pair of alternatives in each vote; the hardness proof is based on the observation that any preference order over three candidates can be made single-peaked with respect to a given axis by a single swap. Further results of this type have been obtained by Erdélyi et al. (2015) for other measures of closeness to the single-peaked domain. However, Erdélyi et al. (2015) also present an easiness result: for k-approval with m candidates, CCWM is polynomial-time solvable for profiles that can be made single-peaked by deleting ℓ voters as long as $\ell < \frac{2k-m}{m-k}$. CCWM for nearly single-peaked profiles is also considered by Menon and Larson (2016), who are interested in the complexity of this problem when voters are allowed to submit partial orders of a certain form, namely *top-truncated ballots*.

Another type of strategic behavior considered by Faliszewski et al. (2014) is (constructive) control: here, the goal is to make a certain candidate an election winner by adding or deleting a given number of voters or candidates; the difference between control by adding voters and coalitional manipulation is that in the former problem the voters to be added have to be selected from a given pool of voters. Faliszewski et al. (2014) investigate the complexity of these forms of control for several voting rules, including Plurality and t-approval; they identify several scenarios where a control problem is hard for general preferences, but can be solved in polynomial time for preferences that are single-peaked or can be made single-peaked by removing a constant number of voters or performing at most a constant number of candidate swaps in each vote. Yang and Guo (2014a,b, 2015) continue this line of inquiry for some other measures of closeness to the single-peaked domain, and obtain several fixed parameter tractability results with respect to the number of modifications needed to make a profile single-peaked. See also the survey by Hemaspaandra et al. (2016).

10.6 Elicitation of Structured Preferences

While much of the work in (computational) social choice deals with aggregating the collective preferences into a joint decision, sometimes the goal is simply to *elicit* the voters' preferences over the alternatives. It is typically assumed that we know the number of voters n and the set of alternatives A, $|A| = m$, and have access to an oracle that, given a triple $(i, a, b) \in N \times A \times A$, outputs 1 if the ith voter prefers a to b and 0 otherwise. The goal is then either to fully determine the preference order of each voter or to obtain enough information to determine the winner(s) under a given voting rule. For unrestricted preferences, the complexity of the former task can be easily seen to be $\Theta(nm \log m)$: effectively, we have to 'sort' the m alternatives in the correct order for each of the n voters.

Perhaps unsurprisingly, this problem, too, becomes easier when voters' preferences belong to a restricted domain. In this section, we provide a brief summary of three papers on this topic: an early paper by Conitzer (2009), who considers single-peaked and 1-Euclidean preferences, and two very recent papers by Dey and Misra (2016a,b), which deal with, respectively, single-crossing preferences and preferences that are single-peaked on a tree.

We start by considering the single-peaked domain. Suppose first that the axis is known; assume without loss of generality that it is given by $a_1 \lhd a_2 \lhd \cdots \lhd a_m$.

Consider a voter i. We know that her least preferred alternative is either a_1 or a_m. Thus, by asking the oracle whether i prefers a_1 to a_m, we can determine the alternative ranked last in i's preference order. We can then continue recursively, building up i's preference order from the bottom to the top. Clearly, $m-1$ queries suffice to elicit the full preference order, so for n voters the number of queries reduces from $O(nm \log m)$ to $O(nm)$. Conitzer (2009) describes an alternative $O(m)$ elicitation algorithm. His algorithm uses binary search to identify the voter's top alternative a^*. If $a^* = a_t$ for some $t \in [m]$, we know that the voter orders the alternatives in $\{a_1, \ldots, a_{t-1}\}$ and $\{a_{t+1}, \ldots, a_m\}$ as $a_{t-1} \succ \ldots \succ a_1$ and $a_{t+1} \succ \ldots \succ a_m$, respectively, so it remains to merge these two orders; this can be accomplished in linear time.

To see that the number of queries for a single voter cannot be reduced to $o(m)$, suppose that $m = 2t - 1$ and consider the weak order $a_t \succ \{a_{t-1}, a_{t+1}\} \succ \ldots \succ \{a_1, a_m\}$. Every linear order that refines this weak order is single-peaked with respect to $a_1 \triangleleft \cdots \triangleleft a_m$. Thus, to identify a specific linear order from this set, we would have to query the oracle about each of the $\frac{m-1}{2} = \Omega(m)$ pairs $(a_{t-1}, a_{t+1}), \ldots, (a_1, a_m)$.

Now, suppose that the axis is not known. Then there is not much we can do for a single voter: saying that her preferences are single-peaked with respect to *some* axis provides no information whatsoever. However, Conitzer (2009) shows that if the number of voters is large, the number of queries can be essentially as low as in the case where the axis is known. His algorithm elicits the ranking of a single voter (using the trivial $O(m \log m)$ algorithm) and then uses it as a guiding order to elicit the preferences of the remaining voters; each additional ranking can be elicited in $O(m)$ queries given the first ranking. The overall number of queries is then $O(m \log m + nm)$.

For the 1-Euclidean domain, knowing the positions of the alternatives on the axis provides an impressive reduction in the number of queries: Conitzer (2009) demonstrates that eliciting a single voter's preferences only requires $2\lceil \log m \rceil$ queries. To see why this is the case, suppose that alternative a_j appears in position x_j on the axis, with $x_1 < \cdots < x_m$. Then voter i prefers a_j to a_ℓ, $j < \ell$, if and only if she is positioned to the left of $\frac{x_j + x_\ell}{2}$. Thus, to determine a voter's ranking, it suffices to determine her position with respect to each of the $\binom{m}{2}$ points of the form $\frac{x_j + x_\ell}{2}$, $j, \ell \in [m]$, $j < \ell$. These points divide the axis into $\binom{m}{2} + 1$ intervals, with voters in each interval having the same preference order. The appropriate interval for each voter can be identified by asking $\lceil \log \binom{m}{2} + 1 \rceil \le 2\lceil \log m \rceil$ queries using binary search. However, Conitzer (2009) shows that if the embedding of the alternatives into the line is not known, then it is not possible to do better than in the single-peaked case.

For single-crossing preferences, the relevant additional information is the single-crossing order of the voters. Dey and Misra (2016a) observe that when this order is known and we can query the voters in any order, all we need to do is to elicit the preferences of the first voter and then find a 'crossing point' for each pair of alternatives (i.e., if the first voter ranks a above b, we need to find the first voter in the single-crossing order who ranks b above a). Indeed, before the crossing point, all voters agree on that pair of alternatives with the first voter, and from that point on they disagree with her on that pair. The first voter's ranking can be elicited using $O(m \log m)$ queries, and the crossing point for each of the $\binom{m}{2}$ pairs can be found using binary search over N. Altogether, we need $O(m^2 \log n)$ queries; while this bound is incomparable with the $O(nm \log m)$ bound for general preferences, it provides a significant improvement for the setting where the number of voters is much larger than the number of alternatives.

The analysis above assumes that one has full control over the order of queries. However, it may be the case that the voters arrive one by one (in the single-crossing order or in an arbitrary order) and one has to elicit a voter's preferences when she arrives (i.e., by the time we start querying voter i, we must have elicited the full rankings of all voters who arrived before i). For the sequential model, Dey and Misra (2016a) propose an algorithm that 'expects' the preference order being elicited to be similar to the nearest ranking among the ones elicited so far. If this is indeed the case, the current order can be elicited quickly, as the number of disagreements with the neighboring order will be small. Each disagreement contributes to the elicitation cost, but the total number of disagreements can be bounded by above for any single-crossing profile. The resulting algorithm asks $O(nm + m^2)$ queries if the voters arrive in the single-crossing order and $O(nm + m^2 \log n)$ queries if the arrival order can be arbitrary.

If the single-crossing order is not known, one can use the fact that the number of distinct preference orders in a given single-crossing profile is bounded by $\binom{m}{2}+1$ (Bredereck et al., 2013). Thus, throughout the elicitation process, there may be at most $\binom{m}{2} + 1$ voters whose preference orders are different from all rankings elicited so far (and are therefore costly to elicit), and in all other cases we can quickly find a 'match' among the already elicited rankings. This approach leads to an algorithm that makes $O(nm + m^3 \log m)$ queries. Dey and Misra (2016a) also provide lower bounds for each of their models; for most (though not all) models these bounds are tight when $n = \Omega(m^3 \log m)$.

We now consider the case when voters' preferences are single-peaked on a tree. If there are no additional constraints on the structure of the tree, we cannot expect to have an asymptotic improvement over the general case, even if the tree and the assignment of the alternatives to the vertices of that tree are known. Indeed, observe that all $(m-1)!$ rankings that place some alternative $a \in A$ first are single-peaked on a star with a in the center, so it may take $\log((m-1)!) = O(m \log m)$ queries to identify a specific ranking in this set. However, Dey and Misra (2016b) show that one can obtain improved bounds when the tree is, in some sense, close to a path. Specifically, for trees that can be covered with k paths, they bound the number of queries by $O(nm \log k)$; in particular, this implies an upper bound of $O(nm \log \ell)$ for trees with ℓ leaves. The algorithm proceeds by eliciting each voter's preferences along each path in the cover, and then merging the results using the standard k-way merging algorithm. A similar argument shows that if a tree can be turned into a path by removing d vertices, the query complexity can be bounded by $O(nm + nd \log d)$. However, Dey and Misra (2016b) show that we still need $\Omega(nm \log m)$ queries if the tree has bounded degree (in fact, the lower bound holds even if the degree of each vertex is at most 3). Moreover, our analysis for the star shows that the same lower bound applies if the tree in question has bounded pathwidth or bounded diameter.

10.7 Further Directions and Trends

At the end of this chapter we would like to highlight a few research directions that we consider promising. First, most of this chapter has focused on domain restrictions that are in some sense one-dimensional: single-peaked, single-crossing and 1-Euclidean preferences are all defined by a linear order or a an embedding into the real line. Multidimensional analogues of these notions have received much less attention in the computational social choice literature. In particular, little is known about computational benefits of such higher-dimensional restrictions. For example, it is not known whether the Kemeny rule is computable in polynomial time on two-dimensional single-peaked profiles (for definitions, see Sui et al., 2013). Other natural higher-dimensional restricted domains arise from 1-Euclidean preferences—their definition can easily be extended to more dimensions. More dimensions also make the choice of metric interesting: apart from the Euclidean ℓ_2-metric, the ℓ_1- or ℓ_∞-metrics are sensible choices as well (Peters, 2017). Even if NP-hard voting problems remain hard for these domains, it might be that better approximation algorithms can be found than for general preferences. Multidimensional domain restrictions offer many challenging research questions, but faster algorithms for these classes are very desirable: these algorithms would be applicable to a much larger class of preferences than algorithms for one-dimensional restrictions.

We have presented a number of results for one-dimensional dichotomous preference domains. More broadly, one can consider trichotomous or even k-chotomous preferences (see, e.g., Ju, 2005; Zwicker, 2016). An example for trichotomous preferences would be the distinction between satisfying, acceptable, and unsatisfying candidates, thus allowing for the indication of compromise outcomes. Notions of structure specifically for k-chotomous preferences have not yet been studied, but some of the concepts discussed in this chapter can easily be adapted to this setting.

Another direction is to consider completely new domain restrictions. Domains suggested in the social choice literature usually guarantee the existence of a Condorcet winner, but this is not a necessarily relevant property for algorithmic purposes. Inspiration could be found by adapting structural concepts from graph theory, such as restrictions resembling treewidth. For a systematic study of domain restrictions, the framework of *forbidden subprofiles* (Ballester and Haeringer, 2011; Bredereck et al., 2013) could prove to be valuable. Preference profiles (sets of linear orders) are mathematically rich structures and there is hope for a similarly diverse and powerful classification of structure as exists for graph classes—along with algorithmic applications of these structural restrictions.

Finally, the work on structured preferences has mostly focused on voting-related topics: winner determination, manipulation, control, etc. Given the advances that have been made in these fields, it could prove to be worthwhile to investigate the impact of structured preferences in other fields of social choice; fair division and judgment aggregation are natural candidates.

Acknowledgments

This work was supported by ERC Starting Grant ACCORD (GA 639945). A shorter version of this survey, with a slightly different focus, is Elkind et al. (2016).

Bibliography

K. J. Arrow. A difficulty in the concept of social welfare. *The Journal of Political Economy*, 58(4):328–346, 1950.

K. J. Arrow. *Social Choice and Individual Values*. John Wiley and Sons, 1951.

H. Aziz, S. Gaspers, J. Gudmundsson, S. Mackenzie, N. Mattei, and T. Walsh. Computational aspects of multi-winner approval voting. In *Proceedings of the 14th International Conference on Autonomous Agents and Multiagent Systems (AAMAS)*, pages 107–115, 2015.

M. A. Ballester and G. Haeringer. A characterization of the single-peaked domain. *Social Choice and Welfare*, 36(2):305–322, 2011.

J. Bartholdi III and M. A. Trick. Stable matching with preferences derived from a psychological model. *Operation Research Letters*, 5(4):165–169, 1986.

N. Betzler, A. Slinko, and J. Uhlmann. On the computation of fully proportional representation. *Journal of Artificial Intelligence Research*, 47(1):475–519, 2013.

D. Black. On the rationale of group decision-making. *The Journal of Political Economy*, 56(1):23–34, 1948.

K. S. Booth and G. S. Lueker. Testing for the consecutive ones property, interval graphs, and graph planarity using PQ-tree algorithms. *Journal of Computer and System Sciences*, 13(3):335–379, 1976.

S. Brams and P. C. Fishburn. *Approval voting*. Springer, 2007.

F. Brandt, M. Brill, E. Hemaspaandra, and L. A. Hemaspaandra. Bypassing combinatorial protections: Polynomial-time algorithms for single-peaked electorates. *Journal of Artificial Intelligence Research*, 53:439–496, 2015.

R. Bredereck, J. Chen, and G. J. Woeginger. A characterization of the single-crossing domain. *Social Choice and Welfare*, 41(4):989–998, 2013.

R. Bredereck, J. Chen, and G. J. Woeginger. Are there any nicely structured preference profiles nearby? *Mathematical Social Sciences*, 79:61–73, 2016.

B. Chamberlin and P. Courant. Representative deliberations and representative decisions: Proportional representation and the Borda rule. *American Political Science Review*, 77(3):718–733, 1983.

V. Conitzer. Eliciting single-peaked preferences using comparison queries. *Journal of Artificial Intelligence Research*, 35(1):161–191, 2009.

V. Conitzer and T. Walsh. Barriers to manipulation in voting. In F. Brandt, V. Conitzer, U. Endriss, J. Lang, and A. D. Procaccia, editors, *Handbook of Computational Social Choice*. Cambridge University Press, 2016.

C. H. Coombs. Psychological scaling without a unit of measurement. *Psychological review*, 57(3):145, 1950.

D. Cornaz, L. Galand, and O. Spanjaard. Bounded single-peaked width and proportional representation. In *Proceedings of the 20th European Conference on Artificial Intelligence (ECAI)*, pages 270–275, 2012.

G. Demange. Single-peaked orders on a tree. *Mathematical Social Sciences*, 3(4):389–396, 1982.

P. Dey and N. Misra. Preference elicitation for single crossing domain. In *Proceedings of the 25th International Joint Conference on Artificial Intelligence (IJCAI)*, pages 222–228, 2016a.

P. Dey and N. Misra. Elicitation for preferences single peaked on trees. In *Proceedings of the 25th International Joint Conference on Artificial Intelligence (IJCAI)*, pages 215–221, 2016b.

F. Dietrich and C. List. Majority voting on restricted domains. *Journal of Economic Theory*, 145(2):512–543, 2010.

J.-P. Doignon and J.-C. Falmagne. A polynomial time algorithm for unidimensional unfolding representations. *Journal of Algorithms*, 16(2):218–233, 1994.

E. Elkind and P. Faliszewski. Recognizing 1-Euclidean preferences: An alternative approach. In *Proceedings of the 7th International Symposium on Algorithmic Game Theory (SAGT)*, pages 146–157. Springer, 2014.

E. Elkind and A. Ismaili. OWA-based extensions of the Chamberlin–Courant rule. In *Proceedings of the 4th International Conference on Algorithmic Decision Theory (ADT)*, pages 486–502. Springer, 2015.

E. Elkind and M. Lackner. On detecting nearly structured preference profiles. In *Proceedings of the 28th AAAI Conference on Artificial Intelligence (AAAI)*, pages 661–667, 2014.

E. Elkind and M. Lackner. Structure in dichotomous preferences. In *Proceedings of the 24th International Joint Conference on Artificial Intelligence (IJCAI)*, pages 2019–2025, 2015.

E. Elkind, P. Faliszewski, and A. Slinko. Clone structures in voters' preferences. In *Proceedings of the 13th ACM Conference on Electronic Commerce (EC)*, pages 496–513. ACM, 2012.

E. Elkind, P. Faliszewski, and P. Skowron. A characterization of the single-peaked single-crossing domain. In *Proceedings of the 28th AAAI Conference on Artificial Intelligence (AAAI)*, pages 654–660, 2014.

E. Elkind, P. Faliszewski, M. Lackner, and S. Obraztsova. The complexity of recognizing incomplete single-crossing preferences. In *Proceedings of the 29th AAAI Conference on Artificial Intelligence (AAAI)*, pages 865–871, 2015.

E. Elkind, M. Lackner, and D. Peters. Preference restrictions in computational social choice: Recent progress. In *Proceedings of the 25th International Joint Conference on Artificial Intelligence (IJCAI)*, pages 4062–4065, 2016.

G. Erdélyi, M. Lackner, and A. Pfandler. Manipulation of k-approval in nearly single-peaked electorates. In *Proceedings of the 4th International Conference on Algorithmic Decision Theory (ADT)*, pages 71–85. Springer, 2015.

G. Erdélyi, M. Lackner, and A. Pfandler. Computational aspects of nearly single-peaked electorates. *Journal of Artificial Intelligence Research*, 58:297–337, 2017.

B. Escoffier, J. Lang, and M. Öztürk. Single-peaked consistency and its complexity. In *Proceedings of the 18th European Conference on Artificial Intelligence (ECAI)*, pages 366–370, 2008.

P. Faliszewski, E. Hemaspaandra, L. A. Hemaspaandra, and J. Rothe. The shield that never was: Societies with single-peaked preferences are more open to manipulation and control. *Information and Computation*, 209(2):89–107, 2011.

P. Faliszewski, E. Hemaspaandra, and L. Hemaspaandra. The complexity of manipulative attacks in nearly single-peaked electorates. *Artificial Intelligence*, 207:69–99, 2014.

A. Gibbard. Manipulation of voting schemes: A general result. *Econometrica: Journal of the Econometric Society*, 41(4):587–601, 1973.

G. Gottlob and G. Greco. Decomposing combinatorial auctions and set packing problems. *Journal of the ACM*, 60(4):24, 2013.

E. Hemaspaandra, L. A. Hemaspaandra, and J. Rothe. The complexity of manipulative actions in single-peaked societies. In J. Rothe, editor, *Economics and Computation*, pages 327–360. Springer, 2016.

B.-G. Ju. An efficiency characterization of plurality social choice on simple preference domains. *Economic Theory*, 26(1):115–128, 2005.

K. H. Kim and F. W. Roush. Special domains and nonmanipulability. *Mathematical Social Sciences*, 1(1):85–92, 1980.

V. Knoblauch. Recognizing one-dimensional Euclidean preference profiles. *Journal of Mathematical Economics*, 46(1):1–5, 2010.

M. Lackner. Incomplete preferences in single-peaked electorates. In *Proceedings of the 28th AAAI Conference on Artificial Intelligence (AAAI)*, pages 742–748, 2014.

M.-L. Lackner and M. Lackner. On the likelihood of single-peaked preferences. *Social Choice and Welfare*, 48(4):717–745, 2017.

J.-F. Laslier and M. R. Sanver. *Handbook on Approval Voting*. Springer, 2010.

R. LeGrand, E. Markakis, and A. Mehta. Some results on approximating the minimax solution in approval voting. In *Proceedings of the 6th International Conference on Autonomous Agents and Multiagent Systems (AAMAS)*, pages 1185–1187, 2007.

C. List. A possibility theorem on aggregation over multiple interconnected propositions. *Mathematical Social Sciences*, 45(1):1–13, 2003.

H. Liu and J. Guo. Parameterized complexity of winner determination in minimax committee elections. In *Proceedings of the 15th International Conference on Autonomous Agents and Multiagent Systems (AAMAS)*, pages 341–349, 2016.

V. Menon and K. Larson. Reinstating combinatorial protections for manipulation and bribery in single-peaked and nearly single-peaked electorates. In *Proceedings of the 30th AAAI Conference on Artificial Intelligence (AAAI)*, pages 565–571, 2016.

H. Moulin. *Axioms of Cooperative Decision Making*. Cambridge University Press, 1991.

K. Nehring and C. Puppe. The structure of strategy-proof social choice—part I: General characterization and possibility results on median spaces. *Journal of Economic Theory*, 135(1):269–305, 2007.

D. Peters. Single-peakedness and total unimodularity: Efficiently solve voting problems without even trying. *arXiv preprint arXiv:1609.03537*, 2016.

D. Peters. Recognising multidimensional Euclidean preferences. In *Proceedings of the 31st AAAI Conference on Artificial Intelligence (AAAI)*, pages 642–648, 2017.

D. Peters and E. Elkind. Preferences single-peaked on nice trees. In *Proceedings of the 30th AAAI Conference on Artificial Intelligence (AAAI)*, pages 594–600, 2016.

D. Peters and M. Lackner. Preferences single-peaked on a circle. In *Proceedings of the 31st AAAI Conference on Artificial Intelligence (AAAI)*, pages 649–655, 2017.

P. Rothstein. Representative voter theorems. *Public Choice*, 72(2-3):193–212, 1991.

M. A. Satterthwaite. Strategy-proofness and Arrow's conditions: Existence and correspondence theorems for voting procedures and social welfare functions. *Journal of Economic Theory*, 10(2):187–217, 1975.

P. Skowron, L. Yu, P. Faliszewski, and E. Elkind. The complexity of fully proportional representation for single-crossing electorates. *Theoretical Computer Science*, 569:43–57, 2015.

P. Skowron, P. Faliszewski, and J. Lang. Finding a collective set of items: From proportional multirepresentation to group recommendation. *Artificial Intelligence*, 241:191–216, 2016.

X. Sui, A. Francois-Nienaber, and C. Boutilier. Multi-dimensional single-peaked consistency and its approximations. In *Proceedings of the 23rd International Joint Conference on Artificial Intelligence (IJCAI)*, pages 375–382, 2013.

M. A. Trick. Recognizing single-peaked preferences on a tree. *Mathematical Social Sciences*, 17(3):329–334, 1989.

T. Walsh. Uncertainty in preference elicitation and aggregation. In *Proceedings of the 22nd National Conference on Artificial Intelligence (AAAI)*, pages 3–8, 2007.

Y. Yang and J. Guo. The control complexity of r-approval: from the single-peaked case to the general case. In *Proceedings of the 13th International Conference on Autonomous Agents and Multiagent Systems (AAMAS)*, pages 621–628, 2014a.

Y. Yang and J. Guo. Controlling elections with bounded single-peaked width. In *Proceedings of the 13th International Conference on Autonomous Agents and Multiagent Systems (AAMAS)*, pages 629–636, 2014b.

Y. Yang and J. Guo. How hard is control in multi-peaked elections: A parameterized study. In *Proceedings of the 14th International Conference on Autonomous Agents and Multiagent Systems (AAMAS)*, pages 1729–1730, 2015.

L. Yu, H. Chan, and E. Elkind. Multiwinner elections under preferences that are single-peaked on a tree. In *Proceedings of the 23rd International Joint Conference on Artificial Intelligence (IJCAI)*, pages 425–431, 2013.

W. S. Zwicker. Cycles and intractability in social choice theory. In *Proceedings of the 6th International Workshop on Computational Social Choice (COMSOC)*, 2016.

CHAPTER 11

Having a Hard Time? Explore Parameterized Complexity!

Britta Dorn and Ildikó Schlotter

11.1 Motivation

More often than not, life teems with difficult problems. This is not less true if you happen to be a researcher in computational social choice; however, in this case you can spend considerable time focusing only on *computational* hardness.

Collective decision making has been studied from various aspects. Political science, economics, mathematics, logic, and philosophy have all contributed to the area of social choice. With the advance of computer science, computational issues have become more and more important. Taking a casual look at the landscape of computational problems in social choice, we find an abundance of hard problems. Within the theory of voting, already winner determination is NP-hard for several voting rules like Dodgson, Young, or Kemeny voting. Considering certain forms of manipulation, control, or bribery in elections, or dealing with partial information results in computationally hard problems as well. We can find examples in every area of social choice, let it be judgment aggregation, fair division of goods, or matching under preferences.

Computational complexity: the classical approach. When considering the computational tractability of a given problem, we focus on the time and space necessary for an algorithm to solve it. In most cases, however, space is not the scarcest resource, and therefore whether an algorithm is considered tractable or not depends on its running time. Of course, running times depend on the actual input, and to overcome this rather cumbersome difficulty, classical complexity theory teaches us to view the running time of an algorithm as a function of the *length* of its input. More precisely, the running time $T(n)$ of a given algorithm $\mathcal{A}$ is defined as the maximum number of computational steps performed by $\mathcal{A}$ on any input of length n. Using this notion, a broadly accepted rule of thumb is to consider $\mathcal{A}$ (and the problem solved by $\mathcal{A}$) tractable if $T(n)$ is a *polynomial* of n.

To grasp the notion of *computational intractability*, classical complexity theory offers a hierarchy of complexity classes, but here we only focus on the central concept of NP-hardness. Instead of repeating the formal definition here, we only would like to recall its most vital property. Namely, there is strong evidence indicating that NP-hard problems are *not* solvable in polynomial time. From a practical point of view, this means that we cannot expect to find an algorithm solving an NP-hard problem that runs in reasonable time for large inputs.

Over the years, researchers facing NP-hard problems have come up with numerous strategies to deal with intractability. Sometimes focusing on easy special cases can be enough. In many areas, approximation algorithms turned out to be extremely useful. Randomization and parallel computing might also help us reduce the running time, especially when combined with other approaches. Lately, ever-growing computational capacities have made exponential-time (exact) algorithms a viable choice in some cases. And when theory does not seem to offer any help, heuristics still play an important role.

All of these strategies might be useful in computational social choice too. However, there is one crucial aspect shared by these approaches which dooms them inefficient in a certain way: they are all *one-dimensional* in the sense that they regard the running time merely as a function of the input length. In reality, there are several properties of the input, explicit or implicit, that heavily influence the complexity of the problem, and to neglect these is a deep source of inefficiency.

Parameterized complexity. So far the only well-developed framework that uses a multidimensional approach to deal with computationally hard problems is *parameterized complexity*. This approach, developed first by Downey and Fellows (1999), considers the complexity of a given problem with respect to several so-called *parameters*, and views the running time of a given algorithm as the function of both the input length and the parameters. This simple idea allows us to draw a much more detailed map of the complexity of a problem.

Each instance of a parameterized problem P is a pair $(\mathcal{I}, k)$ consisting of an input $\mathcal{I}$ and a parameter k, which is usually an integer (we will explain later how to handle multiple parameters within this framework). Since we are mostly dealing with NP-hard problems, we cannot expect a polynomial-time algorithm for P. Instead, what we are interested in is whether the exponential explosion in the running time can be, in a sense, attributed to the parameter. More precisely, we ask if P admits an algorithm that, on an instance $(\mathcal{I}, k)$ runs in time

$$f(k) \cdot |\mathcal{I}|^{O(1)}$$

for some computable function f. Such an algorithm is called *fixed-parameter tractable* (FPT), and the class of parameterized problems solvable by an FPT algorithm is denoted FPT. Usually, the function f is exponential (or worse), but observe that the dependency of the running time on the input length $|\mathcal{I}|$ is a polynomial of constant degree. Hence the essential property of an FPT algorithm: it works fast whenever the parameter value k is a small integer. Intuitively, this indicates that the source of the computational hardness of P is the parameter: if k is small, our instance is tractable, but as k grows, it quickly becomes intractable.

This approach has great potential from a practical perspective: if some parameter is likely to be small in typical real-world instances, then an FPT algorithm can be highly efficient in practice. We can examine the computational complexity of our problem from many different aspects by choosing different parameters and searching for FPT algorithms with each parameterization—we hence exploit the structure of the problem that is given in the input.

Why use parameterized complexity in social choice? Apart from the general advantages of the parameterized framework, there are two additional reasons why it might be particularly helpful in the field of computational social choice.

First, a typical problem in collective decision making contains a handful of natural parameters that, in certain realistic scenarios, are likely to have small values. The most obvious examples are the number of agents or alternatives present, but for a typical problem we can easily detect several natural possibilities for parameterization that may lead to efficient FPT algorithms. This phenomenon can be explained by the fact that most problems in social choice model some real-world situation, and such models tend to have a composite nature, involving various entities and relations between them. Examples include the amount of variety in a voting profile, the budget in a bribery scenario, or the 'distance' from an instance with a certain desirable property, such as single-peakedness for voting profiles, stability for a matching, or envy-freeness of an allocation.

Second, certain problems in the area of social choice have the curious property that their computational hardness might be, in fact, desirable. Such situations often arise when the computational problem models actions of a malicious agent; to name some examples, we can think about bribery, manipulation, or control of some decision making process. For such a problem, computational hardness means that the given process (e.g., a voting rule) is *safe* in the sense that a malicious agent necessarily faces a computationally intractable situation.

Note, however, that simple NP-hardness might not prevent malicious acts in reality: as we have argued earlier, even NP-hard problems might admit efficient algorithms that are applicable in practice. Thus, in such cases a more detailed complexity analysis can become crucial—and this is exactly what we can accomplish by studying our problem from the parameterized aspect. Using the intractability theory of the parameterized framework (see Section 11.3), we can provide evidence that certain problems are not fixed-parameter tractable.

Parameterized complexity can hence contribute to a better evaluation of the hardness of the problem in two ways: on the one hand, fixed-parameter tractability with respect to a parameter shows that NP-hardness might only constitute a theoretical barrier, in particular in applications where the value of this parameter is small. On the other hand, parameterized complexity theory may help to justify the shield provided by computational complexity: if a problem belongs to one of the parameterized hardness classes with respect to a parameter k, it is unlikely that an efficient algorithm can be found to solve it, even for small values of k.

Relation to existing literature and goal of this chapter. In the last decade, parameterized complexity has been applied with great success to many problems in computational social choice. We refer to several surveys overviewing this process, starting with the work by Lindner and Rothe (2008), followed by the work of Betzler et al. (2012) on voting problems, the article by Bredereck et al. (2014) presenting challenges in parameterized algorithmics for computational social choice, and the recent article by Faliszewski and Niedermeier (2015). The goal of this chapter is not to add another survey of current results, trends and challenges, but to provide a comprehensive introduction for anyone interested to get into to this attractive area of research, tailored to applicability in computational social choice, and illustrated with helpful examples.

The classical reference on parameterized complexity is the book by Downey and Fellows (1999), see also the new edition (Downey and Fellows, 2013). The emphasis in the book by Flum and Grohe (2006) is on complexity, and in the book by Niedermeier (2006) on algorithmic techniques. For the most recent advances in parameterized algorithmic techniques, we refer to the book by Cygan et al. (2015).

Organization. We will first present in Section 11.2 some of the basic algorithmic techniques for obtaining fixed-parameter tractability results, such as bounded search trees, data reduction and problem kernels, integer linear programming, and color-coding. We will also explain how to handle multiple parameters. We then turn to parameterized intractability in Section 11.3 where we deal with FPT reductions and the most common parameterized complexity classes. Some more advanced techniques like lower bounds for kernelization and the relation between approximation and parameterized algorithms are presented in Section 11.4. We finish with our conclusions in Section 11.5.

11.2 Basic Algorithmic Techniques

To illustrate some basic techniques for designing FPT algorithms, we will use the classical VERTEX COVER problem. Given a graph G, a *vertex cover* is a set S of vertices in G such that each edge of G has at least one endpoint in S.

> VERTEX COVER:
> Input: An undirected graph G, and an integer k.
> Question: Does G contain a vertex cover of size at most k?

Although this problem itself is not about collective decision making, we believe that its importance as a graph problem renders VERTEX COVER essential also to the researchers of this area. VERTEX COVER is a graph problem belonging to the 21 problems proved to be NP-complete by Karp in his seminal paper (Karp, 1972). Thus, we obviously cannot hope to solve this problem by a polynomial-time algorithm. Given the central role of VERTEX COVER in graph theory, several researchers have attempted to design algorithms for it that would perform well in practical situations. In recent decades, VERTEX COVER became one of the most prominent problems in parameterized complexity, showing how successfully this framework can be applied in practice.

Brute force approach. Let (G, k) be an instance of VERTEX COVER with G having n vertices. The most simple, brute force approach is the following: try every possible set S of at most k vertices, and check if S is indeed a vertex cover. Since this latter condition for a given set S can be checked in $O(|E(G)|)$ time, the whole process can be performed in $\binom{n}{k}O(|E(G)|)$ time.[1]

Clearly, we can assume that G is a simple graph, and we may also assume $|E(G)| \leq k(n-1) = O(nk)$: since k vertices can *cover* (i.e., be adjacent to) at most $k(n-1)$ edges, $|E(G)| > k(n-1)$ would immediately prove (G,k) to be a 'no'-instance. Using this, the brute force algorithm described above has running time $\binom{n}{k}O(nk) = O(kn^{k+1})$, which becomes intractable already for relatively small graphs: it cannot even deal with an instance where $n = 100$ and $k = 10$.

In what follows, we shall see some basic techniques in parameterized complexity that can be used to design much more efficient algorithms. Currently the fastest algorithm for VERTEX COVER, developed by Chen et al. (2010), runs in time $O(1.2738^k + kn)$. This renders VERTEX COVER solvable even for instances as large as $n = 10^6$ and $k = 40$.

11.2.1 Bounded Search Tree

Let us start with a simple observation that allows us to create a more efficient algorithm for VERTEX COVER: if S is a vertex cover for G, then for any edge e of G, at least one of its endpoints must belong to S. The basic idea is to *'guess'* which endpoint of e belongs to S. Of course, 'guessing' means that we have to check both possible outcomes of such a guess, which can be thought of as creating a *branching* in our algorithm. The key to the efficiency of such an approach is the following: if S contains at most k vertices, then we need to perform at most k such guesses, resulting in at most 2^k possibilities in total.

Before elaborating these ideas in a more general form, let us discuss in detail how this approach works for VERTEX COVER.

Example: Bounded Search Tree for VERTEX COVER

Let us be given an instance (G, k) of VERTEX COVER. Our algorithm starts with an empty set S, and adds vertices to S one by one to create a vertex cover. The general step is to pick an edge $e = \{u, v\} \in E(G)$ that is not yet covered by S, and guess which endpoint of e should be put into S. In other words, the algorithm performs a branching into two directions, adding u to S in the one branch, and adding v to S in the other. Then the algorithm proceeds recursively in both branches, decreasing the parameter k to $k-1$ in both branches. The algorithm stops if either all edges are covered by S in which case it outputs S as a solution, or if the parameter reaches 0 in which case it stops without producing a solution. If no solution is found in any of the branches, then the algorithm returns 'no'.

Let VC-BST(G, k, S) denote a call for the above algorithm with input graph G, parameter k and a set $S \subseteq V(G)$ which is the partial solution found so far; see Algorithm 1 for a more formal description.

---

[1] Here and later on, we will rely on the standard notation in graph theory, as used for example in the book by Diestel (2005). In particular, $V(G)$ denotes the set of vertices of G, and $E(G)$ denotes the set of edges of G.

Algorithm 1 Search tree algorithm for VERTEX COVER

    procedure VC-BST(G, k, S)
        if there exists an edge $\{u, v\} \in E(G)$ with $\{u, v\} \cap S = \emptyset$ **then**
            if $k > 0$ **then**
                Branch 1: VC-BST($G, k-1, S \cup \{u\}$);
                Branch 2: VC-BST($G, k-1, S \cup \{v\}$);
            else output 'no';
        else output S;

Algorithms with a recursive structure that use branchings similarly as in VC-BST are called *search tree algorithms*. A useful representation is to think of each call of the given algorithm as a node in a rooted tree T, where the children of a node are the recursive calls performed in the given call as a result of branching.

The expression *bounded search tree* refers to the fact that to obtain an efficient algorithm, we need to bound the size of T (that is, $|V(T)|$). If $F(|\mathcal{I}|, k)$ is an upper bound on the time necessary for the computations in any given node of the search tree (where $\mathcal{I}$ and k are the input and the parameter values provided for the initial call), then the running time of the whole search tree algorithm is at most $F(|\mathcal{I}|, k) \cdot |V(T)|$. Hence, if both the size of the search tree and $F(|\mathcal{I}|, k)$ are fixed-parameter tractable, then the resulting running time is also FPT. In a typical scenario, $F(|\mathcal{I}|, k)$ is simply a polynomial in $|\mathcal{I}|$, and the size of the search tree is bounded by a function of the parameter k. The bound on $|V(T)|$ is often achieved by providing a limit both on the maximum number of branches, say b, and the depth of the search tree, say d, implying $|V(T)| \leq \sum_{i=0}^{d} b^i = O(b^{d+1})$.

In our example for VERTEX COVER, the size of the search tree associated with a run of Algorithm VC-BST($G, k, \emptyset$) is at most $2^{k+1} - 1$. Since the computation in each node takes time $O(|E(G)|)$, we obtain a running time of the form $O(2^k |E(G)|)$. This shows that VERTEX COVER is FPT with respect to parameter k.

Example: Bounded Search Tree for MINIMAL APPROVAL VOTING

MINIMAX APPROVAL VOTING models a situation in voting where we aim to find a committee of pre-defined size that minimizes the maximum distance between any vote and the given committee. Formally, an *approval election* is a pair $(\mathcal{C}, \mathcal{V})$ where $\mathcal{C}$ is a set of *candidates* and $\mathcal{V}$ is a collection of *votes*. Each vote is a subset of the candidates approved by the given voter. We call a subset $C \subseteq \mathcal{C}$ a *committee*, and we define the distance of a vote v and the committee C as their symmetric difference $\text{dist}(C, v) = |C \setminus v| + |v \setminus C|$.

> MINIMAX APPROVAL VOTING:
> Input: An approval election $\mathcal{E} = (\mathcal{C}, \mathcal{V})$, integers k and d.
> Question: Does there exist a committee $C \subseteq \mathcal{C}$ with $|C| = k$ such that $\text{dist}(C, v) \leq d$ for any $v \in \mathcal{V}$?

Let us present a bounded search tree algorithm for MINIMAX APPROVAL VOTING proposed by Misra et al. (2015) that is fixed-parameter tractable with respect to the parameter d (see also Cygan et al. (2016) for a note on the running time).

The algorithm starts from an appropriate candidate committee C_0 of size k, and tries to find a fixed solution S by iteratively modifying C_0. Initially, we take any vote $v_0 \in \mathcal{V}$, and either add or delete at most d candidates from it to obtain a committee C_0 of size k (if this is not possible, then v_0 cannot be at distance at most d from *any* size-k committee, so we can output 'no'). By the triangle inequality, we get $\text{dist}(C_0, S) \leqslant \text{dist}(C_0, v_0) + \text{dist}(v_0, S) \leqslant 2d$.

The algorithm then calls a recursive procedure MAV-BST(C, δ) that keeps track of our candidate committee C and an upper bound δ on $\text{dist}(C, S)$, initially set to C_0 and $2d$, respectively; see Algorithm 2 for a description.

Algorithm 2 Search tree algorithm for MINIMAX APPROVAL VOTING

procedure MAV-BST(C, δ)
  if $\delta < 0$ **then** output 'no';
  else if $\text{dist}(C, v) > d + \delta$ for some $v \in \mathcal{V}$ **then** output 'no';
  else if $\text{dist}(C, v) \leqslant d$ for each $v \in \mathcal{V}$ **then** output C;
  else
    choose $v \in \mathcal{V}$ such that $\text{dist}(C, v) > d$;
    if $|v \setminus C| \leqslant d + 1$ **then** $P_1 \leftarrow v \setminus C$;
    else fix any $P_1 \subseteq v \setminus C$ with $|P_1| = d + 1$;
    if $|C \setminus v| \leqslant d + 1$ **then** $P_2 \leftarrow C \setminus v$;
    else fix any $P_2 \subseteq C \setminus v$ with $|P_2| = d + 1$;
    for all $c_1 \in P_1$ and $c_2 \in P_2$ **do**
      Branch (c_1, c_2): MAV-BST$(C \cup \{c_1\} \setminus \{c_2\}, \delta - 2)$;

At each step, MAV-BST first checks certain simple stopping conditions: assuming $\text{dist}(C, S) \leqslant \delta$, neither $\delta < 0$ nor $\text{dist}(C, v) > d + \delta$ for some $v \in \mathcal{V}$ can hold (the latter follows from $\text{dist}(C, v) \leqslant \text{dist}(C, S) + \text{dist}(S, v)$). So if one of these conditions holds, then the algorithm returns 'no' correctly. Otherwise, MAV-BST searches for a vote $v \in \mathcal{V}$ whose distance from C is more than d. If no such vote exists, then it outputs C as a solution; otherwise, $\text{dist}(C, v) > d$ implies that S must be 'closer' to v than C. The algorithm tries to decrease the distance of C from v by adding a candidate $c_1 \in v \setminus C$ to C and deleting a candidate $c_2 \in C \setminus v$ from C; note that this way the size of the committee remains k. In fact, by $|v \setminus S| \leqslant d$, any subset P_1 of $v \setminus C$ of size $d + 1$ must contain a candidate in S. Similarly, we can use any subset P_2 of $C \setminus v$ of size $d + 1$ instead of $C \setminus v$. Hence, for some $c_1 \in P_1$ and $c_2 \in P_2$, branch (c_1, c_2) is correct in the sense that $c_1 \in S$ and $c_2 \notin S$.

To analyze the running time of MAV-BST, let us calculate the size of the search tree. At each branching step, there are at most $(d + 1)^2$ ways to choose c_1 and c_2. Let us give an upper bound on the depth of the search tree: initially, we have $\delta \leqslant 2d$, and we decrease δ by 2 with each recursion, stopping whenever it becomes negative. Hence, the depth of the search tree is at most d, and thus contains at most $((d+1)^2)^{d+1}$ nodes. Since the computations in each node of the search tree require polynomial time, we obtain an overall running time $O^\star(d^{2d})$.[2]

---
[2] The notation $O^\star$ suppresses polynomial factors.

11.2.2 Kernelization

A great tool in parameterized algorithmics is data reduction by kernelization. One can think of it as a preprocessing procedure: The problem at hand is a hard one, but it might contain some relatively easy parts. The idea is to get rid of these in a (polynomial-time) preprocessing step and to obtain the 'really hard' core, the so-called *problem kernel*, of the problem. If the size of this kernel does not depend on the input size $|\mathcal{I}|$ of the original problem any more, but is bounded by a function depending on the parameter k only, we are done: applying any brute force algorithm on this hard kernel leads directly to an FPT running time where the combinatorial explosion only happens in k. The existence of a problem kernel whose size is bounded by a function of k hence implies for a problem to be in FPT with respect to k, and one can show that the converse holds as well.

More formally, we say that a parameterized problem admits a problem kernel with respect to parameter k, if an instance $(\mathcal{I}, k)$ can be transformed in polynomial time (measured in the input size $|\mathcal{I}|$) into an equivalent instance $(\mathcal{I}', k')$ such that $|\mathcal{I}'| + k' \leqslant g(k)$ for a computable function g only depending on k. The rules describing the transformation are then called *data reduction* rules, and the new instance $(\mathcal{I}', k')$ is called the *problem kernel*. For practical applicability, one is in particularly interested in kernels of polynomial size.

Example: Data Reduction and a $O(k^2)$ Kernel for VERTEX COVER

For the VERTEX COVER problem, one can immediately think of two easy reduction rules. Let (G, k) be our input. First, it is obvious that we can safely delete isolated vertices (i.e., vertices without incident edges) from G, as they cannot cover any edge. Second, if there is a vertex $v \in V(G)$ having more than k incident edges, then v clearly has to belong to any solution S of size k—a vertex cover *not* containing v must contain all its (more than k) neighbors, which is too much. Hence, it is safe to put any vertex of degree strictly greater than k into S, delete all its incident edges, and decrement the value of k by one. This rule is known as the *Buss rule*. If G admits a vertex cover of size k, then after applying these two rules exhaustively, we end up with a graph G' having at most k^2 edges (as the Buss rule is not applicable anymore, G' has maximum degree at most k, and hence k vertices in G' can cover at most k^2 edges) and at most $k^2 + k$ vertices (as there are no isolated vertices in G'). This yields a kernel of size $O(k^2)$ for VERTEX COVER.

Example: Polynomial Kernel for COALITIONAL MANIPULATION for Copeland

Given a voting profile consisting of the voters' preference orders over the set $\mathcal{C}$ of candidates, the COALITIONAL MANIPULATION problem asks if a set of m manipulators is able to make a given candidate win the election by casting their votes in an appropriate way. A *Copeland winner* of the election is a candidate who maximizes the number of candidates that he beats in pairwise comparisons (for simplicity, we assume that the number of voters is odd). Dey et al. (2016) show that if m is polynomial in the number $|\mathcal{C}|$ of candidates, then COALITIONAL MANIPULATION for Copeland voting admits a polynomial kernel with respect to $|\mathcal{C}|$.

They consider the weighted majority graph of the election where vertices correspond to the candidates, and for any two candidates x and y, the weight of the edge (x, y) is the number of voters who prefer x to y minus the number of voters who prefer y to x. The idea of the reduction rule is to replace large edge weights (those greater than m) by smaller ones ($m + 1$ or $m + 2$, so that the parity of the weight is preserved). This guarantees that each weight in the new majority graph is in $O(m)$, that the parities of the weights are unchanged, and that the Copeland score of each candidate remains the same after the application of the rule. Using a construction by McGarvey (1953), such a new majority graph can be realized by a voting profile of size $O(|\mathcal{C}|^2 \cdot m)$, giving us a kernel of size polynomial in $|\mathcal{C}|$.

We remark that Dey et al. (2016) show for the more general POSSIBLE WINNER problem that no kernel of size polynomial in $|\mathcal{C}|$ is likely to exist (cf. Section 11.4.1).

Example: Trivial Kernel for EEF ALLOCATION

Bliem et al. (2016) study the problem of assigning a set $\mathcal{O}$ of indivisible objects to a set N of agents in a Pareto efficient and envy-free way. An instance of EEF ALLOCATION can be described as a triple $\mathcal{I} = (N, \mathcal{O}, \succsim)$ where $\succsim$ contains a preference relation $\succsim_i$ for each agent $i \in N$. The task is to find an allocation of the objects to the agents that is envy-free and Pareto efficient. Naturally, each object must be allocated to only one agent, so any allocation $\pi: N \to 2^{\mathcal{O}}$ must satisfy $\pi(i) \cap \pi(j) = \emptyset$ for any two different agents $i, j \in N$. We say that an allocation π is *envy-free* if for any two agents i, j we have $\pi(i) \succsim_i \pi(j)$. We call π *Pareto efficient*, if there is no allocation π' such that $\pi'(i) \succsim_i \pi(i)$ for each agent i, and at least one agent is strictly better off in π' than in π (for more precise definitions, see Bliem et al. (2016)).

Assuming *monotonic additive preferences*, each agent i has a non-negative utility function $w_i: \mathcal{O} \to \mathbb{R}_0^+$ such that $Y \succsim_i X$ exactly if $\sum_{o \in X} w_i(o) \leq \sum_{o \in Y} w_i(o)$ for any two sets X, Y of objects. In such a model, we can safely assume that each agent assigns a positive utility to at least one object, and similarly, each object has positive utility for at least one agent. However, this implies that if $|N| > |\mathcal{O}|$, then no allocation can be envy-free: any agent that obtains no objects at all envies at least one other agent. This yields a trivial kernel for parameter $|\mathcal{O}|$, the number of objects: if $|N| > |\mathcal{O}|$, then we can replace the instance $\mathcal{I}$ with any small 'no'-instance; otherwise, $|N| \leq |\mathcal{O}|$ and thus the size of the whole instance $\mathcal{I}$ is bounded by a function of the parameter $|\mathcal{O}|$.

We remark that another promising approach is to consider (the weaker concept of) *partial* kernels. Roughly speaking, this means that for problems featuring several dimensions of the input (such as the number of voters and the number of candidates in a voting problem), one can also try and reduce at least one of the dimensions such that its size only depends on the parameter value. For more details, we refer to Section 3.5 of the article by Bredereck et al. (2014).

11.2.3 Integer Linear Programming

Many problems can be formulated in terms of an optimization task with a linear objective function and several constraints given by linear (in)equalities. These *linear programs* can be described in their canonical form as follows:

Linear Programming (LP):
Input: Matrix $A \in \mathbb{R}^{m,n}$, two vectors $b \in \mathbb{R}^m$, $c \in \mathbb{R}^n$.
Task: Find a vector $x \in \mathbb{R}^n$ with $x \geq 0$ that fulfills $Ax \leq b$ and, among all such vectors, maximizes the dot product $c^T x$.

The problem can equivalently be formulated in other variants, e.g., as a minimization problem, or with equalities.

LP problems are known to be solvable in polynomial time. If the variables can only take integral values, one speaks of an *ILP (Integer Linear Program)*. This makes the problem more difficult in general: the corresponding decision problem is NP-complete (Karp, 1972). However, an ILP formulation of a problem can help us obtain an FPT result: A famous theorem by Lenstra (1983) states that solving an ILP is fixed-parameter tractable if the parameter is the number of variables or the number of constraints. Lenstra's running time was later improved by Kannan (1987) and Frank and Tardos (1987), yielding that an ILP with p variables can be solved in $O(p^{2.5p+o(p)} \cdot |\mathcal{I}|)$ time, where $|\mathcal{I}|$ is the input size.

However, we shall remark that the combinatorial explosion of the running time shown by Lenstra is terrible, rendering it impractical. Lenstra's result should therefore be seen as a classification theorem in the first place. We refer to a more detailed discussion about ILP-based fixed-parameter tractability by Bredereck et al. (2014, Section 3.1).

Example: ILP for VERTEX COVER

We start by giving a negative example for VERTEX COVER. For each vertex $v \in V(G)$, we create a binary variable $x_v \in \{0,1\}$: including some vertex v in the vertex cover corresponds to setting the value of variable x_v to 1. The following ILP computes a minimum vertex cover for G:

Minimize $\sum_{v \in V(G)} x_v$
subject to $x_u + x_v \geq 1 \quad \forall \{u,v\} \in E(G);$
$x_v \in \{0,1\} \quad \forall v \in V(G).$

However, the number of variables here is $|V(G)|$, and thus depends not only on the parameter k but on the input size, so Lenstra's result is not applicable.

Example: ILP for EEF ALLOCATION

Bliem et al. (2016) encode an instance $\mathcal{I} = (\{1, \ldots, n\}, \mathcal{O}, \succsim)$ of EEF ALLOCATION as an ILP, assuming *0/1 preferences*. In such a model, the preferences of each agent $i \in \{1, \ldots, n\}$ are determined by a utility function $w_i \colon \mathcal{O} \to \{0,1\}$.

To formulate this problem as an ILP, we define the *fingerprint* of an object $o \in \mathcal{O}$ as the (binary) vector $f_o = (w_1(o), \ldots, w_n(o))$; let $F = \{f_o \mid o \in \mathcal{O}\}$ be the set of

Exploring Parameterized Complexity

all fingerprints. We can then describe any allocation by the number x_i^f of objects with fingerprint f assigned to agent i, for any $f \in F$ and $i \in \{1, \ldots, n\}$. Using the variables x_i^f, formulating envy-freeness is straightforward; to express efficiency, we need to observe that Pareto efficiency under 0/1 preferences is equivalent to assigning each object to an agent for whom it carries utility 1. Hence, an allocation is EEF if it fulfills the following constraints:

$x_i^f = 0$ for each $f \in F$ and $i \in \{1, \ldots, n\}$ with $f[i] = 0$;

$\sum_{i=1}^{n} x_i^f = |\{o \in \mathcal{O} \mid f_o = f\}|$ for each $f \in F$;

$\sum_{f \in F} x_i^f \cdot f[i] \geqslant \sum_{f \in F} x_j^f \cdot f[i]$ for each $i, j \in \{1, \ldots, n\}$ with $i \neq j$.

As each fingerprint is a binary vector of length n, we get $|F| \leqslant 2^n$. The number of variables in our ILP is therefore at most $n2^n$, implying that EEF ALLOCATION is FPT with respect to parameter n, the number of agents.

11.2.4 Color-coding

Let us discuss here an elegant technique called *color-coding*, introduced by Alon et al. (1995), originally developed to solve certain cases of SUBGRAPH ISOMORPHISM. This randomized method is helpful when introducing constraints on a solution enables us to find them more easily. Instead of giving formal definitions, let us illustrate how color-coding works through the following example.

Example: Color-coding for MINIMAL APPROVAL VOTING

Let $\mathcal{I} = (\mathcal{E}, k, d)$ be an instance of MINIMAX APPROVAL VOTING with $\mathcal{E} = (\mathcal{C}, \mathcal{V})$ (cf. the example in Section 11.2.1). We present a randomized FPT algorithm MAV-CC with parameter $|\mathcal{V}| + k$ proposed by Misra et al. (2015); see Algorithm 3. Let us assume that $\mathcal{I}$ is a 'yes'-instance, and S is a solution committee of size k.

Algorithm 3 Color-coding algorithm for MINIMAX APPROVAL VOTING

  procedure MAV-CC($\mathcal{E} = (\mathcal{C}, \mathcal{V}), d, k$)
    choose a coloring $\kappa : \mathcal{C} \to \{1, \ldots, k\}$ randomly;
    for all $v \in \mathcal{V}$ **do**
      choose a set $X_v \subseteq \{\kappa(x) \mid x \in v\}$ with $|X_v| \geqslant (|k + |v| - d)/2$ randomly;
    $S' \leftarrow \emptyset$;
    for all $c \in \{1, \ldots, k\}$ **do**
      $A_c \leftarrow \bigcap \{\text{candidates of } v \text{ with color } c \mid v \in \mathcal{V}, c \in X_v\}$;
      if $A_c \neq \emptyset$ **then** put any $a_c \in A_c$ into S';
    if $|S'| = k$ **then** output S';
    else output 'no';

First, we color our candidates with k colors randomly (independently, with a uniform distribution). Given a coloring $\kappa : \mathcal{C} \to \{1, \ldots, k\}$, for each color $c \in \{1, \ldots, k\}$ we define the *color class* $\mathcal{C}_c = \{x \in \mathcal{C} \mid \kappa(x) = c\}$ as the set of candidates receiving color c. We call the coloring κ *good*, if it makes our solution S *colorful*, meaning that $S \cap \mathcal{C}_c \neq \emptyset$ for each color c; clearly, a colorful solution must contain *exactly* one candidate from each color class.

Let us assume that κ is a good coloring. Next, for each vote $v \in \mathcal{V}$ we guess the set X_v of *consensus colors* for v, containing the colors of the candidates in $v \cap S$. Notice that the consensus colors for a vote determines its distance from S, namely $\text{dist}(S,v) = |S \setminus v| + |v \setminus S| = k + |v| - 2|X_v|$. Hence, we can immediately discard those guesses where $\text{dist}(S,v) > d$ for some vote $v \in \mathcal{V}$.

Given the consensus colors for each vote, finding a colorful solution is easy: for each color c, we need to check whether all sets $v \cap \mathcal{C}_c$ where $v \in \mathcal{V}, c \in X_v$ have at least one common candidate. If so, we put one such candidate a_c into our solution S' for each c. Observe that S' is indeed a solution, as each vote contains at least $|X_v|$ candidates from S'. Since S always yields some $a_c \in S$ contained in all votes which have c as a consensus color, we are bound to find a solution (supposing we guessed the consensus colors correctly).

Let us consider the running time of MAV-CC. Given a good coloring, we need to consider all possible consensus color sets for each vote, which means $(2^k)^n$ possibilities (where $n = |\mathcal{V}|$). For each of these cases, looking for a solution takes $O(kn|\mathcal{C}|)$ time. But how can we obtain a good coloring? Clearly, our random coloring κ is good with probability $\frac{k!}{k^k} \geq e^{-k}$. Thus, repeating the whole procedure e^k times guarantees that we will obtain a good coloring, and hence a solution, with high probability. This yields a total running time of $e^k 2^{nk} O(kn|\mathcal{C}|)$, which is fixed-parameter tractable with respect to parameter $n+k$.

To de-randomize the above algorithm, we need to deterministically construct a family of coloring functions such that any given committee of size k becomes colorful in at least one of the colorings. This can be achieved by so-called *k-perfect families of hash functions*; an explicit construction of such a family of size $e^k k^{O(\log k)} \log |\mathcal{C}|$ is given by Naor et al. (1995).

11.2.5 Multiple Parameters

For a truly detailed insight into a problem's computational complexity, one can typically determine several parameters that might influence its tractability. Allowing for multiple parameters is thus crucial in the parameterized framework.

Suppose we want to handle t parameters in our problem, so each instance $\mathcal{I}$ is associated with parameters $k_1, \ldots, k_t$. Intuitively, a fixed-parameter tractable algorithm in such a model is one that runs in time $f(k_1, \ldots, k_t)|\mathcal{I}|^{O(1)}$ for some computable function f. However, instead of extending the formalism of the original framework, it suffices to define the parameter as the t-tuple $(k_1, \ldots, k_t)$; such composite parameters are usually called *combined parameters*. Equivalently, we can simply define the sum $k_1 + \cdots + k_t$ or the maximum $\max\{k_1, \ldots, k_t\}$ as the parameter; either of these choices yields the same notion of fixed-parameter tractability.

To exploit the full power of parameterized complexity, allowing for multiple parameters is just the first step. Looking for an FPT algorithm with parameters $k_1, \ldots, k_t$ amounts to searching for an algorithm that is efficient if *all* of the values $k_1, \ldots, k_t$ are small. A much more informative approach is to adopt a *multidimensional* view (also called *multivariate algorithmics*; see the paper by Niedermeier

(2010)), and regard each value k_i as either (i) a fixed constant, (ii) a parameter, or (iii) unbounded. This yields 3^t variants of the original problem, and determining the (parameterized) complexity for each of these variants offers a detailed landscape of its computational tractability.

A nice example for such a multidimensional analysis is the work by De Haan (2016a) who investigated the complexity of judgment aggregation based on the Kemeny rule with respect to five parameters and all their possible combinations.

11.3 Parameterized Intractability

In the previous sections, we have gotten to know some basic techniques for showing fixed-parameter tractability of a hard problem. But what can we do if none of these techniques seems to be applicable to our problem at hand? There are many more techniques that we could give a try; see the literature referred to in the introduction. However, it might also happen that the problem on hand simply is *not* in FPT. For such cases, we can try to provide evidence that the problem does not admit an FPT algorithm: similarly to the theory of NP-hardness, parameterized complexity offers an intractability theory which provides the possibility to compare the computational hardness of parameterized problems. For a more detailed view on this topic, we refer to the books by Downey and Fellows (1999, 2013), and by Flum and Grohe (2006).

Before we start, let us introduce two well-known notions from graph theory. Given a graph G, an *independent set* is a set $I \subseteq V(G)$ of vertices in G such that no two of them are adjacent to each other in G. A *clique* is a set $C \subseteq V(G)$ of vertices that are pairwise adjacent in G. The notions of vertex cover, independent set, and clique are closely related: $S \subseteq V(G)$ is a vertex cover of G if and only if $I := V(G) \setminus S$ is an independent set of G, which in turn holds if and only if I is a clique in the complement graph $\overline{G}$.[3]

> INDEPENDENT SET:
>   Input: An undirected graph G, and an integer k.
>   Question: Does G contain an independent set of size at least k?

> CLIQUE:
>   Input: An undirected graph G, and an integer k.
>   Question: Does G contain a clique of size at least k?

The two problems above were proved to be NP-complete by Karp (1972), so their classical complexity is the same as that of VERTEX COVER. However, when parameterized by k, they exhibit a great difference: despite the relentless effort to design efficient algorithms for these problems, neither CLIQUE nor INDEPENDENT SET has been shown to admit an FPT algorithm.

---
[3] The complement graph of G is the graph $\overline{G}$ which has the same set of vertices as G, and there is an edge between two different vertices in $\overline{G}$ if and only if there is no edge between them in G.

11.3.1 FPT Reduction

In classical complexity theory, a polynomial-time many-to-one (or Karp) reduction from problem P to problem P' transforms—in polynomial time—an instance $\mathcal{I}$ of P into an equivalent instance $\mathcal{I}'$ of P', meaning that $\mathcal{I}$ is a 'yes'-instance of P if and only if $\mathcal{I}'$ is a 'yes'-instance of P'. We now describe a similar notion of reduction for parameterized problems that can transfer fixed-parameter tractability.

Let P and P' be two parameterized problems. An *FPT reduction* (also called *parameterized reduction*) from P to P' is an algorithm that runs in FPT time (i.e., in time $f(k) \cdot |\mathcal{I}|^{O(1)}$ for a computable function f) and transforms an instance $(\mathcal{I}, k)$ of P into an equivalent instance $(\mathcal{I}', k')$ of P' such that $k' \leq g(k)$ for some computable function g. The difference from a polynomial-time reduction is thus two-fold: we have to ensure that the parameter of the new instance only depends on the original parameter, but the transformation may take FPT time. The key property of an FPT reduction is the following: if $P' \in$ FPT, then an FPT reduction from P to P' implies $P \in$ FPT as well.

The classical polynomial-time reduction from INDEPENDENT SET to CLIQUE transforms an instance (G, k) of INDEPENDENT SET into an equivalent instance $(\overline{G}, k)$ of CLIQUE. Thus, if we regard k as the parameter in both problems, then this transformation becomes an FPT reduction. Applying the same reduction the other way around shows that CLIQUE to INDEPENDENT SET are equally hard, even in the parameterized form.

By contrast, the classical polynomial-time reduction from INDEPENDENT SET to VERTEX COVER is not an FPT reduction: it transforms an instance (G, k) of INDEPENDENT SET into an equivalent instance $(G, k' = |V(G)| - k)$ of VERTEX COVER, but the new parameter k' depends not only on k but also on $|V(G)|$. Hence, this does *not* prove fixed-parameter tractability of INDEPENDENT SET.

11.3.2 Parameterized Complexity Classes

Parameterized complexity offers a whole hierarchy of hardness classes, called the *weft hierarchy*, based on weighted variants of the satisfiability problem for Boolean circuits. It contains the classes FPT $\subseteq$ W[1] $\subseteq$ W[2] $\subseteq \cdots \subseteq$ W[t] $\subseteq \cdots \subseteq$ W[SAT] $\subseteq$ W[P], where all inclusions are believed to be strict. All these classes are closed under FPT reductions, and are contained in the class XP of *slicewise polynomial* problems, containing parameterized problems that, given an instance $(\mathcal{I}, k)$, can be solved in time $|\mathcal{I}|^{f(k)}$, where f is a computable function only depending on k. The class XP is known to be strictly larger than FPT.

> WEIGHTED 2-CNF-SATISFIABILITY (W-2-CNF-SAT):
> Input: A Boolean formula F in conjunctive normal form (CNF) with at most two literals per clause, and an integer k.
> Question: Does F have a satisfying truth assignment of weight exactly k, i.e., with exactly k variables set to true?

The class W[1] contains all problems that can be reduced to the above defined W-2-CNF-SAT problem (parameterized by k) by an FPT reduction. If *all* problems in W[1] are FPT reducible to a parameterized problem P, then P is called W[1]-*hard*. If in addition P is contained in W[1], then it is W[1]-*complete*.

To prove that P is W[1]-hard, and consequently is not likely to admit an FPT algorithm, it suffices to provide an FPT reduction from an already known W[1]-hard problem to P. Besides W-2-CNF-SAT—which is W[1]-complete by definition—both CLIQUE and INDEPENDENT SET are W[1]-complete with respect to the parameter k (Downey and Fellows, 1999). The following useful variant of CLIQUE is also W[1]-complete with respect to the number k of colors.

> MULTICOLORED CLIQUE:
> Input: An undirected graph G whose vertices are colored with k colors.
> Question: Is there a clique in G containing one vertex from each color class?

As another example, UNARY BIN PACKING, defined as below, is also W[1]-hard with respect to the number b of bins, even if the total weight of the items equals the total bin capacity, i.e., $\sum_{i=1}^{m} w_i = b \cdot C$ (Jansen et al., 2013).

> UNARY BIN PACKING:
> Input: Positive integers $w_1, \ldots, w_m$, b, C, all in unary encoding.
> Question: Is there a packing of m items with weights $w_1, \ldots, w_m$ to b bins such that each bin has total weight at most C?

Analogously to W[1], the definition of the class W[2] is based on the WEIGHTED CNF-SATISFIABILITY problem where the clauses of the input formula can be of any size. A typical W[2]-complete problem is DOMINATING SET, asking if a graph G has a *dominating set* of size k, i.e., a subset $D \subseteq V(G)$ of k vertices such that each vertex in $V(G) \setminus D$ is adjacent to at least one vertex of D; the parameter is k.

> DOMINATING SET:
> Input: An undirected graph G, and an integer k.
> Question: Does G contain a dominating set of size at most k?

Example: W[1]-hardness of EEF ALLOCATION

Bliem et al. (2016) give a parameterized reduction from UNARY BIN PACKING to show W[1]-hardness for EEF ALLOCATION with respect to the number of agents (see the examples in Sections 11.2.2 and 11.2.3 for the definitions), even if agents express their utilities encoded in unary. Given an instance $(w_1, \ldots, w_m, b, C)$ of UNARY BIN PACKING with $\sum_{i=1}^{m} w_i = b \cdot C$, we construct an instance of EEF ALLOCATION as follows: the set of objects is $\{o_1, \ldots, o_m\}$, and there are b agents with identical preferences, each assigning utility w_i to object o_i, for $i \in \{1, \ldots, m\}$.

Observe that an allocation is Pareto efficient and envy-free exactly if the total utility assigned to each agent is $(\sum_{i=1}^{m} w_i)/b = C$: each agents needs to be assigned the same total utility, and each object must be allocated. Therefore, an EEF-allocation of the objects to the b agents immediately gives a packing of all items into the b bins respecting the bin capacities (where assigning object o_i to the j-th agent corresponds to packing the item w_i into the j-th bin), and vice versa.

Clearly, the instance of EEF ALLOCATION can be constructed in polynomial time, and the parameter b in the UNARY BIN PACKING instance equals the number of agents in the constructed EEF ALLOCATION instance. Thus, we obtain W[1]-hardness with respect to the number of agents. We remark that if agents express their utilities in binary encoding, then the problem is NP-hard already for two agents (Bouveret and Lang, 2008).

11.4 Advanced Techniques

Here we briefly mention a few of the more advanced techniques of parameterized complexity which can help us investigate the complexity of a computationally hard problem. For further reading, we refer to the book by Cygan et al. (2015) on lower bounds for kernelization and on lower bounds assuming ETH; the latter topic is also covered by Lokshtanov et al. (2011). The survey by Marx (2008) offers an excellent summary on the connection between fixed-parameter tractability and approximation. For an extension of the parameterized framework dealing with problems beyond NP, see the recent PhD thesis by De Haan (2016b).

11.4.1 Lower Bounds for Kernelization

As already mentioned in Section 11.2.2, a parameterized problem is FPT if and only if it admits a kernel. But an exponential-size kernel may not be very useful in practice, and so the more interesting question is whether a given (FPT) problem admits a kernel of polynomial size.

Recently the field of kernelization has undergone exciting improvements: a series of new results have established a framework for proving lower bounds for the existence of polynomial kernels. This breakthrough started with a paper by Fortnow and Santhanam (2008), followed by Bodlaender et al. (2009) who proved the following: if a parameterized problem Q whose unparameterized version is NP-hard admits an OR-composition, then it does not admit a polynomial kernel, unless NP $\subseteq$ coNP/poly (considered very unlikely in complexity theory). Here, an *OR-composition* for Q is an algorithm that, given t instances $(\mathcal{I}_1, k), \ldots, (\mathcal{I}_t, k)$ of Q, in time polynomial in $\sum_{j=1}^{t} |\mathcal{I}_j| + k$ computes a new instance $(\mathcal{I}', k')$ with $k' = k^{O(1)}$ such that $(\mathcal{I}', k') \in Q$ if and only if $(\mathcal{I}_j, k) \in Q$ for at least one index $j \in \{1, \ldots, t\}$.

OR-cross-compositions offer a more flexible method (Bodlaender et al., 2011a). Roughly speaking, an OR-cross-composition algorithm takes as input t instances of *any* NP-hard problem L, and produces an instance $(\mathcal{I}, k)$ such that $(\mathcal{I}, k) \in Q$ if and only if one of the t instances is in L; the parameter k must be polynomially bounded in the maximum size of the input instances plus $\log t$. Using this extended framework, Bliem et al. (2016) proved that EEF-ALLOCATION with monotonic dichotomous preferences parameterized by the number of objects does not admit a polynomial kernel (unless NP $\subseteq$ coNP/poly).

We remark that instead of OR-(cross-)compositions, one can also use AND-(cross-)compositions, defined analogously, due to a result by Drucker (2012).

Bodlaender et al. (2011b) proposed another tool that can be used to prove the non-existence of polynomial kernels. Given two parameterized problems Q and Q', a *polynomial parameter transformation* (PPT) from Q to Q' is a function that for any instance $(\mathcal{I}, k)$ of Q computes in polynomial time an equivalent instance $(\mathcal{I}', k')$ of Q', where k' is bounded by a fixed polynomial of k. Essentially, if there is a PPT from Q to Q' and Q admits no polynomial kernel, then Q' does not admit a polynomial kernel either.[4] Using this concept, Dey et al. (2016) showed for various voting rules that POSSIBLE WINNER is not likely to admit a polynomial kernel if the parameter is the number of candidates.

Finally, let us mention the technique of *weak compositions* by Dell and van Melkebeek (2010); Hermelin and Wu (2012); Dell and Marx (2012) which can be used to derive more refined lower bounds, ruling out not polynomial kernels in general, but kernels of a certain size (such as, say, a linear kernel).

11.4.2 Lower Bounds Assuming ETH

Impagliazzo et al. (2001) formulated the Exponential Time Hypothesis (ETH) that, roughly speaking, states that 3-SAT cannot be solved in subexponential time. Assuming ETH, one can obtain stronger lower bounds for various computational problems than only assuming the weaker assumption $\mathsf{P} \neq \mathsf{NP}$.

As shown by Chen et al. (2006), ETH implies that CLIQUE, INDEPENDENT SET, and DOMINATING SET cannot be solved in $f(k)n^{o(k)}$ time for any function f on n-vertex graphs with parameter k. This shows that ETH is a stronger assumption than $\mathsf{W}[1] \neq \mathsf{FPT}$. One can obtain lower bounds also for problems in FPT; as an example, Cai and Juedes (2003) proved that VERTEX COVER cannot be solved in $2^{o(k)}n^{O(1)}$ time on an n-vertex graph with parameter k, unless ETH fails.

Such lower bounds can be transferred by appropriate reductions; the obtained lower bound depends on how the reduction changes the parameter. With this method, Cygan et al. (2016) proved that MINIMAX APPROVAL VOTING admits no algorithm running in $O^\star(2^{o(d \log d)})$ time, showing that the algorithm by Misra et al. (2015) described in Section 11.2.1 is essentially optimal.

11.4.3 Approximation and Parameterized Algorithms

Approximation algorithms have a polynomial running time, but produce only suboptimal solutions; by contrast, parameterized algorithms provide optimal solutions, but at a cost of increased running time. Combining these two approaches yields a variety of methods to deal with computationally hard problems; here we only highlight a few ideas and results connected to computational social choice.

Given an optimization problem Q, we can ask whether Q admits an *FPT-approximation algorithm*: one that produces an approximate solution and runs in FPT time with respect to a given parameter. This idea can be extended to *FPT-approximation schemes*; an example is the algorithm by Cygan et al. (2016) for MINIMAX APPROVAL VOTING that for any $\varepsilon > 0$ in time $O^\star((3/\varepsilon)^{2d})$ produces an ε-approximation (i.e., a committee with distance at most $(1+\varepsilon)d$ from any vote).

---

[4]In fact, we also need a polynomial reduction from Q' to Q, which is guaranteed if Q is NP-hard and Q' is in NP.

Another strong connection between approximation schemes and parameterized complexity was observed by Bazgan (1995), and independently, Cesati and Trevisan (1997): if Q admits an EPTAS[5], then deciding whether an instance of Q admits a solution with value at least (or, if Q is a minimization problem, at most) k is FPT with parameter k. This fact is often used in negative form: e.g., as observed by Gurski and Roos (2014), the W[2]-hardness of constructive control by adding/deleting candidates in Lull or Copeland elections implies that these problems do not admit an EPTAS, unless W[2] = FPT.

11.4.4 Parameterized Complexity for Problems Beyond NP

Recently, a new theoretical framework has been developed that combines the idea of parameterized complexity with the practice of converting hard problems into well-studied, standardized problems like SAT and using already existing solvers to deal with the transformed instance; the thesis by De Haan (2016b) offers a thorough introduction to this framework. SAT solvers are highly efficient in practice, but their use is limited by the fact that only problems belonging to NP admit a polynomial-time reduction to SAT. Hence, for problems that lie in higher classes of the Polynomial Hierarchy (so, are 'beyond' NP), it might be helpful to allow transformations into SAT that take FPT time with respect to some parameter.

This idea can be formalized in different ways, leading to various new methods and complexity classes; we only mention two prominent concepts. The first is to consider parameterized problems that admit a many-to-one FPT reduction to SAT; the corresponding complexity class is called para-NP, a direct parameterized analog of NP.[6] Another possibility is to use Turing reductions instead of many-to-one reductions when converting a parameterized problem into SAT. This leads to the definition of complexity classes like $FPT^{NP}[few]$, containing problems solvable by an FPT algorithm that has access to a SAT oracle, with the restriction that the number of oracle queries must be upper-bounded by a function of the parameter. An example from social choice is the agenda safety problem for the majority rule in judgment aggregation which was shown to be $FPT^{NP}[few]$-complete with respect to the agenda size as parameter by Endriss et al. (2015).

11.5 Conclusion

This chapter is meant to be a gentle introduction to parameterized complexity for researchers in computational social choice. We have presented the basic approach, several standard techniques and ideas, and tried to give some simple examples that allow for a quick start in parameterized complexity. We also wanted to give some glimpse of what there is beyond the basic techniques in order to provide a good starting point for the interested reader to get into this

---

[5] An *Efficient Polynomial-Time Approximation Scheme* or EPTAS is an algorithm that produces an ε-approximate solution in $f(\varepsilon) \cdot |\mathcal{I}|^{O(1)}$ time for any instance $\mathcal{I}$.

[6] The class para-NP can be alternatively defined as the set of parameterized problems solvable by a nondeterministic Turing machine in FPT time.

beautiful research area. In this context, we also refer to the collection of PhD theses in computational social choice (www.illc.uva.nl/COMSOC/theses.html)—several of them use parameterized complexity and can serve as a signpost for future directions and trends.

The area of parameterized complexity has experienced an immense boom in recent years, and many new results and techniques have made this area a very active and exciting one. We are convinced that this development also means a big chance for the analysis of problems from computational social choice. Shedding some more light on the complexity landscape of hard problems, parameterized complexity does not only offer a possibility to face the criticism that complexity theory is only a worst-case analysis and hence not suitable to serve as a barrier against manipulative behavior. It might also contribute to make you see the many faces of a hard problem and to gain a better feeling of what really makes it hard. We admit that parameterized complexity cannot always save you from having a hard time with your problems—but probably it can make you enjoy them more!

Acknowledgment

We thank Ulle Endriss for inviting us to write this chapter, and we are indebted to Ronald de Haan for carefully reading a preliminary version of it and providing us with helpful advice. Ildikó Schlotter was supported by the Hungarian Scientific Research Fund (OTKA grants no. K-108383 and no. K-108947).

Bibliography

N. Alon, R. Yuster, and U. Zwick. Color-coding. *Journal of the ACM*, 42(4):844–856, 1995.

C. Bazgan. Schémas d'approximation et complexité paramétrée. Technical report, Université Paris Sud, 1995. Mémoire de DEA.

N. Betzler, R. Bredereck, J. Chen, and R. Niedermeier. Studies in computational aspects of voting—a parameterized complexity perspective. In H. L. Bodlaender, R. Downey, F. V. Fomin, and D. Marx, editors, *The Multivariate Algorithmic Revolution and Beyond*, pages 318–363, Berlin, Heidelberg, 2012. Springer.

B. Bliem, R. Bredereck, and R. Niedermeier. Complexity of efficient and envy-free resource allocation: Few agents, resources, or utility levels. In *Proceedings of the 25th International Joint Conference on Artificial Intelligence (IJCAI)*, pages 102–108, 2016.

H. L. Bodlaender, R. G. Downey, M. R. Fellows, and D. Hermelin. On problems without polynomial kernels. *Journal of Computer and System Sciences*, 75(8): 423–434, 2009.

H. L. Bodlaender, B. M. P. Jansen, and S. Kratsch. Cross-composition: A new technique for kernelization lower bounds. In *Proceedings of the 28th International Symposium on Theoretical Aspects of Computer Science (STACS)*, pages 165–176, 2011a.

H. L. Bodlaender, S. Thomassé, and A. Yeo. Kernel bounds for disjoint cycles and disjoint paths. *Theoretical Computer Science*, 412(35):4570–4578, 2011b.

S. Bouveret and J. Lang. Efficiency and envy-freeness in fair division of indivisible goods: Logical representation and complexity. *Journal of Artificial Intelligence Research*, 32(1):525–564, 2008.

R. Bredereck, J. Chen, P. Faliszewski, J. Guo, R. Niedermeier, and G. J. Woeginger. Parameterized algorithmics for computational social choice: Nine research challenges. *Tsinghua Science and Technology*, 19(4):358–373, 2014.

L. Cai and D. W. Juedes. On the existence of subexponential parameterized algorithms. *Journal of Computer and System Sciences*, 67(4):789–807, 2003.

M. Cesati and L. Trevisan. On the efficiency of polynomial time approximation schemes. *Information Processing Letters*, 64(4):165–171, 1997.

J. Chen, X. Huang, I. A. Kanj, and G. Xia. Strong computational lower bounds via parameterized complexity. *Journal of Computer and System Sciences*, 72(8):1346–1367, 2006.

J. Chen, I. A. Kanj, and G. Xia. Improved upper bounds for vertex cover. *Theoretical Computer Science*, 411(40-42):3736–3756, 2010.

M. Cygan, F. V. Fomin, L. Kowalik, D. Lokshtanov, D. Marx, M. Pilipczuk, M. Pilipczuk, and S. Saurabh. *Parameterized Algorithms*. Springer, 2015.

M. Cygan, Ł. Kowalik, A. Socała, and K. Sornat. Approximation and parameterized complexity of minimax approval voting. *CoRR*, abs/1607.07906, 2016. arXiv:607.07906 [cs.DS].

H. Dell and D. Marx. Kernelization of packing problems. In *Proceedings of the 23rd Annual ACM-SIAM Symposium on Discrete Algorithms (SODA)*, pages 68–81, 2012.

H. Dell and D. van Melkebeek. Satisfiability allows no nontrivial sparsification unless the polynomial-time hierarchy collapses. In *Proceedings of the 42nd Annual ACM Symposium on Theory of Computing (STOC)*, pages 251–260, 2010.

P. Dey, N. Misra, and Y. Narahari. Kernelization complexity of possible winner and coalitional manipulation problems in voting. *Theoretical Computer Science*, 616:111–125, 2016.

R. Diestel. *Graph Theory*, volume 173 of *Graduate Texts in Mathematics*. Springer, Berlin, Heidelberg, 2005.

R. G. Downey and M. R. Fellows. *Parameterized Complexity*. Monographs in Computer Science. Springer, New York, 1999.

R. G. Downey and M. R. Fellows. *Fundamentals of Parameterized Complexity*. Texts in Computer Science. Springer, London, 2013.

A. Drucker. New limits to classical and quantum instance compression. In *Proceedings of the 53rd Annual Symposium on Foundations of Computer Science (FOCS)*, pages 609–618, 2012.

U. Endriss, R. de Haan, and S. Szeider. Parameterized complexity results for agenda safety in judgment aggregation. In *Proceedings of the 14th International Conference on Autonomous Agents and Multiagent Systems (AAMAS)*, pages 127–136, 2015.

P. Faliszewski and R. Niedermeier. Parameterization in computational social choice. In M.-Y. Kao, editor, *Encyclopedia of Algorithms*. Springer, 2015.

J. Flum and M. Grohe. *Parameterized Complexity Theory*. Texts in Theoretical Computer Science. An EATCS Series. Springer, New York, 2006.

L. Fortnow and R. Santhanam. Infeasibility of instance compression and succinct PCPs for NP. In *Proceedings of the 40th Annual ACM Symposium on Theory of Computing (STOC)*, pages 133–142. ACM, 2008.

A. Frank and É. Tardos. An application of simultaneous diophantine approximation in combinatorial optimization. *Combinatorica*, 7:49–65, 1987.

F. Gurski and M. Roos. Binary linear programming solutions and non-approximability for control problems in voting systems. *Discrete Applied Mathematics*, 162:391–398, 2014.

R. de Haan. Parameterized complexity results for the Kemeny rule in judgment aggregation. In *Proceedings of the 22nd European Conference on Artificial Intelligence (ECAI)*, volume 285 of *Frontiers in Artificial Intelligence and Applications*, pages 1502–1510, 2016a.

R. de Haan. *Parameterized Complexity in the Polynomial Hierarchy*. PhD thesis, Technische Universität Wien, 2016b.

D. Hermelin and X. Wu. Weak compositions and their applications to polynomial lower bounds for kernelization. In *Proceedings of the 23rd Annual ACM-SIAM Symposium on Discrete Algorithms (SODA)*, pages 104–113, 2012.

R. Impagliazzo, R. Paturi, and F. Zane. Which problems have strongly exponential complexity? *Journal of Computer and System Sciences*, 63(4):512–530, 2001.

K. Jansen, S. Kratsch, D. Marx, and I. Schlotter. Bin packing with fixed number of bins revisited. *Journal of Computer and System Sciences*, 79(1):39–49, 2013.

R. Kannan. Minkowski's convex body theorem and integer programming. *Mathematics of Operations Research*, 12:415–440, 1987.

R. M. Karp. Reducibility among combinatorial problems. In R. E. Miller and J. W. Thatcher, editors, *Complexity of Computer Computations*, pages 85–103. Plenum Press, 1972.

H. Lenstra. Integer programming with a fixed number of variables. *Mathematics of Operations Research*, 8:538–548, 1983.

C. Lindner and J. Rothe. Fixed-parameter tractability and parameterized complexity applied to problems from computational social choice. In A. Holder, editor, *Mathematical Programming Glossary*. INFORMS Computing Society, 2008.

D. Lokshtanov, D. Marx, and S. Saurabh. Lower bounds based on the Exponential Time Hypothesis. *Bulletin of European Association for Theoretical Computer Science*, 105:41–71, 2011.

D. Marx. Parameterized complexity and approximation algorithms. *The Computer Journal*, 51(1):60–78, 2008.

D. C. McGarvey. A theorem on the construction of voting paradoxes. *Econometrica*, 21:608–610, 1953.

N. Misra, A. Nabeel, and H. Singh. On the parameterized complexity of minimax approval voting. In *Proceedings of the 14th International Conference on Autonomous Agents and Multiagent Systems (AAMAS)*, pages 97–105, 2015.

M. Naor, L. J. Schulman, and A. Srinivasan. Splitters and near-optimal derandomization. In *Proceedings of the 36th Annual Symposium on Foundations of Computer Science (FOCS)*, pages 182–191, 1995.

R. Niedermeier. *Invitation to Fixed-Parameter Algorithms*, volume 31 of *Oxford Lecture Series in Mathematics and its Applications*. Oxford University Press, Oxford, 2006.

R. Niedermeier. Reflections on multivariate algorithmics and problem parameterization. In *Proceedings of the 27th International Symposium on Theoretical Aspects of Computer Science (STACS)*, pages 17–32, 2010.

CHAPTER 12

Approximation Algorithms and Hardness Results for Fair Division with Indivisible Goods

Evangelos Markakis

12.1 Introduction

Fair division problems have attracted the attention of various scientific disciplines in the last decades, including among others, mathematics, economics, computer science, and political science. Ever since the first attempt for a mathematical treatment by Steinhaus, Banach, and Knaster (Steinhaus, 1948), many interesting and challenging questions have emerged. Over the years, a vast literature has developed, see e.g., Brams and Taylor (1996), Robertson and Webb (1998), and Moulin (2003), considering several notions of fairness. For more recent surveys, see also Bouveret et al. (2016), and Procaccia (2016).

The objective in fair division is to allocate a set of resources to a set of agents in a way that leaves every agent satisfied, to the extent that is feasible. To model the preferences of the involved agents, the standard assumption in the literature is that every agent is associated with a valuation function on the set of resources. In most settings, valuation functions are further restricted to be additive functions, but non-additive scenarios are also discussed in some works. Under this setup, various solution concepts have been proposed as to what constitutes a fair allocation, including e.g., *proportionality* and *envy-freeness*, along with several variants, strengthenings and relaxations.

The models that have been studied so far, can essentially be grouped into two classes. The first one concerns *continuous* models, where it is assumed that the resources are infinitely divisible. This is appropriate when items can be split into arbitrarily smaller pieces, or in settings where the resources correspond to the percentage of time an agent can use a shared good, or even further in land division. The second class contains *discrete* models, where the resources are seen as *indivisible* goods. This means that the items to be allocated cannot be divided further; each item has to be entirely allocated to one agent. Although the same solution concepts apply well to both models, the picture is quite different when it comes to existence and computation of fair outcomes. Under continuous models, we can guarantee existence of most standard fairness concepts, and in some cases, we can also have very efficient algorithms, such as the algorithm of Even and Paz (1984) for proportional allocations. On the contrary, in the presence of indivisible goods, we cannot guarantee existence anymore for most fairness concepts, and it is even NP-hard to decide whether a given instance admits a fair allocation.

Undoubtedly, establishing NP-hardness is not encouraging news. However, as with many other optimization problems, one can still resort to algorithms that produce approximation guarantees with respect to the criteria under consideration. Clearly, the solution we would expect from an approximation algorithm depends on the fairness concept that we try to approximate. As an example, if envy is our fairness criterion, then our goal would be an algorithm that always returns an allocation such that the pairwise envy is never more than a small factor away from the optimal envy achievable. Such algorithms provide to us solutions that we could be willing to settle with, given the difficulty of finding an exact optimal solution.

Motivated by this discussion, the purpose of this chapter is to highlight the role of approximation algorithms and inapproximability results for discrete models, towards understanding what we can hope to achieve by polynomial-time algorithms. Consequently, the exposition will be based on presenting recent results published within the last years, along with open problems and trends in allocating indivisible items.

The structure of the remaining chapter is as follows. In Section 12.2, we provide the necessary definitions and we present the fairness concepts that we are interested in. In Section 12.3, we demonstrate problems that admit polynomial-time algorithms and also establish why most interesting problems are NP-hard. Finally in Section 12.4, we present approximation algorithms along with hardness of approximation results, classified according to the fairness criteria under consideration. We conclude with interesting open questions in Section 12.5.

12.2 Preliminaries

In this section, we first provide the general setup and the notation that we will be using. We then define the notions of fairness that will form the backbone of this exposition.

12.2.1 Notation and Terminology

We assume we have a set of n agents, $N = \{1, 2, \ldots, n\}$, and a set of m indivisible goods $M = \{1, 2, \ldots, m\}$. For every agent $i \in N$, the preferences for the items are expressed through a valuation function $v_i(\cdot)$. In its general form, this is a monotone set function $v_i : 2^M \to \mathbb{R}$, defined on subsets of items, such that for $S \subseteq M$, $v_i(S)$ denotes the value derived by agent i, when he obtains the set S. Monotonicity simply means that for $S \subseteq T \subseteq M$, we have that $v_i(S) \leq v_i(T)$. Following the usual assumptions in the majority of the fair division literature, and unless otherwise stated, we consider that each agent has an *additive* valuation function. Hence, for every $S \subseteq M$, $v_i(S) = \sum_{j \in S} v_i(\{j\})$. For $j \in M$, we will use

v_{ij} instead of $v_i(\{j\})$ for simplicity. Note that monotonicity for additive functions implies that $v_{ij} \geq 0$ for every $i \in N$ and $j \in M$.

Under additive valuations, it suffices to specify the value of an agent i for each individual item, in order to fully specify the valuation function. Hence, we can represent the relevant information for agent i by the vector $v_i = (v_{i1}, v_{i2}, \ldots, v_{im})$. The input then to any algorithm for fair division can be encoded by the matrix $V = (v_{ij})$, where for each $i \in N$, the i-th row of V corresponds to the valuation of agent i.

We are interested in solutions that allocate the whole set of goods M to the agents. An allocation of the goods to the agents is therefore a partition denoted by $S = (S_1, \ldots, S_n)$, where S_i is the subset allocated to agent i, $S_i \cap S_j = \emptyset$ and $\bigcup_{i \in N} S_i = M$. Given any set T, we denote by $\Pi_n(T)$ the set of all partitions of T into n bundles. Hence, all the solution concepts we will encounter, seek to produce an element of $\Pi_n(M)$.

12.2.2 Fairness Concepts

Clearly, one cannot hope to have a unique, universally accepted notion of fairness that can be equally applicable to all problems. Several notions have emerged throughout the years as to what can be considered a fair allocation. As it is infeasible to enumerate all these concepts in this exposition, we will only focus on the notions that are most relevant to recent algorithmic research in this area.

We start with two of the most dominant solution concepts in fair division, namely proportionality and envy-freeness.

Definition 12.1. *An allocation $S = (S_1, \ldots, S_n)$ is*

1. *proportional, if $v_i(S_i) \geq \frac{1}{n} v_i(M)$, for every $i \in N$.*

2. *envy-free, if for every $i, j \in N$, $v_i(S_i) \geq v_i(S_j)$.*

Proportionality was considered in the very first work on fair division (Steinhaus, 1948). Envy-freeness seems to have been initially suggested by Gamow and Stern (1958), and was considered more formally later by Foley (1967) and Varian (1974).

It can be easily seen that envy-freeness is a stricter notion than proportionality, i.e., harder to achieve. But even for proportionality, existence cannot be guaranteed under indivisible goods. This gives rise to considering relaxations of these definitions, with the hope of obtaining more positive results.

One first such relaxation is the concept of envy-freeness up to one good, where each player may envy another player, but only by an amount which does not exceed the value of a single item in the other player's bundle. Formally:

Definition 12.2. *An allocation $S = (S_1, \ldots, S_n)$ is envy-free up to one good, if for every pair of agents $i, j \in N$, there exists an item $a_j \in S_j$, such that*

$$v_i(S_i) \geq v_i(S_j \setminus \{a_j\})$$

Note that envy-freeness up to one good is a relaxation of envy-freeness but not of proportionality. There exist allocations that are proportional but not envy-free up to one good, and vice versa.

A relaxation of proportionality, namely the notion of maximin share allocations, was recently proposed by Budish (2011), building on concepts by Moulin (1990). Motivated by the question of what can we guarantee in the worst case to the agents, the rationale of this concept is to think of a generalization of the well-known cut-and-choose protocol to multiple agents as follows: suppose that agent i is asked to partition the goods into n bundles and then the rest of the agents choose a bundle before i. In the worst case, agent i will be left with her least valuable bundle. Hence, a risk-averse agent would choose a partition that maximizes the minimum value of a bundle in the partition. This value is called the maximin share of agent i, and for $n = 2$, it is precisely what he could guarantee to himself in the discrete form of the cut-and-choose protocol, by being the cutter. The objective then is to find an allocation where every agent receives at least his maximin share.

Definition 12.3. *Given a set of n agents, a set of goods M, and a valuation matrix V,*

1. *the maximin share of an agent i, is:*

$$\mu_i := \mu_i(n, M, v_i) = \max_{S \in \Pi_n(M)} \min_{S_j \in S} v_i(S_j).$$

2. *an allocation $S = (S_1, ..., S_n) \in \Pi_n(M)$ is called a maximin share (MMS) allocation, if $v_i(S_i) \geq \mu_i$, for every agent $i \in N$.*

Note that the maximin share of an agent does not depend on the whole valuation matrix V, but solely on v_i.

A related approach on determining worst case guarantees was taken by Hill (1987). His work examined the guarantee that a player can have as a function of two parameters: the number of players and the maximum value of an item across all players. As a result, the following function was identified, under the assumption that the valuation functions are normalized such that $\sum_{j \in M} v_{ij} = 1$ for every $i \in N$.

Definition 12.4. *Given any integer $n \geq 2$, let $V_n : [0, 1] \to [0, n^{-1}]$ be the nonincreasing function satisfying $V_n(\alpha) = 1/n$ for $\alpha = 0$, and for $\alpha > 0$:*

$$V_n(\alpha) = \begin{cases} 1 - k(n-1)\alpha & \text{if } \alpha \in I(n, k) \\ 1 - \frac{(k+1)(n-1)}{(k+1)n - 1} & \text{if } \alpha \in NI(n, k) \end{cases}$$

where for $k \geq 1$, $I(n, k) = \left[\frac{k+1}{k((k+1)n-1)}, \frac{1}{kn-1}\right]$, and $NI(n, k) = \left(\frac{1}{(k+1)n-1}, \frac{k+1}{k((k+1)n-1)}\right)$.

Although this function seems complicated and hard to motivate at first sight, we will establish that it has a very interesting interpretation, and plays an important role in understanding what is feasible to achieve with indivisible goods.

Fair Division with Indivisible Goods

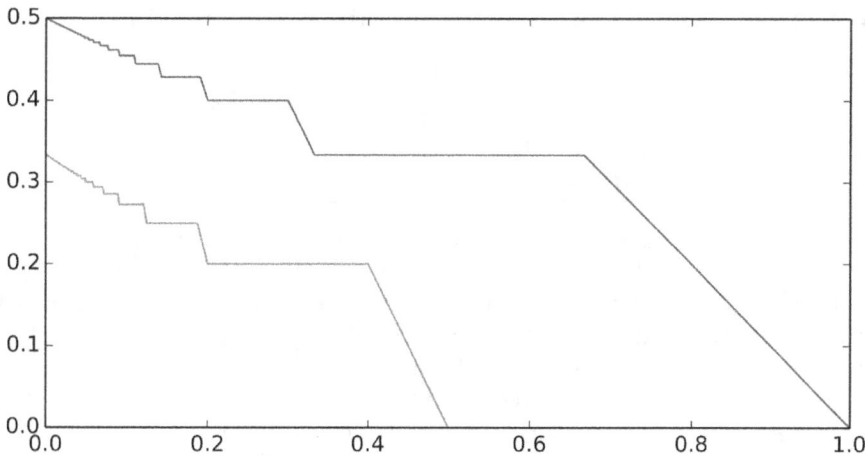

Figure 12.1: The function $V_n(\cdot)$ for $n = 2$ (upper curve) and $n = 3$ (lower curve).

Definition 12.5. *We will call an allocation $S = (S_1, ..., S_n)$ V_n-fair, if for every agent i, it holds that $v_i(S_i) \geq V_n(\alpha_i)$, where $\alpha_i = \max_{j \in M} v_{ij}$.*

In Figure 12.1, one can see the function $V_n(\cdot)$ for $n = 2$ and $n = 3$. For larger n, it has a similar form. The function alternates between segments where it is strictly decreasing (and the decrease is linear in α), and segments where it is constant and equal to the value at the left endpoint of the previous decreasing segment. For example, for $n = 2$, looking at the function from right to left, we can see that the rightmost decreasing segment is $[2/3, 1]$, and the function is equal to $1 - \alpha$ within this interval. This means that for two agents, if there exists an item with value $\alpha \geq 2/3$ for an agent, we can only guarantee to him an allocation with value $1 - \alpha$, since in worst case the other person will receive that item. In a similar manner, we see that $V_2(1/3) = 1/3$. This means that as long as the maximum value of a good for an agent is at most $1/3$, we can always find an allocation guaranteeing at least $1/3$ to him. The worst case for this is when we have 3 items of value $1/3$ each for both players.

It is not hard to see that this function forms a lower bound for μ_i. Therefore, V_n-fairness is a relaxation of maximin share fairness, which is itself a relaxation of proportionality.

Lemma 12.1. *For every additive valuation function v_i for which $\alpha_i = \max_{j \in M} v_{ij}$, it holds that*

$$\frac{1}{n}v_i(M) \geq \mu_i(n, M, v_i) \geq V_n(\alpha_i)$$

More recently, Gourvès et al. (2015) introduced a refined version of the function $V_n(\cdot)$, which leads to slightly stronger guarantees in some cases. As this definition is even more complex, we refer the reader to Gourvès et al. (2015) for the exact definition of their refinement.

An Example. To illustrate some of these concepts, let us consider an example. Suppose we have the following instance with three agents and five items:

	a	b	c	d	e
Agent 1	1/2	1/2	1/3	1/3	1/3
Agent 2	1/2	1/4	1/4	1/4	0
Agent 3	1/2	1/2	1	1/2	1/2

If $M = \{a,b,c,d,e\}$ is the set of items, one can see that $\mu_1(3, M, v_1) = 1/2$, $\mu_2(3, M, v_2) = 1/4$, $\mu_3(3, M, v_3) = 1$. E.g., for agent 1, no matter how she partitions the items into three bundles, the worst bundle will be worth at most $1/2$ for her, and she achieves this with the partition $(\{a\}, \{b,c\}, \{d,e\})$. Similarly, agent 3 can guarantee a value of 1 (which is best possible as it is equal to $v_3(M)/n$) by the partition $(\{a,b\}, \{c\}, \{d,e\})$. This instance admits a maximin share allocation, e.g., $(\{a\}, \{b,c\}, \{d,e\})$, and in fact this is not a unique such allocation.

Let us look now into an allocation with better fairness properties, namely $S = (\{a,e\}, \{b,d\}, \{c\})$. Obviously this is also a MMS allocation. But furthermore, it is also a proportional and envy-free allocation. It is easy to check that each agent is happy with her bundle and would not envy any of the other two bundles.

12.3 Boundaries of Polynomial Time Tractability

In this section, we first examine which fairness criteria admit efficient algorithms. As we will see, two of the concepts defined in Section 12.2 fall into this class. We then proceed to understand the source of computational difficulty for the remaining criteria, and establish NP-hardness for a variety of problems. The main conclusion of this section is that the majority of the problems being studied in the literature are computationally hard.

12.3.1 Efficient Algorithms

One of the easiest criteria that we can satisfy is envy-freeness up to one good. There are several algorithms that produce such allocations. Perhaps the most intuitive one is a simple round robin algorithm (see Algorithm 1). In describing algorithms, we assume that they take as input the set of players N, the set of goods M, and the valuation matrix V that encodes the valuation functions.

Theorem 12.2. *The allocation produced by Algorithm 1 is envy-free up to one good.*

Proof. This is quite easy to establish. Fix an agent i, and let $j \neq i$. We will upper bound the difference $v_i(S_j) - v_i(S_i)$. If j comes after i in the order chosen by the algorithm, then agent i cannot envy j, since i always picks an item at least as desirable as the one j picks. Suppose that j precedes i in the ordering. The algorithm proceeds in $\ell = \lceil m/n \rceil$ rounds. In each round k, let r_k and r'_k be the items allocated to j and i respectively. Then

$$v_i(S_j) - v_i(S_i) = (v_{i,r_1} - v_{i,r'_1}) + (v_{i,r_2} - v_{i,r'_2}) + \cdots + (v_{i,r_\ell} - v_{i,r'_\ell}).$$

ALGORITHM 1: Greedy Round-Robin(N, M, V)
---
1 Set $S_i = \emptyset$ for each $i \in N$
2 Fix an arbitrary ordering of the agents
3 **while** $\exists$ *unallocated items* **do**
4 $\quad$ Let $i \in N$ be the next agent to be examined in the current round (proceeding in a round-robin fashion)
5 $\quad$ Let $j \in M$ be the most desired item for i, among the currently unallocated items
6 $\quad$ $S_i = S_i \cup \{j\}$
7 **return** $(S_1, ..., S_n)$

Note that there may be no item r'_ℓ in the last round if the algorithm runs out of goods but this does not affect the analysis (simply set $v_{i,r'_\ell} = 0$).

Since agent i picks her most desirable item when it is her turn to choose, this means that for two consecutive rounds k and $k+1$ it holds that $v_{i,r'_k} \geq v_{i,r_{k+1}}$. This directly implies that $v_i(S_j) - v_i(S_i) \leq v_{i,r_1} - v_{i,r'_\ell} \leq v_{i,r_1}$. But then, if we remove item r_1 from the bundle of j, agent i will not be envious. $\square$

As we will see, the round-robin algorithm can be useful for other criteria as well. Interestingly, there are more algorithms that also achieve envy-freeness up to one good. For example, see the algorithm by Lipton et al. (2004), based on a graph-theoretic modeling of the problem.

We now move to the notion of V_n-fairness. As already mentioned, the function $V_n(\cdot)$ defined in the previous section, expresses the worst possible guarantee for an agent as a function of the maximum value across all items. Even though it was proved by Hill (1987) that there always exists an allocation providing such guarantees, the proof does not yield an efficient algorithm. Later on, a greedy algorithm was proposed by Markakis and Psomas (2011), which provides an interesting interpretation; the function $V_n(\cdot)$ describes precisely the value guaranteed to an agent by the simple greedy process stated in Algorithm 2.

This algorithm tries to greedily find an agent i who can exceed $V_n(\alpha_i)$ with the least number of items. After doing so, it removes agent i with the goods allocated to her, it normalizes the reduced valuation matrix and continues in the same fashion. The following result about the preformance of the algorithm was proved by Markakis and Psomas (2011).

Theorem 12.3. *Algorithm 2 produces an allocation* $S = (S_1, \ldots, S_n)$ *such that, for each player* i, $v_i(S_i) \geq V_n(\alpha_i)$, *where* $\alpha_i = \max_j v_{ij}$.

Further improvements have been obtained regarding such greedy outcomes, summarized in the following discussion.

Remark 12.4. *The result of Theorem 12.3 is tight on the decreasing segments of the function* $V_n(\cdot)$ *(see Figure 12.1). In Gourvès et al. (2015), a refined version of* $V_n(\cdot)$ *was defined and it was established that one can have a slightly higher guarantee when* α_i *lies in the segments of* $[0, 1]$ *where* $V_n(\cdot)$ *is constant.*

ALGORITHM 2: V_n-FAIR(N, M, V)

1. Set $S_i = \emptyset$ for each $i \in N$, and let $n = |N|$, $\alpha_i = \max_{j \in M} v_{ij}$
2. **while** *for every* $i \in N, v_i(S_i) < V_n(\alpha_i)$ **do**
3.   **for** *each* $i \in N$ **do**
4. $S_i = S_i \cup \{$next most desired item in $M\}$
5.   //we add one item at a time to each person's bundle till we find an agent satisfiable with the least number of items
6. Pick an agent i with $v_i(S_i) \geq V_n(\alpha_i)$ //arbitrarily in case of ties
7. Allocate S_i to agent i
8. **if** $n = 2$ **then**
9.   Allocate all other items to the remaining agent
10. **else**
11.   **for** $k \in N$, $k \neq i$ **do**
12. $v_{kj} = v_{kj}/(1 - v_k(S_i))$
13.   //normalization before going to next round
14. $V' = $ new matrix after removing row i and columns corresponding to S_i
15.   run V_n-FAIR$(V', N \setminus \{i\}, M \setminus S_i)$

12.3.2 Hardness Results

The results in the previous subsection hit essentially the boundaries of what is feasible to achieve by polynomial time algorithms. Most other algorithmic problems regarding fair allocations turn out to be NP-hard. The reason is that a special case of all these problems is the well known PARTITION problem. This has been observed already, among others, by Demko and Hill (1988), and by several other works.

Theorem 12.5. *Even for two agents, it is* NP*-complete to decide if there exists an envy-free allocation. It is also* NP*-complete to decide the existence of a proportional allocation.*

Proof. Deciding the existence of fair allocations clearly belongs to the class NP. To establish NP-hardness, consider an instance I of the PARTITION problem. Such an instance is described by a set of n numbers $A = \{a_1, ..., a_n\}$ and we are asked whether we can split A into two sets of equal value, i.e., whether there exists a set $S \subseteq A$ such that $\sum_{i \in S} a_i = \sum_{i \in A \setminus S} a_i$.

Starting from I, we can define now an instance of our problem, with two agents and n goods. Each number a_i in the PARTITION instance corresponds to a good in our instance with value a_i for both agents. Hence, a proportional or an envy-free allocation exists if and only if both players can receive a bundle of value at least $\sum_{i \in A} a_i/2$. But since the total value of the goods is exactly $\sum_{i \in A} a_i$, we conclude that a proportional allocation exists if and only if there exists a solution to the PARTITION problem. $\square$

One might initially feel more hopeful for the notion of MMS allocations, since this is a relaxation of proportionality. Indeed, for two agents, the existence of MMS allocations is a trivial problem, since they always exist (we note though that the status of existence for higher values of n and m is not completely clear, see Kurokawa et al. (2016)). However, when it comes to computing the actual allocations, even for the case of two agents, we still have an NP-hard problem to solve. The same reduction as in the previous theorem can show the following.

Theorem 12.6. *Even for two agents, finding a MMS allocation is an* NP-*hard problem.*

12.4 Approximation Guarantees: Algorithms and Impossibility Results

Motivated by the hardness results, we will now examine ways to construct approximately fair allocations. As it is not a priori clear what it would mean to be approximately fair, we examine each fairness concept separately and argue about possible approximation versions of each criterion. We summarize in each of the following subsections both positive (in terms of approximation algorithms) and negative (in terms of inapproximability) results that have been established.

12.4.1 Allocations with Maximin Share Guarantees

Apart from the computational difficulty, we know that for $n \geqslant 3$, there exist examples showing that MMS allocations do not always exist (Procaccia and Wang, 2014; Kurokawa et al., 2016). Although these examples are rather extreme, they show that even if we disregard time complexity, we cannot construct algorithms that always compute a MMS allocation.

It is then natural to explore what would be the best guarantee we can give. I.e., how close to a MMS allocation can we come? Can we construct an allocation where every agent receives a bundle of goods with a total value that is "close" to her MMS value? In order to quantify the distance from an actual MMS allocation, we use the notions of *additive* and *multiplicative* approximation. By an additive ρ-approximation, we mean an allocation $(S_1, \ldots, S_n)$, where $v_i(S_i) \geqslant \mu_i - \rho$, for some $\rho \leqslant \mu_i$. As for multiplicative approximations, which is the most common approach used in approximation algorithms, we will mean that we demand an allocation such that $v_i(S_i) \geqslant \rho \mu_i$, for some $\rho \leqslant 1$.

Let us first look for an additive approximation. We claim that the round robin algorithm presented in Section 12.3 provides such a guarantee. In particular, recall that we have defined α_i to be the maximum value of any good for agent i. Let also $\alpha = \max_{i,j} v_{ij} = \max_i \alpha_i$.

Theorem 12.7. *If $(S_1, \ldots, S_n)$ is the output of Algorithm 1, then for every $i \in N$,*

$$v_i(S_i) \geqslant \frac{v_i(M)}{n} - \alpha_i \geqslant \mu_i - \alpha_i \geqslant \mu_i - \alpha.$$

Proof. By Theorem 12.2, we know that the round robin algorithm is envy-free up to one good. This implies that for any $i, j \in N$, we have $v_i(S_i) \geqslant v_i(S_j) - \alpha_i$.

If we now sum up these inequalities over every $j \in N$, we get: $nv_i(S_i) \geq \sum_j v_i(S_j) - n\alpha_i$, which implies

$$v_i(S_i) \geq \frac{\sum_j v_i(S_j)}{n} - \alpha_i = \frac{v_i(M)}{n} - \alpha_i \geq \mu_i - \alpha_i,$$

where the last inequality holds since the maximin share guarantee is a relaxation to proportionality. □

This is already a positive result, as it reveals that when no item has a very high value for any agent, we can get an approximately fair allocation.

If we now try to obtain a multiplicative rather than an additive guarantee, we see that we would need somehow to handle carefully the goods that are valued highly, even by one agent. Obviously, such goods should end up at one of the agents who have a high value for them. What is interesting here is that if we do take care of highly valuable goods in this manner, we end up with an instance, where running the round robin algorithm provides a multiplicative guarantee since the maximum value now is quite small. Quantifying "highly valuable" to mean at least half of the total value of an agent for the set of available goods, we obtain Algorithm 3, for which we can establish a $1/2$-approximation.

ALGORITHM 3: APX-MMS$_{1/2}(N, M, V)$

---

1 Set $S = M$
2 **for** $i = 1$ *to* $|N|$ **do**
3 $\quad$ Let $\beta_i = \frac{\sum_{j \in S} v_{ij}}{|N|}$
4 **while** $\exists i, j$ s.t. $v_{ij} \geq \beta_i/2$ **do**
5 $\quad$ Allocate j to i.
6 $\quad$ $S = S \setminus \{j\}$
7 $\quad$ $N = N \setminus \{i\}$
8 $\quad$ Recompute the β_is
9 Run Algorithm 1 on the remaining instance

Theorem 12.8. *Let N be a set of n agents, and let M be a set of goods. Algorithm 3 produces an allocation $(S_1, ..., S_n)$ such that*

$$v_i(S_i) \geq \frac{1}{2}\mu_i, \ \forall i \in N$$

Proof. The important ingredient of the proof is a simple monotonicity property, which says that we can allocate a single good to an agent without decreasing the maximin share of other agents. Recall that μ_i is defined with respect to the number of agents, the set of goods and the valuation function of i, i.e., $\mu_i := \mu_i(n, M, v_i)$. This means that an analogous quantity can be defined for any sub-instance of an initial instance, hence, for any $S \subseteq M$ or for a smaller number of agents. The following property is then very easy to establish.

Claim 12.9 (Monotonicity property). *For any agent i and any good j, it holds that*

$$\mu_i(n-1, M \setminus \{j\}, v_i) \geq \mu_i(n, M, v_i).$$

We will distinguish two cases. Consider an agent i who was allocated a single item during the first phase of the algorithm (lines 4 - 8). Suppose that at the time when i was given her item, there were n_1 active agents, $n_1 \leqslant n$, and that S was the set of currently unallocated items. By the design of the algorithm, this means that the value of what i received is at least

$$\frac{\sum_{j \in S} v_{ij}}{2n_1} \geqslant \frac{1}{2}\mu_i(n_1, S, v_i).$$

But now if we apply the monotonicity property $n - n_1$ times, we obtain that $\mu_i(n_1, S, v_i) \geqslant \mu_i(n, M, v_i) = \mu_i$, and we are done.

Consider now an agent i, who gets a bundle of goods according to Greedy Round-Robin, in the second phase of Algorithm 3. Let n_2 be the number of active agents at that point, and S be the set of goods that are unallocated before Greedy Round-Robin is executed. We know that the maximum value of any remaining good at that point is less than half the current value of β_i for agent i. Hence by the additive guarantee of Greedy Round-Robin, i.e., the first inequality in Theorem 12.7, we have that the bundle received by agent i has value at least

$$\frac{\sum_{j \in S} v_{ij}}{n_2} - \frac{\beta_i}{2} = \frac{\sum_{j \in S} v_{ij}}{2n_2} \geqslant \frac{1}{2}\mu_i(n_2, S, v_i).$$

Again, after applying Claim 12.9 repeatedly, we get that $\mu_i(n_2, S, v_i) \geqslant \mu_i(n, M, v_i) = \mu_i$, which completes the proof. □

In trying to obtain a better approximation for this problem, one needs to take a different approach. This direction was investigated first by Procaccia and Wang (2014), and followed up by Amanatidis et al. (2015). By using matching arguments in a bipartite graph representation of the problem, and exploiting a more involved monotonicity property underlying the maximin shares, a better approximation factor was obtained, initially in exponential time by Procaccia and Wang (2014), and later in polynomial time by Amanatidis et al. (2015). The following statement summarizes the results of these two works.

Theorem 12.10. *For any n and m, and any constant $\epsilon > 0$, there exists a polynomial time algorithm producing an allocation $(S_1, ..., S_n)$ such that $v_i(S_i) \geqslant (\frac{2}{3} - \epsilon)\mu_i$.*

It is interesting to note that up to now it is still an open question whether a better approximation guarantee is possible for this notion. The impossibility results that have been established by Kurokawa et al. (2016), and Procaccia and Wang (2014) do not rule out even an approximation very close to 1.

Finally, the problem is also nontrivial to understand even with a small number of agents. For $n = 2$, it is pointed out by Bouveret and Lemaître (2014) that maximin share allocations always exist via an analog of the cut-and-choose protocol. Using the result of Woeginger (1997), we can then have a Polynomial Time Approximation Scheme (PTAS), i.e., a $(1 - \epsilon)$-approximation in polynomial time, for any constant $\epsilon > 0$. Hence, despite the NP-hardness, we can still have the best possible positive result we could hope for, when $n = 2$. In contrast, as soon as we move to $n = 3$, it has been proved that there exist instances where no maximin share allocation exists (Procaccia and Wang, 2014). The best known approximation guarantee is roughly 8/9 and was very recently obtained by Gourvès and Monnot (2017). Surprisingly, it is still unclear what is the best we can achieve for 3 agents. All these findings are summarized in the following statement.

Theorem 12.11. *For any number of items m, and*

- *for $n = 2$, there exists a PTAS, i.e, we can produce in polynomial time an allocation (S_1, S_2) such that $v_i(S_i) \geq (1 - \epsilon)\mu_i$, for any constant $\epsilon > 0$.*

- *for $n = 3$, there exists a polynomial time algorithm producing an allocation (S_1, S_2, S_3), such that $v_i(S_i) \geq (8/9 - \epsilon)\mu_i$, for any constant $\epsilon > 0$.*

12.4.2 Proportionality

As soon as we move away from maximin shares towards proportionality, the problems become computationally much harder.

For the concept of proportionality, let us start again with additive approximations. One way to define here such a notion of approximation would be as follows: we can say that an algorithm achieves an additive ρ-approximation if it produces an allocation where every agent i receives a bundle worth at least $\frac{1}{n}v_i(M) - \rho$.

By Theorem 12.7, we directly have the following corollary.

Corollary 12.12. *Algorithm 1 achieves an additive α-approximation for proportionality, where $\alpha = \max_{i,j} v_{ij}$.*

It can be easily seen that this guarantee is tight and cannot be further improved.

In analogy to the approximate versions of maximin share allocations, we will say that an algorithm achieves a multiplicative ρ-approximation for proportionality if it produces a partition $(S_1, S_2, \ldots, S_n)$ such that $v_i(S_i) \geq \rho \cdot \frac{1}{n} \cdot v_i(M)$.

In the previous subsection we saw that combining the round-robin algorithm with a careful handling of the most valuable goods, we obtained an approximation ratio of $1/2$ for the maximin share guarantees. Unfortunately, this does not carry over to approximate proportionality. In fact, it has been established that we cannot hope to have any decent approximation. The following result, proved by Markakis and Psomas (2011) shows that we cannot even decide in polynomial time, if an instance admits an allocation that achieves a constant approximation, hence we cannot possibly compute one for every instance. The proof is based on a reduction from the 3D-Matching problem.

Theorem 12.13. *For any constant $\rho \leq 1$, it is NP-complete to decide if there exists an allocation where every player receives a bundle worth at least $\rho \cdot \frac{1}{n} \cdot v_i(M)$.*

Theorem 12.13 reveals that proportionality is a much stronger concept to satisfy (even approximately), than maximin share fairness under indivisible goods.

12.4.3 Envy-freeness

Coming now to the strongest among the concepts we have considered so far, one might not be so optimistic about obtaining algorithmic results. Nevertheless, we will see that in certain cases, some positive results are feasible.

In order to define approximate versions, let us start with some notation. Given an allocation $S = (S_1, S_2, \ldots, S_n)$, let $e_{ij}(S) = \max\{0, v_i(S_j) - v_i(S_i)\}$ be the envy experienced by agent i towards agent j. When i does not envy j, we have $e_{ij}(S) = 0$. Let also $envy(S) = \max_{i,j \in N} e_{ij}(S)$ be the envy of the allocation S, i.e., we care for the maximum envy between any pair of agents.

Given an instance I, let $OPT(I)$ denote the minimum possible envy that can be achieved over all possible partitions,

$$OPT(I) = \min_{S \in \Pi_n(M)} envy(S)$$

If we look at the notion of envy from an optimization viewpoint, we can define the minimum envy problem as the problem of finding $OPT(I)$ for every instance I. We can now define approximate versions of our problem. Namely, we will say that an algorithm achieves an additive ρ-approximation for the minimum envy problem, if it produces a partition S such that $envy(S) \leq OPT(I) + \rho$. We can now easily have the following observation.

Corollary 12.14. *Any algorithm that is envy-free up to one good achieves an additive α-approximation to the minimum envy problem.*

This is true since any algorithm that is envy-free up to one good produces envy at most equal to α. Hence Algorithm 1 in particular obtains this guarantee.

Suppose now that we try to get a multiplicative guarantee. This would mean that we want an allocation such that the envy within this allocation should be at most $\rho OPT(I)$, at a given instance I. We claim that this particular type of multiplicative approximation is problematic for the minimum envy problem. To illustrate this, consider an instance I that admits an anvy-free solution. Hence $OPT(I) = 0$. An algorithm with a multiplicative ρ-approximation in this case means that it would produce an allocation S such that $envy(S) \leq \rho OPT(I) = 0$. Hence the algorithm is forced to compute an envy-free allocation whenever there exists one, i.e., this algorithm can be used to decide if an envy-free allocation exists. But since we showed in Theorem 12.5 that deciding existence of envy-free allocations is NP-complete, we then immediately have the following corrolary:

Theorem 12.15. *Unless P = NP, there is no finite multiplicative approximation algorithm for the minimum envy problem.*

The discussion above is an artifact of the nature of the problem. In particular, it is a consequence of the fact that the objective function in the optimization problem we try to solve can take the value zero. This is what prevents us from having a multiplicative approximation. We claim that a more suitable objective function for approximating envy is the envy-ratio, defined as taking the ratio rather than the difference between a pair of bundles. More formally, given an allocation $S = (S_1, S_2, \ldots, S_n)$, the envy-ratio of S is defined as the quantity $\max_{i,j \in N} \{1, \frac{v_i(S_j)}{v_i(S_i)}\}$. The minimum envy-ratio then asks for a partition that achieves the best such ratio.

Obviously this problem is still NP-complete. It is however more amenable to multiplicative approximations. Even though we are not aware of any good positive result for general additive valuation functions, it has been established that when the agents have identical preferences, any constant approximation is achievable. The following was established by Lipton et al. (2004).

Theorem 12.16. *Under identical additive valuation functions, there exists a PTAS for the minimum envy-ratio problem.*

It is still an open problem whether we can have positive results for a richer class of additive valuation functions.

12.5 Conclusions and Future Research

In this chapter, we have provided an overview of algorithmic and hardness results, with an emphasis on approximation algorithms. We believe this will continue to be a very active research area over the coming years, as there are still several unexplored problems that are worth further investigation.

To begin with, there are still some challenging open problems regarding the solution concepts we presented. We find the approximability status for MMS allocations one of the most intriguing questions. Is there a better than a 2/3-approximation to the maximin share guarantee of each agent? This question seems to require radically new ideas. Another interesting question concerns a stronger version of envy-freeness up to one good. Suppose that we require an allocation that would be envy-free up to any single good, meaning that an agent i does not envy any other agent j, after throwing away *any* item from the bundle of j. Recall that the standard definition of envy-freeness up to one good only requires that there exists a good that we can throw away from the bundle of agent j, so that i does not envy her. Can we always guarantee the existence of this stronger notion or can we disprove that?

Coming to other notions, there has recently been a surge of interest in the Maximum Nash Welfare (MNW) solution, which denotes an allocation that maximizes the product of the agents' valuations. It has been argued in Caragiannis et al. (2016) that the MNW solution provides certain fairness guarantees, i.e., it yields an allocation that is envy-free up to one good and is also an approximate MMS allocation. Computing this solution is a hard problem and approximation algorithms have also been suggested (Cole and Gkatzelis, 2015). Unfortunately, as soon as we move to approximations, we lose the fairness guarantees. Hence, the question of interest is whether one can have new approximation algorithms that can retain some of the fairness properties of the MNW solution.

Another approach on fair division is to combine fairness with incentive compatibility. Typically in the fair division literature, monetary payments are not allowed when studying strategic settings. Hence, this becomes a mechanism design problem without money. It has been quite challenging to understand which are the truthful mechanisms in such a setting. Up until recently, the only characterization result that was known concerned two agents and two items, due to Caragiannis et al. (2009). Lately, some further results have been obtained by Amanatidis et al. (2016), and a complete characterization of truthful mechanisms for two agents and any number of items was provided by Amanatidis et al. (2017). These results imply several consequences on the interplay between fairness and incentive compatibility. Undoubtedly, the main open question here is to understand and characterize truthful mechanisms for more than two agents.

Finally, over the years, the vast majority of the related literature has focused on additive valuation functions. In many cases, this assumption is crucial for obtaining positive results. It is true, however, that in some scenarios additivity is not the right assumption, since the goods may exhibit complementarities or substitutabilities. Very recently, new results for finding MMS allocations under submodular valuation functions have been obtained by Barman and Murthy (2017). We believe that further extensions to non-additive valuation functions would be very valuable for making this field even more credible and applicable.

Bibliography

G. Amanatidis, E. Markakis, A. Nikzad, and A. Saberi. Approximation algorithms for computing maximin share allocations. In *Proceedings of the 42nd International Colloquium on Automata, Languages, and Programming (ICALP), Track A*, pages 39–51, 2015.

G. Amanatidis, G. Birmpas, and E. Markakis. On truthful mechanisms for maximin share allocations. In *Proceedings of the 25th International Joint Conference on Artificial Intelligence (IJCAI)*, pages 31–37, 2016.

G. Amanatidis, G. Birmpas, G. Christodoulou, and E. Markakis. Truthful allocation mechanisms without payments: Characterization and implications on fairness. In *Proceedings of the 18th ACM Conference on Economics and Computation (EC)*, pages 545–562, 2017.

S. Barman and S. K. K. Murthy. Approximation algorithms for maximin fair division. In *Proceedings of the 18th ACM Conference on Economics and Computation (EC)*, pages 647–664, 2017.

S. Bouveret and M. Lemaître. Characterizing conflicts in fair division of indivisible goods using a scale of criteria. In *Proceedings of the 13th International Conference on Autonomous Agents and Multiagent Systems (AAMAS)*, pages 1321–1328, 2014.

S. Bouveret, Y. Chevaleyre, and N. Maudet. Fair allocation of indivisible goods. In F. Brandt, V. Conitzer, U. Endriss, J. Lang, and A. D. Procaccia, editors, *Handbook of Computational Social Choice*, chapter 12. Cambridge University Press, 2016.

S. J. Brams and A. D. Taylor. *Fair Division: From Cake Cutting to Dispute Resolution*. Cambridge University Press, 1996.

E. Budish. The combinatorial assignment problem: Approximate competitive equilibrium from equal incomes. *Journal of Political Economy*, 119(6):1061–1103, 2011.

I. Caragiannis, C. Kaklamanis, P. Kanellopoulos, and M. Kyropoulou. On low-envy truthful allocations. In *Proceedings of the 1st International Conference on Algorithmic Decision Theory (ADT)*, pages 111–119, 2009.

I. Caragiannis, D. Kurokawa, H. C. Moulin, A. D. Procaccia, N. Shah, and J. Wang. The unreasonable fairness of maximum Nash welfare. In *Proceedings of the 17th ACM Conference on Economics and Computation (EC)*, pages 305–322, 2016.

R. Cole and V. Gkatzelis. Approximating the Nash social welfare with indivisible items. In *Proceedings of the 47th Annual ACM Symposium on Theory of Computing (STOC)*, pages 371–380, 2015.

S. Demko and T. Hill. Equitable distribution of indivisible items. *Mathematical Social Sciences*, 16:145–158, 1988.

S. Even and A. Paz. A note on cake cutting. *Discrete Applied Mathematics*, 7:285–296, 1984.

D. Foley. Resource allocation and the public sector. *Yale Economics Essays*, 7:45–98, 1967.

G. Gamow and M. Stern. *Puzzle-Math*. Viking Press, 1958.

L. Gourvès and J. Monnot. Approximate maximin share allocations in matroids. In *Proceedings of the 10th International Conference on Algorithms and Complexity (CIAC)*, pages 310–321, 2017.

L. Gourvès, J. Monnot, and L. Tlilane. Worst case compromises in matroids with applications to the allocation of indivisible goods. *Theoretical Computer Science*, 589:121–140, 2015.

T. Hill. Partitioning general probability measures. *The Annals of Probability*, 15(2):804–813, 1987.

D. Kurokawa, A. D. Procaccia, and J. Wang. When can the maximin share guarantee be guaranteed? In *Proceedings of the 30th AAAI Conference on Artificial Intelligence (AAAI)*, pages 523–529, 2016.

R. J. Lipton, E. Markakis, E. Mossel, and A. Saberi. On approximately fair allocations of indivisible goods. In *Proceedings of the 5th ACM Conference on Electronic Commerce (EC)*, pages 125–131, 2004.

E. Markakis and C. A. Psomas. On worst-case allocations in the presence of indivisible goods. In *Proceedings of the 7th Workshop on Internet and Network Economics (WINE)*, pages 278–289, 2011.

H. Moulin. Uniform externalities: Two axioms for fair allocation. *Journal of Public Economics*, 43(3):305–326, 1990.

H. Moulin. *Fair Division and Collective Welfare*. MIT Press, Cambridge, Massachusetts, 2003.

A. D. Procaccia. Cake cutting algorithms. In F. Brandt, V. Conitzer, U. Endriss, J. Lang, and A. D. Procaccia, editors, *Handbook of Computational Social Choice*, chapter 13. Cambridge University Press, 2016.

A. D. Procaccia and J. Wang. Fair enough: guaranteeing approximate maximin shares. In *Proceedings of the 15th ACM Conference on Economics and Computation (EC)*, pages 675–692, 2014.

J. M. Robertson and W. A. Webb. *Cake Cutting Algorithms: Be fair if you can*. AK Peters, 1998.

H. Steinhaus. The problem of fair division. *Econometrica*, 16:101–104, 1948.

H. Varian. Equity, envy and efficiency. *Journal of Economic Theory*, 9:63–91, 1974.

G. Woeginger. A polynomial time approximation scheme for maximizing the minimum machine completion time. *Operations Research Letters*, 20:149–154, 1997.

CHAPTER 13

Computer-Aided Methods for Social Choice Theory

Christian Geist and Dominik Peters

13.1 Introduction

The Four Color Theorem is a famous early example of a mathematical result that was proven with the help of computers. Recent advances in artificial intelligence, particularly in constraint solving, promise the possibility of significantly extending the range of theorems that could be provable with the help of computers. Examples of results of this type are a special case of the Erdős Discrepancy Conjecture (Konev and Lisitsa, 2014), and a solution to the Boolean Pythagorean Triples Problem (Heule et al., 2016). The proofs obtained in these two cases are only available in a computer-checkable format, and have sizes of 13 GB and 200 TB, respectively. Proofs like these do not have any hope of being human-checkable, and make the controversy about the proof of the Four Color Theorem pale in comparison. The computer-found proofs of results we discuss in this chapter, on the other hand, will have the striking property of being translatable to a human-readable version.

Social choice theory studies group decision making, where the preferences of several agents need to be aggregated into one joint decision. This field of study has three characteristics that suggest applying computer-aided reasoning to it: it uses the axiomatic method, it is concerned with combinatorial structures, and its main concepts can be defined based on rather elementary mathematical notions. Thus, Nipkow (2009) notes that "social choice theory turns out to be perfectly suitable for mechanical theorem proving." In this chapter, we will present a set of tools and methods first employed in papers by Tang and Lin (2009) and Geist and Endriss (2011) that, thanks to the aforementioned properties, will allow us to use computers to prove one of social choice theory's most celebrated type of result: *impossibility theorems*.

An impossibility theorem posits that there does not exist a preference aggregation procedure that satisfies a given set of desirable axioms, and that these axioms are therefore incompatible. For example, the Gibbard–Satterthwaite Theorem says that no voting rule is simultaneously non-dictatorial, onto, and strategyproof. (A *voting rule* takes as input a collection of preference rankings and selects a winning alternative.) How to prove such a theorem? If we begin by limiting the number of alternatives and voters involved to a finite number, this task reduces to iterating through all possible voting rules and checking that none of them satisfies all axioms. However, this task invites an amazing combinatorial explosion, and a naïve search would be hopeless.

The main piece in our toolkit is a *SAT solver*, which can use our axioms to make logical inferences that make the search feasible. SAT solvers are computer programs that apply powerful reasoning strategies to decide whether a given propositional formula has a satisfying assignment or not. The last two decades have seen dramatic speedups in solving times, with regular 'SAT competitions' producing faster and faster solvers, despite the intimidating NP-completeness of the problem. Most solvers are freely available for use by researchers.

Here is the proof technique in a nutshell: Fix some finite number n of voters and m of alternatives, say $n = m = 3$. Produce a formula of propositional logic saying "there exists a voting rule for n voters and m alternatives satisfying such and such axioms" and decide its satisfiability using any state-of-the-art SAT solver. If, on the one hand, the formula is satisfiable, we can extract a voting rule that satisfies the desired axioms. If, on the other hand, the formula is unsatisfiable, we have the beginnings of an impossibility theorem. Usually, we now want two more things: find a *proof* of the unsatisfiability (human-readable if possible), and to extend the result to larger n and m. To achieve the first goal, we will present an exciting method using *minimal unsatisfiable sets*. For the second goal, we can often prove a relatively straightforward *induction step*, establishing an impossibility for arbitrarily large n and m.

This technique has been successfully applied by Tang and Lin (2008, 2009) to find new proofs of Arrow's and of the Gibbard–Satterthwaite Theorem, by Geist and Endriss (2011) to find new impossibilites in the space of set extensions, by Brandt and Geist (2016) and Brandl et al. (2015) to study strategic properties of tournament solutions, by Brandt et al. (2017) to study the no-show paradox, and by Brandl et al. (2016) to study probabilistic social choice. Many other applications of the technique are imaginable.

Related Work. Using logic solvers has proven to be useful for other problems in economics, too. Examples are the work by Fréchette et al. (2016), in which SAT solvers are used for the development and execution of the FCC's reverse spectrum auction, and recent results by Drummond et al. (2015), who solve stable matching problems via SAT solving. Closely related to our approach is an article by Tang and Lin (2011), who apply SAT solving to identify classes of two-player games with unique pure Nash equilibrium payoffs. In another recent paper, Caminati et al. (2015) verified combinatorial Vickrey auctions via higher-order theorem provers.

In some respects, our approach is similar to *automated mechanism design* (see, e.g., Conitzer and Sandholm, 2002), where desirable properties are also encoded as constraints, but mechanisms are computed to fit specific problem instances (rather than being applicable generally). In a similar spirit, Mennle and Seuken (2016) run linear programs in order to compute optimal (randomized) choice mechanisms that satisfy approximate versions of strategyproofness and efficiency.

A related line of work is directed towards formalizing and verifying *existing* results of social choice theory, such as Arrow's Impossibility Theorem, through logical formalizations (see, e.g., Nipkow, 2009; Grandi and Endriss, 2013; Ciná and Endriss, 2016).

The method we are going to survey in this chapter has also been discussed in articles by Chatterjee and Sen (2014) and Kerber et al. (2016).

Chapter Outline. This chapter comes in two main parts. First, in Section 13.2 we go through an application of the method step-by-step using a simple toy impossibility. Second, in Section 13.3, we give a detailed survey of several papers that have applied the method, emphasising key extensions to the basic technique as described in Section 13.2. We close by discussing the potential and the limits of the method, and sketch some possibilities for future work.

13.2 Case Study: Strategyproofness and the Majority Criterion

In this section, we showcase the method by going through a toy example in detail. We will use SAT solvers to find a human-readable proof of the following result:

Theorem 13.1. *For $n = 3$ voters and $m \geqslant 3$ alternatives, no (resolute) voting rule satisfies both strategyproofness and the majority criterion.*

Let $N = \{1, 2, 3\}$ be a set of 3 voters, let $A = \{a, b, c\}$ be the set of alternatives, let $\mathcal{L}(A)$ be the set of linear orders over A, and let $\mathcal{R} = \mathcal{L}(A)^N$ be the set of profiles over A. Thus, a profile is a function assigning a preference ordering to each voter.

A resolute voting rule $f : \mathcal{R} \to A$ is a function mapping every preference profile of linear orders to a winning alternative.

The voting rule f satisfies the *majority criterion* if whenever R is a profile so that a strict majority of voters ranks some alternative $x \in A$ in top position, then $f(R) = x$.[1] For convenience, for each $x \in A$, we write $\mathcal{M}(x) \subseteq \mathcal{R}$ for the set of profiles where x is ranked top by a majority.

We say that f is *manipulable* if there is a voter $i \in N$ and two profiles $R, R' \in \mathcal{R}$ such that $R(j) = R'(j)$ for every voter $j \in N \setminus \{i\}$, but $f(R') \succ_i f(R)$, where $\succ_i = R(i)$ is i's vote in R. Thus, voter i can achieve a better outcome by misreporting her preferences as $\succ'_i = R'(i)$. Conversely, f is *strategyproof* if f is not manipulable.

Note that the Gibbard–Satterthwaite Theorem immediately implies our Theorem 13.1: if a voting rule satisfies the majority criterion, then it is also onto and non-dictatorial. Thus, proving Theorem 13.1 is not a breakthrough result; however, we hope that this section illustrates the SAT approach.

Step 1: Encoding into SAT. We start by constructing a formula φ of propositional logic that is satisfiable if and only if there exists a resolute voting rule f for $n = 3$ voters and $m = 3$ alternatives satisfying both strategyproofness and

---

[1]Thus, the majority criterion is a much weaker axiom than Condorcet-consistency. The Borda count is a notable example of a rule which fails the majority criterion.

the majority criterion. So that the formula can be processed by standard SAT solvers, we will ensure that our encoding produces a formula in *conjunctive normal form* (CNF). Thus, φ will be a conjunction of *clauses*. Recall that a clause is a disjunction of literals, and a literal is either a variable or its negation. In our example, it will be very natural to phrase our problem as a CNF formula. For some other settings or axioms, we might need to transform a non-CNF formula into CNF first. This is best done using Tseitin transformations (Tseitin, 1983; see Kroening and Strichman, 2016, p. 12–14, for examples).

The propositional variables used in φ will describe the voting rule f explicitly, i.e., they will specify the output of f for every possible profile with $n = m = 3$. Precisely, we will use one variable $v_{R,x}$ for each such profile $R \in \mathcal{R}$ and each $x \in A$. The intended interpretation is that

$$f(R) = x \iff v_{R,x} \text{ is true.}$$

With this interpretation, any satisfying assignment of φ will give rise to a voting rule satisfying our axioms. Thus, Theorem 13.1 will be true (for $n = m = 3$) if and only if φ is unsatisfiable.

We now describe the formula φ as the conjunction of several subformulas. We start out by formalising the requirement that f be a function, that is, $f(R)$ needs to correspond to exactly one alternative. This requirement can be broken down into two statements: that there be *at least* one such alternative, and *at most* one such alternative. The first of these is easy to encode:

$$\varphi_{\text{at least one}} \equiv \bigwedge_{R \in \mathcal{R}} (v_{R,a} \lor v_{R,b} \lor v_{R,c}).$$

The second part can be phrased in CNF by requiring that $f(R)$ does not correspond to two distinct alternatives:

$$\varphi_{\text{resolute}} \equiv \bigwedge_{R \in \mathcal{R}} \bigwedge_{\substack{x,y \in A \\ x \neq y}} (\neg v_{R,x} \lor \neg v_{R,y}).$$

Next, we encode our axioms. The majority criterion is relatively easy to put into logic; we just identify all profiles R for which the majority criterion implies a restriction on f. Recall that $\mathcal{M}(x)$ is the set of profiles in which a majority of voters puts x in top position.

$$\varphi_{\text{majority}} \equiv \bigwedge_{x \in A} \bigwedge_{R \in \mathcal{M}(x)} (v_{R,x}).$$

Strategyproofness is an axiom relating the output of f at two different profiles. The encoding below interprets strategyproofness as "if $f(R) = y$, and voter i can change profile R into R' by misrepresenting her preferences, then $f(R')$ cannot be better for i than y".

$$\varphi_{\text{strategyproof}} \equiv \bigwedge_{i \in N} \bigwedge_{R \in \mathcal{R}} \bigwedge_{\substack{R' \in \mathcal{R} \\ R'(j) = R(j) \\ \forall j \neq i}} \bigwedge_{\substack{x,y \in A \\ x \succ_i y}} (v_{R,y} \to \neg v_{R',x}).$$

```
c reading input file majority-resolute.cnf
c no embedded options
c found 'p cnf 648 12048' header
c read 648 variables, 12048 clauses, 24144 literals in 0.00 seconds
s UNSATISFIABLE
c
c    0.000  36% simplifying
c    0.000   0% search
c ===================================
c    0.000 100% all
c
c 0 conflicts, 0.0 conflicts/sec
c 241 propagations, 1.2 megaprops/sec
c
c 0.0 seconds, 0.1 MB
```

Figure 13.1: Command-line output of the `lingeling` SAT solver when run on the formula produced for our example. The line `s UNSATISFIABLE` states the result.

(Implications "$a \to b$" can be rewritten as the disjunction $\neg a \vee b$.) Putting all the subformulas together, we finally obtain

$$\varphi = \varphi_{\text{at least one}} \wedge \varphi_{\text{resolute}} \wedge \varphi_{\text{majority}} \wedge \varphi_{\text{strategyproof}}.$$

Step 2: SAT Solving. Now that we have an encoding of our problem into CNF, we can pass it on to a SAT solver to decide whether φ is satisfiable. For this we will need to choose a specific solver, and write φ in a file format that the solver can understand. A common source for finding powerful solvers is the series of "SAT competitions" (`satcompetition.org`), where solvers by different researchers are compared on a benchmark set. Two good choices at the time of writing are `lingeling` (developed by Biere, 2013) and `glucose` (developed by Audemard and Simon, 2009).

All common SAT solvers accept input formulas as text files in the DIMACS format. To produce a CNF formula in this format, identify the propositional variables using integers $1, 2, \ldots, v$. Each clause of the formula is represented by a line in the text file; for example, the clause $1 \vee \neg 2 \vee 3$ is represented by the line

```
1 -2 3 0
```

Literals are separated by spaces and lines are terminated with a 0 and a newline character. The first line of a DIMACS file is a header which contains the number of variables and clauses used in the formula. For example, the formula we produced to encode our problem here contains 648 variables and 12,048 clauses, and so the associated file would start with the line

```
p cnf 648 12048
```

The DIMACS file should usually be produced using a script which keeps track of the mapping from variables to integers, so that a possible satisfying assignment can be translated back into an actual model.

When running our chosen SAT solver on the formula produced, we obtain a report that φ is unsatisfiable in much less than 1 second[2] (as in the screenshot in Figure 13.1).

Step 3: MUS Extraction. Still, we would like to know a *reason* for the unsatisfiability, and preferably a human-readable proof. For these purposes it will be useful to know where the unsatisfiability comes from, and which profiles and constraints were responsible for it. The relevant tool for this goal is a *minimal unsatisfiable set (MUS)*, which is a subset of the clauses of φ that is already unsatisfiable, and is minimally so, in the sense that removing any of the clauses results in a satisfiable formula. Thus, each of the clauses in an MUS encodes a 'proof step' that cannot be skipped. The fewer clauses an MUS contains, the easier it is to understand, and so we are hoping to find an MUS of small cardinality.

The number of available tools for extracting an MUS is substantially smaller than the number of SAT solvers. For our purposes the currently best tool available is MUSer2 by Belov and Marques-Silva (2012), which internally uses the solver glucose as a SAT oracle. MUSer2 takes an unsatisfiable DIMACS file as input and returns an MUS. MUSer2 also supports the computation of *group MUSes*: in this setting, the clauses of a CNF formula are partitioned into groups, and we are looking for an inclusion-minimal set of groups that are unsatisfiable. In our experience, it can be useful to group together the clauses referring to a single profile, as this can lead to smaller MUSes that are easier to interpret. A group-CNF formula is specified by a DIMACS file with clause lines like {6} 1 -2 3 0, where 6 is the number of the group that corresponds to this clause, and has header line p gcnf 648 12048 100, where 100 is the number of groups used. Clauses in group 0 are never removed by MUSer2.

Another useful tool is MARCO (Liffiton et al., 2016), which enumerates *all* MUSes of a given (group-)CNF formula. This can be helpful to find smaller MUSes, or ones that have a simpler structure.

The MUS obtained in our example contains just 9 clauses, which refer to a total of 5 profiles, which we label $R_\alpha, R_\beta, R_\gamma, R_\delta, R_\epsilon$ and show in Figure 13.2. In particular, the MUS contains 2 clauses from $\varphi_{\text{at least one}}$ for R_α and R_γ, 3 clauses from $\varphi_{\text{majority}}$ for R_β, R_δ, and R_ϵ, and 4 clauses from $\varphi_{\text{strategyproof}}$ for manipulations from R_α to R_γ, from R_α to R_β, from R_γ to R_δ, and from R_γ to R_ϵ. Interestingly, the MUS does not contain any clauses from $\varphi_{\text{resolute}}$.

Step 4: Interpreting the MUS. Now we will translate the MUS obtained in the previous step into a human-readable proof. The MUS we have obtained can be displayed in a graphical fashion, as in the right-hand half of Figure 13.2. Producing such "proof diagrams" can make it much easier to produce a human-readable proof. To see how this diagram can be obtained, it is useful to distinguish between *intra-profile* and *inter-profile* axioms (cf. Fishburn, 1973). An intra-profile axiom refers to the allowed voting outcomes at a *single* profile; examples are Pareto optimality, the majority criterion, and Condorcet-consistency. Any clauses

---

[2] For our example problem, the strategy of *unit propagation* turns out to be enough to solve the formula, but this is not the case for all problems of this type.

Computer-Aided Methods

	voter 1	voter 2	voter 3
R_α	$a \succ b \succ c$	$b \succ a \succ c$	$c \succ a \succ b$
R_β	$a \succ b \succ c$	$b \succ a \succ c$	$a \succ b \succ c$
R_γ	$a \succ b \succ c$	$b \succ c \succ a$	$c \succ a \succ b$
R_δ	$a \succ b \succ c$	$c \succ a \succ b$	$c \succ a \succ b$
R_ϵ	$b \succ a \succ c$	$b \succ c \succ a$	$c \succ a \succ b$

R_α at least one
— 3 manip. → R_β majority for a
— 2 manip. → R_γ at least one
 — 2 manip. → R_δ majority for c
 — 1 manip. → R_ϵ majority for b

Figure 13.2: The 5 profiles used in the MUS, and a graphical representation of the clauses in the MUS.

in the MUS referring to an intra-profile axiom can be written next to the node of the diagram representing the profile under consideration. An inter-profile axiom *connects* the voting outcomes at multiple profiles; examples are strategyproofness, participation, anonymity and neutrality. Note that these four examples can be phrased so as to refer to *exactly two* profiles. As such, they can be displayed as a (possibly directed) edge connecting two profile-nodes in the diagram. In our example, directed edges correspond to clauses specifying that a certain manipulation is not successful. Proof diagrams of this sort, first used by Brandt et al. (2017), can serve as a unifying 'language' of impossibility proofs.[3]

We will now translate the 'proof' shown in Figure 13.2 into English. In reading the following proof, it is useful to refer to the diagram to see how the two objects correspond to each other.

Theorem 13.2 (Base Case). *For $m = n = 3$, there is no voting rule that satisfies strategyproofness and the majority criterion.*

Proof. Suppose f is a voting rule satisfying both axioms. We proceed in a bottom-up fashion, establishing which value f must take for each profile, and find that there is no possible value $f(R_\alpha)$ for the root node, contradiction.

Consider the profile R_γ, where $f(R_\gamma)$ needs to take some value. If $f(R_\gamma) = a$, then voter 2 can manipulate to obtain profile R_δ. By the majority criterion, $f(R_\delta) = c$, and so we have $f(R_\delta) \succ_2 f(R_\gamma)$, and this was a successful manipulation, contradicting strategyproofness of f. Hence $f(R_\gamma) \neq a$.

If $f(R_\gamma) = c$, then voter 1 can manipulate to obtain profile R_ϵ. By the majority criterion, $f(R_\epsilon) = b$. Thus $f(R_\epsilon) \succ_1 f(R_\gamma)$, and this was a successful manipulation, contradicting strategyproofness of f. Hence $f(R_\gamma) \neq c$. Hence $f(R_\gamma) = b$.

By the majority criterion, $f(R_\beta) = a$. Now consider profile R_α. In case $f(R_\alpha) = b$, then voter 3 can manipulate to obtain profile R_β. Since $f(R_\beta) = a$, this would be a successful manipulation for voter 3. Hence $f(R_\alpha) \neq b$.

---

[3]Inter-profile axioms that refer to more than two profiles, such as non-dictatorship or non-imposition, cannot be represented as edges in a proof diagram. The MUS-based approach is less suited for problems using these axioms, since any MUS will need to contain clauses referring to *every* profile. In such situations, it can be useful to replace these axioms by related ones that refer to at most two profiles. For example, non-imposition is often equivalent to unanimity in the presence of strategyproofness.

Thus, $f(R_\alpha) \in \{a,c\}$. But voter 2 can manipulate at R_α to obtain profile R_γ. We have seen that $f(R_\gamma) = b$. Hence $f(R_\gamma) \succ_2 f(R_\alpha)$ according to voter 2's preferences in R_α, contradicting strategyproofness of f. Hence such an f cannot exist. □

In this example, the MUS corresponds to a short and elegant proof. For more complicated impossibilities, it is sometimes useful to hand-optimize the MUS found. MUS extractors typically use essentially a greedy algorithm to find an MUS, and the result may well only be a local optimum with respect to cardinality of the MUS, or indeed with respect to simplicity of the resulting proof.

Step 5: Induction Step. We have found a proof of the finite fact that for $n = m = 3$, no voting rule can satisfy the axioms of strategyproofness and of the majority criterion. This alone is perhaps not completely satisfying, since we would like to say something about larger values of n and m. Often, it is possible to prove a *reduction argument* which consists of statements of the form

- If there is a voting rule satisfying a given set of axioms for $n + 1$ voters and m alternatives, then there is also a voting rule satisfying these axioms for n voters and m alternatives.

- If there is a voting rule satisfying a given set of axioms for n voters and $m + 1$ alternatives, then there is also a voting rule satisfying these axioms for n voters and m alternatives.

Viewed contrapositively, these statements are *induction steps*. If we can prove these statements, given our proof of the base case above, it immediately follows that the impossibility result also holds for all larger values of n and m. Sometimes it can be difficult to establish this induction step; in such cases it may be possible to manually extend the proof obtained for the base case to go through for larger n or m. In some settings, the induction step may turn out to be false (for example, an impossibility could only hold in profiles with an odd number of voters). For our example, it is easy to prove an induction step for m, but we do not know of a way to prove the induction step for n (except, of course, by cheating and appealing to the Gibbard–Satterthwaite Theorem directly).

Lemma 13.3. *Let $m \geqslant 3$ and $n = 3$. If f is a resolute voting rule satisfying strategyproofness and the majority criterion for $m + 1$ alternatives, then there exists a voting rule f' for m alternatives with the same properties.*

Proof. Let f be defined for the alternative set $A \cup \{x\}$, where $|A| = m$. For every profile R with n voters and on alternative set A, define the profile R^{+x} derived from R by putting alternative x at the bottom of each preference order. Thus, for each voter i and all $a, b \in A$, we have $a \succsim_i^{+x} b$ if and only if $a \succsim_i b$, and we have $a \succsim_i^{+x} x$ for each $a \in A$. Then define the rule f' on alternative set A by

$$f'(R) := f(R^{+x}).$$

Clearly, f' satisfies the majority criterion, for if x is the majority winner in R, then x is also majority winner in R^{+x}, so $f'(R) = f(R^{+x}) = x$, since f satisfies the majority criterion. Also, f' satisfies strategyproofness, because any successful manipulation of f' from R to R' is a successful manipulation of f from R^{+x} to R'^{+x}, which would contradict strategyproofness of f. □

The technique of adding new alternatives to the bottom of the profile is a standard tool for reducing the number of alternatives. Often-used moves for reducing the number of voters, on the other hand, include cloning a specific voter, adding an all-indifferent voter, or adding two voters with completely reversed preferences.

Having established both base case and induction step, this concludes the proof of our modest impossibility theorem.

13.3 Applications and Advanced Techniques

We will now survey several papers that have used this style of technique to prove much more complex results, and discuss ways in which they deviate from the recipe.

13.3.1 Arrow's and the Gibbard–Satterthwaite Theorem

The two most famous impossibility theorems in social choice theory are Arrows' Impossibility Theorem and the Gibbard–Satterthwaite Theorem. Tang and Lin (2008, 2009) used these theorems to introduce the idea of proving impossibilities in social choice by induction on n and m, and by verifying the base case using a SAT or constraint-programming solver. It should be clear how to adapt the method of Section 13.2 to prove the base case of the Gibbard–Satterthwaite Theorem; to encode non-imposition one could use $\bigwedge_{x \in A} \bigvee_R v_{R,x}$, and to encode non-dictatorship one could use $\bigwedge_{i \in N} \bigvee_R \neg v_{R,\text{top}(R,i)}$, where $\text{top}(R, i)$ denotes the most-preferred alternative of voter i in profile R. Note that both of these axioms use very long clauses, which can be tough for solvers to use. Similar ideas can be used to encode the base case of Arrow's Impossibility Theorem; for this, one would probably introduce a variable $v_{R,\succsim}$ for each profile R and each possible output relation $\succsim$.

While establishing the base case for both of these theorems is straightforward, establishing the induction steps is rather involved. This is in contrast to the results we will see below, where establishing the base cases is the main technical difficulty. This is because the number of variables in the encoding grows exponentially with n and m, and the results below need base cases with $m > 3$.

13.3.2 Irresolute SCFs and Fishburn's Set Extension

In this section we will see two modifications to the technique we saw in Section 13.2: here, we will consider voting rules that are *majoritarian* and *set-valued*. Both of these changes have impacts on the encoding technique.

A *set-valued* (or *irresolute*) voting rule assigns to every preference profile a non-empty subset of A; the usual interpretation is that the alternatives returned are tied for winner, and that some external tie-breaking mechanism will later be applied. This approach raises some problems for defining axioms such as strategyproofness; to extend the definition of the resolute case, we need to extend a voter's preference order to a preference order over *sets* of alternatives. Several different ways to do this (so-called *set extensions*) have been proposed. In this section, we will focus on Fishburn's set extension.[4] Suppose i is a voter with preference relation $\succsim_i$, and suppose i expects the ties in the voting rule to be broken according to some linear tie-breaking order; however, i does not know which order will be used. Now, if $X, Y \subseteq A$ are non-empty subsets of alternatives, set X is weakly preferred to Y according to the Fishburn extension (written $X \succsim_i^F Y$) if the tie-broken outcome from X is guaranteed to be weakly better (according to $\succsim_i$) than the outcome from Y, no matter the tie-breaking order used. For a more explicit definition, see Brandt and Geist (2016). Note that the relation $\succsim_i^F$ is incomplete: not all pairs of sets can be compared using the criterion given.

In a similar way to the resolute case, we say that an irresolute rule f is *Fishburn-manipulable* if for some voter $i \in N$ and for two profiles R and R' that differ only in i's vote, we have $f(R') \succ_i^F f(R)$, where $\succ_i$ is i's vote in profile R. Then f is *Fishburn-strategyproof* if it is not Fishburn-manipulable. Now let $R - i = R|_{N \setminus \{i\}}$ denote the profile obtained from R by removing voter i. We say that an irresolute rule f (defined over profiles with variable electorates) satisfies *Fisburn-participation* if there is no profile R and voter i such that $f(R - i) \succ_i^F f(R)$. Thus, voters never strictly regret having voted.

Further, f is said to be *majoritarian* if it is neutral and selects the same set of alternatives for any two profiles with the same majority relation, and it is *Pareto optimal* if whenever x is a Pareto dominated alternative in R, then $x \notin f(R)$.

Finally, we can state the two impossibilities of this section.

Theorem 13.4 (Brandt and Geist, 2016). *There is no majoritarian and Pareto optimal set-valued voting rule that satisfies Fishburn-strategyproofness if $m \geqslant 5$ and $n \geqslant 7$.*

Theorem 13.5 (Brandl et al., 2015). *There is no majoritarian and Pareto optimal set-valued voting rule that satisfies Fishburn-participation if $m \geqslant 4$ and $n \geqslant 6$.*

Both of these results were proved using the method presented in Section 13.2. Let us sketch how the encoding can be adapted to the new setting. In order to encode the irresoluteness of the voting rules, it is useful to choose a variable $v_{R,X}$ for every profile R and every non-empty $X \subseteq A$ indicating that $f(R) = X$. While this might seem like a wasteful encoding, requiring $2^m - 1$ variables for each profile, it makes it much easier to encode Fishburn's set extension, because we can evaluate the relation $\succsim^F$ at encoding time, rather than having to translate its definition into propositional logic.[5] To encode that f should be majoritarian, one

---

[4] Some authors refer to this set extension as Gärdenfors' extension. We follow the terminology of the survey by Gärdenfors (1979), who uses his own name for a different set extension.

[5] If one uses the optimistic or pessimistic preference extension (like in Brandt et al., 2017, Section 7), using variables $v_{R,x}$ for $x \in X$ can often be made to work directly.

could use clauses enforcing an if-and-only-if relation between the outputs of two profiles with the same majority relation. However, a much more efficient possibility exists: for each possible majority relation (represented by a tournament T), introduce variables $v_{T,X}$. Since there are vastly fewer tournaments than there are profiles, this uses many fewer variables, and clearly, this is enough to define any majoritarian voting rule. However, with this choice of encoding, one needs to take care to encode Fishburn-strategyproofness and neutrality only in terms of tournaments; see Theorem 1 and Lemma 1 of Brandt and Geist (2016).

13.3.3 The No-Show Paradox and Incremental Proof Discovery

A stunning result of Moulin (1988) establishes that no Condorcet extension satisfies participation, an axiom that requires that no voter can be worse off by participating and voting honestly. Moulin's proof requires 4 alternatives and 25 voters to go through. Since the maximin rule (with some fixed tie-breaking rule) is a Condorcet extension satisfying participation if $m = 3$ (Moulin, 1988), we see that 4 alternatives are required for the result to hold. However, it seems unlikely that exactly 25 voters are required. We will use SAT solvers to find an optimal bound.

Formally, in this section we consider voting rules that are defined for *variable electorates*, i.e., that are defined for profiles that contain different numbers of voters. Given a profile R of linear orders, an alternative $a \in A$ is called a *Condorcet winner* if for every other alternative $b \in A \setminus \{a\}$, there is a strict majority of voters who prefer a to b. A voting rule is a *Condorcet extension* if it selects the Condorcet winner for all profiles that have one. As in the previous section, we say that a voting rule f satisfies *participation* if for all profiles R, and for all voters i who participate in R, we have $f(R) \succsim_i f(R - i)$. Thus every voter weakly prefers submitting their truthful preference order to abstaining. Again, $R - i = R|_{N \setminus \{i\}}$ is the profile obtained from R by removing voter i.

Theorem 13.6 (Brandt et al., 2017). *While there is no Condorcet extension that satisfies participation for $m \geqslant 4$ and $n \geqslant 12$, there exists such a voting rule for $m = 4$ and $n \leqslant 11$.*

In principle, it should be no mystery how to achieve such a result using the technique of Section 13.2. Inconveniently, there are $4!^{12} \approx 10^{16}$ profiles with $m = 4$ and $n = 12$, and it is impractical to enumerate them all in order to write down (let alone solve) the SAT formula we would produce.

One could try something similar to the approach of Section 13.3.2 and only consider majoritarian voting rules. In fact, if we restrict attention to *pairwise* (C2) voting rules (those that depend only on the *weighted* majority relation), then one gets a positive result for $n = 11$ and a negative one for $n = 12$. This result for $n = 11$ is useful as it implies the second part of Theorem 13.6; the result for $n = 12$, however, is weaker than desired because it uses the additional "axiom" that the voting rule is pairwise. However, obtaining this proof with an additional axiom could still be useful. Brandt et al. (2017) propose using what they call *incremental proof discovery*: using proofs of weaker statements to make educated guesses about a restricted domain over which to look for an impossibility result. In particular, they noticed that the impossibility proof for $n = 12$ using pairwiseness had some interesting structure. The profiles in the proof did contain all $4! = 24$ possible preference orders, instead using only 10 different orders. They then produced a formula including only profiles that were built up using only these 10 orders; a much smaller formula. This formula turned out to be already unsatisfiable, establishing the first part of Theorem 13.6.

Brandt et al. (2017) then used information gleaned from the proof for $n = 12$ to search for impossibility results to look for impossibilities for set-valued voting rules (with participation defined using the *optimistic* and *pessimistic* set extensions) and found optimal bounds of $n = 17$ and $n = 14$ for impossibility results in this setting. Later, Peters (2017) used similar techniques to find such results for Condorcet extensions satisfying *half-way monotonicity*, which is a weaker condition than participation.

13.3.4 Probabilistic Voting Rules

Let $\Delta(A)$ be the set of lotteries (probability distributions) over A. A *probabilistic voting rule* (also known as a *social decision scheme*) assigns a lottery to each preference profile; for example, the voting outcome might be a fair coin toss between a and b. As usual, such a voting rule is anonymous and neutral if it is invariant under renaming voters and alternatives, respectively. For defining other axioms, it is useful to have a way of comparing different lotteries in terms of their desirability to a given voter. Here, we will use the notion of stochastic dominance: If a voter i has preferences $\succsim_i$, and $p, q \in \Delta(A)$ are lotteries, we say that $p \succsim_i^{SD} q$ if

$$\sum_{y \succsim_i x} p(y) \geqslant \sum_{y \succsim_i x} q(y) \quad \text{for all } x \in A.$$

The main appeal of stochastic dominance stems from the following equivalence: $p \succsim^{SD} q$ if and only if p yields at least as much von-Neumann-Morgenstern utility as q under *any* utility function that is consistent with the ordinal preferences $\succsim$. We can now say that a probabilistic voting rule f is *SD-strategyproof* if we do not have $f(R') \succ_i^{SD} f(R)$ for any profiles R and R' that differ only in voter $i \in N$, where $\succsim_i$ is i's preference according to R. Further, we say that f is *SD-efficient* if there never exists a lottery $p \neq f(R)$ such that $p \succsim_i^{SD} f(R)$ for all voters $i \in N$ and $p \succ_i^{SD} f(R)$ for some voter $i \in N$.

It turns out that these two axioms are incompatible in the presence of symmetry axioms.

Theorem 13.7 (Brandl et al., 2016). *If $m \geqslant 4$ and $n \geqslant 4$, and allowing weak orders with indifferences as individual preferences, there is no anonymous and neutral probabilistic voting rule that satisfies SD-efficiency and SD-strategyproofness.*

This result is notable because it implies several other previously found impossibility results in probabilistic social choice (see Chapter 1 of this book). Since this result appears in a chapter on computer-aided methods, it is unsurprising that it, too, was obtained using solving techniques. However, this may seem puzzling: even fixing $n = m = 4$, the search space of probabilistic voting rules is infinite. This suggests that we will need a different solving technique, which can deal with real-valued (rather than Boolean) variables. Integer Programming comes to mind, and indeed one can encode the axioms of Theorem 13.7 using Integer Programming.

Another option in this context, though, are *SMT solvers* ("satisfiability modulo theories"). These solvers are very flexible and are used mainly in software verification. When we use linear arithmetic as our underlying theory, we can think of the input formula given to the SMT solver as a propositional formula whose atoms are linear (in)equalities of real-valued variables. Encoding our axioms into this language is relatively straightforward, though SD-efficiency requires some further analysis (see Brandl et al. (2016) for details). We have found that SMT solvers frequently solve problems like the ones discussed here faster than commercial Integer Programming solvers. This may be because branch-and-cut is less appropriate than conflict-driven approaches for our problems.

Unfortunately, the infinite search space involved seems to make this problem significantly tougher, and Brandl et al. (2016) found it prohibitive to search over the entire space of about 1 million profiles. Thus, they looked for a similar reduction in the size of the search space as was successful for participation (Section 13.3.3). They noticed that many impossibility results take the form of starting at some initial profile R and then considering "nearby" profiles that can be obtained from R through few manipulations (i.e., few voters changing their reported preferences). They identified a promising profile R in which the popular probabilistic rule *Random Serial Dictatorship* returned an *SD*-inefficient lottery, and then generated a "ball" of about $10,000$ profiles around R which could be reached by at most 4 successive manipulations. They also only considered "small" manipulations, where the reported preference was close to the truthful one (according to the Kendall-tau distance). Finally, they incorporated the anonymity and neutrality axioms by only introducing variables for *canonical profiles* which represent all profiles obtainable by renaming voters and alternatives. The resulting domain was small enough for the solver to terminate, and to yield an unsatisfiability result. Many SMT solvers allow for the extraction of minimal unsatisfiable sets, which allow obtaining a human-readable proof, though this is much more involved in this case (see Eberl, 2016).

13.3.5 Other Applications

Set Extensions. There is a well-developed literature about how to extend a preference order over alternatives to a preference order over *sets* of alternatives; see Barberà et al. (2004) for a survey. Much of the work in this area focuses on axiomatic characterisations and impossibility results. Geist and Endriss (2011) introduce a logic for capturing many of the axioms used in the field, and prove a universal induction step for all (conjunctions of) axioms that can be represented as an "existentially set-guarded" formula in this logic. They then considered 20 of such axioms, and used a solver to check base cases for all combinations of these axioms, finding a total of 84 (axiom-minimal) impossibilities, several of which were not previously known.

Proof Verification. One way to gain more confidence in the correctness of computer-generated (and also human-generated) proofs is to formally check them. One tool to do so is ISABELLE/HOL (Nipkow et al., 2002), which is a generic *interactive theorem prover*, where *interactive* indicates that the process of proof discovery is guided by a human operator who indicates a sequence of steps to follow, with most gaps filled automatically by the theorem prover. For examples of this applied to social choice, see Nipkow (2009) and Eberl (2016). In particular, the latter paper verifies the result from Section 13.3.4.

Solving-based Algorithms. There are a few examples of algorithms for computational problems in social choice theory that are powered by SAT solving. For instance, mostly by computing counterexamples, Brandt et al. (2016) explore the boundaries of the connection between the McKelvey uncovered set and the notion of Pareto optimality, Bachmeier et al. (2017) improve our understanding of the notions of k-majority digraphs, and Geist (2014) computes minimal preference profiles with Condorcet dimension 3. Interestingly, using solvers outperforms existing tailor-made algorithms in many applications.

13.4 Discussion and Future Work

New Insights. A perhaps surprising feature of computer-aided proofs is that they may give new and unexpected insights into the problems considered. For example, in studying the no-show paradox, Brandt et al. (2017) found proofs that exploit symmetries that were not present in Moulin's (1988) original proof. A related feature of the computer-aided methods discussed in this chapter are that they allow searching through various related conjectures. For example, it is easy to replace axioms by weaker versions to see whether the impossibility still holds. Brandt and Geist (2016) extensively used this technique to find several weakenings of Fishburn-strategyproofness that sill produce an impossibility. Geist and Endriss (2011) used this technique to find an exhaustive list of impossibility results in their domain of set extensions.

Better Usability. In their current form, applying solving methodologies to social choice theory remains a task for expert users with programming skills. While this does not impact the overall power of the approach, it limits the degree to which it can be broadly used by any researcher in social choice. Still, one may hope for the development of user-friendly tools that help formalizing concepts of social choice theory in the languages of solvers.

However, in our experience, the design of efficient encodings has to follow the requirements of—and needs to be optimized for—the concrete problem. This follows the observation that for general proof assistants with highly expressive input languages, such as ISABELLE, many problems can be easily and intuitively formalized, but the ability of these systems to discover *new* results is rather limited due to the high complexity of the general problem.

Yet, some basic toolsets to assist *expert users* when formalizing concepts from social choice are certainly desirable and should be achievable based on the similarities of existing approaches. It remains an interesting question to which extent such tools can take the role of an automatic proof assistant which allows researchers to quickly test hypotheses on small domains without giving up too much generality and efficiency.

Limitations of the Approach. The vision that Tang (2010) had when he invented the basis for the methods presented here was computer-aided *theorem discovery*, which in his words includes two aspects: "to come up with reasonable conjectures automatically" and "to prove or disprove the conjectures automatically". While these targets turned out to be achievable in the domain of set extensions (Geist and Endriss, 2011), for more complex settings, we will usually need to come up with reasonable conjectures manually, and often the proving process cannot reasonably be described as "automatic". Based on this experience, we believe that the key for successful application of computer-aided methods will be a close collaboration between subject matter experts (who formulate the questions and provide theoretical tools) and experts on the method (who answer the questions with the help of machine support). This enables faster testing of conjectures, and also helps to explore similar statements as well as limits of the hypotheses. When applied interactively, such collaboration might even guide the search for new results in cases where the conjectures are not clearly formulated yet, for instance by quickly providing counterexamples to some ideas.

Regarding the types of theorems that can be proven with the presented approach, there neither is an obvious classification nor are there strict limiting factors that are easily recognizable. An intuitive limit is the question of whether a given problem can be fruitfully reduced to a finite instance—but note that in the probabilistic setting we were able to deal with an infinite domain.

New Application Domains. Most of the results we have surveyed in this chapter focussed on voting rules. The method we presented is flexible enough to apply to other types of objects. Let us briefly sketch some ideas for future applications.

In Chapter 2 of this book, we have seen several axiomatic results in the theory of *multiwinner elections*; however impossibility theorems are notably missing. This could be a promising opportunity. To keep formula sizes tractable, it would be useful to consider only small committee sizes (such as $k = 2, 3$). It may also be fruitful to consider the approval setting, where voters submit dichotomous orders (see Chapter 2). In particular, the approval-based rules AV, MAV, and PAV all have different axiomatic strengths, and combining any two may lead to an interesting impossibility.

Matching theory is another plausible domain. In standard two-sided matching problems, there are known strategyproof mechanisms (such as one side of Gale–Shapley), and one could aim for impossibilities of a combination of strategyproofness with other axioms. Similarly, impossibility results could inform the theory of popular matchings (see Chapter 6). Finally, there is a large literature on the random assignment problem (see Chapter 1), which already contains several impossibilities. Computer-aided approaches could help strengthen and extend those results.

Judgement aggregation is about combining judgements about the truth-values of multiple logical formulas. The field has a rich axiomatic theory (see Endriss, 2016). Logic-based solvers may be particularly useful in this domain. A plausibly helpful tool would be the use of SMT solvers using a bitvector theory.

Argumentation theory is a further possible application domain. See, for example, the work by Booth et al. (2014), in which three-valued logics are applied to directed graphs, reminiscent of tournament solutions.

In addition to impossibility theorems, it may also be possible to use solvers to help obtain axiomatic characterizations of aggregation rules, that is, results that identify a *unique* rule f satisfying a certain collection of axioms. Such characterization results can be turned into impossibility statements by adding an axiom requiring that the rule be different from f.

13.5 Conclusions

In the papers surveyed in this chapter, the application of computer-aided methods has lead to new insights for a range of questions in social choice theory that are of independent interest to the social choice community and unlikely to have been found without the help of computers.

Given the universality of the presented methods and their ease of adaptation (such as to "testing" of similar conjectures with minimal effort by replacing or altering some axioms), we anticipate these and similar techniques to yield further insights and to solve other open problems in social choice theory and related research areas in the future. The breadth of results obtained so far supports this hypothesis.

Furthermore, we hope that the tutorial in this chapter will make the method accessible to many more researchers. It will be exciting to see it applied to new areas.

Acknowledgments

We thank Felix Brandt and Ulle Endriss for helpful comments.

Bibliography

G. Audemard and L. Simon. Predicting learnt clauses quality in modern SAT solvers. In *Proceedings of the 21st International Joint Conference on Artificial Intelligence (IJCAI)*, pages 399–404, 2009.

G. Bachmeier, F. Brandt, C. Geist, P. Harrenstein, K. Kardel, D. Peters, and H. G. Seedig. k-majority digraphs and the hardness of voting with a constant number of voters. *arXiv preprint arXiv:1704.06304*, 2017.

S. Barberà, W. Bossert, and P. K. Pattanaik. Ranking sets of objects. In S. Barberà, P. J. Hammond, and C. Seidl, editors, *Handbook of Utility Theory*, volume II, chapter 17, pages 893–977. Kluwer Academic Publishers, 2004.

A. Belov and J. Marques-Silva. MUSer2: An efficient MUS extractor. *Journal on Satisfiability, Boolean Modeling and Computation*, 8:123–128, 2012.

A. Biere. Lingeling, Plingeling and Treengeling entering the SAT competition 2013. In *Proceedings of the SAT Competition 2013*, pages 51–52, 2013.

R. Booth, E. Awad, and I. Rahwan. Interval methods for judgment aggregation in argumentation. In *Proceedings of the 14th International Conference on Principles of Knowledge Representation and Reasoning (KR)*, pages 594–597. AAAI Press, 2014.

F. Brandl, F. Brandt, C. Geist, and J. Hofbauer. Strategic abstention based on preference extensions: Positive results and computer-generated impossibilities. In *Proceedings of the 24th International Joint Conference on Artificial Intelligence (IJCAI)*, pages 18–24. AAAI Press, 2015.

F. Brandl, F. Brandt, and C. Geist. Proving the incompatibility of efficiency and strategyproofness via SMT solving. In *Proceedings of the 25th International Joint Conference on Artificial Intelligence (IJCAI)*, pages 116–122. AAAI Press, 2016.

F. Brandt and C. Geist. Finding strategyproof social choice functions via SAT solving. *Journal of Artificial Intelligence Research*, 55:565–602, 2016.

F. Brandt, C. Geist, and P. Harrenstein. A note on the McKelvey uncovered set and Pareto optimality. *Social Choice and Welfare*, 46(1):81–91, 2016.

F. Brandt, C. Geist, and D. Peters. Optimal bounds for the no-show paradox via SAT solving. *Mathematical Social Sciences*, 2017. Special Issue in Honor of Hervé Moulin. Forthcoming.

M. B. Caminati, M. Kerber, C. Lange, and C. Rowat. Sound auction specification and implementation. In *Proceedings of the 16th ACM Conference on Economics and Computation (ACM-EC)*, pages 547–564. ACM Press, 2015.

S. Chatterjee and A. Sen. Automated reasoning in social choice theory — some remarks. *Mathematics in Computer Science*, 8(1):5–10, 2014.

G. Ciná and U. Endriss. Proving classical theorems of social choice theory in modal logic. *Journal of Autonomous Agents and Multiagent Systems*, 30(5):963–989, 2016.

V. Conitzer and T. Sandholm. Complexity of mechanism design. In *Proceedings of the 18th Annual Conference on Uncertainty in Artificial Intelligence (UAI)*, pages 103–110, 2002.

J. Drummond, A. Perrault, and F. Bacchus. SAT is an effective and complete method for solving stable matching problems with couples. In *Proceedings of the 24th International Joint Conference on Artificial Intelligence (IJCAI)*, pages 518–525. AAAI Press, 2015.

M. Eberl. A formal proof of the incompatibility of SD-efficiency and SD-strategy-proofness. Bachelor's thesis, Technische Universität München, 2016.

U. Endriss. Judgment aggregation. In F. Brandt, V. Conitzer, U. Endriss, J. Lang, and A. D. Procaccia, editors, *Handbook of Computational Social Choice*, chapter 17. Cambridge University Press, 2016.

P. C. Fishburn. *The Theory of Social Choice*. Princeton University Press, 1973.

A. Fréchette, N. Newman, and K. Leyton-Brown. Solving the station repacking problem. In *Proceedings of the 30th AAAI Conference on Artificial Intelligence (AAAI)*. AAAI Press, 2016.

P. Gärdenfors. On definitions of manipulation of social choice functions. In J. J. Laffont, editor, *Aggregation and Revelation of Preferences*. North-Holland, 1979.

C. Geist. Finding preference profiles of Condorcet dimension k via SAT. Technical report, http://arxiv.org/abs/1402.4303, 2014.

C. Geist and U. Endriss. Automated search for impossibility theorems in social choice theory: Ranking sets of objects. *Journal of Artificial Intelligence Research*, 40:143–174, 2011.

U. Grandi and U. Endriss. First-order logic formalisation of impossibility theorems in preference aggregation. *Journal of Philosophical Logic*, 42(4):595–618, 2013.

M. J. H. Heule, O. Kullmann, and V. W. Marek. Solving and verifying the Boolean Pythagorean triples problem via cube-and-conquer. In *Proceedings of the 19th International Conference on Theory and Applications of Satisfiability Testing*, volume 9710 of *Lecture Notes in Computer Science (LNCS)*, pages 228–245. Springer, 2016.

M. Kerber, C. Lange, and C. Rowat. An introduction to mechanized reasoning. *Journal of Mathematical Economics*, 66:26–39, 2016.

B. Konev and A. Lisitsa. A SAT attack on the Erdős discrepancy conjecture. In *Proceedings of the 17th International Conference on Theory and Applications of Satisfiability Testing (SAT)*, pages 219–226. Springer, 2014.

D. Krocning and O. Strichman. *Decision Procedures: An Algorithmic Point of View*. Texts in Theoretical Computer Science. Springer, 2016.

M. H. Liffiton, A. Previti, A. Malik, and J. Marques-Silva. Fast, flexible MUS enumeration. *Constraints*, 21(2):223–250, 2016.

T. Mennle and S. Seuken. The Pareto frontier for random mechanisms. In *Proceedings of the 17th ACM Conference on Economics and Computation (ACM-EC)*, pages 769–769. ACM Press, 2016.

H. Moulin. Condorcet's principle implies the no show paradox. *Journal of Economic Theory*, 45:53–64, 1988.

T. Nipkow. Social choice theory in HOL: Arrow and Gibbard-Satterthwaite. *Journal of Automated Reasoning*, 43:289–304, 2009.

T. Nipkow, L. C. Paulson, and M. Wenzel. *Isabelle/HOL – A Proof Assistant for Higher-Order Logic*, volume 2283 of *Lecture Notes in Computer Science (LNCS)*. Springer, 2002.

D. Peters. Condorcet's principle and the preference reversal paradox. In *Proceedings of the 16th Conference on Theoretical Aspects of Rationality and Knowledge (TARK)*, pages 455–469, 2017.

P. Tang. *Computer-aided Theorem Discovery - A New Adventure and its Application to Economic Theory*. PhD thesis, The Hong Kong University of Science and Technology (HKUST), 2010.

P. Tang and F. Lin. A computer-aided proof to Gibbard–Satterthwaite theorem. Technical report, mimeo, 2008. URL http://iiis.tsinghua.edu.cn/~kenshin/GS_proof.pdf.

P. Tang and F. Lin. Computer-aided proofs of Arrow's and other impossibility theorems. *Artificial Intelligence*, 173(11):1041–1053, 2009.

P. Tang and F. Lin. Discovering theorems in game theory: Two-person games with unique pure nash equilibrium payoffs. *Artificial Intelligence*, 175(14–15): 2010–2020, 2011.

G. S. Tseitin. On the complexity of derivation in propositional calculus. In J. H. Siekmann and G. Wrightson, editors, *Automation of Reasoning*, pages 466–483. Springer, 1983.

CHAPTER 14

An Introduction to Voting Rule Verification

Bernhard Beckert, Thorsten Bormer, Rajeev Goré,
Michael Kirsten, and Carsten Schürmann

14.1 Introduction

Social choice functions (or more specifically voting rules) form the backbone of modern democracies. They are often expressed as algorithms palatable for machine implementation and execution, and simultaneously they control the transfer of power from the people to a government. Social choice functions vary in complexity and exhibit different behaviors and properties. For scientists, they are perfect objects of study, in particular, to predict the way they behave, to understand corner cases, or to check that they comply with the law. Conversely, for agents (or voters) the functions' behavior and which properties they satisfy or violate is often hard to discern and difficult to understand.

Program verification technology, which is based on formal logic and deduction, provides a powerful toolset for the analysis of algorithms and their properties. The reach and power of software verification methods and tools has increased tremendously over the last decade. Following their earlier successes, for example for hardware design, formal verification methods today are routinely applied to catch design errors at early stages of software and protocol development processes. There has been considerable progress in the verification of real-world software written in languages such as C and Java, as the core technologies of deductive program analysis have matured (Ahrendt et al., 2014; Clarke et al., 2004; Falke et al., 2013).

But as of yet, to our knowledge, little work has been done to combine formal program verification with social choice theory, even though the two go well together: Voting rules are mathematical constructs and formal program verification techniques are optimised to analyse those. Thus, these techniques can help to uncover the hidden secrets of voting rules. For example, they allow us to check whether a voting rule matches its specification, and help determine how many votes must be changed to cause a change in the outcome of an election.

In this chapter, we give an overview about the role that formal program verification can play in social choice research. In particular, we focus on one such technique, namely software bounded model checking (SBMC), which statically analyses the implementation of a voting rule by exhaustively looking for counterexamples in a finitely bounded search space. In order to use a software bounded model checker, the voting rule implementation together with the property to be shown are translated into a formula in propositional or first-order logic before processing. The checker then tries to construct either a proof or a counterexample, which can then be used to understand why the voting rule violates the property.

SBMC techniques can be applied to prove that an implementation of a voting rule satisfies a property for all inputs of bounded size (e.g., up to a certain limit on the number of voters and alternatives) by exhaustively checking the space of all possible inputs. SBMC tools are fully automatic, fast, and easy to use, but their drawback is that they will not be able to identify counterexamples that lie outside these bounds. There are other more complete approaches to program verification that ensure that a property holds for all inputs, but these techniques require significantly more effort and are not covered in this chapter (see Section 14.5 for references to related work).

The role of program verification in social choice research is based on the power of the axiomatic approach, which in modern social science was largely initiated by Arrow's impossibility theorem (Arrow, 1963). His findings imply that the perfect voting rule does not exist. Therefore, developing a voting rule that satisfies a given set of axiomatic properties is cumbersome as the trade-off between any such properties is inherently difficult and error-prone.

The experiences presented in this chapter document that errors in voting rules are easy to make and formal program verification methods greatly enhance the chances of finding such errors. Furthermore, we document that there are formal program verification techniques that provide proof that a voting rule—and its algorithmic implementation—meets a given property. Moreover, we show that these techniques can also produce quantitative statements such as, e.g., changing how many votes can change the election result.

Concretely, we conduct three case studies, namely, (1) checking the properties of the voting rule known as single transferable vote (STV), designed in particular for the election of members of the board of the Conference on Automated Deduction (CADE), (2) using the power of SBMC techniques for verifying properties of voting rules (demonstrated on simple examples), and (3) computing election margins for the purpose of auditing election results.

The rest of this chapter is structured as follows: We start by giving insights into the logical models and formalisations used and also present formalisation techniques specially tailored to axiomatic properties of voting rules (Section 14.2). Then, we describe and compare tools and techniques used for performing formal program verification of voting rules (Section 14.3). In the main part of this chapter, we present experiences and case studies showing the reach and power of formal program verification (Section 14.4). We conclude with a summary of this chapter and a brief overview of related work (Section 14.5).

14.2 Logic-based Formalisation of Properties

In this section, after giving some basic definitions, we classify different types of properties for voting rules. These concepts provide the basis for logic-based formalisations.

14.2.1 Basic Definitions: Ballots, Profiles, Voting Rules

We consider voting rules where the individual preferences of voters are aggregated to produce an election result. Throughout this chapter, to simplify the presentation, we only consider scenarios where each voter casts exactly one ballot and the ballots are (partial) linear orders over the alternatives (or candidates), i.e., linear orders over subsets of the set of alternatives.

Definition 14.1. *Let $N = \{1, \ldots, n\}$ be a finite set of voters, let A be a finite set of m alternatives, and let W be a set of possible election results.*

Then, a ballot *is a (partial) linear order $\succ_i$ on A; and a* profile $\langle \succ_1, \ldots, \succ_i \rangle$ *(with $i \leq n$) is a sequence containing one ballot for each voter. The set of all possible ballots is denoted with $\mathcal{B}$, and the set of all possible profiles is denoted with $\mathcal{B}^*$.*

A voting rule *is a total function $f : \mathcal{B}^* \to W$, assigning an election result to each profile. An individual pair $(p, w) \in (\mathcal{B}^* \times W)$ consisting of a profile and an election result is called an* evaluation. *The set of all evaluations is $\mathcal{E} = \mathcal{B}^* \times W$.*

The concrete structure of possible election results in W depends on the voting rule that is being investigated. In the following, we assume that election results $\langle a_1, \ldots, a_s \rangle \in W$ are sequences of alternatives, denoting that alternatives $a_1, \ldots, a_s$ have been elected (the order of the elected alternatives may or may not be significant). The empty sequence $\langle \rangle$ can be used to denote that there is no "valid" result (e.g., in case of a tie). In case the result is a singleton, we write a instead of $\langle a \rangle$.

14.2.2 Functional and Relational Properties

We distinguish between *functional* and *relational* properties. Functional properties, such as the majority criterion, refer to single election results while relational properties, such as anonymity, compare two (or more) results. In the literature, functional and relational properties are also called *intra-* and *inter-profile* properties, as defined by Fishburn (1973).

Definition 14.2 (Functional property). *Given a set $\mathcal{B}$ of possible ballots and a set W of possible results, a* functional property *F for voting rules is a set of evaluations, i.e., $F \subseteq \mathcal{E} = (\mathcal{B}^* \times W)$ is a relation between profiles and results.*

A voting rule $f : \mathcal{B}^* \to W$ satisfies a functional property F iff $f \subseteq F$, i.e., all evaluations of f are elements of F. Intuitively, a functional property F is the set of those evaluations that a voting rule may contain if it is to have that property.

Example 14.1 (Majority criterion, majority winner). *Given a profile $p \in \mathcal{B}^*$, a* majority winner *for $p = \langle \succ_1, \ldots, \succ_n \rangle$ is an alternative $a \in A$ that is preferred over all other alternatives in more than half of the ballots:*

$$|\{\succ_i \in p \mid a \succ_i a' \text{ for all } a' \in A, a' \neq a\}| > \frac{n}{2} .$$

A voting rule satisfies the majority criterion iff, for all profiles p, either the majority winner for p is elected or there is no majority winner for p. This criterion is formalised by the functional property

$$Maj \;=\; \{(p,a) \mid \text{if } a' \text{ is a majority winner for } p \text{ then } a' = a\} \;.$$

Definition 14.3 (Relational property). *Given a set $\mathcal{B}$ of possible ballots and a set W of of possible results, a relational property R for voting rules is a set of pairs of evaluations, i.e.,*

$$R \subseteq \mathcal{E} \times \mathcal{E} = (\mathcal{B}^* \times W) \times (\mathcal{B}^* \times W) \;.$$

A voting rule $f \colon \mathcal{B}^* \to W$ satisfies a relational property R iff, for all evaluations $e \in f$ and $e' \in f$, the pair (e, e') is in R.

Intuitively, a relational property R consists of those pairs of evaluations that—by definition of that property—are allowed to "coexist" in a voting rule.

Example 14.2 (Monotonicity criterion). *For the monotonicity criterion, we need to compare profiles that are identical up to one ballot. By $b^{\uparrow c} \subset \mathcal{B}$ we denote the set of all ballots that are identical to b except that now $c \in A$ is given a higher rank.*

The relational property of monotonicity is

$$Mono \;=\; (\mathcal{E} \times \mathcal{E}) \setminus \{((p,w),(p',w')) \mid \text{there is an alternative with } a \in w,\, a \notin w',\, \text{and} \\ p' \text{ results from } p \text{ by replacing} \\ \text{a single ballot } b \in p \text{ by a ballot } b' \in b^{\uparrow a}\}$$

That is, $Mono$ contains all pairs of evaluations except those where a winning alternative is given higher preference in one of the ballots (denoted by b') which results in the alternative a no longer being elected.

A functional property consists of single evaluations, namely those evaluations that are considered "good" by the property. A voting rule is judged against the functional property for every evaluation separately. In contrast, a relational property is a relation between two evaluations of the voting rule. Satisfaction is hence judged by considering each of its evaluations in the context of the other evaluations. Thus, the concept of relational properties is stronger and more expressive. In fact, every functional property can also be represented as a relational property.

The classes of functional and relational properties do not cover all interesting properties of voting rules, but only those that can be checked by looking at one (functional) or two (relational) evaluations at a time. However, there are properties that require a comparison of three or more evaluations.

Example 14.3 (Consistency criterion). *A voting rule satisfies the consistency criterion if, for any three profiles p, p_1, p_2 such that p is the concatenation of p_1 and p_2: if $f(p_1) = f(p_2)$ then $f(p) = f(p_1) = f(p_2)$.*

Properties such as consistency[1], which can (only) be defined by comparing three evaluations are called 3-properties. This concept can be extended to generalised k-properties for $k \in \mathbb{N}$, which does—however—still not cover all properties.

---
[1] Sometimes also referred to as *reinforcement* or *convexity*.

For example, the surjectivity[2] property, which requires that for each possible election result there is a profile leading to that result, is a rather simple property that is not a k-property for any k. Surjectivity is an *existential* property, requiring the existence of (combinations of) certain evaluations, while k-properties are universal in nature, requiring all k-tuples of evaluations are "good" in some sense.

14.2.3 Formalisation in First-order Logic with Theories

To formalise properties of voting rules, we use first-order logic over the theories of natural numbers and arrays. Using these theories, on the one hand, allows to easily represent profiles and election results and, on the other hand, is supported by most SMT solvers and program verification tools (Section 14.3.1).

Arrays and numbers allow to encode profiles and election results as follows:

- A profile $p = \langle \succ_1, \ldots, \succ_n \rangle$ is represented as a two-dimensional array P, where $P[i,j] \in \{1, \ldots, m\}$ is the alternative that is ranked by ballot $\succ_i$ in the jth place, i.e., $P[i,1] \succ_i P[i,2] \succ_i \cdots \succ_i P[i,m]$.

- An election result $w = \langle a_1, \ldots, a_m \rangle$ is represented as a one-dimensional array W, where $W[i] = a_i$. If less than s alternatives are elected, then $W[i] = 0$ for the empty places.

A functional property (Definition 14.2), which is a set of evaluations (p,w), can be characterised by a formula $\phi(P,W)$ that has exactly two free variables P, W of type array. The property F_ϕ, characterised by $\phi(P,W)$ consists of all (p,w) such that F_ϕ evaluates to true when assigning the values p to P and w to W and interpreting the formula in the canonical model where the functions and predicates related to theories have their canonical meaning ('+' is interpreted as addition on natural numbers, '<' is the less-than relation etc.).

Example 14.4. *The majority criterion (Example 14.1) can be characterised using the following formula:*

$$\phi(P,W) = \forall a (\exists i (\forall k \forall k' ((1 \leqslant k \wedge k < k' \wedge k' \leqslant \lfloor \tfrac{n}{2} \rfloor + 1) \to \\ (i[k] \neq i[k'] \wedge P[i[k]] = a)) \\ ) \to a = W[1])$$

This formula expresses that, for all alternatives a, if there is an array i of size $\lfloor \tfrac{n}{2} \rfloor + 1$ (which is the required majority) such that (1) the elements of i are pairwise distinct indices $i[k]$ and, for all these indices, (2) $P[i[k],1] = a$, i.e., alternative a is the most preferred alternative in the $i[k]$th ballot in the profile, then $a = W[1]$, i.e., a is elected.

Note, that P, W are the only free variables but there can be any number of additional quantified variables in ϕ. Moreover, the number n of voters is not a variable, but either a concrete number or an uninterpreted constant.

Correspondingly, a relational property (Definition 14.3), which is a set of pairs of evaluations, can be characterised by a formula $\phi(P_1, W_1, P_2, W_2)$ that has four free variables.

---

[2]Sometimes also referred to as (strict) non-imposition property.

14.3 Program Verification Methods

In the following, we apply the insights for classifying and formalising axiomatic properties from Section 14.2 in the field of computer-aided automated verification of voting rules, where these rules are validated against functional and relational properties. We argue that this is an important step towards a process for the design and development of verified tailor-made voting rules with clear and trustworthy axiomatic characterisations.

14.3.1 SMT Solvers and Software Bounded Model Checking

SAT solvers are programs that decide the satisfiability of a given set of formulas in propositional logic. SMT solvers go beyond SAT in that they can handle formulas in first-order logic with quantifiers and theories. They provide domain-specific and highly optimised solvers for arithmetics, arrays, uninterpreted functions, and so on. SMT solvers have evolved into powerful reasoning tools that are successfully used in model checking and software verification. As will be reported during the course of this chapter, SMT solvers can be used to check a voting rule with respect to a formalised property for particular input/output pairs, i.e., for testing the rule, without the need to implement a checker for the particular property.

SMT solvers also form the basis of modern software bounded model checking (SBMC), which goes beyond mere testing and allows to verify voting rules for all inputs of a particular size. SBMC statically analyses programs up to a predefined number of loop iterations and recursions. Programs are symbolically executed and checked for errors up to the given bound. Beyond the bound, no formal correctness guarantee can be obtained. Nevertheless, the restriction to a finite scope is justified because (1) it allows for fully automated proof search, and (2) typical faults manifest themselves already in small instances (small-scope hypothesis (Jackson, 2006)).

14.3.2 Relational Verification

Relational properties (Definition 14.3) relate the behaviour of a voting rule for two independent inputs (profiles). For verification, two runs of the same program α, implementing the voting rule, need to be analysed and their results compared. A common technique, called *self-composition* (Darvas et al., 2005; Barthe et al., 2011), for proving a relational property for a program α is to show a functional property for the concatenation "$\alpha_1 \, ; \, \alpha_2$", combining the behaviour of two variants α_1 and α_2 of α that are identical up to variable names, hence operating on disjoint variable sets, and storing the outputs in disjoint variable sets as well. Based on Hoare logic (Hoare, 1969), we then verify a relational property R by running "$\alpha_1 \, ; \, \alpha_2$" with (symbolic) inputs p_1, p_2 with the results w_1, w_2, and proving $((p_1, w_1), (p_2, w_2)) \in R$.

Formal verification of relational properties using self-composition is challenging in general since it requires static analysis of two independent program runs; the exploration space that needs to be analysed is potentially exponentially larger than the exploration space for analysing a single program run. Moreover, for this type of relational verification, sufficiently strong program specifications (in particular, loop invariants and postconditions) are required to prove non-trivial properties.

Another way to handle relational verification, which improves on self-composition, is to weave the two variants into a single combined program. Since α_1 and α_2 have disjoint variable sets, reordering statements cannot have an effect on the result as long as the execution order of statements is preserved. Details about the possibilities of flexibly weaving programs can be found in the work by Felsing et al. (2014) and Barthe et al. (2011). Consider for instance the program "while($cond$) { $body$ }" consisting of a single while-loop. It is easy to see that, instead of concatenating two variants of this code (one with $cond_1/body_1$ and one with $cond_2/body_2$), one can use the single-loop program

    while($cond_1$ || $cond_2$) { if($cond_1$){$body_1$} if($cond_2$){$body_2$} }

This weaved program does not require separate loop invariants for the loops in α_1 and α_2 but only a single so-called *coupling invariant* for the weaved loop that sets variables $\bar{x}_1$ and $\bar{x}_2$ into relation. In many cases, the coupling invariant is significantly simpler than the (functional) loop invariants. As long as the two loop executions behave similarly, it is easier to express how the two states are related after each step than to specify what it is that the loops actually compute.

14.3.3 Symmetry Breaking

An important kind of relational properties are those expressing that, if two profiles are symmetric (or in some way similar) to each other, then they lead to symmetric (similar) election results. Many fairness criteria are of this type.

In practice, the number of possible ballots is very large and the number of possible profiles even larger. Correspondingly, there is a huge number of possible execution paths through implementations of voting rules. Exploiting symmetries is an important technique to make testing or formal verification more feasible.

The idea is to only prove that a voting rule f satisfies a functional property F for a small subset $X \subseteq \mathcal{B}^*$ of the possible profiles, i.e., $(x, f(x)) \in F$ for all $x \in X$, and to then make use of the symmetry property to conclude that the same holds for all profiles $p \in \mathcal{B}^*$, i.e., f has property F in general. This, of course, is only useful if the subset X is much smaller than $\mathcal{B}^*$ and if it is easy to prove that f is symmetric with respect to a given symmetry relation S—or if we can assume an existing proof because the symmetry is an interesting property in its own right (anonymity, neutrality, monotonicity etc.).

In the specification used for verification, the restriction to the set X is achieved by a first-order logic predicate ψ, called a *symmetry-breaking predicate* (SBP), a term originating from the field of constraint satisfaction (Crawford et al., 1996). The formula $\psi(P)$ has a free variable P, and $X_\psi \subseteq \mathcal{B}$ is the set of profiles that satisfy $\psi(P)$.

In addition to establishing $(x, f(x)) \in F$ for all $x \in X$, we also have to establish (1) that f has symmetry property S, i.e., it produces symmetric outputs for symmetric inputs, (2) all elements in $\mathcal{B}^*$ are represented by (i.e., are symmetric to) at least one element in $\mathcal{B}^*$ which satisfies ψ, and (3) for any evaluation (p,w) satisfying property F, all evaluations (p',w') symmetric to (p,w) also satisfy F. Note, that only (1) needs to be proven for the specific voting rule f, while (2) and (3) only depend on F, S, and X. Propositions (2) and (3) can hence be verified either via a manual proof, or using an automated theorem prover that can deal with first-order logic and set theory (including transitive closure). The proof for $(x, f(x)) \in F$ can be done using program verification techniques, using ψ as an assumption in the proof. More details on this technique may be found in Beckert et al. (2016a).

14.4 Experiences

In this section, we report on experiences applying program verification to analyse voting rules w.r.t. axiomatic properties. We also present an application for aiding in auditing processes by automatically computing election margins.

14.4.1 Checking Properties of Single Transferable Vote

Seemingly innocuous revisions to a voting rule can have serious implications on its properties. In this case study, we show that undesired implications can be uncovered using an SMT solver to check the rule's properties (Beckert et al., 2013, 2014b). The application target is a particularly interesting variant of the single transferable vote (STV) algorithm (CADE-STV) used to elect the board of trustees of the International Conference on Automated Deduction (CADE).

The property to be checked is a tailor-made criterion that is intended to capture the essence of *proportional representation*, stating that "there must be enough votes for each elected alternative". This criterion only considers the number of votes for an alternative and ignores the order of preferences within ballots. More specifically, this property requires that the input profile can be partitioned into (disjoint[3]) groups of ballots such that each elected alternative is supported by one voter group of sufficient size:

Definition 14.4 (Criterion: Enough votes for each elected alternative). *Let q be the quota and s the number of alternatives to be elected (e.g., the number of seats in a parliament). The property $Enough_{q,s}$ consists of all evaluations $(p, \langle a_1, \ldots, a_{s'} \rangle)$ for which there are multisets $m_1, \ldots, m_{s'}, m_{rest}$ ($s' \leqslant s$) that form a partition of the ballots in the profile p, i.e.,*

$$\{b \mid b \text{ is a ballot in } p\} = m_1 \mathbin{\dot\cup} \ldots \mathbin{\dot\cup} m_{s'} \mathbin{\dot\cup} m_{rest}$$

such that, for $0 < i \leqslant s'$ (i.e., not taking m_{rest} into account), the following holds:

1. *$|m_i| = q$ (there are exactly q voters in each class that support an elected alternative),*

2. *for all $b \in m_i$, there is a preference position j such that $b_j = a_i$ (each vote b in the class m_i supports alternative a_i, i.e., the alternative occurs at some position j among the preferences in b).*

---
[3]Hence, we will use the operator $\mathbin{\dot\cup}$ for disjoint unions.

Example 14.5. *Assume there are four alternatives A, B, C, D for two vacant seats, the profile p consists of five ballots $[A, B, D]$, $[A, B, D]$, $[A, B, D]$, $[D, C]$ and $[C, D]$, and the quota is $q = 2$. The evaluation $(p, \langle A, D \rangle)$ satisfies property $Enough_{2,2}$ using the partition consisting of $\{[A, B, D], [A, B, D]\}$, $\{[C, D], [D, C]\}$ and $\{[A, B, D]\}$, where the first group supports alternative A and the second one supports alternative D.*

Formalisation. We formalise property $Enough_{q,s}$ by a formula $\phi(P, W)$, which uses an existentially quantified variable *part* of type array that represents the partition and the assignment of classes in the partition to elected alternatives as follows:

$$part[i] = \begin{cases} k & \text{if the } i\text{th vote supports the } k\text{th elected alternative } W[k] \\ 0 & \text{if the } i\text{th vote does not support any elected alternative} \end{cases}$$

Then, the formula $\phi(P, W) = \exists m (\phi_1 \wedge \ldots \wedge \phi_4)$ is the existentially quantified conjunction:

$$\forall i (0 < i \leqslant n \rightarrow 0 \leqslant part[i] \leqslant s) \tag{ϕ_1}$$

$$\forall i (0 < i \leqslant n \rightarrow (part[i] \neq 0 \rightarrow W[part[i]] \neq 0)) \tag{ϕ_2}$$

$$\forall i ((0 < i \leqslant n \wedge part[i] \neq 0) \rightarrow \exists j (0 < j \leqslant m \wedge P[i,j] = W[part[i]])) \tag{ϕ_3}$$

$$\forall k ((0 < k \leqslant s \wedge W[k] \neq 0) \rightarrow \tag{ϕ_4}$$
$$\exists count\, (count[0] = 0 \wedge$$
$$\forall i (0 < i \leqslant n \rightarrow (part[i] = k \rightarrow count[i] = count[i-1] + 1) \wedge$$
$$(part[i] \neq k \rightarrow count[i] = count[i-1])) \wedge$$
$$count[n] = q))$$

Formulas ϕ_1 and ϕ_2 express well-formedness of the partition. Formula ϕ_3 expresses that for every vote supporting an alternative, that alternative must be ranked somewhere in that vote. Formula ϕ_4 expresses that each class supporting a particular elected alternative has exactly q elements. To formalise this, we use an array *count* such that $count[i]$ is the number of supporters among votes $1, \ldots, i$ that support the kth elected alternative.

Checking the Property Using an SMT Solver. To check the property, we generated input profiles (a) randomly and (b) exhaustively starting from small profiles. The corresponding election results were computed using an implementation of CADE-STV in Python. The formula $\phi(P, W)$ was then evaluated for pairs of profiles and results using the SMT solver Z3 (De Moura and Bjørner, 2008). Note, that the evaluation is not trivial because of the existential quantifier in ϕ. Using an SMT solver in this way amounts to testing.

CADE-STV differs from standard STV in that, after an alternative is elected, all ballots are still in play. In standard STV, however, ballots that have been used to elect an alternative are not available for the next round. Moreover, CADE-STV uses a quota different from standard STV, namely the absolute majority of votes. Because of its non-standard behaviour, CADE-STV does not satisfy property *Enough* from Definition 14.4.

Example 14.6. *Let us run CADE-STV on Example 14.5. First, we compute the majority quota $q = 3$. In the first iteration, alternative A has three first preferences, so that A is the majority winner and is seated. Since CADE-STV uses restart[4], A's votes are not deleted but are redistributed at the end of the first iteration. Now the ballot box contains $[B, D], [B, D], [B, D], [D, C], [C, D]$. Following the algorithm, we observe that now alternative B has the majority with 3 first preference votes and is seated. The election is over, and the election result is $[A, B]$ (which is different from the possible results $[A, D]$ or $[A, C]$ of standard STV). Obviously, there is no partition of the votes to support both alternatives A and B with 3 ballots each, i.e., property* Enough *does not hold.*

Indeed, our checker based on Z3 easily finds smaller counterexamples than the one shown in Example 14.6, but these are not as illustrative. Run-times of Z3 for checking the property for a single evaluation (i.e., performing a single test) are in the range of a few seconds for profile sizes of up to about 30 ballots and 30 alternatives. Thus, random testing for small ballot boxes is easily possible. Exhaustive testing quickly becomes infeasible because of the exponential number of possible profiles. In Beckert et al. (2013), we report on more details using an SMT solver for checking this and other properties of STV, as well as possible solutions to the undesired effects in CADE-STV.

14.4.2 Property Verification for Voting Rules

Below, we report on experiences with relational verification and symmetry breaking techniques (see Section 14.3). For our case study, we used the automated software model checker CBMC (Clarke et al., 2004), which takes C/C++ programs as input that are annotated with specifications in the form of assertions and assumptions.

For our experiments, we use CBMC 5.3 with the built-in solver based on MiniSat 2.2.0 (Eén and Sörensson, 2003), combined with an efficient bit-vector refinement procedure (Bryant et al., 2007), performing computations on an Intel(R) Core(TM) i5-3360M CPU at 2.80 GHz with 4 cores and 16 GB of RAM.

Relational Verification Using CBMC. As explained in Section 14.3.2, relational verification with weaved programs and coupling invariants is more efficient than just composing two variants of the program. We evaluate the impact of coupling invariants on performance and feasibility using as an example the verification of simple first-past-the-post plurality voting with respect to the anonymity property. For plurality voting, anonymity can be written as follows:

$$\forall b_1, b_2 (\ (\ \forall i (0 < i \leqslant n \to (0 < P_1[i] \leqslant m \land 0 < P_2[i] \leqslant m)) \land$$
$$0 < b_1 < b_2 \leqslant n \land$$
$$P_1[b_1] = P_2[b_2] \land P_2[b_1] = P_1[b_2] \land$$
$$\forall i ((0 < i \leqslant n \land i \neq b_1 \land i \neq b_2) \to P_1[i] = P_2[i])$$
$$) \to W_1 = W_2)$$

---

[4] A deviation from textbook STV, where whenever a seat gets assigned by electing a candidate in the counting procedure, the next seat is to be assigned based on the original ballot profile (only having the already elected candidates removed), i.e., resurrecting already eliminated weak candidates.

```
1  void anonymity(int p1[N], int p2[N]) {
2      for (int i = 1; i <= N; i++) {
3          assume (0 < p1[i] ⩽ M ∧ 0 <p2[i] ⩽ M) }
4      int b1, int b2; assume (0 < b1 ⩽ N ∧ 0 < b2 ⩽ N ∧ b1 < b2);
5      assume (p1[b1] == p2[b2] ∧ p2[b1] == p1[b2]);
6      for (int i = 1; i <= N; i++) {
7          if (i != b1 && i != b2) assume (p1[i] == p2[i]); }
8      int w1 = plurality(p1);
9      int w2 = plurality(p2);
10     assert (w1 == w2);
11 }
```

Listing 1: Anonymity property as a C program

Anonymity is a relational property (see Section 14.2.3). It is formalised as a first-order logic formula $\phi_{Anon}(P_1, W_1, P_2, W_2)$, using four free variables denoting two profiles and two election results, respectively. Since plurality voting is a single-choice voting rule (it is not preferential), we assume the profiles to be one-dimensional arrays, i.e., the ith ballot $p[i]$ of profile p equals the ith voter's single choice and is not itself an array. Moreover, we assume that, in case of a tie, no alternative is elected and that this is indicated by the election result of $w = 0$.

Listing 1 shows the corresponding CBMC specification, expressing that the voting rule implemented in the C function plurality satisfies the anonymity property. Lines 2 and 3 express the assumption that the profiles are well-formed. The universal quantification of variable i is expressed using a for-loop. The variables b_1, b_2 introduced by the assumption in Line 4 are implicitly universally quantified as CBMC carries out the proof for all values satisfying the assumptions. The profiles p_1, p_2 are assumed to only differ in ballots of voters b_1, b_2 in that the ballots of these two voters are exchanged. This is expressed in Lines 5 to 7. The function plurality is invoked in Lines 8 and 9 to compute the election result for the two profiles p_1, p_2. Finally, Line 10 makes the assertion that the two election results are identical. CBMC will prove that this assertion holds for all inputs (a) whose size is within a given bound and that (b) satisfy the assumptions from Lines 2 to 7.

We used CBMC to verify the anonymity property for plurality voting using (a) simple composition of two variants without coupling invariants and (b) weaved programs with coupling invariants for the loops (the implementation of plurality voting has two loops, one counting the ballots for each alternative and one for finding the alternative with the maximum number of votes).

Figure 14.1 shows the run-times (in seconds) for between 1 and 12 alternatives and 1 to 15 ballots. For the missing data points, the run-times exceed our predefined time-out of 30 minutes. The results show that the verification without weaving and coupling invariants becomes infeasible for rather small bounds. Verification with coupling invariants fares considerably better; the time-out, here, is finally reached for about 10 alternatives and 25 ballots (in contrast to only 10 alternatives and 7 ballots without coupling invariants).

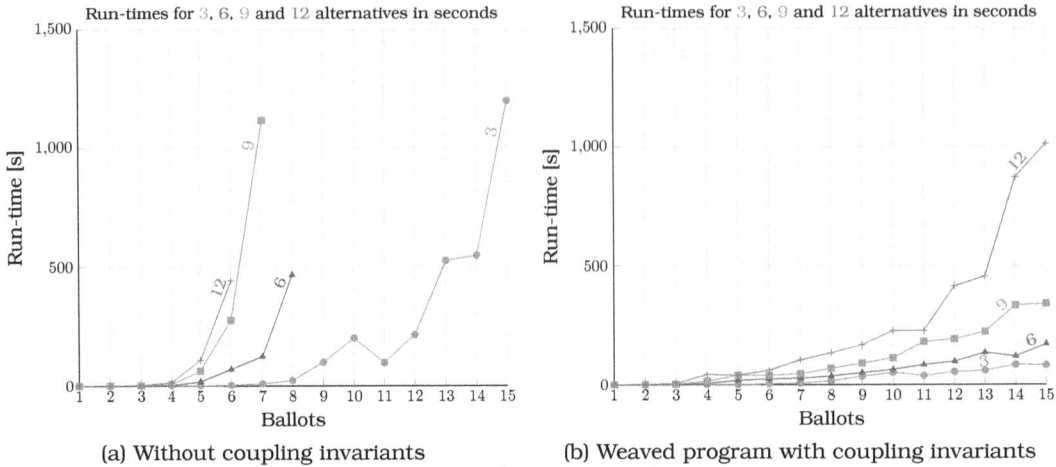

Figure 14.1: Verification of the anonymity property for plurality voting

Symmetry Breaking. We continue the case study, now with the goal to verify the majority criterion (Example 14.1) for plurality voting.

Using CBMC in a straightforward manner, verification is possible for small bounds on the numbers of voters and alternatives, but becomes infeasible for higher numbers. For example, a time-out of 30 minutes is reached with 5 alternatives and 45 voters resp. with 10 alternatives and 20 ballots. Considering the small-scope hypothesis and the simple structure of plurality voting, these bounds are high enough. The run-times (in seconds) for 10 alternatives are shown in the second column of Table 14.1 ('t/o' indicates time-out). The full data can be seen in Beckert et al. (2016a).

Using symmetry breaking, however, the efficiency of verification can be considerably increased—and, thus also, the reachable bounds. Assuming anonymity, which is a symmetry property, by applying the symmetry breaking predicate

$$\forall i (0 < i < n) \rightarrow P[i-1] \leqslant P[i],$$

the situation improves dramatically. This predicate requires the ballots to be sorted according to which alternatives they prefer. Intuitively, this is a valid assumption as anonymity allows to re-order the ballots.

The much lower run-times are shown in the right column of Table 14.1. Experiments show that handling more than 100 ballots for 10 alternatives becomes feasible, when adding predicates for further symmetry properties.

14.4.3 Margin Computation

A method to create confidence in the outcome of an election is to audit the election result against the physical evidence, i.e., the ballots. Some auditing methods require the computation of a margin (Stark and Teague, 2014). Below, we present

Ballots	Without Symm. Red.	With Symm. Red.
5	1.2	0.2
10	41.7	0.9
15	84.3	3.8
20	t/o	6.9
50	t/o	194.2
80	t/o	747.9
85	t/o	855.4
90	t/o	1,369.6
95	t/o	t/o

Table 14.1: Verification of the majority property for plurality voting for 10 alternatives (run-times in seconds)

a technique based on software bounded model checking for computing the margin of an election (consult the work in Beckert et al. (2016b) for more details). This application is different from verification as it provides information about particular elections instead of the voting rule in general.

The margin is the minimal number of votes that would need to be misfiled in order to change the election outcome. The margin is identical to the number of votes that would have had to be miscounted or tampered with during tabulation. If the election margin is large, only a small sample needs to be drawn and audited. The smaller the margin, the larger the sample. In the worst case, the audit will trigger a full manual recount. We assume that a voting rule is given (as an implementation in C) as well as a concrete input, which consists of a table aggregating the initial profile by the alternatives running for election. This table is the result of vote counting and tabulation. We model it as an integer array of size m, which is effectively the number of different stacks into which identical votes are accumulated during counting.

The idea of our approach is to use an SBMC tool to check an assertion claiming that, when the ballots are changed by putting at most a certain number x of votes on other stacks than they were on, the outcome of the election is *not* changed. If that assertion is provable, we know that the actual election margin is greater than x. If the assertion is not provable, we know that the actual election margin is less than or equal to x. In the latter case, the SBMC tool generates a counterexample to the assertion demonstrating that the election outcome can be changed by changing x votes. Having this proof obligation as a basis, we can use binary search to find a value for x such that the assertion holds for $x-1$, but fails for x, i.e., x is exactly the election margin. The main advantage of this method is that it can be uniformly and automatically applied to arbitrary rules without any adaptation.

In contrast to our work, there has been a lot of research on how to compute margins for *specific* voting rules, for which that problem is particularly hard (Bartholdi and Orlin, 1991; Cary, 2011; Sarwate et al., 2013; Magrino et al., 2011; Blom et al., 2016).

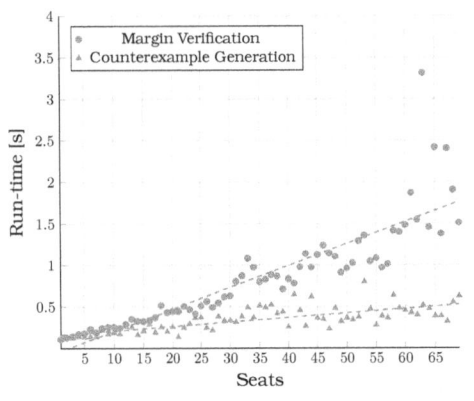 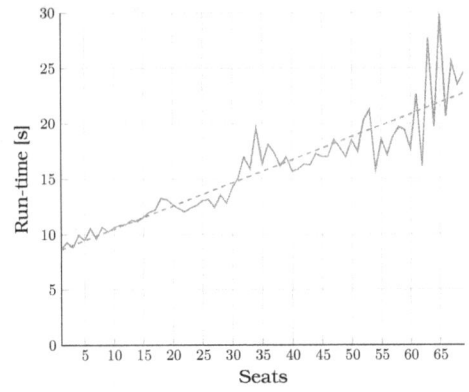

(a) Time for last step in computation. (b) Accumulated time for whole computation.

Figure 14.2: Run-times of automatic margin computation for the Jefferson method with various values for the total number of seats to be allocated.

If the implementation of a voting rule is based on choosing or searching for some parameter, then margin computation can be made much more efficient by replacing the search for the parameter by a non-deterministic choice to be resolved by the SBMC tool. An example is the Jefferson's method, similar to *largest-remainder* methods such as the Hare-Niemeyer method. Here, a quota is chosen, i.e., a number of votes needed to "buy" one seat, such that the resulting seats per alternative, when rounded down to the next natural number, sum up to the required total number of seats.

We demonstrate our approach on the 2005 Schleswig-Holstein state elections with various values for s, the total amount of seats to be allocated. The results are shown in Fig. 14.2a and Fig. 14.2b. The run-times for all computations stay well below 30 seconds. The election margin for the original number of seats (69) is 634 ballots. The computed margins range from only 42 (for $s = 62$) to $177,863$ (for $s = 2$). Performing our method for various values of s scales well on the Jefferson method, as we got rid of the loop depending on the value of s. However, further experiments also indicated a non-exponential dependency on the value for m. For example, an allocation of 69 seats to 10 alternatives takes about 55 seconds, whereas for 20 alternatives, the analysis takes about 300 seconds.

We also demonstrated the applicability of our approach to a further, more complex real-world election: the Danish parliamentary elections in 2015. The Danish elections use a two-tier system, allocating 135 seats using the D'Hondt/Jefferson method for each of the lower-tier electoral districts (Elklit et al., 2011 (accessed August 23, 2016), and allocating the remaining 40 seats using the Saint-Laguë method. We performed our analysis on the first tier for the first 135 seats.

Using the Jefferson version of D'Hondt, we compute a margin of 10 votes within $7,815$ seconds, i.e., around 2 hours and 10 minutes. The final verification (proving that a change in 9 votes cannot change the election outcome) takes 53 seconds and a counterexample for 10 votes (i.e., an example preference profile that does change the election outcome) can be found within 27 seconds.

14.5 Summary and Related Work

Summary. We have seen that SMT solvers and software bounded model checking can be effectively used for the verification of voting rules w.r.t. functional and relational properties as well as for finding violations of such properties. In particular, we have shown that the formalisation of semantic criteria in first-order logic over the theories of integers and arrays is a good choice regarding formal analysis. Moreover, verification techniques can be important parts in a process for the design and development of verified tailor-made voting rules with clear and trustworthy axiomatic characterisations, eventually leading to reliable electoral laws. For this purpose, semantic criteria need to be explicitly stated instead of a mere discussion of voting rules using anecdotal descriptions of individual scenarios.

Our experiences with bounded model checking demonstrated that bounded verification up to bounds of about 20–30 ballots is possible in practice, which can be increased to about 100 ballots using symmetry reduction techniques. Taking the small-scope hypothesis into account, these bounds are sufficiently high, even if the structure of profiles and election results and the operations that make up the voting rule implementation are more complex than in the simple case of plurality voting. In addition, modularisation and decomposition techniques can be used to handle even more complex rules by verifying their components individually (e.g., phases or rounds in the counting process).

Beyond a formal analysis of voting rules with respect to semantic criteria, we presented a further application of bounded model checking in the domain of social choice research: computing election margins fully automatically. It can be applied to arbitrary implementations of voting rules without understanding or even knowing how the election result is computed. Our approach scales for implementations of real-world voting rules in real elections if the number of loop iterations in the voting rule does not go beyond a few hundred.

Related Work. In this chapter, we have discussed the use of program verification technology based on first-order logic for the verification of voting rules. There are also other approaches using tactical theorem provers and higher-order logic. Dawson et al. (2015) specify a complex voting rule according to legal text in higher-order logic and verifies its SML implementation against this specification. Moreover, Pattinson and Schürmann (2015) encode voting rules into axioms for a tactical theorem prover, which is then used to produce certificates for election results by their implementions. Examples which verify voting rules against axiomatic properties are proofs carried out by Goré and Meumann (2014) and Beckert et al. (2014a). Verification using tactical theorem provers may lead to even higher confidence levels, but the task is inherently difficult and time-consuming, resulting in huge and laborious interactive proofs. In Beckert et al. (2016a), we have also used the semi-interactive deductive theorem-prover KeY (Ahrendt et al., 2014) for a case study proving axiomatic properties regardless of the input size using the technique of relational verification as covered in Section 14.3.2. Conducting proofs in KeY is less automatic than SBMC and requires additional specifications like loop invariants and further user interaction, but it enables full proofs for all inputs without any bounds.

Furthermore, there is research on the verification of concrete voting systems, i.e., considering concrete voting rules and software (Dennis et al., 2008; McGaley and Gibson, 2005; Kiniry et al., 2007; Cochran, 2012; Goré and Meumann, 2014; Dawson et al., 2015). With a focus on security, we have conducted an extensive case study on an electronic voting system by using a combination of different program verification techniques (Küsters et al., 2015). Finally, a multitude of theoretical work on proving and finding new incompatibilities of voting rule properties has been done using SAT solvers (Tang and Lin, 2009; Geist and Endriss, 2011; Brandt et al., 2016; Chatterjee and Sen, 2014; Brandt and Geist, 2016). They analyse only properties while encoding or generating abstract voting rules meeting some given assumptions, i.e., an encoding of a mapping from profiles to sets of alternatives is further constrained to form a manageable subset in order to mitigate state-space explosion. More on this topic can be found in Chapter 13 of this book.

Acknowledgments

This research has been funded in part by the DemTech research grant CCR-0325808 awarded by the Danish Council for Strategic Research, programme commission Strategic Growth Technologies. This publication was made possible by NPRP grant NPRP 7-988-1-178 from the Qatar National Research Fund (a member of Qatar Foundation). The statements made herein are solely the responsibility of the authors.

Bibliography

W. Ahrendt, B. Beckert, D. Bruns, R. Bubel, C. Gladisch, S. Grebing, R. Hähnle, M. Hentschel, M. Herda, V. Klebanov, W. Mostowski, C. Scheben, P. H. Schmitt, and M. Ulbrich. The KeY platform for verification and analysis of Java programs. In *Proceedings of the 6th International Conference on Verified Software: Theories, Tools and Experiments (VSTTE)*, 2014.

K. J. Arrow. *Social Choice and Individual Values*. Yale University Press, 1963.

G. Barthe, J. M. Crespo, and C. Kunz. Relational verification using product programs. In *Proceedings of the 17th International Symposium on Formal Methods (FM)*, 2011.

J. Bartholdi and J. Orlin. Single transferable vote resists strategic voting. *Social Choice and Welfare*, 8:341–354, 1991.

B. Beckert, R. Goré, and C. Schürmann. Analysing vote counting algorithms via logic - and its application to the CADE election scheme. In *Proceedings of the 24th International Conference on Automated Deduction (CADE)*, 2013.

B. Beckert, T. Bormer, R. Goré, M. Kirsten, and T. Meumann. Reasoning about vote counting schemes using light-weight and heavy-weight methods. In *Proceedings of the 8th International Verification Workshop (VERIFY) in connection* with the 7th International Joint Conference on Automated Reasoning (IJCAR), 2014a.

B. Beckert, R. Goré, C. Schürmann, T. Bormer, and J. Wang. Verifying voting schemes. *Journal of Information Security and Applications (JISA)*, 19(2):115–129, 2014b.

B. Beckert, T. Bormer, M. Kirsten, T. Neuber, and M. Ulbrich. Automated verification for functional and relational properties of voting rules. In *Proceedings of the 6th International Workshop on Computational Social Choice (COMSOC)*, 2016a.

B. Beckert, M. Kirsten, V. Klebanov, and C. Schürmann. Automatic margin computation for risk-limiting audits. In *Proceedings of the 1st International Joint Conference on Electronic Voting — formerly known as EVOTE and VoteID (E-Vote-ID)*, 2016b.

M. L. Blom, V. Teague, P. J. Stuckey, and R. Tidhar. Efficient computation of exact IRV margins. In *Proceedings of the 22nd European Conference on Artificial Intelligence (ECAI), Including Prestigious Applications of Artificial Intelligence (PAIS)*, 2016.

F. Brandt and C. Geist. Finding strategyproof social choice functions via SAT solving. *Journal of Artificial Intelligence Research (JAIR)*, 55:565–602, 2016.

F. Brandt, C. Geist, and D. Peters. Optimal bounds for the no-show paradox via SAT solving. In *Proceedings of the 15th International Conference on Autonomous Agents & Multiagent Systems (AAMAS)*, 2016.

R. E. Bryant, D. Kroening, J. Ouaknine, S. A. Seshia, O. Strichman, and B. A. Brady. Deciding bit-vector arithmetic with abstraction. In *Proceedings of the 13th International Conference on Tools and Algorithms for the Construction and Analysis of Systems (TACAS)*, 2007.

D. Cary. Estimating the margin of victory for instant-runoff voting. In *Proceedings of the Electronic Voting Technology Workshop / Workshop on Trustworthy Elections (EVT/WOTE)*, 2011.

S. Chatterjee and A. Sen. Automated reasoning in social choice theory: Some remarks. *Mathematics in Computer Science*, 8(1):5–10, 2014.

E. Clarke, D. Kroening, and F. Lerda. A tool for checking ANSI-C programs. In *Proceedings of the 10th International Conference on Tools and Algorithms for the Construction and Analysis of Systems (TACAS)*, 2004.

D. Cochran. *Formal Specification and Analysis of Danish and Irish Ballot Counting Algorithms*. PhD thesis, IT University of Copenhagen, Copenhagen, Denmark, 2012.

J. M. Crawford, M. L. Ginsberg, E. M. Luks, and A. Roy. Symmetry-breaking predicates for search problems. In *Proceedings of the 5th International Conference on Principles of Knowledge Representation and Reasoning (KR)*, 1996.

Á. Darvas, R. Hähnle, and D. Sands. A theorem proving approach to analysis of secure information flow. In *Proceedings of the 2nd International Conference on Security in Pervasive Computing (SPC)*. Springer, 2005.

J. E. Dawson, R. Goré, and T. Meumann. Machine-checked reasoning about complex voting schemes using higher-order logic. In *Proceedings of the 5th International Conference on E-Voting and Identity (Vote-ID)*, 2015.

L. De Moura and N. Bjørner. Z3: An efficient SMT solver. In *Proceedings of the 14th International Conference on Tools and Algorithms for the Construction and Analysis of Systems (TACAS)*, 2008.

G. Dennis, K. Yessenov, and D. Jackson. Bounded verification of voting software. In *Proceedings of the 2nd International Conference on Verified Software: Theories, Tools, Experiments (VSTTE)*, 2008.

N. Eén and N. Sörensson. An extensible SAT-solver. In *Proceedings of the 6th International Conference on Theory and Applications of Satisfiability Testing (SAT)*, 2003.

J. Elklit, A. B. Pade, and N. Nyholm Miller. The parliamentary electoral system in Denmark, 2011 (accessed August 23, 2016). URL http://www.ft.dk/Dokumenter/Publikationer/Engelsk/The_Parliamentary_Electorial_System_Denmark.aspx.

S. Falke, F. Merz, and C. Sinz. The bounded model checker LLBMC. In *Proceedings of the 28th IEEE/ACM International Conference on Automated Software Engineering (ASE)*. IEEE Computer Society, 2013.

D. Felsing, S. Grebing, V. Klebanov, P. Rümmer, and M. Ulbrich. Automating regression verification. In *Proceedings of the 29th IEEE/ACM International Conference on Automated Software Engineering (ASE)*, 2014.

P. C. Fishburn. *The Theory of Social Choice*. Princeton University Press, 1973.

C. Geist and U. Endriss. Automated search for impossibility theorems in social choice theory: Ranking sets of objects. *Journal of Artificial Intelligence Research (JAIR)*, 40:143–174, 2011.

R. Goré and T. Meumann. Proving the monotonicity criterion for a plurality vote-counting program as a step towards verified vote-counting. In *Proceedings of the 6th International Conference on Electronic Voting: Verifying the Vote (EVOTE)*, 2014.

C. A. R. Hoare. An axiomatic basis for computer programming. *Communications of the ACM*, 12(10):576–580, 1969.

D. Jackson. *Software Abstractions: Logic, Language, and Analysis*. MIT Press, 2006.

J. R. Kiniry, D. Cochran, and P. E. Tierney. Verification-centric realization of electronic vote counting. In *Proceedings of the USENIX/ACCURATE Electronic Voting Technology Workshop (EVT)*, 2007.

R. Küsters, T. Truderung, B. Beckert, D. Bruns, M. Kirsten, and M. Mohr. A hybrid approach for proving noninterference of Java programs. In *Proceedings of the 28th IEEE Computer Security Foundations Symposium (CSF)*, 2015.

T. R. Magrino, R. L. Rivest, E. Shen, and D. Wagner. Computing the margin of victory in IRV elections. In *Proceedings of the Electronic Voting Technology Workshop / Workshop on Trustworthy Elections (EVT/WOTE)*. USENIX Association, 2011.

M. A. McGaley and J. P. Gibson. Electronic voting: An analysis of the safety critical issues. In *Proceedings of the National Symposium of The Irish Research Council for Science, Engineering and Technology*, 2005.

D. Pattinson and C. Schürmann. Vote counting as mathematical proof. In *Proceedings of the 28th Australasian Joint Conference on Advances in Artificial Intelligence (AI)*, 2015.

A. Sarwate, S. Checkoway, and H. Shacham. Risk-limiting audits and the margin of victory in nonplurality elections. *Statistics, Politics, and Policy*, 4(1):29–64, 2013.

P. B. Stark and V. Teague. Verifiable European elections: Risk-limiting audits for D'Hondt and its relatives. *USENIX Journal of Election Technology and Systems (JETS)*, 1(3):18–39, 2014.

P. Tang and F. Lin. Computer-aided proofs of Arrow's and other impossibility theorems. *Artificial Intelligence*, 173(11):1041–1053, 2009.

CHAPTER 15

A PREFLIB.ORG Retrospective: Lessons Learned and New Directions

Nicholas Mattei and Toby Walsh

15.1 Introduction

The Internet enables computers and (by proxy) humans to communicate at distances and speeds previously unimaginable. Many of the benefits from this technology are derived from the ability to connect more decision makers (in computer science (CS) we call these *agents*) into groups, composed of human agents, computer agents, or a mix of the two. These groups of agents must make collective decisions subject to external and internal constraints and preferences in many important real-world settings including: selecting leaders by voting (Faliszewski and Procaccia, 2010), kidney exchanges (Dickerson et al., 2012), matching students to seats in schools (Abdulkadiroğlu et al., 2005), allocating work or resources (Budish and Cantillon, 2012; Aziz et al., 2016), and distributing food to charities (Aleksandrov et al., 2015). In all of these settings, self-interested agents formalize and submit their preferences to a centralized or de-centralized authority and outcomes (kidney matchings, leaders, etc.) are decided by a mechanism. Each mechanism for group decision making may (or may not) satisfy various criteria, e.g., fairness and/or efficiency, that a system designer deems important. Within CS, the study of mechanisms including algorithmic, axiomatic, and practical issues, broadly fall in into the artificial intelligence (AI) related subfields of algorithmic game theory (Nisan et al., 2007), preference reasoning (Domshlak et al., 2011), and computational social choice (ComSoc) (Brandt et al., 2016; Rothe, 2015). Results from these research areas have impact within CS as well as across the sciences and daily life, with applications in recommender systems, data mining, and machine learning (Chevaleyre et al., 2008; Domshlak et al., 2011).

Game theory is an important mathematical framework used to analyze strategic behavior of self-interested agents with applications across a number of domains including economics, biology, and computer science (Maschler et al., 2013). A game-theoretic analysis typically provides an idea of how agents *may* act, within a given context, under assumptions about the rationality of and information available to them. However, as researchers have found, there are many instances in economics and biology (Goeree and Holt, 2001) where the predictions of game theory are contradicted by data or experiment, giving rise to the school of behavioral and experimental economics (Kagel and Roth, 1995; Camerer, 2011). Indeed, many important research results for mechanisms and social choice in economics has come from the development of theory that is specifically informed by real-world data and/or practical application that is then rigorously tested (e.g., Budish and Cantillon, 2012; Dickerson et al., 2012).

Much of the work in ComSoc centers on collective decision making; with a special emphasis on understanding manipulative or strategic behavior by the participating agents. This line of inquiry answers questions about incentives and security: participants in an mechanism should be incentivized to report the truth and/or be unwilling (computationally) or unable (axiomatically) to find a misreporting of their information that is beneficial. For voting and aggregation schemes this most often means studying how agents can strategically misreport their preferences given worst-case assumptions about the knowledge of the manipulators, e.g., complete information, nicely structured preferences of the other agents, or limiting assumptions on the responses of other agents (Brandt et al., 2016). Consequently, these studies provide only limited information about the reasoning complexity in many real-world settings; manipulation is often trivially easy given complete information and strict preferences; or NP-hardness proofs may rely on huge instances or vary particular structures which do not frequently occur in real life (Davies et al., 2011; Mattei and Walsh, 2016).

Indeed, in the paper that laid the intellectual foundation for complexity theoretic analysis of voting and aggregation procedures, Bartholdi, III et al. (1989) warned against this direction: *"The existence of effective heuristics would weaken any practical import of our idea. It would be very interesting to find such heuristics."* While there has been robust work on moving beyond the worst-case in theory, leveraging tools such as fixed parameter tractability (Conitzer, 2010; Faliszewski and Procaccia, 2010; Betzler et al., 2012); average case analysis (Erdélyi et al., 2007; Rothe, 2015; Xia and Conitzer, 2008); and other approximation and heuristic techniques (Skowron et al., 2013); until recently there has not been a similar emergence of *data-driven* research programs that directly questions these worst-case assumptions.

The first goal we had in mind when founding PREFLIB was to address what we see as two fundamental questions in ComSoc that can be addressed with data:

1. How wide is the gap between theoretical intractability results and practical, real-world instances? If the constructions required to prove theoretical intractability are rare, what does this tell us about the practical applicability of these results?

2. Models of agent behavior and rationality seem to be largely driven by intuitive feeling (e.g., a left to right political spectrum) or mathematical expediency (preferences are complete, strict linear orders). How realistic are these assumptions? Do we ever see them in real-world data? Can we derive or learn the assumptions we should use from data?

The first push of data to PREFLIB: A Library for Preferences (Mattei and Walsh, 2013) was completed on March 15th, 2013. It contained 40 data files from 5 different sources totaling about 10MB, all from our prior publications. Since that time PrefLib has grown to encompass three distinct types of data and includes over 100,000 data files from 40+ sources totaling more than 10GB. We have organized four instances of the EXPLORE Workshop, held at the International Conference on Autonomous Agents and Multiagent Systems (AAMAS), which focuses on the use of data in ComSoc. Through this effort we have seen a sharp rise in the number of papers using experiments to validate or inform worst-case assumptions. There has also been an increase in the number of tools being built and deployed within the ComSoc community — a sure sign that the community is looking to translate research into impact.

The second goal behind creating PrefLib was to help social choice and preference research in computer science walk the same road that Kagel and Roth (1995) describe for experimental economics: evolving from theory, to simulated or re-purposed data, to full fledged laboratory and field experiments. This progression enables a "conversation" between the experimentalists and the theoreticians which allowed the field to expand, evolve, and have the impact that it does today (Camerer, 2011). We want data work to feedback into basic theoretical research in CS creating a virtuous circle: if we can verify preference models and input languages, we can build more computational tools, if we can rule out certain behaviors in practice then we can be more confident when deploying tools and mechanisms. Closing this feedback loop will enable practitioners to rigorously test their theoretical assumptions before deployment, providing concrete guidance and adding methods to the theoretical analysis toolbox that are built on well studied, practical foundations. We have seen this progression within other fields in computer science, including machine learning fueled by the UCI Machine Learning Repository (Bache and Lichman, 2013); constraint programming fueled by CSPLib (Gent and Walsh, 1999), and most recently the explosion of deep learning fueled by resources like ImageNet (Deng et al., 2009).

In this chapter we look back at the process of designing, building, supporting, and promoting PrefLib. We discuss the basic ideas used and challenges overcome in creating the website and dataset itself including some (hard) lessons learned for others who wish to create and maintain community resources. We then look at some of the publications that have leveraged PrefLib as well as new tools and services related to or using PrefLib, surveying the new impact and research directions. We finally look ahead to the next few years of PrefLib and detail our (biased) view of important research challenges we see on the horizon including expanding the coverage of library and tool chain; using the library to learn well-founded domain restrictions or trends in preferences; expanding the scope of empirical testing and evaluation in social choice; and encouraging stronger links with other aspects of computer science.

15.2 Looking Back: Motivations and Challenges

In our paper that introduced PrefLib we outlined a set of motivations for building PrefLib and a set of challenges that we saw on the horizon. Taking each of these sets in turn we discuss the current priorities of PrefLib and how we think we did agains the challenges. As discussed in the introduction of this chapter there were a number of motivations behind building PREFLIB. While our thinking has changed over the years we remain true to a number of our original motivations.

Challenges and Competitions. When we started out we had intentions of establishing the library itself as a set of data on which to run competitions and challenges, much like the MAX-SAT Competition hosted at http://www.maxsat.udl.cat/ or the Netflix Prize Challenge (Bennett and Lanning, 2007). This explicit motivation has fallen away given privacy concerns around releasing data, e.g., the lawsuits surrounding the sequel to the Netflix Prize Challenge, and the fact that the research priorities of ComSoc are not explicitly amenable to competitions. While we could imagine competitions around various preference reasoning algorithms, given that the majority of PREFLIB contains voting data and multi-attribute preference data, it is not clear what kinds of goals this competition would have.

Benchmarking. We feel that PREFLIB has just recently crossed the threshold where we can begin using the library as a benchmark for various algorithms in the ComSoc community. We have started to see some of this work, for instance the work of Skowron et al. (2015) on approximating hard to compute proportional representations. We see a this type of research expanding as benchmarking could be very interesting for looking at average case or approximation ratios for various voting and assignment objectives that are computationally hard to compute, see, e.g., (Aziz et al., 2017) and (Bouveret et al., 2016).

Realism. Perhaps the key motivating factor behind assembling PREFLIB was a desire to have realistic data. Many of the models studied in classical social choice seem to be chosen because they *seem* reasonable or were explicitly chosen for mathematical expediency. Perhaps nothing is more of an exemplar here than the fact that out of over 300 profiles containing strict, complete preference relations, absolutely none are single-peaked, a common profile restriction that has been called "natural" or "well-motivated" numerous times since its introduction by Black (1948). Collecting data has helped us to quantify what is reasonable. Now we have to start using the data.

Insularity. The final motivation was that many groups within ComSoc were rather insular: most groups worked on their own problems and their own datasets. Additionally these resources were dispersed and not well interconnected through common portals. An additional concern was that we were not collecting data and interacting with more data-centric communities such as the Data Mining and Machine Learning communities, where we think much of the work in ComSoc has applications. We have started to bridge these gaps in big ways: we survey the large selection of tools now available in ComSoc which are mostly interlinked on the web. While PREFLIB was not the impetus for all of this, we like to think we helped.

In addition to the motivations behind building PREFLIB we also foresaw a number of hurdles and challenges that we would face on establishing the library.

Variety and Over-fitting. We painted these two challenges as two sides of a coin. Variety meant there were too many shapes and forms that preferences came in, while over-fitting is a challenge if PrefLib was too small. Rather than try to cover the entire gambit of preference formalisms we focused more tightly on some of the more common formalisms: preference orders and ratings on combinatorial domains. This allowed us to gather a large amount of data across voting, allocation, and matching domains where many groups are doing research. In this way we have (hopefully) addressed both of these concerns.

Elicitation and Modeling. Eliciting and modeling user preferences are both hard problems. Finding the proper formalism and then devising a structure to encode that formalism are both necessary and difficult research problems. We wanted to ensure that while collecting available data into a large database we did not take focus away from these other problems. We may have been overthinking our ambitions at the beginning. There are still rich and ongoing research programs on both of these topics. However, like before, most of this research takes place in other fields like psychology and machine learning (Allen et al., 2015); and we must admit that perhaps some of the formal preference reasoning research in ComSoc has fallen away, evidenced by the lack of such a chapter in the Handbook (Brandt et al., 2016).

Privacy and Data-Silos. We wrote that others may be reluctant to share data for a number of reasons or it may require serious effort to put data in common formats. On the latter point, we even underestimated the challenge; ball-parking the man hours required to put everything in sane and common formats is beyond us at this point. However, we have been encouraged by all the groups, both within ComSoc and beyond, that have approached us to donate their data (even more when they convert it before sending to us). However, we will never overcome the challenge of releasing data and the inherent tension it brings between privacy, exclusivity, and the advancement of science. We have been happy so many have been willing partners.

15.3 Building PrefLib

PrefLib is technically three different systems corresponding to two different GitHub repositories and several thousand individual text files. The first GitHub repository is code and templates for generating the website itself, including the scripts to build the indexing and cross-linking. The second GitHub repository is the tools, useful not only for conducing experiments but also for reading and writing the text files in the various PrefLib formats. The final and largest piece is the several thousand text files which make up the "database" of preferences. We will discuss each of these three core components in turn and discuss the design decisions, technologies, and lessons learned from creating them.

The heart and soul of PrefLib is the data itself. We started off with data files from various projects that we had done in the past, devised a common file format, converted our existing files into those formats, uploaded them to the web, and boom, PREFLIB was born... almost.

From the beginning we wanted to design for both extensibility and ease of use across not only researchers in the ComSoc community but also researchers from psychology, sociology, and political science. Most projects that upload data to the web and walk away are doomed to fail; it requires sustained effort and intentional maintenance to translate a pile of data on the web into something that can be used. The UCI Machine Learning Repository (Bache and Lichman, 2013) and high impact toolkits like scikit-learn (Buitinck et al., 2013) have required full-time developers and committed support; we had two people.

15.3.1 The Data and Website

From the beginning we wanted to integrate files donated by a wide variety of researchers in social choice and beyond. This was the driving force behind using simple, comma separated value based file formats. We hoped that this would mean that others could easily translate their files and send them to us when they heard about the project. Hence, the construction of the database is about as old school as it gets. When we see cool experiments or datasets, we ask to host them. We think of data we would like to have and either go out and collect it or we look for partners (like IFAAMAS) who are willing to help us collect and then publish the data online. We organize the EXPLORE series of workshops as a way to get the word out and hopefully attract even more submissions.

The website and the data are inextricably linked and we cannot explain one without explaining the other. PREFLIB is a series of static pages that are uploaded onto a private server that we maintain along with a large directory structure containing the data. We chose this approach over something more complex, e.g., keeping the text files in a large database and dynamically generating the pages when people loaded the site, because (1) we honestly do not update the text files that often and (2) we are not web designers.

Typically our data is collected when either we get in touch with someone, or they contact us about hosting data on PREFLIB. We collect the requisite information about our ability to publish the data, the required citations from the collector/author, and any special notes they would like distributed. We[1] then convert the data into one or more of the various PREFLIB formats and add it to our index.

In the first iteration of the site, which was online between 2013 and 2015, a Python script read one giant .csv file which contained meta-data and the path for every data file within PREFLIB. In retrospect this was not the best design choice as the file quickly became large and unmaintainable. The only practical upside was that the entire database index was in a single file that we could put under version control easily.

We moved to the current design in 2015, motivated by a number of factors, but mostly due to the size and time it took to maintain the index file. We essentially redesigned the entire process with the design goal that researchers could download a single archive file which would be entirely self-indexing, with no special soft-

---

[1] Not always and thanks to everyone who sends in correctly formatted files!!

ware required. To this end we decided to use the directory structure itself as the index method, with each folder representing a complete dataset and meta-data. The new indexing script simply walks the directory structure of the /data/ folder, builds index.html pages within each folder given the info.txt file in that folder, and builds a top level index page to interlink with the main static portion of the site. This entire structure is then rsynced to the web server. The entire set of scripts and static webpage files is available at https://github.com/nmattei/PrefLib-www.

A current major design challenge we are facing is how to revision the data files themselves. There over 5000 uncompressed data files in the index that range from a few KB to several GB in size. We currently have some "manual" versioning that happens in the form of pushing a dated archive of the entire /data/ directory to the /archive page of PrefLib. However, this solution is not optimal and we hope to move to something more inline with modern development practice in the near term like git-lfs or some another system for versioning both extremely large and extremely numerous files.

15.3.2 The Tools

The PrefLib Tools project, available at https://github.com/nmattei/PrefLib-Tools, was not originally planned as part of PrefLib. However, after looking at the framework that we needed to build just to merge our two datasets, not to mention the amount of code that we needed to write in order to translate the various formats that we had coming in as donations, we decided that maybe a Python module that could read and write the file formats was in order.

The initial launch of the code was just functions in Python that could read and write the file formats listed on PrefLib. We also included the functions necessary to convert between some of the different formats on the site, e.g., turn a strict order into a set of pairwise comparisons. We packaged this up as a single file and posted it on the site.

Over the first years we kept getting requests for more data that was generated according to a particular distributions (also known as cultures in the wider social choice arena, see e.g. Mattei (2011) for more discussion) or had different numbers of candidates. Adding to the pressure to publish more code was reading about experiments which claimed (incorrectly) to generate profiles or structures at random (for a longer example see Allen et al. (2016)). Finally, since our goal was to expand and facilitate a culture of empirical experimentation (Cohen, 1995) in ComSoc we felt the community needed at least some tools to support those just starting out. So we published generators and a command line script to generate unlimited data according to many of the statistical distributions that have been used in social choice research in the past.

After finishing most of the generators we moved the code to GitHub in 2015 in order to make it more accessible and allow others to contribute to the code base. Along with this move we added functions to check for domain restrictions such as single-peakedness (Black, 1948), functions to compute various randomized allocations (Aziz et al., 2015), and have uploaded examples and tutorials that we have given at various conferences over the past several years.

After five years we still have a long way to go to make the tools more generally useable. While they are reasonably well documented, they were never "designed." We have begun a process of refactoring the code to bring some consistency to the objects and call structures we use. We hope that this process will make the code more useable and more extensible for others to use in the future.

15.4 More Tools in ComSoc

While we see PREFLIB as a library and platform to enable research there have been a number of tools developed and deployed online by members of the ComSoc community. We see the broader movement towards implementation and providing useful apps as a sign of budding maturity within ComSoc. We highlight some of the most interesting and useful tools in this section. For a more comprehensive list of other tools in ComSoc as well as other public datasets please visit http://www.preflib.org where we maintain a comprehensive list.

- Whale3, which stands for WHich ALternative is Elected, is an open source web application created by Sylvain Bouveret and is available at http://strokes.imag.fr/whale3/. Whale3 is one of the first online polling systems developed by members of the ComSoc community and put online. The app allows for a number of input preference types including approval voting and rank order ballots, and a number of voting rules including Plurality, Borda, and STV. There are also a number of visualizations to analyze the output of a particular poll. You can read more about Whale3 in Chapter 20 of this book.

- The Spliddit project run by Goldman and Procaccia (2014), available at http://www.spliddit.org/ is a web-based tool to facilitate the splitting of a variety of divisible and indivisible goods from rent to cab fares. It is a front end to a variety of game theoretic and social choice algorithms developed over the years including the Shapley Value (Shapley, 1953), for splitting cabs, and the Dollar Share (de Clippel et al., 2008), for dividing credit.

- The Pynx project run by Brandt et al. (2015), available at https://pnyx.dss.in.tum.de is an easy to use web based tool for preference aggregation. It is designed to run decentralized surveys or polls and automatically selects from a variety of rules including Kemeny's Rule (Kemeny, 1959) and Fishburn's Rule (Fishburn, 1984), also known as maximal lotteries. The inclusion of Fishburn's rule makes Pynx the only online tool to offer randomized rules (Brandl et al., 2016).

- The UNOS Kidney Paired Donation Pilot Program creates a matching market where a donor/receiver pair that are incompatible are matched with different donor/receiver pair that are incompatible such that the cycle (or longer chain) is compatible. Hence, if a husband cannot donate to his wife due to incompatibly, he may be able to donate to another woman whose husband can donate their kidney back. Finding cycles of these possible donations in large groups of people is a computationally difficult problem.

The Kidney Exchange research program run by Dickerson et al. (2012) provide deep technical expertise and custom tools to support the UNOS in this effort. This research program has led to a number of fundamental advances in matching theory (Dickerson et al., 2014) and the group has released a number of tools (and provided datasets to PREFLIB); an overview of these tools is available on John P. Dickerson's GitHub page at https://github.com/JohnDickerson/KidneyExchange.

- The Votelib project run by Tal et al. (2015), available at http://votelib-hdm.ise.bgu.ac.il/ is a collection of data about strategic voting behavior. The group conducted a number of studies with properly incentivized participants in their lab. These participants attempted to vote strategically on a number of tasks. The group then attempted to evaluate the types of strategies used by these voters to solve manipulative voting problems.

- The CRISNER project, which stands for Conditional & Relative Importance Statement Network PrEference Reasoner, was developed by Santhanam et al. (2010) and available at http://www.ece.iastate.edu/~gsanthan/crisner.html. The goal of the project was to provide fast software to solve dominance queries for CP-nets using advances from the model checking community. Since then CRISNER has expanded to other preference formalisms and provides fast solutions to many problems proven to be NP-hard or harder in the preference reasoning literature (Domshlak et al., 2011).

- The Democratix project is run by Charwat and Pfandler (2015) and is available at http://democratix.dbai.tuwien.ac.at/. This project consists of ASP implementations of many voting rules, including some that are computationally hard such as Kemeny's and Dodgson's voting rules. The ASP implementations are very fast and capable of computing solutions for fairly large instance sizes. The website itself is a nice interface to the system and even takes PREFLIB formats as input! The code is open source and allows others to create new voting rules using ASP statements.

- The RoboVote project is run by Ariel Procaccia and his team at Carnegie Mellon University and is available at http://robovote.org/. The site is an elegant and easy to use interface for a number of voting and selection rules divided into the two traditional views of voting: aggregating subjective preferences or aggregating objective preferences subject to noise. To this end the site implements a number of new voting rules that are optimal for these two views of voting given certain noise functions and/or assumptions about the views of the voters (Caragiannis et al., 2017; Boutilier et al., 2015; Procaccia et al., 2016).

15.5 Leveraging PREFLIB

In this section we survey some of the papers that have used data to explore topics in ComSoc. In each of these papers, empirical experiments were run that compliment comprehensive theoretical results. We feel that each of these papers is made stronger, and the results more impactful, by the inclusion of experiments run on real-world data.

- In "Achieving Fully Proportional Representation: Approximability Results", by Skowron et al. (2015), the authors study the complexity of approximate winner determination under the Monroe and Chamberlin-Courant multi-winner voting rules. Though the outcomes of these rules are hard to compute in theory, the approximation algorithms presented in the paper are often tractable and give good results in theory. The empirical experiments use data collected by the authors, and donated to PrefLib, to show that in practice, the approximation ratios are often significantly better than those guaranteed by the theoretical results. This should give implementers confidence in using approximation algorithms to achieve good results in practice.

- In "Voting with Rank Dependent Scoring Rules", by Goldsmith et al. (2014), the authors detail a new class of voting rules which combine Order Weighted Averages with traditional scoring rules. The main thrust of the theoretical work in the paper is the axiomatic characterization of these rules, which show that they have a mix of properties, some better, some worse, than existing rules. To compliment these axiomatic results, there are also empirical experiments on data from PrefLib, showing that in practice, the rules perform better than traditional scoring rules at being robust to noise, a stated design goal of rank-dependent scoring rules.

- In "Optimal Aggregation of Uncertain Preferences", by Procaccia and Shah (2016), the authors provide polynomial time algorithms to aggregate complete rankings of agents when their preferences are expressed as distributions over rankings. This is an important step in relaxing the common strict assumptions over the preference orders of agents. The algorithms presented are complex but yield polynomial time results for minimizing the expected sum of Kendall tau distances between the set of input rankings and the final output ranking. The experiments in this paper are designed to show that *ignoring* this uncertainty can lead to very sub-optimal results. Here we see experiment bolstering the impact of theoretical work by showing how bad things can get when one ignores uncertainty.

- In "Elections with Few Candidates: Prices, Weights, and Covering Problems", by Bredereck et al. (2015), the authors detail algorithms and empirical experiments for problems that occur when voters have prices associated with changing their votes, known as the bribery problem in ComSoc. The authors close a number of open problems in the literature and provide a high level algorithm that encompasses many of the known results. The algorithmic results are mostly in FPT, which provides one measure of computational hardness. Nicely complementing these results is a set of empirical experiments using custom algorithms and MILP formulations, on data from PrefLib, that shows tractability on real-world instances.

- In "Empirical Analysis of Plurality Election Equilibria," by Thompson et al. (2013), the authors design and run a series of comprehensive experiments to investigate the equilibrium states that occur under a variety of information assumptions on the parts of the voters. This work nicely encapsulates the idea that though voters may be strategic, they may not be able to correctly guess at what equilibria other voters are playing. A variety of test settings are considered and they show that, despite the worst-case assumptions, plurality often still leads to reasonable equilibria. The comprehensive set of tools developed for this paper are available under the PREFLIB site in the /tools/ section.

15.6 Looking Ahead: The Next Five Years

We are entering a period of research in ComSoc where one can grab data from a variety of sites and analyze it using a number of online and offline systems. This new ecosystem of data and tools is opening up new avenues of research and exciting new questions. We broadly consider this ecosystem and suggest new and exciting research directions that can be tackled.

Learning and Using Domain Restrictions: As we have seen, some of the assumptions in ComSoc are made more for mathematical expediency rather than motivated by data or experiment. While traditional game theory tells us what may happen if agents are perfectly rational, lessons from behavioral game theory (Camerer, 2011) into how *humans* typically act has not been leveraged in ComSoc. In mechanism design we are starting to see work along this line (Wright and Leyton-Brown, 2012) and it is helping to deliver better impact in areas including auctions (Hartford et al., 2016). We should work with researchers in preference learning, deep learning, and other fields to mine our available preference data, including VoteLib (Tal et al., 2015) and PREFLIB, for models of how agents are likely to act in the settings under study in ComSoc.

Expanding PREFLIB and Empirical Testing: There is even more room to see the empirical work in ComSoc increase. There does not exist a good culture around experimentation and comparative work such as the research programs for AI outlined by Cohen (1995). While we have attempted to address this gap through the EXPLORE workshop we can expand more. In the coming years it would be good to establish benchmark sets of preferences for the voting and allocation domains and devise a competition around solvers for problems that are known to be NP-hard; e.g., computing Kemeny Winners (Kemeny, 1959) or approximating various hard to compute fairness properties (Bouveret and Lemaître, 2016).

New Communities and Tools: We should continue to expand the publication and use of tools that allow us to translate theoretical results in ComSoc into practice. We have surveyed a number of these tools and research programs around these tools like the work of Qing et al. (2014) are moving these tools into other research areas. New tools are coming online such as the OPRA system from RPI, (https://opra.cs.rpi.edu/polls/main) and we expect this trend to continue. The next step is delivering these tools into research with even more communities outside ComSoc.

Preference Drift: Till now, PREFLIB has largely treated preferences as static, as that is the type of data we have received. There are now datasets like the ANES Vote Survey (ED-00013) and the data from VoteLib (Tal et al., 2015) that have a temporal basis. Using these datasets would allow our users to study preference drift, e.g., models of preference change over time, which we see as an exciting avenue for new research.

Hidden Preferences: Since we started PREFLIB, it has largely dealt in explicit preferences. However, there are many settings when preferences are implicit or must be teased out of other signals. For instance, systems collect the books you buy and the songs you listen to and want to learn from this an overall "preference model" for your tastes. While PREFLIB currently doesn't contain this data, it is an exciting avenue for future research.

15.7 Conclusion

In this chapter we have looked back at the first five years of designing, building, supporting, and promoting PREFLIB. Evaluating ourselves on how we measured up to our original intent goals, we notice that we fulfilled most of our goals, shifting a few so that the project stays more focused. We hope that our discussion of the technology used to deploy the site (and the amount of elbow work required) will help others who are considering undertaking the task of building resources for the research community. We are excited by the new avenues of research and new tools that have come online since we established PREFLIB and we look forward to the next five years of research in computational social choice.

Acknowledgments

We would like to thank everyone who has donated their time, energy, data, or support to the PREFLIB project: Haris Aziz, Robert Bredereck, Rafael Bordini, Carleton Coffrin, Sanmay Das, John P. Dickerson, Edith Elkind, Ulle Endriss, Piotr Faliszewski, Toshihiro Kamishima, Omer Lev, David Manlove, Andrew Mao, Jeffrey O'Neill, Dominik Peters, Florenz Plassmann, Nicolaus Tideman, and Hongning Wang. There are others we have certainly left off this list. We attempt to keep an accurate record at http://www.preflib.org/about.php.

Our research and the development of PREFLIB has been supported by a number of organizations over the years including NICTA, Data61, CSIRO, IBM, UNSW, the Australian Research Council, the European Research Council, and AOARD.

Bibliography

A. Abdulkadiroğlu, P. Pathak, and A. E. Roth. The New York City high school match. *American Economic Review*, 95(2):364–367, 2005.

M. Aleksandrov, H. Aziz, S. Gaspers, and T. Walsh. Online fair division: Analysing a food bank problem. In *Proceedings of the 24th International Joint Conference on Artificial Intelligence (IJCAI)*, 2015.

T. Allen, M. Chen, J. Goldsmith, N. Mattei, A. Popova, M. Regenwetter, F. Rossi, and C. Zwilling. Beyond theory and data in preference modeling: Bringing humans into the loop. In *Proceedings of the 4th International Conference on Algorithmic Decision Theory (ADT)*, 2015.

T. Allen, J. Goldsmith, H. Justice, N. Mattei, and K. Raines. Generating CP-nets uniformly at random. In *Proceedings of the 30th AAAI Conference on Artificial Intelligence (AAAI)*, 2016.

H. Aziz, S. Gaspers, S. Mackenzie, N. Mattei, N. Narodytska, and T. Walsh. Equilibria under the probabilistic serial rule. In *Proceedings of the 24th International Joint Conference on Artificial Intelligence (IJCAI)*, 2015.

H. Aziz, O. Lev, N. Mattei, J. S. Rosenschein, and T. Walsh. Strategyproof peer selection: Mechanisms, analyses, and experiments. In *Proceedings of the 30th AAAI Conference on Artificial Intelligence (AAAI)*, 2016.

H. Aziz, G. Rauchecker, G. Schryen, and T. Walsh. Algorithms for max-min share fair allocation of indivisible chores. In *Proceedings of the 31st AAAI Conference on Artificial Intelligence (AAAI)*, 2017.

K. Bache and M. Lichman. UCI Machine Learning Repository, 2013. URL http://archive.ics.uci.edu/ml. University of California, Irvine, School of Information and Computer Sciences.

J. Bartholdi, III, C. Tovey, and M. Trick. The computational difficulty of manipulating an election. *Social Choice and Welfare*, 6(3):227–241, 1989.

J. Bennett and S. Lanning. The Netflix Prize. In *Proceedings of the KDD Cup and Workshop at ACM Knowledge Discovery and Data Mining (KDD)*, 2007.

N. Betzler, R. Bredereck, J. Chen, and R. Niedermeier. Studies in computational aspects of voting - A parameterized complexity perspective. In *The Multivariate Algorithmic Revolution and Beyond — Essays Dedicated to Michael R. Fellows on the Occasion of His 60th Birthday*, pages 318–363, 2012.

D. Black. On the rationale of group decision-making. *Journal of Political Economy*, 56(1):23–34, 1948.

C. Boutilier, I. Caragiannis, S. Haber, T. Lu, A. D. Procaccia, and O. Sheffet. Optimal social choice functions: A utilitarian view. *Artificial Intelligence*, 227: 190–213, 2015.

S. Bouveret and M. Lemaître. Characterizing conflicts in fair division of indivisible goods using a scale of criteria. *Autonomous Agents and Multiagent Systems*, 30 (2):259–290, 2016.

S. Bouveret, Y. Chevaleyre, and J. Lang. Fair allocation of indivisible goods. In F. Brandt, V. Conitzer, U. Endriss, J. Lang, and A. D. Procaccia, editors, *Handbook of Computational Social Choice*, chapter 12, pages 284–311. Cambridge University Press, 2016.

F. Brandl, F. Brandt, and H. G. Seedig. Consistent probabilistic social choice. *Econometrica*, 84(5):1839–1880, 2016.

F. Brandt, G. Chabin, and C. Geist. Pnyx: A powerful and user-friendly tool for preference aggregation. In *Proceedings of the 14th International Conference on Autonomous Agents and Multiagent Systems (AAMAS)*, pages 1915–1916, 2015.

F. Brandt, V. Conitzer, U. Endriss, J. Lang, and A. D. Procaccia, editors. *Handbook of Computational Social Choice*. Cambridge University Press, 2016.

R. Bredereck, P. Faliszewski, R. Niedermeier, P. Skowron, and N. Talmon. Elections with few candidates: Prices, weights, and covering problems. In *Proceedings of the 4th International Conference on Algorithmic Decision Theory (ADT)*, pages 414–431, 2015.

E. Budish and E. Cantillon. The multi-unit assignment problem: Theory and evidence from course allocation at Harvard. *The American Economic Review*, 102(5):2237–2271, 2012.

L. Buitinck, G. Louppe, M. Blondel, F. Pedregosa, A. Mueller, O. Grisel, V. Niculae, P. Prettenhofer, A. Gramfort, J. Grobler, R. Layton, J. VanderPlas, A. Joly, B. Holt, and G. Varoquaux. API design for machine learning software: Experiences from the scikit-learn project. In *Proceedings of the ECML PKDD Workshop on Languages for Data Mining and Machine Learning*, pages 108–122, 2013.

C. Camerer. *Behavioral Game Theory: Experiments in Strategic Interaction*. Princeton University Press, 2011.

I. Caragiannis, S. Nath, A. D. Procaccia, and N. Shah. Subset selection via implicit utilitarian voting. *Journal of Artificial Intelligence Research*, 58:123–152, 2017.

G. Charwat and A. Pfandler. Democratix: A declarative approach to winner determination. In *Proceedings of the 4th International Conference on Algorithmic Decision Theory (ADT)*, pages 253–269, 2015.

Y. Chevaleyre, U. Endriss, J. Lang, and N. Maudet. Preference handling in combinatorial domains: From AI to social choice. *AI Magazine*, 29(4):37–46, 2008.

P. R. Cohen. *Empirical Methods for Artificial Intelligence*. MIT Press, 1995.

V. Conitzer. Making decisions based on the preferences of multiple agents. *Communications of the ACM*, 53(3):84–94, 2010.

J. Davies, G. Katsirelos, N. Narodytska, and T. Walsh. Complexity of and algorithms for Borda manipulation. In *Proceedings of the 25th AAAI Conference on Artificial Intelligence (AAAI)*, pages 657–662, 2011.

G. de Clippel, H. Moulin, and N. Tideman. Impartial division of a dollar. *Journal of Economic Theory*, 139(1):176–191, 2008.

J. Deng, W. Dong, R. Socher, L. Li, K. Li, and L. Fei-Fei. Imagenet: A large-scale hierarchical image database. In *Proceedings of the IEEE Conference on Computer Vision and Pattern Recognition (CVPR 2009)*, pages 248–255. IEEE, 2009.

J. P. Dickerson, A. D. Procaccia, and T. Sandholm. Optimizing kidney exchange with transplant chains: Theory and reality. In *Proceedings of the 11th International Conference on Autonomous Agents and Multiagent Systems (AAMAS)*, pages 711–718, 2012.

J. P. Dickerson, A. D. Procaccia, and T. Sandholm. Price of fairness in kidney exchange. In *Proceedings of the 13th International Conference on Autonomous Agents and Multiagent Systems (AAMAS)*, pages 1013–1020, 2014.

C. Domshlak, E. Hüllermeier, S. Kaci, and H. Prade. Preferences in AI: An overview. *Artificial Intelligence*, 175(7):1037–1052, 2011.

G. Erdélyi, L. A. Hemaspaandra, J. Rothe, and H. Spakowski. On approximating optimal weighted lobbying, and frequency of correctness versus average-case polynomial time. In *International Symposium on Fundamentals of Computation Theory*, pages 300–311, 2007.

P. Faliszewski and A. D. Procaccia. AI's war on manipulation: Are we winning? *AI Magazine*, 31(4):53–64, 2010.

P. C. Fishburn. Probabilistic social choice based on simple voting comparisons. *The Review of Economic Studies*, 51(4):683–692, 1984.

I. P. Gent and T. Walsh. CSPLib: A benchmark library for constraints. In *Proceedings of the 5th International Conference on Principles and Practice of Constraint Programming (CP)*, pages 480–481, 1999.

J. K. Goeree and C. A. Holt. Ten little treasures of game theory and ten intuitive contradictions. *American Economic Review*, pages 1402–1422, 2001.

J. Goldman and A. D. Procaccia. Spliddit: Unleashing fair division algorithms. *ACM SIGecom Exchanges*, 13(2):41–46, 2014.

J. Goldsmith, J. Lang, N. Mattei, and P. Perny. Voting with rank dependent scoring rules. In *Proceedings of the 28th AAAI Conference on Artificial Intelligence (AAAI)*, 2014.

J. S. Hartford, J. R. Wright, and K. Leyton-Brown. Deep learning for predicting human strategic behavior. In *Advances in Neural Information Processing Systems (NIPS)*, pages 2424–2432, 2016.

J. H. Kagel and A. E. Roth. *The Handbook of Experimental Economics*. Princeton University, 1995.

J. G. Kemeny. Mathematics without numbers. *Daedalus*, 88(4):577–591, 1959.

M. Maschler, E. Solan, and S. Zamir. *Game Theory*. Cambridge University Press, 2013.

N. Mattei. Empirical evaluation of voting rules with strictly ordered preference data. In *Proceedings of the 2nd International Conference on Algorithmic Decision Theory (ADT)*, 2011.

N. Mattei and T. Walsh. PrefLib: A library for preferences. http://www.preflib.org. In *Proceedings of the 3rd International Conference on Algorithmic Decision Theory (ADT)*, 2013.

N. Mattei and T. Walsh. Empirical evaluation of real world tournaments. *CoRR*, abs/1608.01039, 2016. URL http://arxiv.org/abs/1608.01039.

N. Nisan, T. Roughgarden, E. Tardos, and V. V. Vazirani. *Algorithmic Game Theory*. Cambridge University Press Cambridge, 2007.

A. D. Procaccia and N. Shah. Optimal aggregation of uncertain preferences. In *Proceedings of the 30th AAAI Conference on Artificial Intelligence (AAAI)*, pages 608–614, 2016.

A. D. Procaccia, N. Shah, and Y. Zick. Voting rules as error-correcting codes. *Artificial Intelligence*, 231:1–16, 2016.

C. Qing, U. Endriss, R. Fernández, and J. Kruger. Empirical analysis of aggregation methods for collective annotation. In *Proceedings of the 25th International Conference on Computational Linguistics (COLING)*, 2014.

J. Rothe. *Economics and Computation: An Introduction to Algorithmic Game Theory, Computational Social Choice, and Fair Division*. Springer, 2015.

G. R. Santhanam, S. Basu, and V. Honavar. Dominance testing via model checking. In *Proceedings of the 24th AAAI Conference on Artificial Intelligence (AAAI)*, pages 357–362, 2010.

L. S. Shapley. A value for n-person games. In H. Kuhn and A. W. Tucker, editors, *Contributions to the Theory of Games*, volume 2 of *Annals of Mathematical Studies*. Princeton University Press, 1953.

P. Skowron, P. Faliszewski, and A. Slinko. Achieving fully proportional representation is easy in practice. In *Proceedings of the 12th International Conference on Autonomous Agents and Multiagent Systems (AAMAS)*, pages 399–406, 2013.

P. Skowron, P. Faliszewski, and A. Slinko. Achieving fully proportional representation: Approximability results. *Artificial Intelligence*, 222:67–103, 2015.

M. Tal, R. Meir, and Y. Gal. A study of human behavior in online voting. In *Proceedings of the 14th International Conference on Autonomous Agents and Multiagent Systems (AAMAS)*, pages 665–673, 2015.

D. R. M. Thompson, O. Lev, K. Leyton-Brown, and J. Rosenschein. Empirical analysis of plurality election equilibria. In *Proceedings of the 12th International Conference on Autonomous Agents and Multiagent Systems (AAMAS)*, pages 391–398, 2013.

J. R. Wright and K. Leyton-Brown. Behavioral game theoretic models: A Bayesian framework for parameter analysis. In *Proceedings of the 11th International Conference on Autonomous Agents and Multiagent Systems (AAMAS)*, pages 921–930, 2012.

L. Xia and V. Conitzer. Generalized scoring rules and the frequency of coalitional manipulability. In *Proceedings of the 9th ACM Conference on Electronic Commerce (ACM-EC)*, pages 109–118, 2008.

PART III
APPLICATIONS

CHAPTER 16

US vs. European Apportionment Practices: The Conflict between Monotonicity and Proportionality

László Á. Kóczy, Péter Biró, and Balázs Sziklai

16.1 Introduction

In a representative democracy citizens exert their influence via elected representatives. Representation will be fair if the citizens have more or less the same (indirect) influence, that is, if each representative stands for the same number of citizens. This idea was explicitly declared in the 14th Amendment of the US Constitution, but dates back even earlier to the times of the Roman Republic.

> "Representatives shall be apportioned among the several States according to their respective numbers, counting the whole number of persons in each State, excluding Indians not taxed. (14th Amendment, Section 2)

Establishing electoral districts with equal numbers of voters becomes nontrivial, when they must fit into the existing administrative structure of a country. For instance the distribution of three seats between two equally populated regions will necessarily lead to inequalities. This example may seem artificial, but under more realistic circumstances with many regions and a high number of seats to be allocated the problem remains hard. The general problem of allocating seats between regions in a fair way is known as the apportionment problem.

Proportional apportionment is one, but not the only ingredient of fair representation. Other, monotonicity-related issues — studying changes in the allocation subject to changes in the input parameters — emerged in the past 150 years. The most notable one is the so-called Alabama paradox. During the 1880 US census the Chief Clerk of the Census Office considered an enlargement of the House of Representatives and noted that moving from 299 to 300 seats would result in a loss of a seat for the State Alabama. This anomaly together with the later discovered population and new state paradoxes pressed the legislators to revise the apportionment rules again and again. The currently used seat distribution method is free from such anomalies. However, it does not satisfy the so called Hare-quota, a basic guarantee of proportionality (Balinski and Young, 1975).

While virtually every Western-type democracy adopted the principle laid down in the US Constitution, their approaches differ on how they deal with the arising paradoxes and anomalies.

The European Commission for Democracy through Law, better known as the Venice Commission, a recent entrant to this debate, published a comprehensive guidebook on good electoral laws in 2002. The Code of Good Practice in Electoral Matters (Venice Commission, 2002) — consequently used in reviewing Albania's and Estonia's electoral law in 2011 (OSCE/ODIHR, 2011; Venice Commission and OSCE/ODIHR, 2011) and forming an apparent model to the modifications Hungary introduced to its electoral law in 2012 —, contains original recommendations for a good practice of apportionment.

> "**Equality in voting power**, where the elections are not being held in one single constituency, requires constituency boundaries to be drawn in such a way that seats in the lower chambers representing the people are distributed equally among the constituencies, in accordance with a specific apportionment criterion, e.g., the number of residents in the constituency, the number of resident nationals (including minors), the number of registered electors, or possibly the number of people actually voting ... Constituency boundaries may also be determined on the basis of geographical criteria and the administrative or indeed historic boundary lines, which often depend on geography ... The maximum admissible departure from the distribution criterion adopted depends on the individual situation, although it should seldom exceed 10% and never 15%, except in really exceptional circumstances (a demographically weak administrative unit of the same importance as others with at least one lower-chamber representative, or concentration of a specific national minority)." (Venice Commission, 2002, §§13–15 in Section 2.2)

The recommendation leaves some details open. Does the maximum admissible departure refer to the difference of population between any two constituencies or the difference of the population of any constituency from the average constituency size? The latter approach is more permissive and more common around the world (see Table 16.1). Indeed, the final version of the 2012 electoral law of Hungary replaced the former with 10-15% departure limits with the latter with 15-20% departure limits. Without this significant relaxation the rule was mathematically impossible to satisfy (Biró et al., 2012).

Similar thresholds exist in many other countries (Table 16.1), but the values differ greatly from country to country. The strictest limits are set in the United States that permits no inequalities by its Constitution. Zero-tolerance, however, remains a theoretical objective. Real life is widely different: the constituencies of Montana are almost twice as large as the ones in Rhode Island. Assuming that the voters' influence is proportional to the size of the constituencies, the voters of Rhode Island have 88% more influence than the voters of Montana. A shocking gap, but dwarfed by the differences in Georgia where the electoral law of 1999 did not set rules about the sizes of constituencies. The number of voters per (single-seat) constituencies ranged from 3,600 in the Lent'ekhi or 4,200 in the

Country	Thresholds	Country	Thresholds
Albania	5%	New Zealand	5%
Armenia	15%	Papua New Guinea	20%
Australia	10%	Singapore	30%
Canada	25%	Ukraine	10%
Czech Republic	15%	UK	5%
France	20%	USA	0%
Germany	15%	Yemen	5%
Hungary	15% (20%)	Zimbabwe	20%
Italy	10%		

Table 16.1: Thresholds (thresholds under "extraordinary circumstances") for the maximum difference from the average constituency size (Handley, 2007).

Kazbegi districts to over 138,000 in Kutaisi City, hugely favouring voters in the former regions.

Setting a limit on the maximum departure from the average size is a very natural condition, but already such a mild requirement conflicts with well-established apportionment standards: for certain apportionment problems all allocations that respect the given limits violate properties such as Hare-quota and monotonicity (Biró et al., 2015). Furthermore, the recommendation of the Venice Committee does not generally specify a unique solution, so it still leaves possibilities of manipulation. This second problem may be overcome by a new apportionment rule, constructed in the spirit of the recommendation. The Leximin Method efficiently computes a solution where the differences from the average size are lexicographically minimized (Biró et al., 2015).

In this chapter we survey the apportionment methods and the impact of the latest policy recommendation by the Venice Commission. First, in Section 16.2 we give an overview on the classical apportionment methods and the Leximin Method, and discuss their properties. Then we illustrate the usage of the Leximin Method compared to the solutions by the current legislations from a wide range of countries. These examples are based on our own calculations that in turn are made using information on voting systems and population data gathered from a wide range of sources. The details together with a systematic study of voting systems will be published elsewhere.

16.2 Overview of Apportionment Methods

In this section we introduce the apportionment problem; we introduce and characterise methods to solve it.

16.2.1 The Apportionment Problem

In a representative democracy higher level decisions are made by a group of elected representatives. In most countries each representative speaks for citizens living in a certain geographical area and is elected in one of several voting districts or constituencies. Generally a constituency elects a single candidate, although in some countries, like Ireland or Singapore a constituency may elect multiple representatives. Other countries, like the Netherlands or Israel, has no non-trivial constituencies, but all representatives are elected at the national level with no geographical attachment — we regard this as a trivial case with a single constituency. Yet others have combinations of these (Csató, 2015, 2016) — we will focus on the voting districts. The basis of geographical representation is that people living in certain regions, such as New Yorkers or Scotsmen are not just arbitrary voters, but people sharing certain cultural or geographical interests. Constituencies are consequently organised into geographical, political or administrative regions.

We look for a fair an proportional representation. However natural this approach seems, it is not universal. The Cambridge Compromise, an academic-driven proposal for a mathematical method to allocate the seats of the European Parliament among the member states, for instance, takes proportionality as only one of the aspects to be taken into account (Grimmett, 2012). In weighted voting the weights are also not proportional. During the negotiations of the Lisbon Treaty that, among others, reformed voting in the Council of the European Union the Jagellonian Compromise proposed to use the Penrose square-root law, where the allocated weights are proportional to the square root of populations (Penrose, 1946; Słomczyński and Życzkowski, 2006; Kóczy, 2012). While these are examples where proportionality is knowingly violated, but for the purposes of fairness, there are many voting systems (Canada and Denmark are examples) where certain *territories*, such as rural regions, or less populate states, are overrepresented by law.

Our interest thus lies in the allocation of representatives among these regions in a fair way. Allocating seats among parties in party-list proportional representation, the biproportional apportionment problem (see Chapter 3 in this book) or voting with multi-winner approval rules (Brill et al., 2017) is analogous and the general problem of apportionment can go well beyond the districting problem and can deal with the allocation of any finite, indivisible good among heterogenous claimants in a fair, proportional way. While the methodology can be used, for instance for discrete clearing in the bankruptcy literature (Csóka and Herings, 2016), in the following we keep the voting terminology and also take such applications and examples. We assume that the task is to allocate the *seats* of a legislature or *House* among several, n states — and elegantly skip the problem of districting (Tasnádi, 2011; Puppe and Tasnádi, 2015), the laying out of the actual districts, that can introduce additional inefficiencies. Before going any further, we formally define the problem and introduce some of the best known methods to solve the apportionment problem.

An *apportionment problem* (p, H) is a pair consisting a vector

$$p = (p_1, p_2, \ldots, p_n)$$

of state populations, where $P = \sum_{i=1}^{n} p_i$ is the population of the country and $H \in \mathbb{N}_+$ denotes the number of seats in the House (where $\mathbb{N}_+ = \{1, 2, 3, \ldots\}$).

Our task is to determine the non-negative integers $a_1, a_2, \ldots, a_n$ with $\sum_{i=1}^n a_i = H$ representing the number of constituencies in states $1, 2, \ldots, n$.

Let $p \in \mathbb{N}_+^n$ and $a \in \mathbb{N}^n$ be the n-dimensional vectors that contain the population sizes and the allotted number of seats, respectively. An *apportionment method* or *rule* is a function M that assigns an allotment for each apportionment problem (p, H). An apportionment method specifies exactly how many House seats each of the states gets. The resulting apportionment is not necessarily unique although for a good method the multiplicity only emerges in artificial examples. Let $A = \frac{P}{H}$ denote the average size of a constituency. The fraction $\frac{p_i}{P} H = \frac{p_i}{A}$ is called the *respective share* of state i. Let δ_i be the difference in percentage, displayed by the constituencies of state i and let d_i be the *departure*, its absolute value. Formally,

$$\delta_i = \frac{\frac{p_i}{a_i} - A}{A} \quad \text{and} \quad d_i = |\delta_i| \tag{16.1}$$

Throughout the paper we will employ the following notation: let $x, y \in \mathbb{R}^n$, we say that $x \geq y$ if $x_i \geq y_i$ for $i = 1, 2, \ldots, n$.

16.2.2 Apportionment Methods

The fundamental idea of apportionment methods is that a representative should speak for the same number of voters irrespective of the state or region she represents. Ideally a state i should get a proportional part $\frac{p_i}{P} H$ of the seats. This number is the *standard quota*. If not all standard quotas are integers and most of the time they are not, we must diverge from the ideal numbers. Rounding the numbers down does not immediately solve the problem as the total number of seats to be distributed is fixed, so if the standard quota is rounded down for some, it must be rounded up for others, immediately creating inequalities. Many of the best known methods only differ in rounding up or down the standard quotas differently. See also Chapter 3 where some remarkably different methods coming from a different stream of literature are presented.

Largest Remainder Methods

The largest remainder methods all rely on the logic of calculating the "price" of a seat in terms of the number of voters, allocating the fully "paid" seats. The remaining seats are allocated to the states with the *largest remainders*, that is, the states with the largest fractional seat. Several methods exist using different ways to calculate the price, the Hamilton method is the simplest and best known.

The Hamilton method (also known as Hare-Niemeyer or Vinton method) sets the price as the standard or Hare divisor $D_S = \frac{P}{H}$, which is the same as the average constituency size A. By dividing the population of a state by the standard divisor D_S we calculate the ideal number of constituencies in the given state. From this we can calculate how many seats does the state's population suffice for: each state is guaranteed to get the integer part of the quota, the *lower quota*. The remaining seats are distributed in the same way as for other largest remainder methods.

We are not aware of a specification of a tiebreaking rule when the remainders are identical, although with real life data this is a non-issue. The Hamilton method was the first proposal to allocate the seats of the United States Congress between states, but this was vetoed by president Washington.

Other largest remainder methods differ in the way their quotas are calculated. The Hagenbach-Bischoff quota (Hagenbach-Bischoff, 1888) is calculated with the divisor $D_{\text{H-B}} = \frac{P}{H+1}$, while the Droop and Imperiali (named after Belgian Senator Pierre Imperiali) quotas with the only very slightly different $D_{\text{D}} = \lfloor \frac{P}{H+1}+1 \rfloor$ (Droop, 1881) and $D_{\text{I}} = \frac{P}{H+2}$. The Droop quota is typically used in single transferable vote systems, where voters rank candidates and if their top choice has sufficient votes to get elected, the vote goes to the second choice and so on. The Droop divisor is the lowest number satisfying that the number of claimable resources, such as seats does not exceed the House. In this sense the Hagenbach-Bischoff and especially the Imperiali method may allocate seats that must later be taken back.

Divisor Methods

Divisor methods (sometimes called *highest average* or *highest quotient methods*) follow a slightly different logic by adjusting the quotient itself. When the (lower) quotas are calculated there will be some left-over seats. By lowering the divisor — effectively the price of a seat — states will be able to afford more. Divisor methods are mathematically equivalent to procedural apportionment methods such as e.g. the D'Hondt method, which distribute seats one at a time to the state with the highest claim, then update the claims after each iteration until all the seats are allocated.

The Jefferson or D'Hondt method, introduced by Thomas Jefferson in 1791 and by Victor D'Hondt in 1878 in two mathematically very different, though equivalent forms is the simplest of all divisor methods. Under the Jefferson method the standard divisor $D_S = \frac{P}{H}$ is calculated. The lower quotas generally do not add up to the size of the House, so in this method the standard divisor is gradually lowered by "trial and error" until they do. While this is not a precise mathematical algorithm, note that the modified divisor will generally satisfy this for a whole range of values, so an appropriate value is easy to find.

The D'Hondt method uses the following claim function

$$\text{D'Hondt method} \qquad q_i^{\text{H}}(s) = \frac{p_i}{s+1}$$

showing how many voters would a representative, on average, represent if an additional seat were given to the state i already having s seats.

Some voting systems use variants of the D'Hondt method that bias the results in favour or against larger claimants, such as states with larger voting population or parties with many votes in a party-list voting system. These include the following

Adams method	$q_i^{\text{A}}(s) = \dfrac{p_i}{s}$
Danish method	$q_i^{\text{D}}(s) = \dfrac{p_i}{s+1/3}$
Huntington-Hill method/EP	$q_i^{\text{HH}}(s) = \dfrac{p_i}{\sqrt{s(s+1)}}$
Sainte-Laguë/Webster method	$q_i^{\text{SL}}(s) = \dfrac{p_i}{s+1/2}$
Imperiali method	$q_i^{\text{I}}(s) = \dfrac{p_i}{s+2}$
Macau method	$q_i^{\text{M}}(s) = \dfrac{p_i}{2^s}$

displaying an increasing bias against large states with the Adams, Danish Huntington-Hill and Sainte-Laguë methods favouring large states more than the D'Hondt, Imperiali or especially the Macau method (Marshall et al., 2002; Bittó, 2017). The Huntington-Hill method, also known as the Method of Equal Proportions (EP) is the method currently used in the United States House of Representatives.

The Leximin Method

The Leximin Method (Biró et al., 2015) is fundamentally different from the methods discussed so far. While these were based on finding the standard quota and then trying to find a good way to round these numbers, the Leximin Method looks at relative differences. It *minimizes the absolute value of the largest relative difference from the average constituency size* — the *maximum departure* — and does this in a recursive fashion.

To have a more precise definition, we need to introduce some terminology. Lexicographic is like alphabetic ordering where words are compared letter-by-letter and the ordering is based on the first difference. When it comes to real vectors the ordering is based on the first coordinates where these vectors differ. Formally vector $x \in \mathbb{R}^m$ is *lexicographically smaller* than $y \in \mathbb{R}^m$ (denoted by $x \prec y$) if $x \neq y$ and there exists a number $1 \leq j \leq m$ such that $x_i = y_i$ if $i < j$ and $x_j < y_j$.

Returning to our model, given an apportionment problem (p, H) and an allotment a, let $\Delta(a)$ denote a nonnegative n-dimensional vector, where the differences $d_i(a)$ are contained in a *non-increasing order*. A solution a is said to be *lexicographically minimal*, or simply *leximin*, if there is no other allotment a' where $\Delta(a')$ is lexicographically smaller than $\Delta(a)$. The *Leximin Method* chooses an allocation of seats, such that the non-increasingly ordered vector of differences is lexicographically minimal. This method is somewhat more complex than the earlier ones, but while other methods make sure that states do not get too many seats, the Leximin Method takes both under- and overrepresentation into account. Perhaps it is not so obvious here, but the method is well-defined and Biró et al. (2015) gave an efficient algorithm to calculate it.

16.2.3 Properties and Paradoxes

There are several apportionment methods and while in most cases they all produce nearly identical results, we would like to understand the reasons for the small differences that may be observed. The way to argue in favour or against these methods is by looking at their properties. In the following we list some properties that apportionment methods satisfy.

Quota

Exact proportional representation is seldom possible as the respective shares of the states are hardly ever integer numbers. However if such a case occurs, that is, the fractions $a_i = \frac{p_i}{P}H$ are integers for all $i \in \{1, \ldots, n\}$ then the allotment a is said to have the *exact quota* property.

In any other case taking one of the nearest integers to the exactly proportional share is a natural choice or at least some methods explicitly try to allocate seats accordingly. An allotment a satisfies *lower (upper) quotas*, if no state receives less (more) constituencies than the lower (upper) integer part of its respective share, that is $a_i \geq \lfloor \frac{p_i}{P}H \rfloor$ for all $i \in \{1, \ldots, n\}$ and $a_i \leq \lceil \frac{p_i}{P}H \rceil$ for all $i \in \{1, \ldots, n\}$, respectively. An allotment satisfies the *Hare-quota* or simply the *quota* property if it satisfies both upper and lower quota.

Similarly, we say that an apportionment method $M(\mathbf{p}, H)$ satisfies lower (upper) quota if for any apportionment problem $(\mathbf{p}, H)$, $M(\mathbf{p}, H)_i \geq \lfloor \frac{p_i}{P}H \rfloor$ or $M(\mathbf{p}, H)_i \leq \lceil \frac{p_i}{P}H \rceil$ respectively for all $i \in \{1, \ldots, n\}$ and satisfies *Hare-quota* if it satisfies both of them.

Monotonicity

Monotonicity properties describe how changes in the number of available seats or the (relative) claims made by the states should affect the number of allocated seats.

House-monotonicity states that the individual states should not lose seats when more seats are available in the House.

Definition 16.1. *An apportionment method M is* house-monotonic *if $M(\mathbf{p}, H') \geq M(\mathbf{p}, H)$ for any apportionment problem $(\mathbf{p}, H)$ and House sizes $H' > H$.*

A scenario where increasing the House size would decrease the number of seats allotted to a state is often considered undesirable, perhaps even paradoxical. An apportionment rule where this is possible is said to exhibit the *Alabama paradox* referring to a historical occurrence of the phenomenon for state Alabama. House-monotonic apportionment methods are free from this paradox.

There is a related monotonicity requirement and an associated paradox when populations are considered. The *population paradox* arises when the population of two states increases at different rates. Then it is possible that the state with more rapid growth actually loses seats to the state with slower growth. Biró et al. (2015) present an example where the population paradox emerges; Tasnádi (2008) surveys the emergence of this paradox historically in the apportionment among parties in Hungary.

Apportionment Practices

Definition 16.2. *An apportionment rule M is population-monotonic if $M(p', H)_i \geq M(p, H)_i$ for any House size H and population sizes p, p' such that $p'_i > p_i$, $p'_j > p_j$ and $\frac{p'_i}{p_i} \geq \frac{p'_j}{p_j}$ while $p'_k = p_k$ for $k \in \{1, 2, \ldots, n\}, k \neq i, j$.*

Note that there are several alternative definitions of this property. The one presented here is slightly weaker than some others used in the literature (Lauwers and Van Puyenbroeck, 2008; Balinski and Young, 1982). However, as we will see even this weaker property is violated by some rules.

Departure from the Exact Quota

If it is not possible to distribute the seats according to the exact quota there will be necessarily some inequality. *Departure* is the relative difference between the average number of represented voters per representative in a given state and nationwide.

Several countries specify an explicit limit on the permitted departure from the average in their electoral law in accordance with the recommendation of the Venice Commission (2002). An apportionment satisfies the *q-permitted departure property* if all departures are smaller than the given limit q. Then an apportionment method satisfies the *admissible departure property* if for each apportionment problem, for which there exists an apportionment satisfying the permitted departure property, it produces such an apportionment. Formally

An apportionment satisfies the *Venice* or *Smallest maximum admissible departure property* if for apportionment problem it produces an apportionment where the largest departure is the smallest. For a given apportionment problem (p, H) let $\alpha_{(p,H)}$ be the smallest maximum admissible departure that can be achieved with an allotment, i.e.,

$$\alpha_{(p,H)} = \min_{a \in A(n,H)} \max_{i \in \{1,\ldots,n\}} \{d_i\} \tag{16.2}$$

where $A(n, H)$ denotes the set of n-dimensional non-negative vectors for which the sum of the coordinates is H.

Definition 16.3. *An apportionment rule M satisfies the smallest maximum admissible departure property if $\left| \frac{\frac{p_i}{M(p,H)_i} - A}{A} \right| \leq \alpha_{(p,H)}$ for any apportionment problem (p, H) and for each $i \in \{1, \ldots, n\}$.*

16.3 Choosing Methods

The reason for looking at the various properties has been to be able to evaluate the different methods. In Table 16.2 we present some of the known comparison results about these methods. Apportionment has a long history in the United States and the method has already been altered several times. Over the years many new states joined, populations increased dramatically and correspondingly, the House was expanded, too, and we have seen properties violated several

Table 16.2: A comparison of apportionment methods.

	quota	House monotonicity	population monotonicity	Venice
Hamilton	both	no	no	no
Jefferson/D'Hondt	lower	yes	yes	no
Webster/Sainte-Laguë	mostly	yes	yes	no
Huntingdon-Hill/EP	no	yes	yes	no
Leximin	no	no	no	yes

times. While apart from the initial use of the Jefferson method, Hamilton and Webster were used together, Hamilton was found to exhibit both the Alabama paradox, when house-monotonicity is violated, the population monotonicity and also the new state paradox that we did not discuss here. As a result the method has been replaced by the Huntingdon-Hill, or Equal Proportions method that is still used today.

Even if we treat the Venice property separately, notice that there is no method that would satisfy all other requirements. Balinski and Young (1975) introduced the so-called *Quota method* that is house-monotonic and fulfills the quota property as well, but proved that no method that is free from both the Alabama and the population paradoxes satisfies quota (Balinski and Young, 1982). On the other hand Biró et al. (2015) have shown that the Venice property is not compatible with any of the remaining properties. Notice that the result is also true if we look at admissible departures only. For a low enough admissible departure the same counterexamples can be presented. This means that the recommendation of Venice Commission (2002) inherently violates quota and the monotonicity properties.

When we say that a method violates a property we mean that there exists an apportionment problem where the given property is violated. These counterexamples are sometimes artificial. They may for instance rely on symmetries that are extremely unlikely in real life. In the following we look at real apportionment problems gathered from countries all over the world. In the next couple of sections we test the properties on this real data set.

16.3.1 Bounds on the Maximum Departure

Let us fix an apportionment problem (p, H). Obviously d_i is the smallest if state i receives either its lower or upper quota, although it matters which one. Note that the closest integer to the respective share does not always yield the smallest difference from the average. Let us elaborate on this relationship a bit further.

Let $l_i = \lfloor \frac{p_i}{P} H \rfloor$ and $u_i = \lceil \frac{p_i}{P} H \rceil$, respectively, denote the lower and upper quotas of state i and let β_i and ω_i denote the minimum and maximum difference achievable for state i when it gets the lower or upper integer part of its respective share. The maximum of the β_i values, denoted by β (for *best* case), is a natural lower bound on the maximum departure for any apportionment, which satisfies the Hare-quota property. Similarly the maximum of the ω_i values, denoted by

ω (for *worst* case), is an upper bound for any apportionment which satisfies the Hare-quota. Formally:

$$\beta_i = \min\left(\left|\frac{\frac{p_i}{l_i} - A}{A}\right|, \left|\frac{\frac{p_i}{u_i} - A}{A}\right|\right), \qquad \beta = \max_{i \in N} \beta_i. \tag{16.3}$$

$$\omega_i = \max\left(\left|\frac{\frac{p_i}{l_i} - A}{A}\right|, \left|\frac{\frac{p_i}{u_i} - A}{A}\right|\right), \qquad \omega = \max_{i \in N} \omega_i. \tag{16.4}$$

Suppose we would like to minimize the differences from the average constituency size. We calculate the standard quota for every state and start rounding it up or down depending on which one yields a smaller difference. Unfortunately the resulting allotment is infeasible if we have distributed too few or too many seats. The *best case scenario* is when the allotted number of seats add up to the House size. In such cases we can guarantee that the departure is not bigger than β. Even if some states are rounded in the wrong direction, β is achievable if we rounded the critical states well. The *worst case scenario* is when the critical states are rounded in the wrong direction, in such cases the difference will be ω. Note that it is always possible to allocate the seats in such way that the apportionment satisfies the quota property, hence if the goal is to minimize the differences from the average then ω is achievable even in the worst case.

In contrast the maximum difference α can be implemented by the Leximin Method, By design, $\beta \leq \alpha \leq \omega$, thus the Leximin Method always yields an apportionment that falls within these bounds. Somewhat surprisingly, empirical data shows that divisor methods, which are known to violate the quota property never exceed these bounds either (see Figures 16.1 and 16.2).

16.3.2 Monotonicity vs. Quota vs. Maximum Departure

The Leximin Method fails to be monotonic because it focuses solely on reducing the maximum departure from the average constituency size. In effect this means that the Leximin Method will reallocate seats from big states to small ones if the resulting apportionment has smaller departure. Large states with many seats serve as puffers where excess seats can be allocated or seats can be acquired if there are needed elsewhere as these changes do not affect the average size of constituencies dramatically. For the exact same reasons the Leximin Method violates quota as well.

Divisor methods are all immune from the Alabama paradox. The reason is clear: by enlarging the House, the price of a seat decreases, thus each state can afford more. Similarly, divisor methods are immune from both the population- and new state paradoxes. In fact if a method avoids the population paradox it must be a divisor method (Balinski and Young, 1982). As a consequence divisor methods sometimes fail to produce quota apportionments. Interestingly, quota failures just as for leximin affect only large states (see Tables 16.3 and 16.4).

Quota failures are more common for problems with substantially different state/county sizes. In case of Hungary the capital Budapest has eight times more voters than the smallest county, Nógrád. In comparison the Irish administrative

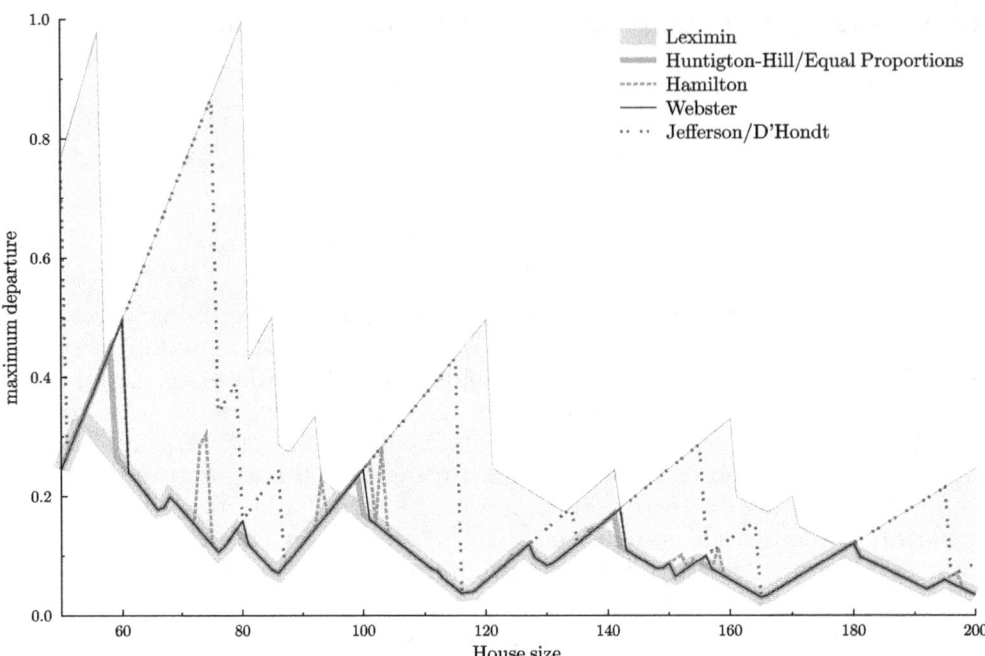

Figure 16.1: Apportionment over Belgian regions. Leximin coincides with β; EP, Webster are near. Ironically, D'Hondt performs poorly, reaching ω several times.

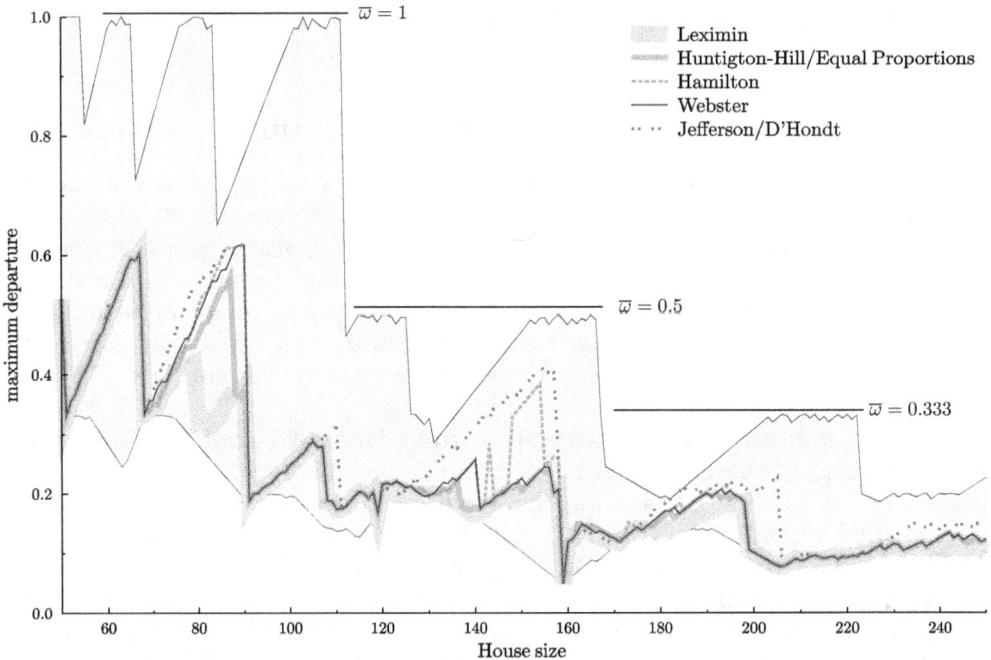

Figure 16.2: Apportionment over Irish counties. Leximin performs best, then EP, Webster, but all struggle to evenly distribute seats due to regular county sizes.

	Leximin	EP	Jeff/D'Hondt	Adams	Webster
Largest county (Budapest)	27	1	74	67	0
2nd largest county (Pest)	4	0	17	21	0
Elsewhere	0	0	0	0	0

Table 16.3: Number of quota failures based on Hungarian constituency data when House size varies between 100 and 200.

	Leximin	EP	Jeff/D'Hondt	Adams	Webster
Largest state (California)	112	2	201	201	0
2nd largest state (Texas)	30	0	198	192	0
3rd largest state (New York)	12	0	120	67	0
4th largest state (Florida)	6	0	105	21	0
Elsewhere	0	0	19	24	0

Table 16.4: Number of quota failures based on US constituency data when House size varies between 335 and 535 (that is current House size ±100).

regions do not vary that much. The population ratio of the largest (Donegal) and the smallest (South-West Cork) county is only 1.83. Even on a broader range of House sizes (50-250) the Adams, EP and Webster methods do not violate the quota property and the leximin and the Jefferson/D'Hondt methods only violate it 3 times each (again at the two largest counties).

The leximin and EP methods, although conceptually very different, in practice tend to produce similar apportionments. They coincide for the apportionment problems in Austria, Denmark, Finland, Ireland, Luxemburg and Portugal, differ for the US House of Representatives and in England by 1 and 2 seats respectively. This small difference, however, accounts for the worse (better) departure statistic and for the (lack of) monotonicity.

The β and ω bounds indicate that proportional representation rests on whether we can round the critical states in a good direction. Enforcing quota ensures that the departure will not exceed ω but the additional constraint also makes it difficult to stay close to β, since it does not allow us to use states as buffers to lend/borrow problematic or desperately needed seats for critical states without creating too much inequality. What are the critical states? Critical states are small states which are only a few times as big as the average constituency size. It is easy to prove the following upper bounds

$$\beta \leq \overline{\beta} \stackrel{def}{=} \frac{1}{2l_{sm}+1} \qquad (16.5)$$

$$\omega \leq \overline{\omega} \stackrel{def}{=} \begin{cases} \frac{1}{l_{sm}} & \text{if } l_{sm} > 0, \\ \infty & \text{if } l_{sm} = 0. \end{cases} \qquad (16.6)$$

where l_{sm} denotes the lower integer part of the smallest state's respective share.

$l_i - u_i$	p_i^*	$\overline{\beta}$	$\hat{p}_i$	$\overline{\omega}$
0 − 1	0	1	$< A$	∞
1 − 2	$\frac{4}{3}A$	1/3	A or $2A$	1
2 − 3	$\frac{12}{5}A$	1/5	$2A$ or $3A$	1/2
3 − 4	$\frac{24}{7}A$	1/7	$3A$ or $4A$	1/3
4 − 5	$\frac{40}{9}A$	1/9	$4A$ or $5A$	1/4
5 − 6	$\frac{60}{11}A$	1/11	$5A$ or $6A$	1/5

Table 16.5: Critical state populations. The first column shows the lower and upper quotas. If state i's population is close to p_i^* then β_i will be close to $\overline{\beta}$. If state i's population is close to $\hat{p}_i$ then ω_i will be close to $\overline{\omega}$.

Figure 16.2 demonstrates the meaning of Table 16.5. As the House size increases from 111 to 112 the average constituency size becomes so small that even the smallest county is at least twice as big as A. As a result ω drops significantly and never anymore exceeds 50%.

The reason why we are interested in $\overline{\beta}$ rather than in $\overline{\omega}$ is that some methods like the EP and Webster can reach β and the Leximin Method often coincides with it even for a wide range of House sizes. Since β is achievable it is a valid question where β takes its maximum and how can we lower it. Equation 16.5 highlights the relationship of β and lower quota of the smallest state. For example, if the average constituency size is sufficiently small, less than half of the smallest state, then the maximum departure will be less than 20% (assuming we achieve β).

The Leximin Method will coincide with β if the House size is not too small and there are puffer states that enable seat reconfiguration. That means there are at least one or two large states.

16.4 Conclusion

Several alternative methods exist for the allocation of seats among states or regions and while all these methods have the same goal, fair representation, each approaches fairness from a different angle. Fairness can be captured by several incompatible properties and our interest lies in uncovering the principles that lead to one or another choice. In particular, we want to understand the incompatibility of the quota and maximum difference properties. The latter is a mathematical formulation of a good practice recommended by the Venice Commission (2002) to ensure near-equal representation. The Quota Property on the other hand puts the states first and guarantees that the states or regions get very close to their fair share. The conflict between the two views is far from obvious, but we soon learned that fairness at the state level contributes to larger inequalities among voters elsewhere.

The actual apportionments in certain European countries fall quite far from both the recommendation of the Venice Commission and the method used in the US. While the differences can, surely be attribute to the lack of a scientific approach, certain countries introduce systematic biases, often to counter the overrepresentation of the urban areas. Corrections are not needed for a country with homogeneous constituencies, but if some share common interest, voting blocks may emerge and proportionality is no longer fair.

For instance the Spanish Congress of Deputies consists of 350 members, but only 248 are apportioned according to the population data. Each of the fifty provinces is entitled to an initial minimum of two seats, while the cities of Ceuta and Melilla get one each. As a result the constituencies of Teruel are roughly 65% smaller, Madrid's are 30% larger than the average; the vote of a Teruelian citizen is worth nearly four times more than that of a Madrilenian. The Danish apportionment, on the other hand, uses the classical D'Hondt method, but based on the sum of the (1) population, (2) voting population, and (3) 20 times the area in square kilometres (as a rural bonus) for each region. Other countries have special clauses specifying the seat allocated to certain states explicitly, outside the apportionment procedure. While this is generally to ensure the fair treatment of a peripheral or underpopulated region, favourable developments of the population often turns such measures unnecessary or even harmful for the region. Such anomalies are very interesting from both a theoretical and practical point of view, but elaborating on them further would be beyond the limits of this paper and we present them in a companion paper with a systematic study of apportionment methods and practices.

Acknowledgments

Biró was supported by the Hungarian Academy of Sciences under its Momentum Programme (LP2016-3/2016) and by OTKA grant no. K108673. Kóczy and Sziklai were supported by OTKA grant no. K109354. Sziklai was supported by the ÚNKP-16-4-I. New National Excellence Program of the Ministry of Human Capacities.

Bibliography

M. Balinski and H. P. Young. The quota method of apportionment. *American Mathematical Monthly*, 82(7):701–730, 1975.

M. Balinski and H. P. Young. *Fair Representation: Meeting the Ideal of One Man, One Vote*. Yale University Press, New Haven, 1982.

P. Biró, L. Á. Kóczy, and B. Sziklai. Választókörzetek igazságosan? *Közgazdasági Szemle*, 59:1165–1186, 2012.

P. Biró, L. Á. Kóczy, and B. Sziklai. Fair apportionment in the view of the Venice Commission's recommendation. *Mathematical Social Sciences*, 77:32–41, 2015.

V. Bittó. Az Imperiali és Macau politikai választókörzet-kiosztási módszerek empirikus vizsgálata. MPRA Paper 79554, Munich Personal RePEc Archive, 2017.

M. Brill, J.-F. Laslier, and P. Skowron. Multiwinner Approval Rules as Apportionment Methods. In *Proceedings of the 31st AAAI Conference on Artficial Intelligence (AAAI)*, pages 414–420, 2017.

L. Csató. Between plurality and proportionality: an analysis of vote transfer systems. Technical report, arXiv, 2015. URL http://arxiv.org/abs/1507.01477.

L. Csató. A mathematical evaluation of vote transfer systems. Technical report, arXiv, 2016. URL http://arxiv.org/abs/1607.02879.

P. Csóka and P. J.-J. Herings. Decentralized clearing in financial networks. Technical Report 14/2016, Corvinus University Budapest, Budapest, 2016.

H. R. Droop. On Methods of Electing Representatives. *Journal of the Statistical Society of London*, 44(2):141–202, 1881.

G. R. Grimmett. European apportionment via the Cambridge Compromise. *Mathematical Social Sciences*, 63:68–73, 2012.

E. Hagenbach-Bischoff. *Die Frage der Einführung einer Proportionalvertretung statt des absoluten Mehres*. H. Georg, Basel, 1888.

L. Handley. Boundary Delimitation. In *Challenging the Norms and Standards of Election Administration*, pages 59–74. International Foundation for Electoral Systems, 2007.

L. Á. Kóczy. Beyond Lisbon: Demographic trends and voting power in the European Union Council of Ministers. *Mathematical Social Sciences*, 63(2):158–152, 2012.

L. Lauwers and T. Van Puyenbroeck. Minimally Disproportional Representation: Generalized Entropy and Stolarsky Mean-Divisor Methods of Apportionment. Working Papers 2008/24, Hogeschool-Universiteit Brussel, Faculteit Economie en Management, 2008.

A. W. Marshall, I. Olkin, and F. Pukelsheim. A majorization comparison of apportionment methods in proportional representation. *Social Choice and Welfare*, 19(4), 2002.

OSCE/ODIHR. Estonia Parliamentary Elections, 6 March 2011. Election assessment mission report, Organization for Security and Co-operation in Europe, Office for Democratic Institutions and Human Rights, Warsaw, May 2011.

L. S. Penrose. The elementary statistics of majority voting. *Journal of the Royal Statistical Society*, 109(1):53–57, 1946.

C. Puppe and A. Tasnádi. Axiomatic districting. *Social Choice and Welfare*, 44: 31–50, 2015.

W. Słomczyński and K. Życzkowski. Penrose voting system and optimal quota. *Acta Physica Polonica B*, 37:3133, 2006.

A. Tasnádi. The extent of the population paradox in the Hungarian electoral system. *Public Choice*, 134(3-4):293–305, 2008.

A. Tasnádi. The political districting problem: A survey. *Society and Economy*, 33(3):543–554, 2011.

Venice Commission. Code of Good Practice in Electoral Matters. *Conseil de l'Europe-AD*, 23(190):1–33, 2002.

Venice Commission and OSCE/ODIHR. On the Electoral Law and the Electoral Practice of Albania. Joint opinion, Venice Commission and Organization for Security and Co-operation in Europe, Office for Democratic Institutions and Human Rights, 2011.

CHAPTER 17

Recent Advances in Large-Scale Peer Grading

Ioannis Caragiannis

17.1 Introduction

Peer grading is the standard practice for evaluating research work and has recently become a necessity in online education. Examples include a program committee that has to decide on the papers that will be accepted for presentation at a scientific conference, the members of a professional society that wish to single out a member that should be given an award, or an instructor of an online course who outsources the evaluation of an exam to the students themselves. In all these cases, the individual inputs provided by each program committee member, society member, or student have to be aggregated in order to get the final result.

The challenge that needs to be addressed is to guarantee an as high as possible level of effectiveness in the evaluation outcome, given that the individual inputs will be, in general, *partial* and *inaccurate*. Typically, the number of submissions in a big scientific conference is a few thousand (e.g., more than 2,000 papers were submitted in the last AAAI and IJCAI conferences). Of course, there is no single program committee member that has a complete view of all submitted papers. Instead, each PC member is given very few papers for review. The source of inaccuracy should be clear in the case of students who grade their peers in an online course but it can be a severe problem even among experts. In a recent experiment,[1] the organizers of the NIPS 2014 conference formed two independent program committees. Among the approximately 900 submitted papers, most were assigned to a single PC, but 166 submissions were reviewed by both committees. This let them observe how consistent the two committees were on which papers to accept. The results have revealed a surprisingly high degree of randomness in the decision process: more than half of the papers accepted by one committee were rejected by the other!

So, it should be clear that there is more than one reason why peer grading can be challenging. In this chapter, we will focus on the extremely challenging scenario that manifests itself when grading an exam in a massive open online

---
[1] See blog.mrtz.org/2014/12/15/the-nips-experiment.html for a detailed discussion on the NIPS experiment.

course (or, simply, MOOC or online course). We will follow the vision of the MOOC enthusiasts and will assume that the number of students participating in the exam is huge (our technical assumption will be that it approaches infinity). In this way, we will have taken scale, partial view, and grading inaccuracy to their extreme. Still, we will present an approach —heavily inspired by social choice theory but also of a machine learning flavour— which has been proved recently to be simultaneously simple and effective.

The rest of the chapter is structured as follows. In Section 17.2, we briefly present the challenge of peer grading in massive open online courses, discuss the current practice and introduce the concept of ordinal peer grading. Then, in Section 17.3, we introduce useful notions and discuss the main tasks that typically take place when ordinal peer grading is used. When particular technical characteristics have to be defined, we follow the recent papers by the author (Caragiannis et al., 2015, 2016b). We identify the important parameters and discuss criteria for selecting their values in Section 17.4. In that section, we also define a natural performance objective for ordinal peer grading. In Section 17.5, we present the approach from (Caragiannis et al., 2016b) for assessing the performance of ordinal peer grading methods in a particular class and for selecting the best such method when statistical information about grading behavior is available. Experimental results follow in Section 17.6. We conclude with directions for future research in Section 17.7.

17.2 Massive Open Online Courses

Platforms supporting online courses like Coursera[2] and EdX[3] have emerged as an education trend and have attracted significant funding from venture capitals and support from leading academics. Based on the data for 2015,[4] the total number of students that enrolled in at least one online course exceeded 35 million, a 100% increase compared to 2014. More than 500 Universities worldwide were involved in more than 4200 online courses in 2016, offering courses not only in popular technology-related subjects such as Computer Science, Business and Management, and Engineering, but also in the Social Sciences and Humanities.

Whether MOOCs will become successful depends on whether they will manage to find a suitable business model and secure revenue sources. It seems that the *verified certificate* that a student participating in such course can get for a few dozens of dollars can serve as such a revenue source. The verified certificate keeps information about the performance of the student in a course or in a chain of courses and can be used to justify the student's quality to potential employers. So, it should contain *reliable information* and achieving this in a popular online course is far from trivial. Enrolment data for the 50 most popular MOOC courses[5] suggests that the vision of the MOOC enthusiasts for courses with several millions of attending students is not very far.

---

[2] www.coursera.org
[3] www.edx.org
[4] www.class-central.com/report/moocs-2015-stats/
[5] www.onlinecoursereport.com/the-50-most-popular-moocs-of-all-time/

How can an exam with over one million of students be graded? With the emergence of MOOCs as a trend a few years ago, and as the number of students started increasing at extremely high rates while the available resources were apparently very limited (e.g., hiring professional graders would be unreasonably costly), a simple first approach that was adopted was to use *automatic grading*, i.e., exams organized around questions with multiple-choice answers that could be graded automatically. Unfortunately, this approach is unsatisfactory in an exam where the student is asked to prepare an essay or express her critical thinking over some issue; exams of this flavour are typical in courses of Social Sciences and Humanities subjects. It is also unsatisfactory in any exam in a Science or Engineering subject where the students are asked to prepare a mathematical proof. Grading in these exams is an inherently *human computation* (Law and von Ahn, 2011) task.

Self-assessment was a next step; each student was asked by the instructor to assess her progress in the course and was also given guidelines on how to do so. Self-assessment may give the student a way to get feedback from her studies but it cannot result to reliable grading information that can be used to compare students in terms of their performance in "class".

Soon, it became apparent that the students should be involved in the grading task. This led to *peer grading* (Kulkarni et al., 2013; Piech et al., 2013; Walsh, 2014), which is widely used in most MOOC platforms today. In addition, several standalone experimental tools such as `crowdgrader.org` (de Alfaro and Shavlovsky, 2014), `peergrading.org` (Raman and Joachims, 2014), and the author's co-rank[6] (Caragiannis et al., 2016a), as well as startup services such as `peergrade.io` are available. The current practice is to use the students as graders, with the traditional meaning of the term. So, each student gets some exam papers by fellow students and grades them by assigning them cardinal scores (and, possibly, giving feedback), in a similar way a professional grader would do this. This results in much noise in the grades. The students are not experienced in assessing the performance of their fellow students in absolute terms and, if they eventually learn how to do so, they will have obvious incentives to use low cardinal grades (hoping that their own grade will look better compared to the student majority). Much of the recent literature in data mining and machine learning studies methods for calibrating cardinal grades; e.g., see the work of Piech et al. (2013), Sajjadi et al. (2016), and Wright et al. (2015).

An approach, that has received much attention recently in the AI and machine learning community (Caragiannis et al., 2015, 2016b; Raman and Joachims, 2014; Shah et al., 2013), does not use cardinal scores and is very close in spirit to voting rules from social choice theory. In a nutshell (the whole process is described in detail in the next section), each student is given a small number of exam papers and is asked to rank them in terms of quality. Then, the partial rankings are combined in an aggregate global ranking that is used as the final grading information that can be stored in the verified certificate of each student. In particular, information of the form "student X was ranked in the top 11% among the 35,000 students that participated in the course Y" can be stored in

---

[6] co-rank.ceid.upatras.gr

the student's verified certificate and already carries much information that can be used by potential employers. If the instructor desires so, the ranking information can be translated to a cardinal score (like 8/10 or A+) using a predefined distribution.

17.3 Organizing Ordinal Peer Grading

We now describe the tasks that are necessary for supporting ordinal peer grading. We will keep the presentation simple by making the simplifying assumptions that *all* students will participate in grading and *no experts* will be used. We do expect however that experts (professional graders or teaching assistants) may be used in practice to calibrate the peer grading outcome; we also expect that some of the students may decide to refrain from grading. These two characteristics will complicate the general structure described below and pose important implementation issues that should be solved when deploying ordinal peer grading in real environments. Since such issues seem to be addressed in *ad hoc* ways until now, we will not incorporate them into the general structure presented below.

So, ordinal peer grading involves three main tasks: First, after the end of an exam, copies of exam papers are distributed to the students. Then, each student acts as grader and ranks the exam papers she received. Finally, the partial rankings are aggregated into a global ranking. Let us denote by n the total number of students participating in an exam (and in its grading).

1. **Distributing the exam papers**. The goal of the first task is to balance the grading load. This can be done by making copies of each exam paper and distributing them back to the students so that each student receives the same number k of exam papers by other students and each paper is given to exactly k students for grading. Following the terminology of Caragiannis et al. (2015), we use the term *bundle* to refer to the set of k exam papers assigned to a student for grading. A *bundle graph* can be used for representing this assignment. In particular, an (n,k)-bundle graph is a bipartite graph[7] $G = ([n],[n],E)$. Both its left and right node sides correspond to the n students; the students are assigned to the integers in $[n]$ randomly. An edge (i,j) indicates that student i's exam paper is in the bundle of student j. Clearly, an (n,k)-bundle graph has all its nodes with degree k while no edge is of the form (i,i).

2. **Grading.** Once the copies of the exam papers have been distributed to the students, each student has simply to rank the k exam papers in her bundle in decreasing order of quality. The instructor may affect the grading process by announcing indicative solutions of the exam and providing detailed grading instructions to the students; in this case, we typically assume that each student acts as a *perfect* grader[8] and ranks the exam papers in her bundle

---

[7]The notation $[n]$ is an abbreviation for the set of integers $\{1,2,...,n\}$.
[8]Admittedly, this assumption is very optimistic as, most probably, in practice some students will make grading mistakes in this case as well. It is useful though as it can be used to obtain upper bounds on grading performance.

correctly. If no such information becomes available from the instructor to the students, it is natural to assume that the grading performance of a student is correlated to her performance in the exam. These assumptions will be made concrete in the next section.

3. **Rank aggregation.** The last task is to take the partial rankings provided by all students as input and compute a global ranking of all exam papers. A very simple way to do this rank aggregation is to use a method inspired by the well-known *Borda* count. Each exam paper gets k points for each appearance in the top position of a partial ranking, $k-1$ points when appearing in the second position, and so on. Its Borda score is simply the total number of points it receives in this way. The final ranking is obtained by ordering the exam papers in terms of their Borda score in non-increasing order, breaking ties randomly. Many other methods can be used as well; a broad class of rank aggregation methods that contain Borda are discussed in the next section.

Despite its apparent similarities to social choice, the ordinal peer grading setting that we just defined has important differences from classical voting rules. First, the rank aggregation task is applied on partial votes only. With the exception of the papers by de Weerdt et al. (2016), Dwork et al. (2001), Sculley (2007), and Caragiannis et al. (2017), this seems to be non-standard in the literature. Second, the decision on the contents of each bundle (and, hence, the exam papers in each partial ranking) is taken by the ordinal peer grading algorithm (and not by each individual providing input as in the four papers above). A third characteristic, which has been used only sporadically in social choice (e.g., see Alon et al., 2011; Holzman and Moulin, 2013), is that the candidates and the voters coincide.

17.4 Problem Parameters and Objectives

From the description of the previous section, the main parameters that have to be decided in order to use ordinal peer grading are the bundle size k, the structure of the bundle graph, and the rank aggregation method.

First, there is a trade-off in deciding the optimal bundle size. On one hand, it should be small so that grading is possible with reasonable effort by each student. As the final grading outcome depends on the quality of the input provided by the students, the number of students that will get frustrated and give grading up or grade at random should be minimized. A small bundle size is an incentive in this direction; additional incentives by the course instructor — such as extra grades depending on the distance between the student's ranking of the exam papers in her bundle and the relative position of them in the final ranking — may guarantee the highest student participation in grading. On the other hand, large bundles imply more grading information that will be given as input to the rank aggregation algorithm. Hence, the larger the bundle size, the more accurate the final grading outcome could be.

Typically, the bundle size will be much smaller than the total number of exam papers. As a result, deciding the structure of the bundle graph is important as well. Note that a global ranking among n exam papers defines the relation between $\binom{n}{2} \in \Theta(n^2)$ pairs. In contrast, each grader provides information for $\binom{k}{2}$ pairs only; this gives a total number of $\Theta(nk^2)$ pairwise relations that can be correctly recovered (with the optimistic assumption that graders provide correct information), plus some additional pairwise relations that can be indirectly inferred by exploiting transitivity (e.g., for exam papers a, b, and c the pairwise comparisons $a \succ b$ and $b \succ c$ by different graders could be combined to conclude that $a \succ c$ as well). However, it should be clear that, as we would like to keep the bundle size small, in order to maximize the amount of information we get from the graders, we do not have the luxury to assign the same pair of exam papers to more than one grader. In graph-theoretic terms, this means that the bundle graph should not contain 4-cycles (as a 4-cycle in a bundle graph would indicate that two different graders have the same pair of exam papers in their bundles). A slightly less restrictive structure is that of a random k-regular bipartite graph as bundle graph (this is guaranteed to contain very few 4-cycles with high probability).

The most important decision is related to the rank aggregation method to be used. A property that sounds highly desirable is to come up with a global ranking of the exam papers that agrees as much as possible with the input provided by the graders. More technically, let us define the distance between the input provided by a grader and a candidate final ranking as the total number of pairwise comparisons among exam papers in which the grader disagrees with the candidate ranking. Then, a global ranking that has minimum total distance from all graders would better aggregate the individual inputs. This is a variation of the well-known Kemeny voting rule, adapted to our setting. Unfortunately, resolving Kemeny (i.e., computing the global ranking with the above property) is a well-known computationally hard problem in voting theory (Bartholdi et al., 1989). In practice, this hardness is magnified by the fact that the total number of exam papers is huge. Hence, simple rank aggregation rules like Borda would be the most desirable from the computational complexity point of view.

But once we have restrict ourselves to simple rank aggregation rule, what is the appropriate objective for selecting the best possible one? There is no single answer here; for simplicity of exposition, we will evaluate rank aggregation rules using as performance objective the expected[9] fraction of corrected recovered pairwise relations between exam papers. Essentially, we assume that there is a true (strict) ranking of the exam papers (i.e., a *ground truth* ranking) and evaluate a rank aggregation rule by measuring the similarity of the ranking produced by the rule to the ground truth.

We are now ready to present a first theoretical statement.

Theorem 17.1 (Caragiannis et al., 2015). *When Borda is used to aggregate the partial rankings provided by perfect graders, the expected fraction of correctly recovered pairwise relations in the final ranking compared to the ground truth is at*

---
[9]The term "expected" is used since the assignment of students to the nodes of the bundle graph is random.

least $1 - \mathcal{O}(k)$ when the (n, k)-bundle graph that is used for distributing the exam papers does not contain 4-cycles, and at least $1 - \mathcal{O}(\sqrt{k})$ in general.

Theorem 17.1 says that performance approaches optimality as the bundle size increases. This is important and suggests that ordinal peer grading can be highly scalable. But, unfortunately, it seems that such a rigorous analysis cannot be more informative than that. For example, fixing a value of k, is Borda the best choice? In other words, is it optimal among simple rank aggregation rules? Theorem 17.1 provides no answer. The constants hidden in the $\mathcal{O}$ notation are rather huge (higher than 50) and, hence, the statement gives only a rough estimation of Borda performance as a function of k. Furthermore, the proof is several pages long and quite involved.[10] It holds specifically for Borda and is based on the particular properties this rule has. It is not at all clear how the analysis could be adjusted to work for other rank aggregation rules and it is even less obvious how imperfect graders could be included in it.

17.5 A Machine Learning Approach

In this section, we present a radically different approach that was originally presented in (Caragiannis et al., 2016b). This approach aims to bypass the limitations of the rigorous theoretical analysis and even get performance estimates of the highest possible accuracy. It can be applied not only to Borda but to the broad class of type-ordering aggregation rules that we will define shortly. Also, it is not restricted to perfect graders but exploits statistical information about grading behavior when computing the performance estimate for a rank aggregation rule. More importantly, following a direction that is typical in modern machine learning literature, the approach can be used to compute the most suitable —the optimal— type-ordering aggregation rule for a given bundle size and statistical information about grading behavior.

17.5.1 Type-Ordering Aggregation Rules

We will use the term *type* of an exam paper to refer to the grading result for it. As each exam paper belongs to the bundles of k different graders, its type is a vector of k integers that contain the position the exam paper has in the k partial rankings provided by the graders that have it in their bundle. We follow the convention that the k entries in a type vector are sorted in monotone non-decreasing order. Then, the set of possible types (for bundle size k) is

$$\mathcal{T}_k = \{\sigma = (\sigma_1, \sigma_2, ..., \sigma_k) | 1 \leqslant \sigma_1 \leqslant ... \leqslant \sigma_k \leqslant k\}.$$

It can be easily seen that the number of different types in $\mathcal{T}_k$ is $\binom{2k-1}{k}$. For example, $\mathcal{T}_6$ contains 462 types.

---

[10]The proof uses martingale theory and Azuma's tail inequality (see standard textbooks on randomized algorithms such as the one by Mitzenmacher and Upfal, 2005) in order to cope with dependencies between the several random variables involved. These dependencies appear due to the restrictions that both the bundle size and the number of students that grade a single paper are fixed.

As another example with $k=6$, an exam paper of type $(1,2,2,2,2,5)$ is ranked first by one of its graders, second by four graders, and fifth by one grader. Now, consider another exam paper of type $(2,2,2,2,3,3)$ and observe that both have the same Borda score of 28. So, Borda does not distinguish any of the two papers as best. Now, consider the two types $(1,1,1,2,5,6)$ and $(2,2,2,3,3,3)$ of Borda scores 26 and 27, respectively. Borda indicates that an exam paper with the second type is better. But looking carefully at the ranks, we could come up with the following interpretation. The first exam paper is very good (and most probably in one of the two top positions in any bundle) and the two low ranks might be due to poor judgement by some of the graders. In contrast, the second exam paper is just above average and this is reflected in all grades. Of course, such interpretations are valid only when they can be supported by information about the graders. But, certainly, there are cases where such interpretations are indeed valid and, in contrast to what Borda does, it might be a good idea to take them into account.

A *type-ordering aggregation rule* uses a strict ordering $\succ$ of all types in $\mathcal{T}_k$. Then, the final ranking of the exam papers follows the ordering $\succ$ of their types, breaking ties uniformly at random. In general, rules of this class seem to be very powerful. Compared to Borda, which partitions the set of exam papers into only $k^2 - k + 1$ different groups (an exam paper can have a Borda score between k and k^2), a type-ordering aggregation rule can distinguish between exponentially many (in terms of k) different types.

17.5.2 Modelling Students' Grading Behavior

The intuition discussed above suggests that the most suitable type-ordering aggregation rule for a particular exam depends on the grading behavior of the students. A simple way to express statistical information about grading behavior is to use a *noise model* for the average grader. This is done through a $k \times k$ *noise matrix* $P = (p_{i,j})_{i,j \in [k]}$, where $p_{i,j}$ denotes the probability that the exam paper with correct rank j among the k exam papers in a bundle is ranked at position i by the grader. Noise matrices are doubly stochastic: the sum of entries in any column and any row is equal to 1. The noise matrix of perfect graders is simply the $k \times k$ identity matrix. Notice that this modelling of grading behavior is very rough; a noise matrix may correspond to many different probability distributions over rankings. As we discuss in the following, this rough representation of grading behavior is enough in order to get accurate estimates of performance for type-ordering aggregation rules and to decide the most suitable rule for exams with a particular student population.

17.5.3 A Framework for Theoretical Analysis

We now present the main ideas in the theoretical analysis presented in (Caragiannis et al., 2016b). We will consider an exam and, taking the vision of the MOOC enthusiasts to the extreme, we will assume that the number of students participating in the exam is infinite. So, the positions of students in the ground truth ranking can be thought of as occupying the continuum of the interval $[0, 1]$.

In the following, we will identify each exam paper by a real number $x \in [0,1]$ that also indicates the position of the student/paper in the ground truth ranking.

Assume that we have fixed the bundle size to k, we have collected statistical information for the grading behavior of our student population in a noise matrix P, and we use a type-ordering aggregation rule that uses the ordering $\succ$ of the types in $\mathcal{T}_k$. Then, the pairwise relations between two exam papers x and y with ranks $x < y$ (i.e., x is ranked higher than y in the ground truth) is correctly recovered in the final ranking produced by the rank aggregation rule (compared to the ground truth) if both exam papers get the exact same type σ and this tie is randomly resolved in favour of exam paper x, or exam papers x and y get types σ and σ' (we use the notation $x \triangleright \sigma$ and $y \triangleright \sigma'$ to represent these events) so that $\sigma \succ \sigma'$. Denoting the expected fraction of correctly recovered pairwise relations by $C(k, \succ, P)$ we obtain

$$\begin{aligned} C(k,\succ,P) &= \int_0^1 \int_x^1 \left(\sum_{\sigma,\sigma':\sigma \succ \sigma'} \Pr[x \triangleright \sigma \wedge y \triangleright \sigma'] + \frac{1}{2} \sum_\sigma \Pr[x \triangleright \sigma \wedge y \triangleright \sigma] \right) dy\, dx \\ &= \sum_{\sigma,\sigma':\sigma \succ \sigma'} \int_0^1 \int_x^1 \Pr[x \triangleright \sigma \wedge y \triangleright \sigma']\, dy\, dx \\ &\quad + \frac{1}{2} \sum_\sigma \int_0^1 \int_x^1 \Pr[x \triangleright \sigma \wedge y \triangleright \sigma]\, dy\, dx \end{aligned}$$

The assumption of infinitely many students nullifies any dependency between the rank vectors two exam papers x and y get after grading (i.e., $\Pr[x \triangleright \sigma \wedge y \triangleright \sigma'] = \Pr[x \triangleright \sigma] \cdot \Pr[y \triangleright \sigma']$). This is due to the fact that the probability that the two exam papers will appear in the bundle of the same grader is zero and different students grade independently. So, by defining the *weight*

$$W(\sigma,\sigma') = \int_0^1 \int_x^1 \Pr[x \triangleright \sigma] \cdot \Pr[y \triangleright \sigma']\, dy\, dx \qquad (17.1)$$

for every pair of types $\sigma, \sigma' \in \mathcal{T}_k$, we obtain

$$C(k,\succ,P) = \sum_{\sigma,\sigma':\sigma \succ \sigma'} W(\sigma,\sigma') + \frac{1}{2}\sum_\sigma W(\sigma,\sigma). \qquad (17.2)$$

So, in order to compute $C(k, \succ, P)$, it suffices to compute the probability $\Pr[x \triangleright \sigma]$ that an exam paper with position x in the ground truth ranking gets type $\sigma = (\sigma_1, ..., \sigma_k)$ after grading. We will now devote some space[11] to show that this probability is nothing more than a polynomial of x and, hence, computing the double integral in equation (17.1) is straightforward.

By considering all ways to distribute the entries of the type vector as ranks of an exam paper by the graders that handle it (ignoring symmetries), there are

$$N(\sigma) = \frac{k!}{d_1! \cdot ... \cdot d_k!}$$

---

[11]The material until the end of this subsection is technical and can be skipped at first reading.

ways that the exam paper can get type σ, where d_i is the number of graders that have the exam paper ranked i-th. Due to our assumption for infinitely many students and the uniform inclusion of them into bundles, the quality of each exam paper included in a bundle does not affect the quality of other exam papers (in the same or different bundles). Clearly, the grading by different students is performed without dependencies either. Denoting by $\mathcal{E}(x, \sigma_i)$ the event that exam paper x is ranked σ_i-th in a bundle, the probability that x is of type σ is

$$\Pr[x \triangleright \sigma] = N(\sigma) \prod_{i=1}^{k} \Pr[\mathcal{E}(x, \sigma_i)].$$

To compute $\Pr[\mathcal{E}(x, \sigma_i)]$, it suffices to consider all possible true ranks that exam paper x may have in a bundle and account for the probability of having such a rank and being ranked σ_i-th by the grader handling the bundle. Let us denote by $\mathcal{E}^*(x, j)$ the event that the true rank of x in a bundle is j. Then,

$$\Pr[x \triangleright \sigma] = N(\sigma) \prod_{i=1}^{k} \sum_{j=1}^{k} p_{\sigma_i, j} \Pr[\mathcal{E}^*(x, j)].$$

Now, the probability $\Pr[\mathcal{E}^*(x, j)]$ is equal to the number of ways we can choose $j-1$ exam papers to be ahead of x times the probability that all of them will indeed be ahead of x in the bundle times the probability that the rest $k - j$ exam papers in the bundle will have true ranks worse than j. The assumption for an infinite population of students allows to safely infer that each of the remaining $k-1$ exam papers in a bundle where exam paper x belongs is selected uniformly at random from the whole student population. We apply this reasoning, using L_k to denote the set of all k-entry vectors $\ell = (\ell_1, ..., \ell_k)$ with $\ell_i \in [k]$ and abbreviating $\sum_{i=1}^{k} \ell_i$ by $|\ell|_1$ for compactness of notation. We have

$$\begin{aligned}
\Pr[x \triangleright \sigma] &= N(\sigma) \prod_{i=1}^{k} \sum_{j=1}^{k} p_{\sigma_i, j} \binom{k-1}{j-1} x^{j-1}(1-x)^{k-j} \\
&= N(\sigma) \sum_{\ell \in L_k} \prod_{i=1}^{k} p_{\sigma_i, \ell_i} \binom{k-1}{\ell_i - 1} x^{\ell_i - 1}(1-x)^{k-\ell_i} \\
&= N(\sigma) \sum_{\ell \in L_k} \left(\prod_{i=1}^{k} p_{\sigma_i, \ell_i} \binom{k-1}{\ell_i - 1} \right) x^{|\ell|_1 - k}(1-x)^{k^2 - |\ell|_1},
\end{aligned}$$

where the second equality is obtained by exchanging the sum and product operators. Hence, $\Pr[x \triangleright \sigma]$ is a univariate polynomial of degree $k^2 - k$. Then, the double integral in the definition of $W(\sigma, \sigma')$ in (17.1) and, hence, $C(k, \succ, P)$ (using equation (17.2)) can be computed analytically with a tedious but straightforward calculation.

The quantity $C(k, \succ, P)$ is the theoretically predicted performance of the type-ordering aggregation rule in an exam with a bundle size of k and student population with grading behavior that is described by noise model P. Crucially, all the derivations above are equalities. Hence, the only reason that could make this prediction inaccurate is the assumption for an infinite number of students participating in the exam. As we discuss later in Section 17.6, no such inaccuracy has been observed in practice and the theoretical analysis presented above is fully justified.

17.5.4 Computing the Optimal Rule

The analysis of the previous section can be used to compute the most suitable type-ordering aggregation rule for grading exams with students from a specific population. Note that, as defined in (17.1), the weights do not depend on the aggregation rule at all. They depend only on the bundle size and on the grading behavior. Instead, the aggregation rule determines the particular weights that should be summed up in the definition of $C(k, \succ, P)$. This means that, once we have information about the bundle size and the grading behavior, we can calculate the weights for every ordered pair of types first and then compute the ordering of types so that the leftmost sum in the equation (17.2) is maximized.

It is not hard to see that the problem is equivalent to solving the feedback arc set (FAS) problem on an edge-weighted complete directed graph. In particular, the input is a complete directed graph that has a node for each type $\sigma \in \mathcal{T}_k$. A directed edge from a node corresponding to type σ towards a node corresponding to type σ' has weight $W(\sigma, \sigma')$. Now, the objective is to find an ordering of the nodes so that the total weight of "consistently directed" edges from a node to a node of higher rank in the ordering is maximized.

Theorem 17.2 (Caragiannis et al., 2016b). *Computing the most suitable type-ordering aggregation rule for a scenario involving specific bundle size and grading behavior is equivalent to solving feedback arc set on an edge-weighted complete directed graph.*

FAS is NP-hard even in its very simple variant on unweighted tournaments (Alon, 2006). Even though the particular weighted version that has to be solved in our case admits a PTAS (Kenyon-Mathieu and Schudy, 2007), the solutions that such a PTAS can guarantee in reasonable time are far from optimality and the resulting type-ordering aggregation rule will consequently have highly suboptimal performance. Fortunately, the instances that have to be solved in order to compute optimal type-ordering aggregation rules have a very nice structure.[12] This structure allows to compute the optimal FAS solution (almost) exactly by a straightforward algorithm that is briefly described in Section 17.6.

Figure 17.1 summarizes the whole approach described above. Using on input the bundle size and a noise model that describes the grading behavior of a student population, the most suitable type-ordering aggregation rule is computed, together with a prediction of the expected fraction of correctly recovered pairwise relations.

---

[12]This is not a formal statement but this has indeed been the case for all the scenarios considered by Caragiannis et al. (2016b). So, it is conjectured therein that it holds in *any* scenario that can appear in practice.

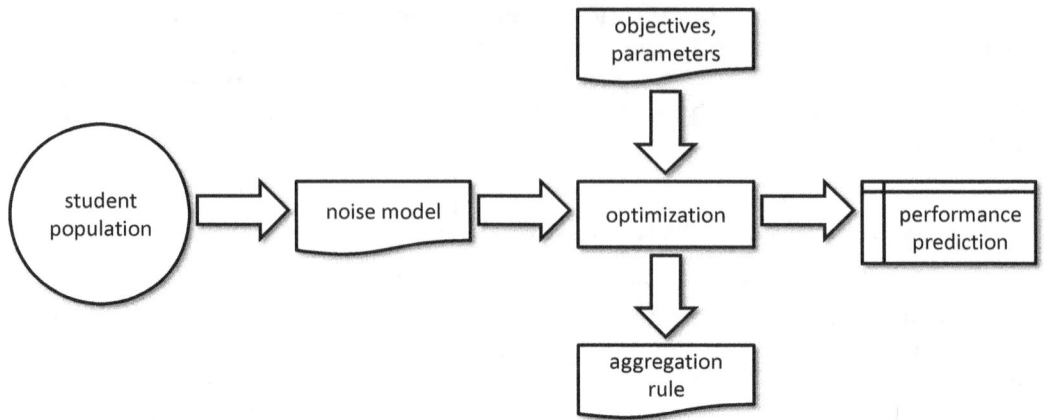

Figure 17.1: A graphical overview of the approach in (Caragiannis et al., 2016b).

Interestingly, the approach described above allows for a general statement that involves Borda. In particular, when perfect grading is used, the noise matrix has 1s only in the main diagonal (and 0s elsewhere). Then, $\Pr[x \triangleright \sigma]$ has a nice simplified form that allows to conclude that the most suitable type-ordering aggregation rule is Borda and, actually, the tie-breaking does not affect the expected fraction of correctly recovered pairwise relations at all.

Theorem 17.3 (Caragiannis et al., 2016b). *For perfect graders, Borda (with any tie-breaking rule) is the optimal type-ordering aggregation rule.*

Theorem 17.3 complements Theorem 17.1 nicely and is much more informative. Furthermore, its proof is short and elegant (see Caragiannis et al., 2016b). The statement is rather surprising as Borda is among the simplest type-ordering aggregation rules; essentially, the statement says that the extra power type-ordering aggregation rules may have compared to Borda is not at all necessary when perfect grading is used.

17.6 Experimental Results

We briefly present a very small set of experimental data from (Caragiannis et al., 2016b) here. The data refer to ordinal peer grading using a bundle size k equal to 6 and grading behavior that is correlated with student quality as follows. Each student has a quality drawn uniformly at random from the interval $[\frac{1}{2}, 1]$ and affects both her performance in the exam (i.e., her position in the ground truth ranking) and her ability to grade. The ground truth is the ranking of the students in decreasing order of quality. A student b of quality q performs the grading task as follows: she considers every pair of exam papers x and y in her bundle, such that x appears ahead of y in the ground truth, and temporarily determines $x \succ_b y$ with probability q and $y \succ_b x$ with probability $1 - q$. If, after considering all pairs of exam papers in the bundle, the pairwise relation $\succ_b$ is cyclic, the whole process is repeated from scratch. Otherwise, the ranking of the exam papers in the bundle induced by $\succ_b$ is the grading outcome of student b. Due to its similarities with the well-known Mallows model (Mallows, 1957) for generating random rankings, we refer to this grading behavior as *Mallows grading*.

The noise matrix P_{mallows} that corresponds to the average Mallows grader is:

$$P_{\text{mallows}} = \begin{bmatrix} 0.6337 & 0.1753 & 0.0824 & 0.0494 & 0.0339 & 0.0253 \\ 0.1753 & 0.5112 & 0.1549 & 0.0768 & 0.0479 & 0.0339 \\ 0.0824 & 0.1549 & 0.4865 & 0.1500 & 0.0768 & 0.0494 \\ 0.0494 & 0.0768 & 0.1500 & 0.4865 & 0.1549 & 0.0824 \\ 0.0339 & 0.0479 & 0.0768 & 0.1549 & 0.5112 & 0.1753 \\ 0.0253 & 0.0339 & 0.0494 & 0.0824 & 0.1753 & 0.6337 \end{bmatrix}$$

The noise matrix has been computed by estimating the probability that a Mallows grader ranks at position i an exam paper with correct rank j among the k exam papers in her bundle; the estimate follows by simulating 10^9 Mallows graders.

Once the bundle size k and the noise model P_{mallows} are available, the approach in Section 17.5.3 is used to compute the weights $W(\sigma, \sigma')$ for every pair of types $\sigma, \sigma' \in \mathcal{T}_k$. For $k = 6$, $\mathcal{T}_6$ contains 462 types. Hence, the type-ordering aggregation rule that is optimal for Mallows graders (as defined above) will follow by solving the feedback arc set problem on a complete directed edge-weighted graph G with 462 nodes.

FAS is then solved as follows. First, notice that if we could compute an type-ordering $\succ$ so that $\sigma \succ \sigma'$ for every pair of types with $W(\sigma, \sigma') > W(\sigma', \sigma)$, then this would definitely maximize the sum of weights in the right hand side of equation (17.2). Clearly, the relative order of a pair of types σ and σ' with $W(\sigma, \sigma') = W(\sigma', \sigma)$ does not affect the sum of weights. So, the algorithm we use for FAS begins with an optimistic pseudo-ordering that requires that $\sigma \succ \sigma'$ for every pair of types σ and σ' with $W(\sigma, \sigma') > W(\sigma', \sigma)$ while it leaves any other pair of types undecided. This pseudo-ordering is represented by a directed graph H that has a node for each type in $\mathcal{T}_k$ and there is a directed edge from type σ to type σ' if $W(\sigma, \sigma') > W(\sigma', \sigma)$. If this graph did not contain any cycles, then the pseudo-ordering could be easily extended to a correct complete ordering. For example, this is indeed the case for perfect graders (as the proof of Theorem 17.3 indicates).

In general, and this is the case with the scenario with Mallows graders we consider here, the graph H will contain cycles, which we have to break in order to compute the desired type-ordering aggregation rule. In order to do this, we first decompose the graph into minimal strongly connected components $C_1, C_2, ..., C_t$ with the following properties. For $i < j$, every edge between a node σ of C_i and a node σ' of C_j has direction from σ to σ'. By definition, within each strongly connected component C_i, there are two opposite directed paths connecting every pair of nodes. So, it remains to "correct" the direction of some edges within each connected component in order to break cycles. This has to be done carefully so that the total weight of directed edges of G that appear in H at the end of this process is maximum. And once this is done, we can complete the ordering of types by adding edges with appropriate direction (so that no cycle is introduced) between nodes that are not connected in H yet.

Of course, if H contains huge strongly connected components, we have made no progress at all in this way. But for the particular experiment, H contains 453 components that consist of a single type only, six components that have size between 3 and 7, two more components of size up to 11, and one additional component with 20 nodes. Clearly, there is nothing we have to do for singleton components. For components of size up to 10, an exhaustive search will give the best correction of the direction of edges so that the contribution of corresponding weights to the sum at the right hand side of equation (17.2) is maximized. For larger components, we order their types according to their Borda score (breaking ties randomly). This yields an almost exact solution to FAS with a predicted expected fraction of correctly recovered pairwise relations equal to 85.15%. Compared to the optimistic upper bound that includes all edges of H and edges between tied types, the loss in the predicted expected fraction of correctly recovered pairwise relations is less than 0.001%.

Interestingly, in spite of the assumption for an infinite population of students in our theoretical analysis, simulations with 10,000 students yield essentially identical results. Figure 17.2 contains data from 1,000 simulated exams with Mallows graders. The coordinates of each point are the fractions of corrected recovered pairwise relations when Borda and the optimal type-ordering aggregation rule (for Mallows graders and bundle size equal to 6) is used, respectively. The average values for both rules are 85.16% and 84.39% (these differ by less than 0.01% from the values predicted using the theoretical framework in Section 17.5.3) while all values are sharply concentrated around their expectation. Furthermore, observe that Borda is always suboptimal (by approximately 0.8%) and hence the whole cloud of points in Figure 17.2 is below the main diagonal.

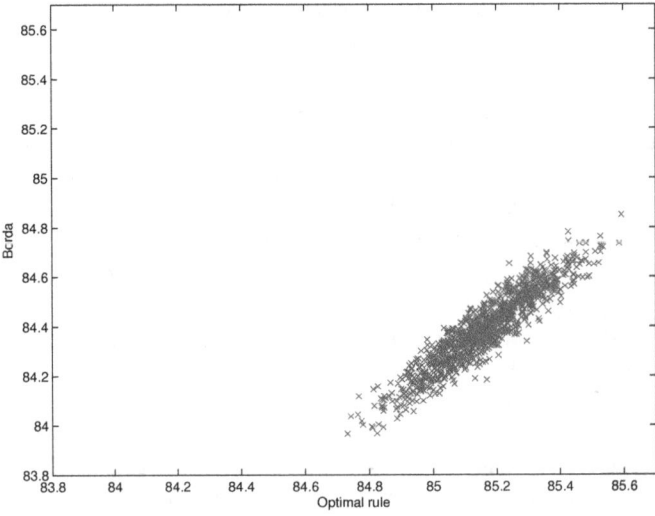

Figure 17.2: Performance of Borda compared to the optimal type-ordering aggregation rule for Mallows graders. Each of the 1,000 points corresponds to a simulated exam with the participation of 10,000 students, whose grading behavior follows the Mallows model.

17.7 Directions for Future Research

We have given a partial view of ordinal peer grading, mostly focusing on recent work by the author. More details about the approach presented in Section 17.5 can be found in (Caragiannis et al., 2016b). Therein, the reader can find a larger set of experiments compared to those presented in Section 17.6. Among other experiments, Caragiannis et al. (2016b) describe an experiment that aims to build a realistic noise model for the grading behavior of real students. This experiment has involved students attending the author's course on Computational Complexity at the University of Patras. A second interesting experiment aims to assess the impact of inaccuracies in the noise matrix to the performance of type-ordering aggregation rules and the selection of the optimal such rule. It turns out that the effect of such inaccuracies is negligible.

There are many interesting open problems regarding theoretical research on ordinal peer grading, experiments, and the deployment of our methods to real MOOCs. Regarding rank aggregation rules, we would like to see efficient implementations of approximations of Kemeny rank aggregation. An implementation in this direction is the random serial dictatorship rule described in (Caragiannis et al., 2015). This rule seems to have amazing performance with perfect graders (clearly outperforming Borda) but is rather poor in the Mallows scenario. Is there a variation of Kemeny that yields good results for imperfect graders?

We have claimed that it is easier for students to come up with a ranking of the exam papers in their bundle compared to assessing their quality in absolute terms. Interestingly, there is an even simpler grading format according to which each student is simply asked to approve a specific number of exam papers from her bundle. Then, a natural rank aggregation rule ranks the exam papers in terms of their approvals, breaking ties randomly. This functionality has already been implemented in our co-rank application. It would be very interesting to have a supporting theoretical analysis of it. The forthcoming paper (Caragiannis and Micha, 2017) is in this direction (but in a slightly different context).

Another thread of interesting research questions is related to incentives. Of course, classical impossibilities in social choice theory imply that students may grade strategically in order to improve their own position in the final outcome. Can this strategic behavior be taken into account when deciding the optimal rank aggregation rule? What about malicious behavior (of students that just want to fool the rank aggregation rule)? We believe that the approach presented in Section 17.5 could be adapted to strategic and malicious graders but this requires challenging technical work.

Of course, during the deployment of ordinal peer grading in real systems, there are several issues that need to be addressed. First, a few professional graders may be available. In the language we have used here, this implies a partial knowledge of the ground truth. How should this partial knowledge be combined with rank aggregation of students' grading in order to get an even better final ranking? Another issue that we have completely neglected here is related to student drop out after their participation in an exam but before its grading. Even though we do not believe that such situations invalidate our theory, there are implementation issues that have to be taken seriously into account in real MOOCs.

Another interesting setting is when grading takes place in steps with all students involved in the first step and only the students that had good performance in the exam involved in the later ones. Besides the obvious implementation issues related to this setting, there are probably nice theoretical questions here. These are open problems that certainly deserve investigation.

Acknowledgments

I am grateful to my co-authors George Krimpas and Alexandros Voudouris for their contribution to our joint related work and for numerous interesting discussions.

Bibliography

N. Alon. Ranking tournaments. *SIAM Journal on Discrete Mathematics*, 20(1): 137–142, 2006.

N. Alon, F. A. Fischer, A. D. Procaccia, and M. Tennenholtz. Sum of us: Strategyproof selection from the selectors. In *Proceedings of the 13th Conference on Theoretical Aspects of Rationality and Knowledge (TARK)*, pages 101–110, 2011.

J. Bartholdi, C. A. Tovey, and M. A. Trick. Voting schemes for which it can be difficult to tell who won the election. *Social Choice and Welfare*, 6:157–165, 1989.

I. Caragiannis and E. Micha. Learning a ground truth ranking using noisy approval votes. In *Proceedings of the 26th International Joint Conference on Artificial Intelligence (IJCAI)*, 2017.

I. Caragiannis, G. A. Krimpas, and A. A. Voudouris. Aggregating partial rankings with applications to peer grading in massive online open courses. In *Proceedings of the 14th International Conference on Autonomous Agents and Multiagent Systems (AAMAS)*, pages 675–683, 2015.

I. Caragiannis, G. A. Krimpas, M. Panteli, and A. A. Voudouris. co-rank: An online tool for collectively deciding efficient rankings among peers. In *Proceedings of the 30th AAAI Conference on Artificial Intelligence (AAAI)*, pages 4351–4352, 2016a.

I. Caragiannis, G. A. Krimpas, and A. A. Voudouris. How effective can simple ordinal peer grading be? In *Proceedings of the 17th ACM Conference on Economics and Computation (EC)*, pages 323–340, 2016b.

I. Caragiannis, X. Chatzigeorgiou, G. A. Krimpas, and A. A. Voudouris. Optimizing positional scoring rules for rank aggregation. In *Proceedings of the 31st AAAI Conference on Artificial Intelligence (AAAI)*, pages 430–436, 2017.

L. de Alfaro and M. Shavlovsky. Crowdgrader: A tool for crowdsourcing the evaluation of homework assignments. In *Proceedings of the 45th ACM Technical Symposium on Computer Science Education (SIGCSE)*, pages 415–420, 2014.

M. M. de Weerdt, E. H. Gerding, and S. Stein. Minimising the rank aggregation error. In *Proceedings of the 15th International Conference on Autonomous Agents and Multiagent Systems (AAMAS)*, pages 1375–1376, 2016.

C. Dwork, R. Kumar, M. Naor, and D. Sivakumar. Rank aggregation methods for the web. In *Proceedings of the 10th International World Wide Web Conference (WWW)*, pages 613–622, 2001.

R. Holzman and H. Moulin. Impartial nominations for a prize. *Econometrica*, 81: 173–196, 2013.

C. Kenyon-Mathieu and W. Schudy. How to rank with few errors. In *Proceedings of the 39th Annual ACM Symposium on Theory of Computing (STOC)*, pages 95–103, 2007.

C. Kulkarni, K. P. Wei, H. Le, D. Chia, K. Papadopoulos, J. Cheng, D. Koller, and S. R. Klemmer. Peer and self assessment in massive online classes. *ACM Transactions on Computer-Human Interaction*, 20(6):33, 2013.

E. Law and L. von Ahn. *Human Computation*. Synthesis Lecture on Artificial Intelligence and Machine Learning. Morgan & Claypool, 2011.

C. L. Mallows. Non-null ranking models. *Biometrika*, 44:114–130, 1957.

M. Mitzenmacher and E. Upfal. *Probability and Computing – Randomized Algorithms and Probabilistic Analysis*. Cambridge University Press, 2005.

C. Piech, J. Huang, Z. Chen, C. Do, A. Ng, and D. Koller. Tuned models of peer assessment in MOOCs. In *Proceedings of the 6th International Conference on Educational Data Mining (EDM)*, pages 153–160, 2013.

K. Raman and T. Joachims. Methods for ordinal peer grading. In *Proceedings of the 20th ACM Conference on Knowledge Discovery and Data Mining (KDD)*, pages 1037–1046, 2014.

M. S. Sajjadi, M. Alamgir, and U. von Luxburg. Peer grading in a course on algorithms and data structures: Machine learning algorithms do not improve over simple baselines. In *Proceedings of the 3rd ACM Conference on Learning at Scale*, pages 369–378, 2016.

D. Sculley. Rank aggregation for similar items. In *Proceedings of the 7th SIAM International Conference on Data Mining (SDM)*, pages 587–592, 2007.

N. B. Shah, J. K. Bradley, A. Parekh, M. Wainwright, and K. Ramchandran. A case for ordinal peer-evaluation in MOOCs. In *Neural Information Processing Systems (NIPS): Workshop on Data Driven Education*, 2013.

T. Walsh. The PeerRank method for peer assessment. In *Proceedings of the 21st European Conference on Artificial Intelligence (ECAI)*, pages 909–914, 2014.

J. R. Wright, C. Thornton, and K. Leyton-Brown. Mechanical TA: Partially automated high-stakes peer grading. In *Proceedings of the 46th ACM Technical Symposium on Computer Science Education (SIGCSE)*, pages 96–101, 2015.

CHAPTER 18

Applications of Matching Models under Preferences

Péter Biró

18.1 Introduction

Matching problems under preferences have been studied widely in mathematics, computer science and economics, starting with the seminal paper by Gale and Shapley (1962). A comprehensive survey on this topic was published also in Chapter 14 of the Handbook of Computational Social Choice (Klaus et al., 2016), and for the interested reader we recommend consulting the following four comprehensive books on the computational (Gusfield and Irving, 1989; Manlove, 2013) and game-theoretical, market design aspects (Roth and Sotomayor, 1990; Roth, 2015) of this topic. In this chapter our goal is to give a general overview of the related applications.

The theory and practice of mechanism design for matching problems have always developed in an interactive way. Practical applications have motivated scientific research and theoretical results have been used for designing new applications and redesigning old ones. The college admission problem was first described and resolved by Gale and Shapley (1962). Their definition of *stable matching* proved to be the most crucial solution concept for two-sided markets. Furthermore, their algorithmic solution, the so-called *deferred acceptance* (DA) mechanism, has been used in many important applications, such as the centrally coordinated schemes for college admissions in Europe (Hungary, Spain, Turkey, Ireland, etc.), school choice programmes (in many US cities, Amsterdam, or Hungary) and for medical resident allocation (US, Japan, UK, etc.). But in fact, in some applications this matching mechanism has been invented and developed independently from the theoretical research. This is certainly the case for the US resident allocation program, NRMP, where the DA algorithm was already implemented in 1952 (Roth, 1984). Moreover, the special features of these applications have been constantly creating new theoretical problems. For an illustrative example we briefly describe the issue of couples in resident allocation problems.

As the proportion of women has increased over time in the medical field, so has the number of married couples among the residents. Most of these couples decided not to participate in the US centralised clearinghouse in the 1970s and

1980s, because they were afraid to get allocated to places far away from each other, which could ruin their partnership during the two-year internship period. So they were looking for pairs of positions outside of NRMP, which started to undermine the efficiency of the mechanism. Therefore in the 1980s the coordinators allowed the couples to submit joint applications within the programme. However, they treated these applications in a special way, asking the couples to nominate a leading person from the couple and only after allocating him/her they tried to find a place for the spouse. This was not satisfactory for the couples, and they kept staying out of the clearinghouse.

The scientific community working in this field took notice of this issue and started to investigate it. First, game theorists showed that if we were to allow the couples to submit joint preferences, which seemed to be inevitable, the existence of a stable matching is not guaranteed anymore (Roth, 1984). Later, the computer science community provided the further bad news that checking the existence of a stable solution is NP-complete (Ronn, 1990). Yet, the coordinators of NRMP decided to allow the couples to submit arbitrary joint preferences and asked two experts to redesign the matching mechanism. Roth and Peranson took an engineering approach and have succeeded to construct a new heuristic mechanism, based on the DA, that could deal with the issue of couples in the NRMP (Roth and Peranson, 1999). This algorithm has been used in many similar applications since (Roth, 2008). In the last two decades both economists and computer scientists have investigated the possible reasons for the tractability of this special feature in real applications, a survey on which was written by Biró and Klijn (2013).

In this chapter we try to give a comprehensive description on the important applications of matching models under preferences without monetary transfers. We focus on applications where central coordination has already been established, but we also mention applications which are not (yet) centrally coordinated, since central coordination can emerge in the future and matching models can also be useful to analyse the decentralised matching processes. We highlight the most relevant special features of the applications and we give pointers to the corresponding theoretical literature, related models and solutions concepts.

Personally, I always found it crucial to understand how the applications are working and what are the main issues to be resolved. Together with colleagues at University of Glasgow we started to collect descriptions of existing applications with references, and we continued this project from 2010 in Budapest (Website on matching practices at Hungarian Academy of Sciences, 2012). In 2010 the Matching in Practice research network has been established in Europe and we also started to collect descriptions of college admission, school choice and early labour allocation practices (Website of the Matching in Practice network, 2014). Finally, in a new COST Action project we are now trying to understand and describe how kidney exchange programmes are operating in Europe (Website of COST Action: European Network for Collaboration on Kidney Exchange Programmes, 2016).

There are also examples from outside of Europe for using a scientific approach to systematically review matching applications and to give policy design advice on their (re-)design. Al Roth has been leading this initiative with his informative blog (Website of Al Roth's blog, 2010), and his new book (Roth, 2015) by giving a comprehensive high level overview on market design together with many real examples. One particularly successful organisation which has emerged also through the work of Roth and his colleagues is the Institute for Innovation in Public School Choice (Website of Institute for Innovation in Public School Choice, 2014), which helps to advise US cities on their school choice practices.

The design of practical applications and the scientific research in multiple disciplines are developing together, and that is what is needed to obtain successful solutions. On the one hand, these successes validate the theoretical findings and boost further research in the newly emerging interdisciplinary fields of Computational Social Choice and Market Design, among others. On the other hand, the scientific results will ultimately lead to better mechanisms that provide fairness and optimality in a transparent and efficient way.

In Section 18.2 we start with the description of classical two-sided matching markets, such as college admission, school choice and resident allocation. We continue with two-sided markets where only one side has preferences in Section 18.3. In Section 18.4 we describe applications based on exchange models. Finally, we consider some further models in Section 18.5 and we study the related applications.

To publish papers in economics or computer science journals, theoretical results are strongly expected, so one cannot just publish a paper merely by describing applications. Indeed, most of the scientific papers cited in this chapter that are motivated by some applications typically focus only on one or two special features of the applications. Therefore, it is hard to judge how relevant these features are and whether there are some further crucial characteristics of the applications which are not mentioned or studied in the scientific papers referenced. So, whenever my descriptions are entirely based on scientific papers the reader must be warned that there may be some missing information. However, I can be more confident in the completeness of my notes when they are based on a description written by an expert and published, e.g., at the Matching in Practice website, or when the knowledge is mostly coming from my personal experience and research. To highlight the latter cases I will use framed environments whenever I had some personal information on the application.

Finally, we note that there are two closely related chapters in this book. In Chapter 15, Mattei and Walsh describe Preflib.org, a data library that also includes some data of matching applications. Cechlárová gives an overview on the theory and practice of trainee teachers in Slovakia in Chapter 19.

18.2 Two-Sided Markets

Stable matchings in two-sided markets were first studied by Gale and Shapley (1962) with title "College admissions and the stability of marriage". Their solution was based on the concept of *stability*. A matching is stable if there is no pair of agents who would be mutually better off by forming a new pair, after abandoning their previous partners. For college admissions the meaning of stability is that an applicant can only be rejected from a college if the college filled its quota with better applicants. This property is easy to check if the rankings by the colleges are based on scores and the so-called cutoff scores are published, which can be the scores of the weakest admitted applicants at the saturated colleges. Such cutoff systems are in use in many European countries, including Hungary, Ireland, Spain and Turkey.

Gale and Shapley gave an efficient algorithm for computing an applicant-optimal stable matching with the DA mechanism. This mechanism can be implemented in such a way that its running time is linear in the number of applications. Moreover, the mechanism is strategy-proof for the students. However, this mechanism is not Pareto optimal for the students, if we consider the set of all possible assignments, and not just the stable ones. The Top Trading Cycles algorithm used for two-sided markets achieves Pareto efficiency, it is strategy-proof, but fails to ensure stability. Finally, in many applications the so-called immediate acceptance (IA) or Boston mechanism is used, where the significant difference compared to DA is that the acceptances are final, so a college does not consider any new applications after its quota becomes filled. This mechanism is highly manipulable, and does not provide stable solutions, but for some special instances it can improve *ex ante* efficiency compared to DA. Nevertheless this first choice first priority system was banned in the UK for use in school choice (Pathak and Sönmez, 2013). See references and further theoretical findings in Section 1 of the chapter by Klaus et al. (2016).

To the best of our knowledge the first usage of the Gale-Shapley algorithm in a centralised matching programme was not for college admissions, but for resident allocation in the US as early as in 1952. Therefore we start our description of applications with resident allocation programmes and early labour applications in general.

Early Labour Markets

Allocating graduates to their first positions in a centrally coordinated way is typical in professions where internships are necessary for learning the practices and getting the licences. Therefore, most of these centralised intern allocation programmes have been established in the medical field, but there are also examples in law studies and army related professions. However, our first, very early example will be related to the famous engineering school of France that has been providing an elite education for the most talented students and a constant resource of trained professionals for the French ministries.

> **Sorting graduates at École polytechnique in 1806.** This institution was founded in 1794, reorganised and named École polytechnique in 1805 under Napoleon, and it is still in operation. The students have always been selected by a highly competitive entrance exam, and after graduation they were sorted to ministries through a coordinated mechanism, called *classement sortie*. After the first three years of a decentralised system (1797-1799) a common final exam and sorting mechanism was established. Between 1799 and 1806 the

students were asked to declare one service of their choice targeted at the beginning of their studies, however, the number of openings at the ministries varied, so many students had to find a different service in an after match period from what they had declared. To resolve this issue, the council approved a new system where the students could declare two choices, but at the end they modified this to a much simpler mechanism. In the implemented mechanism the students were commonly ranked in a master list, and they could choose their services one by one, without making any declaration beforehand. Thus, in mechanism design terms, the one-application system was replaced by a serial dictatorship mechanism based on a common ranking. See more details in Belhoste (2003).

National Resident Matching Program. The allocation of junior doctors to hospitals in the US used to work in a decentralised way until 1950 with various problems, as described in Roth (1984). In 1950 the market participants agreed to establish a central coordination, where the doctors submit their preferences, the hospitals submit their rankings and an algorithm computes the allocation. After the trial run in the academic year 1950/51 (which was not used in the real allocation) some students complained about the fairness of the mechanism, and so they agreed to adjust the mechanism, which was implemented in 1951 and was first used in 1952. This new algorithm was mathematically equivalent to the hospital-proposing Gale-Shapley algorithm (Roth, 1984; Gale and Sotomayor, 1985). In the early 1990s the trust in the central allocation system started to erode, party because of the spreading knowledge over the hospital-optimality (and thus doctor-pessimality and manipulability) of the mechanism and also because of the unsatisfactory way it treated the couples. Thus, the board of NRMP decided to redesign the mechanism on a scientific base, led by Roth and Peranson, as documented by Roth and Peranson (1999). The new algorithm, approved in 1997 and first used in 1998, switched to the applicant-proposing variant (although one of the main findings of Roth and Peranson was that the solutions produced by the two variants were not significantly different, suggesting that in large markets the set of stable solutions may be small in expectation). They also constructed a new heuristic algorithm, based on the Roth-Vande Vate process, to deal with the couples, and also to satisfy some further requirements. The algorithm has remained in operation since, and was subsequently used in many similar applications run by the National Matching Services Inc. (a private company based in Canada, founded by Peranson), see the details and the list of three dozen particular programmes by Roth (2008).

Resident allocation programmes in the UK. In the 1960s the British National Health Service recognised the issues with their decentralised resident allocation processes and thus recommended the usage of centralised schemes. However, the allocations were organised in regions separately, and NHS did not specify the allocation mechanism to be used, so almost every region adopted a different method (Roth, 1990, 1991). An interesting feature of the UK schemes was that the doctors had to apply for a pair of positions, a six-month medical and a six-month surgical post, and they could also indicate their preferences over the order they wanted to take these positions. Yet, if we assume responsive preferences for the doctors (i.e., the preference over two surgical positions is not influenced by the medical position assigned, and vica versa), then stable solutions can be obtained separately for the two kinds of positions leading to pairwise stable solutions for the many-to-two markets. However, if the allocation of either of the two positions fails to be stable then the overall solution is also bound to be blocked by a hospital-doctor pair. Roth has studied the allocation mechanisms of ten regions, and he found that four of them produced stable solutions and all four of them remained in use at the time of writing. However, from those six that could produce unstable solutions only two remained in operation, the other four were abandoned. Therefore this natural experiment provided strong evidence for the importance of stability in two-sided markets.

> **Scottish Foundation Allocation Scheme.** The Scottish scheme was similar in characteristic to the above described UK schemes until 2005, when the programme was named SPA (Scottish PRHO Allocations). The solutions were computed from 2000 by Rob Irving with a sophisticated algorithm which not only provided stable solution for both medical and surgical positions separately, but also satisfied as many seasonal preferences as possible by a flow algorithm (Irving, 1998). In 2006 the programme was renamed SFAS (Scottish Foundation Allocation Scheme) and in the new scheme some characteristics also changed. Instead of the medical and surgical positions the doctors had to apply for a 2-year Foundation Programme that they conducted at one hospital. The hospitals' rankings were not provided independently, but they were deduced from a common scoring method and these also involved ties. The primary goal of the mechanism was to return a (weakly) stable matching of maximum size, which is an NP-hard problem even for master lists (Irving et al., 2008). The computation had been done by a sophisticated heuristic (Irving and Manlove, 2009). From 2009 the programme has also allowed the joint applications of couples, although in a slightly restricted form, so the matching algorithm had to be redesigned accordingly (Biró et al., 2011). In 2012 the Foundation Programme allocation in Scotland started to be handled by the UK Foundation Office, and unfortunately we have no information about the exact mechanism that they use.

Japanese Resident Matching Program. A new allocation system was introduced in 2009 to make the distribution of the residents more balanced in Japan (Kamada and Kojima, 2012). Regional caps have been imposed to reduce the number of doctors allocated in large cities and increase their numbers in rural areas. However, the implementation of the regional caps was strongly criticised from a market design perspective, see, e.g., Kamada and Kojima (2016, 2017), as the ministry introduced artificial quotas for all the hospitals (summing up to the regional quota in each region) which may lead to inefficient solutions with regard to the hard regional constraints.

Teacher allocation in France. Since 1999 the centralised (re-)allocation scheme is organised in two-rounds involving newly tenured teachers and also those teachers who want to change positions. In the first round they allocate the teachers to regions, and in the second round they do the (re-)allocation within each region separately. The priorities of the teachers for positions are based primarily whether they are moving to the region where their spouses are living and then by seniority. The matching mechanism is a combination of the school-proposing DA and the stable improvement cycles algorithm by Erdil and Ergin (2008). See more details by Terrier (2014) and a mechanism design analyses by Combe et al. (2015).

Allocation of lawyers in Germany. Every year more than 8000 graduating lawyers are assigned to legal internship positions, organised separately in each region (Bundesland). At the beginning of the process the set of admitted candidates is determined, where the majority are selected by their First State Exam grades, but some quotas are preserved for applicants with high waiting times and also with low social-economic status. The mechanism used in Berlin is conjectured to be the lawyer-oriented DA. A critical analyses of the mechanism is given by Dimakopoulos and Heller (2015).

Economics job market in the US. This is a partly centralised system, as the application platform is common and the majority of the interviews take place at the annual Allied Social Science Associations (ASSA) meeting, based on which the employers send out the flyouts. An interesting feature is that each candidate can send two signals to the employers, which help them to select the twenty applicants for interview from the hundreds of candidates (Coles et al., 2013). The final offer-rejection part of the process is decentralised.

Allocation in the US Navy. According to Short (2000), Robards (2001) and Yang et al. (2003) more than 300,000 personnel are (re-)assigned with the help of around 300 detailers in every period. Besides the strict eligibility criteria, the presence of couples is also an important feature recognised. Finally, unlike in the resident allocation, all the sailors have to be allocated and also some critical Navy billets must be filled. The latter requirement alone may prevent the existence of a stable matching.

Assigning positions in humanitarian organisations. Similar problems have been identified in the internal assignment process of humanitarian organisations (Soldner, 2014). Here also the goal is to find a complete matching, but instead of using orders, as in the army, they try to modify the preferences of both the staff and the job holders by costly negotiations. The problem of finding a complete stable matching for adjusted preferences with minimum negotiation costs is solved by heuristics and integer programming techniques.

Finally, note that we moved the description of the **resident allocation programme of Israel** to subsection 18.3, since the usage of a single item allocation model is more appropriate for that application.

College Admissions

College admission was the motivating application of Gale and Shapley (1962), and indeed an increasing number of countries have established centrally coordinated higher education admissions. In this section we describe some European, South American and Asian applications.

Europe. In many European countries the college admission is organised via a nationwide scheme involving all kinds of programmes. In **Spain**, cut-off scores have been computed by the student-proposing DA with limited preference lists and university rankings based on the students' grades and entrance exam scores according to Romero-Medina (1998). In **Turkey**, the cutoff score system is similar, but the college-proposing DA was used with tie-breaking by the age of the students, at the time of writing (Balinski and Sönmez, 1999). In **Ireland**, the cut-off scores are also published, but the ties are broken by lottery. The students can apply to at most 10 programmes and their scores are mainly coming from the Leaving Certificate Examinations, but the universities have freedom in choosing their scoring method. In the matching process essentially the college-proposing DA is applied in a manual form, where the students have to accept or reject the offers round by round every week. A further speciality is that the proposal-rejection mechanism is used separately for so-called level 6/7 degree programmes (2-3 year programmes) and for level 8 programmes (4 year programmes), so a student might be admitted to two places from which she can choose one at the end (Chen, 2012).

The **French** admission system is fragmented: there are several small schemes for admission to the elite *Grandes Écoles*, but there is a central clearinghouse, called Admission Post Bac (APB) (Frys and Staat, 2015). In theory, the universities participating in APB are not selective, but due to the overdemand they do select their students and prioritise the students coming from the local region and the first choice applications are also preferred to second choice applications. The latter speciality makes the mechanism similar to IA, thus causing strategic issues. The mechanism is applied in three rounds, and after each round the students can decide whether a) they accept their offer and withdraw their other applications, or b) just tentatively accept the offer and wait for a potentially better offer, or c) reject the offer and wait for better offer, or d) cancel all of their applications.

There are some European countries where the universities should provide open access to education for all students that satisfy the requirements, except in the use of some special fields of study with limited spaces, such as medicine, dentistry, veterinary medicine, and pharmacy. Among these countries, in **Belgium** the universities are divided by language. Flemish universities have common entrance exams for medicine and dentistry, whilst French-speaking universities have entrance exams for civil engineering studies (Cantillon and Declercq, 2012).

In **Italy** each field of study with caps has the entrance exams on the same day, so essentially every student can only apply to one university in each field of study (Merlino and Nicoló, 2013). **Germany** has also centralised admissions in medical studies. The first 20% of the seats are allocated to the students with the best grades, another 20% are allocated to students with long waiting times and the remaining 60% are according to the universities' rankings. In the first two groups the Boston mechanism is used, whilst for the last group the university-proposing DA is employed (Kübler, 2011). The flaws of this sequential mechanism have been studied in several scientific papers (Dwenger et al., 2010; Westkamp, 2013; Braun et al., 2014).

Hungary. In the Hungarian higher education admission scheme around 100,000-150,000 thousand students are allocated to programmes every year. From 1996 a heuristic based on the university-proposing DA was used, and in 2007 the student-oriented DA was implemented with some adjustments to deal with the special features. The students are ranked at most universities based on their exam scores, although different sets of subjects count for different programmes. The allocation is announced by publishing the cut-off scores. One special feature is that the ties are not broken, so students with equal scores are either all admitted or all rejected, which is a tractable feature by an extension of the DA (Biró and Kiselgof, 2015). The universities can also set lower quotas for the number of students admitted for each of their studies separately, which leads to an NP-hard problem, and thus requires a heuristic solution (Biró et al., 2010). Most Hungarian students are eligible for free studies in the majority of the programmes if they are willing to sign a contract, but it is also possible to attend most of the programmes under a different contract where tuition fee must be paid. These two kinds of contracts can be listed in the preference list of the students in any order. Another significant feature is that the government can set a national common quota in each field of study on the number of students admitted under state financed contracts. These common upper quotas together with the faculty quotas (applied to students under both kinds of contracts) make also the problem of finding a stable solution NP-hard (Biró et al., 2010). Paired applications are also allowed for teachers' programmes, which causes similar difficulties to the presence of couples in the resident allocation programmes. In a recent paper we investigated integer programming techniques to deal with the NP-hard cases, and the feature of lower quotas turned out to be tractable even for large real instances (Ágoston et al., 2016). New features of the scheme are the limited length preference lists since 2013, and the possibility of applying to dual university programmes since 2015, where a university programme is linked to an industrial internship. However, the admissions for these internship positions are organised in a decentralised way, causing discrepancies.

Brazil has a college admission system, where affirmative action policies are designated to secure place for racial minorities, low-income families and students coming from public highschools. However, the implementation of this policy is badly designed, separate quotas are devoted to students claiming each possible combination of privileges, sometimes leading to higher cut-off scores for students claiming some privilege than others who do not claim that. This results in unfairness, strategic manipulations on what privileges to claim, and unsatisfactory allocation with regard to the affirmative action goals (Aygün and Bó, 2015). In **Chile** the admission scheme is similar to the Hungarian one with respect to the feature that the ties are not broken, but interestingly their policy is more permissive, as they always admit the last group of students with whom the quota is violated (Ríos et al., 2014).

The largest centrally coordinated college admission system is operating in **China**, however the allocation mechanism runs separately with respect to the students applying from the same province. The universities are partitioned into tiers according to their prestige, and their rankings over the students are based on the national standardised test results. Regarding the allocation mechanism, the so-called sequential mechanism was replaced by the so-called parallel mechanism in 27 from the 31 provinces between 2002 and 2012 (Chen and Kesten, 2013). The sequential mechanism is essentially the IA mechanism used in each tier, whilst in the parallel mechanism the students can submit multiple ordered lists as choices, and for each of their choices the serial dictatorship is used separately.

In **South Korea** the admission system was redesigned in 1994. Until 1994 there were only two admission dates, and a student could only attend the exam of one university on each date, so essentially there were only two possible applications. Moreover, the elite universities all scheduled their exam on the first date. After 1994 the results of the comprehensive exam were published before the application period, and they also introduced an early admission period, where the students could apply to one university and they received binding offers according to their state exams. In the regular admission period each university could choose one from the four potential dates to conduct specialised exams. So the students could apply to four universities, but the elite universities decided to schedule their exams to one of the first two dates in an interesting pattern after an adjustment period. The game-theoretic reasons for the behaviour of the universities have been studied in Avery et al. (2014).

School Choice

Before going into the details of the applications, we note that the model behind school choice applications is considered to be slightly different from the Gale-Shapley college admission model. This is because the school seats can be seen as goods to be allocated, over which the children may have different priorities. Thus the main difference is that the schools are not necessarily strategic agents. The stability of a matching in a school choice setting can be therefore interpreted as the lack of *justified envy*, i.e. no student should have priority over another student assigned to a school if the former student is assigned to a less preferred place (or no place at all). For a comprehensive overview on school choice, we refer to Abdulkadiroğlu and Sönmez (2003).

However, we shall note that the usage of this modified model is not appropriate for every school choice application. In fact, as we will see in the descriptions, in Hungary the elementary and secondary schools are strategic players, as they can rank their applicants in any way they want (Biró, 2012), just like in Estonia (Lauri et al., 2014). Meanwhile, in almost all of the nationwide university admission systems that we have seen, the universities must use a commonly defined ranking method, together perhaps with some special priority structures and constraints imposed by the governments. So the universities cannot always be considered strategic players, as already observed in some early scientific papers on college admissions in Spain (Romero-Medina, 1998) and Turkey (Balinski and Sönmez, 1999). Yet, for university admissions the students are typically ranked by merit, so they can influence their rankings. This model was called *student-placement* problem by Balinski and Sönmez (1999).

To sum up the terminology, the Gale-Shapley college admission model refers to the case where both sides of the market are strategic. In the school choice and student placement models only the students are strategic, and the seats are considered as objects to be allocated. The slight difference between the latter two models is that in the school choice model we consider the priorities to be exogenously given, whilst in the student placement model the rankings are (partly) based on the students' performances, so the students can influence them.

We can actually give examples for the adequate use of each of the three models at any level of application, i.e., for school choice, college admissions and resident allocation. Note that the terminologies of the college admission and school choice models have probably been established with regard to the US context, but as we explained, one should use them with caution in other countries.

US city highschools. The decentralised **New York** school choice system switched to a centralised programme using the student-proposing DA with distance and sibling priorities and lotteries in 2004 (Abdulkadiroğlu et al., 2005a, 2013), immediately reducing the number of administratively assigned students from 30,000 to 3,000. The random tie-breaking was criticised, as the lotteries can create a seemingly artificial stability constraint. It was showed that around 2-3% of the students could have been assigned to a better school without harming anyone if only the original priorities would be considered as binding (Erdil and Ergin, 2008). However, removing the lotteries can cause strategic issues (Abdulkadiroğlu et al., 2009), so the lottery system remained in use. In **Boston** the IA mechanism was replaced with the DA in 2005 (Abdulkadiroğlu et al., 2005b). This was a scientifically proposed redesign that led to much discussion in the literature since. Note that in recent years the Boston school choice system has been transformed again, partly due to the request by the local authority to reduce busing costs (Shi, 2015). In the last decade at least a dozen US cities followed the advice and used the assistance of the Institute for Innovation in Public School Choice to establish a school choice system in the spirit of the successful New York programme. Most programmes adopted the student-proposing DA, except **New Orleans**, where the TTC algorithm was implemented in 2012 for the unified public school admissions (Abdulkadiroğlu et al., 2017).

European school choice. In **Hungary** a nationwide system has been in use for secondary school allocation since 2000. The students apply to study programmes with no limit on the number of applications, and the schools set their quotas for each study programme and rank their applicants strictly according to exam results and interviews (so the selection is merit based). The student-proposing DA is used to compute the solution, thus the classical Gale-Shapley college admission model is followed (Biró, 2012). Similarly, a nationwide system is used in **Finland**, where the schools rank their students separately based on their grades and entrance scores. Every student can apply up to five schools and the school-proposing DA is used for computing the solution (Salonen, 2014).

In **Spain** the admissions are organised separately in each municipality with no common rules (Calsamiglia, 2014). According to Calsamiglia (2011) the IA mechanism is applied everywhere with different priority systems. For elementary schools the location and sibling priorities are used (although in Madrid the distance-based priorities were removed), whilst for secondary schools the priorities are mostly coming from the grades of the students. In Barcelona there was a change in the distance priority criterion in 2007, when the catchment area system was replaced with a personal priority system where every child had priority for at least the six closest schools. This change enabled the study of the strategic aspects of the Boston mechanism (Calsamiglia and Güell, 2014). In **Germany**, school admissions are organised separately in each of the 16 states. In Berlin the IA mechanism is used with 10% of the seats reserved for low-income families first, then 60% of the seats are allocated on the basis of merit (Basteck et al., 2015), and the remaining 30% assigned by sibling priority and lottery.

The **Amsterdam** school choice programme was redesigned in 2015, replacing a sequential version of the IA mechanism by the DA with multiple tie-breaking, where no distance-based priorities are used (de Haan et al., 2015). **Paris** is divided into four sub-districts and the students are required to seek schools within their sub-district by getting 600 points in those schools. This number of points can be obtained for academic performance, whilst 300 points are given to low-income families, and 50 points are awarded for having siblings in the school. A centralized platform called Affelnet is used in all districts with the school-proposing DA, however, extra points are awarded in the first choice schools, so the overall mechanism is actually closer to IA (Hiller and Tercieux, 2013). A scientific paper on preference estimation based on data from one of the sub-districts has been published recently (Fack et al., 2015).

> **Kindergarten allocation in Estonia.** The kindergarten allocation in Estonia is organised in cities usually based on a simple priority system with the application date being the main criterion. This creates unfair and inefficient solutions, since the preferences of the parents may change in the 3-4 years between the birth and the admission, and social objectives are also neglected. In 2015 Harku municipality agreed to redesign their mechanism on a scientific basis, documented by Veski et al. (2017). We tested seven different priority systems based on distance and sibling priorities combined with the student-proposing DA. In the simulation we used the data submitted by the

parents in 2016, which may be assumed to be truthful. We also conducted a sensitivity analysis by adjusting the effect of the distance and sibling factors on the parents' preferences. The municipality decided to use a transitory priority system in 2016, where the importance of application date, age, distance and siblings vary across the seats in a rotating manner.

Further Applications

There are many further centrally coordinated applications of two-sided matching markets, some of which are of smaller size, and some others that are still in preparation. Due to the lack of space we only mention some interesting examples with future potential. In a coordinated **project allocation** university students are assigned to supervisors or to their offered topics (Abraham et al., 2007; Manlove and O'Malley, 2008). **Adoptions** could also be organised via more sophisticated allocation mechanisms, as studied by Slaugh et al. (2016). **Refugee allocation** under preferences is a timely issue discussed in some very recent mechanism design papers (Delacrétaz et al., 2016; Andersson and Ehlers, 2016). Finally, **dating markets** have always worked in a decentralised way, however due to some novel platforms the search and selection may be better coordinated, e.g. by signalling features (Lee and Niederle, 2015). We close this section with a description on an internship project allocation experience.

Internship allocation at Corvinus University of Budapest. As part of a Masters programme at Corvinus University the students are allocated to participating companies to conduct internship projects in groups. In 2016 the allocation mechanism was changed from IA to a stable matching mechanism by requiring the 25 students to rank all of the 5 companies and asking the companies to evaluate and score all of the candidates. The ties in the scores gave us more flexibility to find a (weakly) stable matching that also satisfies some distributional constraints, namely a lower quota on the number of students at each company and also a balanced distribution of foreign students. For the computation we used IP techniques (Ágoston et al., 2017).

18.3 Allocation of Indivisible Goods

Allocation of indivisible goods to strategic agents is a topic discussed in both the matching literature under the name of two-sided markets with one-sided preferences, and it also belongs to the field of fair division and resource allocation, extensively studied by the AI community. See Klaus et al. (2016) for the theoretical background.

Single-Item Allocation

When every agent can get at most one single item, then the classical mechanism is the *serial dictatorship* (SD), where the agents choose their objects one by one according to some specified order, based e.g. on seniority. This mechanism is used, e.g., for **dormitory allocation in Israel** (Perach et al., 2008). When the agents are ordered randomly we call the mechanism *random serial dictatorship* (RSD). RSD is strategy-proof and ex-post efficient, meaning that no set of agents can improve their situation with an after-match exchange. However, this mechanism is not ex-ante efficient: the agents may exchange their marginal probabilities and can sometimes improve their expected welfare. It is always possible to obtain an ex-ante efficient probability distribution by the so-called *Probabilistic Serial* (or eating) mechanism of Bogomolnaia and Moulin (2001), however this mechanism is manipulable.

In the **resident allocation program of Israel** RSD was used until 2014, but in the redesigned mechanism they conduct improving exchanges to increase the expected welfare of the residents, and in the meantime they randomise over assignments in such a way that every couple is guaranteed to get positions in the same hospital, without harming the chances of the single doctors (Bronfman et al., 2015b,a; Roth and Shorrer, 2015).

Online Matchings

In many situations the objects arrive one by one and have to be allocated immediately. This is the case in deceased organ allocation, organised with a common protocol in eight European countries by Eurotransplant and also in Nordic countries by Scandiatransplant. Social housing is another important application, where the recipients may accept or reject offers in a strategic way (Leshno, 2015; Bloch and Cantala, 2017). Further interesting applications are the allocation of parking slots (Ayala et al., 2012) and airport landing slots (Schummer and Abizada, 2017).

Course Allocation

How should we allocate the seats of the courses if some popular courses cannot accommodate all the interested students? The simplest way is perhaps the **serial dictatorship** (SD) mechanism, where students are ordered randomly and they can choose their bundles one by one. This is happening in most of the Hungarian universities, where the central administration website opens the enrollment process and the students can take their turn whenever they manage to log into the website. Perhaps it is more fair and less stressful to create a random order by a transparent lottery and let the students select their courses at scheduled intervals. The advantage of the SD mechanism is that it is Pareto-efficient and strategy-proof, since each student selects the best bundle from the set of available courses. However, the allocation is very unequal. One way to balance this over the years of studies is to have adjusted lotteries favouring those who were less fortunate so far. This is also the main intuition behind the **draft mechanisms**, used e.g. at the Harvard MBA courses (Budish and Cantillon, 2012), where the students are randomly ordered and they can choose their courses one by one, by switching the order of the picking sequence in the rounds. This results in more egalitarian solutions, however the result is not Pareto-optimal, and the students can benefit from strategic manipulations.

In **bidding mechanisms**, which are widely used in US colleges (Sönmez and Ünver, 2010; Krishna and Ünver, 2008), the students have a virtual budget that they can allocate over their targeted courses. The bids are ordered in a unique ranking decreasing in price and they grant the bids one by one whenever possible. The biggest issue with this mechanism is that the students' preferences may not be aligned with their strategically optimal bids, since the most-preferred course of a student may be less popular, so she could potentially get a seat there also by a minor bid, but if she is lucky with her higher bids for most popular, but personally least-preferred courses then she wont get her most-preferred course due to credit limits. A proposed improvement is to collect the preferences of the students together with her bids, which was also shown to be useful in experiments (Krishna and Ünver, 2008).

Finally, another kind of improvement for the bidding mechanism is the usage of a **competitive equilibrium** solution of a combinatorial auction, with the theoretical background prepared by Budish (2011), and implemented recently at Wharton college (Budish et al., 2016). Here the students report their cardinal utilities over the courses and the central coordinator computes the market clearing prices. In this approximate equilibrium solution every student gets her best possible bundle that is possible to buy from her budget under the market clearing prices. Further advantage of this system is that students can also express their valuations on sets of courses, making it possible to improve the selection of the best bundle by stating which courses are substitutes and which ones are complements of each other. However, it is challenging to elicit all the relevant preferences in advance, so the direct revelation mechanisms may have shortcomings when compared with sequential or decentralised mechanisms.

> **Priority mechanism at Eötvös Lóránd University (ELTE).** Setting priorities at each course and then finding a student-optimal stable solution based on the students' submitted linear preferences over the courses has been proposed in the literature (Diebold et al., 2014). However, the course allocation method used at ELTE is decentralised: the students can optimise their bundles during a long enrollment period by seeing their possibilities at the administration website. The priorities of the students are based on reasonable factors, and multiple lotteries are used for breaking ties at every course separately. The students have to submit their ideal bundles in a preregistration phase; the university can use these to adjust their quotas before the enrollment starts, to better satisfy the demand. The only strategic issue might be that the priority at a course also depends on whether the student included that course in her submitted bundle at the preregistration. (This description was based on the presentation by Ferenc Zaka and Tamás Solymos (ELTE) at the 12th Workshop on Matching in Practice in December 2016, Budapest.)

Further Applications

The assignment of papers to reviewers at conferences is coordinated in many conference-administration websites, e.g. EasyChair, based on the reviewers' preferences, but the exact computational goals of these mechanisms are not known. A couple of reasonable approaches were studied theoretically by Garg et al. (2010). Foodbanks are responsible for allocation of unused food to people in need in many countries worldwide. In the US the largest organisation, Feeding America redesigned its allocation mechanism in 2005 following the advice of a group of economists. The new system is based on a combinatorial auction with virtual credits (Prendergast, 2016), and significantly improved the efficiency and overall welfare of the solution. Finally, a new approach was developed by Kurokawa et al. (2015) for allocating sets of indivisible goods via a randomised mechanism, which was successfully applied for room allocation to Charter schools in California.

18.4 Exchange Models

In exchange markets the agents are endowed with objects that they can exchange to improve everyone's situation without using monetary transfers. When every agent owns exactly one object then the so-called housing market always has a core solution, which can be obtained efficiently by Gale's Top Trading Cycles algorithm (Shapley and Scarf, 1974). However, the core property (also called as stability) may not be the only objective of the central organiser and constraints may also apply, e.g. on the lengths of the exchange cycles, so different models and solution concepts may be needed. Furthermore, when the agents own multiple indivisible goods then the exchange problem becomes significantly more complicated, even to decide the Pareto-efficiency of the solution can be challenging under strong restrictions on the preference domain (Aziz et al., 2016).

Exchange of Indivisible Goods

The exchange of houses or rental flats, the original motivating context of Shapley and Scarf (1974), has indeed been organised in ad-hoc exchange cycles without monetary payments in many countries. A Czechoslovakian film, *Ball lightning* from 1979 illustrates this, which also motivated a scientific paper on exchanges with marrying and divorcing couples (Cechlárová et al., 2016). Timeshare exchanges (Wang and Krishna, 2006) are often organised in a coordinated way. There are new platforms for exchanging homes for holiday, but typically allowing only pairwise exchanges which are negotiated in a decentralised way. Finally we shall note that a national exchange programme was established in 1943 for exchanging shoes among those who needed only a half pair or who had feet of significantly different sizes (Website of National Odd Shoe Exchange, 2016).

Kidney Exchange

Kidney exchange is certainly the most important application of the exchange model with indivisible goods, where patients with kidney failure wish to exchange their incompatible donors for compatible ones. The first single-centre exchange programme was established in South-Korea in 1991 and the Netherlands began the first nationwide programme in 2004 (de Klerk et al., 2008). For an overview we refer to two recent survey papers on this topic (Glorie et al., 2014; Ferrari et al., 2015). The most important features of these centrally coordinated schemes are that the lengths of the exchange cycles are bounded, e.g. in the Netherlands (respectively UK) up to four (respectively three) patient-donor pairs can be involved in an exchange cycle. The other distinguishing feature is that the goal of the programmes are typically to save as many patients as possible, so the optimal solution has maximum size under some constraints and priority criteria.

In the **USA** the New England Kidney Exchange Program was the first centralised scheme established in 2005 (Roth et al., 2005a). Currently the three major nationwide programmes are organised by the United Network for Organ Sharing (UNOS), the National Kidney Registry (NKR) and the Alliance for Paired Donation (APD) (Fumo et al., 2015). An important challenge in the US is that the large transplant centres are very influential, and they conduct the majority of the US kidney exchange transplants internally (e.g. the San Antonio centre). They have a tendency not to report their easy-to-match patient-donor pairs to the national schemes, but wait for suitable exchange partners within the hospital, which results in the accumulation of hard-to-match pairs and highly sensitised patients in the pool (Ashlagi and Roth, 2012). The usage of altruistic donors to trigger so-called never ending chains became a common practice in the US and it has improved the number of transplantations in the kidney exchange pool significantly (Stepkowski et al., 2015).

The Dutch and the UK programmes were established in **Europe** in 2004 and 2007, respectively. In recent years new programmes have been developed in Austria, Belgium, the Czech Republic, France, Italy, Poland, Portugal, Spain and Sweden. Moreover, there was already a transnational exchange between Austria and Czech Republic, and Sweden has also started to cooperate with Denmark and Norway via Scandiatransplant. In 2016 September a COST Action was started (Website of COST Action: European Network for Collaboration on Kidney Exchange Programmes, 2016) involving both practitioners and theoretical researchers in multiple disciplines, to study current practices, identify best practices and key challenges, and investigate the possibilities of further transnational collaborations. (A Handbook on the current practices is scheduled to be published in July 2017.) **Canada** and **Australia** also have well established programmes — see the comparison by Ferrari et al. (2015).

> **UK paired donation scheme.** The scheme has been run by NHS Blood and Transplant since 2007 (Johnson et al., 2008) with matching runs conducted every three months. At the beginning only two-way exchanges were allowed, but since 2008 three-way exchanges have also been sought. The optimal so-

> lutions were first computed with an exact graph algorithm (Biro et al., 2009), which was later replaced by a sequential IP solution (Manlove and O'Malley, 2014). Altruistic donors have been used to start chains involving one or two patient-donor pairs from the exchange pool, with the last donor's kidney given to the waiting list. Overall, as if May 2017, from the 1676 patients registered, 1133 were identified for possible exchanges by the matching algorithm based on the virtual cross-match tests, out of which 687 received organs in the end.

Exchange of Multiple Indivisible Goods

Swapping used books without monetary payments is an potential application present in many countries (see e.g. ReadItSwapIt in the UK). The typical decentralised exchange process of such a scheme is to offer the goods first to the community for getting credits, and then spend the credits on other goods later on. This organisation is also typical for timebanks (see e.g. TimebankingUK), where the participants offer their time in the form of providing different services (e.g. teaching math) and receive the same amount of time back in the form of other services (e.g. French class or haircutting). There are many sites also for exchanging babysitting services (e.g. BabysitterExchange).

A more serious application is the exchange of deceased organs among countries. Eurotransplant is an organisation involving eight European countries who share their deceased donors among themselves in a fair way, and Scandiatransplant is a similar organisation for Scandinavian countries. In their online allocation policy it is crucial to find the best suitable recipient(s) for the newly available organs, but in the long run they also ensure the balancedness of the allocation, that is, every participating country should receive about the same number of organs as they offered.

The balancedness of the solution is also crucial in the tuition exchange programmes in the US, such as The Tuition Exchange, Inc, where member colleges award the dependents of their staff with free tuitions that they can use at other colleges. Thus essentially the colleges exchange their students. Although the coordination of the exchanges is semi-centralised, the number of incoming and outgoing students should be roughly equal for every college (Dur and Ünver, 2016). A similar framework is applied in the Erasmus programme, where European higher education institutions exchange their students. These exchanges are based on bilateral contracts, but in the long run every university cares about the balance of the incoming and outgoing students, since every student pays the tuition at her home university.

18.5 Further Matching Models

In this last section we mention some further models that have applications.

Roommates Problem

The roommates problem was defined by Gale and Shapley (1962) as the extension of the marriage problem for non-bipartite graphs – this is also referred to as a one-sided market in the economic literature. Here a stable matching may not exist, but we can decide the existence in linear time. Regarding the corresponding applications, finding roommates for twin rooms is a reasonable one, although we are not aware of any recorded application of this sort. Note that the pairwise exchange problem, i.e. where the length of exchange cycles is bounded by two, is equivalent to the roommates problem, if stability of the solution is the main concern. Therefore, for instance, the initial kidney exchange papers were also concerned with matching problems on non-bipartite graphs, where the Edmonds algorithm can find maximum size or maximum weight matching efficiently (Roth et al., 2005b). A very recent application of the roommates model is speed networking at conferences (Vaggi et al., 2014), where the participants are scheduled for one-to-one discussions on a scientific basis. Finally, we describe the classical application of chess pairings below.

FIDE chess pairings. Chess pairings are used in both individual and team tournaments for allocating the competitors into pairs based on their performance. The most well-known pairing system is the Swiss system, invented by Dr. Julius Müller of Brugg, which was first used in a chess tournament at Zurich in 1895. The goal of a chess tournament is to determine the winner and rank the others based on their results achieved in a fixed number of rounds, typically nine. The common practice in all of the variants used by the World Chess Federation (FIDE) is to try to match the players or teams with those who are similarly ranked based on their performance so far. However, the completeness of the pairing is also required (at most one player can be unmatched, if the number of players is odd), and no two players can play twice against each other. The colours are also important in individual tournament, no player can play with the same colour three times in a row. The main pairing rule used in the Swiss-tournaments has now four official variants, the Dutch, Lim, Dobov, and Burnstein systems (Website of the World Chess Federation, 2016). The description of the pairing methods states that every arbiter should be able to conduct the matching by hand, although official pairing software applications are widely used. For the above reasons, the descriptions of current processes contain some highly inefficient exhaustive search procedures, as the arbiters cannot be expected to find a complete matching, e.g., by using Edmonds' algorithm. Yet, it is an interesting question as to whether the solutions returned by the described processes can be obtained by efficient algorithms, which can be implemented and used in a software tool (Biró et al., 2017).

Coalitional Matchings

Matching problems can be extended to so-called coalition formation problems, where the groups of agents can agree on cooperations. An example that we have already seen is the matching problem with couples, where a couple can form a coalition with two hospitals. Stable 3D-matchings are also widely studied, where the set of agents can be separated into three parties (rather than two, as in the stable marriage problem), see e.g. (Biró and McDermid, 2010). In the group activity selection problem the agents are assigned to activities and they may have preferences also over the number of partners with which they participate in a given activity, see Chapter 5 or this book. Finally, in some national grant agencies (such as the Hungarian and the French ones) researchers can be involved in multiple project proposals, but their contributions must be declared and no one can be involved in projects with a total contribution exceeding 100%. These applications can be described in a general game-theoretic framework, see e.g. Biró and Fleiner (2016).

Matching with Contracts

In many applications two agents can choose from different contracts when cooperating. For instance, as we have seen, in the Hungarian higher education admission scheme the students may be admitted to the same programme under two different contracts, mainly differing in the tuition fees. Cadet branch allocation in the US is another important application, where the number of service years may differ in optional contracts (Sönmez and Switzer, 2013). If multiple contracts are possible in a many-to-one market, then the unit-capacity agents should have the opportunity to order the contracts in their applications in any way, as it is the practice in Hungary (but what is not allowed in the cadet branch matching). With regard to the capacitated side, the preferences of the agents on that side may be more complex over the sets of contracts, but as long as they satisfy the so-called substitutability condition, stable solutions bound to exist (Fleiner, 2003; Hatfield and Milgrom, 2005).

Matching with Payments (not covered)

In this survey we do not cover models where payments are allowed between the agents, such as coordinated auctions, since this would probably double the length of this chapter. However, we note that these applications are based on very similar matching models, with common generalisations including the matching with no payments models, see e.g. Kelso Jr and Crawford (1982). Indeed, some important applications, such as the Google adwords auctions, can also be studied with such hybrid models (Aggarwal et al., 2009). Furthermore, there are also examples for solving the allocation of indivisible goods with virtual auctions to increase the overall efficiency and the fairness of the solution, as we have seen for course allocation (Budish et al., 2016) and in the allocation process of foodbanks (Prendergast, 2016).

18.6 Conclusion

Discovering and describing the current applications based on matching models under preferences is an important task that our research community has also recognised, e.g., in the European research network on Matching in Practice. These findings can help us understand what the main features of the applications are and what the main questions, issues and challenges are. Scientists in several disciplines can then join forces to analyse the performance of the current mechanisms, and come up with ideas for possible improvements. Note though that in many cases the optimisation criteria are not entirely clear, there may be multiple solution methods to consider, and the best practices may highly depend on the context. But our ultimate goal as scientists should be to help the decision makers in the (re-)design of their applications to make them efficient, fair and transparent, by serving the best interests of society.

Acknowledgments

I appreciate the valuable comments of Eric Budish, Estelle Cantillon, Guillaume Haeringer, Bettina Klaus, Dorothea Kübler, David Manlove and Al Roth. I thank the financial support by the Hungarian Academy of Sciences under its Momentum Programme (LP2016-3/2016) and by OTKA grant no. K108673.

Bibliography

A. Abdulkadiroğlu and T. Sönmez. School choice: A mechanism design approach. *The American Economic Review*, 93(3):729–747, 2003.

A. Abdulkadiroğlu, P. A. Pathak, and A. E. Roth. The New York city high school match. *American Economic Review*, 95(2):364–367, 2005a.

A. Abdulkadiroğlu, P. A. Pathak, A. E. Roth, and T. Sönmez. The Boston public school match. *American Economic Review*, 95(2):368–371, 2005b.

A. Abdulkadiroğlu, P. A. Pathak, and A. E. Roth. Strategy-proofness versus efficiency in matching with indifferences: Redesigning the NYC high school match. *American Economic Review*, 99(5):1954–78, 2009.

A. Abdulkadiroğlu, N. Agarwal, and P. Pathak. The welfare effects of coordinated school assignment: Evidence from the NYC high school match. Technical report, MIT, 2013.

A. Abdulkadiroğlu, Y.-K. Che, P. A. Pathak, A. E. Roth, and O. Tercieux. Minimizing justified envy in school choice: The design of New Orleans' OneApp. Technical report, No. w23265, National Bureau of Economic Research, 2017.

D. J. Abraham, R. W. Irving, and D. F. Manlove. Two algorithms for the student-project allocation problem. *Journal of Discrete Algorithms*, 5(1):73–90, 2007.

G. Aggarwal, S. Muthukrishnan, D. Pál, and M. Pál. General auction mechanism for search advertising. In *Proceedings of the 18th International Conference on World Wide Web (WWW)*, pages 241–250, 2009.

K. C. Ágoston, P. Biró, and I. McBride. Integer programming methods for special college admissions problems. *Journal of Combinatorial Optimization*, 32(4): 1371–1399, 2016.

K. C. Ágoston, P. Biró, and R. Szántó. Stable project allocation under distributional constraints. In *Proceedings of the 10th Japanese-Hungarian Symposium on Discrete Mathematics and Its Applications*, pages 43–52, 2017.

T. Andersson and L. Ehlers. Assigning refugees to landlords in Sweden: Stable maximum matchings. Technical report, Lund University, 2016.

I. Ashlagi and A. E. Roth. New challenges in multihospital kidney exchange. *The American Economic Review*, 102(3):354–359, 2012.

C. Avery, S. Lee, and A. E. Roth. College admissions as non-price competition: The case of South Korea. Technical Report No. 20774, National Bureau of Economic Research, 2014.

D. Ayala, O. Wolfson, B. Xu, B. DasGupta, and J. Lin. Stability of marriage and vehicular parking. In *Proceedings of the 2nd International Workshop on Matching Under Preferences (MATCH-UP)*, 2012.

O. Aygün and I. Bó. College admission with multidimensional privileges: The Brazilian affirmative action case. In *Proceedings of the 3rd International Workshop on Matching Under Preferences (MATCH-UP)*, 2015.

H. Aziz, P. Biró, J. Lang, J. Lesca, and J. Monnot. Optimal reallocation under additive and ordinal preferences. In *Proceedings of the 15th International Conference on Autonomous Agents and Multiagent Systems (AAMAS)*, 2016.

M. Balinski and T. Sönmez. A tale of two mechanisms: Student placement. *Journal of Economic Theory*, 84(1):73–94, 1999.

C. Basteck, K. Huesmann, and H. Nax. Matching practices in secondary schools — Germany, MiP country profile 21. http://www.matching-in-practice.eu/matching-practices-for-secondary-schools-germany/, 2015.

B. Belhoste. *La Formation d'une technocratie: L'École polytechnique et ses élèves de la Révolution au Second Empire*. Belin, 2003.

P. Biró. Matching practices in secondary schools — Hungary, MiP country profile 6. http://www.matching-in-practice.eu/secondary-schools-in-hungary/, 2012.

P. Biró and T. Fleiner. Fractional solutions for capacitated ntu-games, with applications to stable matchings. *Discrete Optimization*, 22:241–254, 2016.

P. Biró and S. Kiselgof. College admissions with stable score-limits. *Central European Journal of Operations Research*, 23(4):727–741, 2015.

P. Biró and F. Klijn. Matching with couples: A multidisciplinary survey. *International Game Theory Review*, 15(02):1340008, 2013.

P. Biró and E. McDermid. Three-sided stable matchings with cyclic preferences. *Algorithmica*, 58(1):5–18, 2010.

P. Biro, D. F. Manlove, and R. Rizzi. Maximum weight cycle packing in directed graphs, with application to kidney exchange programs. *Discrete Mathematics, Algorithms and Applications*, 1(04):499–517, 2009.

P. Biró, T. Fleiner, R. W. Irving, and D. F. Manlove. The college admissions problem with lower and common quotas. *Theoretical Computer Science*, 411(34-36): 3136–3153, 2010.

P. Biró, R. W. Irving, and I. Schlotter. Stable matching with couples: An empirical study. *Journal of Experimental Algorithmics (JEA)*, 16:1.2, 2011.

P. Biró, T. Fleiner, and R. Palincza. Designing chess pairing mechanisms. In *Proceedings of the 10th Japanese-Hungarian Symposium on Discrete Mathematics and Its Applications*, pages 77–86, 2017.

F. Bloch and D. Cantala. Dynamic assignment of objects to queuing agents. *American Economic Journal: Microeconomics*, 9(1):88–122, 2017.

A. Bogomolnaia and H. Moulin. A new solution to the random assignment problem. *Journal of Economic Theory*, 100(2):295–328, 2001.

S. Braun, N. Dwenger, D. Kübler, and A. Westkamp. Implementing quotas in university admissions: An experimental analysis. *Games and Economic Behavior*, 85:232–251, 2014.

S. Bronfman, N. Alon, A. Hassidim, and A. Romm. Redesigning the israeli medical internship match. In *Proceedings of the 16th ACM Conference on Economics and Computation (EC)*, pages 753–754, 2015a.

S. Bronfman, A. Hassidim, A. Afek, A. Romm, R. Shreberk, A. Hassidim, and A. Massler. Assigning Israeli medical graduates to internships. *Israel Journal of Health Policy Research*, 4(1):6, 2015b.

E. Budish. The combinatorial assignment problem: Approximate competitive equilibrium from equal incomes. *Journal of Political Economy*, 119(6):1061–1103, 2011.

E. Budish and E. Cantillon. The multi-unit assignment problem: Theory and evidence from course allocation at Harvard. *The American Economic Review*, 102(5):2237–2271, 2012.

E. Budish, G. P. Cachon, J. B. Kessler, and A. Othman. Course match: A large-scale implementation of approximate competitive equilibrium from equal incomes for combinatorial allocation. *Operations Research*, 2016.

C. Calsamiglia. School choice in spain: Theory and evidence. *Els Opuscles del CREI*, 2011.

C. Calsamiglia. Matching practices in elementary and secondary schools — Spain, MiP country profile 17. http://www.matching-in-practice.eu/matching-practices-for-elementary-and-secondary-schools-spain/, 2014.

C. Calsamiglia and M. Güell. The illusion of school choice: Empirical evidence from Barcelona. Technical report, Barcelona Graduate School of Economics, 2014.

E. Cantillon and K. Declercq. University admission practices — Belgium, MiP country profile 9. http://www.matching-in-practice.eu/higher-education-in-belgium/, 2012.

K. Cechlárová, T. Fleiner, and Z. Jankó. House-swapping with divorcing and engaged pairs. *Discrete Applied Mathematics*, 206:1–8, 2016.

L. Chen. University admission practices — Ireland, MiP country profile 8. http://www.matching-in-practice.eu/higher-education-in-ireland/, 2012.

Y. Chen and O. Kesten. From Boston to Chinese parallel to deferred acceptance: Theory and experiments on a family of school choice mechanisms. Technical report, Social Science Research Center Berlin (WZB), 2013.

P. Coles, A. Kushnir, and M. Niederle. Preference signaling in matching markets. *American Economic Journal: Microeconomics*, 5(2):99–134, 2013.

J. Combe, O. Tercieux, and C. Terrier. The design of teacher assignment: Theory and evidence. Technical report, London School of Economics (LSE), 2015.

M. de Haan, P. A. Gautier, H. Oosterbeek, and B. Van der Klaauw. The performance of school assignment mechanisms in practice. Working paper, 2015.

M. de Klerk, M. D. Witvliet, B. Haase-Kromwijk, W. Weimar, and F. Claas. A flexible national living donor kidney exchange program taking advantage of a central histocompatibility laboratory: The Dutch model. *Clinical Transplantation*, 8:69–73, 2008.

D. Delacrétaz, S. D. Kominers, and A. Teytelboym. Refugee resettlement. Working paper, 2016.

F. Diebold, H. Aziz, M. Bichler, F. Matthes, and A. Schneider. Course allocation via stable matching. *Business & Information Systems Engineering*, 6(2):97–110, 2014.

P. D. Dimakopoulos and C. Heller. Matching with waiting times: The German entry-level labour market for lawyers. In *Proceedings of the German Economic Association Annual Conference 2015: Economic Development — Theory and Policy*, 2015.

U. M. Dur and M. U. Ünver. Two-sided matching via balanced exchange? Technical report, Boston College, Department of Economics, 2016.

N. Dwenger, S. Braun, and D. Kübler. Telling the truth may not pay off: An empirical study of centralized university admissions in Germany. *The BE Journal of Economic Analysis & Policy*, 10(1), 2010.

A. Erdil and H. Ergin. What's the matter with tie-breaking? Improving efficiency in school choice. *The American Economic Review*, 98(3):669–689, 2008.

G. Fack, J. Grenet, and Y. He. Beyond truth-telling: Preference estimation with centralized school choice. Working paper, 2015.

P. Ferrari, W. Weimar, R. J. Johnson, W. H. Lim, and K. J. Tinckam. Kidney paired donation: principles, protocols and programs. *Nephrology Dialysis Transplantation*, 30(8):1276–1285, 2015.

T. Fleiner. A fixed-point approach to stable matchings and some applications. *Mathematics of Operations Research*, 28(1):103–126, 2003.

L. Frys and C. Staat. University admission practices — France, MiP country profile 23. http://www.matching-in-practice.eu/university-admission-practices-france/, 2015.

D. Fumo, V. Kapoor, L. Reece, S. Stepkowski, J. Kopke, S. Rees, C. Smith, A. Roth, A. Leichtman, and M. Rees. Historical matching strategies in kidney paired donation: The 7-year evolution of a web-based virtual matching system. *American Journal of Transplantation*, 15(10):2646–2654, 2015.

D. Gale and L. S. Shapley. College admissions and the stability of marriage. *The American Mathematical Monthly*, 69(1):9–15, 1962.

D. Gale and M. Sotomayor. Some remarks on the stable matching problem. *Discrete Applied Mathematics*, 11(3):223–232, 1985.

N. Garg, T. Kavitha, A. Kumar, K. Mehlhorn, and J. Mestre. Assigning papers to referees. *Algorithmica*, 58(1):119–136, 2010.

K. Glorie, B. Haase-Kromwijk, J. Klundert, A. Wagelmans, and W. Weimar. Allocation and matching in kidney exchange programs. *Transplant International*, 27(4):333–343, 2014.

D. Gusfield and R. W. Irving. *The stable marriage problem: Structure and algorithms*. MIT Press, Cambridge, MA, USA, 1989.

J. W. Hatfield and P. R. Milgrom. Matching with contracts. *The American Economic Review*, 95(4):913–935, 2005.

V. Hiller and O. Tercieux. Matching practices in secondary schools — France, MiP country profile 16. http://www.matching-in-practice.eu/matching-practices-in-secondary-schools-france/, 2013.

R. W. Irving. Matching medical students to pairs of hospitals: A new variation on a well-known theme. In *Proceedings of the 6th Annual European Symposium on Algorithms (ESA)*, pages 381–392. Springer, 1998.

R. W. Irving and D. F. Manlove. Finding large stable matchings. *Journal of Experimental Algorithmics (JEA)*, 14:2, 2009.

R. W. Irving, D. F. Manlove, and S. Scott. The stable marriage problem with master preference lists. *Discrete Applied Mathematics*, 156(15):2959–2977, 2008.

R. J. Johnson, J. E. Allen, S. V. Fuggle, J. A. Bradley, and C. Rudge. Early experience of paired living kidney donation in the United Kingdom. *Transplantation*, 86(12):1672–1677, 2008.

Y. Kamada and F. Kojima. Stability and strategy-proofness for matching with constraints: A problem in the Japanese medical match and its solution. *The American Economic Review*, 102(3):366–370, 2012.

Y. Kamada and F. Kojima. Stability and strategy-proofness for matching with constraints: A necessary and sufficient condition. Working paper, 2016.

Y. Kamada and F. Kojima. Stability concepts in matching under distributional constraints. *Journal of Economic Theory*, 168:107–142, 2017.

A. S. Kelso Jr and V. P. Crawford. Job matching, coalition formation, and gross substitutes. *Econometrica*, 50(6):1483–1504, 1982.

B. Klaus, D. F. Manlove, and F. Rossi. Matching under preferences. In F. Brandt, V. Conitzer, U. Endriss, J. Lang, and A. D. Procaccia, editors, *Handbook of Computational Social Choice*, pages 333–355. Cambridge University Press, 2016.

A. Krishna and M. U. Ünver. Improving the efficiency of course bidding at business schools: Field and laboratory studies. *Marketing Science*, 27(2):262–282, 2008.

D. Kübler. University admission practices — Germany, MiP country profile 5. http://www.matching-in-practice.eu/higher-education-in-germany/, 2011.

D. Kurokawa, A. D. Procaccia, and N. Shah. Leximin allocations in the real world. In *Proceedings of the 16th ACM Conference on Economics and Computation (EC)*, pages 345–362, 2015.

T. Lauri, K. Põder, and A. Veski. Matching practices in elementary schools — Estonia, MiP country profile 18. http://www.matching-in-practice.eu/elementary-schools-estonia/, 2014.

S. Lee and M. Niederle. Propose with a rose? Signaling in Internet dating markets. *Experimental Economics*, 18(4):731–755, 2015.

J. D. Leshno. Dynamic matching in overloaded waiting lists. Technical report, Columbia University, 2015.

D. F. Manlove. *Algorithmics of Matching Under Preferences*. World Scientific Publishing Company, 2013.

D. F. Manlove and G. O'Malley. Student-project allocation with preferences over projects. *Journal of Discrete Algorithms*, 6(4):553–560, 2008.

D. F. Manlove and G. O'Malley. Paired and altruistic kidney donation in the uk: Algorithms and experimentation. *Journal of Experimental Algorithmics (JEA)*, 19:2–6, 2014.

L. P. Merlino and A. Nicoló. University admission practices — Italy, MiP country profile 23. http://www.matching-in-practice.eu/higher-education-in-italy/, 2013.

P. A. Pathak and T. Sönmez. School admissions reform in Chicago and England: Comparing mechanisms by their vulnerability to manipulation. *The American Economic Review*, 103(1):80–106, 2013.

N. Perach, J. Polak, and U. G. Rothblum. A stable matching model with an entrance criterion applied to the assignment of students to dormitories at the Technion. *International Journal of Game Theory*, 36(3-4):519–535, 2008.

C. Prendergast. The allocation of food to food banks. Technical report, University of Chicago Booth School of Business, 2016.

I. Ríos, T. Larroucau, G. Parra, and R. Cominetti. College admissions problem with ties and flexible quotas. Technical report, 2014.

P. A. Robards. Applying two-sided matching processes to the united states navy enlisted assignment process. Technical report, Naval Postgraduate School Montrey CA, 2001.

A. Romero-Medina. Implementation of stable solutions in a restricted matching market. *Review of Economic Design*, 3(2):137–147, 1998.

E. Ronn. NP-complete stable matching problems. *Journal of Algorithms*, 11(2): 285–304, 1990.

A. E. Roth. The evolution of the labor market for medical interns and residents: a case study in game theory. *The Journal of Political Economy*, pages 991–1016, 1984.

A. E. Roth. New physicians: A natural experiment in market organization. *Science*, 250(4987):1524–1528, 1990.

A. E. Roth. A natural experiment in the organization of entry-level labor markets: Regional markets for new physicians and surgeons in the United Kingdom. *American Economic Review*, 81(3):415–40, 1991.

A. E. Roth. Deferred acceptance algorithms: History, theory, practice, and open questions. *International Journal of Game Theory*, 36(3):537–569, 2008.

A. E. Roth. *Who Gets What — and Why: The New Economics of Matchmaking and Market Design.* Houghton Mifflin Harcourt, 2015.

A. E. Roth and E. Peranson. The redesign of the matching market for American physicians: Some engineering aspects of economic design. *American Economic Review*, 89(4):748–780, 1999.

A. E. Roth and R. I. Shorrer. The redesign of the medical intern assignment mechanism in Israel. *Israel Journal of Health Policy Research*, 4(1):11, 2015.

A. E. Roth and M. A. O. Sotomayor. *Two-Sided Matching: A Study in Game Theoretic Modelling and Analysis.* Cambridge University Press, 1990.

A. E. Roth, T. Sönmez, and M. U. Ünver. A kidney exchange clearinghouse in new england. *American Economic Review*, pages 376–380, 2005a.

A. E. Roth, T. Sönmez, and M. U. Ünver. Pairwise kidney exchange. *Journal of Economic theory*, 125(2):151–188, 2005b.

M. A. Salonen. Matching practices in secondary schools — Finland, MiP country profile 19. http://www.matching-in-practice.eu/matching-practices-for-secondary-schools-finland/, 2014.

J. Schummer and A. Abizada. Incentives in landing slot problems. *Journal of Economic Theory*, 170:29–55, 2017.

L. Shapley and H. Scarf. On cores and indivisibility. *Journal of Mathematical Economics*, 1:23–37, 1974.

P. Shi. Guiding school-choice reform through novel applications of operations research. *Interfaces*, 45(2):117–132, 2015.

M. M. Short. Analysis of the current navy enlisted detailing process. Technical report, Naval Postgraduate School Montrey CA, 2000.

V. W. Slaugh, M. Akan, O. Kesten, and M. U. Ünver. The Pennsylvania adoption exchange improves its matching process. *Interfaces*, 46(2):133–153, 2016.

M. Soldner. *Optimization and measurement in humanitarian operations: Addressing practical needs.* PhD thesis, Georgia Institute of Technology, 2014.

T. Sönmez and T. B. Switzer. Matching with (branch-of-choice) contracts at the United States Military Academy. *Econometrica*, 81(2):451–488, 2013.

T. Sönmez and M. U. Ünver. Course bidding at business schools. *International Economic Review*, 51(1):99–123, 2010.

S. Stepkowski, D. E. Fumo, L. J. Reese, J. E. Kopke, A. E. Roth, A. B. Leichtman, and M. A. Rees. Advantages of chains vs. cycles in a kidney paired donation program: A 7-year analysis. *Transplant International*, 28:18, 2015.

C. Terrier. Matching practices for secondary public school teachers — France, MiP country profile 20. http://www.matching-in-practice.eu/matching-practices-of-teachers-to-schools-france/, 2014.

F. Vaggi, T. Schiavinotto, J. L. Lawson, A. Chessel, J. Dodgson, M. Geymonat, M. Sato, R. E. C. Salas, and A. Csikász-Nagy. A network approach to mixing delegates at meetings. *eLife*, 3:e02273, 2014.

A. Veski, P. Biró, K. Põder, and T. Lauri. Efficiency and fair access in kindergarten allocation policy design. *Journal of Mechanism and Institutional Design*, 2017. To appear.

Y. Wang and A. Krishna. Timeshare exchange mechanisms. *Management Science*, 52(8):1223–1237, 2006.

Website of Al Roth's blog. http://marketdesigner.blogspot.hu/, 2010. Accessed on 30 November 2016.

Website of COST Action: European Network for Collaboration on Kidney Exchange Programmes. http://www.cost.eu/COST_Actions/ca/CA15210, 2016. Accessed on 30 November 2016.

Website of Institute for Innovation in Public School Choice. http://iipsc.org/, 2014. Accessed on 30 November 2016.

Website of National Odd Shoe Exchange. http://www.fide.com/fide/handbook?id=18&view=category, 2016. Accessed on 30 November 2016.

Website of the Matching in Practice network. http://www.matching-in-practice.eu/, 2014. Accessed on 30 November 2016.

Website of the World Chess Federation. http://www.fide.com/fide/handbook?id=18&view=category, 2016. Accessed on 30 November 2016.

Website on matching practices at Hungarian Academy of Sciences. http://econ.core.hu/english/res/game_app.html, 2012. Accessed on 30 November 2016.

A. Westkamp. An analysis of the German university admissions system. *Economic Theory*, 53(3):561–589, 2013.

W. Yang, J. Giampapa, and K. Sycara. Two-sided matching for the US Navy Detailing Process with market complication. Technical report, Robotics Institute, Carnegie-Mellon University, 2003.

CHAPTER 19

School Placement of Trainee Teachers: Theory and Practice

Katarína Cechlárová

19.1 Introduction

The traditional study programs of teachers-to-be for upper elementary and secondary education in Slovakia and the Czech Republic involve the specialization of each student in two subjects, e.g., Mathematics and Physics, Chemistry and Biology, Slovak language and English, etc. In addition to the study of various topics of these school subjects and principles of Pedagogics and Psychology, each curriculum contains a practical placement in a real school several times during the studies. School placement enables the students to find connections between the theoretical knowledge and its practical use in a class. It can be organized in several modes, each providing a different level and type of support to the trainees and putting different levels of requirements on their competences.

The aim of this work is to describe mathematical models, computational complexity results and proposed algorithms for the tasks connected with the school placement of trainee teachers. They depend on the concrete type of the placements, so now we describe briefly their two types as used at the home university of the author.

During the *group placement (observational)* a group of students (ideally of 4-6 students) visit real classes, they observe the teacher at her work, her didactic methods, reactions to the behavior of pupils, etc, and after the class they engage in common discussion to analyze everything that has happened. The computational difficulty of this placement problem comes from the requirement to assign each student to two different groups (one for each of her specialization subjects) in such a way that a non-conflicting schedule should be possible.

Individual placement means that a student teaches pupils herself, but under a supervision of a qualified teacher. Students of our university teach both their specialization subjects during one placement period, and for practical reasons, the whole placement should take place at the same school. There is a requirement to teach *at least* a certain number of classes for each subject and have a supervising teacher for both specialization subjects, which leads to certain capacity restrictions on the side of schools.

To ensure the quality of practical placements, the university approves of both

Year	1967	1974	1989	2003	2006	2011	2012	2014
# of combinations	3	4	6	9	13	19	26	31

Table 19.1: Two-subject combinations of P.J. Šafárik University graduates

schools and supervising teachers. The university staff also construct the assignment for the whole cohort of students. We shall provide some figures to give an indication of how complicated and time-consuming this task is.

At the time of writing this text (academic year 2016/2017) there are 10 universities in Slovakia providing the teachers' studies. Previously, there was a relatively clear separation of various subjects: Science faculties offered subjects of natural sciences, like Mathematics, Physics, Biology, Chemistry, etc., Philosophical faculties offered languages and humanities, whilst Pedagogical faculties (in addition to primary and special education) offered sports and arts education. In the 1990s many new universities and faculties were established in Slovakia and also the teaching profession became less popular. As a result, universities started to compete for students in several different ways. One approach was to offer a greater degree of flexibility for their studies, namely, to allow a much larger number of different two-subject combinations. To be able to achieve this, most universities joined forces of their faculties. So, for example, at the University of Prešov, a student can choose *any* two subjects offered by 6 faculties (Faculty of Arts, Faculty of Humanities and Natural Sciences, Faculty of Sports, Faculty of Education and two theological faculties) plus three from the Institute of Minority Languages and Culture - Ruthenian, Hungarian and Roma. This means a choice from almost any pair of more than 21 different subjects; the explicit list of study programs for applicants in 2017/2018 contains 135 different two-subject combinations. For Pavol Jozef Šafárik University in Košice, where we conducted our research, we can give more detailed data, based on the official graduates' lists of the University. The first students of the Science faculty graduated in 1967 and originally, the only possible combinations were Mathematics-Physics, Chemistry-Physics and Chemistry-Biology. Year 1974 saw the first graduates of the combination Mathematics-Chemistry; in 1989 Informatics appeared among the specialization subjects and after the Institute of Geography was established, combinations with Geography emerged in 2003. A further important catalyst for the rise in the number of combinations was the foundation of the Faculty of Arts; the first graduates of common study programs were in 2011. Currently, the Faculty of Science offers 6 subjects and the Faculty of Arts 8 subjects; in 2014 the number of different two-subject combinations of graduates was 31.

There are many objections against so many different subject combinations. First, it is very complicated to coordinate so many different study groups (even with the help of the most recent computers and information systems) and to create the timetable for them, but more important are scientific and economic objections. Namely, it is difficult for a future teacher to cope with very distant subject areas at the level required for successful teaching in the school-leaving years. Moreover, complementary subjects, for example Mathematics and Physics, clearly help the teacher to master each of them to a greater depth. Further, for some specific subject combinations the position of the graduates in the labor market is difficult, as most schools do not have enough teaching hours for these subjects. This was demonstrated also during our study, where the most common combination found among the trainees without a place was Geography-Psychology.

Our research responded to the current situation. We wanted to provide a tool for replacing the most time-consuming part of the students' placement management by a user-friendly computer program. The administrative staff can use the list of students with their specializations and the list of schools with their affiliated supervising teachers (the data they always had to deal with) and as the output they receive a list of groups, a list of students with their assigned school, a list of schools with their assigned students and other supporting documents helping them to find an ad-hoc solution to various unexpected cases that can emerge. The data we provided could even be used for a deeper analysis of the current situation of the teachers' studies.

Related Work. Frieze and Yadegar (1981) model the assignment of students of colleges of education to teaching practice in the following way. Each student has to be assigned to one of a set of schools and there she is supervised by a tutor who comes from the college. Each school and tutor have a capacity (i.e., the maximum number of trainee-teachers that they can accept or supervise, respectively). Moreover, there is a cardinal *satisfaction value* for each student-school-tutor triple. Frieze and Yadegar propose an integer linear program to find a schedule with maximum total satisfaction.

A related task is that of assigning students to projects. Each project is supervised by a lecturer, and projects as well as lecturers have their capacities (enabling a lecturer to have a lower total capacity than the sum of capacities of the projects she is supervising). In a series of papers Abraham et al. (2007) and Manlove and O'Malley (2008) suppose that students have preferences over projects, and lecturers have preferences over students, or over projects. The optimality criterion is *stability*, and the authors study the computational complexity of various problems connected with algorithms for finding stable assignments. By contrast, Kwanashie et al. (2015) want to optimize the *profile* of a matching, i.e., a vector whose rth component indicates how many students have their rth-choice project in the assignment.

Recall that in our trainee teacher assignment problem each student needs two places in a specific structure. In the group placement the student practices one of her subjects in the first part of the placement period and the other subject in its second period. This is similar to the problem studied by Irving (1998) in the context of Scottish medical education. Each medical student must take on two positions in two half-years, namely a medical post and a surgical post, respecting the capacities of medical and surgical units in the two half-years. Irving seeks a stable matching maximizing the number of fulfilled seasonal preferences of students. However, while the types of posts are the same for each medical student, in our case, the pairs of subjects may vary for different students, plus in the group assignment problem we need to combine several students with the same specialization subject into groups.

Similarities with the structure of the trainee teacher assignment problem connected with individual placement can be found in the problems associated with the hospitals/residents matching problem. Motivated by the requirement of the couples (pairs of residents) not to be separated, McDermid and Manlove (2010) study the hospitals/residents problem with sizes of residents (a couple is a 'resident' of size 2) and capacities of hospitals. Let us remark that in the trainee teachers assignment problem each student also needs two places at one school, but the school capacities are more structured, related to individual subjects.

Similar 'multidimensional' constraints appear in a recent work of Delacrètaz et al. (2016) modeling the refugee resettlement problem. A refugee family needs a certain number of units of different public services, such as school seats, hospital beds, slots in language classes or employment training programs and each country or municipality has only restricted numbers of those. Delacrètaz et al. (2016) propose several mechanisms for this allocation problem and study their properties.

Let us also mention here further theoretical work connected with teacher placement. While the trainee teachers and the schools do not have (or, at least they are not asked about them) preferences over the other side of the market, when teachers are looking for a job, their preferences and preferences of schools really matter. Cechlárová et al. (2016) use stability as the criterion for the matching and study the computational complexity of various modifications of the basic problem.

19.2 Basic Notation

We shall denote by A the set of n applicants (students, trainee teachers) and by P the set of k subjects. For ease of exposition, elements of the set P will sometimes be referred to using letters such as M, F, I or B, to serve as a reminder of real subjects taught at schools, such as Mathematics, Physics, Informatics or Biology.

Each applicant $a \in A$ is characterized by a pair $p(a) = \{p_1(a), p_2(a)\} \subseteq P$ of different subjects. The subset of applicants whose specialization involves a subject $p \in P$ (while the other subject may be arbitrary) will be denoted by A_p, the subset of applicants with specialization $\{p, q\}$ by $A_{p,q}$. Further notation differs for the two kinds of placement and so it is postponed to the respective sections.

19.3 Group Placement: Observational

During this type of placement, groups of students of size between 4 and 6 visit classes that are led by a teacher. Their task is to observe everything that happens during a class, take notes about how the teacher presents the material, how she reacts to the pupils' behavior, etc. After the class, students together with the teacher analyze her methods, approaches, ask questions, etc. The aim of this type of placement is to see how to apply in practice the principles that students learned so far only theoretically.

Students	Specialization
Anna, Boris	MF
Cyril, Daniel	MI
Eva, František	IF

Table 19.2: Students for group placement

Group	Students
M	Anna, Boris, Cyril, Daniel
I	Cyril, Daniel, Eva, František
F	Anna, Boris, Eva, František

Table 19.3: Minimum number of groups

Although the basic pedagogical and psychological principles are common for all subjects, many methods and approaches are content-dependent, so the requirement is that students should visit classes where their specialization subjects are taught. Therefore this type of placement is divided into two periods. In the first period the student visits classes of one specialization subject of hers and in the second period she visits classes of her other specialization subject. So the task is to create one-subject groups of size 4-6 students in such a way that each student is in exactly two groups in two different periods. The groups are then scheduled in such a way that each group, if possible, visits a class in an elementary school, a general education high school and also in a specialized high school. To save human and financial resources, it is desirable to keep the number of groups as small as possible.

Example 19.1. *To get an idea of the essence of the problem, let us consider six students whose data are given in Table 19.2. If we create exactly one group of students for each subject, we will not be able to schedule them. For, suppose that group M will be scheduled for the first placement period. Then, since Anna's specialization is MF and Daniel's specialization is MI, both I and F groups have to be scheduled for the second placement period. However, in this case, Eva and František cannot visit classes for both their specialization subjects. If, instead, we split M into two 'mathematical' groups M1={Anna, Boris} and M2={Cyril, Daniel}, then a valid schedule could be M1 and I in the first period and M2 and F in the second period.*

Formally, an instance of the MIN-TAP-G problem is $I = (A, P)$ where P is the set of subjects and A is the set of students, where each $a \in A$ is characterized by a pair $p(a) \subset P$. We want to find a family $\mathscr{B} = \mathscr{B}^1 \cup \mathscr{B}^2$ with $\mathscr{B}^1 = \{B_1^1, B_2^1, \ldots, B_k^1\}$ and $\mathscr{B}^2 = \{B_1^2, B_2^2, \ldots, B_k^2\}$ in such a way that

$$B_p^1 \cup B_p^2 = A_p \text{ and } B_p^1 \cap B_p^2 = \emptyset \text{ for each subject } p \in P \quad (19.1)$$

for each $a \in A_{p,q}$ there exists $i \in \{1, 2\}$ such that $a \in B_p^i$ and $a \in B_q^{3-i}$. (19.2)

Sets $B_1^1, B_2^1, \ldots, B_k^1$ are the groups scheduled for the first period, sets $B_1^2, B_2^2, \ldots, B_k^2$ are the groups scheduled for the second period. Requirements (19.1) and (19.2) mean that each student is a member of exactly one group for her first subject and of exactly one group for her second subject and that the family enables a valid schedule, i.e., the two groups containing a given student are never scheduled for the same period. The problem MIN-TAP-G is to find a valid family with the minimum number of groups. The proof of the intractability of this problem uses a reduction that is closely related to the construction of an auxiliary graph presented when designing an algorithm for finding a minimum size odd cycle transversal by Reed et al. (2004).

Theorem 19.1. MIN-TAP-G *is NP-complete even when* $|A_{p,q}| \leq 1$ *for each pair* $\{p, q\} \subset P$.

Proof. We provide a polynomial transformation from the NP-complete problem BIPARTITE GRAPH (Garey and Johnson, 1979). Here, a graph $G = (V, E)$ and an integer t are given; the question is whether it is possible to delete a set W (an odd cycle transversal) of at most t vertices from G in such a way that the subgraph $G = (V \setminus W, E')$ induced on the set of vertices $V \setminus W$ is bipartite.

Let an instance I of MIN-TAP-G for $G = (V, E)$ be defined as follows. The sets of subjects and applicants are $P = \{p(v); v \in V\}$ and $A = \{a(e); e \in E\}$, where the pair of subjects of a student $a(e)$ corresponding to edge $e = \{u, v\}$ is $\{p(u), p(v)\}$.

First suppose that $G = (V \setminus W, E')$ is bipartite with the bipartition $U \cup U'$. We create $|V| + |W|$ groups as follows. For each $v \in U$ we have $B_{p(v)}^1 = \{a(e); v \in e\}$ in $\mathscr{B}^1$ and for each $v \in U'$ the group $B_{p(v)}^2 = \{a(e); v \in e\}$ in $\mathscr{B}^2$. For each vertex $v \in W$ we create two groups: group $B_{p(v)}^1 = \{a(e); e = \{v, w\}; w \in U'\} \in \mathscr{B}^1$ and group $B_{p(v)}^2 = \{a(e); e = \{v, w\}; w \in U\} \in \mathscr{B}^2$. It is easy to see that this a valid partition.

Conversely, suppose that we have a valid partition. It is easy to see that to obtain a bipartite subgraph of G it is enough to delete the vertices that correspond to the subjects p with both sets B_p^1 and B_p^2 nonempty. □

The computer program that is currently in use for group placement was developed by Silvia Bodnárová (2015) for her bachelor thesis. Although an $O(\log n)$ approximation algorithm exists (Garg et al., 1994) for finding a minimum odd cycle transversal, she used a very simple heuristic to find a valid partition that consists of dividing each set $A_{p,q}$ into two halves A' and A'': in the first period the first half A' practices subject p and the second half A'' subject q; for the second period they simply switch the subjects. Although the number of sets in the obtained partition may be very far from the optimum (i.e., for the instance of Example 19.1 it outputs two sets for each of the subjects M,I,F), the fact that the sets still have to be divided into smaller groups implies that the final solution is in practice not so bad. Recall that the size of the final groups should be between 4 and 6 students (smaller groups are tolerated, for example if the total number of students with the given subject is too small). To get the final groups, observe that each integer $g \geq 8$ can be expressed in the form $g = 4x_6 + 5x_5 + 4x_4$ where x_6, x_5, x_4 are nonnegative integers. Table 19.4 lists the values of these coefficients minimizing the sum $x_6 + x_5 + x_4$ according to the division remainder z of g expressed in the form $g = 6y + z$.

Silvia's program applied to the lists of students from years the 2010 to 2016 was able to deal with each cohort of students in milliseconds, whilst for the single merged list of all students from these seven years containing more than 750 students it still needed less than 0.1 seconds. Perhaps surprisingly, the more students were in the list, the 'better' results were obtained. With smaller samples, sometimes groups containing only 2 or 3 students appeared (this only happened if for some p, the number of students in A_p was less than 16), but the members of the administrative staff were happy to find suitable mergers by hand, given that they were dealing with at most 20 students instead of around 100.

Division remainder	0	1	2	3	4	5
x_6	y	$y-2$	$y-1$	$y-1$	y	y
x_5	0	1	0	1	0	1
x_4	0	2	2	1	1	0

Table 19.4: The numbers of groups of sizes 6,5 and 4 for sets in a valid family

19.4 Individual Placement: Teaching

Individual placement means that the trainee teacher is alone with a group of pupils, observed by a supervising teacher. Students of our university teach both their specialization subjects during one placement period and for practical reasons and also to model everyday professional practice, the whole placement should take place at the same school. The requirement to teach *at least* a certain number of classes for each subject and have a supervising teacher for *both* specialization subjects leads to certain capacity restrictions on the side of schools, derived from the number of available supervising teachers, but also from the number of classes scheduled at the given school.

19.4.1 Mathematical Model and Complexity Results

There is a set S of m schools. Each school $s \in S$ has a certain capacity for each subject: the vector of capacities of school s is $c(s) = (c_1(s), \ldots, c_k(s)) \in \mathbb{N}^k$. An entry $c_p(s)$ of $c(s)$ will be referred to as a *partial capacity* of school s for subject p, meaning that it is the maximum number of applicants from A_p that school s is able to accept. Again, we shall sometimes write $c_M(s), c_I(s)$, etc.

We also suppose that an applicant a can provide a subset $S(a) \subseteq S$ of *acceptable* schools, i.e. schools to which he/she is willing to go. This can be justified as follows: a student has already done a placement at an elementary school, so now she would like to visit a different type of school. Or, a school is neither within the town of the student's residence nor in the locality of the university, so the need to commute may be prohibitive.

An instance of TAP is a triple $I = (P, A, S)$ of the sets of subjects, applicants (characterized by their specializations and sets $S(a)$ of acceptable schools) and schools (along with their partial capacities). Given an instance of TAP, an *assignment* $\mathcal{M}$ is a subset of $A \times S$ such that each applicant $a \in A$ is a member of at most one pair in $\mathcal{M}$. We shall write $\mathcal{M}(a) = s$ if $(a, s) \in \mathcal{M}$ and say that applicant a is *assigned* (to school s); if there is no such school, applicant a is *unassigned*. The set of applicants assigned to a school s will be denoted by $\mathcal{M}(s) = \{a \in A; (a, s) \in \mathcal{M}\}$. We shall also denote by $\mathcal{M}_p(s)$ the set of applicants assigned to school s whose specialization includes subject p and by $\mathcal{M}_{p,r}(s)$ the set of applicants assigned to s whose specialization is exactly the pair $\{p, r\}$. More precisely, $\mathcal{M}_p(s) = \{a \in A : (a, s) \in \mathcal{M} \;\&\; p \in p(a)\}$ and $\mathcal{M}_{p,r}(s) = \{a \in A : (a, s) \in \mathcal{M} \;\&\; \{p, r\} = p(a)\}$. An assignment $\mathcal{M}$ is *feasible* if $\mathcal{M}(a) \in S(a)$ for each $a \in A$ and $|\mathcal{M}_p(s)| \leq c_p(s)$ for each $s \in S$ and each $p \in P$.

MAX-TAP denotes the problem of deciding, given an instance J of TAP and an integer ℓ, whether a feasible assignment exists that assigns at least ℓ applicants. A special case of MAX-TAP asking for an assignment that leaves no student unassigned will be denoted by FULL-TAP.

Example 19.2. *Again, to get an idea of the difficulty of the problem, let us have a look at the following example. Trying to assign students one by one may lead to a maximal matching (no other student can be assigned). Clearly, not every maximal matching is maximum. In the TAP instance with the set of subjects $P = \{1, 2, 3\}$, given in Figure 19.5, the maximum matching is $\mathcal{M}_1 = \{(a_1, s_1), (a_2, s_1), (a_3, s_2)\}$ of size 3. Matching $\mathcal{M}_2 = \{(a_3, s_1)\}$ is maximal and its size is 1. This shows that the size of a maximal matching can be only one third of the size of a maximum matching. Cechlárová et al. (2015a) prove that it cannot be less.*

school	capacities for			applicant	type	acceptable schools
	1	2	3			
s_1	2	1	1	a_1	$\{1, 2\}$	s_1
s_2	0	1	1	a_2	$\{1, 3\}$	s_1
				a_3	$\{2, 3\}$	s_1, s_2

Table 19.5: An instance of TAP for Example 19.2

If there are only two subjects in a given instance then all applicants are in a sense equivalent and MAX-TAP reduces to the famous maximum cardinality matching problem in a bipartite graph. In what follows we list several results concerning the intractability of FULL-TAP and MAX-TAP as well as the identified polynomially solvable cases (Cechlárová et al., 2015b).

Theorem 19.2. FULL-TAP *is* NP-*complete even when* $|S(a)| \leq 3$ *for each* $a \in A$ *and*

(i) $|P| = 3$ *and no partial capacity of a school exceeds* 2; *or*

(ii) $|P| = 4$ *and no partial capacity of a school exceeds* 1,

but it is polynomially solvable if either $|P| = 2$, *or* $|P| = 3$ *and no partial capacity of a school exceeds* 1; *or if each applicant is allowed to list at most 2 acceptable schools and all partial capacities are at most* 1.

Theorem 19.3. MAX-TAP *is* NP-*complete, even in the following restricted cases:*

(i) $S(a) = S$ *for each applicant and no partial capacity exceeds 2;*

(ii) *each applicant is allowed to list at most 2 acceptable schools and all partial capacities are at most 1.*

The identified efficiently solvable special cases are of little practical significance. Therefore, the approximability of the optimization version of FULL-TAP was explored by Cechlárová et al. (2015a). Two greedy-like approximation algorithms were proposed. The theoretical approximation guarantees were $1/2$ and $2/k$ respectively, and although computational experiments showed a much better performance on the instances generated, we still preferred an exact algorithm based on integer programming.

19.4.2 Integer Linear Program, its Implementation and Application to Real Data

Taking into account the intractability results for MAX-TAP, we decided to use integer linear programming. This approach allows also for some special features that were encountered in the real data. First, we allow the possibility that some applicants, usually only a small proportion, need a placement for one subject only. This situation occurs if an applicant has received recognition for one of their subjects as a result of some other activity (e.g., teaching the subject in question in a specialized summer camp, working in a counseling center, etc.) or if the applicant has failed an exam that is a prerequisite for a particular subject and cannot therefore study that subject before resiting and passing the exam at a later date. Some placement schools also ask not to be sent more than a certain number of trainees at once, regardless of their specialization. We shall also describe the special treatment used in cases where students specializing in one subject are allowed to do their practical placement in another (related) subject. This is the case for students of Psychology, as the number of supervising teachers for them is not sufficient, moreover, elementary schools and most secondary schools do not teach Psychology as a separate subject. The common practice therefore is to allocate these students to either Ethics or Civics courses instead.

Let J be an instance of TAP with applicants $A = \{a_1, \ldots, a_n\}$, schools $S = \{s_1 \ldots, s_m\}$ and subjects $P = \{p_1, \ldots, p_k\}$. Let us associate with each applicant $a_i \in A$ a vector v^i of length k such that $v^i_p = 1$ if the specialization of a_i involves subject p and $v^i_p = 0$ otherwise. In our context, $v^i_p = 1$ for at most two values of p, for a given i, $(1 \leq i \leq n)$. Further, each applicant a_i has an ordered list of length $\ell(a_i)$ consisting of acceptable schools in $S(a_i)$. Let $pos(i, r, j) = 1$ if position r in the ordered list of applicant a_i contains school s_j, where $i = 1, 2, \ldots, n$, $r = 1, 2, \ldots, \ell(a_i)$, $j = 1, 2, \ldots, m$ and $pos(i, r, j) = 0$ otherwise.

The set of variables will be $X = \{x^i_r := 1, 2, \ldots, n, r = 1, 2, \ldots, \ell(a_i) + 1\}$ with the following interpretation:

$$x^i_r = \begin{cases} 1 & \text{if } a_i \text{ is assigned to the school in position } r \text{ in her list} \\ 0 & \text{otherwise} \end{cases}$$

for $r = 1, 2, \ldots, \ell(a_i)$, and

$$x^i_{\ell(a_i)+1} = \begin{cases} 1 & \text{if } a_i \text{ is unmatched} \\ 0 & \text{otherwise.} \end{cases}$$

We consider the following integer linear program:

$$\sum_{i=1}^{n} \sum_{r=1}^{\ell(a_i)} x^i_r \;\to\; max$$

$$\sum_{r=1}^{\ell(a_i)+1} x^i_r \;=\; 1 \text{ for } i = 1, \ldots, n$$

$$\sum_{i=1}^{n} \sum_{r=1}^{\ell(a_i)} pos(i,r,j) v^i_p x^i_r \;\leq\; c_p(s_j) \text{ for } j = 1, \ldots, m, \; p = 1, \ldots, k$$

$$x^i_r \;\in\; \{0,1\} \text{ for } j = 1, \ldots, n, \; r = 1, \ldots, \ell(a_i) + 1$$

The first set of constraints ensure that each applicant is assigned to exactly one school or is unassigned. The second set of constraints (notice that they are linear, since $pos(i,r,j)$ and v^i_p are constants) ensure that the number of applicants from A_p that are assigned to school s_j does not exceed the partial capacity $c_p(s_j)$ of subject p at school s_j. It is obvious that an optimal solution of this linear integer program corresponds to a solution of MAX-TAP.

Let us now describe how we handled the possibility that it may be acceptable to assign applicants whose specialization involves a certain subject (for simplicity, let us suppose that the index of this subject is 1), to places of some related subjects (here, again for ease of exposition, let us suppose that these related subjects are indexed by 2 and 3). First, let us denote the set of applicants a_i in $A_1 \setminus (A_2 \cup A_3)$, i.e., those with $v^i_1 = 1$ and $v^i_2 = v^i_3 = 0$, by A'. For each $a_i \in A'$ we created two clones a_{i+n} and a_{i+2n}, such that

$$v^{i+n}_1 = 0; \; v^{i+n}_2 = 1; \; v^{i+n}_3 = 0;$$
$$v^{i+2n}_1 = 0; \; v^{i+2n}_2 = 0; \; v^{i+2n}_3 = 1;$$
$$v^{i+n}_j = v^{i+2n}_j = v^i_j \text{ for each } j > 3.$$

The lists of acceptable schools for both clones of a_i are the same as that of a_i. The constraints applied to a_i are applied in similar fashion to a_{i+n} and a_{i+2n}.

Since we require that at most one of the three clones be matched, the unmatched position $\ell(a_i) + 1$ may be 0 for at most one of the three clones. Thus the sum across the 3 unmatched positions must be greater than or equal to 2, i.e. for each $a_i \in A'$ we add a constraint

$$x^i_{\ell(a_i)+1} + x^{i+n}_{\ell(a_i)+1} + x^{i+2n}_{\ell(a_i)+1} \geq 2.$$

The results of the application of an implementation with IP solver CPLEX 12.4 to the list of 175 schools used before 2015 were reported by Cechlárová et al. (2015b). The software that is currently in use at our university was implemented

| | | without replacement for Psychology | | with replacement for Psychology | |
Year	# of students	time	# of assigned	time	# of assigned
2010	103	0.66	95	0.87	101
2011	118	3.42	90	16.18	98
2012	100	0.49	77	8.11	93
2013	138	1.10	114	34.17	116
2014	82	0.38	73	0.60	78
2015	107	0.61	93	0.91	100
2016	102	0.59	94	0.90	100

Table 19.6: Experiments with real data

by Michal Barančík (2015) in Java using the open source library *lpsolve.jar*. Experiments were carried out on a desktop PC with an Intel i5-2500 3.3Ghz processor, with 4GB of memory running Windows 7 Enterprise.

We tested this implementation using the real data of students from the years 2010 to 2016. Their numbers varied from a minimum of 82 to a maximum of 138. The list of schools was in all cases the same, containing 53 schools, all in Košice. The numbers of assigned students and run-times in seconds for individual years are contained in Table 19.6.

However, the free Java LP-solver got close to its limits. When we submitted combined two-year lists, in several cases we did not obtain a solution within 10 minutes, so decided to stop the computation.

Acknowledgments

Putting the theoretical results into practical use would not be possible without the open minds, willingness to cooperate and to change their previous routine of Renáta Orosová and Zuzana Boberová (Nováková). Roman Soták was kind to extract the data from the university information system. People who prepared the user-friendly software packages, promised to maintain them in the future, provided technical support to administrative staff and helped to carry out the numerical experiments are Michal Barančík, Silvia Bodnárová and Lukáš Miňo. David Manlove helped to improve the language of this text.

Bibliography

D. J. Abraham, R. W. Irving, and D. F. Manlove. Two algorithms for the Student-Project Allocation problem. *Journal of Discrete Algorithms*, 5(1):73–90, 2007.

M. Barančík. Integer linear programming in matching problems (in Slovak). BSc thesis, Faculty of Science, P. J. Šafárik University, Košice, 2015.

S. Bodnárová. Flows in networks and matching problems (in Slovak). BSc thesis, Faculty of Science, P. J. Šafárik University, Košice, 2015.

K. Cechlárová, P. Eirinakis, T. Fleiner, D. Magos, I. Mourtos, and E. Oceláková. Approximation algorithms for the teachers assignment problem. In *Proceedings of the 13th International Symposium on Operations Research (SOR)*, pages 479–484, 2015a.

K. Cechlárová, T. Fleiner, D. Manlove, I. McBride, and E. Potpinková. Modelling practical placement of trainee teachers to schools. *Central European Journal of Operations Research*, 23(3):547–562, 2015b.

K. Cechlárová, T. Fleiner, D. Manlove, and I. McBride. Stable matchings of teachers to schools. *Theoretical Computer Science*, 653:15–25, 2016.

D. Delacrètaz, S. D. Kominers, and A. Teytelboym. Refugee resettlement. Manuscript, 2016.

A. M. Frieze and J. Yadegar. An algorithm for solving 3-dimensional assignment problems with application to scheduling a teaching practice. *Journal of the Operational Research Society*, 32(11):989–995, 1981.

M. Garey and D. Johnson. *Computers and Intractability*. Freeman, 1979.

N. Garg, V. V. Vazirani, and M. Yannakakis. Multiway cuts in directed and node weighted graphs. In *Proceedings of the 21st International Colloquium on Automata, Languages and Programming (ICALP)*, pages 487–498. Springer, 1994.

R. W. Irving. Matching medical students to pairs of hospitals: A new variation on a well-known theme. In *Proceedings of the 6th Annual European Symposium of the European Symposium on Algorithms (ESA)*, pages 381–392. Springer, 1998.

A. Kwanashie, R. W. Irving, D. F. Manlove, and C. T. S. Sng. Profile-based optimal matchings in the student/project allocation problem. In *Proceedings of the 26th International Workshop on Combinatorial Algorithms (IWOCA)*, pages 213–225. Springer, 2015.

D. F. Manlove and G. O'Malley. Student-project allocation with preferences over projects. *Journal of Discrete Algorithms*, 6(4):553–560, 2008.

E. McDermid and D. F. Manlove. Keeping partners together: Algorithmic results for the hospitals/residents problem with couples. *Journal of Combinatorial Optimization*, 19(3):279–303, 2010.

B. Reed, K. Smith, and A. Vetta. Finding odd cycle transversals. *Operations Research Letters*, 32(4):299–301, 2004.

CHAPTER 20

Social Choice on the Web

Sylvain Bouveret

In this chapter, we will speak about the development and use of a web application dedicated to social choice, Whale.[1] The chapter is intended to be a compilation of lessons learned from the users of this web application, rather an extensive presentation of it. We will see through specific use cases what concrete problems have been encountered during the development of this web application.

20.1 Introduction

The history of social choice theory is paved with paradoxes. Of course, theoretical peculiarities like the Condorcet Paradox or Arrow's Theorem form the basis of the discipline. But social choice even seems to be inherently paradoxical at the epistemological level.

First example: Social Choice Theory has been being studied in its modern form for two centuries — if we date back the birth of modern social choice to the debates between Condorcet and Borda in the late 18th century. During the history of this discipline, a lot of theoretical knowledge about collective decision making and voting procedures has been accumulated. Yet, until recently, the occasions to really put this knowledge into practice in everyday life were rather infrequent and limited to political elections or particular situations (like scientific committees). As a consequence of this distortion between theory and practice of social choice, lessons and knowledge learned from the theoretical study of collective decision making did not seem to have much influence on the way people practice elections.[2] This can be well explained. In the rare occasions where people really practice voting, the stakes and the exogenous influences (political, cultural, ...) are usually so high that nobody would ever think of questioning the voting process itself.

Second example: although people only seldomly experiment with voting, practical situations of making collective decisions happen every day. A group of friends deciding which movie to watch, colleagues choosing a date for a meeting, a recruitment committee hiring a candidate for a job, ... All these situations that

---

[1] WHich ALternative is Elected. Current version accessible at: https://whale.imag.fr/
[2] The converse can also be observed to some extent, where the models at the heart of social choice are often based on very strong assumptions, the practical relevance of which can be questioned, or at least need to be confronted with experiment.

usually do not require a formal vote are nevertheless collective decision making situations. These everyday life situations would be perfect candidates for applying the formal knowledge brought by voting theorists. Usually the stakes remain quite low, but are still high enough to require an enlightened decision that voting theory can provide.

Bringing voting theory to these kinds of everyday situations was still hardly conceivable until recently. One major reason is that the logistical burden required to implement the least voting procedure (expressing a linear order in practice, tallying the votes, ...) is often too high to be reasonable. Another major reason is that most people are simply not aware of the fact that it is possible to vote other than by simply writing one name on the ballot sheet and choosing as the winner the candidate voted for most often.[3]

Two recent major scientific and technological breakthroughs that have nothing to do with social choice have dramatically changed things. The first one is the advent of computer networks and the World Wide Web. This has a major impact on the democratisation of social choice for several reasons. First, it makes the implementation of light remote voting systems possible. Human computer interfaces make possible the use of ways of expressing preferences that would have been unpractical otherwise, and enable the access to automatic tallying procedures. Second, it multiplies collective decision-making-like situations: social networks, recommender systems, and so on. Finally, computer networks have considerably changed the way knowledge disseminates. This also applies to voting: new citizens' initiatives to promote alternative voting procedures appear every day. They spread much faster and further than they used to, and as a consequence they disseminate in some way ideas from social choice theory.

The second major breakthrough is the advent of mobile devices. Ubiquity has a major impact on social choice. It now becomes possible to use computer-aided collective decision making in virtually every situation. More than that, it has brought connectivity and technology to a substantial part of the population that was before excluded from the technological sphere.

Social choice is facing a unique situation in its history. It is no longer limited to the political and scientific communities, but it is now ready to be widely applied. The goal of this chapter is to analyse the major difficulties that social choice theorists will probably have to face if they want to apply social choice in practice. The considerations proposed in this chapter are inspired by the active development of a web application dedicated to social choice. It is important to note that this is by no means intended to be the description of scientific results obtained by a rigorous experimental approach. It can be seen as nothing more than a compilation of lessons learned from the user experience with this platform. Moreover, this chapter voluntarily excludes the security issues posed by electronic voting. We make the assumption that the collective decision making situations analysed here are uncritical situations (further referred to as low- and middle-stake situations) where the voters can tolerate some lack of guarantees in terms of security, authentication and certification.

This chapter is organised as follows. First, we will quickly explain the main

---

[3]Except for the few countries — like Ireland — where people vote by ranking (or approving / disapproving) candidates for political elections.

features and objectives of the Whale web application in Section 20.2. Then, in Section 20.3, we will describe a particular use case and analyse the users' behaviour and impressions. Finally, in Section 20.4, we try to give more general lessons learned from the everyday use of the platform.

20.2 Whale: A Web Application for Social Choice

20.2.1 Goals and History

The genesis of Whale dates back to 2010 when we started to develop a small and lightweight web application dedicated to voting. At the beginning, this application was just intended to be an alternative to well-known and widely used poll applications like Doodle® or Framadate. The initial observation was that such applications were very efficient tools to help solving collective decision making problems that happen in our everyday life (like choosing a restaurant, a candidate for a position, a date for a meeting, ...), but were sometimes too simple to adequately represent the complexity of the individuals' preferences. For instance, most of these tools are limited to the expression of binary (Yes / No) preferences, but for some applications this is not enough. As an example, in situations where a group of people has to hire someone for a job, it is reasonable to assume that the participants have more in mind than a simple dichotomy between approved and disapproved candidates. When collectively choosing a date for a meeting, we are often faced with the situation where some date is not completely unavailable to us, but is not ideal either, whatever it may mean. In such situations, it could be useful to provide the participants with a way of expressing more subtle preferences than just approving / disapproving alternatives.[4]

Even if there is a clear method to choose the winning option when we deal with approval (Yes / No) ballots, namely the one which consists in choosing the option that is approved by a maximal number of participants, this is not so clear anymore once the participants can choose among strictly more than two possible evaluations for each option.[5] In this case, there exist several collective decision making procedures. All of them satisfy their own properties, but none is always better than the others, so the procedure has to be carefully chosen, depending on the context of the decision making problem.

Hence, as we can see, a lot of people use poll applications to make collective decisions nowadays, but these applications are sometimes too simple to adequately represent preferences and reflect the complexity of collective decision making. On the other hand, social choice theory provides all the mathematical background and models to make well-informed collective decisions. The main rationale of Whale is to try to bridge the gap between these two worlds.

As of January 2017, four versions of Whale have been released. The main reasons for this evolution are mainly technical: technologies tend to evolve more quickly in the context of web applications than in any other context. Developing

---

[4]The best evidence of this affirmation is that popular poll applications now propose to the participants an intermediate level "(Yes)" between Yes and No.

[5]Or as soon as we are in the multiwinner case, which we exclude from the scope of this chapter.

an upgradable, maintainable, reusable and durable code is a real challenge and it is often easier to restart everything from scratch than to make the code evolve.

The first version of Whale was issued in 2010. At this time, it was just a very simple web application, developed in PHP with a Postgres backend for the persistent data storage. The second version was developed by a team of students in 2012, using Java and the web framework Play (`https://playframework.com/`). Both versions had the same functionalities: registered users could create polls (date or classical) with several possible ballot types (approval, scores, rankings with or without ties), users could vote, and the results given by several voting rules where displayed using a simple table (as in Figure 20.1).

	April 2012					
	Monday, 2nd		Tuesday, 3rd		Wednesday, 4th	
	matin	après-midi	matin	après-midi	matin	après-midi
Hide the votes						
Sylvain B.	5	5	4	0	3	2
Herbert	0	0	4	5	4	2
Marvin	4	3	5	5	2	2
Alcybiade	5	5	3	3	5	5
Grogro	2	2	0	0	4	5
Borda	16	15	16	13	18	16
Majority	2	2	1	2	1	2
Veto	4	4	4	3	5	5
Bucklin	2	2	2	4	1	3
Leximin SWO	5	3	3	0	3	2
Leximax SWO	3	0	5	0	5	3
Nash SWO	540	432	600	144	1800	972
Condorcet Winner	(no winner)					
Copeland	3	1	-1	-4	2	-1
Maximin (Simpson)	1	0	1	1	2	1
Display Condorcet matrix						

Figure 20.1: Results of different voting procedures in the first version of Whale.

The third version of Whale was released in 2013, with the clear idea to focus on a better presentation of the results given by different voting rules. For that, we used data visualisation techniques, as we will see later. This version was developed in Scala / Java Servlet Pages and Postgres / JDBC for the backend, and the data visualisation was based on the D3.js library (`https://d3js.org/`). The last version of Whale (Whale 4) is in testing phase since September 2016. For this new version, the main focus was made on the simplicity of use and the responsiveness of the application (adaptation to mobile devices). It was developed in Python with the Django framework (`https://www.djangoproject.com/`), is based on the Bootstrap framework (`http://getbootstrap.com/`) for the responsiveness, and still on D3.js for data visualisation.

20.2.2 Features

Since the first version, the objectives of Whale have slightly evolved and this application now has three main goals:

- to be used by non-specialists as a poll and voting platform;
- to be used by researchers and teachers as a pedagogical resource to illustrate the concepts of voting;
- to be used by researchers as a source of real voting data for experiments.

Whale currently supports two kinds of decision problems, corresponding to two different situations:

- open-ballot polls, where anyone can participate, and everyone can see the preferences of the participants;
- sealed-ballot elections, which are accessible only at the invitation of the poll's creator. Each participant receives an individual 16-characters code that must be used to connect to the poll. A voter can modify her vote any number of times until the poll closes. When the poll closes, the ballots are publicly displayed, just hiding the names of the corresponding voters to guarantee anonymity.

Poll creators can currently choose between five ballot types: approval (Yes / No), scores (from 0 to 10), qualitative scale (--, -, 0, +, ++), rankings with ties, rankings without ties. Depending on the ballot type chosen, several methods are proposed to compute the collective preference and the election winner. Contrary to other voting platforms, the approach chosen was not to force the choice of a particular voting rule, but rather to provide decision makers with all the tools to understand the voters' preferences, discuss them, and make enlightened decisions. Hence, the users can see at any time the results suggested by several relevant voting procedures. In the first two versions of Whale, these results were given as tables of scores (see Figure 20.1). However, we observed that these tables were difficult to interpret, especially when the winners differed from one voting rule to another. In the subsequent versions of Whale, we have put a lot of effort into developing data visualisation modules to present these results in an easily understandable way. Four kinds of modules (illustrated in Figures 20.2, 20.3, 20.4 and 20.5 on the best poster election use case presented in Section 20.3) dedicated to four kinds of voting rules have been developed so far.

- Histogram-based visualisations for scoring rules (see Figure 20.2, left), and a specific view dedicated to approval voting (Figure 20.2, right).
- Representations of the majority graph for Condorcet-consistent methods. Here, we use two different representations of the majority graph: a node-link representation where the thickness of a link encodes the margin information (see Figure 20.3 left), and an incidence matrix representation, with lines and columns ordered according to a particular score chosen among Copeland 0, Copeland 1 and maximin (see Figure 20.3 right). We also use colour to

encode the information about the margin (for a case of the matrix) or the score of a candidate (for a node of the graph). This work on the majority graph has been extended to graph-compressed representations that seem to be quite efficient visualisation ways (Karanikolas et al., 2016), but this work has not been implemented in Whale yet.

- Run-off methods like plurality with run-off or Single Transferable Vote, where we simply display the list of candidates present in each round with the score they obtain in this round (see Figure 20.4).

- Randomized cups, displayed exactly like the board of a sport cup having candidates as participants (see Figure 20.5).

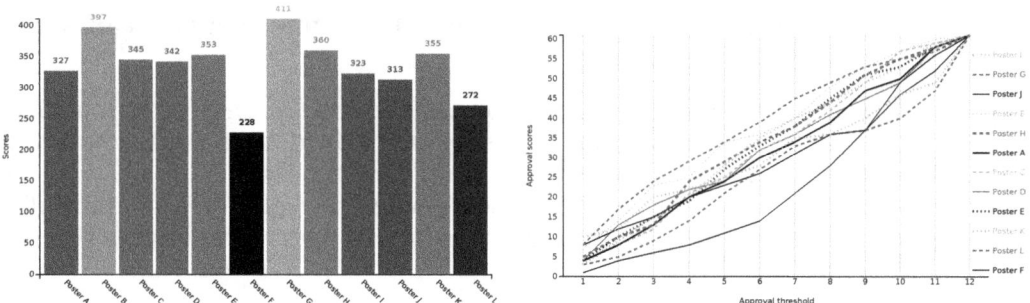

Figure 20.2: Graphical view for scoring functions in Whale 4 (for the best poster election). The left picture shows the Borda scores of the candidates. In the right picture, each curve corresponds to a candidate c and is a graphical representation of the function mapping a rank k to the k-approval score of c.

Beyond data visualisation techniques, the raw data of each poll can be accessed through an HTTP API, and the raw (and anonymous) data of all the polls of the database can be downloaded on the website. Currently three formats are supported: CSV, JSON and Preflib (see Mattei and Walsh, 2013, and Chapter 15 of this book). This data is provided for two main reasons. First, we hope that researchers will find valuable real-world data for their experiments. Second, providing an access to the data independently of any visualisation or aggregation technique gives the opportunity to the developers to extend the visualisation modules of Whale by developing their own representations of the voting profiles.

Other Existing Voting Platforms. Whale is certainly not the only online voting platform project. If we exclude popular aforementioned poll applications, we can cite two interesting and successful projects from academia: Pnyx (https://pnyx.dss.in.tum.de/) and Robovote (http://robovote.org/). Both also aim at bringing social choice theory to ordinary people by providing user-friendly collective decision making interfaces. Pnyx (Brandt et al., 2015) proposes several ways of expressing preferences (first-past-the-post, approval, ranking with ties, rankings without ties, pairwise comparisons), and several outputs are possible: unique winner, lottery, ranking without ties. Depending on the input and output

Social Choice on the Web

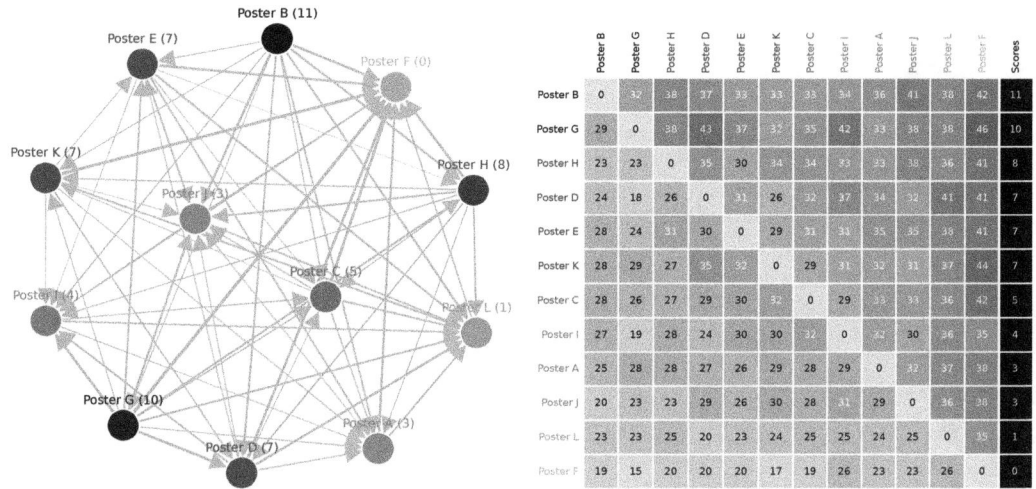

Figure 20.3: The majority graph and its adjacency matrix for the best poster election. In the matrix, the rows and the columns are ordered by decreasing Copeland score.

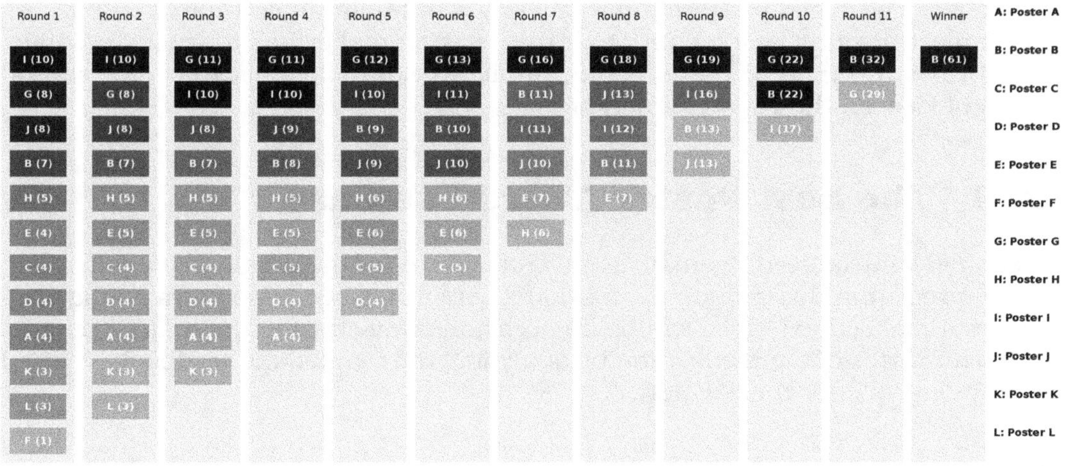

Figure 20.4: Graphical view for run-off methods in Whale 4 (for the best poster election). The picture shows the candidate ordering in the different rounds of the Single Transferable Vote method.

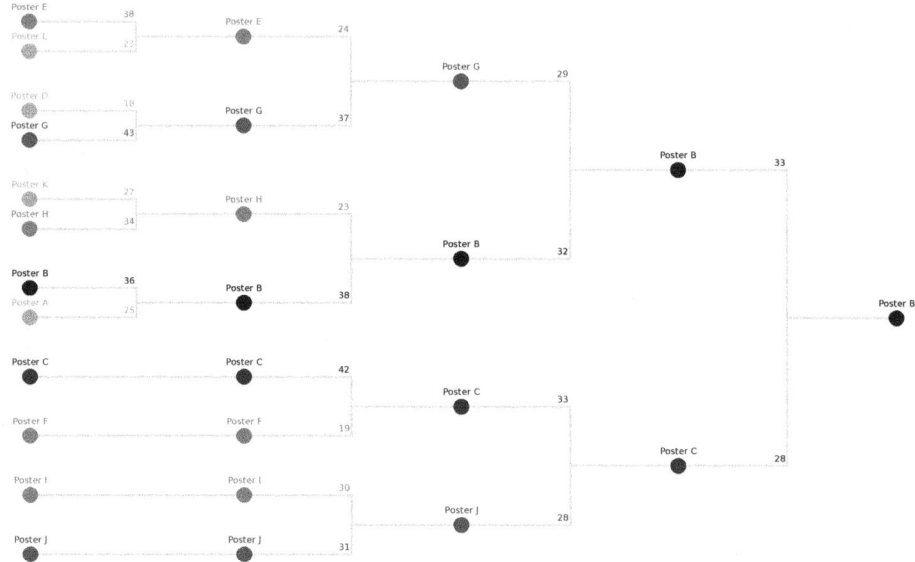

Figure 20.5: Graphical view of randomized cups in Whale 4 (for the best poster election).

types, a different aggregation rule is used. Robovote (Caragiannis et al., 2017) adopts a different point of view. Preferences are always given as rankings, but a different aggregation rule is used according to whether these preferences are supposed to be estimators of a ground truth ("objective" preferences) or totally subjective. These two platforms have clearly a different objective from Whale, as they impose a voting rule *a priori*, that the decision maker has to trust. In Whale, voting rules are more seen as voting profile exploration tools that give several points of view on the voters' preferences.

20.3 The Best Poster Award Use Case

After having introduced the main goals and features of the Whale web application, we will present in this section a situation where it has been used as a voting platform in a real context. This will be an occasion of discussing the main strengths and weaknesses of the application by analysing the results and feedback received from the users after the election.

20.3.1 Organisation

The situation we will speak about in this section is the election of the best poster in the main French-speaking conference in Geomatics, SAGEO'14 (https://sageo2014.sciencesconf.org/). The conference involved about 120 participants, and 12 posters — referred to as Poster A to Poster L — were competing for the best poster award. It is important to note that most of the participants

Social Choice on the Web 395

(*i.e.*, the pool of voters) were from the field of geography, mathematics or computer science, but to the best of our knowledge none of them had a background in collective decision making.

From a practical point of view, each participant was given — together with the conference kit distributed at the registration desk — a voting sheet containing the following information:

- the direct URL to the voting page;

- a personal 16-characters voting code (randomly generated by Whale);

- the list of posters with labels (A...L), authors, titles.

The vote was opened during the first two days of the conference and was closed just a few minutes before the session dedicated to the best poster award (which shows the advantages of automatic tallying). People were free to vote using their own laptops or smartphones, but could also use a computer which was provided by the organisers.

The voting process was presented during the opening session of the conference. During this session, we presented the technical details concerning the connection to the voting page and the voting procedure that would be used to elect the winner. The choice we made was to ask participants to give complete rankings of the posters and to give the best poster award to the Condorcet winner if there is one, and to the Borda winner otherwise. This choice was made both for pedagogical and for simplicity purposes: the goal was mainly to promote alternative voting procedures which are easy to explain, to implement and to understand, and have well-known and good properties. As we will see later, this choice is debatable.

20.3.2 Feedback and Results

In the end, 61 persons took part to the vote, in other words, slightly more than half of the attendees, which is a reasonable score. We collected some feedback on the voting process by directly and informally discussing with the voters. Three kinds of remarks were made by several participants.

- Most people had never voted electronically before for this kind of elections, and had never used rankings to vote for an election. Most of them had not heard at all of the voting procedures we used before the presentation during the opening session. They seemed to be very happy to discover these kinds of methods, and had a real interest in alternative voting procedures. From this point of view, the data visualisation, may they be simple and imperfect, were helpful tools to better understand how these procedures work.

- On the negative side, rather surprisingly, a common remark is that having to type a 16-characters code to access the personal voting page was quite burdensome. This remark speaks for the use of light authentication processes for non-critical settings, at the price of lower security guarantees (see Section 20.4.1).

- Concerning the voting procedure itself, a very important remark is that asking for complete rankings was completely inappropriate in an election setting with 12 candidates where people usually have clear preferences over not more than 4 or 5 candidates.

When the poll closed, we used Whale to tally the votes and determine the winner of the best poster award. The majority graph of the election is shown in Figure 20.3.

It turns out that there was a Condorcet winner — Poster B — that should have been elected according to the voting rule chosen. However, if we have a closer look at the majority margin matrix shown in Figure 20.3, we notice that Poster G is very close to being a Condorcet winner but is not because it loses against Poster B with a margin of 3 votes (32 voters in favour of Poster B, 29 in favour of Poster G).

Let us have a look at the winner given by the most classical scoring voting rules, which are not Condorcet-consistent. Poster B is the (co-)winner only for $\{5,9,10,11\}$-approval (hence Veto), whereas Poster G wins for $\{2,3,4,5,6,7,8,9\}$-approval and for Borda, and defeats Poster B for the plurality rule.

The settings where different voting rules yield different winners are not uncommon, and are simply due to the fact that they are based on different normative definitions of a democratic consensus and on different interpretations of the voters' preferences. However, a basic analysis of the profile reveals that the majority in favour of Poster B might not be only due to a natural interpretation of the voters' rankings.

Namely, if we look at the voting profile, we observe a clear bias in favour of candidates appearing earlier in alphabetical order. This bias seems to increase as candidates approach from the end of the rankings. This impression is confirmed by a numerical analysis of the profile.[6] Table 20.1 shows the normalized Kendall-Tau distance (that is, the number of pairwise disagreements divided by the total number of pairs) between alphabetical orders and voters' rankings for the k worst and the k best candidates in the rankings.

k	2	3	4	5	6
δ (%) for the k worst	34.4	42.6	38.3	40.2	44.3
δ (%) for the k best	57.4	51.4	49.7	49.8	49.5

Table 20.1: Normalized Kendall-Tau distance between alphabetical orders and voters' rankings for the k worst candidates and the k best candidates in the rankings.

This table clearly shows that near the bottom of the ranking, the voters tend to agree more with alphabetical order than near the top. How does it apply to Poster B and Poster G? Table 20.2 shows the number of voters for which B and G both appear amongst the last k candidates of the ranking and preferring Poster B (resp. G) to Poster G (resp. B).

---

[6]This analysis just shows some informal trends, as a rigorous analysis would have required to start from a hypothesis on the probability distribution of the votes and evaluate it as regards to the data obtained during the election.

k	2	3	4	5	6	7	8	9	10	11	12
$\#(B \succ G)$	1	1	2	6	8	8	11	12	20	25	32
$\#(G \succ B)$	0	0	0	0	1	3	6	10	14	21	29
Ratio (%)	0	0	0	0	11.1	27.3	35.3	45.5	41.2	45.7	47.5

Table 20.2: Number of voters preferring Poster B (resp. G) to Poster G (resp. B) when B and G both appear amongst the last k candidates in the rankings.

Since about 47.5% of the voters prefer Poster G to B in general, there is no special reason that this ratio changes a lot when the preferences are limited to the bottom k ranks. Table 20.2 shows exactly the contrary. When B and G are both at the bottom of the ranking, there is a much higher probability that G is ranked after B (hence respecting alphabetical order) than the other way around.

The reasons of this obvious bias are pretty clear and are to be related to the aforementioned feedback on the voting procedure: most people have clear preferences on the first 4 or 5 candidates at most, but tend to order the rest of the candidates randomly.[7] In Whale, the interaction effort required by adding candidates at the end of the ranking is significantly lower if they are added in the same order as they appear on the voting page (in alphabetical order in the case of the best poster election). That clearly explains the bias we observe at the bottom of the rankings. This phenomenon could have been anticipated, since this bias has already been clearly observed and measured by groups of researchers in the context of real political elections (see *e.g.* Krosnick, 2006; Ho and Imai, 2008).

We can learn at least two lessons from this analysis. First, where the context permits it, the voting interface should be designed so as to break any *a priori* order in the presentation of the candidates. A solution can be for instance to shuffle the candidate list every time a new voter accesses to the voting page. Secondly, when the number of candidates exceeds 4 or 5, one should absolutely avoid asking for complete rankings, except in very specific contexts where each voter absolutely knows every candidate and needs to give a clear opinion on each of them.

Epilogue. In the end, it was quite clear from the analysis of the voting profile that even if Poster B was the Condorcet winner, it probably was for exogenous reasons that had nothing to do with the quality of the work perceived by the voters, whereas there seemed to be strong arguments justifying the fact that Poster G is actually a better candidate than Poster B. We hence decided to manipulate the election by changing the rules and giving the best poster award to both Poster B and G. We carefully explained the reasons of this change to the voters. This change was possible because we were in a rather small community of well-intentioned candidates and voters. In a higher-stake context, things would have been very different and it would have been all the more important to carefully choose the procedure and test the interface before proceeding to the election.

---

[7]This is not always the case. For political elections, for instance, we can reasonably assume that people might have a clear idea about both the top and the bottom of the ranking, with a pool of candidates with unclear order in-between.

20.4 Lessons Learned from Ordinary Users

We have described in the previous section the feedback received from the participants to a real election having used Whale as a voting platform. In this section we will now give some informal feedback received from people using Whale on a regular basis for everyday collective decision making. This feedback provides very useful insights on how to improve the user experience on a poll / voting platform. More importantly, it also gives directions and priorities for future research on social choice, by pointing to some practical problems that still need appropriate theoretical models and solutions.

20.4.1 Lighter is (Often) Better

The first important lesson learned from personal experience is that the success of a collective decision making platform like Whale largely depends on a careful analysis of its use cases and of its intended users. At the heart of this analysis, it is especially important to understand the stakes of the typical voting situations that the application will have to process. In the context of voting, we can typically distinguish three kinds of situations:

- high-stake elections like political elections, for which the requirements in terms of confidentiality, verifiability, transparency and availability are so high (and attackers potentially so equipped) that they require specific tools with mathematically provable properties[8] — like Belenios for instance (see Cortier et al., 2013);

- middle-stake elections like local political elections or recruitment for a job, where some mild guarantees must be given on the transparency of the process and the anonymity of the ballots, but where it is acceptable for the users to trust a third-party application and nobody has a high incentive to attack the voting server to manipulate the election;

- low-stake elections where the participants trust each other and the voting platform is just there to help people express their preferences about a set of options and discuss about them.

We can observe that most collective decision making we are faced with in our everyday life falls in the third category. In this case, it is crucial for the process to be as easy, light, and permissive as possible. These features are often contradictory with the standard point of view in voting that usually assumes that: (i) the set of candidates is fixed beforehand and does not evolve in time, (ii) votes are personal, and should not be altered or removed by anyone other than the voter herself, and (iii) it is forbidden for the same person to vote several times. In traditional voting theory, any action contradicting these three assumptions is seen as a (malicious) manipulation, either by the voters or by the chair herself. Experience shows that in many situations, it is perfectly fine for the system to allow these actions, mostly because we are the context of small communities

---

[8]It is even doubtful that any form of electronic or online voting can guarantee these properties.

where participants all know and trust each other and have a strong incentive to find a consensus that is beneficial to everyone. If the system is too restrictive, it can be observed that participants will try to tweak it to do what they want to do (for instance vote several times if they cannot modify votes, create new polls if they cannot add / remove candidates...), or simply not use it and switch to a more permissive system.

These observations thus argue for having two different sets of parameters: one dedicated to middle-stake elections that gives some mild guarantees on the verification of the usual assumptions (fixed set of candidates and voters, one vote for each voter, a vote cannot be altered...), and one dedicated to everyday situations and permitting every action. This last situation has not been studied so much by social choice theorists to the best of our knowledge, which shows a first divergence between theory and what people really do in practice.

20.4.2 Preference Representation

The second divergence concerns preference representation. In practice, voting procedures usually ask for one name on a ballot. There are many reasons for that: it is cognitively simple, easily understandable, and simplifies tallying.

At the other end of the scale, social choice theory is usually based on the assumption that a voting procedure takes a profile of linear orders (complete rankings) as input, and outputs either a collective ranking, a winner, or a set of co-winners. Hence, the traditional assumption is that each voter is able to rank all the candidates. As we have seen in Section 20.3, this assumption is just completely unrealistic as soon as there are more than four or five candidates to rank. As a result, the order given for the candidates at the bottom of the scale (or around the middle, depending on the context) is meaningless, or, worse, can be strongly biased.

There are many intermediate ways of expressing preferences on a ballot. The right level for most applications is probably to ask people to give scores to candidates, scores being taken from a small qualitative or numerical scale (*e.g.*, $\{\text{Yes}, \text{No}\}$, $\{-1, 0, 1\}$, $\{0, \ldots, 5\}$, $\{--, -, 0, +, ++\}$, ...). Even if a setting like approval voting is well understood and has been widely studied, this does not seem to be the case for other score-based ballot settings,[9] in spite of the obvious cognitive interest in this kind of ballots.

20.4.3 Incomplete Preferences

The third divergence that we can observe between theory and practice concerns potentially incomplete preferences. Whereas most work in voting theory assumes that the voters express complete preferences, in the sense that they express a clear opinion (rank, score, ...) on each candidate, we cannot rule out the possibility that a voter is unable to do so in practice, particularly when the number of candidates is high as in the example we have discussed in Section 20.3. Moreover, as soon as we allow the set of candidates to be dynamic and candidates to

---

[9]Apart from work in experimental voting that analyses the behavioural differences induced by different scoring scales.

be added during the election, as we have seen in Section 20.4.1, we need to be able to deal with incomplete ballots, since at the time we add new candidates, we do not know yet the opinion on these candidates of the voters that have already voted.

There are two usual ways of dealing with incomplete preferences. The first possibility is to ignore them and force people to give an opinion for every single candidate (*e.g.*, a complete ranking).

The second way of dealing with incomplete preferences is to use a kind of ballot with possible indifferences between candidates (*e.g.*, rankings with ties, truncated rankings, approval ballots, ...) and use a default value for each candidate not evaluated by the voter (for instance "No" for approval, not-ranked for truncated rankings, 0 for the numerical scale $\{0, \ldots, 5\}$).

None of these methods is satisfactory. We have seen earlier how bad the first method can be. The second method can be seen as a workaround, but turns out to be really unsatisfactory in some contexts, because giving a default value to a given candidate is different from the absence of information concerning this candidate. Let us take for instance the voting situation considered by Karanikolas et al. (2016) about the election of the best movie among the ten most popular movies of the last decades according to IMDB registered users. Most voters only had a partial opinion about the movies, just because they had not watched them all. If we ask their opinion on a $\{0, \ldots, 5\}$ numerical scale, assuming that the default value is 0, we will simply not be able to distinguish between a movie they have not watched and a movie they have not liked at all.

These examples show how crucial it is to provide voters with a way not to give any opinion on some candidates. Otherwise, the process of voting will be painful to them, and the result given by the voting procedure might be biased or irrelevant. However, the ways to deal with incomplete ballots is still not clear. Collective decision making in this context probably comes down to the following question: *between a well-known candidate which is just moderately appreciated by everyone and a candidate that just a few voters know but about which all of them are very enthusiastic, which one should be elected?* The answer to this question probably depends on the context, but incomplete preferences would probably deserve a careful attention from the scientific community.

20.4.4 Multiple Voting Procedures

The final issue we will quickly discuss is a well-known difficulty related to the nature of social choice itself, and that is as old as the scientific discussion between Jean-Charles de Borda and Nicolas de Condorcet about the respective merits of different voting systems. As soon as there are more than two candidates to choose from and we ask the voters for more than approval ballots, there are several ways of electing the winner of the election, all corresponding to a different notion of consensus. Worse, there are extreme cases where each candidate is declared winner of the election by a different voting rule. The problem of choosing the *right* voting rule, whatever it means, is not simple in this case.

There are several possible approaches to this problem. First, we can impose a voting rule *a priori* and choose the winner according to this voting rule. This is the approach used by several voting platforms.[10] We could also think of letting election chairs (or even the voters themselves, see Laslier, 2012) choose amongst several proposed voting rules before the election begins. The real question here is to provide enough explanation to ensure that stakeholders make an informed decision about which voting rule they choose to use. Several recent works in social choice have started to study this question of making people choose the voting rule that most fits their needs (see, *e.g.*, Cailloux and Endriss, 2016).

In the aforementioned context of low-stake elections, another point of view is possible. Since in this context the voting platform is mainly used to elicit preferences and discuss about them, voting rules can be seen as many ways of aggregating the preference information contained in the profile and as many ways of exploring this information. This is the approach we have followed in the first two versions of Whale, where the raw results given by several voting rules were displayed to the user, as shown in Figure 20.1. However, as we might expect, simply displaying the potentially contradictory information given by the different voting rules does not help much making a decision, and people were often lost especially when different voting rules yield different winners.

For the last two versions of Whale, we have tried a different approach based on a literal interpretation of "exploring the voting profile". Namely, we have tried to use information visualisation techniques to provide interactive visualisation of the results given by voting procedures. This has lead to the set of basic graphical views that are proposed in Whale 3 and 4 (see Figures 20.2, 20.3, 20.4 and 20.5). This work is just at the beginning, but we believe that it is a promising approach, both to better understand and analyze the voting profiles, and as pedagogical tools to explain to laypersons how the voting procedures work.

20.5 Conclusion

In this chapter, we have presented a web application dedicated to collective decision making. The aim was not exactly to advertise a particular platform, but rather to put into light some practical problems that have not received a lot of attention by the scientific community yet, or, at least, would deserve more attention. Amongst these topics, the design and analysis of voting rules that are usable in practice for everyday collective decision making seems to be of the utmost importance. That concerns the analysis of voting rules that work on small scales of scores rather than on linear orders and also voting rules that are robust to the absence of information concerning some candidates. It would be also crucial to put some efforts into making voting rules be more than only black boxes or oracles that elect a winner for a given set of ballots. It could mean developing ways of explaining these voting rules and providing people with concrete means to argue to choose the right one, or use them as voting profile exploration tools, through graphical visualisation for instance. It is a safe bet that some of the problems listed above will be amongst the future trends of the discipline.

---

[10]And it is also, to some extent, used by by poll platforms like Doodle® or Framadate, which recommend to choose amongst the set of co-winners that lexicographically maximise the number of "yes" and the number of "(yes)" choices.

Acknowledgments

Most work about information visualization presented in this chapter has been made in collaboration with Renaud Blanch. Several people have contributed to Whale, especially Marie-Jeanne Natete, who was the main developer of Whale 4. Whale is supported by ANR project CoCoRICo-CoDec.

Bibliography

F. Brandt, G. Chabin, and C. Geist. Pnyx: A powerful and user-friendly tool for preference aggregation. In *Proceedings of the 14th International Conference on Autonomous Agents and Multiagent Systems (AAMAS)*, pages 1915–1916, 2015.

O. Cailloux and U. Endriss. Arguing about voting rules. In *Proceedings of the 15th International Conference on Autonomous Agents and Multiagent Systems (AAMAS)*, pages 287–295, 2016.

I. Caragiannis, S. Nath, A. D. Procaccia, and N. Shah. Subset selection via implicit utilitarian voting. *Journal of Artificial Intelligence Research*, 58:123–152, 2017.

V. Cortier, D. Galindo, S. Glondu, M. Izabachene, et al. A generic construction for voting correctness at minimum cost-application to helios. *IACR Cryptology EPrint Archive*, 2013:177, 2013.

D. E. Ho and K. Imai. Estimating causal effects of ballot order from a randomized natural experiment the California alphabet lottery, 1978–2002. *Public Opinion Quarterly*, 72(2):216–240, 2008.

N. Karanikolas, R. Blanch, and S. Bouveret. Edge-compressed majority graph: Where social choice meets information visualization. In *Proceedings of the 6th International Workshop on Computational Social Choice (COMSOC)*, 2016.

J. A. Krosnick. In the voting booth, bias starts at the top. *The New York Times*, November 2006.

J.-F. Laslier. And the loser is... plurality voting. In D. S. Felsenthal and M. Machover, editors, *Electoral Systems: Paradoxes, Assumptions, and Procedures*, pages 327–351. Springer, 2012.

N. Mattei and T. Walsh. PrefLib: A library for preferences. http://www.preflib.org. In *Proceedings of the 3rd International Conference on Algorithmic Decision Theory (ADT)*, Lecture Notes in Artificial Intelligence. Springer, 2013.

www.ingramcontent.com/pod-product-compliance
Lightning Source LLC
Chambersburg PA
CBHW080228180526
45158CB00008BA/1959